CLEAR, CORRECT, CREATIVE

CLEAR, CORRECT, CREATIVE:
A Handbook for Writers of Academic Prose

Karen Taylor
Heather Avery
Lucille Strath

Academic Skills Centre
Trent University
Peterborough, Ontario
Canada

Clear, Correct, Creative: A Handbook for Writers of Academic Prose

Printed by Webcom in Canada
First Edition

Graphic Design: Joanne Ward
Cover Design: Anne Hoover
Typesetting: Barbara Fox
Translation: Peter Northrop

Acknowledgments and permissions appear on pages xiii-xv of this text which constitute an extension of the copyright page.

Canadian Cataloguing in Publication Data

Taylor, Karen (Karen E.)
  Clear, correct, creative : a handbook for writers of academic prose

ISBN 0-9693668-4-1

1. English language - Composition and exercises.
2. English language - Rhetoric - Computer-assisted instruction.
I. Avery, Heather.   II. Strath, Lucille.   III. Trent University.
Academic Skills Centre.   IV. Title.

PE1408.T38 1991   808´.042   C91-094471-7

CONTENTS

INTRODUCTION

WHY WE WROTE THIS HANDBOOK

Why publish yet another book on writing clear, correct, and creative non-fiction prose when there are already many writer's handbooks, grammar texts, usage guides, and style manuals available? This book was written primarily because we (the authors) teach writing, and could not find a book that worked for us or for our students. We found that although current texts present comprehensive lists of the rules of grammar and usage, as well as catalogues of common errors revised, using them did not improve writing greatly. "Why then," we asked ourselves, "should we persist in teaching rules and error identification?" Or, going to the extreme, "Why should we teach grammar at all?" To answer these questions, we began investigating the ways students receive grammar and attempt to put it into practice. In the process, we found ourselves re-examining some of our beliefs about the teaching of composition and grammar.

We came to believe that writers learn to write well by writing frequently. In other words, writers learn to improve their writing best by writing and revising their own work, not by memorizing abstract grammatical rules in isolation from the composing process. Most of the texts we tried to use in the classroom presented exercises that required students to analyze and revise the work of others rather than to generate their own writing. Even the sentences that formed the basis for this revision work seemed artificial. They were taken out of context and were usually too simple to have been written by a university or high school student attempting to write an essay or report. It seemed little wonder that students had difficulty applying the information presented in these texts to their writing; this grammar was not useful grammar. We discovered that useful grammar is grammar that helps writers create prose.

We then began to think that misunderstandings about the nature of grammar result in students' failure to learn how to write well and in teachers teaching grammar ineffectively or not at all. Students, at least many university students, seem to think that grammar is a series of rules, and they want to know the rules. When teachers agree with this definition, they either teach grammar in a traditional way, or they don't teach it at all. Those who teach traditional grammar are going against current research into the teaching of writing, which concludes that "the study of traditional school grammar . . . has no effect on raising the quality of student writing."[1] Of course, these teachers are motivated by the desire to assist student writers. They believe that "people who write should know their tools" and that a knowledge of grammar does not inhibit creativity, but rather "provides the discipline to support and enrich the art" of writing.[2] Teachers who teach no grammar at all are also concerned about students. Many of these teachers are responding to the conclusion, supported by research, that teaching traditional grammar with "a heavy emphasis on mechanics and usage results in significant losses" in the overall quality of writing.[3] Very useful books on freewriting and on teaching writing as a process were written in response to this conclusion. These books, and the teachers who write and use them, empower students by valuing their writing and thinking.[4]

Teachers have another reason for not teaching grammar; when grammar is defined as the way a language is used, rather than the way a language should be used, teaching the conventions of grammar and usage seems unnecessary. Why? The answer goes something like this. Linguistic conventions are not learned formally, but acquired in the process of growing up and living within a society and culture. Therefore, every writer has his or her own grammar, which is conventional enough to be understood because it is the product of his or her environment, that is, because it is socially constructed.

---

[1] George Hillocks, Jr., "Synthesis of Research on Teaching Writing," *Educational Leadership* 44.8 (1986/87): 74.

[2] Gail Lewis Tubbs, "A Case for Teaching Grammar to Writers," *Writing Lab Newsletter* 15.7 (March 1991): 3.

[3] Hillocks 74.

[4] See, for example, Peter Elbow, *Writing with Power* (New York: Oxford U P, 1973); Peter Elbow and Pat Belanoff, *A Community of Writers: A Workshop Course in Writing* (New York: Random House, 1989); Toby Fulwiler, *Teaching with Writing* (Portsmouth, NH: Boynton/Cook, 1987); Ken Macrorie, *Telling Writing*, 4th ed. (Montclair, NJ: Boynton/Cook, 1985); Heather Avery, et al., *Thinking It Through*, 2nd ed. (Peterborough, Ontario: Academic Skills Centre, Trent U, 1989).

Consequently, teaching the conventions of grammar and usage in a formal way appears an impossible and ultimately useless exercise.

As teachers ourselves, the authors of this book agree in part with all the reasons for and against teaching grammar, but with none completely. We recognize that the study of traditional grammar can sometimes dampen creativity and worsen the quality of prose by promoting greater attention to the form and appearance of writing than to its meaning. We have seen how important it is to encourage students to write frequently by convincing them that the knowledge they have acquired about language enables them to write well, that their freely written words are valuable attempts at expressing and discovering thought. Yet we have found that freewriting and inquiry alone do not successfully teach, or even facilitate, clear and correct writing in our classes; when teaching, we constantly need to acquaint students with the way language works. When students are not taught about the conventions of language, they must either pick up this information themselves, or do without. Leaving students to their own devices in this regard reinforces the status quo; students with certain advantages within society will have an easier time acquiring language that is considered proper. Therefore, empowerment should mean enabling students to understand and use conventional grammar as well as encouraging them to realize their own knowledge and creative abilities; teachers must help students become powerful as well as make them feel powerful.

Intuitively, we began to believe that these goals are not mutually exclusive. There is a middle path, one that enables writers to learn conventions without becoming rule-bound, that values creativity without sacrificing clarity and correctness, and, most important, that emphasizes the importance of learning about grammar and usage within the context of a writer's own writing tasks and writing processes. To teach grammar or not to teach grammar: that is not the question. Not teaching traditional school grammar does not mean not teaching grammar at all. It simply means that grammar is learned and should be taught as a means to an end, not as a subject somehow separate from composing and revising writing.

So what is grammar and what is its place in the writing process? To answer we must explain what grammar does and what it can and cannot do for writers.

In the beginning, writing is exploratory; we write for ourselves to discover what we mean. We create preliminary drafts, writer-based prose that need make sense only to its creator. If we pay too much attention to grammatical conventions at this stage, we risk hobbling creativity. Studies show that concern about making grammatical errors during the exploratory stages of writing promotes writer's block and all its attendant problems: disjointed writing, writing that doesn't flow, and writing that, while correct, lacks either style or the depth of analysis necessary in academic prose.[5]

Of course, grammar does have a place in writer-based prose. Writers use grammar whenever they write. Language defines and describes the world. But at this stage, writers use their own private grammar, one that makes sense to them. In fact, being speakers of English, we all know quite a lot about English grammar. We can all choose and arrange words into meaningful patterns. We can all communicate by manipulating language according to conventions. Often, these skills were not taught to us; we acquired them by listening to others speak and by reading. We picked up language in the home, in the playground, on the street. In fact, linguists believe that it is the job of grammarians to investigate and describe the way a language is used by those who were raised speaking it rather than to tell these same people how they should use their native tongue.

---

[5] See, for example, Mike Rose, *Writer's Block: The Cognitive Dimension* (Carbondale: Southern Illinois U P, 1984); Marie Ponsot and Rosemary Deen, *Beat Not the Poor Desk* (Upper Montclair, NJ: Boynton/Cook, 1982); Richard Lanham, *Style: An Anti-Textbook* (New Haven: Yale U P, 1974).

However, grammar does not only mean our own particular way of arranging words, but also a standardized conventional arrangement acceptable to society or to a certain group within society. Errors in grammar and usage are said to occur when our own method of structuring sentences or using words does not correspond to the method agreed upon by our readers.

These considerations led us to five conclusions about how to learn and teach clear and correct writing without dampening creativity. First, practising writing and gaining experience in analyzing, responding to, and revising writing improves writing quality. Second, although a knowledge of grammar is useful in the drafting stage of writing, the way in which language works can be best learned and taught during the revision stage. Third, because learning to write well means, in part, learning to apply the conventions of grammar and usage to one's own prose, writers should learn to revise their own work or the work of their peers. Fourth, because the revision process turns writer-based prose into reader-based prose, collaborative revision, peer-editing, and group discussions about grammatical conventions are good ways in which to learn how to improve one's own writing. Fifth, because the conventions of grammar and usage are socially constructed and differ depending upon the writer's purpose and audience, learning to write well involves considering the context in which your writing will be judged. In other words, writers cannot expect that memorizing rules will help them improve their writing because what some people consider an error, other people consider perfectly acceptable. A good writer, therefore, is a flexible writer, one who thinks about how a particular audience reading a particular text defines correctness, clarity, and creativity.

We have written this book with these conclusions in mind. The importance of learning how to write well by writing frequently made us think to include numerous writing prompts. We also included many learning prompts, designed to stimulate group discussion. The significance of revising one's own or one's peers' writing prompted us to include revision worksheets containing paragraphs of student writing for students to discuss and revise. Whenever possible, we have demonstrated the difficulties student writers have by using actual student prose, not simplistic sentences and paragraphs manufactured by grammarians to exemplify and then correct particular errors. Consequently, teachers should not expect our samples of student prose to be models of flawless writing, even when revised. In fact, we deliberately created all exercises, worksheets, and prompts to encourage investigation into the way language works, or doesn't work. Although we have provided answers to exercises, as well as revisions of problematic sentences and paragraphs, we **do not** consider our answers and revisions to be definitive. They are included only to show students one way of making prose more clear and correct. We expect and hope that arguments will break out.

Because we believe that writing cannot be adequately evaluated out of the context created by the writer's purpose, audience, and subject, a primary concern was to evaluate and revise writing within this context. Specifically, we tried to examine the context typically provided by an academic assignment. What sort of diction is expected in a biology essay, for example? What arrangement of ideas within paragraphs do philosophy professors usually find appropriate? Throughout this book, you will see references to many academic disciplines and to many different writers trying to enter into the discourse of these disciplines. To make the book more personal, and to imitate the gender-neutral language now conventional in most academic disciplines, these different writers are referred to using pronouns that accurately reflect each one's sex, although writers' names are withheld.

WHAT THE CHAPTERS ARE ABOUT AND HOW THE BOOK IS ORGANIZED

Chapter One begins our investigation of the way language works by looking at the patterns and parts of the sentences we compose. In this chapter, we are trying to acquaint students with the information and terminology they will need throughout the text. Although definitions of the parts of speech are provided, experiential learning is stressed. Students are guided toward the general principles of sentence composition in exercises and by examples that show, rather than tell, the way language works.

Chapter Two still looks at sentences, but focuses on their revision rather than their creation. Common sentence problems are discussed and revision strategies are suggested. Whenever possible, the uses, as well as the abuses, of atypical sentences are investigated. We do not want to tell students how to write, but we do want to make them aware of the choices available to them and of the way in which a reader will probably respond to their writing.

Chapter Three is also about sentences, but here sentences are considered within a wider context; the chapter discusses how to make prose interesting and emphatic by varying sentence length, structure, and type within a paragraph. All the sentences of the paragraphs considered are grammatically acceptable, but some are unclear because style of expression interferes with communication. This chapter considers creating a style that is appropriate to the writer's purpose. Which points should be emphasized? Which are tangential? What effect does the writer want to create?

In Chapter Four, the focus broadens. Here, the grammar of paragraphs is investigated. How do we compose a correct, clear, and creative paragraph? We stress choice based on content, context, and purpose, and investigate the qualities of unity, coherence, and development to answer this question. The many writing and learning prompts help students to an understanding of the various types of paragraphs that they may use in their essays.

The many conventions of punctuation are discussed in Chapter Five. We have concerned ourselves with the sorts of punctuation problems students often encounter. Where do commas go? Is end punctuation placed outside or inside quotation marks? Even here, in spite of the fact that punctuation is usually treated as a series of rules to be memorized, we consider it as a way of making meaning clear and of creating special effects.

Chapter Six discusses the three main things writers should consider when choosing words: accuracy, propriety, and efficacy. Of course, because the writer's subject, purpose, and audience determine which words are accurate, appropriate, and effective, each is investigated.

Chapter Seven takes the discussion of words one step further by looking at how many words writers need to be clearly understood. Wordiness and the lack of clarity it induces are examined, and revision strategies warn of the dangers of cutting out too many words.

The last large section of this book is a glossary of commonly misused or overused words and phrases. We included this section because each of us has benefited, at one time or another, from consulting the glossaries provided in other books. (Fowler, Partridge, and Strunk and White come immediately to mind.)[6] We wanted to compile most of the information students need to create clear, correct, effective prose — usage conventions included — and publish it in one book.

We do not expect that all students and teachers of writing will read this book cover to cover, but we hope that you read carefully the sections that interest you. At first, you may feel a little overwhelmed by the amount of writing presented in *Clear, Correct, Creative*, especially if you are used to traditional grammar textbooks that treat grammar as a set of rules to be memorized and provide fairly sketchy (and bossy) descriptions of the dos and don'ts of writing arranged in tidy categories. Our book, because it investigates the options a writer has at the drafting and revising stages of writing, must be less categorical and must have more explanation.

---

[6] H.W. Fowler, *A Dictionary of Modern English Usage*, 2nd ed. (Oxford: Clarendon P, 1968); Eric Partridge, *Usage and Abusage* (Harmondsworth, Middlesex: Penguin, 1973); William Strunk, Jr. and E.B. White, *The Elements of Style*, 2nd ed. (New York: Macmillan, 1972).

Nevertheless, our book is not comprehensive. It does not cover every convention of grammar and usage. It focuses on what its authors see as the key writing problems of senior secondary and post-secondary students. For example, we don't mention that the beginnings of sentences are capitalized, and we don't discuss the conjugation of regular and irregular verbs in any detail. However, we do have thorough sections on maintaining clear pronoun reference and on using commas properly because our experiences indicate that students need to know how to do these things. By keeping our students' needs in mind in this way, we believe we have written a book that is useful because it doesn't waste people's time on already known conventions of writing and because it doesn't simplify the problems students **do** have producing non-fiction prose.

HOW TO USE *CLEAR, CORRECT, CREATIVE*

To Improve Writing

How can you use this book effectively? If your aim is to improve your own writing, you should first try to analyze that writing. What is good about it? What needs improvement? Gathering together the comments friends and instructors have made about your writing will help you answer these questions. Next, use the table of contents, the subject index, and the index of marker's symbols to find the sections of the book that will help you strengthen your writing and correct those errors you most commonly make. Read these sections carefully, paying particular attention to the sample paragraphs and sample paragraph discussions of relevant revision worksheets. Then, respond to the writing and learning prompts, do the exercises, revise the exercise paragraphs. Only by doing do we truly understand how to do something. Buying a book on how to sculpt does not make someone an expert sculptor. Neither does reading it. Likewise, owning and studying this book is not enough. Only by writing and revising our writing do we truly understand how to write.

To Teach Writing

If you teach writing, you will use this book differently. You might read through a section and teach it, using the examples and explanations provided. You might have your students respond to writing prompts and use their responses to generate discussions of common grammatical errors or of certain characteristics of good writing. We have found that a great deal of effective teaching can be done from samples of student writing. If you cannot work from the writing of your students, work from the writing of our students. Feel free to make transparencies of the revision worksheet paragraphs. In fact, these paragraphs were designed to be enlarged and made into overhead transparencies. By working through the sample paragraphs of these revision worksheets with your class interactively and creatively, while still paying attention to the sample paragraph discussions, you can effectively teach much of the material in this book.

We would also suggest that you give your students sufficient class-time to do exercises, to revise exercise paragraphs, and to discuss their answers and revisions. In our experience, the less we lecture and the more students do and say, the more they learn. A useful strategy for encouraging students to think about writing and revising is to get them to work collaboratively. You might divide your class into groups of three and assign each group the task of revising a revision worksheet exercise paragraph, for example. In a small group, an individual often feels less at risk. Also, he or she will be exposed to the knowledge, skills, and perspectives of the other group members. This exposure encourages learning, as does the comforting feeling of being the member of a group of editors rather than the individual solely responsible for editorial decisions. Besides, groups will be more willing than individuals to share answers to exercises and revisions of paragraphs, and it is this sharing that demonstrates the infinite variety of good writing.

To Evaluate and Analyze Writing

Of course, this book can also be used as a reference guide by any instructor commenting on writing and by any writer trying to understand such comments. To assist those commenting on and marking writing, we have included a chart of standard marker's symbols. Once you are familiar with these symbols, you can mark the instances of error and excellence more quickly, more comprehensively, and more appropriately, leaving yourself time to write a substantial comment evaluating the piece of writing as a whole. Following each symbol is a brief explanation of its meaning and a page reference pointing to a more detailed discussion of what these symbols should prompt writers to think or to do about their writing. Thus, by using these symbols, an instructor indicates not only the strengths and weaknesses of a writer's prose but also, indirectly, which part of this text a writer should consult. We provided this chart to give students and instructors a common vocabulary. We wanted to free teachers from providing long explanations of common writing problems over and over again. We wanted to help students understand what their instructors thought about their writing, and we decided that the way to do this was to encourage teachers to comment on rather than to edit or revise student prose.

When we began writing this handbook, our aims were practical, and yes, even self-serving. We were trying to find a way to teach what students needed to know. When we were in the thick of things, collaborating amongst the three of us, we became caught up with the desire to communicate to our students and colleagues some of the excitement we felt as wordsmiths. We hoped that we could encourage students to become actively involved with language and with the way meaning is created through language. Moreover, we wanted writers to know that although grammar implies structure and convention, it is liberating in the choices it presents, choices that allow the writer to take control of expression and communication. What began as a task ended as a keen desire to share with students and teachers our sense that grammar could and should be taught, could and should be learned—and could and should be discovery.

ACKNOWLEDGMENTS

The writers of this book wish to acknowledge the contributions of the students, staff, and faculty of Trent University. Without the inspiration of the students who attend the workshops and individual appointments provided by the Academic Skills Centre of Trent University, this book would not have been possible. Helpful, as well as inspiring, were the many students who gave us permission to reproduce exact or edited passages of their prose. These passages were essential to the composition of *Clear, Correct, Creative.*

The hard work of many of the staff of the Academic Skills Centre, who, although not directly responsible for writing this book, gave of their time and talent, is also appreciated. Maged el Komos read and proofread much of this text, as did Evelyn Cotter. Carol Tomlin helped to format and proofread the text. She also provided invaluable secretarial and moral support to the writers.

Thanks must also go to staff and faculty outside the Academic Skills Centre. Barbara Fox, Peter Northrop, Joanne Ward, and Anne Hoover all assisted in the process of typesetting and designing this book. Both Professor David Glassco and Professor Fred Helleiner took time away from a busy, hot summer to read and comment on drafts of *Clear, Correct, Creative.* These two critical readers offered timely advice and sound recommendations, which were deeply appreciated.

Finally, we must acknowledge that, in an important way, all students and teachers of writing have helped in the creation of this book. Yes, *Clear, Correct, Creative* was written for you, but it was also inspired by you.

Throughout this book we have quoted from published material, and we would like to thank the copyright holders for allowing us to do so. We have made every effort to trace the ownership of all copyrighted material and to secure permission from copyright holders. In the event of any question arising as to the use of any material, we will be pleased to make the necessary corrections in future printings.

Walter Allen, from *The English Novel: A Short Critical History.* Published by Penguin 1954. Used by permission of the author.

Gordon Alley and Donald Deshler, from *Teaching the Learning Disabled Adolescent.* Reprinted by permission of Love Publishing Company, Denver, CO.

Margaret Atwood, "An End to Audience?" from *Second Words: Selected Critical Prose.* Reproduced with the permission of Stoddart Publishing Co. Limited, 34 Lesmill Rd., Don Mills, Ontario, Canada.

Margaret Atwood, "Canadian-American Relations: Surviving the Eighties," from *Second Words: Selected Critical Prose.* Reproduced with the permission of Stoddart Publishing Co. Limited, 34 Lesmill Rd., Don Mills, Ontario, Canada.

Margaret Atwood, "Women's Novels," from *Murder in the Dark: Short Fictions and Prose Poems.* Published by Coach House Press. Reprinted by permission of the author.

Sheridan Baker, from *The Practical Stylist,* 2nd Can. ed. Copyright © 1986 by Harper & Row. Used by permission of HarperCollins Publishers, New York.

Ann Berthoff with James Stephens, from *Forming/Thinking/Writing*, Second Edition, 1988. Reproduced with permission of Boynton/Cook Publishers, Portsmouth, NH.

Joseph Conrad, "A Familiar Preface," from *A Personal Record: Some Reminiscences.* Used by permission of J.M. Dent & Sons.

John W. Dean III, "Haldeman Is No More Innocent Than I Am," from *The New York Times,* April 6, 1975. Copyright © 1975 by The New York Times Company. Reprinted by permission.

Annie Dillard, from *An American Childhood.* Used by permission of HarperCollins Publishers, New York.

Annie Dillard, "Sight into Insight," from *The Norton Reader,* ed. Arthur Eastman, et al., 7th ed., 1988. Reprinted by permission of Blanche C. Gregory, Inc., New York.

Annie Dillard, from *The Writer's Life.* Used by permission of HarperCollins Publishers, New York.

Janet Emig, "Children and Metaphor," from *The Web of Meaning,* 1983. Reproduced with permission of Boynton/Cook Publishers, Portsmouth, NH.

Timothy Findley, from *Not Wanted on the Voyage.* Copyright © Pebble Productions, Inc., 1984. Reprinted by permission of Penguin Books Canada Limited.

E.M. Forster, from *Aspects of the Novel,* ed. Oliver Stallybrass. Published by Penguin 1974. Used by permission of King's College Cambridge and the Society of Authors as the literary representatives of the E.M. Forster Estate.

Northrop Frye, "Conclusion to *A Literary History of Canada*," from *The Bush Garden.* Reproduced with the permission of Stoddart Publishing Co. Limited, 34 Lesmill Rd., Don Mills, Ontario, Canada.

Northrop Frye, "Lawren Harris: An Introduction," from *The Bush Garden.* Reproduced with the permission of Stoddart Publishing Co. Limited, 34 Lesmill Rd., Don Mills, Ontario, Canada.

Northrop Frye, "The Narrative Tradition in English-Canadian Poetry," from *The Bush Garden.* Reproduced with the permission of Stoddart Publishing Co. Limited, 34 Lesmill Rd., Don Mills, Ontario, Canada.

W.F. Garrett-Petts, "Research Notes on George Bowering as Radical Pedagogue and Reading Teacher." Reprinted from *Inkshed* 9.3 (February 1991). Used by permission of the author.

Louis Giannetti, from *Understanding Movies,* 3rd ed. Used by permission of Prentice Hall, Englewood Cliffs, NJ.

Roger Gibbins, from *Conflict and Unity.* Used by permission of Nelson Canada.

Linda Hutcheon, from *The Canadian Postmodern,* copyright © Linda Hutcheon 1988. Reprinted by permission of Oxford University Press Canada.

Walter Laqueur, from *The Terrible Secret.* Used by permission of the author, and George Weidenfeld & Nicolson Limited, London.

Margaret Laurence, from *The Diviners* by Margaret Laurence. Used by permission of the Canadian Publishers, McClelland & Stewart, Toronto.

F.L. Lucas, from *Style,* originally published by Cassell & Co., London. Copyright © 1962, 1955 by F.L. Lucas. Reprinted with permission of Macmillan Publishing Company.

Robert McCrum, William Cran and Robert MacNeil, from *The Story of English.* Copyright © 1986 by Robert McCrum, William Cran, and Robert MacNeil. Used by permission of Viking Penguin, a division of Penguin Books USA Inc.

Farley Mowat, from *Canada North.* Copyright © 1967 by Farley Mowat. Used by permission of Farley Mowat Limited.

Alice Munro, "Thanks for the Ride," from *Dance of the Happy Shades.* Copyright © Alice Munro, 1968. Used by permission of McGraw-Hill Ryerson Limited.

George Orwell, "Politics and the English Language," from *The Penguin Essays of George Orwell.* Used by permission of the estate of the late Sonia Brownell Orwell and Martin Secker & Warburg Ltd.

Michael Peterman, "'All That Happens, One Must Try to Understand': The Kindredness of Tillie Olsen's 'Tell Me a Riddle' and Margaret Laurence's *The Stone Angel*," from *Margaret Laurence: An Appreciation,* edited by Christl Verduyn. Published by the Journal of Canadian Studies and Broadview Press, 1988. Used by permission of the Journal of Canadian Studies.

David Quammen, "Strawberries Under Ice," from *The Best American Essays 1989.* Copyright © David Quammen. Originally published in *Outside Magazine,* 1988. Used by permission of the author's agent, Renee Wayne Golden.

Hugh Rawson, "Euphemisms," from *About Language: A Reader for Writers,* Second Edition, William H. Roberts and Gregoire Turgeon, eds. Copyright © 1989 Houghton Mifflin Company. Adapted with permission.

David Adams Richards, from *Nights Below Station Street* by David Adams Richards. Used by permission of the Canadian Publishers, McClelland & Stewart, Toronto.

Charles Ritchie, from *The Siren Years* by Charles Ritchie. Copyright © 1974. Reprinted by permission of Macmillan of Canada, a Division of Canada Publishing Corporation.

Carl Sandburg, excerpt from *Abraham Lincoln: The War Years,* Volume IV, by Carl Sandburg, copyright 1939 by Harcourt Brace Jovanovich, Inc. and renewed 1966 by Carl Sandburg. Reprinted by permission of the publisher.

Gertrude Stein, from *The Autobiography of Alice B. Toklas.* Published by Vintage Books, 1961. Reprinted by permission of Random House, Inc.

Gertrude Story, "Das Engelein Kommit," from *Black Swan.* Used by permission of Thistledown Press Ltd., Saskatoon, Sask.

Dylan Thomas, "Holiday Memory," from *Quite Early One Morning.* Used by permission of David Higham Associates Limited, London.

Lewis Thomas, "Leech Leech, Et Cetera," from *A Long Line of Cells: Collected Essays.* Published by Viking Penguin. Used by permission of Penguin USA.

Lewis Thomas, "On Societies as Organisms," from *A Long Line of Cells: Collected Essays.* Published by Viking Penguin. Used by permission of Penguin USA.

Barbara Tuchman, "The Historian's Opportunity," from *Practicing History: Selected Essays.* Published by Ballantine Books, 1982. Reprinted by permission of Random House, Inc.

We all learned to speak in sentences before we reached school-age: *The pig says oink.* Once in school, we learned to read sentences: *The pig plays in the mud.* As our knowledge and abilities grew, so did the complexity of the sentences we read and constructed: *Pigs, animals remarkable for their size and appetite, are also uncommonly intelligent.* If we encountered an English teacher who was a traditionalist in matters of grammar, we were taught methods of recognizing and naming the parts of speech which form sentences. This skill was called parsing the sentence and involved analyzing and describing sentences grammatically:

The	black	mud	covered	the	ground,	and	the	pigs
article	*adjective*	*noun*	*verb*	*article*	*noun*	*conjunction*	*article*	*noun*

lay	contentedly	in	it.
verb	*adverb*	*preposition*	*pronoun*

However, for many of us, these formal grammar lessons seemed to have no practical purpose. What did being able to analyze someone else's sentence matter when what we needed to know was how to write and revise our own? How was studying the sentences written by some long-dead author or grammarian supposed to help us create prose that was correct, comprehensible, and interesting? There always seemed to be a chasm between what we could already accomplish with words in sentences and what we were being taught about words, sentences, and language in general. There was a gulf between the creative and the analytical processes. It made grammar lessons, which of necessity concentrated on analysis, boring and irrelevant.

But let's put ourselves in the teacher's position for a moment. Is it possible to explain the conventions of language without analyzing and codifying, without creating and naming names, without grammar? Again, think of a child. How do children learn society's conventions? Of course they copy. They emulate the actions of those around them. But do we not tell, as well as show, children how to act? We might say, "I know that I eat peas with my knife at home, but we are going to Aunt Maria's, and she expects us to have proper table manners," or "Don't do as I do, do as I say." While the latter pronouncement might be objectionable, it does suggest that explication as well as exemplification constitutes education.

When it comes to grammar, however, none of us is a child any more; we all received an education in one way or another, regardless of whether someone told us about parsing sentences or the parts of speech. Therefore, we do not need to learn all the rules of grammar from scratch. Accordingly, the task of this chapter is to bring all the knowledge we have about sentences and their creation to mind. Since we take much of this knowledge for granted, being either unwilling or unable even to name what it is we know, we must arrive at a common vocabulary capable of expressing the various ways of composing and revising sentences.

Obviously, this chapter is a review, and can be skipped by the confident. However, since most of us acquired language in a fairly haphazard way and are often unaware of the gaps in our linguistic knowledge, even the skilled writer can benefit from sampling this chapter. To allow you to nibble at leisure, the primary questions and concerns addressed are listed:

What is a sentence and what are the different types of simple sentence?

What are the basic elements and structures of the declarative sentence, the type of sentence most used in academic writing?

How can the meaning of simple sentences be expanded through the addition of modifying words and phrases?

How can simple sentences be combined using coordination and subordination?

The Sentence

What is a sentence? Definitions multiply. One grammar text claims that a sentence is the expression of a complete thought. Another describes a sentence as a group of words containing a subject and a verb. Both the first, conceptual definition, and the second, grammatical definition, are inadequate.

Writers find the conceptual definition of a sentence difficult to apply because they have trouble judging which thoughts are complete. Are the ideas expressed by single words incomplete? Usually not. Examine the word *liberty*. For many North Americans, the concept of liberty is a complete thought, a description of our culture. However, most of us would recognize that *liberty* is not a sentence. Conversely, one might ask if the ideas expressed in grammatically complete sentences are always complete. They certainly don't seem to be. Sometimes such a sentence depends so strongly upon neighbouring sentences for its meaning that the thought it expresses is incomplete, a fact which forces us to write in paragraphs. Writers might well question, for instance, what is complete about the idea expressed by this grammatically complete sentence: *This follows.*

Just as a sentence does not always express a complete thought, it does not always contain a subject. *Shut the door* has no stated subject, yet we recognize it as a complete sentence. In the preceding paragraph, I punctuated *Usually not* as a sentence, although it has neither subject nor verb. Was I wrong? No. Both *Usually not* and *No* are minor sentences, sometimes called acceptable fragments.

All of this shows just how problematic an accurate definition of a sentence is. Luckily, being unable to define a sentence usually doesn't stop us from being able to create one. We seem to understand intuitively what a complete sentence is, recognizing it as a unit of meaning that is usually larger than a word and smaller than a paragraph. As Richard Grant White states, "In English, words are formed into sentences by the operation of an invisible power, which is like magnetism."[1] For the most part, we possess this power; it is a part of our unconscious mind. If you have any doubts, translate the following nonsense sentences.

---

[1] Richard Grant White quoted in Dennis E. Brown, *Grammar and Good Taste* (New Haven: Yale UP, 1982) 203.

Exercise One: Nonsense Sentences

Substitute English words for the following nonsense words to make meaningful sentences. This exercise is not a cryptogram; the number of letters in a nonsense word has nothing to do with the possible meaning of that word. The position of nonsense words within a sentence, the suffixes (word endings), the punctuation, and the recognizable English words surrounding the nonsense words do afford clues to meaning, however. Be assured that there is no one correct answer to this exercise. You are being asked to create your own sentences following the patterns suggested by the nonsense sentences below.

A brepling vlatage stuzlled quirmorly to haddle a floupen, zledful whurt.

Glump the meklest pizt.

Did the woozes flek the chumped boph greeperly?

Ip's glipperful!

To bech is to trackle Jenny's fleab.

Crafing crums crouster crets.

Again, there are no correct or incorrect answers to this exercise, but we believe that your translations of these sentences will exhibit similarities, correspondences which indicate your understanding of what a sentence is and of the sorts of words that function as parts of speech to form sentences. On page 368, there is a compilation of six different attempts to make sense of these sentences. Compare them to one another and to your own efforts. Do you follow words like *a* and *the* (articles) with names of people, objects, or concepts (nouns) or with words modifying these names (adjectives)? Does your second sentence start with an action word (a verb)? Do you follow the word *to* with a word that is descriptive of an action, forming combinations like *to eat, to sleep,* and *to be* (infinitives)? See? You may not know how to name the parts of speech (the words in brackets), but you do know how to use them. Do your sentences fulfil different functions? Do most make statements? Does one command, another question, and a third exclaim? See? You know a lot about English grammar.

If you still feel uncomfortable with grammatical terms like noun, adjective, verb, and adverb, there is a chart presenting the standard definitions of the eight parts of speech on page 20. Warnings should accompany all such attempts to define grammatical terminology, however, because they are, of necessity, simplifications. As such, they are inaccurate. For this reason, our book attempts to help you discover how words interact with one another to communicate meaning more by giving you examples of different sentence patterns than by defining terms.

To proceed with the task of discovering how words interact, let's investigate our knowledge of different sentence patterns and functions more fully. As Exercise One demonstrates, sentences can fulfil one of four basic functions: they can make statements, pose questions, issue commands or requests, or make exclamatory remarks. A sentence that makes a statement or declares something is called a statement or a declarative sentence; one that poses a question is a question or an interrogative sentence; one that issues a command or a request is a command or an imperative sentence; and one that makes an exclamatory remark is an exclamation or an exclamatory sentence.

By far the most common type of sentence is the **declarative sentence**. Essays are full of statements, of declarations:

Henry Tudor seized the crown.

The declarative sentence first names something or someone (*Henry Tudor*) and then makes a declaration about that something or someone (*seized the crown*). Declarative sentences follow many patterns, and we will examine their most usual patterns later, but it is necessary to understand that a declarative sentence has two parts: a subject and a predicate. Its bare subject is a noun or a noun equivalent (*Henry Tudor*), and the essence of its predicate is a verb or verb phrase (*seized*). Omit one of these elements and you no longer have a complete declarative sentence: *Henry Tudor the crown*.

In academic prose, **interrogative sentences (questions)** are less common than declarative sentences but more common than either exclamatory or imperative sentences. Of course, being questions, interrogative sentences end with question marks. An essayist might ask the following questions:

Is Canada's contribution to NATO sufficient?
Did Dickens attempt to reform Victorian society?
What is radioactive waste?
How should we then live?

The first two sentences invite yes or no answers. They are also similar in order; both begin with a verb or an auxiliary verb (a word that combines with the main verb to form a verb phrase: *did attempt*). The verb or auxiliary verb is followed by a subject. These two interrogative sentences can be parsed — analyzed and described grammatically — in the following way:

Is   Canada's contribution   to NATO sufficient?
verb   *subject*

Did   Dickens   attempt   to reform Victorian society?
auxiliary   subject   main
verb   verb

The last two questions begin with a question-word, a word like *who, whom, whose, which*, and *what* or like *where, when, why*, and *how*. Both sentences invite more than yes or no answers. While the order of the last question is similar to the order of the first two, the third question follows the pattern of most statements or declarative sentences. It can be parsed in this way:

What   is   radioactive   waste?
subject   verb

The similarity between the order of this type of interrogative sentence and the order of a declarative sentence has given rise to a classic baseball joke.

Dexter: Now, on the St. Louis team we have Who's on first, What's on second, I Don't Know is on third — .

Sebastian: That's what I want to find out. I want you to tell me the names of the fellows on the St. Louis team.

Dexter: I'm telling you. Who's on first, What's on second, I Don't Know is on third — .

Sebastian: You know the fellows' names?

Dexter: Yes.

Sebastian: Well, then, who's playin' first?

Dexter: Yes.

Sebastian: I mean the fellow's name on first base.

Dexter: Who.

Sebastian: The fellow playin' first base for St. Louis.

Dexter: Who.

Sebastian: The guy on first base.

Dexter: Who is on first.

Sebastian: Well, what are you askin' me for?

Dexter: I'm not asking you — I'm telling you. **Who is on first.**[2]

And so it goes. But to return to serious matters, an interrogative sentence also needs a subject and a verb to be complete. *Canada's contribution to NATO sufficient?* is not a complete sentence. In certain circumstances, neither is *Who is on first.* The reason Sebastian has such a difficult time recognizing *Who* as the name of the guy playing first base is that many words that act as subjects in interrogative sentences act as conjunctions in declarative sentences: *Ken, who is on first base, plays well.* Poor Sebastian can only interpret Dexter's communication as a complete question (*Who is on first?*) or as an incomplete statement (*who is on first*); he cannot understand the meaning of the declarative sentence.

Imperative sentences, sentences that give commands or make requests, are also occasionally used in essays. Here is an imperative sentence taken from a student essay:

Recognize that the statistics presented in the following chart show a correlation between the centralization of bureaucracies and the increased cost of administration.

Notice that imperative sentences begin with verbs and do not have stated subjects. Their subjects are implied, as are the subjects (*you* in both cases) of the preceding example and of the imperative sentence that follows it. To be complete, then, an imperative sentence needs a verb that relates to an implied subject. Here is a complete imperative sentence: *Do it.* And here is an incomplete sentence: *It.*

---

[2] *Naughty Nineties* dir. Jean Yarbrough, with Bud Abbott and Lou Costello, Universal City Studios Inc., 1945.

Exclamatory sentences express strong emotion; they exclaim. It is customary to end exclamatory sentences with an exclamation point or mark. In fact, if you leave out the exclamation point, you risk writing an incomplete sentence.

Complete	Complete	Incomplete
It's wonderful!	It's wonderful.	Wonderful.
It's marvellous!	It's marvellous.	Marvellous.
Wow!		Wow.
Great!		Great.

Because academic essayists usually want their arguments to appear objective, rational, and considered rather than emotional, they use exclamatory sentences infrequently.

We have now named and described four types of sentence; however, we still have not answered our initial question. We still don't know exactly what a sentence is. We may never know exactly. H.W. Fowler, a respected expert in the field of grammar and usage, writes that a "sentence is defined in every grammar book and every dictionary, but it would not be easy to find two that gave the same definition."[3] He also warns, "Grammarians are free to maintain that no sequence of words can be called a sentence unless it has a grammatical structure, but they should recognize that, except as a term of their art, the word has broken the bounds they have set for it."[4]

Nevertheless, certain grammatical structures or patterns do exist, and by leaving essential elements out of these patterns, a writer risks confusing or irritating a reader. We are now aware of four sentence types, but we need to know more about one of these. We need to examine the various shapes and patterns of simple declarative sentences in greater detail because these sentences are the most common and form the foundation of all others.

The Simple Declarative Sentence

As we have determined, the two essential ingredients of a declarative sentence are a subject and a predicate. The subject names something and the predicate tells something about that named thing.

THE SUBJECT

Subjects can be single words or single grammatical terms. These subjects are nouns or noun equivalents. Noun equivalents include pronouns like *it*, *that*, and *she* and verbals like *to eat* (an infinitive) and *eating* (a gerund). Verbals are so named because they are verbs transformed to fulfil other functions, such as the

---

[3] H.W. Fowler, *A Dictionary of Modern English Usage*, 2nd ed. (Oxford: Clarendon P, 1965) 546.
[4] Fowler 546.

function of a noun. Here are some subjects that are either single words or single grammatical terms:

Bands play. (noun)
Millions were killed. (noun)
Marcos died. (noun)
It is good. (pronoun)
This seems reasonable. (pronoun)
Skipping is great exercise. (gerund)
To rest is my only wish. (infinitive)

Most complete subjects, however, are composed of more than one noun or noun equivalent.

*Two military **bands** from Old Fort Henry* play for tourists.
Millions of civilians were killed during World War II.
Marcos, the former president of the Philippines, died.
*This innovative **idea*** seems reasonable.
Skipping rope for two hours a day is great exercise.
To rest my weary bones is my only wish.

The complete subject of a declarative sentence, then, consists of a bare subject (highlighted in the preceding and following examples) as well as all the words and word groups that describe the bare subject.

A complete subject may also consist of two or more bare subjects joined with a coordinating conjunction (*and, but, or*) or a correlative conjunction (*both . . . and, either . . . or, neither . . . nor, not only . . . but also*) as well as all the words and word groups describing these bare subjects.

*Cancer and heart **disease*** are leading killers. (nouns)
*Neither **you** nor **I*** should pollute. (pronouns)
*Both **Yates** and **Tomlin*** concede to authority. (nouns)
*Opera **singers**, scuba **divers**, and long distance **runners*** have strong lungs. (nouns)
*My **wife**, my **child**, and **I*** took a holiday. (nouns and a pronoun)

A phrase can also function as a subject. A phrase is a group of related words that does not contain both a subject and a predicate.

Jumping in and out of trouble was her specialty. (gerund phrase)
To study diligently is to pass. (infinitive phrase)
Helping students is what we do best. (gerund phrase)
To know her is to love her. (infinitive phrase)
Over the rainbow is too far to go. (prepositional phrase)

A clause (a group of related words that contains both a subject and a predicate) can also be a subject. Things get tricky here since the bare subject of the clause functioning as the complete subject of the sentence may be different from the bare subject of the sentence.

> **Whoever** *pulls the sword from this stone* shall rule England.
> *bare subject of both clause and sentence*

> **That**   **Prime Minister Trudeau** *and* **his government** *were criticized*
> *bare subject*   *bare subject of clause*
> *of sentence*

> *for their invocation of the War Measures Act* is true.

THE PREDICATE

In a declarative sentence, the essential element of a predicate is the verb or the verb phrase that tells what the subject does or that asserts something about the subject. Predicates always include a verb or a verb phrase, and are sometimes composed solely of one or the other.

> God *exists*. (verb)
> Right *will prevail*. (verb phrase)
> The Cabinet *has met*. (verb phrase)

Most often, a predicate is composed of more than just a verb or a verb phrase. Still, as with bare subjects and complete subjects, the verb or verb phrase remains the heart of the predicate.

> God *exists in the minds and hearts of individuals.*
> Right *will prevail in the struggle against the tyranny of the dollar.*
> The Cabinet *has met native representatives from each of Ontario's reservations.*

Two or more verbs or verb phrases may be joined by a coordinating conjunction (*and, but, or*) or by a correlative conjunction (*both . . . and, either . . . or, neither . . . nor, not only . . . but also*) to form a compound predicate.

> Thomas De Quincey *began taking opium to relieve a toothache and* **wrestled** *this habit for years.*
> He *spent five years at Oxford but* **left** *the University without a degree.*
> De Quincey *neither* **achieved** *great fame nor* **wallowed** *in obscurity.*
> He *both* **wrote** *about and* **lived** *the life of a self-involved romanticist.*

Examine the predicates of the preceding examples carefully and you will realize that, although a verb or verb phrase is an essential ingredient of a predicate (and of a sentence), other elements are needed, or at least expected, after some verbs or verb phrases. For example, we expect certain sorts of words to appear in the predicates of the following:

De Quincey *achieved*
De Quincey *was*.
He *helped*.
He *believed*.

What did De Quincey achieve? Who was he? What was he like? Whom did he help? Whom or what did he believe? Because these questions remain unanswered, our expectations are violated and we suspect error. Obviously, a more detailed analysis of the possible patterns of declarative sentences is needed, one that concentrates on the predicate.

To begin, see if you can discover some similarities between the predicates of the sentences grouped together in Exercise Two. These five groups demonstrate the five most common patterns of a simple declarative sentence.

Exercise Two: Sentence Patterns

In your own words, describe the pattern you see when you compare the four sentences in each of the five sentence groups. Pay attention to verbs and to other words in the predicate. How is the subject related to the part of the predicate that is not the verb? What questions are answered by the nouns and adjectives contained in the predicates of certain sentence patterns? Predicates are in bold type to assist you.

1)
Most mammals **communicate**.
Humans **speak**.
Whales **sing**.
Both humans and whales **gesture**.

2)
John Stuart Mill **suffered an acute mental crisis**.
Consequently, he **reconsidered his philosophy**.
The poetry of Wordsworth **influenced this new philosophy**.
It **encouraged Mill's interest in humanity**.

3)
Many Chinese labourers **gave Chinese companies bonds**.
These companies **promised indentured workers passage to North America**.
They **promised North American businesses cheap labour**.
They **sold railway contractors a virtually enslaved labour force**.

4)
Freud **considered every dream a piece of hard work**.
Dreams **made dangerous impulses and experiences harmless**.
Freud **labelled this job dream work**.
He **thought this dream work essential**.

5)
The company's solar heating system **is automatic**.
It **is efficient**.
The system **includes several components**.
These components **are piping, a storage tank, a water pump, a heat exchanger, and a solar collector**.

PATTERNS OF SIMPLE DECLARATIVE SENTENCES

Simple declarative sentences follow one of five basic patterns. One pattern, exemplified by the first group of sentences in Exercise Two, contains only a subject and a verb or verb phrase, as in the following sentences:

Pattern One:
Subject + Intransitive Verb.

He shoots. He scores.

When a verb is used in this pattern, it is called intransitive because it doesn't provide a passage or a transition from a subject (the performer of the action of the verb) to a direct object (the receiver of the action of the verb). Most verbs can be labelled intransitive or transitive depending upon the context in which they are used. Even a verb that seems to be clearly transitive, that seems to require a direct object, can be used intransitively. For example, *shoot* is described in the dictionary as a transitive verb because it usually requires a direct object; for clarity, the reader usually needs to be told what or who is being shot. As Canadians, we know that the shooter described by the preceding sentences is a hockey player shooting a puck. But what if he were an archer shooting an arrow, a gambler shooting craps, a soldier shooting an enemy? It is clear, then, that while *shoot* can be used intransitively (as in the preceding example), it is usually used transitively (as in the following examples).

Pattern Two:
Subject + Transitive Verb
+ Direct Object.

He shoots *groundhogs*.
He shoots *the puck*.
He shoots *the rapids*.
He shoots *pool*.

These sentences are written following another declarative sentence pattern, the pattern exemplified by the second group of sentences in Exercise Two. This pattern includes a subject, a transitive verb, and a direct object. Notice that the direct object tells who or what is being shot, who or what receives the action of the verb.

Sometimes another piece of information must be conveyed. We need to tell not only what is being shot but also to whom.

Pattern Three:
Subject + Transitive Verb
+ Indirect Object +
Direct Object.

He shoots *Gretzky* the puck.

In this example, *Gretzky* is the indirect object. Indirect objects, then, tell to whom or for whom the verb's action is being done. The third pattern of a simple declarative sentence, the pattern illustrated by the third group of sentences in

Exercise Two, includes a subject, a transitive verb, an indirect object, and a direct object. Here are more examples:

Marlow   told   his shipmates   a tale.
subject   *verb*   *indirect object*   *direct object*

My baby   wrote   me   a letter.
subject   *verb*   *indirect object*   *direct object*

Weygand and Petain painted the French Council of Ministers a bleak picture.
subject   *verb*   *indirect object*   *direct object*

Cyrano de Bergerac   wrote   Roxanne   a poem.
subject   *verb*   *indirect object*   *direct object*

A fourth pattern also uses a transitive verb. This sentence pattern, illustrated by the fourth group of sentences in Exercise Two, contains not only a direct object but also a word renaming or describing that object.

Brian Mulroney appointed Ray Hnatyshyn *governor-general*.
George Orwell found writing *difficult*.

Governor-general is a noun renaming the proper noun *Ray Hnatyshyn*, and *difficult* is an adjective describing the noun *writing*. Adjectives and nouns which rename or describe nouns in this fashion are called complements because they complete the meaning of these nouns. In the preceding examples, the complements complete the meanings of direct objects, so they are objective complements.

The last basic pattern of a declarative sentence, exemplified by the fifth group of sentences in Exercise Two, also includes a complement. This complement completes the subject, so is called a subject complement.

Reflectors are *mirrors*.
Whales are *mammals*.
The trial of the Templars remains *enigmatic*.
Shakespeare's fools seem *wise*.

Notice that the subject complement can be a noun (*mirrors* and *mammals*) or an adjective (*enigmatic* and *wise*). In either case, the verb performs the same function; it links the subject to the subject complement. Because it performs this function, it is called a linking verb or a copula. Linking verbs frequently set up an equivalence between the subject and the subject complement: *Newfoundland was the last province to join Canada* or *Newfoundland = the last province to join Canada*. For this reason, *to be* in its various forms (*is, are, was, were, etc.*) is the most common linking verb. Other verbs, however, frequently act as linking verbs (*to appear, to seem, to become, to remain, to taste, to feel*). Be warned that some verbs can be used as linking verbs or as transitive verbs depending on the writer's purpose. For example, a person may feel a cat's fur or feel sick. If someone or something is engaged in the action of touching or feeling an object, the verb used to describe this action is transitive.

The doctor   felt   her arm.
subject   *transitive verb*   *direct object*

Pattern Four:
Subject + Transitive Verb + Direct Object + Objective Complement.

Pattern Five:
Subject + Linking Verb + Subject Complement.

Writing Prompt

Write a series of simple declarative sentences describing a person, an object, a place, an idea, an event, or a circumstance. Try to use all five of the declarative sentence patterns we have identified.

If someone or something is not actively touching an object but is experiencing a feeling (experiencing a state of being), the verb used is a linking verb.

She   felt   ill.
subject   *linking verb*   *subject*
                              complement

Expanding the Meaning of the Simple Declarative Sentence

The sentences used to illustrate the five patterns of a simple declarative sentence probably seem to express ideas in a bare and unlovely way. They appear to be naked because, for the most part, they are composed of only the sentence elements essential to the sentence patterns they exemplify. They are correct, but plain. They resemble a stripped-down but functional Chevy rather than a Lincoln Continental with power steering, swivel seats, and all the other extras. In this regard, they are unusual; most of the sentences we construct contain many more words of description.

As well as seeming unclad, most of these sentences communicate only one or two propositions. In other words, each generally makes only one or two statements affirming or denying something so that this something can be characterized as being true or false. Let's investigate this idea further by examining how many propositions are made by five of these sentences, each of the five illustrating one of the five patterns of a simple declarative sentence.

Sentence	Propositions
He scores.	There is one proposition: he scores.
He shoots groundhogs.	There is one proposition: he shoots groundhogs.
Cyrano de Bergerac wrote Roxanne a poem.	There are two propositions: Cyrano de Bergerac wrote a poem; the poem was to Roxanne.
Brian Mulroney appointed Ray Hnatyshyn governor-general.	There are two propositions: Brian Mulroney appointed Ray Hnatyshyn; the appointment was to the position of governor-general.
Reflectors are mirrors.	There is one proposition: reflectors are mirrors.

As you can see, three of these simple declarative sentences express one proposition only. You might think that a simple declarative sentence <u>can</u> express only one or two propositions, that this is why we call such sentences simple. You would be wrong. Grammatically, a simple declarative sentence contains only one subject and one predicate, but, through the addition of words describing or modifying the words essential to this subject and predicate, the number of propositions expressed by a simple sentence can be increased; the meaning conveyed by a simple sentence can be expanded.

Look at this process in action. As we have seen, the following sentence contains one proposition:

He shoots groundhogs.

With the addition of modifying words and phrases, the number of propositions expressed by a sentence that has the preceding sentence at its core can be increased dramatically:

In the hot, muggy afternoons of August, he regretfully shoots cute but pesky groundhogs persistently destroying farmers' fields.

Propositions

1) He shoots groundhogs.
2) He regrets the shooting.
3) The shooting is in the afternoons.
4) The afternoons are hot.
5) The afternoons are muggy.
6) The afternoons are in August.
7) The groundhogs are cute.
8) The groundhogs are pesky.
9) The groundhogs are destroying fields.
10) The destruction is persistent.
11) The fields belong to farmers.

Modifiers, then, are not simply frills; they expand the meaning conveyed by a sentence.

MODIFIERS

So what are modifiers, you ask. They are words or groups of words that describe or limit other words. Modifiers come in three varieties; they are either adjectival, adverbial, or absolute. Don't let these distinctions worry you. Just remember that **adjectival modifiers** hang around and describe any word, phrase, or clause functioning as a noun. In terms of the basic sentence patterns previously examined, adjectival modifiers can modify subjects, objects, or complements which are nouns.

Adverbial modifiers are used to describe all words, phrases, and clauses not functioning as nouns. In other words, they describe words, phrases, and clauses functioning as verbs, adjectives, and adverbs. They can also modify independent clauses, which can stand as complete sentences. Of course, they modify the verb in the basic sentence patterns we have studied, but they can also modify the complement when that complement is an adjective.

Absolute modifiers are not grammatically connected to any single part of the basic sentence; compared with other modifiers, they are relatively independent, hence absolute. They modify absolutely all the sentence.

Let's look at some of these modifiers.

Nouns as Adjectives

Sometimes, nouns may be used as adjectives. In other words, nouns can modify other nouns.

As *space* travel becomes common, *moon* bases may be established.

Women, men, and *children* colonists might even inhabit *space* stations in distant galaxies one day.

The overuse of modifying nouns, however, makes a sentence confusing. Look at the number of nouns in the following:

Social service employees' *opposition* to proposed *federal government health* and *welfare family allowance payment reductions* is widely known.

Here, the string of nouns beginning with *federal* and broken only by *and* is very difficult to understand. The reader keeps thinking he or she has come to the main noun, only to be disappointed. The intended meaning of the sentence is also hard to determine because a reader cannot quickly put the two main nouns (*opposition* and *reductions*) together.

Adjectives and Adverbs

When modifiers are single words, they are called simply adjectives and adverbs. **Adjectives** modify nouns and pronouns; **adverbs** modify verbs, adjectives, other adverbs, and whole clauses or sentences.

There are two sorts of adjectives: non-descriptive and descriptive. A non-descriptive adjective frequently limits or makes more exact the meaning of the noun or pronoun it modifies. Also, a non-descriptive adjective is often capable of functioning as another part of speech, as a pronoun, for example. These adjectives include the following sorts of words:

Articles (*an* opiate; *a* book; *the* ducks; *the* planet)

Demonstrative, Interrogative, and Relative Pronouns (*That* opiate is dangerous; *Which* book did you enjoy?; *These* ducks eat vociferously; *Whose* planet is this?)

Indefinite and Numerical Pronouns (*Any* opiate is dangerous; *Another* book would be more appropriate; *Two* ducks were tame; Earth is the *third* planet from the sun.)

The Possessive Forms of Pronouns and Nouns (Consumerism is the *people's* opiate; I borrowed *George's* book; *His* ducks won prizes; *Our* planet is threatened by pollution.)

Most of you are probably more familiar with descriptive as opposed to non-descriptive adjectives. Descriptive adjectives describe. They inform readers about the colour, shape, size, look, nature, or quality of the noun or pronoun they modify: a *dangerous* opiate, the *white* ducks, a *good* book, the *endangered* planet.

Adverbs, the other single-word modifiers, describe, limit, or make more exact the meaning of the sentence elements they modify. As stated, adverbs modify verbs, adjectives, other adverbs, and whole clauses.

Adverbs Modifying Verbs (The opiate worked *slowly*; The ducks flew *away*; Your book came *yesterday*; The planet glowed *brightly*.)

Adverbs Modifying Adjectives (the *dangerously* effective opiate; the *grossly* overfed duck; the *exceptionally* important book; the *barely* perceptible planet)

Adverbs Modifying Adverbs (The opiate worked *too* slowly; The ducks flew *very* swiftly; He wrote the book *rather* sloppily; The planet was *quite* thoroughly researched.)

Adverbs Modifying Clauses (*Fortunately*, the opiate did not induce a coma; *Usually*, ducks fly south; The book sold poorly *meanwhile*; *Obviously*, life on our planet is in peril.)

Notice that adverbs answer the questions *how, when*, or *to what extent*. Following are some examples of how students have used adjectives and adverbs to expand the meaning of their sentences.

Adjectives

The *intelligent* manager forestalls *managerial* problems. (*Intelligent* modifies the noun *manager* and *managerial* modifies the noun *problems*.)

Insightful and *sensitive*, she recognizes *unhappy* workers. (*Insightful* and *sensitive* are two adjectives joined with a conjunction and modifying the pronoun *she*. *Unhappy* modifies the noun *workers*.)

Adverbs

Unfortunately, insects *gradually* become *substantially* immune to many pesticides. (*Gradually* modifies the verb *become, substantially* modifies the adjective *immune*, and *unfortunately* modifies the independent clause that follows it.)

The transformation of myths over time is *sluggishly* slow but *very* perceptible.(*Sluggishly* modifies the adjective *slow* and *very* modifies the adjective *perceptible*.)

Most adjectives and adverbs have three forms or degrees: the positive form, the comparative form, and the superlative form.

The Positive Form

The *new* treaty was *effective*. (adjectives)
The *recently* negotiated treaty was *carefully* worded. (adverbs)

The Comparative Form

The *newer* of the two treaties was *more effective*. (adjectives)
The *more recently* negotiated treaty was *less carefully* worded. (adverbs)

The Superlative Form

The *newest* of the three treaties was the *most effective*. (adjectives)
The *most recently* negotiated treaty was the *least carefully* worded of the three. (adverbs)

Here are two sentences that use the three forms of adjectives and adverbs correctly. It is probably more difficult to use the comparative and superlative forms properly because these forms require some sort of comparison.

Adjectives

While the United States has a *large* reflector at Kitt Peak and a *larger* one at Palomar Mountain, the *largest* reflector in the world is at the Special Astrophysical Observatory in the Soviet Union.

Adverbs

In Canada, Polysar Energy stock was *actively* traded in 1988 while Inco Ltd. was *more actively* traded, and Nova Corporation stock was *most actively* traded in that year.

Modifying Phrases

A phrase, or a group of words that does not contain a subject and a predicate but that forms a grammatical unit, can also function as a modifier. There are four sorts of phrases: prepositional phrases, verbal phrases, absolute phrases, and appositives. We will examine each in turn.

PREPOSITIONAL PHRASES

A prepositional phrase begins with a preposition. This preposition connects a noun, a pronoun, or a group of words functioning as a noun to another word or word group. Because prepositional phrases can be connected to nouns, verbs, adjectives, or adverbs, they function as either adjectival or adverbial modifiers. Accordingly, they appear with great frequency in prose. As you can see from the list of the most common prepositions, prepositional phrases are useful for indicating time, place, manner, cause, and condition, as well as a host of other concepts.

about	before	during	off	under
above	behind	except	on	until
across	below	for	onto	up
after	beneath	from	out	upon
against	beside	in	over	with
along	between	inside	past	within
among	beyond	into	since	without
around	by	like	through	
as	despite	near	to	
at	down	of	toward	

Note that although the words in this list are prepositions, they are not exclusively prepositions. In other words, many of these words perform other functions as well. For example, *since* can be an adverb (*I started work yesterday and have been tired ever since*) or a conjunction (*He has been depressed since he retired*).

Adjectival Prepositional Phrases	Adverbial Prepositional Phrases
Hollywood's portrayal *of America at war* emphasizes America's victories *on the land, on the sea,* and *in the air*.	Some film makers manipulate their audience's understanding *by distorting the presentation of a filmed object*.
Film versions *of the First World War* are no exception.	*In 1984*, the Conservatives won the federal election *with 211 seats*.
One always expects to encounter Gary Cooper, *with a rifle in his hand, a kind expression on his face, and a gaggle of German prisoners in tow*.	

VERBALS AND VERBAL PHRASES

Just as a verb is not the same as a verbal, a verb phrase is very different from a verbal phrase. Unlike verbs and verb phrases, verbals and verbal phrases function as nouns or modifiers. We are concerned here with verbals and verbal phrases functioning as adjectival or adverbial modifiers. A verbal phrase consists of a verbal and its modifiers. The verbal modifier will be in one of three forms: the infinitive (*to help*), the present participle (*helping*), or the past participle (*helped*).

Infinitives and Infinitive Phrases

The infinitive is usually made up of the plain form of a verb, the form listed in dictionaries, and a preliminary *to*: *to sleep, to dream, to be*. Infinitives can form phrases: *to sleep soundly, to dream your life away, to be a famous poet*. Both infinitives and infinitive phrases can be either adjectival or adverbial modifiers. While infinitive phrases look similar to prepositional phrases beginning with *to*, they can be distinguished from such phrases by the fact that the *to* which starts an infinitive phrase is followed by a verb in its simple form.

Ride a cock-horse *to Banbury Cross*, (prepositional phrase)

To see a fine lady upon a white horse. (infinitive phrase)

Here are some examples of ways in which infinitives and infinitive phrases can be used as modifiers to expand the basic sentence.

Adjectival Modifiers	Adverbial Modifiers
Stalin's war against the Orthodox Church was a portent of a more sinister persecution *to be initiated by the Kremlin.*	The problem of Canadian unity is too important *to disregard.*
An agreement *to ban production of chlorofluorocarbons by the year 2000* was reached in March 1989.	Businesses advertise *to convince people of the value of their services and products.*

Participles and Participial Phrases

Participles are either in their present form, their past form, or their perfect form. **Present participles** are constructed by adding *-ing* to the simple form of a verb: *sleeping, dreaming, being*. Present participles act as adjectival modifiers.

Memorable sentences are memorable on account of some single *irradiating* word. – Alexander Smith

Past participles are usually formed by adding *-ed* or *-d* to the simple form of a verb: *influenced, shovelled, watched*. Some verbs, however, have an irregular past participle: *slept, dreamt, been, fallen, sung, stood.* Past participles also act as adjectival modifiers.

There is a weird power in a *spoken* word. — Joseph Conrad

While we are not really concerned with the **perfect participle** here, it is probably handy to know that these participles are formed with *having* and a past participle. They are called perfect participles because they describe a completed action.

Having lost in love, he turned to war.

As is obvious from the preceding example, participles can begin phrases. Participial phrases can function as nouns or as adjectival modifiers. We are concerned with the latter here. Notice how the following sentences have been expanded through the use of participles and participial phrases.

Reflecting Sir Arthur Conan Doyle's interest in both science and spiritualism, the series of stories *featuring Sherlock Holmes* shows that this detective is a logical yet creative man *working to find the human agents of crimes that appear to have been perpetrated by spirits*. (present participial phrases acting as adjectival modifiers)

Currently, mystery stories *dealing with what attracts people to criminals* are the rage. (present participial phrase acting as adjectival modifier)

Mesmerizing murderers, *tantalizing* thieves, and *charming* con artists inhabit today's mysteries. (present participles acting as adjectival modifiers)

Compared to Japan and America, Canada is not a technologically *advanced* society. (past participial phrase and past participle acting as adjectival modifiers)

Convinced of this fact, David Suzuki argues that Canadians maintain the illusion of living in an *industrialized, developed* country by exploiting Canada's abundant natural resources. (past participial phrase and two past participles acting as adjectival modifiers)

ABSOLUTE PHRASES

Verbals can be used to expand upon basic sentences in another way as well. Participles and infinitives appear in absolute phrases. These phrases are called absolute because they do not modify any one element in a sentence. By definition, then, absolute phrases are neither adjectival nor adverbial modifiers.

Speaking of inventions, basketball was the brain-child of Canadian James Naismith. (present participle)

To be fair, Naismith was working in Massachusetts at the time. (infinitive)

Some absolute phrases are very close to being complete sentences: they have their own subjects, but, although they may have verbals, they lack verbs. Because the following absolute phrases do have their own subjects, they allow for a shift in focus. This sort of absolute phrase is very useful in sentence expansion and combination.

The New World barn was an adaptation of the Old World barn, *its structure reflecting a break with tradition by no longer providing accommodation for the farmer and his family*.

A nineteenth-century memsahib arrived in India with huge quantities of baggage, *her corset tightly laced, her crinoline and bustle secured, and one of her 36 pocket handkerchiefs waving*.

APPOSITIVES

Appositives usually rename words or word groups functioning as nouns. While appositives are like adjectives in that they describe or modify nouns, they are unlike adjectives in that they can substitute for the nouns they relate to. Appositives are themselves nouns or word groups functioning as nouns. An appositive, then, is an economical way of redefining an already expressed noun.

Female silkworms release a sex attractant molecule, *a scent that male silkworms detect with their antennae*.

Beetles, *insects of the order Coleoptera*, also receive sexual stimulation through their olfactory system.

Appositives are frequently introduced by words and phrases such as *that is, in other words, for example, including, particularly, notably,* and *namely*.

During the 1930s, there was an economic depression, ***that is,*** *a period marked by slackening business activity, widespread unemployment, and falling wages and prices*.

A vault of even curvature built on a circular base, ***in other words*** *a dome*, can be segmental, semicircular, pointed, or bulbous.

Note that an appositive is separated from the noun it relates to by a comma and that, when an appositive is preceded and followed by words, it is set off from the sentence by a closing as well as an initial comma.

Writing Prompt

Write three to five simple sentences about four of the following topics. If none of the following topics appeals to you, choose four of your own. Then, combine the sentences about the same topic without using words like *and, but, because,* or *although*. Instead of these sorts of linking words, try to use the techniques we have already examined, which build simple sentences using modifiers. An example follows the list of topics.

an apple	jewels	saffron
a book	karate	a tent
a clock	lemons	university
doughnuts	money	a vegetable
eggs	napalm	wisdom
a flower	an orange	x-rays
gloves	a park	yo-yos
a hat	quilts	zippers
an insect	rent	a mug

Example:

1) **The mug is white and blue.**
2) **It is old.**
3) **It is ceramic.**
4) **It is stained from overuse.**
5) **It needs washing.**

The old, white and blue ceramic mug, stained from overuse, needs washing.

NOTE: A quick look in any dictionary will tell you that most words can be categorized as belonging to more than one "part of speech." For example, the word *one* can be described as an adjective, a noun, or a pronoun; the word *moderate* can be called an adjective, a noun, or a verb; and the word *only* can be categorized as an adverb, an adjective, or a conjunction.

Writing is the *one* activity I enjoy. (adjective)
One is the lowest whole number. (noun)
One should never give up. (pronoun)

Many Canadians have *moderate* incomes. (adjective)
A *moderate* does not hold extreme views. (noun)
Conciliators *moderate* conflicts. (verb)

It *only* made matters worse. (adverb)
Are you an *only* child? (adjective)
I would have gone, *only* it rained. (conjunction)

Parts of Speech

NOUNS name. They name **people** (*Anne Murray, woman*), **places** (*Halifax, school*), **things** (*meat, words*), **qualities** (*anger, intelligence*), **actions** (*to march, speaking*), and **ideas** (*justice, reality*).

PRONOUNS function like nouns (I like *these*) or they signal that nouns will follow (I like *these* dogs). Unlike a noun, a pronoun does not name a specific person, place, thing, quality, action, or idea. It does, however, stand in for or point to one. There are **personal pronouns** (*I, me, my, mine, etc.*), **relative pronouns** (*which, that, who, whom, whose, etc.*), **interrogative pronouns** (*what, which, who, whose, etc.*), **reflexive and intensive pronouns** (*myself, yourself, etc.*), **demonstrative pronouns** (*this, these, etc.*), **indefinite pronouns** (*all, few, none, such, etc.*), **reciprocal pronouns** (*each other, one another*), and **numerical pronouns** (*one, first; two, second*). See pages 73-82 for more information about pronouns.

VERBS express **action** (*speak, run*), **occurrence**, (*happened, fell*), **state of being** (*is, feel*), and **process** (*grew, become*). All verbs tell or ask something about a noun or a noun equivalent, called the subject of the verb. While a noun can name an action, occurrence, state of being, or process (*To walk* is *to become fit*; *Swimming* is *relaxing*), a verb shows the action being done, the occurrence being experienced, etc. by a specific subject and taking place in a particular time (I *walk*; Brent *was walking* when the accident *happened*; They *had rested* for an hour by the time we *arrived*; It will have *rested* unopened for forty years).

ADJECTIVES modify nouns or noun equivalents. They can be **descriptive** (*graceful* dancing, *raucous* laughter, it is *attractive*) or **non-descriptive** (*second* place, *this* one, *one* idea). **Non-descriptive adjectives** are sometimes called **limiting adjectives** because they seem to limit rather than to describe the quality of the words they modify.

ADVERBS modify verbs, adjectives, other adverbs, or whole clauses. They frequently answer the questions **how?** (He danced *gracefully*; She laughed *attractively*), **when?**, (Fred had an accident *recently*; Reports are issued *occasionally*), or **to what extent?** (We were *quite* upset; They were *very* late). A **conjunctive adverb** modifies a whole clause and expresses the logical connection (**conjunction**) between that clause and a preceding one (Stockholders, *therefore*, are not regularly informed; *However*, they do not seem to mind; *Consequently*, the practice continues).

PREPOSITIONS relate a noun or noun equivalent to another word, and they often refer to location or time (the dancer *on* stage, the raucous laughter *without* joy, singing *at* Christmas, tired *from* walking, everyone *under* the table).

CONJUNCTIONS join words and groups of words together. There are seven **coordinate conjunctions**: *and, but, or, nor, for, so, yet*. There are **correlative conjunctions**: *both...and, not only...but also, neither...nor, etc.* There are **subordinate conjunctions**: *although, because, if, while, etc.* There are **comparative conjunctions**: *as...as, so...that, such...that, etc.* Conjunctions express particular logical relationships. They can indicate an added idea (kind *and* generous), a cause (He fought *because* he was cornered), an alternative (*either* injustice *or* anarchy), a contrast (*Although* the crops received sufficient rain, they died), and many other links.

ARTICLES signal that a noun will follow. There are three articles: *a, an, the* (*the* sunny day, *an* opportune moment, *a* tree).

Coordination and Subordination

So far, we have talked about simple sentences, sentences consisting of one clause. Although it is true that a simple sentence can communicate many propositions, it is also true that at its core is a single statement. The very act of punctuating a group of words as a sentence indicates that you want the reader to see these words as a whole and distinct idea, as an independent thought. Sometimes, however, one clause, one central statement, is not sufficient to express this completeness; rather, the thought itself depends upon specifying the exact relation between two or more clauses, between two or more statements. Because essays necessitate persuasion, interpretation, explanation, and analysis, sentences that show how two or more statements relate are useful. Consequently, many academic sentences have more than one clause, and you need to know about these as well. But I hear you murmuring, "I can't remember what a clause is." A clause is a cluster of words related to and containing a subject and a predicate. "But this sounds like one of the definitions of a sentence," you say. Well, it is. And for now, we can discuss the joining of two or more clauses as the linking of two or more sentences through coordination and subordination.

Coordination makes use of the seven coordinating conjunctions (*and, but, for, nor, or, so, yet*) or of a semicolon to join independent clauses into compound sentences.

Compound Sentence

The joke was funny,	and	it was on me.
independent clause,	*coordinating*	*independent clause.*
(*ic*)	*conjunction* (*cc*)	(*ic*)

Subordination makes use of subordinators (relative pronouns like *who, which, that* or subordinating conjunctions like *after, because, since*) to join dependent clauses to an independent clause, that is, to a clause not preceded by a subordinator. Complex sentences are formed when subordination is used.

Complex Sentence

	subordinator (*s*)	
The joke was funny	although	it was on me.
independent clause (*ic*)	*dependent clause (dc)*	

Of course, coordination and subordination can be used together in the same sentence. A sentence that links clauses through both subordination and coordination is called a compound-complex sentence.

Compound-Complex Sentence

	s		*cc*	
The joke was funny	although it was on me,	but	I could laugh at it.
ic	*dc*		*ic*	

Let's investigate the uses and abuses of coordination and subordination more fully.

COORDINATION

Coordination brings related but separate ideas together in coordinate or compound sentences. As mentioned, these sentences consist of two independent clauses (also known as sentences) joined by one of the seven coordinating conjunctions (*and, but, for, nor, or, so, yet*) or by a semicolon.

Coordination is simply a way to show ideas that are equal in importance, *but* subordination indicates what's powerful and what isn't. — Betty Jean Goodwin

Art is limitation; the essence of every picture is the frame.
    — G.K. Chesterton

Notice that in the first example a comma and a coordinating conjunction join the two independent clauses, which could have been written as two complete and separate sentences. In the second example, a semicolon links independent clauses. In both examples, coordination creates meaning. Coordination allows Goodwin to make a comparison. If she had created two sentences, one defining coordination and the other describing subordination, the difference between the two would have been difficult to see. Chesterton, by combining the expression of a general principle with a statement that makes that principle concrete, adds to the meaning of both.

Coordination, then, is a balancing act. When you write a compound sentence, you balance at least two ideas. You say, "Here is a thought, and here is another." Or you say, "This idea looks good, yet so does this opposite one." Compound sentences are well-balanced and well-coordinated; they don't suggest a fixation, an obsession, nor do they fall off the balance beam because their right sides are weightier than their left. They make you think of a marriage of equals, even if those equals disagree and are in danger of divorce. The well-coordinated sentences of this old lyric, for example, are meant to emphasize a disagreement:

You say po-tay-to, *and* I say po-taht-o
You say to-may-to, *and* I say to-maht-o
Po-tay-to, po-taht-o
To-may-to, to-maht-o
Let's call the whole thing off.[5]

Because compound sentences link equally important ideas, they are useful in describing the unfolding of events, in telling stories. Coordination allows storytellers to write "This happened, and then this happened." We don't have to determine which happening was more significant or which event was a consequence of the other when we write compound sentences; we don't have to write "Because this happened, this happened." Therefore, coordination is useful when we want to show the connection of ideas without making explicit

---

[5] George Gershwin, *The Greatest Songs of George Gershwin* (New York: Chappell, 1979) 71-72.

what that connection implies. The following clauses have been linked in coordinate structures to suggest rather than to state outright that spring has arrived:

> The flowers appear on the earth; the time of the singing of birds is come, *and* the voice of the turtle is heard in our land.

This passage, taken from the King James Version of the Bible, is representative of the predominance of coordination over subordination in that text. Much of the Bible's emotive power comes from making striking symbols and circumstances coordinate, from issuing an array of imagery and experiences through coordination: the almond tree shall flourish, *and* the grasshopper shall be a burden, *and* desire shall fail. This technique can be used in academic writing, especially when describing something.

> Maslow confronts us with paradoxes. He started out as a behaviourist, a skilled experimenter, *and* then went on to demonstrate the crippling limitations of just that kind of psychology in the study of human affairs. He coauthored a textbook on abnormal psychology, a classic in its field, *and* then went on to investigate, not the pathological, but the exceptionally healthy person.[6]

Notice that while coordination is used here to juxtapose Maslow's opposite tendencies, the author doesn't let these coordinate structures speak for themselves. The reader is told the point of this juxtaposition of opposites: Maslow's life as paradox. It is wise to mix this kind of direct explanation, this kind of telling, with the technique of coordination, which shows or demonstrates.

Coordination, because it relates ideas of equal importance, is much more democratic than subordination. Sometimes, by linking two ideas usually considered unequal with a coordinating conjunction, an author jolts us into examining our own or society's priorities. Leonard Cohen achieves this effect in one of his songs: *everybody's got that sinking feeling, like their father or their dog just died.*[7] Fathers and dogs get equal treatment here.

Equality can also mean a levelling, and coordination is a great leveller. In coordinate structures there are no peaks and valleys but only a plain. Therefore, coordination can be used to achieve a monotonous and flat and dead feeling in prose, as it is used by Carl Sandburg to describe reactions to Abraham Lincoln's assassination:

> Men tried to talk about it *and* the words failed *and* they came back to silence.
> To say nothing was best.
> Lincoln was dead.
> Was there anything more to say?

[6] George Leonard, "Abraham Maslow and the New Self," *Fifty Who Made the Difference*, ed. Lee Eisenberg (New York: Villard, 1984) 253.

[7] Leonard Cohen, "Everybody Knows," *I'm Your Man*, Columbia Records, 1988.

Yes, they would go through the motions of grief *and* they would take their part in a national funeral and a ceremony of humiliation and abasement and tears.

But words were no help.

Lincoln was dead.[8]

Sandburg has even left out the commas commonly required after an independent clause linked to another by a coordinating conjunction. If present, they would have lessened the poem's impact by causing a reader to pause between expressions of public despair. Far better just to add and add to the picture of people's grief, without relief.

While coordination can be used effectively, as the preceding examples show, it can also be misused. Excessive coordination and illogical coordination should usually be avoided.

Excessive Coordination

Prose that is littered with coordinating conjunctions tends to appear simple, childlike, and undiscriminating. The writer, like a very young child, seems to be incapable of sorting out the significance of various statements. Ideas are simply catalogued, listed without regard to their import. Think of the stories children tell, and you will understand how you can unintentionally damage your credibility by overusing coordination:

It is Friday, *and* I went to my grandmother's house, *and* she gave me cake and ice cream, *but* I didn't eat too much, *and* it is her birthday, *and* she is eighty-five years old.

While academic writers sometimes want to display a sense of wonder and curiosity by writing fresh, unaffected prose, they rarely want to seem like a naive, unschooled child. Also, because the purpose of essays involves analysis, explanation, persuasion, and interpretation, the essay writer usually has to do more than list things and leave it to the reader to work out the meaning of this list. At the very least, lists in essays should be organized:

This Friday was my grandmother's eighty-fifth birthday, so I went to her house for cake and ice cream. I didn't eat too much though.

While it may still be difficult for the reader to discern which of the ideas here are most important, it is easier to determine the sequence of events.

Excessive coordination, then, makes not only unsophisticated prose, but also jumbled, thoughtless writing. It creates a kind of prattle, a childish babble in which the writer appears to jabber on about anything and everything that comes

---

[8] Carl Sandburg, *Abraham Lincoln: The War Years*, 4 vols. (New York: Harcourt, Brace, 1939) 4:350.

to mind. Readers find prattle annoying, and they should. Prattle doesn't consider readers' needs; writers of prattle either can't or won't sort out their initial impressions and thoughts in order to present them appropriately. Frequently, excessive coordination leads to illogical coordination, to unrelated or unequal ideas being related through coordination.

Illogical Coordination

Unrelated facts and concepts should not be made to appear related by being expressed in a single compound sentence, unless the writer is trying to achieve some special effect. Illogical coordination occurs when the statements expressed in each of the joined independent clauses are correct but not closely enough related.

> Iceberg lettuce is shipped by train, and Pullman made a great contribution to train travel.

Sometimes, illogical coordination results because a writer mistakenly uses a coordinating rather than a subordinating conjunction. (Consult the section on subordination for a list of subordinating conjunctions.) Logically, when one idea is dependent upon another, a subordinating conjunction more adequately reflects this dependence. Make sure that the relationship you set up between clauses is valid.

> Illogical Relationship: Iceberg lettuce can be shipped by train, and refrigerated freight cars have revolutionized salad-eating patterns.

> Revised: Salad-eating patterns have been revolutionized because iceberg lettuce can now be shipped by train in refrigerated freight cars.

Revising Excessive and Illogical Coordination

Sample Paragraph:

1. The buffalo and the buffalo hunt were important to the Plains Indians. **2.** Buffalo meat was used for food, and buffalo hide was used for clothing, and buffalo dung was used for fire, and the bones of buffaloes were made into tools. **3.** All of a buffalo was used after it was killed, and there was not much food or material resources on the Plains, so after a buffalo was killed, it was thanked for giving its life. **4.** The buffalo hunt was important as well. **5.** It gave order to the political life of the Plains Indians, and it produced a yearly political cycle. **6.** One Indian organization involved with the hunt was the Warriors Society. **7.** The most worthy young men sat on the Warriors Society, and it organized the hunt and guarded the camp during the hunt. **8.** The Warriors Society also had a chief, and it was his duty to maintain camp discipline, but there was also a tribal chief who was a peacemaker and an orator.

Exercise One:

Courtesy was a necessary attribute in King Arthur's Court, and King Arthur developed the Knights of the Round Table knowing that the people of his kingdom were important assets. These knights were to protect the people, and in no way were they to make the people uncomfortable, so all the knights were to be courteous. The only reason the knights existed was to protect and keep the people of the kingdom secure, so, obviously, knights had to be courteous. Courtesy worked both ways: the knights were expected to be courteous to the people, and the people were expected to be courteous to the knights in return. We especially see this courtesy in the relationship between Sir Gawain and the people, for the people respected Sir Gawain and Sir Gawain was very considerate and caring of the people.

Exercise Two:

The cost of preventative medicine is low, and there is no need for technological research. Many of the methods have been in practice since the beginning of civilization, and thus they have already had many years of testing and have proven to be effective, so there is no money needed for testing procedures. These methods do not rely on the technology and equipment usually found in a hospital located in an urban centre, and thus are more accessible to a greater portion of the public. Preventative medicine can easily become a part of everyone's life, for it is so accessible and costs little. If this were to happen, less money would have to be put into curative medicine, and fewer people would get sick.

Revising Excessive and Illogical Coordination: Sample Paragraph Discussion

This passage demonstrates the jumbled thinking that often accompanies excessive and illogical coordination. Sorting out the passage is a difficult task requiring more than merely breaking up or rearranging coordinate clauses. Sometimes turning a coordinate clause into a phrase or into a subordinate clause clarifies meaning. Sometimes words or phrases that signal the relation between sentences are needed (e.g., *however, also, in this case,* or *consequently*). Let's work through this passage identifying coordinate clauses and deciding whether there are too many of them and whether the coordinating conjunctions used are logical. To refresh your memory, the coordinating conjunctions are *and, but, or, nor, for, so,* and *yet.*

Although Sentence One contains the coordinating conjunction *and*, it does not contain a coordinate clause. In this instance, the *and* forms a compound subject.

The first time we see a string of coordinate clauses is in Sentence Two. Here, the *ands* stop the reader from seeing this sentence for what it is: a list of the ways in which the Plains Indians used the buffalo. Keeping the commas and getting rid of all but the last coordinating conjunction puts this list in list form (item, item, item, and item).

> Buffalo meat was used for food, buffalo hide was used for clothing, buffalo dung was used for fire, and the bones of buffaloes were made into tools.

Even this revision can be improved upon. Notice how many times *was used for* appears. It is possible to take these words out of the second and third clause because the reader will "borrow" them from the first. When we do eliminate these words, we create elliptical clauses.

> Buffalo meat was used for food, buffalo hide for clothing, buffalo dung for fire, and the bones of buffaloes were made into tools.

Sentence Three is a mess. It is a compound-complex sentence, which means that it contains at least one coordinate clause and at least one subordinate clause. We will disregard the subordinate clauses, which both begin with *after* (if you are really curious about them, skip to the next section). We will concentrate instead on how the three main parts of this sentence are linked together using coordinating conjunctions. The first main part tells us that all of a buffalo was used after it was killed, the second that there was not much food or material resources on the Plains, and the third that a buffalo was thanked for giving its life. While all of these ideas seem related, their relationship is not adequately expressed by the coordinating conjunctions used, by the *and* and the *so*. It is likely that the Plains Indians used all of a slain buffalo *because* there was not much food or material resources on the Plains. They probably thanked the buffalo for giving its life for the same reason. A more logical combination of clauses follows:

> Because there was not much food or material resources on the Plains, the Plains Indians used all of a buffalo after it was killed and thanked it for giving its life.

The next coordinating conjunction (*and*) appears in Sentence Five. We can eliminate the comma and the second coordinate clause by eliminating the subject of the second clause, the pronoun *it*. What we are really doing here is forming a compound predicate, an easy thing to do because the subject of the second clause is the same as the subject of the first.

> It gave order to the political life of the Plains Indians and produced a yearly political cycle.

Although the coordination in Sentence Seven is neither excessive nor illogical, the sentence sounds choppy and immature because the writer has unnecessarily repeated the concept expressed by the words *the Warriors Society* by using the pronoun *it*. Doing this is unnecessary if a writer knows how to use relative pronouns. To make the sentence flow better and to demonstrate syntactic sophistication, the writer could replace *and it* with the relative pronoun *which*.

> The most worthy young men sat on the Warriors Society, which organized the hunt and guarded the camp during the hunt.

Sentence Eight can also be revised using a relative pronoun. In this case, we would use the relative pronoun *whose* or *who*. Additionally, changing the *but* to an *although* subordinates the clause containing information not essential to this writer's argument.

> The Warriors Society also had a chief whose duty was to maintain camp discipline, although there was also a tribal chief who was a peacemaker and an orator.

> The Warriors Society also had a chief who maintained camp discipline, although there was also a tribal chief who was a peacemaker and an orator.

The revised paragraph looks like this:

> The buffalo and the buffalo hunt were important to the Plains Indians. Buffalo meat was used for food, buffalo hide for clothing, buffalo dung for fire, and the bones of buffaloes were made into tools. Because there was not much food or material resources on the Plains, the Plains Indians used all of a buffalo after it was killed and thanked it for giving its life. The buffalo hunt was important as well. It gave order to the political life of the Plains Indians and produced a yearly political cycle. One Indian organization involved with the hunt was the Warriors Society. The most worthy young men sat on the Warriors Society, which organized the hunt and guarded the camp during the hunt. The Warriors Society also had a chief who maintained camp discipline, although there was also a tribal chief who was a peacemaker and an orator.

As a paragraph, this revision is far from perfect. The ideas are not sufficiently developed and too many of them have been crammed together, which just goes to show that one revision usually necessitates another. See the chapter on paragraphs for ways in which to revise faulty paragraphs.

Work through the remaining two paragraphs in a similar way, looking for and revising excessive and illogical coordination.

SUBORDINATION

Subordination brings related but separate ideas together in what are known as complex sentences. These sentences consist of at least two clauses: one independent clause and one dependent clause. The dependent clause is said to be subordinate to the independent clause because it cannot stand alone as a complete sentence; it depends on the independent clause to complete its meaning. Unlike coordination, therefore, subordination does not set up an equivalence. There are two types of subordinate clauses: ones that begin with relative pronouns and ones that begin with subordinating conjunctions. We will examine each in turn.

Subordinate Clauses Beginning with Relative Pronouns

Subordinate clauses starting with relative pronouns are a type of adjective clause known as a relative clause. They are adjective clauses because they perform a function similar to that of an adjectival modifier: they expand the meaning of a noun or a noun equivalent. They are called relative clauses because they relate information to a noun or noun equivalent using a relative pronoun. The most frequently used relative pronouns are *who, which,* and *that. Who* is used to relate information to persons or to animals thought of as persons. *Which* connects information to things, and *that* can link information to either persons or things. (To discover which relative pronoun to use in a particular circumstance, consult the glossary.) Here are some examples of relative clauses:

Louis Riel, *who led the Métis in the North West rebellions of 1870 and 1885*, was hanged for treason in November, 1885.

In societies *that discriminate against minorities*, immigrants naturally feel self-conscious.

Bartolomeo Cristofori, *who was keeper of instruments at the Medici court*, made the first pianoforte, *which he called a harpsichord with loud and soft*.

The forests of eastern Canada, *which contain both coniferous and deciduous trees*, experience rainfall and temperatures *that allow less hardy species to flourish*.

Mephistopheles, *to whom Faustus sells his soul for knowledge and power*, is one of the seven chief devils.

Obviously, a relative clause can be used to give additional information about a noun or to qualify that noun. You can also combine sentences by turning one into a relative clause. Examine the following sentences:

Dismissing the messenger, Lady Macbeth launches into a monologue. This monologue is striking for its demonic ferocity and intensity.

These sentences can be combined by getting rid of the subject of the second sentence (*this monologue*) and replacing it with a relative pronoun (*which*).

Dismissing the messenger, Lady Macbeth launches into a monologue *which is striking for its demonic ferocity and intensity*.

By following this strategy, the writer avoids repeating the noun *monologue* and the demonstrative pronoun *this*, which is there to help the second sentence stick to the first. Relative clauses help eliminate wordiness. Using relative clauses is not only economical; it is often essential. The following passage is in desperate need of relative clauses.

There was a constant battle between the radical Albertans. They wanted to reform the parliamentary system and install group government. They were fighting the more moderate Manitobans. These moderates sought to achieve their goals within the existing governmental framework and looked to the Liberals as the means of obtaining those goals.

This passage doesn't work. The writer wants to demonstrate that there was a never-ending fight between the radical Albertans and the more moderate Manitobans, but supplementary information regarding the positions of each group gets in the way of the clear expression of just who was battling whom. Putting the descriptions of each warring party's stand into relative clauses would clarify this writer's meaning.

There was a constant battle between the radical Albertans, *who wanted to reform the parliamentary system and install group government*, and the more moderate Manitobans, *who sought to achieve their goals within the existing governmental framework and looked to the Liberals as the means of obtaining those goals*.

Subordinate Clauses Beginning with Subordinating Conjunctions

Subordinate clauses beginning with subordinating conjunctions are usually adverb clauses and act like other adverbs: they modify verbs, adjectives, adverbs, or whole independent clauses.[9] Look, for example, at the following complex sentence, composed of an independent clause and a subordinate clause beginning with a subordinating conjunction:

He suffered *because he had a conscience*.

---

[9] Occasionally, a subordinating conjunction, such as *where* or *when*, begins an adjective clause: *The place **where the river narrows** is the site of the new bridge*; *It was a time **when human kindness was scarce**. You will be able to distinguish between adjective and adverb clauses if you remember that, regardless of whether adjective clauses begin with relative pronouns or subordinating conjunctions, these clauses modify nouns or noun equivalents (*place* and *time* in the preceding examples).

The subordinating conjunction *because* introduces the adverb clause *because he had a conscience*, joining it to the independent clause whose verb, *suffered*, it modifies. Here are more examples of adverb clauses:

While some of the Fathers of Confederation advocated complete unification, others favoured a large measure of provincial autonomy.

Realism has the potential to mislead an audience *because it makes viewers think that films are objective presentations of reality*.

Archimedes studied at the Library of Alexandria, *although he was born in Syracuse*.

Notice that three patterns are demonstrated by the preceding three sentences. In sentence one, the adverb clause comes before the independent clause and is separated from it by a comma. In sentence two, the adverb clause comes after the independent clause and no comma separates the two clauses. These are the two most frequently seen patterns of complex sentences containing adverb clauses. The third pattern, exemplified by sentence three, occurs when an adverb clause follows but does not restrict an independent clause. To put this simply, the information contained in the adverb clause of sentence three is not essential to the meaning of the sentence; it doesn't limit or define the independent clause; it doesn't restrict its meaning.

The Uses of Subordination

Subordination is extremely useful in academic writing. It allows writers to arrange information sequentially and spatially, that is, in time and space.

Since Quebec voted "no" to sovereignty-association in 1980, the province's economy has become less dependent upon the rest of Canada. (The two events are related in terms of time.)

Our company must support research *before we can produce a better light-bulb*. (The two ideas are related in terms of time.)

. . . Fools rush in *where angels fear to tread*. — Alexander Pope
    (The two events are related in terms of space or location.)

Subordination also enables writers to distinguish between major and minor points. Often, the main idea of a complex sentence shows up in an independent clause, and lesser ideas appear in dependent clauses. This is particularly true of complex sentences containing relative clauses that are non-restrictive.

Kenneth Grahame, *who worked for the Bank of England*, based <u>The Wind in the Willows</u> on bedtime stories and letters to his son.

Relative Pronouns

which, who, whom, that, what, whose, whatever, whoever, whomever, whichever

Subordinating Conjunctions

Contrasting Ideas:
    although, even though, though, whereas, while

Showing Cause and Effect:
    as, because, since, so that

Placing Ideas in Time:
    after, afterward, as long as, as soon as, before, once, since, until, when, whenever, while

Placing Ideas in Space:
    where, wherever

Establishing Conditions:
    assuming that, if, inasmuch as, insofar as, in case, in order that, provided that, so that, to the extent that, unless, whether

We expect an investigation of the book or of Grahame's relationship with his son to follow. Look at what happens when the information conveyed in the relative clause is switched with that contained in the independent clause.

> Kenneth Grahame, *who based* The Wind in the Willows *on bedtime stories and letters to his son*, worked for the Bank of England.

Now we expect a description of how Grahame's work influenced his book or perhaps of how odd it is that a bank employee managed to retain such a vivid and authentic vision of childhood.

Of course, subordinate ideas do frequently turn up in independent clauses. If you have learned nothing else from reading this book, you have learned that grammar is rarely based on logic. Subordination does, however, allow you to show what specific logical relationships exist among the concepts expressed within a sentence. Therefore, choosing the right subordinating conjunction is important even though deciding what information to put in a subordinate clause and what to put in an independent clause might not be significant.

Subordination, like coordination, can be used to create special effects. Let's use another passage of the King James Bible to demonstrate an effective use of subordination, although, as has been stated, coordination is used more often than subordination in this scripture.

> *Though I speak with the tongues of men and of angels, and have not charity,* I am become as sounding brass, or a tinkling symbol. *And though I have the gift of prophecy, and understand all mysteries, and all knowledge; and though I have all faith, so that I could remove mountains, and have not charity,* I am nothing. *And though I bestow all my goods to feed the poor, and though I give my body to be burned, and have not charity,* it profiteth me nothing.

Notice that while coordinating conjunctions are used to join dependent clauses beginning with *though*, the basic sentence structure here works something like this: Although *x* is true, without charity, *y* is the result. The piling up of subordinate clauses before the short, emphatic main clause which finishes each sentence gives power and significance to the consequences of being without charity, to *y*.

A similar effect is achieved by a student writer describing Reno, Nevada in an essay which compares Jane Rule's The Desert of the Heart to Marie-Claire Blais's Nights in the Underground.

> What is Reno, Nevada? In Rule's terms, it is a place where "the apes could not have survived" (108). Set in the middle of a desert, *where there is no water for industrial production or human consumption, where temperatures can reach 104 at mid-day, where nothing can grow*, it thrives.

Using subordination in this way helps this writer to prove her point: Reno's existence, according to her interpretation of Rule's novel, typifies human creations in that it is unnatural and unrelated to physical needs.

Subordination can also achieve irony. A clause which overturns, undermines, or takes the meaning of the clause it follows in an unexpected direction produces an ironic effect. Look at the following examples.

The heart has its reasons, which reason does not know.
— Blaise Pascal

The best is the best, though a hundred judges have declared it so.
— Sir Arthur Quiller-Couch

In the second example, Quiller-Couch has achieved an ironic effect by using an unexpected subordinating conjunction. We expect him to write that the best is best *because* it has been judged the best. He fools us, and by fooling us jolts us into thought.

The Misuse of Subordination

Sometimes, a writer might produce a complex sentence which is unintentionally ironic. Perhaps she selects an inappropriate subordinating conjunction, or maybe he stresses an idea which is really of secondary importance. The first of these mistakes in judgment is usually called illogical subordination, the second upside-down subordination. Another misuse of subordination, excessive subordination, involves piling up so many subordinate clauses that the sense of the sentence is hard to determine. How fine is the line between excellence and error: a writer may consciously create irony through subordination or unconsciously undermine meaning; a writer may intentionally pile up dependent clauses for emphasis or unintentionally confound the reader by doing the same thing without purpose or control.

ILLOGICAL SUBORDINATION

Illogical subordination usually occurs when a writer chooses the wrong subordinating conjunction, a subordinator that doesn't demonstrate the proper relationship between the dependent clause and the independent clause:

Although it is raining, the grass is wet.

Here, the correct subordinating conjunction is *because*. The grass is not wet *although* it is raining; it is wet *because* it is raining. Here is a more complicated example from a student's essay:

Despite the supreme tactical skill displayed by Napoleon during the Battle of the Three Emperors, he lost only 8,000 men to his enemy's 27,000.

Of course, Napoleon's army suffered fewer losses than its opponent *because of* Napoleon's military skill, not in spite of it. Let's revise this sentence by substituting a logical subordinating conjunction for the illogical one first used.

Because of the supreme tactical skill displayed by Napoleon during the Battle of the Three Emperors, he lost only 8,000 men to his enemy's 27,000.

Now the meaning is clear.

UPSIDE-DOWN SUBORDINATION

Upside-down subordination makes the wrong idea stand out in a complex sentence, often by expressing this idea, which should be secondary or subordinate to an independent clause, in an independent clause. Sometimes it does more than this; sometimes it mixes cause and effect:

Because the ground is wet, it is raining.

In this sentence, it seems as if the wetness of the ground is causing the rain. By subordinating the clause *it is raining*, we arrive at a more logical expression:

The ground is wet because it is raining.

Most instances of upside-down subordination are not as obvious as this, however. Usually, upside-down subordination unintentionally achieves a subtle ironic effect by emphasizing the wrong idea in a complex sentence:

The citizens considered a new house to be affordable, although none of them could afford one.

Here, the subordinate clause *although none of them could afford one* seems to overturn the meaning of the independent clause. It acts like a punch-line. The reader, expecting to be told why these citizens think that new houses are affordable, is confronted suddenly with the idea that the citizens might be wrong. To revise this sentence and to indicate that there is a difference between the citizens' considerations and their experiences, we can move the *although*:

Although the citizens considered a new house to be affordable, none of them could afford one.

EXCESSIVE SUBORDINATION

Excessive subordination is often called tandem subordination. We prefer to call it soap-opera subordination because a writer who indulges in excessive subordination, who strings together numerous, unparallel, and distantly related dependent clauses, reminds us of someone trying to explain all the relationships surrounding a character in a popular day-time drama.

Jill, *who* was married to James, *who* divorced Jean, *who* was having an affair with Jerry, *who* works as a dentist in an office-building *which* is close to the park *where* Jenny met Jeff, *who* died in a train wreck, married Jack.

It's hard to decipher the point of such a sentence. Are we being told that Jill married Jack? If so, it's difficult for us to put Jack and Jill together because they are divided by a series of dependent clauses. Of course, when students make this sort of error, it is less obvious. Here is an example of excessive subordination written by a student:

> *Because* medical science has made advances, children are now more likely to survive the early years of life *since* they are more apt to be born healthy, *which* means that unlike pre-industrial society *where* children were needed to provide help on the farm or to provide some form of insurance *that* one would be taken care of in old age, people today do not have children for economic reasons.

Because of excessive subordination, this sentence loses its way, and loses its reader en route. To revise a sentence like this, break it into bits and recombine those bits in a logical way. The bits might look like this:

> Medical science has made advances.
> These advances enable more children to survive the early years of life.
> These advances enable more children to be born healthy.
> In pre-industrial society, children were needed to provide help on the farm.
> In pre-industrial society, children were needed to provide insurance.
> The insurance was that one would be taken care of in old age.
> People today do not have children for economic reasons.

One possible recombination of these bits would look like this:

> The advances of medical science have enabled more children to be born healthy and to survive the early years of life. Children were needed in pre-industrial society to help on the farm and to insure that one would be taken care of in old age. People today do not have children for economic reasons.

Now that only the logical relationships remain, we can see that the original sentence lacked some essential ideas. What is the relationship between pre-industrial society's need of children and the increased health and survival rate of children? How does pre-industrial society's need of children relate to the fact that today people don't have children for economic reasons? After answering these questions, the writer will be able to convey rather than suggest the desired meaning:

> As advances in medical science enable more children to be born healthy and to survive the early years of life, fewer children need be born into each family to ensure its economic viability. Also, while children were needed in pre-industrial society to help on the farm and to insure that one would be taken care of in old age, they are not needed in this way by industrial societies. People today do not have children for economic reasons.

This revision is far from perfect. It just makes a guess regarding what the original sentence was striving to communicate. Guesswork is the only possible work that can be done in this circumstance because excessive subordination not only confuses the relations among ideas in the original, it masks a lack of relation.

Revising Excessive, Illogical, and Upside-Down Subordination

Sample Paragraph:

1. Henry Tilney, who has the manner, appearance, and speech of a gentleman and whose family is wealthy and prestigious, was Catherine's hero, who could provide her with a life that was "picture perfect." **2.** However, Jane Austen manipulates Henry, as much as this is possible, to show a hero who is also a patronizing, chauvinistic boor, who delights in the ridicule of women, whom he sees as inadequate. **3.** Henry feels that in "every power, of which taste is the foundation, excellence is pretty fairly divided between the sexes" (49). **4.** However, he claims that women have taste, although they are deficient in most other areas. **5.** Henry considers it proof of his nobility and manliness to let himself "sometimes down to the comprehension" (126) of women, whom he attempts to impress with his humble "genius" in choosing and caring for different fabrics and with his excellence in bargain hunting for women's clothes. **6.** Henry's chauvinism, which makes a contribution to the novel by generating feelings of anger in the reader, who consequently recognizes the truth about Henry's character, which is that Henry is an uninventive bore as well as a boor. **7.** Henry infrequently attempts originality, although his only tries seem to be a lively plagiarism of scenes from the novels Udolpho and The Romance of the Forest (12, 165). **8.** Catherine's hero is obviously an unoriginal, boorish bore.

Exercise One:

More common than Dutch barns in Ontario are the Pennsylvania German barns, which are characterized by their size, their cantilevered forebay, and their typical hillside setting. These barns, which are different from the Dutch barns in several respects, are very large. The German barn is typically sixty feet wide by one hundred feet long, more than double the size of the voluminous Dutch barn, which has a lengthy gable roof, similar in its uninterrupted expanse to the German barn's roof, which is sometimes distinguished by the asymmetry of its two slopes. Viewed from the outside, the German barn stands much taller at its eaves than does the Dutch, but its most characteristic feature is its cantilevered forebay, which overhangs the upper mow, improving the Bavarian prototype in which the upper storey was cantilevered a mere foot or so, thereby protecting the windows and walls of the lower storey. Even though the practice of building barns into the sides of hills originated in the hilly country of Upper Bavaria, the Southern Black Forest, and Switzerland, it was followed in the building of Pennsylvania German barns.

Exercise Two:

The reason some issues divide Canadians and become the subjects of political debates while other issues do not is simple: the group that has power, which is either economic or political, that wants to further concerns that are not too delicate for politicians, who will not deal with sensitive problems, will make their concerns the subjects of debate. If an issue is supported by a group that does not have any power, or if supporting an issue is considered political suicide, the chances of that issue becoming the subject of debate are almost non-existent. In conclusion, whether an issue is considered political or not depends on how volatile it is and on how much money is behind it. An issue that is too emotionally charged or that does not have any money pushing it has little chance of becoming political, although an issue that is both volatile and unbacked by capital is not even an issue in the political sense of the word.

Revising Excessive, Illogical, and Upside-Down Subordination: Sample Paragraph Discussion

This passage suffers from an excess of relative clauses. There are eleven, most of which begin with the relative pronoun *who*. Before tackling this obvious problem, however, let's make sure that the relations set up by the relative pronouns and the subordinating conjunctions make sense.

Illogical Subordination

In Sentence One, the main point seems to be that Henry Tilney was Catherine's hero because he could provide her with a *"picture perfect"* life. While the use of the relative pronoun *who* to introduce the last clause in this sentence is not completely illogical, it is imprecise. Also, changing the *who* to *because* would eliminate one of the many relative clauses composing this sentence:

> Henry Tilney, who has the manner, appearance, and speech of a gentleman and whose family is wealthy and prestigious, was Catherine's hero because he could provide her with a life that was "picture perfect."

Sentence Seven also contains a subordinate clause introduced by an illogical subordinator. The first clause tells us that Henry doesn't try to be original very often. The second suggests that even when he does try, he fails. Therefore, the *although* introducing the second clause is illogical because it signals an exception when what follows it is a distinct idea that tends to reinforce the meaning of the first clause. A coordinating conjunction or a semicolon would be more logical here:

> Henry infrequently attempts originality; his only tries seem to be a lively plagiarism of scenes from the novels Udolpho and The Romance of the Forest (12, 165).

Upside-Down Subordination

Sentence Four can be considered an example of upside-down subordination. In it, the exception to the deficiencies of women is the fact that they have taste, so the clause expressing this exception should begin with the *although*:

> However, he claims that, although women have taste, they are deficient in most other areas.

Excessive Subordination

Now we come to our major task: eliminating some of the many relative clauses in this paragraph. We can easily eliminate one in Sentence Two by changing the relative clause beginning with *who delights* into a participial phrase beginning with *delighting*.

> However, Jane Austen manipulates Henry, as much as this is possible, to show a hero who is also a patronizing, chauvinistic boor delighting in the ridicule of women, whom he sees as inadequate.

In Sentence Five, the last relative clause is really an example of how Henry condescends to women. By changing this relative clause into a prepositional phrase, we can more accurately signal this fact:

> Henry considers it proof of his nobility and manliness to let himself "sometimes down to the comprehension" (126) of women by attempting to impress them with his humble "genius" in choosing and caring for different fabrics and with his excellence in bargain hunting for women's clothes.

If we revise only one sentence for excessive subordination in this passage, it should be Sentence Six. Here, the number of relative clauses interferes with the reader's ability to determine which points are essential. One possible revision stresses the contribution Henry's chauvinism makes to the novel as well as the truth about Henry's character:

Henry's chauvinism makes a contribution to the novel by generating feelings of anger in the reader, who consequently recognizes the truth about Henry's character: Henry is an uninventive bore as well as a boor.

The revised paragraph would look like this:

Henry Tilney, who has the manner, appearance, and speech of a gentleman and whose family is wealthy and prestigious, was Catherine's hero because he could provide her with a life that was "picture perfect." However, Jane Austen manipulates Henry, as much as this is possible, to show a hero who is also a patronizing, chauvinistic boor delighting in the ridicule of women, whom he sees as inadequate. Henry feels that in "every power, of which taste is the foundation, excellence is pretty fairly divided between the sexes" (49). However, he claims that although women have taste, they are deficient in most other areas. Henry considers it proof of his nobility and manliness to let himself "sometimes down to the comprehension" (126) of women by attempting to impress them with his humble "genius" in choosing and caring for different fabrics and with his excellence in bargain hunting for women's clothes. Henry's chauvinism makes a contribution to the novel by generating feelings of anger in the reader, who consequently recognizes the truth about Henry's character: Henry is an uninventive bore as well as a boor. Henry infrequently attempts originality; his only tries seem to be a lively plagiarism of scenes from the novels Udolpho and The Romance of the Forest (12, 165). Catherine's hero is obviously an unoriginal, boorish bore.

Notice that the sentences of this paragraph are not substantially shorter than the sentences of the original. Nevertheless, the sentences are tighter because the relationships between the clauses of the revised sentences are more logical and clear.

Work through the remaining two paragraphs looking for and revising illogical, upside-down, and excessive subordination.

Exercise Three: Combining Sentences

Combine related sentences in the following paragraphs using coordination, subordination, and techniques for expanding the basic sentence with modifiers.

1) Acid rain is unnaturally acidic precipitation. It falls to earth downwind from industrial sources of sulphur dioxide and nitric oxides. Composed of approximately two parts of sulphuric acid to one part nitric acid, acid rain is formed when SO_2 and NO_x are dispersed. These chemicals are discharged into the atmosphere. The air also contains water vapour and dust. Heavy metals and other inorganic pollutants are transported along with acid rain in the air. This compounds the ecological damage.

The primary pollutant is SO_2. Canadian sources of SO_2 differ from American sources. There are both differences in the absolute quantities of the emissions in Canada and a different geographic concentration of emission sources. Canadian smelting industries emit the bulk of SO_2 in that country. These industries are large and smelt non-ferrous metals. American sources of SO_2 are dispersed and represent smaller private-sector industries. They are located over a wider geographic area than Canadian sources of SO_2 and are less easily regulated. Canada's contribution to the acid rain problem was over four and a half million metric tons of SO_2. This amount of SO_2 was discharged in 1980 in the area east of Flin Flon. Canadian acid rain has a higher concentration of heavy metals than American acid rain. Canadian acid rain comes from a metallurgic source. American SO_2 emissions are about five times the Canadian total. They add up to roughly 26 million metric tons. American emissions originate primarily from coal-fired electric generating stations.

2) The expansion of hospitals opened the doors to numerous nurturing jobs. These jobs were quickly filled by women. The nursing profession became dominated by women. However, it was soon found that this type of work was exhausting, frustrating, and, of course, alienating. Shapiro points out that nurses have fairly low status in the hospital hierarchy. Shapiro goes on to say that nurses are allowed very little decision making. They must follow orders given by physicians.

The expansion of the government also created jobs for women. Clerical jobs were opened. These quickly pulled women into the labour force. However, these occupations offered women low wages. They also required low skill levels, less responsibility, and fewer hours of work. Women entered and were trapped in degrading jobs. The development of highly specialized machines further degraded women in this field.

Another factor which drew women into the job market was the baby boom from 1946 to 1964. This expanded the number of teaching jobs available. The majority of them were soon filled by women. Women did well in this area. As Armstrong points out, they held most of the full-time jobs. Men were hired on a part-time basis. Women today still occupy elementary and secondary school teaching jobs. A low percentage of females teach in higher education facilities.

In Chapter One, we investigated ways of composing different types and patterns of sentences. We also used and described certain sentence elements. Having done this, we can now begin examining some of the most common problems writers have when trying to create clear and correct sentences. At first, the information in this chapter will be most useful to you when you revise your work. Make a revision checklist noting which sorts of problematic sentences you most frequently compose and in which particular circumstances you create these sentences. Soon you may find yourself composing sentences that avoid the problems once listed in your revision checklist.

The sentence problems discussed in this chapter can be placed into four categories. The first involves not knowing the boundaries of the complete sentence. When writers are unsure of these boundaries, they tend to produce sentence fragments, comma splices, or fused sentences. The second sort of problem sentence is the one whose elements either do not agree with or do not parallel one another. In this chapter, we discuss two sorts of agreement necessary to sentences (subject-verb agreement and pronoun-antecedent agreement) and two problems writers have with parallelism (faulty parallelism and false parallelism). The third type of problem, misplacing sentence elements, is discussed in a section about misplaced modifiers. This section also contains information on dangling modifiers, a type of construction which exemplifies the fourth and last category of problem covered here: sentences that begin in one way and end in another. Really, this category covers sentences whose parts don't agree, sentences whose parts are not parallel, and sentences that have dangling modifiers, as well as many other syntactically dysfunctional constructions. Emulating markers and editors, we have lumped these problematic sentences together and called them awkward.

Sentence Fragments

A sentence fragment is a part of a sentence written as if it were a whole sentence; it is an incomplete sentence punctuated like a complete one. Although fragments start with capital letters and finish with end punctuation, they either lack an essential sentence element—usually a subject or a verb—or they have been turned into dependent clauses by the addition of subordinating words.[1]

Fragments are funny things. They're like the little girl with the curl on her forehead; when they're good they're very very good, and when they're bad they're horrid. Good fragments provide emphasis. In December of 1944, General McAuliffe replied to a German demand for the surrender of the 101st Airborne Division using a clearly understandable and emphatic fragment: *Nuts!* In fact, good fragments appear frequently in conversation because those conversing understand the context in which these fragments exist. Imagine two people talking about using phosphate-free detergent.

Person one: Mom didn't. Do you?
Person two: Sometimes. You?
Person one: Yes.

---

[1] See pages 21-31 for a definition of dependent and independent clauses.

This imaginary conversation contains nothing but fragments. Although people may converse using complete sentences more frequently than the preceding dialogue suggests, conversations that don't contain fragments rarely take place outside of English language classes.

Most advertisements also contain fragments. Again, these fragments are acceptable because they are presented in a context which has been defined. If we see images of furniture flash across our television screen and hear the jingle of a particular department store, we understand that the fragment *No money down* means that this department store will allow customers to purchase furniture on credit without requiring them to pay a deposit.

Because writers must arrange words meaningfully to create context for readers and because writers and readers cannot enter into a dialogue, it is hard to use fragments well in academic prose. If I hadn't described the circumstances surrounding General McAuliffe's fragmented sentence, if I had just written *Nuts!* in the middle of my paragraph, I would have seemed demented, offensive, or both. And I would have turned General McAuliffe's good fragment into a bad fragment.

Writing good fragments, then, is more difficult than speaking them. However, effective fragments are common in the prose of novelists striving for emphatic, descriptive language that matches the rhythms of everyday speech and thought. Examine the following passage taken from Margaret Laurence's The Diviners.

> True. Undoubtedly true. Morag Gunn, country woman, never managing to overcome a quiver of distaste at the sight of an earthworm. Lover of swallows, orioles and red-winged blackbirds. Detester of physical labour. Lover of rivers and tall trees. Hater of axes and shovels. What a farce.[2]

Notice that the detailed description of what Morag Gunn loves and hates accumulates in fragmented sentences but that the reader is left to link these fragments and to reach a general comprehension of this character's attitude toward country life.

Academic writers, because they strive to make the connections between ideas explicit, to explain as well as describe, generally avoid fragments. However, many writers unwittingly create a sentence fragment because they are influenced by the speech patterns of everyday life, by advertisement jingles, or by the writing style common in modern fiction and poetry. These fragments often interfere with the reader's perception of the writer's meaning or ability. The task of this section is to help writers recognize and revise these unintentional fragments.

RECOGNIZING AND REVISING FRAGMENTS

Recognizing Fragments

There are two sorts of fragments common to academic prose. One sort lacks one or both of the essential elements of a grammatically complete sentence: an

[2] Margaret Laurence, *The Diviners* (Toronto: McClelland and Stewart, 1974) 46.

Clip magazine and newspaper advertisements that contain sentence fragments. If neither magazines nor newspapers are handy, write down the advertising slogans you can remember from radio or television and determine which of these slogans are fragments. Next, imagine that you have to express the information communicated by these advertisements using words alone. Revise the advertisements accordingly.

Select a topic of your own or use one of the ones provided and write a dialogue between two people with different perspectives on this topic. Try to make your dialogue true to the patterns of actual conversation. Next, rewrite this discussion, reporting the speech of both dialogue participants in an indirect way. In other words, write something that looks like a film script first; then, write something that looks like a few paragraphs from an essay examining a subject in two different ways.

parental authority
the influence of religion upon society

the uses of art
public education

discrimination
national unity

dress codes
the effective office manager

population control
the possibility of predicting the future

implied or actual subject and a verb. Another sort has all the ingredients necessary to a complete sentence but begins with a subordinating word, which makes it depend upon another, independent clause for its meaning. How can you detect fragments? First, check that all of the word groups you have punctuated as sentences contain the elements needed to complete them.

Does every word group that is not an imperative sentence contain a subject?
If not, you are looking at a fragment.

Does every word group contain a verb that relates to the actual or implied subject?
If not, you are looking at a fragment.

THE MISSING SUBJECT

If a group of words punctuated like a sentence has no subject, it is usually a fragment. To determine if a group of words has a subject, locate the verb and try to find an expression of *who* or *what* the verb is talking about. If you can find no such expression and if the group of words in question is not an imperative sentence which makes a command or a request, you are looking at a fragment.

In the 1970s, Canadian foreign aid to African and Asian nations increased. *Trying to improve social conditions in very poor countries.* (Without the information presented in the first sentence, we don't know *who* or *what* tried to improve social conditions. Since the passage in italics does not contain this information, it is a fragment.)

Non-status Indians do not live on reserves. *And do not usually receive fishing and hunting concessions.* (Again, the italicized passage does not contain an expression of *who* or *what* did not usually receive these concessions, so it is a fragment. This fragment was created by splitting a compound predicate made up of the verbs *live* and *receive*.)

Remember that socialization encourages conformity. (Although there is no stated subject here, this is a sentence, an imperative sentence which requests the reader to remember that socialization encourages conformity. The subject of the sentence (*you*) is implied.)

THE MISSING VERB

If a group of words punctuated like a sentence has no verb relating to an actual or implied subject, it is a fragment, even if it contains a verbal or a verbal phrase.[3] Notice that although many of the following fragments are phrases which also have no subject, we have categorized them as lacking verbs because a missing verb is usually more confusing than a missing subject. Verbs are the

---

[3] See the section in Chapter One entitled "Verbals and Verbal Phrases" (pgs. 17-19) for more information.

real workhorses of the English language; they speak of actions, occurrences, and states of being.

This essay will deal with the opening phase of the First World War. *From the German invasion of Belgium to the First Battle of Ypres.* (There is no verb in this phrase beginning with the preposition *from*. Therefore, it is a prepositional phrase fragment.)

In his work "The Love Song of J. Alfred Prufrock," Eliot makes use of many images and other literary devices. *To depict his desire/inaction paradox.* (Although there is a verbal, the infinitive *to depict*, there is no verb in this phrase. Therefore, it is an infinitive phrase fragment.)

In Paradise Lost, Satan is determined to fight God in any manner open to him. *Even facing him in battle.* (Although there is a verbal, the gerund *facing*, there is no verb in this phrase. Therefore, it is a gerund phrase fragment.)

Running absolutely straight from all directions. All roads led to Rome. (Again, while there is a verbal, the present participle *running*, this phrase has no verb. It is therefore a participial phrase fragment.)

The Winnipeg General Strike was one of Canada's most unusual and significant labour milestones. *A strike possessing the strength of a revolution but the character of a peaceful protest.* (This phrase does not contain a verb; it is simply a restatement and redefinition of the concept represented by the proper noun *Winnipeg General Strike*. Thus, it is an appositive fragment.)

Another problem with the efficiency of the legislation clause in the Ontario Temperance Act which allowed the manufacture and sale of wine within the province. (While this word group does appear to have a verb (*allowed*), this verb is in a dependent clause that modifies the noun *Ontario Temperance Act*. Because there is no verb that relates directly to the subject (*problem*) of this word group, it is a fragment. This fragment was probably created because of its length; the writer packed so much information into the complete subject by piling on modifiers that he felt, erroneously, in need of a period.)

THE DEPENDENT CLAUSE FRAGMENT

If a clause depends upon an independent clause to complete its meaning, it is called a dependent clause. Dependent clauses, unlike independent clauses, cannot stand alone as grammatically complete sentences. A dependent clause usually begins with a subordinating conjunction—such as *because, if, since,* or *when*—or a relative pronoun—such as *that, which,* or *who.* (There is a list of subordinating conjunctions and relative pronouns on page 31.) Therefore, to guard against writing a dependent clause fragment, ask yourself the following question.

Does every word group that begins with a subordinating conjunction or relative pronoun have an independent clause to complete its meaning? If not, you are probably looking at a fragment.[4]

Although battles have to be investigated, there is no need to examine them in detail. *As there are already many volumes of military history covering just about every part of every battle ever fought.* (Although both word groups begin with subordinating conjunctions, only the one in italics starting with *as* is a fragment. The sentence starting with *although* is complete because its dependent clause is joined to an independent clause.)

It can be said that the United States made Canada a nation. *Because the threat of an American invasion just after the American Civil War was one of the reasons for Confederation.* (Again, the italicized clause is a dependent clause fragment beginning with a subordinating conjunction.)

Just after dawn on the day of the winter solstice, sunlight shines down the entire length of the Irish tomb called New Grange. *Which was completed in approximately 3100 B.C.* (This is a dependent clause fragment beginning with a relative pronoun, which means that it should relate to and modify the noun *New Grange*.)

Donald B. Smith describes the life and writings of George Copway, an Ojibwa author. *Who became famous in the United States during the late 1840s.* (This is another dependent clause fragment beginning with a relative pronoun. Notice that if this word group were punctuated with a question mark rather than a period, it would be a complete interrogative sentence: *Who became famous in the United States during the late 1840s?*)

---

[4] An interrogative sentence (a question) often has a relative pronoun as its subject. Therefore, questions that begin with relative pronouns are usually not fragments.

Revising Fragments

In general, there are two ways of eliminating a fragment: combine it with an already complete sentence, or rewrite and complete it, so it can stand alone as a separate sentence.

Passages Containing Fragments	Strategy One: Combining Fragments with Complete Sentences	Strategy Two: Rewriting Fragments as Complete Sentences
In the 1970s, Canadian foreign aid to African and Asian nations increased. *Trying to improve social conditions in very poor countries.*	In the 1970s, Canadian foreign aid to African and Asian nations increased as Canadians tried to improve social conditions in very poor countries.	In the 1970s, Canadian foreign aid to African and Asian nations increased. This aid tried to improve social conditions in very poor countries.
Non-status Indians do not live on reserves. *And do not usually receive fishing and hunting concessions.*	Non-status Indians do not live on reserves and do not usually receive fishing and hunting concessions.	Non-status Indians do not live on reserves. Also, they do not usually receive fishing and hunting concessions.
This essay will deal with the opening phase of the First World War. *From the German invasion of Belgium to the First Battle of Ypres.*	This essay will deal with the opening phase of the First World War, which lasted from the German invasion of Belgium to the First Battle of Ypres.	This essay will deal with the opening phase of the First World War. This phase lasted from the German invasion of Belgium to the First Battle of Ypres.
In his work "The Love Song of J. Alfred Prufrock," Eliot makes use of many images and other literary devices. *To depict his desire/ inaction paradox.*	In his work "The Love Song of J. Alfred Prufrock," Eliot makes use of many images and other literary devices to depict his desire/inaction paradox.	In his work "The Love Song of J. Alfred Prufrock," Eliot makes use of many images and other literary devices. He uses images in particular to depict his desire/inaction paradox.
In Paradise Lost, Satan is determined to fight God in any manner open to him. *Even facing him in battle.*	In Paradise Lost, Satan is determined to fight God in any manner open to him, even facing him in battle.	In Paradise Lost, Satan is determined to fight God in any manner open to him. Even facing him in battle is considered.
Running absolutely straight from all directions. All roads led to Rome.	Running absolutely straight from all directions, all roads led to Rome.	The roads of the Roman Empire ran absolutely straight. All led to Rome from all directions.
The Winnipeg General Strike was one of Canada's most unusual and significant labour milestones. *A strike possessing the strength of a revolution but the character of a peaceful protest.*	The Winnipeg General Strike was one of Canada's most unique and significant labour milestones, possessing the strength of a revolution but the character of a peaceful protest.	The Winnipeg General Strike was one of Canada's most unique and significant labour milestones. It possessed the strength of a revolution but the character of a peaceful protest.
Although battles have to be investigated, there is no need to examine them in detail. *As there are already many volumes of military history covering just about every part of every battle ever fought.*	Although battles have to be investigated, there is no need to examine them in detail as there are already many volumes of military history covering just about every part of every battle ever fought.	Although battles have to be investigated, there is no need to examine them in detail. There are enough volumes of military history, which cover just about every part of every battle ever fought.

It can be said that the United States made Canada a nation. *Because the threat of an American invasion just after the American Civil War was one of the reasons for Confederation.*

Because the threat of an American invasion just after the American Civil War was one of the reasons for Confederation, it can be said that the United States made Canada a nation.

The threat of an American invasion just after the American Civil War was one of the reasons for Confederation. Thus, it can be said that the United States made Canada a nation.

Just after dawn on the day of the winter solstice, sunlight shines down the entire length of the Irish tomb called New Grange. *Which was completed in approximately 3100 B.C.*

Just after dawn on the day of the winter solstice, sunlight shines down the entire length of the Irish tomb called New Grange, which was completed in approximately 3100 B.C.

The Irish tomb called New Grange was completed in approximately 3100 B.C. Just after dawn on the day of the winter solstice, sunlight shines down its entire length.

Donald B. Smith describes the life and writings of George Copway, an Ojibwa author. *Who became famous in the United States during the late 1840s.*

Donald B. Smith describes the life and writing of George Copway, an Ojibwa author who became famous in the United States during the late 1840s.

Donald B. Smith describes the life and writing of George Copway. Copway, an Ojibwa author, became famous in the United States during the late 1840s.

Because one of the examples of a fragment was not given in context, we cannot follow the first strategy and combine it with an already complete sentence. We can, however, follow the second strategy and rewrite it. Notice that the two following revisions of this fragment have different meanings. Only the writer of the original fragment, or perhaps a Canadian history buff, would be able to determine which version was intended.

Fragment: *Another problem with the efficiency of the legislation clause in the Ontario Temperance Act which allowed the manufacture and sale of wine within the province.*

Revision One: Another problem with the efficiency of the legislation clause in the Ontario Temperance Act was that it allowed the manufacture and sale of wine within the province.

Revision Two: Another problem with the efficiency of the legislation clause in the Ontario Temperance Act, which allowed the manufacture and sale of wine within the province, was that no distinction was made between wine and fortified wine.

Notes

My writing strengths:

Things I need to remember:

Things I need to check:

Revising Sentence Fragments

Sample Paragraph:

1. The Holy Grail has been represented in various ways. **2.** For example, as a chalice, a dish, and a cup. **3.** The Grail being the centre of a large amount of medieval legend and romance. **4.** It has received a great deal of scholarly attention. **5.** Scholars have explained the origin of the Grail myth in three different ways. **6.** Because the actual origin of this myth is unknown. **7.** J.D. Bruce believes that stories about the Grail began as Christian legends. **8.** And were altered over time. **9.** In fact, the best known accounts of the Grail refer to Biblical events and people. **10.** So Bruce's theory has support. **11.** These accounts describing the Grail as the cup of the Last Supper and the container in which Joseph of Arimathea caught the blood of the crucified Christ. **12.** J.L. Weston, on the other hand, sees the Grail as a pagan symbol of fertility. **13.** So she relates the Grail legend to Britain's replenishment after the devastation wrought by King Pellam. **14.** Other scholars feel that the Grail myth began as a Celtic story. **15.** Which was transmitted from Ireland through Wales and Brittany to France.

Exercise One:

In looking at the actions taken by Germany in 1914, one must examine the German Army in the age of Moltke. For by doing this one will come to an understanding of why Germany acted the way she did. And what the military believed was possible in the Great War. In looking at the German Army in the age of Moltke, one must first look at Clausewitz. Whom Moltke claimed to be a student of. Then the theories of Moltke have to be examined. And finally the theories of Schlieffen and the plan that bears his name.

Exercise Two:

John Maynard Keynes, in a book entitled The General Theory of Employment, Interest and Money, provided a solution to high unemployment. The government could mechanize the business cycle by means of monetary and fiscal policy. In effect, by increasing public spending and decreasing taxes when times were bad. And by decreasing public spending and increasing taxes when times were good. To acquire a surplus to compensate the economy in the future. When the system reached full employment, it would be able to regulate itself. In Keynes's theory, social programs provide the immediate stimulus to the economy. Because they provide a way of transferring purchasing power to those willing to spend.

Revising Sentence Fragments: Sample Paragraph Discussion

In the sample paragraph, Sentence One is complete; it has a subject (*The Holy Grail*), it has a verb relating to that subject (*has been represented*), and it doesn't begin with a subordinating conjunction. The next word group is a fragment. It is missing a verb. Logic demands that this fragment be joined to the sentence preceding it because it gives examples of the various ways the Holy Grail has been represented. At least two revisions are possible.

> The Holy Grail has been represented in various ways, for example, as a chalice, a dish, and a cup.

> The Holy Grail has been variously represented as a chalice, a dish, and a cup.

Sentence Three is also incomplete. Although it does have a verbal (*being*), it does not have a verb that completes a subject. To complete this sentence, turn the verbal into a verb (*is*), or join this fragment to another complete sentence, like the one following it.

> The Grail is at the centre of many medieval legends and romances.

> The Grail, being at the centre of many medieval legends and romances, has received a great deal of scholarly attention.

Sentence Five is complete. It is not a dependent clause, and it has a subject (*scholars*) and a verb related to that subject (*have explained*). A dependent clause fragment beginning with the subordinating word *because* follows, however. To complete it, join it to Sentence Five.

> Scholars have explained the origin of the Grail myth in three different ways because its actual origin is unknown

Sentence Seven is complete, but Sentence Eight is not. It has no subject. The true subject of this fragment, *stories*, is contained in Sentence Seven, so Sentence Seven and Sentence Eight should be linked.

> J.D. Bruce believes that stories about the Grail began as Christian legends and were altered over time.

The next sentence, Sentence Nine, is complete. Sentence Ten might be considered incomplete by some because it begins with a coordinating conjunction (*so*). However, sentences beginning with coordinating conjunctions are not fragments by definition. As long as a subject and verb follow the coordinating conjunction, the sentence should really be considered complete. To guard against overzealous markers, replace dodgy initial coordinating conjunctions with conjunctive adverbs like *however* or *therefore*.

> Therefore, Bruce's theory has support.

We might also integrate this sentence more completely by linking it to the example of support provided for Bruce's theory:

> Bruce's theory is supported by the fact that the best known accounts of the Grail refer to Biblical events and people.

Next, we have a fragment, sporting a verbal (*describing*) instead of a verb (*describe*). Make the appropriate change and create a complete sentence:

> These accounts describe the Grail as the cup of the Last Supper and the container in which Joseph of Arimathea caught the blood of the crucified Christ.

Sentence Twelve is complete, having a subject (*J.L. Weston*), a related verb (*sees*), and no initial subordinating word. Although the following sentence also has a subject (*she*) and a verb (*connects*), and doesn't start with a subordinator, it feels incomplete. The author seems to want to connect Weston's vision with Weston's theory, or Sentences Twelve and Thirteen. Therefore, even though technically Sentence Thirteen is complete, it might very easily be considered a fragment by a marker responding to the choppy, disjointed style evident in this passage. Either get rid of the tentative connection between Sentences Twelve and Thirteen, the *so*, or make that connection clear.

> J.L. Weston, on the other hand, sees the Grail as a pagan symbol of fertility. She relates the Grail legend to Britain's replenishment after the devastation wrought by King Pellam.

> On the other hand, because J.L. Weston sees the Grail as a pagan symbol of fertility, she relates the Grail legend to Britain's replenishment after the devastation wrought by King Pellam.

Sentence Fourteen is complete, but Sentence Fifteen is not. It begins with the relative pronoun *which*, which relates the information conveyed in this clause to the noun *story*. Combine Sentence Fourteen and Sentence Fifteen:

> Other scholars feel that the Grail myth began as a Celtic story, which was transmitted from Ireland through Wales and Brittany to France.

One possible revision of the sample passage follows:

> The Holy Grail has been variously represented as a chalice, a dish, and a cup. The Grail, being at the centre of many medieval legends and romances, has received a great deal of scholarly attention. Scholars have explained the origin of the Grail myth in three different ways because its actual origin is unknown. J.D. Bruce believes that stories about the Grail began as Christian legends which were altered over time. Bruce's theory is supported by the fact that the best known accounts of the Grail connect it to Biblical events and people. In these accounts, the Grail is described as the cup of the Last Supper and as the container in which Joseph of Arimathea caught the blood of the crucified Christ. J.L. Weston, on the other hand, sees the Grail as a pagan symbol of fertility. She relates the Grail legend to Britain's replenishment after the devastation wrought by King Pellam. Other scholars feel that the Grail myth began as a Celtic story, which was transmitted from Ireland through Wales and Brittany to France.

Work through Exercises One and Two. To recognize fragments, ask yourself the following three questions.

1) Does every word group punctuated as a sentence that is not an imperative sentence have a subject?

2) Does every word group punctuated as a sentence have a verb relating to the subject?

3) Does every word group punctuated as a sentence and beginning with a subordinating conjunction or relative pronoun have an independent clause to complete its meaning?

A negative answer to any of these questions identifies a fragment.

Comma Splices and Fused Sentences

RECOGNIZING COMMA SPLICES AND FUSED SENTENCES

A comma splice, sometimes called a comma fault, occurs when independent clauses are spliced, smashed together with only a comma between them.

> Comma Splice: H.G. Wells was concerned about average people and wished to provide them with some fundamental ideas concerning the workings of the world, the result was The Outline of History.

A fused sentence, often called a run-on sentence, is the same kind of error as a comma splice, except that no punctuation at all appears between independent clauses: these clauses are fused or run together.

> Fused Sentence: The non-logical, instinctive, subconscious part of the mind plays a part in a sculptor's work the conscious mind as well is not inactive.

Comma splices and fused sentences usually occur in three circumstances: when writers misuse conjunctive adverbs and transitional phrases, when they fail to recognize that a clause beginning with a pronoun may be independent, and when two independent clauses are so closely related in meaning that a writer wants to include them in the same sentence and doesn't know what punctuation is necessary to do this correctly.

Misusing Conjunctive Adverbs and Transitional Phrases

Frequently, comma splices and fused sentences happen because writers believe that conjunctive adverbs—like *however, therefore,* and *consequently*—and transitional phrases—like *as a result, in fact,* and *on the contrary*—have the connecting power of coordinating conjunctions. They do not.

> Comma Splice: Sir Gawain's manner of greeting was enough to tell the court that he was a noble knight, *thus* he was courteously received.

> Fused Sentence: Regarding censorship, liberals would remain firm in their conviction to maintain civil liberties *however* socialists would support legislation to protect the public.

> Comma Splice: Alienation can also occur among members of the same class, *in fact*, capitalists are frequently compelled to drive out their competitors, and workers are almost always forced to compete in the selling of their labour.

> Fused Sentence: In 1985, the United States had a divorce rate of approximately 5.0 *in comparison* Canada's divorce rate was 2.4.

Conjunctive Adverbs

accordingly	moreover
also	namely
anyway	nevertheless
besides	next
certainly	nonetheless
consequently	now
conversely	otherwise
finally	rather
furthermore	similarly
hence	still
however	subsequently
incidentally	then
indeed	therefore
instead	thus
likewise	undoubtedly
meanwhile	

Transitional Phrases

all in all	in fact
as a result	in other words
as an illustration	in short
as has been noted	in the future
as we have seen	in the past
as well	in the same way
at that time	of course
at the same time	on the contrary
equally important	on the one hand
for example	on the other hand
for instance	on the whole
for this purpose	otherwise
in any event	that is
in comparison	to illustrate
in conclusion	to this end
in contrast	

The transitional word *also* and the transitional phrase *as well* deserve special mention because they are so frequently confused with the coordinating conjunction *and*. Using *also* or *as well* instead of *and* often creates comma splices or fused sentences.

Comma Splice: These women experienced greater amounts of post-abortion depression when the abortion had been opposed by their parents, *also* peer group opposition increased depression.

Fused Sentence: In 1979, the Conservative Party's television commercials attacked Trudeau's policies *as well* they emphasized the length of the Liberals' term in office.

Independent Clauses Beginning with Pronouns

Pronouns, which by definition replace nouns, often function as subjects. Therefore, a pronoun frequently signals the beginning of an independent clause. When writers fail to understand that a pronoun can start an independent clause, they tend to link all word groups beginning with pronouns to other independent clauses, creating comma splices or fused sentences.

Comma Splice: The physical feature known as the Oak Ridges Moraine is located in Southern Ontario, *it* extends from Trenton to Orangeville covering a distance of over one hundred miles.

Comma Splice: Large doses of cocaine can depress the central nervous system, *this* can result in respiratory arrest.

Fused Sentence: Arguments entirely motivated by self-interest fail to question the fundamental assumptions upon which they are based *they* result inevitably in a loss to humanity as a whole.

Fused Sentence: The human brain is arranged so that emotional life can operate largely independently from thought, according to Dr. Joseph LeDoux *he* is a psychologist at the Center for Neural Science at New York University.

Independent Clauses Closely Related in Meaning

Sometimes two independent clauses are so closely related in meaning that a writer wants to have them together in a sentence. Knowing neither the proper use of colons and semicolons nor the techniques of subordination, he or she links these independent clauses using a comma or uses no punctuation, fusing them. Thus, a comma splice or a fused sentence is created.

Comma Splice: The anti-drug movement is inconsistent, an ideological conflict exists over which drugs are socially acceptable and which are not.

Fused Sentence: Canada and America are not the same each country came to exist in a different way, and each continues to exist in different circumstances.

Exceptions

While fused sentences are almost never acceptable in academic prose, it is sometimes correct to link independent clauses using commas. Independent clauses that can be legitimately joined with a comma are usually short and simple. They should also fulfil one of the following requirements.

a) They should be listed in a series using the following order: a, b, and c.

> Harvey discovered the circulation of the blood, Leeuwenhoek documented the existence of microscopic life, and Vesalius made advances in anatomy.

b) They should be very short, parallel, and climactic.

> I came, I saw, I conquered.

c) They should form an antithesis or use the following formula: it was not merely this, it was this.

> Victorian prisons were not lively places, they were moribund.

> Some of the policies followed in Residential Schools were not only strict, they were abusive.

Professional writers, novelists and poets in particular, frequently expand or contract the boundaries of the grammatically complete sentence to suit their purposes; they break sentences into fragments and they run sentences together. You will find many comma splices and fused sentences used for effect in modern prose, especially in the prose of novelists writing in a stream-of-consciousness style. Unless your writing exudes a mastery of grammar, it is unwise to emulate the unconventional punctuation evident in the following writing samples.

> Yet all those years I thought it was an accident and I'm sure Papa did, too. I think Mama knew. I do not want to do the thinking sometimes, there is a danger in it. But I think now Mama knew because it raised a real uproar the way she went to bed and stayed there the day it happened and wouldn't even get up for the funeral.[5]

---
[5] Gertrude Story, "Das Engelein Kommt," *Black Swan* (Saskatoon, Saskatchewan: Thistledown P, 1986) 17.

Writing Prompt

Think of the three circumstances in which it is acceptable to link independent clauses with commas, and compose sentences patterned on the three sample sentences provided to exemplify these circumstances (marked a, b, and c). Try to create at least two sentences for each pattern.

It is already July. The fireflies will soon be out. My death flashes across my afternoon like a nun in white, hurrying, evanescing, apparitional as the rise of heat off boulevards, the parched white of sails across cement, around the corner, fleeing the sun. I have not yet seen the face, it is hooded, perhaps wrapped, but I know the flow, the cloth of her, moving always in diagonals, in waves toward me, then footlessly away again.[6]

The absence of a Canadian identity has always seemed nonsense to me, and the search for it a case of the dog chasing its own tail. What people usually mean by a national identity is an advertising gimmick. Everything has an identity. A stone has an identity, it just doesn't have a voice. A man who's forgotten who he is has an identity, he's merely suffering from amnesia, which was the case with the Canadians. They'd forgotten. They'd had their ears pressed to the wall for so long, listening in on the neighbours, who *were* rather loud, that they'd forgotten how to speak and what to say. They'd become addicted to the one-way mirror of the Canadian-American border—we can see you, you can't see us—and had neglected that other mirror, their own culture.[7]

REVISING COMMA SPLICES AND FUSED SENTENCES

There are five ways to correct comma splices or fused sentences. You can separate the two spliced or fused clauses into two sentences; you can join these clauses correctly using coordination, subordination, or proper punctuation; or you can eliminate one of the clauses and tighten up the sentence.

1) **Separate**. Use a period to separate the spliced or fused clauses into two distinct sentences. Because this revision strategy works best when at least some sort of pause between independent clauses seems natural, it can be more readily applied to comma splices than to fused sentences. However, fused sentences resulting from the misuse of conjunctions and transitional phrases can often be corrected in this way. This correction strategy works best when long independent clauses have been spliced or fused because separating short independent clauses, while creating a grammatically correct set of sentences, also produces choppy, disjointed prose.

> Comma Splice: H.G. Wells was concerned about average people and wished to provide them with some fundamental ideas concerning the workings of the world, the result was The Outline of History.

> Revised: H.G. Wells was concerned about average people and wished to provide them with some fundamental ideas concerning the workings of the world. The result was The Outline of History.

[6] Lorrie Moore, "Go Like This," *Self-Help* (London: Faber and Faber, 1985) 77.

[7] Margaret Atwood, "Canadian-American Relations," *Second Words: Selected Critical Prose* (Toronto: Anansi, 1982) 385.

Comma Splice: Alienation can also occur among members of the same class, in fact, capitalists are frequently compelled to drive out their competitors, and workers are almost always forced to compete in the selling of their labour.

Revised: Alienation can also occur among members of the same class. In fact, capitalists are frequently compelled to drive out their competitors, and workers are almost always forced to compete in the selling of their labour.

Fused Sentence: In 1985, the United States had a divorce rate of approximately 5.0 in comparison Canada's divorce rate was 2.4.

Revised: In 1985, the United States had a divorce rate of approximately 5.0. In comparison, Canada's divorce rate was 2.4.

Comma Splice: These women experienced greater amounts of post-abortion depression when the abortion had been opposed by their parents, also peer group opposition increased depression.

Revised: These women experienced greater amounts of post-abortion depression when the abortions had been opposed by their parents. Peer group opposition also increased depression.

Fused Sentence: In 1979, the Conservative Party's television commercials attacked Trudeau's policies as well they emphasized the length of the Liberals' term in office.

Revised: In 1979, the Conservative Party's television commercials attacked Trudeau's policies. As well, they emphasized the length of the Liberals' term in office.

2) **Coordinate**. Use coordination to link the two independent clauses correctly. Placing a comma and a coordinating conjunction after the first independent clause joins it to the second. This strategy should be used when the two ideas expressed in the two independent clauses are of equal importance. Coordination is also more appropriate than separation when the two clauses are short.

Fused Sentence: The non-logical, instinctive, subconscious part of the mind plays a part in a sculptor's work the conscious mind as well is not inactive.

Revised: The non-logical, instinctive, subconscious part of the mind plays a part in a sculptor's work, but the conscious mind is not inactive.

Fused Sentence: In 1985, the United States had a divorce rate of approximately 5.0 in comparison Canada's divorce rate was 2.4.

Revised: In 1985, the United States had a divorce rate of approximately 5.0, and Canada's divorce rate was 2.4.

Fused Sentence: In 1979, the Conservative Party's television commercials attacked Trudeau's policies as well they emphasized the length of the Liberals' term in office.

Revised: In 1979, the Conservative Party's television commercials attacked Trudeau's policies, and they emphasized the length of the Liberals' term in office.

3) **Subordinate**. Use a subordinating conjunction or a relative pronoun to turn one of the independent clauses into a dependent clause. This revision strategy is particularly useful when correcting sentence faults resulting from the misuse of conjunctive adverbs, transitional phrases, and pronouns because misusing these sentence parts as joining words and phrases often signals a more basic problem: a poorly thought-out relationship between the ideas expressed in the two spliced or fused clauses. Subordination helps express the exact relationship between the ideas and clauses of a sentence.

Comma Splice: Sir Gawain's manner of greeting was enough to tell the court that he was a noble knight, thus he was courteously received.

Revised: Because Sir Gawain's manner of greeting was enough to tell the court that he was a noble knight, he was courteously received.

Fused Sentence: Regarding censorship, liberals would remain firm in their conviction to maintain civil liberties however socialists would support legislation to protect the public.

Revised: Regarding censorship, liberals would remain firm in their conviction to maintain civil liberties while socialists would support legislation to protect the public.

Fused Sentence: Arguments entirely motivated by self-interest fail to question the fundamental assumptions upon which they are based they result inevitably in a loss to humanity as a whole.

Revised: Arguments entirely motivated by self-interest fail to question the fundamental assumptions upon which they are based which results inevitably in a loss to humanity as a whole.

Fused Sentence: The human brain is arranged so that emotional life can operate largely independently from thought, according to Dr. Joseph LeDoux he is a psychologist at the Center for Neural Science at New York University.

Revised: The human brain is arranged so that emotional life can operate largely independently from thought, according to Dr. Joseph LeDoux, who is a psychologist at the Center for Neural Science at New York University.

4) **Punctuate**.[8] While two independent clauses cannot be strung together without punctuation or linked using a comma, they can be joined with a semicolon or a colon. Semicolons are the more usual way to join independent clauses closely related in meaning. However, colons can be used if the second independent clause is an example or explanation of the first. Obviously, this means of correction is useful in revising spliced or fused independent clauses which express similar or associated ideas. A semicolon can also be used to link an independent clause beginning with a conjunctive adverb or transitional words to the independent clause preceding it.

Comma Splice: The anti-drug movement is inconsistent, an ideological conflict exists over which drugs are socially acceptable and which are not.

Revised: The anti-drug movement is inconsistent; an ideological conflict exists over which drugs are socially acceptable and which are not.

Fused Sentence: Regarding censorship, liberals would remain firm in their conviction to maintain civil liberties however socialists would support legislation to protect the public.

Revised: Regarding censorship, liberals would remain firm in their conviction to maintain civil liberties; however, socialists would support legislation to protect the public.

Fused Sentence: Canada and America are not the same each country came to exist in a different way, and each continues to exist in different circumstances.

Revised: Canada and America are not the same: each country came to exist in a different way, and each continues to exist in different circumstances.

---

[8] Much more information on the use of semicolons and colons is available in Chapter Five.

5) **Tighten**. Sometimes a comma splice or fused sentence can be revised by turning one of its independent clauses into a modifying phrase. This means of correction is especially useful in cases where a pronoun has been used to link the second clause to the first. A pronoun misused in this way may signal information (qualifications or modifications) incorrectly integrated. Another way of revising spliced or fused clauses through tightening involves creating compound subjects or predicates (subjects or predicates joined by coordinating conjunctions). This revision strategy is useful in cases where transitional words and phrases have been used to splice or fuse clauses.

Comma Splice: The physical feature known as the Oak Ridges Moraine is located in Southern Ontario, it extends from Trenton to Orangeville, covering a distance of over one hundred miles.

Revised: Located in Southern Ontario, the physical feature known as the Oak Ridges Moraine extends from Trenton to Orangeville, covering a distance of over one hundred miles.

Comma Splice: Large doses of cocaine can depress the central nervous system, this can result in respiratory arrest.

Revised: Large doses of cocaine can depress the central nervous system, resulting in respiratory arrest.

Fused Sentence: In 1979, the Conservative Party's television commercials attacked Trudeau's policies as well they emphasized the length of the Liberals' term in office.

Revised: In 1979, the Conservative Party's television commercials attacked Trudeau's policies and emphasized the length of the Liberals' term in office.

Notes

My writing strengths:

Things I need to remember:

Things I need to check:

Revising Comma Splices and Fused Sentences

Sample Paragraph:

1. When Schlieffen considered Moltke's experience in the Austrian war, he felt that Moltke had achieved not an ordinary victory, but a decisive one. **2.** It might also be said that Moltke achieved a decisive victory in the French War when Napoleon III surrendered at Sedan. **3.** When Schlieffen looked at the victories won by Moltke, he did not notice that both had been achieved within a very narrow political context, all he noticed was that they had been achieved by encircling the enemy. **4.** The Schlieffen plan, consequently, called for German forces to sweep down the west coast of Europe, take Paris, and fall on the rear of the French army this would catch the French unaware because they would be busy fighting the weaker forces of the German right wing. **5.** The two wings of the German army would thus surround the French troops. **6.** Schlieffen forgot one thing, in the victory over France, Moltke had a superior force, however, in the war to come, Schlieffen would not.

Exercise One:

The courts' predilection to grant divorced mothers custody of children stems from a variety of factors, in most cases the mother has already been the primary child-rearer, regardless of the father's emotional attachment to his children, this usually means that she has better child-care skills and that her dependence on the children is greater, it has also established patterns within the family that would require a major adjustment for all family members if they were to change. Men are more likely to be employed full time, to be making a larger income, to have higher status jobs, and to be in career progression. Thus, following the divorce it is usually easier for the father to continue his occupation than for a non-working mother to leave the home and start a new career, in addition, the social pressures on mothers to take custody are overwhelming.

Exercise Two:

There are vast differences among all the major regions of Canada, therefore, these regions are brought into conflict. Some reasons for conflict are as simple as the terms under which provinces entered Confederation, such was the case with the western provinces when they entered Confederation the federal government kept control over natural resources. In the Maritime provinces the story is different, they joined Confederation in order to boost the sagging industrial sector, this did not happen.

Revising Comma Splices and Fused Sentences: Sample Paragraph Discussion

The sample paragraph contains three comma splices and one fused sentence.

Independent Clauses Beginning with Pronouns

The first comma splice, which occurs in Sentence Three, probably resulted from a failure to recognize the pronoun *all* as the subject of the independent clause *all he noticed was that they had been achieved by encircling the enemy*. It is difficult to see quickly that this clause is independent and that it should not be linked to the clause that precedes it by a comma. One way to determine whether tricky clauses, like this one, are independent is to try to make up a simple sentence that follows the pattern of the clause in question. If such a sentence is possible, the clause is independent. The pattern of this independent clause is similar to the pattern of this sentence: *All he noticed was me*. Therefore, the clause is independent.

Many revisions of this comma splice are possible. The writer might want to keep these two independent clauses in the same sentence because they have closely related meanings:

> When Schlieffen looked at the victories won by Moltke, he did not notice that both had been achieved within a very narrow political context; all he noticed was that they had been achieved by encircling the enemy.

Sentence Four also runs into trouble because a pronoun subject goes unrecognized. The demonstrative pronoun *this* forms the subject of the sentence *this would catch the French unaware because they would be busy fighting the weaker forces of the German right wing*. In other words, Sentence Four is really two sentences fused together. One way to guard against overlooking demonstrative pronoun subjects is to use these pronouns (*this, that, these, those*) not as pronouns but as demonstrative adjectives (*this book, that girl, these clocks, those thoughts*). If our writer had written *this sweeping movement* instead of *this*, it would have been easier for him to recognize that he was writing a noun which formed the subject of a new sentence.

A revision strategy that separates these two sentences would probably be best:

> The Schlieffen plan, consequently, called for German forces to sweep down the west coast of Europe, take Paris, and fall on the rear of the French army. This sweeping movement would catch the French unaware because they would be busy fighting the weaker forces of the German right wing.

Independent Clauses Closely Related in Meaning

In Sentence Six, the writer tries to put an independent clause stating that Schlieffen forgot one thing with an independent clause describing what Schlieffen forgot. The result is a comma splice. Replacing the first comma in this sentence with a colon would be an appropriate revision strategy because a colon is a mark of anticipation that first halts the reader and then directs him or her forward from an initial statement to a following one. In other words, colons both separate and connect. Here is Sentence Six partially revised.

> Schlieffen forgot one thing: in the victory over France, Moltke had a superior force, however, in the war to come, Schlieffen would not.

Misusing Conjunctive Adverbs

Even when its first comma is replaced with a colon, Sentence Six is incorrect. A conjunctive adverb (*however*) is misused to join two independent clauses, creating a comma splice. These independent clauses are fairly similar in importance and grammatical structure, so they should probably be kept in the same sentence. Replacing the *however* with the coordinating conjunction *but* would demonstrate the equality of these independent clauses while allowing them to remain together. Here is a more complete revision of Sentence Six.

> Schlieffen forgot one thing: in the victory over France, Moltke had a superior force, but in the war to come, Schlieffen would not.

Notice that the changed punctuation makes the revised sentence easier to read but remains faithful to the meaning and the rhythm of the original sentence. Similarly, the following revision of the sample paragraph enhances rather than alters the writer's cadence by using correct and more emphatic punctuation:

> When Schlieffen considered Moltke's experience in the Austrian war, he felt that Moltke had achieved not an ordinary victory, but a decisive one. It might also be said that Moltke achieved a decisive victory in the French War when Napoleon III surrendered at Sedan. When Schlieffen looked at the victories won by Moltke, he did not notice that both had been achieved within a very narrow political context; all he noticed was that they had been achieved by encircling the enemy. The Schlieffen plan, consequently, called for German forces to sweep down the west coast of Europe, take Paris, and fall on the rear of the French army. This sweeping movement would catch the French unaware because they would be busy fighting the weaker forces of the German right wing. The two wings of the German army would thus surround the French troops. Schlieffen forgot one thing: in the victory over France, Moltke had a superior force, but in the war to come, Schlieffen would not.

Work through Exercise One and Exercise Two looking for comma splices and fused sentences. Revise each in an appropriate way.

Subject-Verb Agreement

In a sentence, a verb should agree with a subject in person (first, second, or third) and in number (singular or plural). Commonly, writers have little difficulty making subjects and verbs agree. *I work, we work, you work, he works, she works, it works, one works,* and *they work* come tripping off the tongue and dripping from the pen. Agreement is easy when the subject is clear and is placed right beside the verb, but odd couplings can occur because the writer misidentifies the number of the subject or loses sight of the subject completely.

MISTAKING THE NUMBER OF A SUBJECT

Tricky Plural Forms

Most nouns demonstrate their plurality by sporting an *-s* (*apples, books, cats*). Some English nouns, however, especially those originating from Greek and Latin, have plural forms that seem singular to the modern ear and eye. When these nouns are subjects, subject-verb agreement is often lacking.

Incorrect: In judging managerial style, the most important *criteria is* concern for relationships with people.

Revised: In judging managerial style, the most important *criterion is* concern for relationships with people. (*Criterion* is singular, and *criteria* is plural. Since a singular subject is required here, we have changed the subject rather than the verb.)

Incorrect: The *data indicates* a correlation between alcohol consumption and suicide rates.

Revised: The *data indicate* a correlation between alcohol consumption and suicide rates. (Again, *data* is plural. Its singular form is *datum*.[9])

Incorrect: Ancient Egyptian engineering *phenomena is* remarkably durable, graceful, and impressive.

Revised: Ancient Egyptian engineering *phenomena are* remarkably durable, graceful, and impressive. (Again, *phenomena* is plural. Its singular form is *phenomenon*.)

Number and Person

First Person

Singular	Plural
I walk	We walk
I am	We are

Second Person

Singular	Plural
You walk	You walk
You are	You are

Third Person

Singular

** The boy (he) walks
The girl (she) walks
The dog (it) walks
A person (one) walks

The boy (he) is
The girl (she) is
The dog (it) is
A person (one) is

Plural

The boys (they) walk
The girls (they) walk
The dogs (they) walk
People (they) walk

The boys (they) are
The girls (they) are
The dogs (they) are
People (they) are

**Notice that singular third person forms of regular verbs like *to walk* have an *-s* while plural third person regular verbs do not. This fact sometimes confuses students because they associate plurals with the addition of an *-s*. Remember that nouns and verbs are opposite in this regard, that while a plural noun often sports an *-s*, a plural verb usually does not.

---

[9] It should be noted that there is some debate over whether *data* should be treated as a plural noun or as a collective singular noun. Since *data* means *givens* in Latin, it is usually treated as a plural in formal and technical writing, although it is clearly on its way to becoming singular in informal speech and writing.

Unusual Plurals

Singular	Plural
antenna	*antennae
formula	*formulae
vertebra	vertebrae
analysis	analyses
crisis	crises
hypothesis	hypotheses
thesis	theses
appendix	*appendices
index	*indices
criterion	criteria
phenomenon	phenomena
curriculum	curricula
datum	data
medium	media
stratum	strata
alumnus/alumna	alumni/alumnae
nucleus	nuclei
stimulus	stimuli

*While these plurals are correct, other plural forms of these words are becoming increasingly acceptable. Conductors of electromagnetic waves may be called *antennas*, fixed rules for doing something may be called *formulas*, and it is possible to have *appendixes* and *indexes* in books.

Compound Subjects

When the subject of a sentence consists of two or more nouns or pronouns joined by *and*, it is usually plural.

> Incorrect: *Film and television influences* the attention span of adolescents.

> Revised: *Film and television influence* the attention span of adolescents.

Usually, a writer easily recognizes compound subjects like *film and television* as being plural. However, when the normal order of a sentence is inverted, when the verb of a sentence comes before the compound subject, mistakes are common.

> Incorrect: Enclosed *is a report* of my original research *and a review* of related literature.

> Revised: Enclosed *are a report* of my original research *and a review* of related literature.

If this revision sounds awkward, try reordering the sentence or changing its subject.

> Revised: *A report* of my original research *and a review* of related literature *are* enclosed.

> Revised: *I have enclosed* a report of my original research and a review of related literature.

It is possible for two nouns joined by *and* to describe one single thing or person (*my friend and confidante, peanut butter and jelly*). Consider such subjects to be singular.

> Correct: *Peanut butter and jelly* is a good sandwich combination.

A compound subject preceded by *every* or *each* is also singular.

> Correct: *Every immunologist and molecular biochemist seems* obsessed with how cell membranes function.

> Correct: *Each subtle shift and dramatic change in policy was* scrutinized.

When *each* follows a compound subject, however, that subject may be plural or singular.

> Correct: *Toronto and Montreal each claim* (or *claims*) to be the financial heart of Canada.

Alternative Subjects

When a subject is formed by joining two singular nouns with *or* or *nor*, a singular verb is required. Of course, if *or* or *nor* joins two plural nouns to form a subject, the verb should be plural as well. The easiest rule to remember is that verbs of sentences whose subjects contain two nouns linked by *or* or *nor* should agree with the nearer noun.

Correct: Adaptation or *extinction faces* all living things.

Correct: The study fails to state whether eclipses or full *moons are* the most publicized astronomical occurrences.

Correct: An individual's self-esteem or individual *experiences* of social interaction *determine* the ability to love.

Likewise, when using some correlative conjunctions (*either . . . or, neither . . . nor, not . . . but, not only . . . but also*), the verb should usually agree with the noun closest to it.

Correct: Not only hockey but also other *sports were developed* in Canada.

Correct: Not only other sports but also *hockey was developed* in Canada.

Collective Subjects

Collective nouns—like *government, group, team, variety*, and *number*—can be singular or plural depending on context. Such nouns are singular if they denote a single unit and plural if they denote the individuals or items making up the unit. Let logic be your guide. It would be illogical to write the following sentence, for example.

Illogical: *Faculty takes* sabbaticals at different times of the year. (Here the faculty members are being discussed, not the group of professors known as the faculty.)

Revised: *Faculty take* sabbaticals at different times of the year.

If you are worried about when to consider a collective subject plural, try adding the word *members* after every subject denoting a group of people. When this addition seems to fit, use a plural verb. When determining how to make a verb agree with a collective subject that does not denote a group of people, follow the general principle that a collective subject referring to a single whole takes a singular verb, and a collective subject referring to the items making up a whole takes a plural verb. Sometimes articles can help you make these decisions. *A number* and *a variety* take plural verbs while *the number* and *the variety* take singular verbs.

Correct: *A number* of humourists *try* to change society by mocking the idiocy of societal norms.

Phrases like *as well as, in addition to,* and *together with* do not add one subject to another. Treat these phrases and the nouns following them as asides, as irrelevant interrupters not capable of changing the number of the subject. Do not treat them as conjunctions. A singular subject preceding such a phrase still requires a singular verb, even if the noun following the phrase is plural. A plural subject preceding such a phrase and its noun requires a plural verb. In other words, ignore such phrases when determining subject-verb agreement.

Incorrect: *A red-winged blackbird*, along with most other birds, *communicate* through a complicated system of sounds and actions.

Revised: *A red-winged blackbird*, along with most other birds, *communicates* through a complicated system of sounds and actions.

Writing Prompt

Write a paragraph about one of the subjects listed below. This list contains collective nouns. Remember that you will have to think carefully about when to treat collective nouns as wholes or parts to determine when to use singular or plural verbs.

family	jury
Senate	peer group
House of Commons	The Rolling Stones
faculty	army
staff	gang
flock	public
choir	orchestra
Blue Jays	government

Correct: *The number* of dramatic techniques used by Bergson *is* staggering.

Following the same principle, expressions describing a whole amount or a single entity are treated as singular, even if their form is plural.

Correct: While wheat was selling at $1.60 a bushel in 1929, *thirty-eight cents* a bushel *was* the price in 1932.

Correct: One third of the land's produce was kept by the serf, and *two thirds was* given to the lord.

Correct: <u>*Great Expectations*</u> *chronicles* the life and learning of Pip.

Tricky Pronouns as Subjects

INDEFINITE PRONOUNS

Generally, an indefinite pronoun, one that does not by itself refer to a specific thing or person, takes a singular verb. However, some indefinite pronouns—like *all, any, more, most, none,* and *some*—may be singular or plural. The verb you use with these pronouns depends on the meaning of the noun or pronoun referred to. These exceptional indefinite pronouns sometimes give writers trouble.

Incorrect: While *most remains* unaccomplished, some of the goals of Canada's aboriginal people have been reached.

Revision One: While *most remain* unaccomplished, some of the goals of Canada's aboriginal people have been reached.

Revision Two: While *most* of the goals of Canada's aboriginal people *remain* unaccomplished, some have been reached.

Incorrect: *All* the revolutionaries wanted *were* power and a redistribution of wealth.

Revision One: *All* the revolutionaries wanted *was* power and a redistribution of wealth.

Revision Two: *Power and redistribution of wealth were* all the revolutionaries wanted.

RELATIVE PRONOUNS

Because relative pronouns like *who, which,* and *that* do not have different singular and plural forms, writers must check that each verb in a relative clause agrees with the noun or pronoun represented by the relative pronoun.

Incorrect: <u>Twelfth Night</u> is one of Shakespeare's plays *that depends* upon mistaken identity to create comical situations.

Plural and Singular Pronouns

Always Singular

he, she, it
each one
anybody, anyone, anything
everybody, everyone, everything
somebody, someone, something
this, that
whatever, whichever, whoever
nobody, no one, nothing

Almost Always Singular

one, another
each, other
either, neither
much

Always Plural

we, they
these, those
both, others
few, several, many

Singular or Plural

all, any, more, most, none, some

Here the writer probably thought the verb in the relative clause should be singular to agree with *Twelfth Night* or with *one*. Since *that* stands in for *plays*, however, the verb *to depend* should be plural. Twelfth Night is one of many plays that use this comedic device.

Correct: Twelfth Night is one of Shakespeare's plays *that depend* upon mistaken identity to create comical situations.

Look at what happens in the following sentence, which also contains the words *one of*.

Correct: Twelfth Night is the only one of Shakespeare's plays *that makes* several jokes about yellow stockings.

Here the pronoun *that* does refer to *one* and the proper verb to use is consequently singular.

THE LOST SUBJECT

Writers will occasionally lose track of the subjects of their sentences. When this happens, subject-verb agreement is difficult to maintain. A writer may be distracted from the true subject of a sentence by a complement (see page 11 for a definition). The distracting power of a complement obviously caused the writer of the following sentence to make the verb agree with *sandstorms* instead of *thing*.

Incorrect: The most difficult *thing* about living in the desert *are* the sandstorms.

Revised: The most difficult *thing* about living in the desert *is* the sandstorms.

If this revision seems awkward, switch the complement and the subject.

Revised: *Sandstorms are* the most difficult thing about living in the desert.

Another reason for losing the subject and consequently failing to make a subject and verb agree involves inverted sentence order. When placing a verb in front of a subject, check for subject-verb agreement. We have already seen how inverted word order can cause mistakes when the subject coming after the verb is composed of two nouns joined by *and*. There are two other inverted sentence patterns that also cause trouble. One pattern begins with the word *what* and the other with the word *there*.

Incorrect: What *is*, after we have examined the question carefully, the possible *answers*?

Revised: What *are*, after we have examined the question carefully, the possible *answers*?

Incorrect: Additionally, there *are* a wide *range* of other external factors which can increase individual sensitivity to a given carcinogen.

Revised: Additionally, there *is* a wide *range* of other external factors which can increase individual sensitivity to a given carcinogen.

Incorrect: There *is* a few *reasons* why Flowerpot Island became a part of the Bruce National Park.

Revised: There *are* a few *reasons* why Flowerpot Island became a part of the Bruce National Park.

Probably the most common reason for making an error in subject-verb agreement is that words, modifiers in particular, intervene between the bare subject and the verb, causing the writer to lose track of the subject. These interrupting words frequently distract writers who react by making the verb agree with an adjacent noun that is not the subject.

Incorrect: In The Rape of the Lock, Pope implies that stiffened *hoops* bound with whalebone *is* not enough to guard a young lady's virtue. (The writer has made the verb agree with *whalebone* rather than *hoops*.)

Revised: In The Rape of the Lock, Pope implies that stiffened *hoops* bound with whalebone *are* not enough to guard a young lady's virtue.

Incorrect: In other words, the initial *change* in the DNA of cells *seem* impermanent and reversible. (Here the verb agrees with the noun *cells*, which is the object of a prepositional phrase, not the subject of the sentence. This sort of error is common. The verb should agree with the subject *change*.)

Revised: In other words, the initial *change* in the DNA of cells *seems* impermanent and reversible.

Incorrect: *Support* from local governments and businesses for building projects *have* added considerably to the university's financial stability. (The verb should agree with *support*, not with *projects*.)

Revised: *Support* from local governments and businesses for building projects *has* added considerably to the university's financial stability.

It is particularly easy to overlook a singular subject like *anyone, each, neither,* or *one* when it is followed by a prepositional phrase having a plural object. In the following example, the writer has made the verb agree with the object of the prepositional phrase starting with *of*.

Incorrect: *Neither* of these organizations *deliver* effective aid to developing African countries. (The subject is *neither*, so the verb should be singular, not plural.)

Revised: *Neither* of these organizations *delivers* effective aid to developing African countries.

Learning Prompt

Examine old essays noting all instances where subjects and verbs do not agree. Determine in which circumstances you usually have difficulty making subjects and verbs agree. As you may recall, we have divided these circumstances into two main categories: mistaking the number of the subject and losing sight of the subject. The circumstances grouped under the first category include using tricky plural forms, compound subjects, alternative subjects, collective subjects, and tricky pronouns.

Revising for Subject-Verb Agreement

Sample Paragraph:

1. On the increase in today's society is technology and mechanization. **2.** The increasing use of technology and machinery in the work place and the resulting impact on capitalistic society has been well-documented. **3.** Therefore, emphasized here is the impact of technology and machinery upon workers and, in particular, the influence of both factors upon women workers. **4.** Workers, forced to operate machines and subjected to working in an impersonal situation, require enhanced skills and self-reliance. **5.** Instead of seeking out skilled labour or retraining workers, however, bosses often use mechanization as an excuse to cut labour and staff development costs. **6.** For women, who are often clerical workers, the effects have been great. **7.** Since the jobs once assigned to a female secretary, for example, is now taken over by machines, she finds herself doing repetitive, boring work. **8.** As seen in the movie, "Good Monday Morning," women are becoming exasperated because they feel left out of their jobs. **9.** A woman's employers want her to perform a function rather than to exist as an individual. **10.** There is a few very obvious and clear messages being sent here, but one of these many messages are being stressed: leave respect and dignity at home before coming to work.

Exercise One:

It has been suggested that the disparity between costs and benefits underlie the difficulty in arriving at a comprehensive agreement. Two camps, each composed of memberships that cuts across party, national, and even ideological lines, have been unable to reconcile their different perspectives. Both seek to avoid the costs; neither quantify the benefits. One of the sides seem to enjoy a burgeoning mass support while the other fights a holding action of counter-information and rely on the prevalence of conservative economic attitudes during periods of economic downturn.

Exercise Two:

Uncertainty regarding the costs of abatement are dwarfed by the great controversy over quantifying the environmental costs of inaction. In many ways, the problem of proving dose-response relationships are analogous to the difficulties encountered in proving cigarettes cause cancer. In the same way that the tobacco industry challenged medical evidence, many industrial polluters hope to defeat the issue by funding "research" that fail to make the obvious conclusions. Equally dishonest is the rearguard actions fought by such groups as the Coalition for Energy-Environment Balance. This group run full page ads in major American daily newspapers calling into question Canadian motives for opposition to coal-fired plant emissions. In providing a position paper on the Clean Air Act, the National Environmental Development Association, whose members include the Allied Chemical Corporation, Standard Oil, General Electric, and General Motors, make the case for more research.

Revising for Subject-Verb Agreement: Sample Paragraph Discussion

Determining the bare subjects and verbs of the clauses of the sample paragraph is a good way to recognize errors in subject-verb agreement. Let's start with the first three sentences.

These sentences incorrectly combine compound subjects, which are plural by definition, with singular verbs. The bare subject of Sentence One is *technology and mechanization*, and the verb is *is*; the bare subject of Sentence Two is *use and impact*, and the verb is *has been*; and the bare subject of Sentence Three is *impact and influence*, and the verb is *is*. Either this writer did not understand that compound subjects are plural and take plural verbs, or she failed to realize that she had created compound subjects because of the length and complexity of her complete subjects. An additional reason for her mistake might have been that two of the sentences (Sentence One and Sentence Three) are not in the usual subject-verb-object order; their verbs come before their compound subjects. When this happens, the writer must forecast the number of the subject before he or she has written it down, a difficult task. Here is one revision of the first three sentences:

> On the increase in today's society are technology and mechanization. The increasing use of technology and machinery in the work place and the resulting impact on capitalistic society have been well-documented. Therefore, the impact of technology and machinery upon workers and, in particular, the influence of both factors upon women workers are emphasized here.

The next three sentences are correct. In Sentence Four, the plural subject (*workers*) is followed by a plural verb (*require*), even though many words intervene between subject and verb. In Sentence Five, the plural subject (*bosses*) is followed by a plural verb (*use*). Sentence Six also has a plural subject (*effects*) and a plural verb (*have been*).

There are errors in some of the sentences that follow, however, and these errors probably resulted from an inability to recognize the subject.

In Sentence Seven, the singular verb (*is*) has been made to agree with the singular noun (*secretary*) instead of with the plural subject (*jobs*) of the dependent clause beginning with the subordinating conjunction (*since*). Here is a revision.

> Since the jobs once assigned to a female secretary, for example, are now taken over by machines, she finds herself doing repetitive, boring work.

Sentence Eight and Sentence Nine are correct. In both, a plural subject is followed by a plural verb: the subject of Sentence Eight is *women* and the verb is *are becoming*; the subject of Sentence Nine is *employers* and the verb is *want*.

Sentence Ten is not correct. There are two subject-verb agreement errors here. The first might have been caused by the inverted order of the initial independent clause or by the distance between its subject (*messages*) and its verb (*is*). Whatever caused this error, it can be corrected by making the verb plural. The second mistake was probably made because the writer thought that the subject of the second independent clause was *messages* instead of *one*. The plural verb in this clause (*are*) should be singular (*is*). Here is Sentence Ten revised:

> There are a few very obvious and clear messages being sent here, but one of these many messages is being stressed: leave respect and dignity at home before coming to work.

Here is one possible revision of the whole paragraph:

On the increase in today's society are technology and mechanization. The increasing use of technology and machinery in the work place and the resulting impact on capitalistic society have been well-documented. Therefore, the impact of technology and machinery upon workers and, in particular, the influence of both factors upon women workers are emphasized here. Workers, forced to operate machines and subjected to working in an impersonal situation, require enhanced skills and self-reliance. Instead of seeking out skilled labour or retraining workers, however, bosses often use mechanization as an excuse to cut labour and staff development costs. For women, who are often clerical workers, the effects have been great. Since the jobs once assigned to a female secretary, for example, are now taken over by machines, she finds herself doing repetitive, boring work. As seen in the movie, "Good Monday Morning," women are becoming exasperated because they feel left out of their jobs. A woman's employers want her to perform a function rather than to exist as an individual. There are a few very obvious and clear messages being sent here, but one of these many messages is being stressed: leave respect and dignity at home before coming to work.

Now work through Exercise One and Exercise Two. First, find the subject and verb of each clause and sentence. Next, see if these subjects and verbs agree in number. If you find a subject-verb agreement error, make the revision suggested by the context of the other sentences in the paragraph.

Pronoun-Antecedent Agreement

Except for some indefinite pronouns used in some contexts (Many are called, but few are chosen) and for pronouns used in an impersonal way (It is snowing), a pronoun stands in for a noun or another pronoun. This function as a place holder is revealed in the etymology of the term pronoun; it comes from the Latin word *pronomen* which means for (*pro*) a name (*nomen*). In other words, a pronoun is a replacement for something already named, for another noun or pronoun. The named thing that a pronoun replaces is called an antecedent. While the word antecedent means that which goes before, an antecedent may either precede or follow its pronoun.

> Correct: Although *totalitarianism* can be defined as any dictatorship, including the autocratic governments of ancient history, in reality, *it* is a modern phenomenon, a logical extension of industrial society.

> Correct: Because *they* helped create and maintain a feeling of fellowship among all Greeks, the four Panhellenic *festivals* were supported by advocates of Greek unity.

It is important to be able to identify a pronoun's antecedent because, like a subject and its verb, an antecedent and its pronoun must agree in person (first, second, or third) and number (singular or plural). Also, a third-person singular pronoun (*she, he, it*) must agree with its antecedent in gender (feminine, masculine, neuter).

SHIFTS IN PERSON

It is unlikely that you will mistake the gender of an antecedent. Sometimes, a shift in person slips by, however, especially when a pronoun has another pronoun as its antecedent.

> Incorrect: If *we* depend upon external things for *our* happiness, whether they be material possessions, the respect of others, or good health, *we* risk *our* peace of mind because these things are outside of *your* control and may always be taken away from *you*.

> Correct: If *we* depend upon external things for *our* happiness, whether they be material possessions, the respect of others, or good health, *we* risk *our* peace of mind because these things are outside of *our* control and may always be taken away from *us*.

> Incorrect: Not only were the salons the sole places where *one* could become a recognized artist, they were the only places where *one* could show *your* work. (This shift probably occurred either because the writer didn't know that *one* has a possessive form (*one's*) or because she felt that *one's* sounded overly formal.)

Learning Prompt

Collect and examine examples of business writing: letters, memos, and reports written by the administration of your school, university, or place of business. Underline every pronoun and its antecedent. Are there pronoun-antecedent agreement errors? Revise any errors you find.

Correct: Not only were the salons the sole places where *one* could become a recognized artist, they were the only places where *one* could show *one's* work. (This does sound stilted. Another revision attempt is obviously needed.)

Better: Not only were the salons the sole places where an artist could become recognized; they were the only spots available for displaying art.

SHIFTS IN NUMBER

Most errors in pronoun agreement have to do with number and occur in circumstances similar to those in which subject-verb agreement problems take place. Compound antecedents, alternative antecedents, collective-noun antecedents, and indefinite pronouns are all potential troublemakers.

Compound Antecedents

A compound antecedent joined by *and* requires a plural pronoun.

Incorrect: When Juliet puts aside her fears and drinks to her Romeo, she abandons *reason and logic*, substituting passionate love in *its* place.

Correct: When Juliet puts aside her fears and drinks to her Romeo, she abandons *reason and logic*, substituting passionate love in *their* place.

A compound antecedent preceded by *each* or *every*, however, takes a singular pronoun.

Incorrect: When constitutional amendments are being discussed, *every period and comma* raises such deep and intense personal feelings that *they* must be carefully scrutinized.

Correct: When constitutional amendments are being discussed, *every period and comma* raises such deep and intense personal feelings that *it* must be carefully scrutinized.

A singular pronoun is also required when the compound antecedent refers to a single thing or person.

Incorrect: In part because of Confucianism's influence, *the philosopher and thinker* was assured of *their* place in ancient Chinese society. (Using the article *the* in front of *philosopher* and not in front of *thinker*, as well as using the singular form of the verb *to be* (*was*), signals that a single, general concept is being described here, rather than two different types of people. Therefore, the writer has mistaken the number of the subject and used a plural instead of a singular pronoun.)

Correct: In part because of Confucianism's influence, *the philosopher and thinker* was assured of *his* place in ancient Chinese society. (A singular possessive pronoun (*his*) was substituted for the incorrect plural possessive pronoun (*their*). The use of *his* (a sexually specific pronoun) is accurate here because only a male individual was granted the title philosopher and thinker in ancient China.)

Alternative Antecedents

Antecedents joined by *or* or *nor* require a singular pronoun if both are singular, and a plural pronoun if both are plural.

Incorrect: *A cow or any other ruminant* has a third stomach, called an omasum, between *their* reticulum and *their* abomasum.

Correct: *A cow or any other ruminant* has a third stomach, called an omasum, between *its* reticulum and *its* abomasum.

Incorrect: Because *it* was often the centre-piece around which people gathered, the *open fireplaces or cast iron stoves* in pioneer homes were usually attractively decorated.

Correct: Because *they* were often the centre-piece around which people gathered, the *open fireplaces or cast iron stoves* in pioneer homes were usually attractively decorated.

When there is a mix of singular and plural antecedents, a pronoun should agree with the number of the antecedent closest to it.

Incorrect: Neither the Nasty Boys nor *Madonna* is too concerned about promoting feminism through *their* lyrics.

Correct: Neither the Nasty Boys nor *Madonna* is too concerned about promoting feminism through *her* lyrics.

While correct, this revision sounds awkward and illogical; it sounds as if everyone in the sentence is female. Because the writer is so obviously talking about both males and females, a better revision puts the noun *Nasty Boys*, which can be considered plural, closer to the pronoun.

Revised: Neither Madonna nor the *Nasty Boys* are too concerned about promoting feminism through *their* lyrics.

As indicated, *Nasty Boys* can be considered plural. However, a case can also be made for regarding this proper noun as singular. When considering the Nasty Boys as a single unit, as one band, a singular pronoun should be used.

Correct: With *its* latest album causing controversy among some people, the *Nasty Boys* has become a well-known rap band.

Nasty Boys is an example of what grammarians call a collective noun, a noun that can be regarded as describing either a single unit or a collection of members or items.

Collective-Noun Antecedents

When a collective-noun antecedent (*audience, board, chorus, committee, flock, herd, triumvirate*) describes a single whole, it requires a singular pronoun.

Incorrect: The *Senate* can hold up legislation, and *they* have exercised this power.

Correct: The *Senate* can hold up legislation, and *it* has exercised this power.

When a collective noun describes the individuals or items collected into a unit, a plural pronoun is needed.

Incorrect: The *Senate* took *its* seats and began arguing among *itself*.

Correct: The *Senate* took *their* seats and began arguing among *themselves*.

To avoid confusion, some writers insert a word like *members* after a collective noun requiring a plural pronoun: *The Senate **members** took **their** seats and began arguing among **themselves***. Alternatively, if one exists, a word denoting the members of a particular group may be substituted for the collective noun: *The **Senators** took **their** seats and began arguing among **themselves***.

Indefinite Pronouns

As discussed in the section on subject-verb agreement, many indefinite pronouns are always singular, some are almost always singular, a few are obviously plural, and others may be plural or singular depending on their context.

Anyone is always singular.

Correct: *Anyone* failing to pay taxes by the deadline must explain *his* or *her* reasons. (Because either a man or a woman might have to explain his or her failure to pay taxes, alternative pronouns have been used.)

Much is almost always singular.

Correct: *Much* of the tax money went to pay the salaries of those who collected *it*.

Both is always plural.

Correct: *Both* of the buildings had elaborate carvings around *their* doorways.

Some may be plural or singular, depending on context.

Correct: *Some* of the owners restored *their* homes.

Correct: *Some* of the restoration work was criticized for *its* impracticality.

Mistakes in making pronouns agree with indefinite pronoun antecedents usually occur when inexperienced writers try to use gender-neutral language. While traditionally a singular indefinite pronoun antecedent that includes both sexes, such as *everyone, someone,* and *anyone,* has taken a masculine pronoun, conventions have changed. Today, it is conventional to avoid what many people consider to be the sexual bias implied by traditional usage practices through the use of gender-neutral language. Of course, this does not mean that past writers were consciously sexist in their use of pronouns; the meanings of words are determined by a society and should be considered in historical context. In the past, the use of masculine pronouns to refer to singular antecedents was considered appropriate and grammatically correct by the academy. However, the contemporary context often demands gender-neutral language.

When writers try, simultaneously, to use gender-neutral language and to avoid graceless compounds (*his or her, s/he, herself or himself*), pronoun-antecedent agreement is often sacrificed. It need not be. In fact, it should not be. Usually writers can both use gender-neutral language and avoid awkwardness. In one of the preceding examples, the compound pronoun *his or her* is used to refer to *anyone*, an indefinite pronoun. While this example doesn't violate the rules of pronoun agreement, it isn't very elegant. It can be easily revised. Simply eliminate all the words after *explain*; they are redundant anyway.

Revised: *Anyone* failing to pay taxes by the deadline must explain.

Here are some other errors in pronoun agreement made in an attempt to use gender-neutral language. Notice that they have been revised in two ways; the first revision makes the disagreeable pronoun more agreeable, while the second changes the number of the antecedent or eliminates the need for a referent pronoun.

Writing Prompt

Write a paragraph that uses gender-neutral language to define the general characteristics and role of one of the following sorts of people. In other words, your first sentence might resemble the old chestnut "Happiness is a hug," except it will focus on defining a type of person rather than a feeling.

a friend	an adult
a teacher	a monarch
a writer	a follower
a child	a liar
a student	a politician
a thief	a conservative
a leader	a party animal
a rebel	

Incorrect: *Anyone* who is poor cannot participate in sports like horseback riding or cycling because *they* have no leisure time and no extra finances.

Revised: *Anyone* who is poor cannot participate in sports like horseback riding or cycling because *she or he* has no leisure time and no extra finances.

Revised: The *poor* cannot participate in sports like horseback riding or cycling because *they* have no leisure time and no extra finances.

 Incorrect: Because the *scientist* must be aware of both the potential advantages and disadvantages of discoveries, *theirs* is a difficult role.

Revised: Because the *scientist* must be aware of both the potential advantages and disadvantages of discoveries, *his or her* role is difficult.

Revised: Because *scientists* must be aware of both the potential advantages and disadvantages of discoveries, *theirs* is a difficult role.

Notes

My writing strengths:

Things I need to remember:

Things I need to check:

Revising for Pronoun-Antecedent Agreement

Sample Paragraph:

1. Everyone wants to obtain a job, wealth, and the social status necessary for them to enter a higher class within society. **2.** However, class plays a definite role in determining what type of job someone can obtain. **3.** If one falls into the category which permits "ascribed attributes" by finding themselves born into a wealthy family, they will find a considerable number of doors open to them. **4.** Connections or a wealthy father plays a prominent role in getting a job, since they determine status in today's society. **5.** Also, the children of upper-class families have more access to education and a better chance of entering the family business. Because of this, they receive greater attention from all members of society, who award them "badges of ability." **6.** It is relevant here to remember that one is usually unable to escape one's class. **7.** Someone might be able to drop from the upper class to the lower class, but they will very rarely be able to go in the other direction. **8.** The class one belongs to defines the way people perceive you.

Exercise One:

Every woman of this period became alienated from physical exercise because society and the medical profession took it upon itself to tell them what they could and could not participate in. Medical experts directed females toward a safe recovery from her menstrual cycle. They believed that because a woman experienced menstruation, a time of physical renewal was absolutely necessary. For this, outdoor exercise was of utmost importance. Consequently, doctors advised women in both Canada and the United States to partake of fresh air and moderate physical activity because it would allow for a healthy alleviation of the emotional and physical stress brought on by menstruation. Improving a woman's emotional well-being became as important as developing her physical strength in doctors' decisions regarding exercise. Physicians believed light exercise was an absolute necessity in order to develop a healthy character and a strong mind, attributes that would make a woman into a "fit mother." This attitude pushed women into believing that her only purpose in life was to bear children. As a result of this belief, a woman's exercise was curtailed, and social and medical attitudes toward a woman's biological and psychological make-up made competitive sports or overexertion impossible since they might damage her capacity to fulfil her primary role.

Exercise Two:

During the 13th century, the jury had two functions: they presented the accused to the bench, and they tried him on his conviction. Each jury was formed of twelve men of stature from the community they served. These men took an oath before becoming jury members, and they were kept honest by being subjected to fines and imprisonment for concealment of pleas. The trial was simple; the jury informed itself. No evidence was presented and no witness was called, because the jury's job was to discover the facts of each case without it. Jury members judged the accused based on his character and his reputation within the community. By considering the offense committed and by witnessing the prisoner's confrontation with the bench, it determined its verdict. If anything was unclear, it asked questions. One can only marvel that despite the paucity of protection afforded the accused, neither the prisoner nor the judge usually challenged the jury's verdict; they considered most judgments fair. We can surmise that this arose more from the fact that the jury held the majority of power within the system than from their effective dispensation of justice.

Revising for Pronoun-Antecedent Agreement: Sample Paragraph Discussion

We can check for pronoun-antecedent agreement by identifying all pronouns in the sample paragraph and by determining which noun or pronoun each relates to.

In Sentence One, the pronouns are *everyone* and *them. Everyone* is an indefinite pronoun, which forms the subject of the sentence. *Them* is meant to refer to this subject. Since *everyone* is singular and *them* is plural, there is an agreement problem here. In this case, eliminating the referent pronoun, the *them*, is the best revision strategy:

> Everyone wants to obtain a job, wealth, and the social status necessary to enter a higher class within society.

There is only one pronoun in Sentence Two: the indefinite pronoun *someone*. Sentence Three, however, is loaded with pronouns: *one, themselves, they,* and *them*. As this list demonstrates, the writer begins by using a singular pronoun, probably as a result of the singular indefinite pronoun used in Sentence Two, and then switches to plural pronouns. One way to revise Sentence Three would be to make all the pronouns singular: *If one falls into the category which permits "ascribed attributes" by finding one's self born into a wealthy family, one will find a considerable number of doors open to one*. This revision sounds stuffy and stilted. A better strategy involves changing Sentence Two as well as Sentence Three; replacing the indefinite pronoun *someone* in Sentence Two with a plural noun like *people* makes us feel that a plural rather than a singular pronoun should start Sentence Three. We are then able to make all the pronouns in Sentence Three plural. Here is a more graceful revision:

> However, class plays a definite role in determining what type of job people can obtain. If they fall into the category which permits "ascribed attributes" by finding themselves born into a wealthy family, they will find a considerable number of doors open to them.

There is one pronoun (*they*) in Sentence Four. Because this pronoun is referring to the last noun (*father*) in an alternative subject (*connections or a wealthy father*), it should be singular: *Connections or a wealthy father plays a prominent role in getting a job, since he determines status in today's society*. This sounds odd. A better revision would leave the pronoun alone and switch the order of the alternative subject, making *connections* (a plural noun) the antecedent of *they* (a plural pronoun):

> A wealthy father or connections play a prominent role in getting a job, since they determine status in today's society.

There are no pronouns in Sentence Five, but there are three in Sentence Six: *this, they,* and *them*. The *they* and the *them* agree in number with one another and with the noun *children* in Sentence Five. Both are correct. However, because we are not sure which noun the *this* refers to, it is difficult to determine its correctness. Does the writer mean *this access to education* or *this chance of entering the family business*? Perhaps both are meant. If both constitute the antecedent, a more accurate pronoun would be *these*. Also, in order to avoid ambiguity, a noun descriptive of just what is being referred to should follow the *these*. Here is a possible revision:

> Also, the children of upper-class families have more access to education and a better chance of entering the family business. Because of these advantages, they receive greater attention from all members of society, who award them "badges of ability."

Sentence Six is correct. The pronouns *one* and *one's* agree. The next two sentences, however, run into pronoun-antecedent agreement trouble. In Sentence Seven, we see the singular indefinite pronoun (*someone*) referred to with a plural pronoun (*they*). In Sentence Eight, there is a shift in person; the sentence starts out using a third person pronoun (*one*) and ends up using a second person pronoun (*you*). Again, if we attend only to correctness, we will produce an awkward revision. Watch:

Someone might be able to drop from the upper class to the lower class, but he or she will very rarely be able to go in the other direction. The class one belongs to defines the way people perceive one.

Here is a better revision:

People might be able to drop from the upper class to the lower class, but they will very rarely be able to go in the other direction. The class a person belongs to defines the way that person is perceived.

A revision of the whole paragraph might look like this:

Everyone wants to obtain a job, wealth, and the social status necessary to enter a higher class within society. However, class plays a definite role in determining what type of job people can obtain. If they fall into the category which permits "ascribed attributes" by finding themselves born into a wealthy family, they will find a considerable number of doors open to them. A wealthy father or connections play a prominent role in getting a job, since they determine status in today's society. Also, the children of upper-class families have more access to education and a better chance of entering the family business. Because of these advantages, they receive greater attention from all members of society, who award them "badges of ability." It is relevant here to remember that people are usually unable to escape their class. They might be able to drop from the upper class to the lower class, but they will very rarely be able to go in the other direction. The class a person belongs to defines the way that person is perceived.

Correct the pronoun-antecedent agreement errors in the two exercise paragraphs. First, identify each pronoun and its antecedent. Then, determine whether each pronoun agrees with its antecedent in number and person. Be sure to consider the purpose and style of the writers of the two paragraphs when deciding how to revise errors.

Faulty and False Parallelism

Parallelism is a fancy name for a simple concept. It means expressing related ideas in closely similar and balanced arrangements of words. Usually, these ideas are expressed using parallel parts of speech or grammatical structures to allow a reader to see conceptual relationships quickly. For example, the following children's rhyme names various occupations and social positions in a series of parallel nouns, making it easy for us to remember and compare these names: *tinker, tailor, soldier, sailor, rich man, poor man, beggar man, thief. . . .*

Often, using parallel structures comes naturally; the ear seems to demand that sentence elements parallel in thought be parallel in grammatical function and form. Perhaps we employ parallel structures intuitively because memorable sentences so frequently use parallelism. Think of proverbs. It is likely that at least a few of the ones that come to mind contain parallel structures. Here are some examples, with parallel elements indicated and described.

A penny saved is *a penny earned.* (two parallel noun phrases)

Forgive and *forget.* (two parallel verbs)

Something old, something new, something borrowed, something blue. . . . (four parallel pronouns and adjectives)

Everything passes, everything perishes, everything palls. (three short parallel independent clauses)

So most of the time, most of us use parallel structure without thinking because parallelism is part of what Winston Churchill calls "the essential structure of the ordinary British sentence." If you forget what parallelism is, think of any one of Churchill's famous speeches.

Never in the field of human conflict was *so much* owed by *so many* to *so few*.

I have nothing to offer but *blood, toil, tears*, and *sweat*.

Notice that parallelism seems most essential when writers list, add, or compare concepts. Parallelism is so habitual in these circumstances that failure to use parallel structures jars by violating a reader's expectations. This lapse from custom is sometimes called **faulty parallelism**.

In more precise terms, faulty parallelism results when two or more sentence elements of different grammatical form or function appear together in lists, in series, or in compound or coordinate structures. Here are some examples:

Faulty: Scrooge is *a curmudgeon* and *miserly*. (Here a noun is in faulty parallelism with an adjective.)

Parallel: Scrooge is *a curmudgeon* and *a miser*.

Learning Prompt

Write down as many proverbs, adages, and sayings as you can remember. In a small group or on your own, determine which sayings have parallel elements. Then, make these parallel elements as unparallel as you can, without losing the sense of the sentence completely.

Faulty: The ideal forest ranger has studied *biology, ecology,* and *how to plant and take care of forests.* (Here two parallel nouns are in faulty parallelism with a phrase.)

Parallel: The ideal forest ranger has studied *biology, ecology,* and *forestry.*

Faulty: The politician had a successful visit, *kissing babies* and *he dodged reporters.* (Here a participial phrase is in faulty parallelism with an independent clause.)

Parallel: The politician had a successful visit, *kissing babies* and *dodging reporters.*

Faulty: Some critics consider A Tale of Two Cities not only *to be sentimental,* but also *superficial.* (Here the misplacement of *not only* causes an infinitive phrase to be in faulty parallelism with an adjective.)

Parallel: Some critics consider A Tale of Two Cities to be not only *sentimental,* but also *superficial.*

Faulty: Several dissenting City Councillors *were at the midnight meeting* but not *agreeing to change their minds.* (Here a sentence predicate is in faulty parallelism with a participial phrase.)

Parallel: Several dissenting City Councillors *were at the midnight meeting* but *did not agree to change their minds.*

As you can see, some examples of faulty parallelism seem more faulty than others. The last of the preceding examples is the most awkward, illogical, and incorrect. We know this sentence is very wrong because, when we substitute the second sentence element for the first, we create a sentence that sounds incorrect or incomplete: *Several dissenting City Councillors agreeing to change their minds.* The ability to substitute one sentence element for another does not guarantee that these elements are expressed using parallelism, however. The first of the preceding examples is faulty even though it is possible to write *Scrooge is miserly.*

Just to confuse things, it is sometimes acceptable to make sentence elements that are different in grammatical structure but identical in grammatical function parallel. Here is an example:

The runner was *exhausted* but otherwise *in good condition.*

In this sentence, the adjective *exhausted* is paired with the prepositional phrase *in good condition,* but most people would not consider this an example of faulty parallelism because the prepositional phrase functions exactly as the adjective does. In these circumstances, making meaning is more important than making sentence elements parallel in both grammatical form and function: do not sacrifice meaning to enhance parallelism. Nevertheless, if the parallelism of such sentences can be improved without a change in meaning that is unacceptable to you (the writer), make the needed revisions: *The runner was **exhausted** but otherwise **fit**.*

As you can see, there are degrees of faulty parallelism. This does not really matter. What does matter is knowing what parallelism does. To avoid faulty parallelism, remember that parallelism clarifies and confirms the relationship between two or more equally important sentence elements by expressing them in equal grammatical constructions. Therefore, without damaging your meaning, try to make sentence elements that appear in lists, pairs, and comparisons parallel in form if they are of the same order.

Don't, however, force unparallel concepts into parallel structures. A writer's purpose and meaning should determine sentence structure, so don't use parallel structures to express concepts that are not sufficiently similar to be grouped together or compared. This misuse of parallelism is called **false parallelism**:

False Parallelism: The heroine trudged home in *damp clothes, wet shoes,* and *a bad mood*.

Revised: The heroine was in a bad mood as she trudged home in her damp clothes and wet shoes.

When you read the preceding example of false parallelism, what did you think? Did you, by chance, think it was an effective sentence? Well, if its purpose is to show the underlying similarity between seemingly dissimilar things, it is effective. If the writer is suggesting that the heroine's bad mood can be thrown off as easily as her wet shoes and damp clothes, if the items in this list are being compared in a figurative way, then there is no problem. In other words, distinguishing false parallelism from unusual comparisons made for special effect is difficult. It means determining the writer's purpose.

As mentioned, parallelism is most needed when writers list, add, or compare concepts. So let's examine and revise sentences that either fail to use or misuse parallelism in these circumstances.

LISTS

Words, phrases, and clauses listed in a series should be parallel. In the following example of faulty parallelism, two adjectives are followed by a clause instead of by another adjective.

Not Parallel: Governor Murray found his allies *polite, respectful, and that they had a pleasant disposition*.

The last clause creates a problem not only because it destroys the symmetry of the list but also because it is not connected to the beginning of the sentence: we cannot write *Governor Murray found his allies that they had a pleasant disposition*. Simply eliminating all words in this clause but the adjective *pleasant* achieves parallelism.

Revised: Governor Murray found his allies polite, respectful, and pleasant.

While the preceding example of faulty parallelism upsets, it doesn't confuse; we understand the meaning of the sentence. The next example, as well, can be understood, even though it is awkward.

Not Parallel: I asked the chief executive officer *whether she believed in William Ouchi's approach to management, about her own managerial style,* and *to recommend some texts on current organizational theory.*

This series contains a noun clause, a prepositional phrase, and an infinitive phrase. The writer probably placed these dissimilar constructions together because they all describe things that he asked the chief executive officer. In fact, if we read the first part of the sentence with any one of the three items listed, it makes sense: *I asked the chief executive officer whether she believed in William Ouchi's approach to management; I asked the chief executive officer about her own managerial style; I asked the chief executive officer to recommend some texts on current organizational theory.* However, these elements are not parallel in form. Here is a revision:

Revised: I asked the chief executive officer if she believed in William Ouchi's approach to management, if she would describe her own managerial style, and if she might recommend some texts on current organizational theory.

Following is another example of faulty parallelism that disturbs more because it is awkward than because it is unclear. However, in this instance, faulty parallelism makes the reader unsure of emphasis. How much importance is the writer giving the last item in this list?

Not Parallel: As a result of abuse, children may become *withdrawn, too eager to please, aggressive, demanding,* or *have suicidal tendencies.*

The last sentence element in this series is the least parallel. The first four all function as adjectives, and the last functions as a predicate. Besides this major problem, there is the awkwardness of listing three single adjectives in a series with an adjectival phrase. Parallelism would be improved by substituting a word like *fawning* for the phrase *too eager to please.* We can correct the major fault in parallelism in two ways. We can make the list end right after *demanding* by inserting an *or* between *aggressive* and *demanding,* or we can turn the predicate beginning with the verb *have* into an adjective. Notice that the last sentence element receives different emphasis in each of the following revisions.

Revision One: As a result of abuse, children may become withdrawn, fawning, aggressive, or demanding, or have suicidal tendencies.

Revision Two: As a result of abuse, children may become withdrawn, fawning, aggressive, demanding, or suicidal.

In the following sentence, the first two phrases are nicely balanced, but the last phrase is sadly out of sync. The writer probably had trouble finding the vocabulary to make the last phrase parallel the first two.

Not Parallel: The ideal nurse was supposed to show *wifely obedience to the doctor, motherly devotion to the patient*, and *sexless teacher/servant to those outside the medical community*.

Revised: The ideal nurse was supposed to show wifely obedience to the doctor, motherly devotion to the patient, and schoolmarmish serviceability to those outside the medical community.

The revised phrase now parallels the other two: an adjective formed from a noun is followed by a noun that can act as an object of the infinitive *to show*, and that noun is followed by a prepositional phrase.

In the next example of faulty parallelism, unparallel clauses are listed in a series. We know from the punctuation and the placement of the coordinating conjuction *and* that the writer was making a list: *a, b, and c*. However, he does not make the items in this list parallel. Two parallel noun clauses listing Bercuson's arguments are matched with an independent clause. The last item in the list should also be a noun clause; it should also begin with the relative pronoun *that*.

Not Parallel: Bercuson argues *that the OBU played no role in initiating the Winnipeg General Strike, that the Strike did influence the development and perpetuation of the OBU*, and *labourers trying to achieve real control over their lives caused the Strike*.

Revised: Bercuson argues that the OBU played no role in initiating the Winnipeg General Strike, that the Strike did influence the development and perpetuation of the OBU, and that labourers trying to achieve real control over their lives caused the Strike.

While the above revision eliminates faulty parallelism by turning the last clause into a noun clause, it still seems unbalanced. This lack of balance relates to the ideas themselves and not to their grammatical expression; it exists because the ideas are not really equal, although the syntax used to convey these ideas is now parallel. False parallelism, expressing unrelated or unequal ideas in parallel grammatical structures, has replaced faulty parallelism. A better revision follows.

Better: Bercuson argues that, while the OBU played no role in initiating the Winnipeg General Strike, the Strike did influence the OBU's development and perpetuation. Furthermore, he states that labourers trying to achieve real control over their lives caused the Strike.

Since items following a colon comprise a list, they should also be in parallel form.

> Not Parallel: The successful candidate will possess the following qualifications:
>   1) *an M.A.*
>   2) *achieved good grades in university*
>   3) *will be able to get along with people and communicate well*
>   4) *effective in group situations*

> Revised: The successful candidate will possess the following qualifications:
>   1) an M.A.
>   2) a strong academic background
>   3) a high level of interpersonal and communication skills
>   4) the ability to work effectively with groups

As you can see, it is a good idea to keep parallel structure in mind when working on a resume or a job description.

ADDITION AND COMPARISON

Sentence parts that are added together to form pairs or that are compared should also be parallel. After all, a pair is simply a list with two elements, and a comparison is a juxtaposition of elements made to judge similarities and differences. You can often tell when you are adding or comparing ideas by observing when you use coordinating and correlative conjunctions.

Coordinating Conjunctions and Parallelism

The coordinating conjunction *and* is frequently used to create compound structures: double-barrelled subjects, verbs, objects, complements, or modifiers. When the parts of a compound are not expressed in parallel form, faulty parallelism is created.

> Not Parallel: The Victorian Order of Nurses was founded *to give homecare to the sick* and *cottage hospitals in remote areas.* (Here, an infinitive phrase is followed by a noun phrase, and this lack of parallelism makes the sentence illogical and ambiguous. We can guess that the V.O.N. was not founded to give cottage hospitals in remote areas to someone and that the V.O.N. did not give homecare to cottage hospitals in remote areas, but we can't determine the relationship between the V.O.N. and cottage hospitals. Perhaps the V.O.N. was founded to give something to cottage hospitals, like personnel.)

> Revised: The Victoria Order of Nurses was founded to give homecare to the sick and to staff cottage hospitals in remote areas.

Writing Prompt

Write a paragraph comparing/ contrasting two or more people, places, things, or ideas. Examine the paragraph yourself or have a friend examine it to see how effectively you use parallel structures. Improve the parallelism of your paragraph after this examination. Following are lists of things to compare/contrast. Of course, these are only suggestions.

apples/oranges/bananas/pineapples
women/men/girls/boys
reading/writing/listening/speaking
dogs/cats/birds/fish
Clint Eastwood movies/Chuck Norris
   movies/James Bond movies
hockey/curling/figure skating/skiing
pizzas/hamburgers/fried chicken
country & western music/rock 'n'
   roll/rhythm & blues/rap
Halifax/Montreal/Toronto/Calgary/
   Vancouver
primary school/secondary school/
   community college/university

As mentioned, when unrelated or unequal concepts are expressed in grammatically parallel structures, false parallelism is a danger. Unless striving for a special effect, you should avoid forming compounds using coordinating conjunctions when the components of these compounds do not have sufficient features in common to be logically joined. Let us assume that no special effect was intended in the following sentence.

False Parallelism: The expedition led by Roald Amundsen successfully reached the South Pole on December 14, 1911 by *dogsled* and *determination*. (*Dogsled* and *determination* are both nouns; they are grammatically parallel. However, it would be difficult to reach the South Pole by riding on a determination, no matter how determined you were. These nouns should not have been expressed using parallel structure.)

Revised: The determined expedition led by Roald Amundsen successfully reached the South Pole on December 14, 1911 by dogsled.

Coordinating conjunctions are used to compare or contrast ideas as well as to add them together. In general, it is wise to use parallel structures on either side of any coordinating conjunction that adds or compares ideas because, if elements connected by a coordinating conjunction are not expressed using parallelism, the relationship between them can be missed or misconstrued.

Not Parallel: The proposal *offers tax incentives to employers who hire young people,* but *still is neglecting companies that provide unemployed youth with training programs.*

Revised: The proposal offers tax incentives to employers who hire young people, but still neglects companies that provide unemployed youth with training programs.

Not Parallel: In 1891, sullen, hungry Russians could *watch passively as trainloads of grain disappeared into Germany,* or, *risking suppression at the hands of the Cossacks by protesting violently.* (This writer got pulled away from his original intent. He probably wanted to finish his sentence like this: *or, risking suppression at the hands of the Cossacks, protest violently.* This finish still does not achieve parallelism since the syntax of the last element is different from that of the first. It would have been an improvement, however.)

Revised: In 1891, sullen, hungry Russians could watch passively as trainloads of grain disappeared into Germany, or protest violently, risking suppression at the hands of the Cossacks.

Be particularly careful when writing a clause beginning with *and who, and whom,* or *and which* that your sentence already has a *who, whom,* or *which* clause.

Not Parallel: Typhoid fever is a disease *transmitted by polluted water* and *which is cured by antibiotics.*

Revised: Typhoid fever is a disease transmitted by polluted water and cured by antibiotics.

Not Parallel: Cezanne is an artist *famous for his use of colour* and *who paints landscapes.*

Revised: Cezanne is an artist famous for his use of colour and for his landscape paintings.

Not Parallel: <u>Waiting for Godot</u>, *written by Samuel Beckett* and *which typifies the theatre of the absurd,* combines humour with existential anguish.

Revised: <u>Waiting for Godot</u>, which was written by Samuel Beckett and which typifies the theatre of the absurd, combines humour with existential anguish.

Correlative Conjunctions and Parallelism

Watch for unparallel sentence elements linked with correlative conjunctions, such as *either . . . or, neither . . . nor, not only . . . but also,* and *both . . . and.*

Not Parallel: When living with an abusive parent, a child must either *abide by the family's rules of proper conduct* or *violence as a means of disciplining will be risked.*

Revised: When living with an abusive parent, a child must either abide by the family's rules of proper conduct or risk being violently disciplined.

Not Parallel: In arid lands, water is needed in great amounts not only *for consumption* but also *the agricultural industry needs it to irrigate crops.*

Revised: In arid lands, water is needed in great amounts not only for consumption but also for irrigation.

When comparing or joining two ideas with correlative conjunctions, make sure that the parts of the conjunction are correctly positioned. As the following example shows, faulty parallelism often results because a writer misplaces a part of a correlative conjunction and unwittingly relates two dissimilar or unequal sentence elements.

Not Parallel: Ammonia is used for softening both *water* and *dissolving grease*. (The misplacement of *both* causes the noun *water* to be mismatched with the phrase *dissolving grease*. Is ammonia used for softening dissolving grease? Probably not.)

Revised: Ammonia is used for both softening water and dissolving grease.

Other Comparisons

Of course, we can compare concepts without using a coordinating or correlative conjunction. Words like *as, along with, among, between, than, together with*, and *rather* often signal these comparisons. In general, parallelism helps clarify any comparison because, if the two or more ideas being compared are expressed in grammatically equivalent structures, they will be easily recognized and their similarities and differences will be readily apparent. In the following comparison, the parallel infinitive phrases can be quickly spotted and contrasted.

It is better *to live rich* than *to die rich*.[10]

Sometimes, however, illogical comparisons are made because of faulty parallelism. The following sentence compares *actions* to *commanders*, something the writer obviously didn't want to do.

Not Parallel: In guerrilla conflict, *the actions of regional commanders* may be more important than *battalion or brigade commanders*.

Revised: In guerrilla conflict, the actions of regional commanders may be more important than those of battalion or brigade commanders.

Like the preceding example, other sentences making inexact comparisons because of faulty parallelism can easily slip by even the most careful writer. Such sentences are difficult to spot because usually only one or two missing words are needed to make the comparison exact. The preceding example needed only the words *those of*. Sometimes, a missing apostrophe is enough to skew a comparison, as in the first of the following examples of inexact comparisons.

Not Parallel: In 1987, *Pakistan's infant mortality rate* was higher than *most other countries*. (*Pakistan's infant mortality rate* is being compared with *most other countries* instead of with *the infant mortality rate of most other countries*.)

Revised: In 1987, Pakistan's infant mortality rate was higher than most other countries'. (The possessive apostrophe enables the reader to borrow the phrase *infant mortality rate*, making the comparison logical and the two sentence elements compared parallel.)

---

[10] As you can see, parallelism is aesthetically pleasing. However, we are more concerned with recognizing and revising faulty and false parallelism than with using parallelism to create special effects. If you are interested in parallelism as a stylistic choice, Chapter Three will be more to your taste.

Not Parallel: The vigilantes who stormed the Donnelly farm house in 1880 were more fearful *of letting this family live* than *the authorities*. (Here *of letting this family live* is compared with *the authorities*. This sentence lacks clarity as well as parallelism. We are not sure whether the vigilantes were more fearful of letting the Donnelly family live than they were of the authorities or whether they were more fearful of letting this family live than the authorities were.)

Revision One: The vigilantes who stormed the Donnelly farm house in 1880 were more fearful of letting this family live than of the authorities. (Parallel prepositional phrases make the meaning clear.)

Revision Two: The vigilantes who stormed the Donnelly farm house in 1880 were more fearful than the authorities of letting this family live. (Here the comparison is between two parallel nouns *the vigilantes* and *the authorities*.)

Notes

My writing strengths:

Things I need to remember:

Things I need to check:

Revising Faulty and False Parallelism

Sample Paragraph:

1. The author paints a picture not of uncivilized black Africans but of the uncivilized Europeans and a continent that both through its people and geographically does not welcome invasions. **2.** Marlow, the narrator of <u>Heart of Darkness,</u> is responsible for most of this picture. **3.** He criticizes the people working for the Company, describing them as "conquerors. . . . They grabbed what they could get for the sake of what was to be got. It was just robbery with violence . . ."(10). **4.** It is the European imperialists who are portrayed as barbarous people. **5.** The only two European characters not strongly criticized by Marlow are the Russian because he is selfless, and Kurtz because he seems to be a man with morals, and the natives because they are not to be blamed.

Exercise One:

The late nineteenth century brought many changes to Alberta. The coming of the North-West Mounted Police did not end the misfortunes of the Indians and Métis. Their strength and the way they had spirit had been taken away by the white man's ways. In 1876 and 1877, the Indians signed away their heritage of parklands, plains, and freedom. In exchange, they were given small amounts of treaty money, forced onto reserves, and had to try to farm instead of hunting for their livelihood. With the bison gone and now that the Indians were on reserves, Alberta was ready for settlement. At first, growth was slow; a few settlers tried ranching in the south and others lived around Fort Edmonton, Fort Saskatchewan, Fort Calgary, and Fort Macleod. According to the Dominion census of 1881, there were only 18,072 whites and Métis living in what would soon be Alberta. Nonetheless, surveyors and scientists were reporting on routes for roads and railways, fertility of the soil, and prospecting for coal, oil, gas, and minerals. During this time, thousands of square miles of prairie were divided into neat square parcels of 160 acres each, free to any male over eighteen or a widow who was head of a family (Hardy, 1967, 310-12).

Exercise Two:

The possibilities of the Western genre become most apparent when films within the genre are compared. <u>My Darling Clementine</u> (1947), <u>The Man Who Shot Liberty Valance</u> (1962), and the work <u>The Left-Handed Gun</u> (1959) are essentially the same film in terms of plot. In each, a stranger enters town, decides to act in accordance with his own moral code, and some change is made, and who then leaves town. Nonetheless, the films are not indistinguishable. If the earliest of the three, <u>My Darling Clementine</u>, is taken as the prototype by which the other two can be considered, it soon becomes apparent that John Ford's <u>Liberty Valance</u> is a self-conscious commentary on the nature of the Western hero, while Arthur Penn's <u>The Left-Handed Gun</u> criticized the manner in which society understands that hero. <u>Liberty Valance</u> rises above its restricted structure to comment on the form itself; <u>Left-Handed Gun</u>, to examine the darker origins of this form, reaches under its limited structure. The artistry in these two films, then, is created by each director's exploration of the possibilities within the genre; not simply are variations on a standard theme demonstrated.

Revising Faulty and False Parallelism: Sample Paragraph Discussion

Since parallelism is most essential when comparing or listing, determining where such comparisons and lists occur in the sample paragraph is a good way to begin to check it for faulty or false parallelism. Next, we should consider whether the items in these comparisons and lists are or should be parallel.

In Sentence One, the writer lists what the author of Heart of Darkness does and does not describe. There are three main items in this list: the author does not paint a picture *of uncivilized black Africans*; he does paint a picture *of the uncivilized Europeans*; and he does paint a picture of *a continent*. By comparing the italicized phrases, which are taken directly from the sample paragraph, we can see immediately that the last item in this list (*a continent*) needs to have the word *of* in front of it to parallel the other two. Also, the first two items in the list could be made to parallel each other more closely: *of uncivilized black Africans* could be followed by *of uncivilized white Europeans*. One additional list is made in this sentence. The writer describes the ways in which Africa does not welcome invasions: *through its people* and *geographically*. These items should be expressed using parallelism as well. Here is one possible revision of Sentence One.

> The author paints a picture not of uncivilized black Africans but of uncivilized white Europeans and of a continent that, through both its people and its geography, does not welcome invasions.

Sentence Two does not list or make comparisons that necessitate employing parallel structure. Sentence Three and the quoted sentences that follow it maintain parallelism. Notice, in particular, Conrad's juxtaposition of the clauses *what they could get* and *what was to be got*. Sentence Four suffers from neither faulty nor false parallelism, but Sentence Five suffers from both. The first two elements in the list of European characters that Marlow criticizes belong there. However, because the noun *natives* is not representative of a European character in Heart of Darkness, it has no business being tacked on to the end of this sentence. Let's eliminate false parallelism by splitting this sentence in two:

> The only two European characters not strongly criticized by Marlow are the Russian, because he is selfless, and Kurtz, because he seems to be a man with morals. The natives are not criticized either because they are not to be blamed for the barbarity of the Europeans.

The first sentence of this revision is in need of further revision. The expressions of why each character was not criticized should be made parallel:

> The only two European characters not strongly criticized by Marlow are the Russian, because he is selfless, and Kurtz, because he seems moral.

Here is one possible revision of the complete paragraph:

> The author paints a picture not of uncivilized black Africans but of uncivilized white Europeans and of a continent, that through both its people and its geography, does not welcome invasions. Marlow, the narrator of Heart of Darkness, is responsible for most of this picture. He criticizes the people working for the Company, describing them as "conquerors. . . . They grabbed what they could get for the sake of what was to be got. It was just robbery with violence. . ." (10). It is the European imperialists who are portrayed as barbarous people. The only two European characters not strongly criticized by Marlow are the Russian, because he is selfless, and Kurtz, because he seems moral. The natives are not criticized either because they are not to be blamed for the barbarity of the Europeans.

Identify the lists and comparisons made in Exercise One and Exercise Two. Are the elements of these lists and comparisons expressed in parallel grammatical structures? Should they be? Revise both exercise paragraphs for faulty and false parallelism.

Misplaced and Dangling Modifiers

MISPLACED MODIFIERS

We now know that modifiers come in many varieties and sizes: they can be adjectival, adverbial, or absolute; they can be words, phrases, or clauses. What, then, is a misplaced modifier? Obviously, it is a modifier that is in the wrong place. It might be too far from the sentence element it is supposed to be wedded to; it might be positioned between two sentence elements, either of which could be its intended; or it might act to break up sentence elements that should be paired by sitting awkwardly between them, like an unwanted chaperon. The thing to remember about a modifier is that it will usually follow the philosophy Crosby, Stills, Nash, and Young set out in their song "Love the one you're with": if it can't be with the one it modifies, it modifies the one (or ones!) it's with.

Misplaced modifiers cause confusion and often unintentional humour. So if you don't want your reader to be frustrated or to laugh at you rather than with you, position your modifiers carefully.

Distant Modifiers

Modifiers that are too far from the words, phrases, or clauses they are supposed to modify end up seeming to modify another sentence element. Both adjectives and adverbs can be positioned at too great a distance from the sentence elements they are meant to modify.

> Misplaced Adjectives: In the seventies, women protested against the *patriarchal* and *hierarchical* injustices being perpetuated by society. (These adjectives seem to modify *injustices* when they are probably meant to modify *society*.)

> Revised: In the seventies, women protested against the injustices being perpetuated by a patriarchal and hierarchical society.

> Misplaced Adverb: As usual, the politicians argued amongst themselves *loudly* surrounded by aides who were calmly reaching an agreement. (This sentence seems to say that the politicians were surrounded loudly. Of course, the adverb *loudly* was supposed to modify *argued*.)

> Revised: As usual, the politicians argued loudly amongst themselves while surrounded by aides who were calmly reaching an agreement.

Notice that both of the preceding sentences were revised by moving the modifier closer to the word it was supposed to modify.

[13] Richard Lederer, *Anguished English* (New York: Bantam Doubleday Dell, 1989) 151.

Phrases which modify can also be misplaced. Prepositional phrases are particularly hard to position correctly since they can function either as adjectives or adverbs. Some of the most troubling prepositional phrases are those starting with *by, for, in,* and *with*.

Misplaced Prepositional Phrase: Mary Shelley wrote a futuristic novel describing the gradual destruction of the human race by plague *in 1826*. (Mary Shelley wrote the novel in 1826; the human race was not destroyed by plague in 1826.)

Revised: In 1826, Mary Shelley wrote a futuristic novel describing the gradual destruction of the human race by plague.

Misplaced Prepositional Phrase: A representative from the tourist board discussed the possibility of stocking the area's rivers *with fishing enthusiasts*. (The discussion was with fishing enthusiasts, not about stocking the rivers with fishing enthusiasts.)

Revised: A representative from the tourist board held a discussion with fishing enthusiasts about the possibility of stocking the area's rivers.

The last example was corrected by doing more than moving the offending modifier. Often, this strategy is best since it doesn't force the writer to correct the problem of a misplaced modifier by creating another problem: an awkward sentence like *A representative from the tourist board discussed with fishing enthusiasts the possibility of stocking the area's rivers.*

Participial phrases also require careful placement. They can easily attach themselves to the wrong nouns.

Misplaced Participial Phrase: *Connecting the toes of the feet*, aliped creatures have a winglike membrane. (Obviously, aliped creatures do not connect the toes of the feet, but a winglike membrane does.)

Revised: Aliped creatures have a winglike membrane connecting the toes of the feet.

Misplaced Participial Phrase: Doctors worried about the legal ramifications of a bill to limit abortions *approved by the House of Commons*. (The abortions were not approved by the House of Commons; the bill, however, was.)

Revised: Doctors worried about the legal ramifications of a bill to limit abortions, which was approved by the House of Commons.

Turning the participial phrase (*approved by the House of Commons*) into a relative clause (*which was approved by the House of Commons*) cues the reader as to which noun this modifier modifies. If the writer wanted to modify the noun *abortions* using a relative clause, the verb in that clause would have to be plural. Since the verb in the relative clause is singular, we know that *bill* and not *abortions* is modified.

A clause may also be placed too far from the sentence element it is intended to modify, as the two following examples demonstrate.

Misplaced Clause: The Iroquois made combs for their hair from the bones of animals *which had very strong teeth*. (The combs, not the animals, had strong teeth.)

Revised: The Iroquois made combs for their hair from the bones of animals. These combs had very strong teeth.

Misplaced Clause: Terry Fox told reporters that he planned to run across Canada *after he lost his leg to cancer*. (The implication here is that Fox planned to lose his leg to cancer.)

Revised: After he lost his leg to cancer, Terry Fox told reporters that he planned to run across Canada.

The suggested revision of the first sentence containing a misplaced clause involves breaking apart the sentence. Since it is difficult to place the clause *which had very strong teeth* close to the word *combs* because the modifying phrase *for their hair* intrudes, the writer has chosen to repeat the noun *combs* and to place the idea that these combs had strong teeth in another sentence. Another possible revision follows: *The Iroquois made hair combs, which had very strong teeth, from the bones of animals*.

Squinting Modifiers

A squinting modifier is cross-eyed from looking both ways at once. Because it doesn't focus on one particular sentence element, it can be interpreted as modifying the words preceding it or the words following it.

Squinting Modifier: In 1917, Henri Bourassa rallied anti-conscription supporters *actively* arguing that Canada had already done enough to support the Great War. (We are not sure whether the anti-conscription supporters were actively rallied or whether the arguing was being done actively.)

Revision One: In 1917, Henri Bourassa actively rallied anti-conscription supporters by arguing that Canada had already done enough to support the Great War.

Revision Two: In 1917, Henri Bourassa rallied anti-conscription supporters by actively arguing that Canada had already done enough to support the Great War.

The modifiers that usually squint are adverbs. This is because an adverbial modifier can attach itself to so many more sentence parts than an adjectival modifier. So be sure that your adverbs don't make unacceptable attachments.

Be particularly careful when placing limiting modifiers, adverbs like *almost, even, exactly, hardly, just, merely, nearly, only, scarcely,* and *simply.* In speech, many of these limiting modifiers occur directly before the verb, regardless of which sentence element they are intended to modify. In our oral language, this placement of a limiting modifier is acceptable and clear because of the ability of the human voice to stress certain words. In our written language, however, we cannot rely upon intonation to clarify our meaning; we must rely upon word order, not upon a rising and falling human voice, to make connections. Writers must consequently make sure that when limiting modifiers fall into their normal, idiomatic place in front of verbs, no ambiguity is created.

Squinting Limiting Modifier: Acting simply is not valued by those who grant Academy Awards.

We don't know whether acting the part of a simpleton is not valued or whether *simply* is being used to intensify the meaning of the verb, whether good acting of any sort goes unrecognized on Oscar night. Let's assume that the writer wanted to express the first concept. Moving *simply* to the head of the sentence would not solve the problem.

Poor Revision: Simply acting is not valued by those who grant Academy Awards.

This sentence suggests that, while the performances of actors and actresses are considered by the Academy, acting ability alone will not guarantee the receipt of an Oscar. Also, the sentence is awkward.

Better Revision: Acting in a simple manner is not valued by those who grant Academy Awards.

Notice that getting rid of a limiting modifier is sometimes more effective than repositioning it. Whatever you do, check your first attempts to revise the placement of limiting modifiers to make sure that in solving one problem you have not created another.

Awkwardly Placed Modifiers

Some modifiers are awkwardly rather than incorrectly positioned. Since we expect grammatically related sentence elements to stay together, placing modifiers between the components of an infinitive or the components of a verb phrase can confuse and irritate. We also expect sentences to be arranged in certain ways. One of the most common arrangements moves from the subject with all its modifiers to the verb with all its modifiers to the verb's objects or complements with all their modifiers. When this movement is interrupted by long modifying phrases or clauses, awkwardness or confusion may result. Consequently, long modifiers coming between the subject and the verb or between the verb and its object or complement should be avoided.

SPLIT INFINITIVES

Infinitives are verbals consisting of *to* and a verb: *to be, to drink, to go, to live.* When a modifier comes between the *to* and its verb (*to boldly go*), the infinitive is said to have been split. Some split infinitives are effective, some are acceptable, but many are awkward. When the Enterprise announces that its mission is *to boldly go* where no one has gone before, the boldness of this mission is stressed by the unconventional placement of the word *boldly*. This splitting of an infinitive could be considered effective because it provides appropriate emphasis. When a student writes *The Board of Directors met to quickly review next year's budget*, he avoids an awkward sentence (*The Board of Directors met to review quickly next year's budget*) and he avoids conveying an incorrect meaning (*The Board of Directors met quickly to review next year's budget*). Such a split infinitive could be considered acceptable.

When it comes to splitting infinitives, however, writers must know their readers. Some readers never consider a split infinitive to be either effective or acceptable. Don't worry. Most split infinitives can be eliminated through careful rewriting: *The Board of Directors quickly reviewed next year's budget in a meeting called for that purpose.* Most rewriting is more easily accomplished, as the following revisions of awkwardly split infinitives demonstrate.

Split Infinitive: *To completely revise* current teaching strategies is difficult to accomplish with the minimal amount of parental resistance.

Revised: To revise current teaching strategies completely is difficult to accomplish with the minimal amount of parental resistance.

Split Infinitive: Lithuania, Latvia, and Estonia, the three Baltic republics of the U.S.S.R. determined *to eventually win* independence, were provinces of Imperial Russia before World War One.

Revised: Lithuania, Latvia, and Estonia, the three Baltic republics of the U.S.S.R. determined to win independence eventually, were provinces of Imperial Russia before World War One.

Split Infinitive: By hunting, trapping, and developing energy and agricultural resources, Canadians have begun *to severely reduce* the population of wolverines.

Revised: By hunting, trapping, and developing energy and agricultural resources, Canadians have begun to reduce the population of wolverines severely.

INTERRUPTED VERB PHRASES

Be careful of inserting modifiers in the middle of verb phrases like *is writing, was writing, has written, had written, has been writing, had been writing.* Interrupting modifiers that do not relate to the time sequence being set up by a verb phrase cause a bumpy sentence rhythm and unnecessary havoc.

Poor: Albert Camus *was, in 1913, born* in Algeria, which provides the setting for many of his writings.

Revised: Albert Camus was born in 1913 in Algeria, which provides the setting for many of his writings.

Poor: Camus already *had, when he was awarded the Nobel Prize for literature in 1957, written* his most famous works: L'Étranger, La Peste, Le Myth de Sisyphe, and L'Homme révolté.

Revised: When he was awarded the Nobel Prize for literature in 1957, Camus already had written his most famous works: L'Étranger, La Peste, Le Myth de Sisyphe, and L'Homme révolté.

INTERRUPTED SENTENCE MOVEMENT

When the movement of a sentence from subject to verb is interrupted by a long, complicated modifier, it is likely that the writer will lose both the reader and the natural flow of the sentence.

Poor: William Lyon Mackenzie King, *managing to stay in office because of support from Progressive and Labour members and in spite of the fact that Arthur Meighen's Conservatives won a plurality of seats in the general election of October 29, 1925*, resigned in 1929 following the furor created by the disclosure that the Customs Department was corrupt.

Revised: Because William Lyon Mackenzie King was supported by Progressive and Labour members, he managed to stay in office despite losing a plurality of seats to Arthur Meighen's Conservatives in the general election of October 29, 1925; nevertheless, he resigned in 1929 following the furor created by the disclosure that the Customs Department was corrupt.

A sentence in which a modifier comes between the verb and its object or complement is often unclear and graceless.

Poor: A few months after his resignation, Mackenzie King regained and held *until 1930* power in another general election.

Revised: In another general election held a few months after his resignation, Mackenzie King regained power and held it until 1930.

DANGLING MODIFIERS

A dangling modifier modifies a concept that is implied but not stated in a sentence. Think of dangling modifiers as loners who, although alienated from the sentences they inhabit, hang around. Dangling modifiers, then, because they are hangers-on with nothing to hang on to, simply hang out, usually at the beginning or end of a sentence. Unlike loners, dangling modifiers are hard to spot. Since writers are so familiar with what they mean to write, their brains usually supply the missing sentence element, the friend or relation able to bring the loner back into the fold. The reader, on the other hand, does not have this advantage and is forced to make an educated guess as to the missing link. Here is an example of a dangling modifier.

Incorrect: *To manage corporations effectively*, good communication skills are essential.

Obviously, good communication skills are not managing corporations effectively. Something is missing. There are three ways to fix this dangling modifier, and most others. You can leave the modifier as it is and supply the missing sentence element.

Revised: To manage corporations effectively, business people have an essential need: good communication skills.

You can turn the modifier into a complete clause and leave the rest of the sentence as it is.

Revised: If business people want to manage corporations effectively, good communications skills are essential.

You can rewrite the whole sentence to integrate the modifier more fully.

Revised: Good communication skills are essential to the effective management of corporations.

A common dangler is an elliptical clause, a clause from which the subject, verb, or both have been omitted. An elliptical clause dangles unless the omitted subject or verb is the same as that of the main clause.

Incorrect: *While protesting the Vietnam War by journeying to Hanoi on a peace mission*, Tom Hayden's reputation as a social activist grew. (The first clause is a dangling elliptical clause because its omitted subject (*Tom Hayden*) and its omitted verb (*was*) are different from the subject (*reputation*) and the verb (*grew*) of the main clause.)

Revised: While Tom Hayden was protesting the Vietnam War by journeying to Hanoi on a peace mission, his reputation as a social activist grew.

Incorrect: *When a child*, his love for animals and flowers was expressed through the collections Vincent Van Gogh made rather than through art. (Again, the first clause is a dangling elliptical clause missing the subject *Vincent Van Gogh* and the verb *was*. The subject of the main clause is *love* and the verb is *was expressed*.)

Revised: When a child, Vincent Van Gogh expressed his love for animals and flowers through the collections he made rather than through art.

Besides elliptical clauses, the most common danglers are adverbs, prepositional phrases, and verbal phrases (participial, infinitive, and gerund phrases). These common dangling modifiers are also the most commonly misplaced modifiers.

As you may have noticed, you can usually use one of three strategies to revise danglers:

1) Change the subject of the main clause so that the modifier has a noun or pronoun to hang on to.

2) Change the dangler into a phrase or clause that clearly modifies an existing part of the main clause.

3) Recast the whole sentence.

Here are some examples of the most common dangling modifiers revised.

Dangling Adverb: *Satisfactorily*, novelist Robertson Davies almost always describes the lives of his characters fully. (Who is satisfied by this circumstance?)

Revision Strategy Two: To the readers' satisfaction, novelist Robertson Davies almost always describes the lives of his characters fully.

Revision Strategy Three: Novelist Robertson Davies's readers are satisfied because this author almost always describes the lives of his characters fully.

Dangling Prepositional Phrase: *As a young girl*, Marian Engel's father was in and out of work during the Depression, a fact that caused her to learn the virtues of self-sufficiency and determination. (Marian Engel's father was never a young girl. This dangler was caused because the writer did not realize that a possessive noun like *Marian Engel's* cannot be the subject of a main clause. Watch for danglers when using the possessive form of nouns and pronouns.)

Revision Strategy One: As a young girl, Marian Engel learned the virtues of self-sufficiency and determination from her father who was in and out of work during the Depression.

Revision Strategy Two: When Marian Engel was a young girl, her father was in and out of work during the Depression, a fact that caused her to learn the virtues of self-sufficiency and determination.

Revision Strategy Three: Marian Engel learned the values of self-sufficiency and determination as a young girl because her father was in and out of work during the Depression.

Dangling Participial Phrase: *Staying in England*, the blooming of the first daffodils inspired Norman Levine to write "Thin Ice" because it made him nostalgic for Canadian winters. (The blooming of the first daffodils was not staying in England.)

Revision Strategy One: Staying in England, Norman Levine was inspired to write "Thin Ice" by the blooming of the first daffodils, which made him nostalgic for Canadian winters.

Revision Strategy Two: While Norman Levine was staying in England, the blooming of the first daffodils inspired him to write "Thin Ice" because it made him nostalgic for Canadian winters.

Revision Strategy Three: The first daffodils to bloom in England inspired Norman Levine's "Thin Ice" by making this author nostalgic for Canadian winters.

Dangling Infinitive Phrase: According to W.O. Mitchell, *to create effective prose*, "the left side of the brain—the assessor, the critic" must be told "to bugger off." (The left side of the brain is not creating effective prose; it is being told to bugger off.[11])

Revision Strategy One: According to W.O. Mitchell, to create effective prose, the writer must tell "the left side of the brain—the assessor, the critic—to bugger off."

Revision Strategy Two: According to W.O. Mitchell, if a writer wants to create effective prose, he or she must tell "the left side of the brain—the assessor, the critic—to bugger off."

Revision Strategy Three: W.O. Mitchell states that the writer must tell "the left side of the brain—the assessor, the critic—to bugger off" in order to create effective prose.

---

[11] This dangling modifier was written because its author chose to use the passive voice. This voice allows the true actor of the sentence, in this case the person doing the telling, to escape notice. For more information about the passive voice, see pages 291-294 of Chapter Six.

Dangling Gerund Phrase: *In deciding what to write*, the ability of poetry to renew language is considered. (Who is doing the deciding? The writer obviously needs to provide more information, to name the individual doing the considering and the deciding.[12])

Revision Strategy One: In deciding what to write, Margaret Atwood considers the ability of poetry to renew language.

Revision Strategy Two: When Margaret Atwood decides what to write, she considers the ability of poetry to renew language.

Revision Strategy Three: The ability of poetry to renew language is a consideration in Margaret Atwood's decision concerning what she will write.

Dangling Elliptical Clause: *When two years old*, Al Purdy's father died of cancer.

Revision Strategy One: When two years old, Al Purdy lost his father to cancer.

Revision Strategy Two: When Al Purdy was two years old, his father died of cancer.

Exceptions

Some modifiers are not considered danglers even though they seem to dangle. One such modifier is an absolute phrase, usually a participial phrase with its own subject:

His plurality turned into a clear majority, Prime Minister Diefenbaker faced the House of Commons with confidence.

Another modifier that is not considered a dangler although it appears to dangle is an idiomatic phrase that relates to a whole sentence. These modifiers are often verbal phrases:

Strictly speaking, Diefenbaker won 208 of the 265 seats in the 1958 general election.

Although idiomatic expressions such as *strictly speaking* are not considered to dangle when used in circumstances like those in the preceding example, a professor might think these expressions too informal for academic writing. It is probably best to avoid such idioms.

Writing Prompt

Write a few short paragraphs describing an event or an action. Next, combine the sentences of these paragraphs without using coordination or subordination; try to pack as much description and information into each sentence as is possible. Read through these "packed" sentences to see that you have correctly placed all modifiers.

---

[12] Here is another example of a writer creating a dangler by using the passive voice.

Revising Misplaced and Dangling Modifiers

Sample Paragraph:

1. In spite of evidence that points to the need to quickly make the transition to a system of sustainable agriculture, we are circumscribed by an economic system based on continuous growth and by the pressures created by world hunger and inflation. **2.** Immediate sacrifices are still viewed as myopically disastrous by many farmers. **3.** Looking to the future, the tunnel vision of farmers is not hard to understand. **4.** They probably fear that they will be the only ones to pay for change. **5.** Change is also discouraged by the dominating force of the multinationals and by the dogma of technological optimism actively. **6.** In spite of these seemingly insurmountable external pressures, we should be optimistic. **7.** Optimism lies in the alternatives that do exist and in the ability of a self-aware species to eventually recognize the limitations of the present system of agriculture.

Exercise One:

Consequently, it would seem, having not maintained an impartial position, it was decided that Fulton was needed by the federal government no longer and subsequently Crombie was shuffled out of Indian and Northern Affairs to another ministry also. Roger Tasse, appointed as the new Federal Negotiator soon after Fulton's departure, limited the possibility of fruitful discussion decisively by refusing to ever work from the discussion paper compiled by Fulton or to involve him as a mediator. Once again, no headway was made in negotiations for a couple of years.

Exercise Two:

There are several reasons that the character of Herbert is not memorable. First, we are only introduced to Herbert in an incident comprising one and a half pages. Encountering a "milk toast" young man referred to as the "pale young gentleman" (70), the first meeting could only be considered memorable because of the occurrence of a fight, which is unprovoked and unimpassioned. An exchange of pleasantries in fact showing Herbert's distinct lack of passion follows the fight. Second, Herbert is equally unimpassioned and unmemorable in his love relationships. Clara only seems moderately enamoured of Herbert, although the two are supposed to eventually marry.

Revising Misplaced and Dangling Modifiers: Sample Paragraph Discussion

In order to revise the sample paragraph, we must be able to recognize distant, squinting, awkwardly placed, and dangling modifiers. Let's begin by looking through the paragraph for awkwardly placed modifiers because this sort of misplacement occurs in fewer circumstances than other sorts do. Specifically, let's look for times when a modifier splits an infinitive.

Split Infinitives

There are four infinitives in this passage: *to make* (in Sentence One), *to understand* (in Sentence Three), *to pay* (in Sentence Four), and *to recognize* (in Sentence Seven). Two of these infinitives are split by adverbs: *to quickly make* and *to eventually pay*. The first split infinitive, which is located in Sentence One, can be eliminated by moving the word *quickly*:

> In spite of evidence that points to the need to make the transition to a system of sustainable agriculture quickly, we are circumscribed by an economic system based on continuous growth and by the pressures created by world hunger and inflation.

If *quickly* seems too far away from the infinitive *to make* in this revision, we could rewrite the sentence like this:

> In spite of evidence that points to the need to make a quick transition to a system of sustainable agriculture, we are circumscribed by an economic system based on continuous growth and by the pressures created by world hunger and inflation.

The second split infinitive occurs in Sentence Seven. It is much more difficult to eliminate. In fact, we could argue that this is an effective split infinitive; the adverb *eventually* receives appropriate emphasis by being placed where it is. One way to maintain the writer's emphasis on *eventually* while avoiding a split infinitive would be to use this word as an interrupter:

> Optimism lies in the alternatives that do exist and in the ability of a self-aware species to recognize, eventually, the limitations of the present system of agriculture.

Let's look for dangling modifiers next because, as we have discovered, they also generally occur in particular circumstances; they usually hang off the beginning or the end of a sentence.

Dangling Modifiers

Sentence One, Sentence Three, and Sentence Six all begin with introductory phrases, perfect places for dangling modifiers to hide. The prepositional phrases beginning Sentence One and Sentence Six both have a noun to cling to; they both modify the noun *we*. The introductory phrase in Sentence Three, however, does not modify any noun. This phrase (*looking to the future*) certainly doesn't modify *the tunnel vision of farmers*; *tunnel vision* can't look to the future. We can revise this sentence by making its introductory phrase into a dependent clause that contains an expression of who is looking to the future:

> When one looks to the future, the tunnel vision of farmers is not hard to understand.

Misplaced Modifiers

Sentence Two contains a misplaced modifier. To discover it, identify the nouns and verbs in the sentence and ask yourself whether the words that appear to modify these nouns and verbs can modify them logically. For example, can we have *sacrifices* that are *immediate*? Yes. Can we have *immediate sacrifices* that are *myopically disastrous*? Can a disaster be myopic? Can a sacrifice? Probably not, so we have identified the misplaced modifier. Which noun or verb do you think the writer meant to modify? Farmers can be myopic. Could the writer have meant *myopic farmers*? Probably the writer meant to be less literal. She might have wanted to express the idea that the viewing was myopic. Here is one possible revision:

Immediate sacrifices are still viewed myopically as disastrous by many farmers.

This revision isn't very graceful; the word *myopically* now sits in the middle of the phrase *viewed as disastrous*, breaking this phrase awkwardly. Here is a better revision:

Many farmers still myopically view immediate sacrifices as disastrous.

There are no misplaced modifiers in Sentence Four. Sentence Five, however, does contain an adverb (*actively*) that is too distant from the word it modifies. Simply reposition this adverb:

Change is also actively discouraged by the dominating force of the multinationals and by the dogma of technological optimism.

We have now revised every faulty sentence in the paragraph. Here is the complete revision:

In spite of evidence that points to the need to make a quick transition to a system of sustainable agriculture, we are circumscribed by an economic system based on continuous growth and by the pressures created by world hunger and inflation. Many farmers still myopically view immediate sacrifices as disastrous. When one looks to the future, the tunnel vision of farmers is not hard to understand. They probably fear that they will be the only ones to pay for change. Change is also actively discouraged by the dominating force of the multinationals and by the dogma of technological optimism. In spite of these seemingly insurmountable external pressures, we should be optimistic. Optimism lies in the alternatives that do exist and in the ability of a self-aware species to recognize, eventually, the limitations of the present system of agriculture.

Work through Exercise One and Exercise Two, revising misplaced, awkwardly placed, and dangling modifiers.

Awkward Sentences

Often, when an essay is returned to a student, sentence problems are not clearly labelled as dangling modifiers, split infinitives, or faulty parallelism. Most instructors will mark sentence fragments as *frag* or comma splices as *c.s.*, but often other sentence difficulties will simply be circled and *awk* or *awkward* written in the margin.

What do instructors mean when they label a sentence *awkward*? Well, awkward comes from the Old Norse word *ofugr*, meaning *turned the wrong way*, and this definition provides a useful clue to what happens in an awkward sentence. In one way or another, an awkward sentence begins with an arrangement of words that leads the reader to expect the sentence to proceed in a particular way. Somewhere, however, the sentence will take a wrong turn, either not following through with an idea or following through in a way that seems to permit more than one meaning. When this happens, the sentence may be labelled awkward.

At the most rudimentary level, we could say that sentences in which the subject does not agree with the verb are awkward:

Ginger Rogers and Fred Astaire dances together.

In this sentence, the compound subject, *Ginger Rogers and Fred Astaire*, leads the reader to expect that the verb will be *dance*, not *dances*. Between the subject and the verb, the sentence shifts focus, and the result is a crack down the middle of the sentence.

The shift in agreement between subject and verb is such an easily identified sentence problem that it is usually clearly labelled an error. Likewise, a shift in the way in which one of two or more coordinate elements is expressed creates such a recognizable problem that we call it faulty parallelism. And when a modifier at the beginning of a sentence leads us to expect a certain subject, yet that subject isn't in place, we say that someone has created a dangling modifier.

Sentences can shift in other ways as well, ways that are often described as awkward, even though they too have a more specific grammatical label. Consider these sentences:

Awkward: The industrial designer *gave* a brief description of her new design, and then she *demonstrates* the product.

Awkward: When *a person* fails to dress warmly, *you* can expect to get a cold.

Awkward: Howells believes *that there* is a connection between nationality and gender, *and "there* are close parallels between the historical situation of women and of Canada as a nation" (2).

In the first sentence, the reader expects *demonstrate* to be *demonstrated*, because the beginning of the sentence suggests that the writer is reporting something that happened in the past. In this case, the verb tense shifts in a way that confuses.[14] In the second sentence, the writer begins by talking about *a person*, but shifts to talking about *you*. The reader expects the writer to continue discussing the person referred to in the opening part of the sentence. In this case, a shift in pronoun creates awkwardness.[15] Finally, the writer of the last sentence begins by reporting indirectly what Howells has claimed. In the second part of the sentence, the writer begins to report directly what Howells has said, but the reader expects the indirect reporting to continue. In this case, then, there is a shift between direct and indirect discourse, one that creates faulty parallelism.

If you are a careful reader, you are probably noting right now that we have already discussed these types of sentence problems under a different name. We have, but since these sentences might also be labelled awkward, we included them here. You will probably agree that all three sentences do sound less awkward when these shifts are eliminated:

Better: The industrial designer *gave* a brief description of her new design, and then she *demonstrated* the product.

Better: When *a person* fails to dress warmly, *that person* can expect to get a cold.

Better: Howells believes *that there* is a connection between nationality and gender, *and that* "*there* are close parallels between the historical situation of women and of Canada as a nation" (2).

Once the crack is repaired, the sentences move smoothly from beginning to end.

In the preceding examples, the shifts occur at the level of words: a certain word choice in the first part of a sentence makes the reader expect a similar word choice in another part of the sentence. In another sort of awkward sentence, the writer seems to lose track of the sentence altogether, starting it in one way and ending it in another:

Awkward: Although most consumers are overly influenced by advertising does create an informed customer.

Awkward: In a society where, as Gilbert asserts that there are weakening family values, the influence of the church declines.

Awkward: When this situation arises one is forced to ask why do we not have a better transit system?

---

[14] Note that a shift in tense is not necessarily awkward. For example, consider the following sentence: *After we have finished our lab reports, we will celebrate.* Here the tense shifts, but the arrangement of the sentence (with the preposition *after* introducing the element of time) leads the reader to expect the shift.

[15] For more information about this particular kind of shift, see pages 73-74 of the section on pronoun-antecedent agreement.

Awkward: The new municipal tax system has flaws in which cause great anxiety among property owners.

Let us consider these examples one by one. In the first sentence, we begin with a subordinate clause: *Although most consumers are overly influenced by advertising*. The reader expects an independent clause to follow and *advertising does create an informed consumer* is an independent clause. The problem is that *advertising* cannot be both places at once; it must either finish the subordinate clause or begin the independent clause. The writer has used it for both purposes and has created an awkward sentence. To revise, we need another word to replace *advertising* in one of the clauses.

Better: Although most consumers are overly influenced by it, advertising does create an informed customer.

The crack in the second example comes between *asserts* and *that*. The reader expects that *as Gilbert asserts* will be an interruption, and that what follows *asserts* will be a continuation of the clause that *where* sets in motion. But the sentence doesn't work that way: the reader cannot make *In a society where that there are weakening values* work, because we have two subordinating conjunctions, *where* and *that*, in a row. One needs to be eliminated.

Better: In a society where, as Gilbert asserts, there are weakening family values, the influence of the church declines.

Note that the commas around the interjection *as Gilbert asserts* help to establish the interruption more clearly. If your use of commas is not exemplary, you, too, may create this kind of awkward structure.

In the third example, the grammatical arrangement at the beginning of the sentence indicates that a statement is being made, but, by the end of the sentence, a question is being asked. The writer could report the question directly by enclosing it in quotation marks, or could change the syntax of the sentence so that the question section is rephrased as a statement.

Better: When this situation arises, one is forced to ask, "Why do we not have a better transit system?"

Better: When this situation arises, one is forced to ask why we do not have a better transportation system.

In the second revision, the *why* does the work of introducing a questioning mood without creating a shift in the type of sentence.

The final sentence loses the reader in the gap between *in* and *which cause*. The problem is the *in*: *in* is a preposition, so the reader expects it to have an object, a noun following it. What follows it is *which cause great anxiety*, but that part of the sentence is connected to *flaws*. What the flaws are in is the system, but the word *system*, or a pronoun taking its place, does not follow *in*. We could revise two ways:

Better: The new municipal tax system has flaws in it, which cause great anxiety among property owners.

Better: The new municipal tax system has flaws, which cause great anxiety among property owners.

In the first revision, *it* substitutes for *system*, so *in* has an object. The second revision, probably the better of the two because it is less wordy, eliminates the *in*. The *which* gets placed beside *flaws*, and the reader is kept on track.

As you may have guessed from the explanations, these mixed constructions, as they are called, are examples of a grammatical awkwardness: parts of a sentence do not align grammatically, either because an element is missing, in the wrong place, or doing double duty. Dangling modifiers, misplaced modifiers, and squinting modifiers are common forms of grammatical awkwardness as well.

Another type of awkwardness results, not from grammatical non-alignment, but from non-alignment in terms of meaning, of making sense.

Awkward: An example of the problem with current pay equity plans is the garment worker.

Awkward: Haiku is when a poem has three lines.

Awkward: The terms of the agreement expect all parties to comply with health regulations.

Let's consider the first two examples. Note that both contain the verb *is*, a form of the verb *to be*. In Chapter One, we discussed the notion of the linking verb, and in both these sentences, *is* plays the role of a linking verb, connecting the subject and its complement. The awkwardness in the first two sentences comes about because the complement does not align with the subject. It isn't really *the garment worker* who is an example of the problem with pay equity; the garment worker is blameless. *Haiku* is not *when a poem has three lines*; haiku is a type of poetry.

Better: An example of the problem with current pay equity plans is the way in which these plans fail the garment worker.

Better: Haiku is a poem that has three lines.

This pattern of awkwardness may seem acceptable because it frequently occurs in speech. However, it is not permissible in written prose.

In the final example, the awkwardness arises because the subject does not align in meaning with the verb. *Terms of an agreement* cannot *expect* anything;

only people (and perhaps some other animals) can expect. To revise, we need to place *expect* with *parties*.

Better: The terms of the agreement state that all parties are expected to comply with health regulations.

All the preceding examples are only a beginning. Sentences can fall apart anywhere; we have just named a few of the more common stress points. The longer your sentences are, the more clauses they contain, the greater the chances will be for a fissure. If you tend to be wordy, the problem may be compounded, because the use of many small words, including prepositions and relative pronouns, invites grammatical non-alignment.

If awkwardness is a problem for you, however, take heart. Many researchers feel that awkwardness is a result of writers trying to expand their vocabulary and their sentence repertoire. Most of the time, the writer will successfully express complex ideas, but sometimes the complexity of thought will exceed writing ability, and awkwardness occurs. Keep in mind Robert Browning's words, "Ah, but a man's reach should exceed his grasp, / Or what's a heaven for?"

REVISING AWKWARD SENTENCES

Though awkward sentences may be an indication of scholarly virtue, they are still unsightly, and you must try to avoid them in your prose. Fortunately, we can often hear awkwardness even when we cannot see it. For this reason, the best way to begin revising awkward sentences is to read your prose aloud. We would even advocate that you read an essay backwards so that you are forced to consider each sentence on its own, as it is written. In our experience, writers often do not read what is on the page when they read from start to finish; they read what should be on the page. Taking sentences out of context helps the writer to see each sentence independently.

Begin, then, by reading aloud. Focus in particular on long sentences, especially those containing several clauses. You are not likely to lose your way in a short sentence. As you read, listen for sentences that you stumble over, ones that don't ring true.

When you find these sentences, examine them carefully. Is there a shift? Do you change tense somewhere? Do you change pronouns? Or is the problem that parts of the sentence are not aligning grammatically? Is one word playing two roles in the sentence? To revise, take the sentence apart and look at its component parts. See what needs to be added or deleted. In some cases, you will need only to eliminate one word; in other circumstances, you may have to add several words or even create two sentences. As you revise, continue to read aloud (try versions of the sentence aloud before you write them down). Eventually you will discover a version that moves smoothly.

Revising Awkward Sentences

Sample Paragraph:

1. For many scholars of popular music, the question remains how can we define what country and western music is. **2.** The musician would argue that country and western music is when standard rock 'n' roll rhythms are softened by the whine of steel guitars, which seems accurate but that ignores the matter of lyrics. **3.** It is crucial to remember that lyrics tend to make or break the success of a c&w single. **4.** A fan's definition, then, would also have lyrics, probably saying that country and western music has a distinctive sound and lyrics focus on love affairs and the problems of the ordinary man. **5.** Such a definition is still unsatisfying because the lyrics of country and western music are different from rock 'n' roll even though both are about love, c&w lyrics focus more on betrayal, rock 'n' roll lyrics more on unrequited love.

Exercise One:

From this it is clearly seen that the future holds an increase in the amount of elderly people within the province. At the same time, the younger people will rapidly decrease. This is because couples, if they choose to have children, view that the ideal number to have are one or two or three at the most. In 1901, seniors made up 5.5 per cent of the total population in Ontario, and, as the baby boom hit the nation, Ontario's population increased to 8.7 per cent. During the 1970s, the younger generation decreased and this is because of two simple facts: parents were reducing the size of their families and the baby boom generation was growing up and reaching older ages. It seems evident to believe then that Ontario will rapidly age within the next twenty years.

Exercise Two:

It is still important to consider the question how education was viewed in the pre-industrial period. All education was within the walls of a child's home. In fact, many parents believed that there were necessary things a child needed to learn were sewing, farming, and other such skills. However, with the emergence of industrialization, Canadians became empowered in the technological era. For parents who did not have their children enrolled in schools their attitudes changed, and they began to feel that it was very important for a child to grow and develop inside a classroom. Another factor promoting schools were the street urchins. In the 1840s and 1850s, social leaders feared social disorder because so many young adolescents were left with idle hands.

Revising Awkward Sentences: Sample Paragraph Discussion

Probably you had little difficulty understanding the meaning of the sample paragraph but recognized that points are not made very smoothly. Indeed, each of the sentences in the paragraph contains some type of awkwardness. Let's consider each sentence separately.

Sentence One

The awkwardness in this sentence is easy to recognize: the sentence begins as a statement but ends as a question. What we need to do is somehow eliminate the entire question *how can we define what country and western music is*. We can do it by describing the question rather than stating it.

> For many scholars of popular music, the question of defining country and western music remains.

In the revision, we have rephrased the question as a prepositional phrase.

Sentence Two

This sentence has two problems. The first is the *is when* construction, easily revised by deleting the *when* and *are*.

> The musician would argue that country and western music is standard rock 'n' roll rhythms softened by the whine of steel guitars, which is accurate, but that ignores the matter of lyrics.

The second problem is the *which* and the *that*. The *which* is awkward because it has too much work to do; it is unclear in the sentence exactly what *which* stands for. In fact, it stands for *definition*, a word that does not precede it in the sentence. It would be better to use *definition* and eliminate the *which*. You can see in our revision that making this change necessitates breaking the sentence in two.

Furthermore, there are two ways of interpreting how *that* is being used here. It could be a pronominal adjective: the writer could mean *but that definition ignores the matter of lyrics*. On the other hand, it might be a relative pronoun beginning a subordinate clause, in which case it would be parallel to the which in *which is accurate*. This ambiguity, although it does not interfere much with meaning, creates awkwardness because the reader is unsure how the sentence should be read, what words need to be stressed. We want to draw your attention to the problem with *that*; however, correcting the *which* forces a revision that solves the *that* problem anyway.

> The musician would argue that country and western music is standard rock 'n' roll rhythms softened by the whine of steel guitars. This definition is accurate, but it ignores the matter of lyrics.

Using *this definition* permits us to substitute *it* for *that*, and thereby lessens ambiguity.

Sentence Three

Think about this sentence for a minute. Can you make or break success? You can make or break a single, but the writer does not mean that lyrics will break the success of the single; she means that lyrics will, figuratively, make or break the single. The problem here results from wordiness; the extra phrase confounds rather than clarifies.

> It is crucial to remember that lyrics tend to make or break a c&w single.

Sentence Four

If this sentence is read literally, it is quite funny. The writer is saying, literally, that a fan's definition would be poetic, that it would *have lyrics*. Probably what she means is that a fan would define lyrics as being an important element of country and western music.

> A fan, then, would claim that the lyrics of country and western music help to define it, probably saying that country and western music has a distinctive sound and lyrics focus on love affairs and the problems of the ordinary man.

The sentence is still awkward. There is a crack between *lyrics* and *focus*; the writer is using *lyrics* to end one clause and begin another. A pronoun like *that*, substituting for *lyrics*, should help.

> A fan, then, would claim that the lyrics of country and western music help to define it, probably saying that country and western music has a distinctive sound and lyrics that focus on love affairs and the problems of the ordinary man.

Sentence Five

This sentence actually contains a comma splice but is included here because it is an extreme example of part of a sentence playing "double duty." *Even though both are about love* either ends one sentence or begins another, but it cannot do both. The sentence needs to be broken into two sentences.

Before we do that, let's fix two other problems. First, consider the clause *the lyrics of country and western music are different from rock 'n' roll*. The comparison here is not in parallel form, so it is awkward: the lyrics of c&w are not different from rock 'n' roll; they are different from the lyrics of rock 'n' roll. We don't want to repeat the word *lyrics*, but we can use the pronoun *those* to achieve parallelism.

Second, the word *more* will always suggest to the reader that the word *than* is going to follow because *more* is a comparative. Note that there is no *than* in the sentence. The two *mores* should be eliminated so the reader does not expect a direct comparison.

> Such a definition is still unsatisfying because the lyrics of country and western music are different from those of rock 'n' roll. Even though both are about love, c&w lyrics focus on betrayal, rock 'n' roll lyrics on unrequited love.

Here is the entire paragraph in less awkward form:

> For many scholars of popular music, the question of defining country and western music remains. The musician would argue that country and western music is standard rock 'n' roll rhythms softened by the whine of steel guitars. This definition seems accurate, but it ignores the matter of lyrics. It is crucial to remember that lyrics tend to make or break a c&w single. A fan, then, would claim that the lyrics of country and western music help to define it, probably saying that country and western music has a distinctive sound and lyrics which focus on love affairs and the problems of the ordinary man. Such a definition is still unsatisfying because the lyrics of country and western music are different from those of rock 'n' roll. Even though both are about love, c&w lyrics focus on betrayal, rock 'n' roll lyrics on unrequited love.

Read both exercise paragraphs aloud and mark the sentences that sound awkward. Consider them carefully and try to determine the problem with each sentence. Revise accordingly.

In Chapter Two, we provided strategies for creating grammatically correct sentences. Knowing grammatical conventions, however, is only the foundation for writing well. Once your sentences are correct, you need to consider how they interact: you must assemble sentences and groups of sentences that are not only grammatically acceptable but that also make meaning clear and keep the reader, if not entertained, at least attentive.

Such goals are accomplished in part through varied prose, an element of style that addresses three writing problems. First, varied prose alleviates boredom: prose that plods along, sentence after sentence following the same pattern, is not very exciting to read. Second, varied prose provides emphasis, making it easy for the reader to recognize your main concerns. Finally, varied prose permits clarity. Certain types of unvaried prose (passages consisting of all short sentences or all simple sentences, for example) simply cannot communicate properly the complex ideas and connections of academic writing. Interesting prose, then, satisfies the reader both by maintaining interest and by helping to make meaning clear.

Producing interesting prose, however, is frequently seen as requiring what many people would term natural writing ability, for the best stylists often appear to have an innate sense of the rhythm of words. Read a Lewis Lapham editorial or a Jay Scott movie review: the sentences lift off the page with a life of their own. We would argue, however, that to view such writing a result of natural ability is to venture into that murky territory of biological determinism from which most careful thinkers of the twentieth century have been struggling to escape. Interesting prose is generally produced through thinking about words and sentences and meaning. Although that thinking may often occur unconsciously (because the writer has spent years reading and listening to how other people arrange words), variety and emphasis can be achieved consciously, too, through a critical examination of one's own writing.

This chapter, in fact, focuses on helping you to think consciously about creating varied, interesting prose. Many of you will already have a repertoire of strategies for creating variety; in an initial draft, you might vary openings frequently or make interesting use of punctuation. It is unlikely, however, that you have internalized all the strategies possible for creating variation: few writers have, and so this chapter will provide you with information and examples about those primary strategies for creating interest. Once you know your own writing well, you can work to improve variety and emphasis generally by using the new strategies you discover in this chapter.

Your ultimate goal – the goal of all serious writers – is to produce sentences and paragraphs that are rich and textured, diverse, yet harmonious. Your immediate goal – again the goal of all serious writers – is to make your meaning clear. These objectives are identical, although for some students they will seem a contradiction in terms: how can one write clearly yet create prose that is rich and diverse? Do not confuse diversity with obscurity. As the samples of professional writing in this chapter illustrate, rich and diverse prose can often be written using everyday vocabulary and simple structures; the diversity is created, not from elaborate constructions, but from simple interjections and qualifications, interesting punctuation marks, unexpected but effective interruptions. But do not automatically equate clarity with simplicity either. Often, elaborate syntactic structures are necessary, and they do not have to obscure meaning; used properly, they can illuminate rather than confound.

One of our colleagues has noted, "The problem with most essays is not that the language is too simple. The problem almost always is that the language is bloated, tortured into strange shapes, pretentious." As you revise, keep this in mind. One does not vary prose in order to make it more difficult to read but rather to make it more comprehensible. The aim is to make every word, every punctuation mark, tell. Preserve clarity of meaning as your first aim, and vary your writing only to improve it.

Exercise One: Discovering Sentence Variety

The following passages are all written by professional writers famous for their particular styles. Look at the individual sentences. How would you describe each one? How do the sentences differ from one another? How do they interconnect? How is the particular "variety" of each writer created? Which style do you prefer?

> When I was six or seven years old, growing up in Pittsburgh, I used to take a penny of my own and hide it for someone else to find. It was a curious compulsion; sadly, I've never been seized by it since. For some reason I always "hid" the penny along the same stretch of sidewalk up the street. I'd cradle it at the roots of a maple, say, or in a hole left by a chipped-off piece of sidewalk. Then I'd take a piece of chalk and, starting at either end of the block, draw huge arrows leading up to the penny from both directions. After I learned to write I labelled the arrows "SURPRISE AHEAD" or "MONEY THIS WAY." I was greatly excited, during all this arrow-drawing, at the thought of the first lucky passerby who would receive in this way, regardless of merit, a free gift from the universe. But I never lurked about. I'd go straight home and not give the matter another thought, until, some months later, I would be gripped by the impulse to hide another penny.
>
> — Annie Dillard[1]

> . . . Where do I start?
>
> With personal relationships. Here is something comparatively solid in a world full of violence and cruelty. Not absolutely solid, for Psychology has split and shattered the idea of a "Person," and has shown that there is something incalculable in each of us, which may at any moment rise to the surface and destroy our normal balance. We don't know what we are like. We can't know what other people are like. How, then, can we put any trust in personal relationships, or cling to them in the gathering political storm? In theory we cannot. But in practice we can and do. Though A is not unchangeably A or B unchangeably B, there can still be love and loyalty between the two. For the purpose of living one has to assume that the personality is solid, and the "self" is an entity, and to ignore all contrary evidence. And since to ignore evidence is one of the characteristics of faith, I certainly can proclaim that I believe in personal relationships.
>
> — E.M. Forster[2]

---

[1] Annie Dillard, "Sight into Insight," *The Norton Reader,* ed. Arthur Eastman, et al., 7th ed. (New York: Norton, 1988) 1182.

[2] E.M. Forster, "What I Believe," *The Norton Reader* 1163.

My daughter was making, that day in Chicago, an entirely unconscious but quite basic assumption about people and the work they do. She was assuming that the glory she saw in the work reflected a glory in its maker, that the painting was the painter as the poem is the poet, that every choice one made alone—every word chosen or rejected, every brush stroke laid or not laid down—betrayed one's character. *Style is character.* It seemed to me that afternoon that I had rarely seen so instinctive an application of this familiar principle, and I recall being pleased not only that my daughter responded to style as character but that it was Georgia O'Keefe's particular style to which she responded: this was a hard woman who had imposed her 192 square feet of clouds on Chicago.

—Joan Didion[3]

For three thousand years, poets have been enchanted and moved and perplexed by the power of their own imagination. In a short and summary essay I can hope at most to lift one small corner of that mystery; and yet it is a critical corner. I shall ask, What goes on in the mind when we imagine? You will hear from me that one answer to this question is fairly specific: which is to say, that we can describe the working of the imagination. And when we describe it as I shall do, it becomes plain that imagination is a specifically *human* gift. To imagine is the characteristic act, not of the poet's mind, or the painter's, or the scientist's, but of the mind of man.

—Jacob Bronowski[4]

Some people think a women's novel is anything without politics in it. Some think it's anything about relationships. Some think it's anything with a lot of operations in it, medical ones I mean. Some think it's anything that doesn't give you a broad panoramic view of our exciting times. Me, well, I just want something you can leave on the coffee table and not be too worried if the kids get into it. You think that's not a real consideration? You're wrong.

—Margaret Atwood[5]

Strategies for Creating Interest

Sentences can vary in an extraordinary number of ways. They can vary in their length, in their function (statements, exclamations, questions, commands), in their grammatical structure (simple, compound, complex, compound-complex), and in their rhetorical arrangement (cumulative, periodic, parallel, climactic). Creating interesting prose, therefore, cannot be reduced to a mechanical act: there are an almost infinite number of possible choices for re-arranging a sentence, so the writer seeking to create interesting prose must tinker with word arrangement, adding, subtracting, shifting, rearranging, until meaning emerges clearly and with grace.

[3] Joan Didion, "Georgia O'Keefe," *The Norton Reader* 1098.

[4] Jacob Bronowski, "The Reach of Imagination," *The Norton Reader* 194.

[5] Margaret Atwood, "Women's Novels," *Murder in the Dark: Short Fictions and Prose Poems* (Toronto: Coach House, 1983) 35.

Furthermore, as the passages of Exercise One make clear, there is no need to use eighteen varieties of sentence in one paragraph to achieve interest or clarity of meaning. Creating interest is a subtle and complex operation; often an aptly placed word or phrase is all that is needed to give a lifeless paragraph some vigour. For this reason, it is important that you read what follows in the proper spirit. We discuss length, grammatical function, grammatical structure, and rhetorical arrangement only in order to make you aware of possibilities for tinkering. We are not prescribing rigorous re-styling for all paragraphs but are presenting options for you to play with, possibilities to keep in mind when you are staring at the computer screen trying to revise a passage so that it sounds "just right."

As you begin to work through the exercises, you will realize that, although we present strategies for creating variety one by one, in practice, the strategies work together to produce interesting prose. Change the length of a sentence and you will often change its structure; change the punctuation and you may change the rhetorical arrangement to match. We would encourage you to be creative in your revisions. Do not be afraid to step outside the boundaries of the exercises and experiment with other forms of variety while focusing on one particular strategy.

VARYING SENTENCE LENGTH

Regardless of how long your sentences are, if they are all the same length, you run the risk of boring your reader. A paragraph consisting entirely of short sentences often receives negative comments because the lack of variety produces a choppy effect. The reader feels as if she were being dealt blows, rather than being led gently through an argument. Conversely, too many long sentences can create confusion. Generally speaking, the longer the sentences, the more difficult the prose is to read; this is why one measure of "readability" involves simply counting the number of words in each sentence. In fact, even neutral, medium-length sentences can present problems if the main point of a paragraph becomes obscured by their uniform length.

The paragraphs in Exercise One illustrate the corollary to this point: sentences that are varied in length do create interest. Because end punctuation inevitably brings the reader to a definite halt, sentences, no matter what their length, if they are the same length, have the staccato monotony of robot language: they are stilted, jerky, unemphatic. Above all, professional writers want their prose to sound human, so they vary sentence length, trying to capture the patterns of spoken language, its sudden stops and starts, its melodic outpourings, in effect, its infinite variety.

Even the most untutored reader will recognize, therefore, that varying sentence length is not a mechanical process. One cannot simply alternate between short and long sentences: short/long/short/long. Instead, the writer must focus on two elements when revising for length: voice and emphasis.

To consider voice, you must begin by reading your prose aloud, coming to a full stop at the end of every sentence. What do you hear? An essay that contains no variety in sentence length will have a steady, mechanical beat: tick, tick, tick, tick, tick. Varied sentences will produce a more complex and seemingly human rhythm—a voice. The Annie Dillard passage in Exercise One, for example, has quite an intricate and conversational cadence. There is a voice

Learning Prompt

Very few people write short, choppy sentences in one paragraph and overly long sentences in another. Read aloud an old essay and try to determine your particular predilection. Are there passages where the rhythm is mechanical? If so, are the sentences all short? all long? Select three or four paragraphs which have sentences all about the same length. Rewrite them, altering the sentences so that a less staccato rhythm emerges and points are more clearly emphasized.

here, a pleasant, casual voice describing, adding details and qualifiers to some sentences, stating facts simply in others. And there is a voice in the E.M. Forster passage, too, although the voice is different from Dillard's. Forster's short stops and starts, combined with his more lengthy ponderings, let the reader hear a reflective human being mulling over the intellectual puzzle of faith. Both passages — indeed all the passages in Exercise One — achieve this effect in part by varying the lengths of sentences so that the reader is never lulled by predictability. (Of course, the writing is varied in several other ways as well, and it is the overall effect, not simply the variety in length, that creates memorable prose.)

If your reading indicates that your own prose has a mechanical rather than a human voice, consider how you might change the rhythm of the prose. Can you add qualifiers, transitional phrases, or details to make certain sentences longer? Can some sentences be combined? The operative word again is tinker. Play around with the sentences, combining them, rearranging them, splitting them, until the mechanical beat disappears, and a more human rhythm emerges.

While you play, keep the second element, emphasis, in mind. From your own experience with language, you will immediately recognize that short sentences are usually the most emphatic, especially when they occur in a passage of long sentences. The content of the short sentence is instantly foregrounded for the reader. This principle is demonstrated nicely in the passage written by Joan Didion; her three-word sentence "*Style is character*" catches the reader's attention and stresses the theme of the paragraph. Likewise, Atwood's closing "You're wrong" more convincingly makes the point that women take many things, including their children's needs, into account when reading.

This principle could be extended to the simple claim that variety creates emphasis: place a long sentence in the middle of a series of short sentences and it, too, will stand out in contrast, a peacock among the peafowls. When you revise your work, therefore, consider your main points. Can they be brought into focus by using a sentence of contrasting length to express them?

❧ ❧ ❧

Varying Sentence Length

Sample Paragraph:

1. The water plants that developed the necessary features to live on land would all have come from similar environments. **2.** The appropriate locale must have been an area that had some aquatic features and some periods of dryness. **3.** Proximity to water would have been necessary because some events in the life cycle would still depend on an external water supply (Bower, 1967). **4.** Some periods of dryness would have to occur, however, to force the plants to adapt to land conditions. **5.** Areas affected by tides, for example, contained plants that had to be adapted to both an aquatic and a gaseous environment.

Exercise One:

The railway lines had enlisted men to kill the buffalos. These men did not spare any buffalo herds. They killed more buffalo than were needed for meat. The buffalo were also killed for their fur. Buffalo robes were not only practical but also fashionable. Supplying people with robes contributed greatly to the extinction of the buffalo. Furthermore, some killed for the mere joy of watching the beasts fall.

Exercise Two:

Meanwhile, in the United States, Jimmy Carter announced in January 1980 his support for the EPA plan to force a ten-billion-dollar conversion from oil to coal-fired electric generation. The lack of provisions for pollution abatement equipment attached to these mandatory conversions aroused suspicions in Canada that the Carter Administration was promoting relaxed air quality standards while appearing to move toward an international agreement. Despite immediate concern over what appeared to be one step forward and two steps back, there was little doubt that if Reagan were elected a much more pronounced retreat would be in the offing. As one American environment official, reacting to the strong lobbying of coal producers and utilities, said, "It's a good time to circle the wagons and protect what environmental legislation we have." Clearly his choice of a homespun metaphor that the next holder of the Oval Office could understand if not appreciate reflected a change to the defensive on the part of environmentalists.

Varying Sentence Length: Sample Paragraph Discussion

Read the first passage aloud. Can you hear the staccato effect (point.point.point.point.point) created as a result of the sentences being consistent in length? Now think about the passage. Is it easy to see what the main point of the passage is? Or do you find that no one idea is emphasized?

This passage, although comprehensible, illustrates some of the difficulties caused by lack of variety in sentence length. Although it is without grammatical flaws, the prose is a little boring, a little mechanical and uninspired, and the message a little obscure.

The Wrong Approach

Reconstructing these sentences, however, is not an easy matter. You need to realize that making medium-length sentences shorter or longer involves more than the mechanical recombining of sentences. You can't just break one medium sentence in two to create two short sentences or combine two medium sentences into one to create a long sentence. The resulting passage would be entirely unsatisfactory:

> The water plants developed the necessary features to live on land. They would all have come from similar environments. The appropriate locale must have been an area that had some aquatic features and some periods of dryness, and proximity to water would have been necessary because some events in the life cycle would still depend on an external water supply (Bower, 1967). Some periods of dryness would have to occur, however. These force the plants to adapt to land conditions. Areas affected by tides, for example, contained plants that had to be adapted to both an aquatic and a gaseous environment.

You can see for yourself that this revision is hardly an improvement. It separates items that are related (for example, the idea that periods of dryness were necessary is separated from the reason for dryness being necessary), connects items that are unrelated, and has too many short sentences to flow gracefully.

Determining Meaning and Emphasis

Varying length of sentences through splitting and combining can be done effectively only if one looks at meaning, combining concepts that are connected and setting off items that need emphasis. You will also remember that often it is necessary to make a sentence only slightly longer or slightly shorter to achieve that essential human voice. This can be accomplished by embedding or deleting words, phrases, and clauses, ensuring that clear meaning is always preserved. Indeed, as you add words, endeavour to make your meaning more clear. Consider this second revision:

> The water plants that adapted to life on land would all have come from similar environments. Our knowledge of evolution would suggest that the appropriate locale must have been an area that had some aquatic features and some periods of dryness. Proximity to water would have been necessary because some events in the life cycle would still depend on an external water supply (Bower, 1967); some periods of dryness would have to occur, however, to force the plants to adapt to land conditions. A tidal area would be one such location. There, plants would have to adapt to both an aquatic and a gaseous environment.

The occasional addition of transitions and explanatory phrases in this revision makes meaning more clear. The first sentence, a topic sentence, is justifiably short since we want the reader to understand easily the point being made. A few words were added to the second sentence to ease the transition into the long third sentence. In the third sentence, it was possible to combine Sentences Three and Four of the original since the ideas in the two sentences are very closely connected, and the semicolon invites the reader to connect the two statements. Breaking the last sentence into two — naming the example in one sentence, explaining it in the next — is a good strategy for helping the reader to remember tidal areas. You can see from the revision that, in changing sentence length, we also have added interrupters and pronouns, and changed punctuation. These alterations also contribute to the interest of the paragraph.

Although five sentences still remain, then, the rhythm has been slightly altered: altering length does improve the passage. However, the prose still isn't as inspired as that of Annie Dillard or E.M. Forster. To achieve a more lively passage, the writer would also need to consider varying rhetorical arrangement, because, even after revising for length, the sentences still share the same rhetorical pattern. After you have read about varying rhetorical arrangement, you may want to return to this paragraph and rewrite it.

Of course, there are several other possibilities for sentence combining here. You might be able to think of another way of rewriting this paragraph that would preserve meaning but produce variety. Other strategies are fine, as long as meaning is clear and the important points are emphasized.

You can see at a glance that the two exercise paragraphs also suffer from a lack of variety in sentence length. Read the two passages aloud, then rewrite them, recreating the sentences in each to add variety and emphasis.

VARYING SENTENCE FUNCTION

Most sentences in academic prose are declarative statements: this happened, it happened for these reasons, this is what we can conclude. Skim through any academic journal and you will discover that exclamatory sentences are almost non-existent, and that questions occur only rarely and usually in introductions and conclusions. The imperative is also uncommon, even though academic writers, in trying to persuade, do have a tendency to order their readers around a little. What this should tell you is that there isn't a good deal of room for creating variety in your prose by varying sentence function. Most of the time, you will have to make statements. But if there are points you wish to have strongly emphasized, using questions and commands can cleverly single them out.

Questions

A question can be used to draw a reader in, to focus on a particular issue or concept, as in the following passage from The Story of English:

> The logic of this global approach has led us to make a basic descriptive decision: rather than talk about *accents* and *dialects* of English, we talk of *varieties*. Again and again we found that the line between *accent, dialect,* and *language* is not a sure or a steady one and is often disputed, even by specialists. Is Scottish English, for instance, a language or a dialect? The experts find it hard to be certain. It has been said that "a language is a dialect with an army and a navy," but *my* accent often turns out be *your* dialect.[6]

Here, the authors use a question to provide a concrete example of the puzzle they are trying to solve. The reader, in being invited to address the same puzzle, is thus drawn into the debate much more effectively than if the authors had said, "We wondered, for example, whether Scottish English was a language or a dialect."

Commands

The question creates emphasis or interest because it addresses the reader directly; so do commands, imperative sentences. In this text, commands are often used to give emphasis and to create connections with the reader: we are continually telling you to "Consider this passage" or "Think about these paragraphs." In this way, we direct you forward, invite you to be actively involved in making meaning. We jolt you out of passively accepting our word, demanding that you participate with us in understanding the way written language works. The authors of The Story of English use this strategy as well, although their commands are less direct:

---

[6] Robert McCrum, William Cran, and Robert MacNeil, *The Story of English* (New York: Viking Penguin, 1986) 13.

Writing Prompt

Think for a moment about the topic of the next essay you must write. Compose six commands and six questions you might use at some point in the essay.

Ask a Jamaican what he or she speaks and you will have the best expression of the paradox that underlies Caribbean attitudes towards English — and a clue to the future. Jamaicans will say anything from "the dialect" to "patois" to "Caribbean creole" to "Jamaican English" to "the Jamaican language." Caribbean nationalism will prompt them to put as much distance as possible between what they speak and the Standard English of the ex-colonial visitor. On the other hand, if you suggest to the Jamaican that he or she does *not* speak English, they will be insulted or outraged.[7]

In the opening sentence of this passage, the reader is indirectly invited to speak with a Jamaican, and thus again is made to feel part of the ongoing investigation into the nature of Jamaican English.

Exclamations

Exclamations are rare in academic prose perhaps because, unlike questions and commands, they do not have the power to invite readers into a passage. The exclamation mark tells the reader that the sentence is exciting and leaves no room for the reader to make that decision independently. Exclamations do draw attention to sentences, but not in a very useful way. Their presence is so lacking in subtlety that they seem juvenile, and most academic writers avoid them.

---

[7] McCrum, et al., *The Story of English* 317.

Notes

My writing strengths:

Things I need to remember:

Things I need to check:

Varying Sentence Function

Sample Paragraph:

1. This research has implications for the university in that it establishes the need to make learning-disabled students more aware of the aids and services available to them. **2.** Even the university student group devoted to the special needs of disabled students must find a way to make itself more visible. **3.** Although university aids and services for the learning-disabled student are listed in guide books, published in articles in the university newspaper, and advertised on posters and in pamphlets, still many students are not aware of them. **4.** Perhaps people are trying to attract the attention of learning-disabled students by making them read. **5.** This would seem to indicate the lack of sensitivity society has toward the academic difficulties of learning-disabled students.

Exercise One:

By reflecting on the various comments made by these authors, it is possible to infer the following two points. First, society has viewed learning-disabled individuals as undesirable deviants from the norm. Secondly, the lack of a positive self-image and self-esteem is a major problem for these individuals. These observations led to the formation of this study, which will explore how learning-disabled students' behaviour is modified by their perception of society's view of them.

Exercise Two:

Hamlet does undoubtedly delay. Whether he delays consciously or not, one cannot ascertain. There is significant evidence that Hamlet has other matters to think over as well. J. Dover Wilson, for example, has convincingly shown that the perplexing question of the ghost's true nature was a real enough concern. Elizabethans themselves were in disagreement about this issue: they could not decide whether apparitions were really ghosts or merely devils trying to confuse the living. In this light, Hamlet's recourse to the play as a means of getting at the truth seems not as ridiculous as Dr. A.C. Bradley would have us believe: "It is an unconscious fiction, an excuse for his delay — and for its continuance" (104). Although there is some truth in Bradley's comment, it would seem unwise to dismiss Hamlet's plan as purely "fiction."

Varying Sentence Function: Sample Paragraph Discussion

Questions and commands should be used to focus the reader on the most important point of a passage, so decisions about incorporating these types of sentences must be made on the basis of what needs to be stressed in a paragraph.

Determining Emphasis

What do you think the main point of this paragraph is? We believe that in this passage, the writer is trying to stress that there are problems with the way information about services is being presented to the learning-disabled student; even though the information is available, students do not seem to be receiving it. If we consider the writer's key point to be that this information is being presented in the wrong way, here is how our attention might be more directly focused on this point:

> This research has implications for the university in that it establishes the need to make learning-disabled students more aware of the aids and services available to them. Even the university student group devoted to the special needs of disabled students must find a way to make itself more visible. Although university aids and services for the learning-disabled student are listed in guide books, published in articles in the university newspaper, and advertised on posters and in pamphlets, still many students are not aware of them. **Let us think about this for a minute. Could it be that people are trying to attract the attention of learning-disabled students by making them read?** If so, this would seem to indicate the lack of sensitivity society has toward the academic difficulties of learning-disabled students.

The use of both a gentle command and a question brings the writer's point into focus much more dramatically than one declarative statement can, especially since the reader is invited to ponder the problem with the writer. In your own prose, you can use questions and commands to communicate your main points to the reader.

The exercise paragraphs consist entirely of declarative statements. Consider each carefully. Should any of the statements be changed to questions, commands, or exclamations to provide better emphasis? Rewrite the paragraphs, changing sentence function where you think it might be appropriate.

VARYING GRAMMATICAL STRUCTURE

There are several grammatical types of sentences. First, there are simple sentences, consisting of one independent clause:[8]

> <u>Hill Street Blues</u> is considered a classic television program.

Then, there are compound sentences, consisting of two or more independent clauses:

> This police drama was popular among a certain group of TV viewers, but unfortunately those viewers tended to be a fickle audience.

Next are complex sentences, consisting of an independent clause and one or more dependent clauses (also known as subordinate clauses):

> Rather, these viewers were young, middle-class professionals, who watched TV only rarely when they had nothing better to do.

Finally, there are compound-complex sentences, consisting of two or more independent clauses and one or more dependent clauses:

> Consequently, <u>Hill Street Blues</u> rarely got high ratings and it was dropped, despite the critical acclaim it received.

Just describing these various types makes one aware of their dizzying possibilities: varying grammatical structure allows a writer to construct a range of sentences, from very simple to enormously complex. This is useful to know because, when the sentences of a passage are all the same grammatical type, the reader has difficulty determining emphasis. All ideas seem to have equal weight. Since the writer rarely intends all the sentences of a passage to be weighted equally (usually sentences in a passage operate on different levels of generality), the lack of variety can hinder meaning. Too many simple sentences will suggest an immaturity of thought; too many compound-complex sentences will make reading tortuous.

By looking at two paragraphs, both of which fail to vary grammatical structure, you will see the problems that can arise. Consider this passage first:

> Another determining factor was the baby boom from 1946 to 1964. This expanded the number of teaching positions available and the majority of them were filled by women. Women did well in education. They held most of the full-time jobs, and men were hired usually only on a part-time basis. Women today still occupy positions at elementary and secondary schools, but only a low percentage of females teach at higher education facilities. The future in this field appears to be stable.

Learning Prompt

Read through an old essay, examining your sentences carefully. Do the grammatical types of sentences you choose always convey your meaning well? Do you favour a particular grammatical type of sentence? What type? Pick a paragraph that seems to suffer from lack of variety in grammatical sentence type and revise it to reflect your meaning more accurately.

---

[8] For an explanation of independent and dependent clauses, see pp. 21-31.

This passage uses only simple and compound sentences, and although the use of compound constructions prevents choppiness to some extent, the avoidance of complex sentences limits development of ideas. The reader is unsure whether the author wants to stress how well women have done in teaching or how limited they have been by it. The passage is not hard to read, but it is difficult to extract the main point.

Now compare the previous passage with the structure of the passage which follows:

> The two developments that strained the bonds of business unionism were the increased fragmentation of skills and the standardization of construction details, which eliminated much site-built woodwork, and these provided the thin edge of the wedge threatening symbiotic relations. Large companies, aware of the potential for profits implicit in piece work, especially when a reserve pool of semi-skilled labour existed, were torn between their eagerness for profit and their dependence on stable wages and uninterrupted job progress to bring their project in under bid. The absence of strikes on large Peterborough projects suggests that employers saw the wisdom of the latter. A ramification of technological change in building that was beyond local control was the new trades' usurping of carpenters' traditional sphere. Inventions such as sheet metal roofing, siding, and trim, and the question of who was to install them, became the focus for jurisdictional disputes between national and international unions.

This passage suffers from a different problem. Because all its sentences are complex, the content is more difficult to retain. Varying length creates some relief in the prose, but the first two sentences, both of which contain several clauses, are quite taxing to read. Sentence One is particularly difficult. It should serve as a topic sentence but contains too many ideas for the reader to determine focus.

Which passage sounds better? As a student, you might guess that an instructor would prefer that you err toward the complex. It is true that much more can be said, and relationships can be made more clear, when the writer uses complex sentence structures. The first passage tells us very little about female teachers, but the second passage provides a substantial amount of detail about construction work. However, not all the points you wish to make will require complex structures. You should also recognize, as the second passage shows, that making a reader work hard is something to avoid. A variety of grammatical sentence types will always be more interesting than the same type repeated, even if the type is complex. Furthermore, a variety of sentence types almost always will express your meaning more appropriately, since any essay contains both simple and complex points.

Writing Prompt

Once you have determined the grammatical type of sentence you favour, practise writing other types. Pick a topic — recycling or alligators if you cannot think of something more useful — and write four simple sentences, four compound sentences, four complex sentences, and four compound-complex sentences about it. Write another four sentences of the type you use least often in your own work.

Varying Grammatical Structure

Sample Paragraph:

1. The last aspect of this paper focuses on work and status opportunities for females. **2.** Women are highly concentrated in low-status jobs. **3.** These types of jobs are usually either clerical work, or retail work, or teaching, or nursing. **4.** Derber views such jobs as invisible employment. **5.** Women become further alienated in them and they receive attention only from their supervisors (1979:78). **6.** According to Derber, women in these jobs suffer from attention-deprivation, an affliction far more painful than negative attention (1979:78). **7.** The work and status opportunities for women, therefore, do not help them.

Exercise One:

The whole work environment at university was very impersonal. Human relations were not considered important. This was evident in the student identification system. Students were numbers, not names. All correspondence was conducted by means of the student identification number. It was the only personal identification required on assignments and exams. Prisoners are likewise identified by a number. Guards do not generally know every prisoner by name. They identify them by the numbers stitched on their uniforms.

Exercise Two:

The book reviews of the era, both native and foreign, reflect these assumptions about national culture. Most reviewers of this era supposed Canada to have its own culture; that the New York Times employed Stuart Keates, a Canadian and the editor of the Victoria Times, to write most of its Canadian literature reviews, supports this statement. The assumption is implicit; only a Canadian could fully comprehend the subtleties of Canadian literature. Canadian culture was an unknown entity; foreign reviewers were considered too ignorant to provide knowledgeable reviews. The action of the New York Times not only indicates a willingness to admit ignorance of Canadian culture; it also suggests that Canada is supposed to be different in some vital way from the United States. The nation should have its own culture; the literature it produces should not be simply universal.

Varying Grammatical Structure: Sample Paragraph Discussion

Revising the grammatical structure of sentences within a passage involves two steps: considering the current grammatical structures and then deciding which points can be subordinated and which require emphasis.

Considering Grammatical Types

Usually, you will be able to determine at a glance what grammatical types of sentences you favour. However, if you are uncertain, you might begin by looking carefully at each sentence in a paragraph to determine grammatical type. The sample passage follows this pattern: 1. simple   2. simple   3. simple   4. simple   5. compound   6. simple   7. simple

Such a pattern does not necessarily indicate that the paragraph is uninteresting or monotonous; indeed, shifts in length and the use of interrupters such as *therefore* do help to create a voice in the passage. However, the paragraph does exhibit some problems. The voice sounds unpolished since the simplicity of the sentences does not match the complexity of the vocabulary. Furthermore, and probably more important, the avoidance of complex sentences prevents the reader from being able to see exact relations between ideas. The sentence structure gives all ideas equal weight; hence the whole passage seems slightly flat.

Making Revisions: Subordination and Emphasis

Consider this revision (revised sentences have been highlighted):

> **1.** The last aspect of this paper focuses on work and status opportunities for females. **2. Women are highly concentrated in low-status jobs, which are usually either clerical work, or retail work, or teaching, or nursing. 3.** Derber views such jobs as invisible employment. **4. Women become further alienated in them because they receive attention only from their supervisors (1979:78). 5.** According to Derber, women in these jobs suffer from attention-deprivation, an affliction far more painful than negative attention (1979:78). **6.** The work and status opportunities for women, therefore, do not help them.

Two simple changes were made here. Sentences Two and Three were combined to create one complex sentence. In Sentence Five, the word *and*, which made that sentence compound, was changed to *because* to create a complex sentence. The passage now has this grammatical pattern: 1. simple   2. complex   3. simple   4. complex   5. simple   6. simple

The changes are small (tinkering again), but in terms of emphasis, the revisions make a substantial difference. The examples of low-status jobs are now subordinated to the notion that women are highly concentrated in this kind of work; the use of *because* permits the reader to understand better the connection between alienation and contact only with a supervisor.

When shifting grammatical types of sentences, then, focus first on meaning. Are there ideas in your passage that should be subordinated to other ideas (creating complex sentences)? Are there ideas that should stand alone for emphasis (in simple sentences)? Once you have determined your meaning, shape the sentences to reflect that meaning. Your paragraphs will become both more interesting and more meaningful.

Read the exercise paragraphs carefully. What kind of sentence (simple, compound, complex, compound-complex) dominates each paragraph? Do these sentences adequately reflect the thought of the writer, or are the ideas made overly simple or overly complex by the choice of sentence type? If necessary, rewrite the paragraphs, changing the grammatical type of the sentences when necessary to reflect meaning better. Remember to focus on what items can be subordinated and on what items should be emphasized.

VARYING RHETORICAL ARRANGEMENT

Making sentences long or short, simple or complex, is not very difficult; all the options available are familiar to most adult writers, and the choice that provides the appropriate emphasis can be determined quickly. Varying the arrangement of a sentence is slightly more complicated, for the choices do not always occur to us readily, and the shift in emphasis can be quite subtle. If you have a natural ear for rhythmic language, certain rhetorical patterns may occur to you automatically; otherwise, you may have to work consciously to inject this type of variety into your prose. (It seems that about as many people have a natural ear for language as can play the piano by ear – not an overwhelmingly large percentage of the world population, but more people than you might think.) Whether or not you have a good ear, playing around with word order is worthwhile. Artful rhetorical arrangement can lend style and emphasis to a passage and can also help your reader remember the point being made.

To understand arrangement, think about famous speeches. Often, the means of arranging language in these speeches, although compelling, is somewhat odd and – despite the fact that a speech is spoken communication – does not at all resemble the way people usually talk to one another. For example, when John F. Kennedy said to Canadians, "Geography has made us neighbours. History has made us friends. Economics has made us partners. And necessity has made us allies. Those whom nature hath so joined together, let no man put asunder," we know he was making a speech. Had he been chatting casually, he would more likely have said, "We have lots in common, so we shouldn't argue." However, to stir his audience, Kennedy deliberately chose arrangements that would create interest and that had a certain rhythm his listeners could retain.

There are several ways to sustain a reader's interest through the arrangement of a sentence.

Cumulative and Periodic Sentences

First, a writer can exercise control over the point where meaning is attained in a sentence. Meaning will come clear to a reader as soon as the basic elements of the sentence (the subject, the verb, and perhaps the object or complement) are known. As a writer, you can play around with this point of clarity by arranging your sentences in particular ways.

Cumulative sentences provide the reader with a subject and verb at the beginning, and add details afterward:

> But there is a certain unity of impression one gets from it [Canadian literature], an impression of gentleness and reasonableness, seldom difficult or greatly daring in its imaginative flights, the passion, whether of love or anger, held in check by something meditative.[9]

> Mallarmé shakes words loose from their attachments and bestows new meanings upon them, meanings which point not toward the external world but toward the Absolute, acts of poetic intuition.[10]

---

[9] Northrop Frye, "Conclusion to *A Literary History of Canada*," *The Bush Garden: Essays on the Canadian Imagination* (Toronto: Anansi, 1971) 246-47.

[10] Donald Barthelme, "Not-Knowing," *The Best American Essays 1986,* ed. Elizabeth Hardwick (New York: Ticknor and Fields, 1986) 14.

There is something brooding, somber here, the memory of bright hopes dashed by first encounters with magnificent lands and seascapes, paradise poisoned by dreams saved from a fantastic pettiness only by their size and tragic consequences, of death and utter disappointment, of blighted seaboards and blasted rainforests, of entire native cultures, fragile as feathers, that disappeared.[11]

In all three of the preceding examples, the reader is provided with the basic elements of the sentence quickly: *There is a certain unity of impression; Mallarmé shakes words loose from their attachments; There is something brooding, somber here.* But the sentences don't stop there. Phrases and clauses accumulate, qualifying, sharpening, elaborating on the meaning of the initial clause. As a reader, you can see easily the advantages and disadvantages of the cumulative sentence. There is one primary disadvantage: because the reader is given the independent clause in the opening, there is no need to pay attention to the rest of the sentence because vital information for making meaning has already been given. The advantage, however, is that cumulative sentences, like cumulous clouds, have a certain billowy air about them. Details are piled on softly, building gently to an overall impression. The reader, knowing the main point to be made, can enjoy the accompaniments at leisure without having to scurry to the end of the sentence to find meaning. A cumulative sentence is like going to see a movie for the second time: when you already know the plot, you can begin to examine cinematic technique.

Periodic sentences are opposite to cumulative, and are very much like going to see a movie for the first time. In periodic sentences, the basic elements of the sentence are withheld until the end of the sentence, so that the reader cannot know the full meaning of the sentence until the last word is read. Our three writers again:

For the artist, whatever may be true of the scientist, the real world is not the objective world.[12]

If the writer is taken to be the work's way of getting itself written, a sort of lightning rod for an accumulation of atmospheric disturbances, a St. Sebastian absorbing in his tattered breast the arrows of the Zeitgeist, this changes not very much the traditional view of the artist.[13]

Of their crafts no single bit survives.[14]

Writing Prompt

Write six cumulative sentences about oranges. Write six periodic sentences about apples.

[11] Frederick Turner, "Visions of the Pacific," *The Best American Essays 1986* 250.

[12] Northrop Frye, "Lawren Harris: An Introduction," *The Bush Garden* 208.

[13] Donald Barthelme, "Not-Knowing" 17.

[14] Frederick Turner, "Visions of the Pacific" 242.

You can see easily that meaning is suspended in each sentence until its end. Barthelme's sentence illustrates the periodic arrangement most completely. The subject, *the traditional view of the artist*, is the last piece of information given. In the case of periodic sentences, then, the reader is compelled to keep reading until the end of the sentence just to see "whodunit." The rhetorical advantage is clear: the reader is forced to be interested. But be careful here: too many periodic sentences and your reader will become irritated at constantly being held in suspense.

Partly Periodic Sentences

Very few sentences are as completely periodic or cumulative as the examples listed previously. Most sentences are partly periodic: the kernel of meaning, the basis of the sentence, is revealed somewhere in the middle. Partly periodic sentences can be accomplished either by varying the opening of a sentence or by using interrupting elements, both of which delay the completion of the independent clause. If you are in doubt about what partly periodic sentences might look like (or about what effect they might have) return to Exercise One at the beginning of this chapter. The passage by Jacob Bronowski contains several partly periodic sentences.

VARYING THE OPENING

The ordinary way to open a sentence is with its subject:

> English Canadians currently, in predictable fashion, view Eastern bloc problems of ethnicity with great interest while regarding the Meech Lake battle with a boredom verging on disgust.

But there are all sorts of other ways to open this particular sentence. It could be opened with an adverb:

> *Currently*, English Canadians, in predictable fashion, view Eastern bloc problems of ethnicity with great interest while regarding the Meech Lake battle with a boredom verging on disgust.

Or it could be opened with a prepositional phrase (or a verbal phrase or an absolute phrase):

> *In predictable fashion*, English Canadians currently view Eastern bloc problems of ethnicity with great interest while regarding the Meech Lake battle with a boredom verging on disgust.

Or it could be opened with a subordinate clause:

> *While regarding the Meech Lake battle with a boredom verging on disgust*, English Canadians currently, in predictable fashion, view Eastern bloc problems of ethnicity with great interest.

Meaning in all these sentences is suspended while the reader gets through the opening, causing readers both to absorb the information in the opening (which might otherwise be ignored) and compelling them to read forward to get the complete meaning of the sentence. Be forewarned, however, that a long opening clause can be confusing:

> However, while the matter that had captivated the attention of few Canadians was being debated among the premiers and their constitutional legal advisers in their plush quarters in the nation's capital, the Oka crisis, an event that would excite many Canadians interested in human rights, began.

This sentence seems a little unbalanced, and its main point is almost lost. As a writer, you will need to determine when an opening other than the subject is appropriate — and when a varied opening only confuses the reader.

Remember, when you do begin a sentence with something other than the subject, the opening is usually followed by a comma.

USING INTERRUPTERS

When we talk, quite often we interrupt the flow of our own sentences to add information or asides, to clarify points or to develop them. If we do this too much, we can bore our audience ("I was talking to Joe — you know, Franca's son, the one who went to Queen's and whose sister went to Guelph — what was her name? Anna, I think — named after her grandmother who is still in Ottawa — and Joe said . . ."). The listener rebels against this sort of verbal assault. The judicious use of interrupters, however, maintains the reader's interest, feeding tidbits of relevant details and qualifying declarations, but still keeping the reader attentive for the primary message of the sentence.

There are many means of interrupting the flow of a sentence. You can use single words (adverbs, conjunctive adverbs, exclamations), or phrases (appositives and absolutes), or clauses even. Dashes and parentheses can be used to insert interrupting information that doesn't conform easily to any of these categories. Here's a passage by Northrop Frye to think about:

> **1.** The "framework" of Lampman, for instance, is that of a placid romantic nature poet beating the track of Wordsworth and Keats. **2.** But there are also in Lampman many very different characteristics. **3.** He has, for instance, a spiritual loneliness, a repugnance to organized social life, which goes far beyond mere discontent with his provincial environment. **4.** This is a quality in Lampman which links him to the great Canadian explorers, the solitary adventurers among solitudes, and to the explorer-painters like Thomson and Emily Carr who followed them, with their eyes continually straining into the depths of nature. **5.** And in the terrible clairvoyance of "The City of the End of Things," a vision of the Machine Age slowly freezing into idiocy and despair, something lives again of the spirit of the Old English Wanderer, who, trudging from castle to castle in the hope of finding food and shelter in exchange for his songs, turned to the great Roman ruins, the "eald enta geweorc" (the ancient work of giants), to brood over a greater oppression of man by nature than his own.[15]

---

[15] Northrop Frye, "The Narrative Tradition in English-Canadian Poetry," *The Bush Garden* 147.

If you are feeling ambitious, compose eight sentences on your own about going to the movies (or another topic). Then, make them more interesting and more informative by varying the opening or adding mid-sentence interrupters. If you prefer, use the sentences below as your core sentences, and add openings or interrupters to them. You will need to add some information, and you can feel free to change the meaning of the sentences. Don't be afraid to have some fun: the purpose of the exercise is to encourage you to play with language.

1) Watching movies at home will never replace the social act of "going to the show."
2) The big screen and the complete darkness allow immersion in a film.
3) It is true that the small screen in most Cineplex theatres is slightly irritating because details are obscured.
4) That might be the reason that teenagers are the only people who go to the movies in Peterborough.
5) Going to the movies still costs less than going to dinner or to the theatre or to the ballet or to a baseball game.
6) It is important to support the careers of multimillionaires like Madonna, Dustin Hoffman, and Meryl Streep.
7) Every small town needs an independent cinema.
8) No small town needs to see sequel movies for an entire summer.

This passage typifies the prose style of Northrop Frye: he likes to add phrases and clauses, particularly appositives, and the result is prose which reads with a conversational, reflective tone. We sense that his mind is engaged constantly, that he thinks new thoughts even as he writes.

The first two sentences, however, where Frye is beginning to develop his topic, have few interrupters. Sentence One is punctuated by the short phrase *for instance*, but otherwise the two sentences move smoothly from beginning to end. This choice makes sense since Frye is trying to introduce the reader to his subject and therefore wants his opening to be accessible. When Frye warms to his topic, he uses interrupters with greater frequency. Look at Sentences Four and Five. Phrases such as *the solitary adventurers among solitudes,* and *a vision of the Machine Age slowly freezing into idiocy and despair* are insertions of tone as well as information. They permit Frye's personal comments to interrupt the general argument of the piece, thus breaking the narrative line, taking the reader, for a brief time, in a new direction. And in Sentence Four, interrupters interrupt other interrupters, particularly where *the great Roman ruins* is followed by the two appositives *the "eald enta geweorc,"* and *(the ancient work of giants)*. Again, we see the rhythm, the variety of the spoken word, imitated here as Frye inserts comments that create different layers of meaning, points of clarification, as if he were responding to a puzzled face or a raised eyebrow.

How does all of this apply to you as a writer? The passage from Frye isn't meant to be read as a definitive example of exactly how interrupters work. In fact, if you return to Exercise One at the beginning of this chapter and examine the passage written by Annie Dillard, you will find that she uses interrupters to create quite a different, though no less appealing, effect. Both passages establish that interrupting your sentences, whether with appositives, prepositional phrases, or dependent clauses, commas, dashes, or brackets does help to keep prose interesting: the breaks in the prose add tone and pitch to the voice and allow key ideas to be stressed.

Parallel Structure and Climactic Arrangement

Variety in general can keep a reader interested; particular sorts of variety can make a passage memorable. You probably remember from books you have read on study tips that giving anything a rhythm or a rhyme, a pattern of some sort, from the parts of the crayfish to the reasons for the conscription crisis, is a good strategy for retaining that information. Likewise, sentences that have some sort of rhythmic movement or balance will linger in a reader's mind, pleasing the reader with their harmony, long after the less musical passages have been forgotten.

Parallel structure, for example, can create a balance between two or more phrases or clauses that both connects the items, yet holds them separate. As Jane Siberry notes, "You can't chop down symmetry." The appeal of grammatically balanced elements strikes the reader immediately, as in this passage from

Annie Dillard's An American Childhood:

> We were blond, we were tan, our teeth were white and straightened, our legs were brown and depilated, we shuffled the cards fast and dealt four hands. It was not for me.[16]

The parallel structure here is carefully composed; not only are there pairs of parallel clauses, but certain words — we, we, we — echo throughout the passage. The second sentence, although not parallel, is worthy of comment: consider the emphasis created by this short sentence — *It was not for me* — coming after the long one. Breaking a parallel structure can also be emphatic, and so middle-class conformity is not just rejected; it is rejected definitively.

Parallel structure can add a good deal of grace and emphasis to a passage. Compare the following two paragraphs:

> Everyone wants to be glamorous, though it isn't that easy. We would all like to look like models, but even "covergirls" sometimes need help. When Michelle Pfeiffer's picture recently appeared on the cover of Esquire magazine, several adjustments had to be made. In fact, photo retoucher Diane Scott charged Esquire $1,525 for her work on the photograph.

> Everyone wants to be glamorous, though not everyone can be. Even "covergirls" need help occasionally. When Michelle Pfeiffer's picture recently appeared on the cover of Esquire magazine, her laugh lines were erased, her forehead was altered, and her hair colour was changed. In fact, photo retoucher Diane Scott charged Esquire $1,525 for her work on the photograph.

The second paragraph reads more vividly, more memorably, than the first, all because the second version uses parallel structure to add details and bring rhythm to the paragraph.

An extended version of parallel structure is climactic structure: good, better, best; important, more important, most important. Here, parallel elements build to a climax, so that the sentence rises to end with the message of greatest import:

> There is a common superstition that "self-respect" is a kind of charm against snakes, something that keeps those who have it locked in some unblighted Eden, out of strange beds, ambivalent conversations, and trouble in general. It does not at all.[17]

Here, Joan Didion allows strange beds and ambivalent conversations to add up to the climax of trouble in general. Note her use, also, of the short sentence immediately after the parallel structure. Like Dillard, she recognizes the emphatic possibilities of the short sentence.

Writing Prompt

Pick a topic to which you are emotionally or politically committed: Temagami forests, access to abortion, American domination of popular culture, steady employment, the need for the CBC. Write four sentences about that topic that exhibit parallel or climactic structure.

---

[16] Annie Dillard, *An American Childhood* (New York: Harper and Row, 1987), 215.

[17] Joan Didion, "On Self-Respect," *Slouching Towards Bethlehem* (New York: Washington Square, 1981) 147.

Varying Rhetorical Arrangement

Sample Paragraph:

1. A structural approach is dominant in the hierarchy of the organization. **2.** There is a very definite communication flow. **3.** Administrators run the financial end of the university. **4.** Professors primarily play an informant role, although they have some say in financial decisions. **5.** They relay their needs and make proposals about what changes they see necessary. **6.** The professor's key responsibilities are to control the material being taught and outlining methods used to teach it. **7.** They have teaching assistants and secretaries who carry through their commands. **8.** These assistants make no decisions; they are simply conveyors of information. **9.** The students are at the bottom of this hierarchy. **10.** They accept what is given to them, as it is presented, without question. **11.** Students do not speak directly with professors if there is a problem. **12.** Any help required is to be sought from teaching assistants. **13.** The student is to see the professor only if the teaching assistants cannot help.

Exercise One:

The bricklayer/stonemason and carpenter/joiner once represented the apogee of artisanal autonomy. The long craft traditions of these two trades meant that both carpenters and bricklayers were able to react to threats of craft degradation without perceiving their actions as class-oriented or radical in any way. Threats to craft autonomy occurred first for the carpenters during the 1880s, and, about two decades later, problems slowly started to occur for the bricklayers. This gradual yet differential rate of degradation seems to have been determined at least as much by the persistence of producer-conscious unionism as by the building aristocracy's craft-conscious reaction to technological change. These peculiar strains of "consciousness" alone might not have been enough to stay the building trades from resorting to confrontational class-conscious action; however, the town's leading promoters had adopted an industrial strategy that successfully stabilized the normal boom-and-bust building cycles. The context within which these aristocrats of the building trades operated determined the range of possible responses to changes in the industry.

Exercise Two:

The majority of Canadians against conscription were from Quebec. Other people, however, also opposed it. There were people from rural communities who were against conscription. These people were farmers and could not afford to have their sons do the actual fighting. Their sons were an economic asset to them, and crops could not be grown if they were sent to war. Municipalities were also against the Conscription Act. They felt that conscription was interfering with their economies and their regular duties.

Varying Rhetorical Arrangement: Sample Paragraph Discussion

Varying rhetorical arrangement requires thought, not only about the types of changes possible, but also about the meaning of the passage. Begin revising by thinking about content. What points need to be emphasized? An unusual sentence order such as the periodic arrangement will help to stress these points. Are there any points that need to be connected? Parallel structure can help to make connections; one lengthy cumulative sentence can combine points made over two sentences.

Identifying Existing Rhetorical Strategies

The sample passage expresses meaning adequately, but flatly. The sentences are mostly cumulative; they all open in a conventional way; and opportunities for parallel structure are missed. The net effect is a passage without rhythm or voice, and it is difficult to determine what ideas are being stressed.

Revising for Rhetorical Effect

Playing a little with rhetorical arrangement can produce a passage like this:

1. Dominant in the hierarchy of the organization is a structural approach, exemplified here by a very definite communication flow. **2.** Administrators run the financial end of the university. **3.** Although professors have some say in financial decisions, they primarily play an informant role, relaying their needs and making proposals about what changes they see necessary. **4.** Maintaining control of the material being taught and the methods being used to teach it, however, are their key responsibilities. **5.** Professors have teaching assistants and secretaries who, in turn, carry through their commands. **6.** These assistants make no decisions; they simply convey information. **7.** At the bottom of this hierarchy are the students. **8.** They accept what is given to them, as it is presented, without question. **9.** If students have problems, they do not speak directly with professors. **10.** Any help required is to be sought from teaching assistants. **11.** Only if the teaching assistants cannot help does the student consult the professor.

You will recognize that many changes have been made. Sentences have been combined, items interjected, openings varied, clauses rearranged. In particular, look at Sentences One, Three, Four, Six, Seven, and Eleven in the revised passage.

Sentence One combines the first two sentences of the sample passage. Originally, Sentences One and Two both followed the usual order of a simple sentence. In our revision, we have combined the two to create a partly periodic sentence. The order of Sentence One has been reversed: *dominant*, the complement, now begins the independent clause, and *approach*, the subject, completes it. This structure pulls the reader into the passage by deferring meaning. Sentence Two now operates as a modifier rather than a complete sentence, thereby connecting two closely related points.

Sentence Three is now partly periodic. Placing the subordinate clause beginning with *although* at the beginning of the sentence allows for better connection of ideas between Sentence Two and Sentence Three, placing the information about responsibility for finances in each sentence closer together.

Sentence Four in the revised version differs from the original sentence in three ways. The sentence is now periodic: its complete subject, *their key responsibilities*, is placed at the end of the sentence. To reinforce the two responsibilities being discussed, these items have been arranged in parallel order. Finally, the insertion of *however* helps to create interest and preserve unity.

Small changes in Sentence Six have made the elements more clearly parallel, creating a more forceful and rhythmic statement.

Sentence Seven has been revised to a periodic sentence, a good rhetorical revision. The writer would want to emphasize the place of students, so keeping the reader in suspense helps to reinforce the students' lowly status. Likewise, Sentence Eleven has been revised to a semi-periodic structure. This revision pulls the reader toward the end of the paragraph, keeping our attention until the last word.

Altogether, the use of periodic or semi-periodic structures and of parallel structures makes the sentences more interesting, breaking the predictability of the passage. The varied rhetorical arrangements also help to reinforce meaning. You may have made quite different revisions, creating another sort of effect. Your revision is sound if the passage reads more gracefully and if what you consider the key points are stressed.

Examine the exercise paragraphs carefully. What strategies (cumulative vs. periodic sentences, varied openings, interrupters, parallel and climactic arrangements) are used to create interest? What strategies are not used? Rewrite the paragraphs, making any changes in rhetorical arrangement that you think might make the paragraphs more interesting and the meaning more clear.

VARYING PUNCTUATION

A quick glance at a typewriter or computer keyboard lets any writer see the punctuation choices available to the skilled composer: the period, the question mark, and the exclamation mark for ending sentences; the comma, the semi-colon, the colon, and the dash for internal punctuation; slashes and brackets, ampersands and cross-hatches even, should anyone want to use them. Much of what is communicated in academic prose, however, could be expressed satisfactorily using only the period and the comma, the period to indicate a full stop, the comma to separate and set off items so that meaning is clear.

But the world would seem a joyless place if we used only what we needed, ate only fruits, vegetables, grains, and proteins (instead of exotics like Twinkies, Mars Bars, and marinated mushrooms). So it is with punctuation. You don't want a completely unbalanced diet of exclamation marks and asterisks, unless you are writing a comic strip (Kapow!!@**##!), but a sprinkling of interesting punctuation can give writing a texture, clarity, and depth – a joy, really – it might not otherwise have.

The writer who wishes to create variety through punctuation has two options. Punctuation can be varied either within the framework of the conventions which dictate its use or outside that framework by violating rules. Either option depends on a sound knowledge of conventional punctuation, so students who are a little hesitant about proper punctuation should make themselves familiar with those conventions (outlined in the chapter on punctuation) before experimenting with variety.

Working within Punctuation Conventions

Many students depend almost solely on the comma and the period for punctuation, ignoring the possibilities of the colon, the semicolon, and the dash. If you are not accustomed to these more unfamiliar punctuation marks, it probably won't occur to you to use them as you draft. However, when you begin to revise, you can punctuate creatively to create variety.

Certain conventions, of course, must be followed: semicolons cannot simply replace commas; a colon can't be replaced automatically by a period. Indeed, to vary punctuation, you often may need to alter the structure of a sentence altogether or combine two sentences into one. Furthermore, colons, semicolons, dashes, and parentheses should not appear in your prose with as great a frequency as commas and periods: like Mars Bars, these punctuation marks are a treat if the reader gets them only occasionally; otherwise, they can be nauseating.

Nonetheless, alternative punctuation can be useful to vary pace in a long paragraph. What follows is a passage from Adrienne Rich's "When We Dead Awaken: Writing as Re-Vision," slightly altered so that only commas and periods are used as punctuation. As you can see, the passage is readable, even enjoyable, with unvaried punctuation:

> In closing I want to tell you about a dream I had last summer. I dreamed
> I was asked to read my poetry at a mass women's meeting, but when I began
> to read, what came out were the lyrics of a blues song. I share this dream

with you because it seemed to me to say a lot about the problems and the future of the woman writer, and probably of women in general. The awakening of consciousness is not like the crossing of a frontier, one step and you are in another country. Much of women's poetry has been of the nature of the blues song, with a cry of pain, of victimization, or a lyric of seduction. And today, much poetry by women, and prose for that matter, is charged with anger. I think we need to go through that anger, and we will betray our own reality if we try, as Virginia Woolf was trying, for an objectivity, a detachment. That would make us sound more like Jane Austen or Shakespeare. We know more than Jane Austen or Shakespeare knew, more than Jane Austen because our lives are more complex, more than Shakespeare because we know more about the lives of women, Jane Austen and Virginia Woolf included.

Even the most grammar-conscious of instructors wouldn't find much fault with this passage, although the sentence beginning with *The awakening of consciousness* contains a comma splice.[18] However, improvement is possible. Here is the way Rich actually wrote the passage:

In closing I want to tell you about a dream I had last summer. I dreamed I was asked to read my poetry at a mass women's meeting; but when I began to read, what came out were the lyrics of a blues song. I share this dream with you because it seemed to me to say a lot about the problems and the future of the woman writer, and probably of women in general. The awakening of consciousness is not like the crossing of a frontier—one step and you are in another country. Much of women's poetry has been of the nature of the blues song: with a cry of pain, of victimization, or a lyric of seduction. And today, much poetry by women—and prose for that matter—is charged with anger. I think we need to go through that anger, and we will betray our own reality if we try, as Virginia Woolf was trying, for an objectivity, a detachment; that would make us sound more like Jane Austen or Shakespeare. We know more than Jane Austen or Shakespeare knew: more than Jane Austen because our lives are more complex, more than Shakespeare because we know more about the lives of women, Jane Austen and Virginia Woolf included.[19]

Writing Prompt

Compose a paragraph about your parents (or your children) using only commas and periods. Then, rewrite the paragraph, using at least two of the following: colons, semicolons, dashes, parentheses. Invent new sentences if necessary.

The changes in punctuation are highlighted here. You can see for yourself that the changes, which do alter meaning slightly, also help to create variety in the prose. The semicolon in the second sentence makes a more reflective pause than a comma would. The dashes allow Rich to insert a more casual tone into a fairly serious passage. The other semicolons and colons also help to break up long sentences that already contain several commas. In all, the passage reads more easily, more clearly, because the additional punctuation marks grant Rich more opportunities to direct the way the reader reads the passage.

Again, Rich's prose is not presented here as a definitive example of how to vary punctuation. Rather, it serves as a model to illustrate the possibilities for depth that alternative punctuation affords.

---

[18] For more information about comma splices, see Chapter Two.
[19] Adrienne Rich, "When We Dead Awaken: Writing as Re-Vision," *The Norton Reader* 422-23.

Notes

My writing strengths:

Things I need to remember:

Things I need to check:

Varying Punctuation: Working within Conventions

Sample Paragraph:

1. Victory is regarded as a possibility rather than a foregone conclusion among our present-day heroes. **2.** The question is not how much glory the hero will receive in the span of his lifetime, but whether he will survive at all. **3.** Of course the poem <u>Beowulf</u> incorporated this uncertainty of victory into each battle. **4.** It was, however, expressed in a radically different way. **5.** It really didn't matter very much when Beowulf died. **6.** He was still destined to get glory because of the heroic way it was known he would die. **7.** Because the modern hero rarely gets glory, the idea of winning or losing, whether the form is tragic or otherwise, is far more important.

Exercise One:

<u>My Darling Clementine</u> is not a simple film, but its presentation of the typical aspects of the Western plot is precise and vivid. Wyatt Earp is the usual Western hero. He simultaneously upholds violence and law by becoming marshal in order to avenge the murder of his younger brother. Earp takes the law into his own hands, both figuratively and literally, and shoots the Clanton brothers, who are the archetypal Western bad guys. The Clanton family obviously represents the savagery of the West which must be quelled and conquered. Its members are unkempt, illiterate barbarians. The Earp family, conversely, is good. The brothers are clean, neat, and, above all, fair. In fact, Wyatt is quite preoccupied with baths and shaving. When the shoot-out at the O.K. Corral is over, and the dust settles on dead Clanton bodies, no viewer would dispute that justice has been served.

Exercise Two:

Joseph Conrad's <u>Victory</u> is a novel about belief, about belief, trust, faith, confidence, and fidelity, all those qualities that give life meaning and purpose when the necessary knowledge, evidence, and hard facts do not exist. It is a novel about those things upon which belief is founded, things such as a word, an instinct, a smile, a code, a tradition, a religion, a voice. It is also a novel about those things that destroy belief, things such as a word, many words, gossip, doubt, suspicion, fear, apathy, and cynicism. Finally, it is a novel about the absence of belief, about a man, to paraphrase Professor Frye, who attempts to live directly, nakedly in nature without illusions, myths, religions, or beliefs. It is about a "disarmed man." Wandering Heyst substitutes detachment for piety, the island Heyst substitutes need for love, and in both cases, he endures by stoically, fastidiously, refusing to surrender to belief.

Varying Punctuation Working within Conventions: Sample Paragraph Discussion

This sample passage contains only periods and commas. However, other punctuation marks could give more depth and clarity to the passage.

Colons

Sentences One and Two could easily be joined by a colon, since Sentence Two actually restates the principle of Sentence One in a more concrete way.

> Victory is regarded as a possibility rather than a foregone conclusion among our present-day heroes: the question is not how much glory the hero will receive in the span of his lifetime, but whether he will survive at all.

Semicolons

Sentences Three and Four could be joined by a semicolon, thereby allowing the reader to see that these two sentences are closely connected, the latter being a qualification of the former.

> Of course the poem Beowulf incorporated this uncertainty of victory into each battle; it was, however, expressed in a radically different way.

Dashes

Sentences Five and Six might be joined by a dash, thereby drawing attention to the reason for glory.

> It really didn't matter very much when Beowulf died — he was still destined to get glory because of the heroic way it was known he would die.

Parentheses

The clause *whether the form is tragic or otherwise* in Sentence Seven could be enclosed in parenthesis rather than commas since it is really an aside.

> Because the modern hero rarely gets glory, the idea of winning or losing (whether the form is tragic or otherwise) is far more important.

Here is the revised paragraph:

> Victory is regarded as a possibility rather than a foregone conclusion among our present-day heroes: the question is not how much glory the hero will receive in the span of his lifetime, but whether he will survive at all. Of course the poem Beowulf incorporated this uncertainty of victory into each battle; it was, however, expressed in a radically different way. It really didn't matter very much when Beowulf died — he was still destined to get glory because of the heroic way it was known he would die. Because the modern hero rarely gets glory, the idea of winning or losing (whether the form is tragic or otherwise) is far more important.

As was the case in the passage by Adrienne Rich, the use of other punctuation marks adds a vitality, a voice, to this prose. The colon in the first sentence draws the reader's attention and focuses it on the question at hand; the semicolon in the second sentence invites the reader to hold the two ideas on either side together. The dash in the third sentence and the parenthesis in the fourth create more lively writing as the author addresses possible questions at the point the reader might pose them.

The exercise paragraphs again are punctuated only by commas and periods. Consider how each passage might be made more interesting by the use of other punctuation marks (colons, semicolons, dashes, parentheses). Rewrite each paragraph, inserting your own punctuation choices. Feel free to combine sentences or alter wording if necessary.

Violating Punctuation Conventions

Most writers assume that grammar texts and usage books detail all the possible ways punctuation marks can be used, but the next time you read a novel or essay, look at the punctuation carefully. You will discover that professional writers do not always use punctuation in the ways outlined in this text. Semicolons are used, not to separate two complete sentences, but to separate one complete sentence and one subordinate clause; colons are scattered in front of almost anything; dashes occur much more frequently in academic prose than most handbooks would deem appropriate.

Furthermore, you will probably also notice that these "errors" did not distract you at all. On the contrary, you may have had to fight to pay attention to punctuation, so strongly was the writer's voice persuading you to focus on content and argument. Yet a punctuation violation in a student paper rarely goes uncircled; often, it distracts the instructor to the extent that he or she finds it difficult to keep reading unless the transgression is circled or corrected.

"What is the difference here?" you might well ask. "Are instructors willing to tolerate errors in the work of professional writers—even in their own work—that would not be tolerated in my student prose?" To a certain extent, the answer is probably yes. Student papers are often graded, in part at least, according to how well they meet a fairly rigid standard of conformity. The overuse of dashes may well elicit the comment, "Style too casual—C+"; violating comma conventions often results in advice to "Visit the Academic Skills Centre." But that's not the whole story. There is a qualitative difference between distracting student errors and the less visible transgressions of professional writers. In one sense, the errors committed by professional writers are not really errors at all. Rather, they are what could be called interpretative uses of punctuation, uses that depend on a thorough knowledge of how punctuation marks are used effectively in terms of both meaning and timing.

Each punctuation mark gives a signal, conveys some sort of meaning, to the reader. As well, each punctuation mark denotes a certain pause or breath to be taken. The semicolon, for example, suggests to the reader that what comes on either side of it is too closely related to be separated by something so final as a period, and invites the reader to hold the two ideas together, weighing them against one another; it also indicates that the reader should pause for a more definitive break than a comma would permit. An inventive writer like Margaret Atwood, therefore, can compose a sentence such as this one:

> Canada sees itself as part of the world; a small sinking Titanic squashed between two icebergs, perhaps, but still inevitably a part.[20]

Some fairly sophisticated editing choices are being made here. Clearly, the section of the sentence after the semicolon is not an independent clause and technically should be introduced either by a colon or a comma. So what's Atwood doing? First, she is gently drawing the reader's attention to the last part of the sentence. Had she used a comma, the "sinking Titanic" analogy—the fun

---

[20] Margaret Atwood, "Canadian-American Relations: Surviving the Eighties," *Second Words: Selected Critical Prose* (Toronto: Anansi, 1982) 379.

part of the sentence — would have been lost in a non-restrictive clause tacked to the end of a statement about Canada. A colon, probably a more apt choice than a comma, perhaps would make the sentence more bossy than Atwood wanted — the equivalent, perhaps, of saying "Get it?" and nudging the reader in the ribs. The semicolon, though, lets the reader hear a voice pausing slightly for effect before the punch line; the choice is perfect, though "incorrect."

This example shows readily what must be understood about punctuating for emphasis: that it requires a sound knowledge of the conventions, of the use of punctuation marks, and, beyond that, fairly careful deliberation about the choices being made. For these reasons, students wishing to use punctuation for emphasis should proceed cautiously. Commas or semicolons must be placed with care and skill, and the student must be ready, not only to defend any unconventional punctuation, but also to be reprimanded for it. Many academics would circle even Atwood's semicolon as an error.

MAKING CHOICES ABOUT COMMAS

Adding Emphasis

As Chapter Five suggests, commas are used primarily to set off or separate items in a sentence. As a writer, you can take advantage of this generality to create subtle distinctions in meaning or to dictate the pace of a passage.

You can use the comma, first of all, to set off or emphasize items not usually set off. Introductory elements and non-restrictive clauses are examples of items conventionally set off in sentences: by setting off elements of a sentence not usually set off, you draw attention to them. Think about these two sentences:

The new tax caused concern and anger.
The new tax caused concern, and anger.

The first sentence follows the standard pattern of punctuation: two items are joined by *and*, so there is no need for a comma. The meaning indicated is that the two reactions are equal and occurred at the same time. In the second sentence, however, the comma gives *and anger* extra emphasis. Without a comma, the two items are a pair of equal weight, happening at the same time. With the comma, one can hear the speaker pause for dramatic effect. The comma thus suggests that *anger* is separate from *concern* in some way — that it came later or that it is more important.

Changing Pace

Because commas indicate a pause, using a great number of them can slow a passage down, making the reader hear a voice which draws breath for emphasis frequently. Conversely, few or no commas can create a breathless voice. The following two passages, each written by a professional writer, exemplify the extremes of comma usage. The first is written by Gertrude Stein, an author well known for her violation of grammatical conventions to achieve a particular effect:

> We saw a great deal of Edith Sitwell at this time and then she went back to London. In the autumn of that year nineteen twenty-five Gertrude Stein had a letter from the president of the literary society of Cambridge asking her to speak before them in the early spring. Gertrude Stein quite completely upset at the very idea quite promptly answered no. Immediately came a letter from Edith Sitwell saying that the no must be changed to yes. That it was of the first importance that Gertrude Stein should deliver this address and that moreover Oxford was waiting for the yes to be given to Cambridge to ask her to do the same at Oxford.[21]

As you can see, Stein has omitted several necessary commas here. What one hears through reading the passage is the voice of someone reporting an incident quickly, conversationally. In contrast, the following passage from G.V. Carey's Mind the Stop: A Brief Guide to Punctuation suggests the voice of someone speaking with great deliberation and authority:

> I feel, therefore, that before getting down to details, which must necessarily involve some degree of laying down the law, I may be excused for stating some personal views on the general principles of punctuation. Readers who are anxious to "cut the cackle" may prefer to skip this chapter, but if, having done so, they find themselves at loggerheads with me later on, they must remember that they have missed part of the plot.[22]

There are no extra commas in this passage; Carey has simply included every comma that convention deems permissible, and the result is a very academic voice, although still conversational.

As a writer of academic prose, you probably will want to imitate G.V. Carey's comma style more frequently than Gertrude Stein's. Stein's style forces the reader to concentrate very carefully on the logic of the sentence, whereas Carey's use of commas makes the logic apparent.[23] However, you can make a passage move slightly more swiftly by working out a happy medium, omitting only optional commas. This style is very common in academic prose, as this passage, written by Janet Emig, establishes:

> This is not to say that metaphor as a phenomenon has been ignored. For centuries philosophers have speculated richly and diversely about the nature of metaphor. More recently—roughly within the last century—

[21] Gertrude Stein, *The Autobiography of Alice B. Toklas* (1933; New York: Vintage, 1961) 232.

[22] G.V. Carey, *Mind the Stop: A Brief Guide to Punctuation* (1939; Harmondsworth, Middlesex: Penguin, 1971) 15.

[23] Incidentally, Stein would agree with this interpretation. In her essay "Poetry and Grammar," she writes, "And what does a comma do, a comma does nothing but make easy a thing that if you like it enough is easy enough without the comma" (*Lectures in America* [1935; Boston: Beacon Press, 1985] 221).

psychologists, psychiatrists, and linguists have also made metaphor an object for scrutiny. But as yet no one has connected the work on metaphor from such disciplines with speculations and studies about how children deal with metaphor.[24]

In this paragraph, we see that Emig does not omit all commas, but she does omit a few where meaning can be clear without them. In particular, she leaves out the optional comma after the introductory element *for centuries* and omits the two commas that could be placed around the interrupting phrase *as yet*. The result is that her prose moves at a slightly faster pace, and the reader isn't distracted by commas that create a pause around fairly inconsequential information.

If you choose to omit commas, do so with care. Be absolutely certain that meaning is still clear without the commas, and keep most commas so that the passage can be read without difficulty. If you are trying to slow down your prose, remember that you can use commas only where conventions dictate. Extraneous commas may be added to create emphasis, but not to vary pace.

MAKING CHOICES ABOUT SEMICOLONS

Semicolons and colons, as you know, are fairly formal punctuation devices, and the reader is likely to give more attention to them than, say, to a comma or period. Many writers take advantage of this fact and use semicolons and colons to create more forceful pauses than a comma or no punctuation at all would make possible. The Margaret Atwood example discussed in the introduction to this section illustrates this tendency. Although violating a convention, Atwood did create the effect she desired. Here is another example of Atwood using the semicolon in a similar way:

> The exceptions to this prevailing climate are, of course, the poets from the ethnic minority groups; and women.[25]

Here again, we certainly can recognize that *and women* is not an independent clause. Using the semicolon, however, creates a deliberate pause before this key phrase on which Atwood wishes the reader to focus.

MAKING CHOICES ABOUT COLONS

When colons are used creatively, the author is often taking advantage of the semantics of the colon: it directs the reader forward, saying, "Look at this, pay attention to this." Colons are often used emphatically, therefore, when the writer wants to give a direct command to the reader. Lorrie Moore uses this strategy to good effect in her short story "How," which is written for the most part in the imperative:

> After dinners with the actor: creep home.[26]

---

[24] Janet Emig, "Children and Metaphor," *The Web of Meaning: Essays on Writing, Teaching, Learning, and Thinking* (Portsmouth, N.J.: Boynton/Cook, 1983) 99.

[25] Margaret Atwood, "Adrienne Rich: *Poems, Selected and New*," *Second Words: Selected Critical Prose* 205.

[26] Lorrie Moore, "How," *Self-Help* 61.

The conventions of punctuation would dictate a comma here, but the use of a colon makes the command seem more imperious, more urgent.

Cynthia Ozick illustrates the same rhetorical strategy in this climactic sentence:

Call it density, call it intensity, call it continuity: call it, finally, society.[27]

When writing academic prose, you will rarely need to use the colon in this way. Remember that such emphatic use will draw your reader's attention to the punctuation, so make sure that you are not making a more forceful statement than you wish.

MAKING CHOICES ABOUT DASHES

Most grammar handbooks say that dashes are not very common in academic prose. In our research for this text, we found quite the opposite to be true: while many academic writers used few colons, dashes occurred frequently — often more than one per page.

Dashes are used, like parentheses and commas, to set items off. They are the most forceful of the punctuation marks that set off because they draw attention to the material enclosed by the dashes, rather than de-emphasizing it, as parentheses do, or presenting it neutrally, as do commas. However, dashes can be overused, and when they are, they make writing seem fragmented and offhand; too much is emphasized, and the reader will view the prose as scattered, incoherent. Timothy Findley, in his novel <u>Not Wanted on the Voyage</u>, deliberately overuses dashes to create this very impression, describing the distress felt by a character:

Mrs Noyes went running — headlong down the darkening hall — her skirts and aprons yanked above her thighs — running with the blank-eyed terror of someone who cannot find her children while she hears their cries for help. Smoke was pouring through the house from one open end to the other — and at first Mrs Noyes was certain the fire must be inside, but when she reached the door and saw the blazing pyre, she knew it was not the house but something else — alive — that was in flames.[28]

Here, not all the dashes are used according to standard textbook conventions, but Findley manages to express Mrs Noyes's confusion and anxiety by using dashes to show her distraction.

[27] Cynthia Ozick, "First Day of School: Washington Square, 1946," *The Best American Essays 1986* 244.

[28] Timothy Findley, *Not Wanted on the Voyage* (Toronto: Penguin, 1985) 4.

Of course, you will rarely want to give your reader the impression that you are distressed to distraction (although dashes do permit that possibility). As the above example establishes, the dash must normally be used sparingly; too many dashes and you will sound neurotic rather than casual, light-headed rather than lively. Still, dashes can be used in academic prose to recreate a personal, emphatic voice (which is probably why academics choose to use them — they add tone and emphasis). Louis Giannetti, in his textbook Understanding Movies, makes good use of the dash to create emphatic conversational prose:

> Deren believed that in certain cases, it's possible — though very difficult — to combine these two types of structures. In the greatest plays of Shakespeare, for example, the story moves along on a horizontal plane of development. But occasionally, this forward action stops, thus permitting the dramatist to explore a given feeling within a kind of timeless void. The Shakespearean soliloquy is essentially a vertical exploration of an idea or emotion — somewhat like an aria in an opera which temporarily suspends time, space, and movement. Deren believed that, in film, such "arias" or set pieces are sometimes found in works that employ loose horizontal structures — the famous Odessa Steps sequence from Eisenstein's Potemkin, for example.[29]

Giannetti could have used commas instead of dashes at all three points where dashes occur in this passage. However, the dashes help to create a voice by placing stress on Giannetti's explanations, examples, and asides.

Learning Prompt

Take a good look at one of your course readings for this week. How does the author use commas, colons, semicolons, and dashes? Are conventions violated? If so, are the violations effective?

---

[29] Louis Giannetti, *Understanding Movies,* 3rd ed. (Englewood Cliffs, N.J.: Prentice-Hall, 1982) 387.

Making Choices about Violation of Punctuation Conventions

Sample Paragraph:

1. Success or failure, in a world where expanding horizons are the order of the day, becomes a relative condition. **2.** In the seventeenth century the nation that only held its own and secured for itself a fixed position was, in relation to those advancing their station a failure. **3.** It was the Netherlands' inability, in the face of jealous competition from seafaring neighbours, to further its economic dominance during the last half of the seventeenth century that signalled its slow decline in the nineteenth. **4.** This gradual reversal was less an outcome of the series of indecisive wars fought between England and the Netherlands, than the reflection of a host of differences between combatants. **5.** This is not to belittle the importance of war, for the seventeenth century was a period of almost continuous war; the maritime nature of which was of particular concern to Europe's major seaborne traders.

Exercise One:

Gigantism was close to the Russian heart—and who represented the Russian heart and soul better than that Georgian, Joseph Stalin? Whether it was a hydro-electric dam, the numbers in its standing army, the ego of its leader, or merely the plans on paper the Stalinist regime admired size in a way that would have done America proud; like Texans, only bigger! The rich ores and hydro potential of the Ural-Kuznet area, lacking only good coking coal, were developed in plans of gigantic scale. Workers went hungry, disastrous accidents occurred, but the work went on.

Exercise Two:

It seems inappropriate to attribute human susceptibilities to Stalin, but both the Soviet planners and their leader were unexceptional in one respect: they like everyone else (Canadians often exhibit this quality) could not leave a resource untapped—it seemed to burn a hole in the national pocket. The reason "because it is there" seems enough for most progressive-minded materialist developers; and, if anything, the five-year planners were developers. Economic planners in their establishment of a centralized, hierarchical bureaucracy were forced to look beyond economics—military and especially ideological imagery became a powerful inducement for the exploitation of immense resources of hydroelectricity, oil, copper, gold, lead, nickel, zinc, platinum, and coal.

Making Choices about Violation of Punctuation Conventions:
Sample Paragraph Discussion

To decide about violation of punctuation conventions, begin by focusing on the sentences where conventions are violated. In Sentence One, for example, the punctuation follows standard rules and need not be considered.

Sentence Two

Normally, a comma would follow the word *century*. However, if the writer wanted the passage to move quickly, this comma could be omitted since the introductory phrase is short, and few readers would fail to recognize the need for a break between *century* and *the*.

A comma would also normally follow the word *station*, setting off the prepositional phrase *in relation to those advancing their station*. If the first comma (after *was*) remains, then a second comma is also necessary: we need either two commas or no commas at all. It might be possible to omit the first comma as well as the second, although the sentence would be more difficult to read then. Our preference is for the following revision:

In the seventeenth century the nation that only held its own and secured for itself a fixed position was, in relation to those advancing their station, a failure.

Sentence Three

The commas enclosing *in the face of jealous competition from seafaring neighbours* could be viewed as optional: it is difficult to determine whether the phrase is an essential or non-essential modifier. However, since this sentence is quite long and the more important meaning is contained in the independent clause, it is probably appropriate to enclose the phrase in commas, giving the reader a break and emphasizing the important clause. We will leave this sentence as is.

Sentence Four

In Sentence Four, a comma has been placed after *Netherlands* that is technically incorrect. The writer obviously placed the comma there in an attempt to improve clarity in a long sentence, although the sentence reads fairly easily without the comma. Probably it would be better to leave this comma out rather than run the risk of having it circled as an error.

This gradual reversal was less an outcome of the series of indecisive wars fought between England and the Netherlands than the reflection of a host of differences between combatants.

Sentence Five

One might make the same argument about the semicolon here as about the comma in Sentence Four. The clause following the semicolon is not an independent clause, so the semicolon is technically incorrect. Furthermore, there is no particular emphatic advantage in placing a semicolon at this point. However, since the sentence is quite long, replacing the semicolon with a comma is perhaps not the wisest revision choice. It might be more appropriate to rewrite the sentence, keeping the semicolon and changing the subordinate clause to an independent clause.

This is not to belittle the importance of war, for the seventeenth century was a period of almost continuous war; and the maritime nature of these wars was of particular concern to Europe's major seaborne traders.

Here is the revised passage:

Success or failure, in a world where expanding horizons are the order of the day, becomes a relative condition. In the seventeenth century the nation that only held its own and secured for itself a fixed position was, in relation to those advancing their station, a failure. It was the Netherlands' inability, in the face of jealous competition from seafaring neighbours, to further its economic dominance during the last half of the seventeenth century that signalled its slow decline in the nineteenth. This gradual reversal was less an outcome of the series of indecisive wars fought between England and the Netherlands than the reflection of a host of differences between combatants. This is not to belittle the importance of war, for the seventeenth century was a period of almost continuous war; and the maritime nature of these wars was of particular concern to Europe's major seaborne traders.

In the exercise passages, several punctuation conventions have been violated. Find the violations and decide which are acceptable and what purpose they serve.

A Closing Note

Much student writing — such as the exercise passages cited here — expresses ideas quite adequately and would not bore the average reader so much that an essay would be thrown down in dismay. The strategies for variety we have just worked through, therefore, do not need to be applied to every single paragraph you write. Nevertheless, learning to analyze your work for variety, so that you can recognize a dead paragraph and bring it back to life, is a useful skill. Reread this chapter from time to time as you work at revising and polishing your written assignments. If you use variety to work with content, to make your ideas more clear, more vivid to the reader, then you will be using variety well.

You are now familiar with the grammatical conventions of the sentence and also with ways to make sentences varied, emphatic, and clear. Many of the conventions and choices that guide the composition of sentences also guide the composition of paragraphs because all linguistic forms — whether a word, a sentence, a paragraph — are alike in that each represents a thinking process, an expression of meaning.

The Paragraph

Do you remember the difficulty we had arriving at a definition of a sentence? Do you think we will have any greater success defining a paragraph? How do you create an all-inclusive definition of articulated thought? Perhaps it is best not to try. Recalling the standard definition of a paragraph, that a paragraph is made up of several sentences that can be read as a single unit of meaning, is not very helpful when drafting your own paragraphs. But it is helpful to know what paragraphs contain and what paragraphs do, that is, the features and functions of paragraphs.

FEATURES

Paragraphs, like sentences, have identifiable features. While sentences express ideas, paragraphs organize ideas and develop thought. We can point to the subject and predicate of a sentence. However, it is more difficult to identify the parts of a paragraph because whole sentences are sequenced in a way that allows them to create meaning in relation to each other. Nonetheless, just as the parts of a sentence work together to form an idea, the parts — the sentences — of a paragraph work together to develop one thought, one topic, one unit of meaning. Therefore, the sentences of a paragraph are complete and accurate within the context of the paragraph that contains them; paragraphs are complete and accurate and create meaning within the context of a single chapter,[1] and chapters are complete and accurate in the context of a book as a whole.

Just as the period ends a sentence, the paragraph break allows the reader to pause, focus on one point at a time, assimilate that information, and move on. The signal for the break — first line indentation or an additional space between the last line of one paragraph and the first line of the next (sometimes both line space and indentation) — acts as the punctuation mark of the paragraph.

How long should a paragraph be? How many sentences does it take to develop a thought? How many angels can dance on the head of a pin? Again, the answers can be found by looking at what we now know about sentences. A sentence can be one word or several hundred. We know, too, from our reading, that a paragraph can be almost any length except too long or too short: a paragraph that is too long contains too much information and strays from a single topic; a paragraph that is too short contains too little information and is insufficiently developed. When we write, we discover what we want to say, and in the process, we discover the length that is best for a chosen purpose. Sometimes

---

[1] This chapter is a discussion of paragraphing. For a full discussion of the paragraphs of an essay, see *Thinking It Through: A Practical Guide to Academic Essay Writing*, Heather Avery, et al. (Peterborough, Ontario: Academic Skills Centre, Trent U, 1989).

a paragraph is only a sentence, or just an emphatic fragment; sometimes a single paragraph can go on for a whole page. In either case, the length is determined by subject, style, and purpose.

In addition, paragraphs have grammatical structure, just as sentences do; within a wide range of choices, they have semantic and syntactic form: semantic, in the way they are shaped by meaning, and syntactic, in the way that form is governed by the conventional use of language. Knowing the forms and studying the relations between ideas provide the writer with the strategies needed to compose effective prose. The writer's aim is always to have language convey meaning—through words, sentences, paragraphs—and paragraphs are the main purveyors of developed thought.

Does this discussion of features bring us any closer to a practical definition of the paragraph? Perhaps not. Knowing what a paragraph is is not nearly so important as knowing what a paragraph can do, the functions it serves.

FUNCTIONS

A paragraph is a paragraph if it functions to present a coherent, unified thought and to form prose into comprehensible portions. The definition need be no more rigid than this. If it is, we miss the importance of a paragraph's receptiveness to choice and its infinite flexibility.

To understand what a paragraph can do, and to grasp a sense of the process of paragraphing, we need to understand that flexibility is necessary to accommodate the convergent and recursive nature of thought. What we need in order to explore the functions of a paragraph is not a definition of paragraphs but a definition of paragraphing; what we need is an understanding of the process of creating a paragraph that communicates meaning.

Paragraphing

Just as a sentence is more than a linear string of words, a paragraph is more than a string of sentences. The mechanical paragraph break does more than help the reader catch his or her mental breath; it is, as well, an indicator of the cognitive processes of the writer. Paragraphing is not bricklaying; those neat blocks of sentences on a page are formed more by thought than design. As the writer writes, ideas are formed, and the logical shifts of thought from one topic, or subtopic, to the next are indicated by paragraph breaks. Each new paragraph signals that the writer's thought pattern is shifting, or that a new thought is being introduced, or that another perspective is being taken. Each paragraph shapes and builds the writer's thoughts, and together the paragraphs form a logical, coherent progression of thoughts and ideas.

Writers often say that they do not pay much attention to paragraphs when drafting, that they rely on instinct and a kind of mental rhythm to guide them to the paragraph breaks. Certainly, sentences often seem to utter themselves, and the process of invention makes paragraphing seem intuitive. "When you write, you lay out a line of words," Annie Dillard tells us. "The line of words is a miner's pick, a woodcarver's gouge, a surgeon's probe. You wield it, and it digs a path you follow."[2] Your mind directs you to get the message across, point by point, paragraph by paragraph. As we write, the paragraphs seem to discover themselves; ideas shape them. Certainly this seems to be the way paragraphs are created at the drafting stage of writing.

At the revision stage, however, paragraphs must be scrutinized for clarity, coherence, and completeness. At this stage, writers make their work comprehensible for the reader. Sentences are added, reorganized, or deleted; paragraphs are developed, reorganized, or restructured. In the initial draft, there are always those sentences that are not much more than exploratory babble, and the freely written paragraphs are seldom developed enough, coherent and integrated enough, to communicate clearly and accurately all that the writer sets out to say and all that the reader needs to know.

Through revision, the writer responds to the reader's need to know and understand. With time, practice, and increased awareness, the writer will be able to anticipate and meet those needs. The grammatical conventions of paragraphing assist the writer to do this: they are short-cuts to meaning. They organize language and thought patterns so that the reader recognizes and comprehends the writer's intended meaning.[3]

Wise writers know that readers, the recipients of their communication, are demanding. They know that readers expect certain things to happen in a paragraph: readers are on the lookout for information, examples, solutions. Most of all, they anticipate movement. Just as a sentence has a verb to activate the subject, a paragraph has an idea undergoing change. Although the unexpected often happens, readers expect <u>something</u> to happen: a topic or subtopic to be introduced; a concept to evolve; data to be organized; purpose to be shaped. Readers want to know what they are reading (the subject and its significance), why they are reading (the importance or relevance of the subject and the writer's stance), and where their reading will take them (the direction and development of the writer's thought). If the writer is mindful of the reader's expectations and tries to satisfy them, then he or she will revise first drafts for clarity, coherence, and sufficient development.

Every decision a writer makes in paragraphing is, ultimately, an attempt to communicate the writer's ideas clearly to a reader. Therefore, all the choices a writer makes have twin foci: one is the writer's expression of thought, and the other is the reader's comprehension of that thought. These choices are based on **content, context,** and **purpose**. The choices surrounding content determine paragraph unity, those based on context connect ideas logically, and those choices arising from a writer's purpose are made to develop the writer's ideas and to express that development in a way that meets the reader's expectations. Therefore, the time-honoured requirements of the paragraph—those of unity, coherence, and development—remain as valid as ever, but in this discussion, these requirements are based firmly on choices the writer makes about content, context, and purpose. Now we are going to explore and exercise some of these choice-making opportunities.

---

[2] Annie Dillard, *The Writing Life* (New York: Harper & Row, 1989) 3.

[3] While the writer controls the writing (the meaning-making process), the reader, ultimately, determines meaning. The text " . . . remains literally 'meaningless' until the reader activates its significance. Meaning resides in reading, not in texts" (W.F. Garrett-Petts, "Research Notes on George Bowering as Radical Pedagogue and Reading Teacher," *Inkshed* 9.3 [February 1991] 3).

MAKING CHOICES ABOUT PARAGRAPH CONTENT

Since sentences make up paragraphs, the writer must decide which sentences to include and which to exclude. Such decisions are based on several concerns, all of which determine unity: the controlling thought or **topic** which creates unity, **irrelevancies and digressions** which destroy unity, and **paragraph breaks** which define the paragraph boundaries that preserve unity.

The Topic

Each paragraph contains a **topic**, a single controlling idea. The topic may be expressed in a **topic sentence**, but most often the topic is implied in several sentences. Whether explicit or implied, the topic is the focus of all the sentences in the paragraph; in other words, each sentence is tied, or is related, to the topic by an invisible thread of meaning.

A complex paragraph may include **subtopics** as well as the main topic, but these too have a clear relation to the topic. When a paragraph is unified, all its sentences, including topic and subtopic sentences, fit within the boundaries of a single thought; they add up to some thing: one thing. That is why a collection of sentences only related by a single subject may not make a unified paragraph: they do not add up to one main thought but to many thoughts. For example, consider this group of sentences related to the subject of reconstructing a house:

> The roofers finished the roof with new shingles. The masons re-set the brickwork. The carpenters rebuilt the main frames. Drywall was installed.

The subject is clearly implied, but the ideas or points are not controlled by a single thought. You will see paragraphs such as this. Sometimes they appear to have sufficient unity to work within the context of the paragraphs that come before and after them, but most often they are too unfocused to develop one complete thought. Such paragraphs risk being confusing. Adding a topic sentence and, perhaps, combining sentences to clearly indicate direction of thought will help bind the ideas together. Here is the paragraph with three of the original sentences combined to make one compound sentence and a topic sentence added:

> The reconstruction of the old house was underway. The roofers finished the roof with new shingles, the masons re-set the brickwork, and the carpenters rebuilt the main frames. After the structure was made secure, workers installed the drywall.

In this revised paragraph, the topic is explicitly stated in the first sentence. The topic sentence states the subject (the reconstruction of the old house) and focuses the thought (that reconstruction was underway).

The following paragraph does not have a topic sentence either; nevertheless, notice how the implied topic evolves:

A shot rang out in the dark alleyway. The silhouette of a man could be seen running through a shaft of murky light cast from the rooming-house window. I ran to the back of the building, up the stairs, into my room, and, panting with fear and relief, bolted the door. As I reached for the light switch, a gloved hand sprang from the darkness and clamped firmly over my mouth.

Again, we have a series of sentences; this time the subject is a suspected crime. However, in this example, the sequencing of the sentences links the ideas, and the topic is clearly implied. The sentences relate to one another and lead to a single, unified thought: the criminal is in the same room as the witness. Here is another example from a short story by Alice Munro:

There was only the one waitress, a pudgy girl who leaned over the counter and scraped at the polish on her fingernails. When she had flaked most of the polish off her thumbnail she put the thumb against her teeth and rubbed the nail back and forth absorbedly. We asked her what her name was and she didn't answer. Two or three minutes later the thumb came out of her mouth and she said, inspecting it: "That's for me to know and you to find out." [4]

What is the topic here? We know the paragraph is "about" a waitress, but is there a topic sentence? Even though we cannot point to one, this paragraph is an example of the way some of the very best stories get told, with each paragraph opening the way for the next. The scope and flexibility of the well-written paragraph seem to be endless despite the need for a controlling topic. Munro's paragraph is a unified, vivid character sketch (a thumbnail sketch?) of a waitress who refuses to give her name.

Although the two paragraphs quoted are examples of creative narrative, paragraphs containing implied topics occur frequently in all types of prose. The paragraph usually presents details and facts that add up to something, the implied topic, as is the case in the following paragraph:

H.C. Nixon announced the appointment of four extra provincial licensing inspectors. They were given unlimited resources to hire as many men as were needed to fight the unusually large amount of liquor traffic still taking place in the province (Howell: 119). The government also appointed several commissioners to inquire into those law enforcers who were accused of not upholding the prohibition legislation, such as the one who inquired into the charges against David Hastings, police magistrate at Dunnville (Ontario Temperance Legislation, Doc. 6: 10). The government also put greater restrictions on obtaining liquor by legal means through a pharmacy.

[4] Alice Munro, "Thanks for the Ride," *Dance of the Happy Shades: Stories by Alice Munro* (Toronto: Ryerson P, 1968) 45.

Learning Prompt

Pick up several textbooks in the library and examine the paragraphs in each for topic sentences. Do all paragraphs have topic sentences? Are there more implied topics than explicitly stated topic sentences? Is there a difference between the construction of paragraphs in literary texts and those in scientific texts? Examine the length of the paragraphs on several pages. Do you find that length varies? Can you detect each writer's reasons for the positioning of topic sentences?

¶   ¶   ¶

Dig out one or two of your old essays. Look at the paragraphs and analyze each one for topic. In the margins, write a phrase or sentence that sums up the main point of each paragraph. Do you find that most of the topics are implied or explicitly stated? Do the topic statements contain all the necessary key words and phrases to project a unified paragraph? If you have the opportunity, exchange an essay with a classmate, asking him or her to analyze your paragraphs. In this way you will find out if a new reader recognizes the main point of each of your paragraphs.

The implied topic of this paragraph is the ways in which the Ontario Temperance Act was enforced.

A paragraph containing sentences which list items (often, a list of examples) all relating to one main point may also be considered a unified paragraph, as in the following example:

Several authors (Earp, 1970; Forase, 1968; Goodstein, circa 1972; LeBlanc, 1977; Sims, 1969; Vos, 1976) have suggested either general or specific procedures to aid in teaching mathematical verbal problem solving. LeBlanc stated four procedures in problem solving:

1. Understanding the problem
2. Planning the solution
3. Solving the problem
4. Reviewing the solution in the context of the problem.[5]

In this paragraph, the subject *problem solving* is explicitly stated, as is the topic *general or specific procedures to aid in teaching mathematical verbal problem solving.* The list develops the paragraph by itemizing four procedures.

Initially, then, the writer has only two choices to make concerning topic: whether it is to be implied throughout the paragraph or made explicit in a sentence or two. The decisions about topic seem to come about naturally as we write. When we revise, we check to make sure that if the topic is implied, we have taken every opportunity to make that implication clear, and if it is explicitly stated, the topic statement contains the key ideas that control the paragraph.

INTRODUCING THE TOPIC

When explicitly stated, the topic sentence may appear at the beginning, the middle, or the end of a paragraph. The writer chooses the most effective juncture to state the controlling idea of the paragraph, the point when focusing assists the overall meaning with maximum emphasis and clarity.

Most paragraphs have the topic sentence at the beginning and they function in much the same way as cumulative sentences do. The cumulative paragraph opens with a topic sentence which is usually followed by sentences that elaborate that topic. The advantages of this arrangement are twofold: the main points are made directly, and the reader is able to recognize them immediately. This arrangement is especially useful when writing the paragraphs of a speech, a report, a memo, an essay examination, or an argumentative essay. In the following paragraph, the opening sentence states the topic which is followed by explanatory statements about the economic development of Canada:

For over two centuries Canada developed steadily as an industrial state, passing from a colonial dependency on British mercantilism to a national economic system based on reciprocity with the United States. Trade patterns changed from east-west and trans-Atlantic to north-south and intercontinen-

---

[5] Gordon Alley and Donald Deshler, *Teaching the Learning Disabled Adolescent: Strategies and Methods* (Denver: Love, 1979) 174.

tal. This change came about gradually, and for a long time, Canada, in its infancy as a manufacturing country, depended heavily on the availability of United States' goods and on the impetus given by American investment capital. The development of a nationally directed trading system with strong US financial support was motivated by Canada's belief in the virtues of progress, expansion, and material growth.

The student announces in the first sentence that the topic is Canada's economic development. The following sentences explain the pattern of this development. Note the key words and key phrases in the topic sentence: *Canada, industrial state, British mercantilism, national economic system, reciprocity with the United States.* The key words and phrases describe the boundaries of the paragraph, while the supporting sentences clearly relate to the subject area defined by the topic sentence. We can assume that British mercantilism is not mentioned again in the subsequent sentences because the paragraph focuses on changes that occurred after the period of economic mercantilism.

Students write fewer paragraphs that place the topic at the end; however, the periodic paragraph, like the periodic sentence, can effectively add variety and emphasis. In the periodic paragraph, specific details lead to a closing generalization, or a series of general statements may lead to a specific point. In the following paragraph, sentences containing details lead to a general statement which sums up the main idea:

The plan of 1899 called for the German army to cut through the corner of Belgium. In subsequent revisions to this strategy, the amount of movement through Belgian territory was increased so that in the final plan, authored by Schlieffen himself, the whole of Belgium was involved. In that final plan of 1905, Schlieffen envisioned the right wing moving into Belgium as far as Flanders before turning to attack Paris. Schlieffen reasoned that taking the long way to Paris would be faster than laying siege to the French fortresses. *German strategic planning emphasized that the approach through Belgium contained the key to the quick defeat of France and, hence, to German victory.*

In this paragraph the student writer has chosen to give the details of a series of plans, including the Schlieffen plan, before closing with the topic statement indicating the aim of all the German strategic plans and their importance. The key phrases are *German strategic planning, approach through Belgium, quick defeat of France, German victory.* The supporting sentences give the dates of the plans, the name of the author of the final plan, and specific details of the plans.

The two examples show but two possible locations of topic sentences. In all, the topic sentence may be stated:

at the beginning,
at the end,
in the middle, or
at the beginning and amplified and reaffirmed at the end of a paragraph.

Writing Prompt

1) Make a list of three types of music. Beside each type, write a phrase describing how that type of music affects you.
2) Add to the list, naming specifically an artist, band, vocalist, group, or song associated with each type of music. Beside each name, write a phrase describing the qualities of the artist, group, or song. You may want to include when or where you listen to each type of music.
3) Next, develop each item on the list into a topic sentence. Each sentence should include the relevant key ideas expressed in your added phrases.
4) Using the three topic sentences, create three paragraphs, one with an opening topic sentence, one with a closing topic sentence, and one with the topic sentence appearing at mid-point in the body of the paragraph.

Write a one-paragraph mini-essay. Choose your own topic. The topic may be implied or explicitly stated. Make certain that all sentences relate to your chosen topic, that the sentences develop the key ideas, and that the topic is moved to a point of closure or completion. If you have difficulty getting started, begin with one of the following opening sentences:

1) _____ was the kind of person who _____.

2) **Let me tell you how to _____ in five easy steps.**

3) **Driving a car at night is more difficult than driving in daylight.**

Learning Prompt

Keep the paragraph from the previous writing prompt and revise it as you proceed through this chapter. As you make changes, list the revisions you have made and comment on your reasons for making them. When you have completed the chapter and made revisions, exchange paragraphs with a classmate. Respond and comment on all the features of paragraph composition you recognize in your partner's sample of writing. When your paragraph is returned to you, study the responses that have been made and continue to make revisions to your paragraph.

Or the topic may be implied:

in several, or all, of the sentences that make up the paragraph.

It is important to remember that paragraphs are not fixed by definition, and prescribing exactly when or where a topic should be introduced in a paragraph would not assist the writing process. Paragraphs are composed of ideas undergoing change, development, and clarification. Therefore, form is shaped by meaning and by the relationships created within and between paragraphs, not by rules.

Regardless of when a topic is introduced, every paragraph must have one. If there is no implied or explicit topic, the paragraph will be unfocused. The ideas in the paragraph will have nothing to unite them, and nothing to relate them to the ideas and topics of neighbouring paragraphs. Moreover, without a topic to guide them, readers will lose their way; they will not know how to "read" the paragraph.

Irrelevancies and Digressions

It makes sense that if the topic unites the sentences that make up a paragraph, then sentences or phrases that stray from that topic destroy unity and obscure meaning. In first-draft writing, writers often let ideas spill onto the page. They write quickly to get ideas down so that they can decide later which ideas and details are relevant. When a writer has written enough to establish a clear purpose, he or she goes over the draft examining how the thoughts support one another.

As you revise your first drafts, ask yourself if all the information contained in each paragraph is necessary for the development of your overall purpose. Know, too, that some tangential material may be retained for stylistic purposes, but be careful that such digressions add to, rather than subtract from, the effectiveness of your composition. A paragraph has a job to do. A stray sentence derails meaning. The writer's aim in paragraphing is to compose whole units of meaning containing supporting sentences which are linked logically to a topic.

Notes

My writing strengths:

Things I need to remember:

Things I need to check:

Irrelevancies and Digressions

Sample Paragraph:

1. For centuries, people have been amazed at the camel's ability to go without water for long periods of time. **2.** Many tales have been told about the long journeys successfully completed and the hard work endured by the camel (Schmidt-Nielsen, 1964, p. 40). **3.** It is evident that this animal must have adaptive mechanisms to endure these harsh conditions. **4.** The kangaroo rat does not appear to drink water at all, and this phenomenon has captured the interest of researchers.

Exercise One:

Native people have lived in Canada for thousands of years. When the Europeans set out to discover the New World in the early sixteenth century, they landed in Canada and found the native people already there. The native people belonged to tribal groups; the tribes comprised nations. In order to survive, the Europeans had to depend on the natives to show them how to live off the land, to kill animals, and to fish for food.

Exercise Two:

When the Europeans decided to remain in the New World, they formed their own government which included an Indian agent who organized the fur trade. Soon more missionaries joined the Europeans already here and without hesitation set up residential schools for native boys and girls. Sharing an attitude of racial and cultural superiority, both the government and the missionaries decided they were going to assimilate the Indians to European government, religion, and culture. They went about this by forcing Indian families to give up their children, telling them that truant children would be put in jail. Native parents wanted their children to have an education but were not aware of the complications involved.

Irrelevancies and Digressions: Sample Paragraph Discussion

This paragraph appears to deal exclusively with the camel, not with the kangaroo rat. Without an emphasis on both animals' ability to survive without water, there is no clear link to Sentence Four which seems to be the beginning of a new thought. If the writer wanted to establish that these two desert animals share an ability to go without water for long periods of time, then the revised paragraph must link this last sentence to the topic of the paragraph:

> For centuries, people have been amazed by the camel's ability to go without water for long periods of time. Many tales have been told about the long journeys successfully completed and the hard work endured by the camel *unreplenished with water* (Schmidt-Nielsen, 1964, p. 40). It is evident that this animal must have adaptive mechanisms to endure harsh, *dry* conditions. *However, there is another desert animal at least as remarkable as the camel for its ability to go without water: the kangaroo rat does not appear to drink water at all, a phenomenon that has captured the interest of researchers.*

This revision still seems unsatisfactory because Sentence Three, *It is evident that this animal must have adaptive mechanisms to endure these harsh conditions,* sets up reader expectations that remain unmet, even when the word *dry* has been added. The reader is led to expect that the camel's ability to adapt to desert conditions will be discussed, but the next sentence, Sentence Four, alters that expectation and focuses the paragraph on the adaptive mechanisms of the kangaroo rat. What we need is one more small revision to the last sentence to make a connection between the adaptive mechanisms of the camel and those of the kangaroo rat:

> However, there is another desert animal at least as remarkable as the camel for its ability to go without water: the kangaroo rat *adapts well to desert conditions* and does not appear to drink water at all, a phenomenon that has captured the interest of researchers.

It is worth noting that the writer is employing a very useful device to introduce a topic: she is creating interest by proceeding from the known (the camel) to the unknown (the kangaroo rat), the latter being even more remarkable than the camel for its ability to go without water and for the way it has adapted to desert conditions.

Here is a revision of the whole paragraph:

> For centuries, people have been amazed by the camel's ability to go without water for long periods of time. Many tales have been told about the long journeys successfully completed and the hard work endured by the camel unreplenished with water (Schmidt-Nielsen, 1964, p. 40). It is evident that this animal must have adaptive mechanisms to endure harsh, dry conditions. However, there is another desert animal at least as remarkable as the camel for its ability to go without water: the kangaroo rat adapts well to desert conditions and does not appear to drink water at all, a phenomenon that has captured the interest of researchers.

Examine the exercise paragraphs for digressions and irrelevant sentences. Search for sentences or phrases that lead nowhere, that confuse, or that add information which is irrelevant to the main topic of the paragraph. Rewrite the exercise paragraphs deleting the stray sentences, clauses, or phrases. Make any changes and additions you think necessary to strengthen unity.

A few years ago, some textbooks and writing instructors guided students through an exercise called writing-the-five-paragraph-theme. Even if students did not know precisely what a paragraph was, they knew they needed five of them. They needed an introductory paragraph that included a thesis statement (the main point or purpose of the theme); three body paragraphs, each with topic sentences and details to develop the main point; and a concluding paragraph to restate and sum up the thesis just covered. This formulaic writing exercise taught student writers form—what sentences clustered in five groups looked like on a page, how the mind shaped an argument into a beginning, a middle, and an end. Let's try the exercise.

Write a five-paragraph theme (approximately 500 words or two double-spaced typewritten pages) on the topic of endangered species. As you draft your theme, pay particular attention to the pattern of your paragraphs: one introductory paragraph, three body paragraphs, and one concluding paragraph. No, you may not choose your own topic. You may even have to do a little research. If possible, get together with a learning partner to discuss your ideas and to hear your partner's responses. You may choose your own topic on a second attempt of this exercise, but try the one given first. Do you find that the prescribed topic and form (and my bossy instructions) make writing easier or more difficult than other forms of writing? Do you have difficulty restricting your theme to only five paragraphs?

Paragraph Breaks

How do we determine the boundaries of a paragraph? Sometimes it is very difficult to detect when one thought ends and another one begins. A general subject which binds together a whole prose passage tends to obscure internal paragraph divisions. Often when we draft, we cannot distinguish separate thoughts; we cannot see the trees for the forest.

Where I choose to end a paragraph may not be the same point you do, yet both of us could have valid reasons for our choices. Both choices could be considered correct. However, there are times when one or both of us would be decidedly wrong. Incorrect paragraph divisions are likely to occur when thoughts are developed carelessly, when they are scrambled, combined, or overlapped in a single long paragraph, or when a single thought is not developed enough before the paragraph break occurs.

Exercise One: Creating Paragraph Breaks

Here is a paragraph that is too long. There is a topic: the student wants to make some points, backed up by subtopics, about the soliloquy given by Lady Macbeth in her first appearance in the play Macbeth. However, the passage clearly exemplifies the work of a writer who has chosen too broad a controlling idea. This type of commentary on a soliloquy could form an entire section of an essay! There is too much information, too many points in the paragraph. Read the paragraph carefully, then re-read and restructure the passage to provide the number of paragraphs that you believe are necessary for clarity. Check to see if each new paragraph has one implied or explicit controlling thought. You may have to create a sentence that states the controlling thought. For now, do not worry about your knowledge of Shakespeare's Macbeth; just concentrate on making sound paragraphs and logical breaks.

1. The entrance of Lady Macbeth in Scene 5 comes as a strong dramatic contrast to all the preceding scenes. **2.** Until this scene, we have had only the vaguest mention of her, and her appearance is all the more forceful because of this. **3.** Alone on the stage, she has a chance to state her frankest and most hidden thoughts, uncomplicated by the social compromises of dialogue. **4.** She begins to speak by reading Macbeth's letter aloud. **5.** In the letter's opening line, Shakespeare subtly reveals the crucial flaw in the couple's plans: "They met in the day of success . . ." (Macbeth 1.5.1). **6.** There is no mention here of Banquo, and it is his presence at the meeting with the witches that so undermines the couple's success. **7.** The audience is made more aware that Lady Macbeth does not realize Banquo's full involvement in Macbeth's plans. **8.** Finishing his letter, she then begins a forceful soliloquy in which she discusses her husband's character. **9.** Apparent here is her repressed disgust and automatic assumption of superiority over him. **10.** In this passage, she categorically outlines his flaws and his obvious inadequacy to fulfil their shared ambitions. **11.** In doing so, she is unconsciously convincing herself that only she is capable of perpetrating the murder of Duncan. **12.** In her mind a vision is already forming of herself as controller of their joint destiny. **13.** The clarity of her vision and the completeness of her commitment to this destiny has strong dramatic impact, for she is not once besieged by the moral doubts which have left Macbeth completely indecisive. **14.** Plainly she sees action rather than passivity as the only means to the throne, and it is this preference which determines the role she will play in the struggle. **15.** Shakespeare reveals this passionate intent in a brilliantly subtle stroke. **16.** When the messenger interrupts her reverie with the words "The King comes here tonight" (Macbeth 1.5.29), he is referring to Duncan. **17.** For Lady Macbeth, who already is unconsciously associating Macbeth with the throne, it is as though someone read her innermost thoughts. **18.** Her amazed reaction, "Thou art mad to say it!" is hastily covered up with the weak rejoinder, "Is not the master with him?" (Macbeth 1.5.30-31), for she quickly realizes whom the messenger really means. **19.** This nervous misjudgment plainly reveals the depth of her guilty thoughts and the earnestness of her intent.

¶   ¶   ¶

MAKING CHOICES ABOUT CONTEXT

A writer makes choices about the order in which ideas are presented. The sequencing of ideas and the organization of thought into passages of written discourse are ways a writer communicates meaning, sentence by sentence, paragraph by paragraph, to a reader. But neither a single sentence nor a single paragraph carries meaning in isolation. Exact meaning is derived from the relations set up between sentences and between paragraphs: meaning created by context. Ideas, like people, are known by the company they keep.

Gaining a sense of control over contextual meaning is one of the greatest challenges facing any writer. We are never absolutely certain that the relations set up and the links provided are clear enough for complete understanding. Nevertheless, the accuracy of contextual meaning depends to a large extent on paragraph coherence, that is, on the way ideas, explanations, and details fit together, link up, and support the topic of the paragraph.

Coherence

Paragraph coherence can be achieved by the following devices and strategies:

1) repetition, substitution, and ellipsis;
2) pronoun reference;
3) parallel constructions;
4) transitions;
5) effective organization.

REPETITION, SUBSTITUTION, AND ELLIPSIS

Repetition

Repetition of key words and phrases, often with slight modification, can help the reader follow a thought as it unfolds, hold important details in memory, and remain engaged in the line of inquiry that the writer is pursuing. Consequently, repetition, by making the sentences of a paragraph cohere, can be used to demonstrate the unity of the meaning expressed within a paragraph. Notice how Roger Gibbins uses repetition in the following paragraph on language politics, taken from his book Conflict and Unity: An Introduction to Canadian Political Life:

> The examination of *Canadian language politics* can be compared to opening a carved *set of* Russian *dolls*; *within* the first *doll* is *another*, and *within* that *another*, and so forth until one is left with a table covered in *doll parts* but no *doll*. Like the *set of dolls*, the *components* of *language politics* are nested *within* one *another*. Thus we must consider not only each *component* in turn but the interplay among them in coming to grips with the *language policies* pursued by the governments of Canada, Quebec, and the other nine provinces. The controversies that have swirled about these *policies* provide a useful window through which to view the broader *Canadian* political process.[6]

[6] Roger Gibbins, *Conflict and Unity: An Introduction to Canadian Political Life* (Toronto: Methuen, 1985) 39.

Of course, the main subject of the paragraph is indicated by the repetition of words like *language, Canadian, politics,* and *policies.* The repetition of words like *doll, set, component(s), within,* and *another* suggests the complexity and intricacy of the relations between the various constituent elements of language politics and language policies. In other words, this repetition helps the reader understand the main point of the paragraph: each of the components of language politics, which are nested within one another, must be considered separately and in relation to one another.

While selective repetition creates coherence and demonstrates unity, excessive repetition can be monotonous, even irritating. (See Chapter Seven to distinguish between repetition that strengthens prose and repetition that weakens it.)

Substitution

One way of repeating concepts without repeating words is substitution. To create coherence, the writer repeats an idea expressed in a preceding sentence using different words. In effect, the writer substitutes a word or words that mean the same as, mean something similar to, or refer to the words originally used to express the idea. In the following example, substitution avoids monotony and creates ties between the three sentences:

> *Modern African Socialism* appears to be a highly flexible, vague set of ideas and beliefs having little coherence or direction. However, *this political ideology* must be seen in the light of *Africa's political structures* and *conditions.* Both proponents of *the doctrine* and members of *African governments* are struggling to meet a wide range of formidable *problems.*

In this paragraph, the words *this political ideology* and *the doctrine* are substitutes for *modern African Socialism. African governments* is related in meaning to *Africa's political structures,* and *problems* refers to the word *conditions.*

Frequently, substitution and repetition work together to create coherent paragraphs. Examine the following two sentences:

> *The proximal layer* is called *the pia,* and *the distal layer* is called *the dura mater.* Imposed between *the two layers* is a fibrous mass called the arachnoid.

The words *the two layers* in the second sentence are a substitute for *the proximal layer* and *the distal layer,* and for *the pia* and *the dura mater.* Here, the repetition of the word *layer(s)* makes the substitution clear and connects all the information given in the first sentence to the information given in the second. The reader, holding in memory the information given in the first sentence, knows the answer to the embedded question "What two layers?"

Certain words, like pronouns, are particularly useful in substitution. In fact, pronouns are substitutes by definition; they stand in for nouns. Note the links created in the following example when pronouns are substituted for nouns:

> The white manager of the Central Station is described as having few organizational skills and little intelligence or initiative. *His* only redeeming feature is that *he* is able to survive so far from the civilization of *his* birthplace.

The pronoun *he* refers to the manager, and the possessive pronoun *his* indicates those things that the manager has. (Substituting pronouns for nouns to create cohesion is a particular form of referential tie that will be discussed more fully under the heading Pronoun Reference.)

The definite article (*the*) and comparatives (words that refer to a preceding element by comparison) are also helpful to writers creating coherence through substitution. Because the definite article indicates the substitution of a specific noun for a general noun, it creates a connection between these two nouns. Comparatives, by making a comparison, also tie words and thoughts together. Whether using pronouns, the definite article, or comparatives, the writer makes the interpretation of a sentence element depend on information given elsewhere. By doing this, the writer creates referential ties that can create cohesion within a single sentence or within a single paragraph. Study the following paragraph:

> **1.** When *a student* begins to learn all the parts of the brain, *he* or *she* will have *to memorize many unfamiliar names, terms, and details.* **2.** *This* may seem *difficult at first.* **3.** *Later*, when *these* facts become relevant to the understanding of neuroanatomy, the student will retain *the nomenclature and definitions more easily.*

In this passage, we find examples of ties created by substituting pronouns for nouns. In Sentence One, the pronoun *he* or the pronoun *she* is a substitute for the noun *student.* In Sentence Two, the demonstrative pronoun *this* refers to the memorization of *many unfamiliar names, terms, and details* while in Sentence Three, the demonstrative pronoun *these* refers to the *names, terms,* and *details* themselves.

Ties are created by substituting specific, concrete terms for general, abstract terms. In Sentence Three, *the nomenclature and definitions* refers specifically to the more general *many unfamiliar names, terms,* and *details* in Sentence One. The reader is alerted to this specificity by the switch from the general *many* to the definite article *the.*

In addition, there is a comparative reference which helps tie the sentences within the paragraph together to create meaning. The *more easily* at the end of Sentence Three prompts the reader to compare this sentence to Sentence One and Sentence Two. Note the progression of thought within the paragraph: *When . . . begins . . . difficult; Later . . . more easily.* The movement in the paragraph is maintained by the use of chronological order and by the comparison.

You can see how important it is that the referents are present and clearly identifiable. If, for example, the reader asks "he or she who?" or "more easily than what?" the answers to these questions must be contained in the text of the paragraph.

Ellipsis

Instead of repeating or substituting words and phrases to maintain paragraph coherence, a writer may choose to omit a word or a phrase that is clearly understood in context. This type of omission, called *ellipsis*, makes it necessary for the reader to recall the information given in a previous sentence. In the following example, note the deletion of the word *layers* in the second sentence without any loss of meaning:

The *proximal layer* is called the pia, and the *distal layer* is called the dura mater. Imposed between *the two* is a fibrous mass called the arachnoid.

Note, also, the ellipsis created by these two sentences:

Each axon is enclosed in a myelin sheath. A bundle of axons is not.

The second sentence is elliptical. Omitted from the sentence are the words *enclosed in a myelin sheath*. However, the missing words are clearly understood in context. The referential tie created by the ellipsis assists, almost forces, the reader to hold in memory information gathered from the first sentence and to carry it forward to the next.

Examine the following paragraph to see how repetitions, substitutions, and ellipses can work together to create coherence:

1. *Dean Rusk* was unassuming and loyal. **2.** Because *he* was a follower, not a leader, *his* appointment as *head of the State Department* suited *President Kennedy's* purpose: *Kennedy* intended to assume command of *foreign affairs himself.* **3.** Before *Rusk* was nominated, *the president* had decided on the membership of the *Department of State.* **4.** Later, when *President Kennedy* had *the Department* completely under *his* control, *he* referred to *it* as *"a bowl of jelly"* (Fairlie 321).

In terms of substitution, Dean Rusk is referred to as *he, head of the State Department,* and *Rusk.* President Kennedy becomes *Kennedy, himself, the president,* and *he.* (Note that *his,* a pronominal adjective, is also a substitute for *Rusk's* and *Kennedy's*). Finally, the key words *foreign affairs, Department of State, Department, it,* and *bowl of jelly* refer in various ways to the same entity. Substitution is effective in these examples because the referents are easily traceable. Ellipsis also contributes to coherence in the paragraph. Sentence Three, beginning *Before Rusk was nominated,* is elliptical in its omission of the words *as head of the State Department.* The phrase does not need to be repeated because this information is carried forward from Sentence Two. Also, Sentence Three begins with the introductory phrase *Before Rusk was nominated.* Sentence Four begins simply with the word *Later.* For the reader, there is the embedded question "Later than when?" *Later* is elliptical, but the answer to the question is known: *Later* refers to the time after Rusk was nominated, when President Kennedy had the Department completely under his control.

Ellipses, substitutions, and repetitions without referential ties are weak or faulty constructions; however, when carefully planned and constructed with referential ties, they add to the integrity and coherence of paragraphs. For the writer, referential ties allow ideas to build, take shape, and bind together; for the reader, they make meaning clear. Meaning is not created word by word but by words, phrases, and sentences in context.

Exercise Two: Repetition and Substitution

Study the following paragraph, marking repeated key words and substitutions. Note that repeated, synonymous words and phrases help to sustain the main thought. Circle the pronouns and connect them with a pencilled line to the nouns to which they refer.

The comparatively sudden appearance at the turn of the seventeenth century of the novel as we know it was a manifestation of a marked change in the direction of men's interests. Comparable and related changes, sometimes resulting in new forms in art and literature, had of course occurred in the arts before. Until about the fifteenth century, for instance, there was no such thing as portrait painting as we know it. It began as representations of the Virgin or the Holy Family. Then, as the Renaissance advanced, the painter's attitude to his subject changed; he went on painting Virgins, but more and more his model is obviously a flesh-and-blood and not-at-all-virginal peasant girl or great lady. After a space of years the pretext disappeared entirely: to paint a woman it was no longer necessary for the painter to pretend that he was painting the image of the Mother of God.[7]

PRONOUN REFERENCE

Because pronouns are the most common referential ties and are so frequently used as noun substitutes, let us examine their use more closely to understand clearly when pronoun substitutions create coherence and when they create confusion.

For pronoun reference to be clear, readers must know what noun each pronoun stands for or which noun each pronoun refers to. In other words, the antecedent of each pronoun must be obvious to readers. Four things can interfere with clear pronoun reference. The antecedent may be missing from the paragraph (**missing antecedent**), or it may be too far away from the pronoun (**remote reference**). Also, the pronoun may appear to refer to any one of two or more antecedents (**ambiguous reference**), or it may refer in a general way to some idea (the reader is not quite sure what, or which) expressed previously (**vague reference**). Some examples might help you to recognize and to avoid these four pronoun reference problems.

[7] Walter Allen, *The English Novel: A Short Critical History* (Harmondsworth, Middlesex: Penguin, 1954) 21.

Missing Antecedent

A pronoun must have a noun or a noun equivalent as its specific antecedent. Words and phrases that merely suggest appropriate nouns or noun equivalents cannot function as antecedents. For example, the possessive pronoun *her* in the sentence *Her ear hurt* cannot function as the antecedent of the pronoun *she* in the sentence *She went to the doctor*. There is no *she* in the first sentence, only the *ear* of a she. Similarly, an adjective cannot function as the antecedent of a pronoun, even if the adjective is a noun functioning as an adjective. Look at the problem created here:

Moon shots are now common. *It* is a familiar planetary satellite.

In the first sentence, *moon* is a noun functioning as an adjective: *Moon shots are now common*. Because *moon* is used as an adjective, it cannot be the antecedent for the pronoun *it* of the following sentence: *It is a familiar planetary satellite*. Now, examine this paragraph:

Hagget's theory allows for the differentiation of two population systems. *He* defines the closed population system as one in which birth, death, and other natural changes increase or decrease population. *He* defines the open population system as one that responds to migration patterns, as well as to natural changes.

There is no antecedent for the pronoun *he*. *Hagget's theory*, not Hagget himself, is the subject of the first sentence. When using possessives, be careful that your pronouns do not refer to a noun or noun equivalent that is implied rather than explicitly expressed.

Remote Reference

A pronoun should not be too distant from its antecedent because you do not want to force your reader to search through your paragraph to discover what the pronoun is referring to. In general, the closer a pronoun is to its antecedent, the more obvious the connection between the two. Here is a pronoun at too great a distance from its antecedent:

As defined by James McCroskey (1982), *communication apprehension* is the level of fear or anxiety that an individual feels upon communicating or upon thinking about having to communicate. People who are anxious or fearful of communicating are more likely to be in jobs that require little communication, to believe themselves less competent than other workers, to experience greater dissatisfaction than others in similar jobs, and to remain at a lower occupational level than their intelligence and skills warrant. In other words, *it* is meaningfully associated with choice of occupation, perception of competence, job satisfaction, and occupational advancement.

The pronoun *it* is too remote from its antecedent *communication apprehension*. Confusion rather than clarity and coherence results.

Ambiguous Reference

A pronoun that might refer to either of two possible antecedents, or to any one of three or more possible antecedents for that matter, is ambiguous. Its meaning is not clear because the reader does not know the specific antecedent that the writer intends the pronoun to replace. The following paragraph reveals clearly the ambiguity created when personal pronouns do not have clear antecedents:

> First, Iago engineers the brawl between Cassio, Roderigo, and Montano. Then, he paints *him* in the worst possible light when describing the event to Othello. Being entirely deceived by this account, *he* dismisses *him* from *his* service, and values Iago all the more.

In the first sentence we have the proper names of four male characters: Iago, Cassio, Roderigo, and Montano. It is fairly clear that the first pronoun in the second sentence, the *he*, stands for the proper noun *Iago*. The structure of both sentences indicates this: first *Iago* does one thing, and then *he* does something else. The second pronoun in the second sentence, however, is ambiguous. Which one of the other three male characters mentioned in the first sentence is being referred to by the pronoun *him*? Someone familiar with the play <u>Othello</u> would know that *him* is a stand-in for Cassio, but other readers would not. The next three pronouns are also ambiguous. The reader is not completely sure which of the five male characters mentioned in the paragraph is being referred to by the *he, him,* or *his.*

Vague Reference

In informal English, we often use the pronoun *this, that,* or *which* to refer to a general idea expressed in a preceding sentence. We might write this sentence: *Jack felt sick because it was raining.* Then we might follow it with this sentence: *This caused Jill pain.* What caused Jill pain? Probably the whole miserable situation, but we are not sure. Therefore, the pronoun *this* is vague. As you can see, broad references run the risk of confusing the reader. They should be avoided. If the writer means *this miserable situation caused Jill pain,* that is what she should write. Notice that vague references can often be corrected by supplying a noun after the pronoun. Here is another example of vague reference:

> Class identity is the first element in the development of class consciousness because individuals must recognize that they belong to a class before they can attain true solidarity with other members of their class. *This* poses problems. For example, manual workers often do not consider themselves a part of the working class, even though their formal status indicates that they are members of this class. *This* is because people want to see themselves as members of the middle class, a class more valued within society's class structure.

Could the first *this* mean *that class consciousness depends upon class identity*? What does the second *this* refer to? Perhaps the student meant *this failure of class consciousness happens* instead of *this is*.

Sometimes pronouns can be both ambiguous and vague; that is, the pronoun can refer to any number of possible antecedents and one or more of the antecedents are indefinite referents. Often ambiguity and vagueness go together to create additional pronoun reference problems, such as missing antecedents and remote references. The paragraph that results is quite a conundrum for the poor reader. In the following paragraph, notice that the italicized pronouns do not have clear antecedents. The words in parenthesis are needed to make meaning clear:

> The transition from ignorance to knowledge is a major theme in both Frankenstein and Northanger Abbey. *This* (transition) generally occurs through some formal education or life experience. When in the early stage of ignorance and ingenuousness, one is blinded to reality and injustice: life appears to be naturally fair. As one acquires knowledge however, *it* (life) is looked at from a different perspective. *This* (new perspective) can make the world a better or a worse place in which to live. In Northanger Abbey, the increased knowledge is desirable for the heroine, but in Frankenstein, acquiring knowledge is dangerous because *he* (the creature) begins to detest life and perform evil acts.

The pronouns must be replaced by the words in parentheses or have the parenthetical words added to the pronouns to make meaning clear. When only the pronouns are read, the meaning is impossible to decipher accurately. The first pronoun *this* has two possible antecedents, *transition* and *theme*; the pronoun *it* could refer to *knowledge* or *life*; in the second occurrence of *this*, the pronoun could refer to one of three things: *acquiring knowledge, looking from a different perspective,* or *perspective.* Finally, the pronoun *he* has a missing antecedent, as *he* cannot refer to the novel Frankenstein, but only to *the creature* in the novel Frankenstein.

¶   ¶   ¶

Revising Pronoun Reference

Sample Paragraph:

1. A decrease in government activity and size is demanded by the neo-conservatives, who believe that the growth of government in the 1930s and after the Second World War was unprincipled, excessive, and harmful. **2.** The liberals and the social democrats, on the other hand, believe that this was a recognition of collective responsibility for the economic and social well-being of the state and the people. **3.** According to them, governments can and should maintain levels of employment by spending during recessions. **4.** The others feel that this leads to higher taxes and reduced profits for business, which, among other things, tend to stifle growth and wealth creation. **5.** Therefore, it is not "necessary or beneficial" (Mishra 30).

Exercise One:

Vienna, during Franz Schubert's short life, experienced major political, economic, and social upheavals. The Holy Roman Empire, which was ruled from it for at least one thousand years, effectively came to an end in 1806, when Emperor Franz II relinquished his title to Napoleon. Vienna's aristocracy had lost much money and status since the abolition of serfdom and the institution of new land taxes in the 1780s. Consequently, it was no longer in a position to patronize musicians as extensively as in the past. As a result, the middle class emerged as a new factor in the music industry of Vienna. They desired published music that could be performed by small groups of amateur musicians. This increased the number of publishing houses and made composing certain types of music a viable occupation. Beethoven, who settled there in 1792, lived through this. So did Haydn. They were older men, however, with defined personalities and musical styles. Unlike them, Schubert was born into it in 1797, and his personality and musical talent were defined by this. Musical historians argue that his music can only be correctly understood and interpreted when placed in this historical context: he lived and matured in Vienna between 1797 and 1828, when this was in a state of flux.

Exercise Two:

Alcohol profoundly alters the structure and functioning of the central nervous system. It interferes with the supply of oxygen to the brain. This may cause blackout or temporary amnesia. It destroys brain cells, causing the deterioration and atrophy of the brain. It is possible that this can be reversed, but research is insufficient to prove this. Also, it alters the brain's production of RNA, an important genetic "messenger." Finally, it causes vitamin B deficiencies. This can result in a neurological disorder called Wernicke-Korsakoff's syndrome, although it may be the result of the direct action of alcohol on the brain. It includes amnesia, loss of short-term memory, disorientation, hallucinations, double vision, and loss of muscle control. This is why one should think very carefully about even moderate alcohol consumption.

Revising Pronoun Reference: Sample Paragraph Discussion

It is quite easy to spot unclear pronoun references in someone else's prose because you, as reader, are the one needing to receive the accurate, clear, and complete communication. Readers almost automatically ask the right questions when they cannot locate the antecedent of a pronoun. If you, as writer, have trouble maintaining clear pronoun reference, try getting a friend to read your drafts. Ask this reader to mark unclear pronouns with questions: which? what? who? To give you an idea of what you want your reader to do (and of what most readers will probably do whether you want them to or not), we will work through the sentences of the sample paragraph, asking similar questions.

Sentence One has only one pronoun (the relative pronoun *who*) which refers clearly to *neo-conservatives*. However, in Sentence Two, a reader might well ask *this what?* upon reading the pronoun *this*. This pronoun is vague, although it probably refers to the growth in the size and activity of governments that occurred in the 1930s and after the Second World War: the general idea expressed in Sentence One. Here is a revision:

> The liberals and the social democrats, on the other hand, believe that this growth in the size and activity of governments was a recognition of collective responsibility for the economic and social well-being of the state and the people.

The next question pops into the reader's mind when he or she reads the pronoun *them*: *which them?* Does the writer mean *liberals* or *social democrats,* or both *liberals* and *social democrats*? This pronoun is ambiguous; it could be a substitute for either or both antecedents. Let us imagine that both *liberals* and *social democrats* are being referred to:

> According to both liberals and social democrats, governments can and should maintain levels of employment by spending during recessions.

Sentence Four is the most problematic of all the sentences in this paragraph. You may find that as you proceed in the writing of a paragraph, maintaining clear pronoun reference gets more difficult because there are many more antecedents and ideas to which a pronoun might refer. After reading Sentence Four, the reader will probably have three questions: *which others? this what?* and *which which?* The pronoun *others* is too distant from its antecedent *neo-conservatives* to be clear, the pronoun *this* is vague in that it refers broadly to an idea expressed in Sentence Three (government spending to *maintain levels of employment during a recession*), and the pronoun *which* is ambiguous in that it could refer to *higher taxes, reduced profits*, or both of the consequences of government spending. Here is one possible revision:

> Neo-conservatives feel that government spending for this purpose leads to higher taxes and reduced profits for business, consequences which, among other things, tend to stifle growth and wealth creation.

The pronoun *it* in the last sentence is missing its antecedent. The student meant to refer to an antecedent implied but not directly stated in Sentence Three: a government spending its way out of a recession. Notice that the following revision not only avoids unclear pronoun reference but also links the idea stated in the first sentence to the idea reaffirmed in the last sentence. The pronoun *they* has a clear antecedent in *Neo-conservatives*, the subject of the revised version of Sentence Four:

> Therefore, they argue that for a government to spend its way out of a recession is not "necessary or beneficial" (Mishra 30).

Here is one revision of the whole paragraph:

A decrease in government activity and size is demanded by the neo-conservatives, who believe that the growth of government in the 1930s and after the Second World War was unprincipled, excessive, and harmful. The liberals and the social democrats, on the other hand, believe that this growth in the size and activity of governments was a recognition of collective responsibility for the economic and social well-being of the state and the people. According to both liberals and social democrats, governments can and should maintain levels of employment by spending during recessions. Neo-conservatives feel that government spending for this purpose leads to higher taxes and reduced profits for business, consequences which, among other things, tend to stifle growth and wealth creation. Therefore, they argue that for a government to spend its way out of a recession is not "necessary or beneficial" (Mishra 30).

Inspect the two paragraphs for unclear pronoun references. Make the changes necessary for clarity of meaning.

PARALLEL STRUCTURE

Parallel structure is created by using equivalent forms within a sentence or among the sentences of a paragraph. At the sentence level, parallel structure is usually defined fairly precisely: grammatical forms must be almost equivalent. At the paragraph level, we define parallel structure a little more loosely. The grammatical structure of phrases and clauses need not be replicated exactly; in fact, to parallel only a few words or the opening of a clause in a paragraph helps ideas cohere and produces rhythm in language. The reader recognizes, and subconsciously expects, symmetry or balance. Therefore, the writer who uses matched, harmonious, grammatical structures skillfully helps the reader grasp meaning and make intended connections. Sometimes, especially in literary works, content is secondary to pattern and rhythm. In his discussion of the novel, E.M. Forster points out that "[d]etails of the intrigue may be forgotten, but the symmetry created is enduring."[8]

While parallel structure can create coherence in all forms of writing, it is clearly exemplified in fictional writing. Here is a paragraph going about its business in David Adams Richards's Nights Below Station Street. The parallelism is subtle and sure:

Now he was here, beneath the earth. So instead of collecting and analyzing soil samples and taking water samples of streams and ponds, he was carrying blasting caps in his pocket, shovelling ore and placing dynamite, playing pranks on the other men — sometimes crawling up into a chute with a ton of ore above his head. And all of this made him feel special, why he did not know, and since he had grown into it, it was something he would do.[9]

Balance is created most obviously at the sentence level by the use of parallel verb forms: *collecting, analyzing, taking, carrying, shovelling, placing, playing, crawling.* Note also the rhythm of *now he was here. . . . So instead of . . . he was. . . . And all of this. . . .* The repeated *he* carries the reader through the paragraph: *he was, he was, he did, he had,* as does the tie that binds the opening phrase of the paragraph with the close: *he was here* with *he would do.* The construction of this paragraph is unobtrusive and natural. It establishes a connection from past, to present, to future; the balance makes meaning clear.

Here is another paragraph, written by Joseph Conrad, that makes abundant use of parallel structures of various forms:

And we all nodded at him: the man of finance, the man of accounts, the man of law, we all nodded at him over the polished table that like a still sheet of brown water reflected our faces, lined, wrinkled; our faces marked by toil, by deceptions, by success, by love; our weary eyes looking still, looking always, looking anxiously for something out of life, that while it is expected is already gone — has passed unseen, in a sigh, in a flash — together with the youth, with the strength, with the romance of illusions.[10]

---

[8] E.M. Forster, *Aspects of the Novel,* ed. Oliver Stallybrass (Harmondsworth, Middlesex: Penguin, 1974) 137. Forster is referring specifically to Henry James's *The Ambassadors.*

[9] David Adams Richards, *Nights Below Station Street* (Toronto: M&S Paperback-McClelland and Stewart, 1988) 220.

[10] Joseph Conrad, *Youth,* in *"Youth" and "The End of the Tether"* (Harmondsworth, Middlesex: Penguin, 1975) 39.

Surprisingly, this paragraph, filled with imagery and movement, consists of only one long sentence. The first instance of parallel structure is the obvious repetition *we all nodded* which occurs twice, before and after the parallel noun phrases: *the man of finance, the man of accounts, the man of law.* Then we have the parallel phrases *by toil, by deceptions, by success, by love,* followed by the rhythmic repetition of the verbals and adverbs *looking still, looking always, looking anxiously.* Finally, note the closing parallel prepositional phrases *in a sigh, in a flash,* and *with the youth, with the strength, with the romance.* Note also the broader parallelism of *our faces, our faces, our weary eyes.*

An interesting aspect of this paragraph is that in the place where one most expects parallel structure, Conrad does not have it. A less skilled writer might have written *while it is expected, already it is gone* to create another parallel, instead of *while it is expected is already gone.* Conrad's elliptical avoidance of parallelism makes this reflective sentence shine forth as a focal point.

"Very nice," you murmur, "but how does this help me with academic writing?" Be assured that parallel constructions strengthen all writing in different ways. In academic writing, whenever we compare or contrast two things or several things, whenever we examine cause and effect, whenever we consider several things and set up a relation between them, we have an opportunity to create parallel structures.[11]

Thus, although parallel structure at the paragraph level occurs frequently in fiction, it is also used in non-fiction to bridge gaps between sentences and to tie complex ideas together. Linda Hutcheon, a theorist well known for her ability to explain complex ideas clearly, uses parallel structure for this purpose in the following passage:

> To accept responsibility as an active agent in culture is to accept that there must always be considerable open debate among writers, theorists, and readers about the value and even the meaning of these various postmodernist challenges. For example, there are writers like Kroetsch who are happy to call themselves postmodern, arguing further that the national discontinuities of Canada have made it particularly ripe for the discontinuities of postmodernism. On the other hand, there are novelists like Matt Cohen who argue that postmodernism lives only as a theory and not as a reality in fiction. I think the numbers are against him here, though. There are other, more internal, debates as well. Postmodern George Bowering sees, at long last, the demise of the realist novel in Canada. But the numbers are against him too, I fear. What is striking and particular about Canadian postmodernist fiction is that the very real challenge to the conventions of realism has always come from within those conventions themselves.[12]

---

[11] For more information about parallelism, see Chapters Two and Three.

[12] Linda Hutcheon, *The Canadian Postmodern: A Study of Contemporary English-Canadian Fiction* (Toronto: Oxford, 1988) 20.

In this passage, parallel structure helps the reader see the details which support Hutcheon's initial claim that there must be debate about postmodernism. First we have *there are writers like Kroetsch who,* then *there are novelists like Matt Cohen who,* and finally, in a slight departure from true parallel structure, we have *there are other, more internal, debates as well.* Because each of these sentences starts with the same grammatical structure, the reader understands how they are connected, even when there are intervening sentences.

Furthermore, parallel structure also lets us know the point of view for which Hutcheon has the most sympathy. After describing Cohen's position, Hutcheon writes *I think the numbers are against him here, though.* The summary of Bowering's position is followed by an almost parallel comment: *But the numbers are against him too.* Because there is no corresponding comment after the sentence on Kroetsch, the reader is left with the impression that Hutcheon must feel that the numbers are "with" Kroetsch.

In this passage, the parallel structures within the paragraph are helped by the parallel structures within the sentences. In the first sentence, *To accept [this]* is balanced by *to accept that.* In the third sentence *only as a theory* is balanced with *not as a reality.* Can you spot any other sentence-level parallel structures?

Parallel structure can be particularly useful when we create an outline or draw up a list that will provide the scaffolding for a paragraph. If the forms are parallel, both the writer and the reader will be able to determine the category and the importance of each entry. Consider this list:

The Byzantine Empire survived because:
— the Byzantine emperors preserved the traditions of Roman justice
— the Byzantine generals organized and led the armies well
— the Byzantine statesmen possessed great diplomatic skill
— religion

The list contains three almost parallel clauses (following the general grammatical pattern of article, adjective, noun, verb, object) describing the reasons the Byzantine Empire survived. The final item on the list, *religion*, is not a clause and departs from the structure. The reader does not know the relation of religion to the other items or to the overall idea of Byzantine survival. Suppose the last item were *the Byzantine religion united the people of the Empire.* This clause, containing the noun *religion* and the verb *united,* would be parallel to the other items in the list.

An absence of parallel construction indicates a writer's inattention to rhythm and to the possibilities for coherence in balanced forms, while faulty parallelism often reflects accidental shifts in form.

Exercise Three: Recognizing Parallel Structure

In the following paragraph, identify the ways the writer has created parallel structure. Try to suggest reasons for the author's use of these structures. Do you think the structures are used effectively? Can you suggest other ways that parallel structure might have been used?

¶ ¶ ¶

Personal alienation is compounded by the inability of the characters portrayed in the stories to communicate their feelings. They construct mental walls which confine and distort their sense of reality. They struggle like some forgotten race for perpetuation and for freedom to reveal the truth that lies just beneath the surface of their prosaic lives. The brief exposure of the characters in single episodes, in mere fragments of commonplace "adventures," intensifies the portrayal of isolated, unhappy souls. They do not grow or change. The reader leaves many of them as they are found: Wing Biddlebaum will continue to walk his veranda, Enoch Williams will remain alone with the phantom people of his dreams; the Reverend Curtis Hartman will continue to preach. Only George Willard, as the one who sees and listens, is present in every episode; only he passes the milestones of growth from adolescence to young adulthood. The presence of George unites the separate lives. He is the natural confidant of all the lonely people of the town; he is "the young thing" referred to in "The Book of the Grotesque" (Anderson 24). He is the singular manifestation of renewal, rebirth, and hope; even so, Elmer Cowley feels that George Willard "belonged to the town, typified the town, represented in his person the spirit of the town" (Anderson 194).

Notes

My writing strengths:

Things I need to remember:

Things I need to check:

Improving Coherence through Parallel Structure

Sample Paragraph:

1. There are several excellent reasons for encouraging community newspapers. **2.** Newspapers that focus on the interests of a small group of people can cover many issues well. **3.** Profit is also a factor here, since, as Hendricks claims, people are more likely to subscribe to a newspaper that has articles on people they know (342). **4.** It also is not very profitable for a small town business to advertise in a large-circulation newspaper when its advertisements are aimed only at the local market. **5.** Finally, community spirit is created by a community newspaper since interest groups can be formed and issues raised through the newspaper itself.

Exercise One:

The adolescent female wants both security and freedom, and therefore demands made by her are often contradictory. She may request a personal set of keys for the family car one week. Nevertheless, later, she might want one of her parents to take the car for an oil change. Similarly, she might insist that she be allowed to stay out until two a.m. But the next night, she might become angry because when she got home, both her parents were in bed. These fluctuations in mood are to be expected. Parents will often find them irritating, but must learn to endure them.

Exercise Two:

When all indicators are taken into consideration, Ontario emerges as the best province in which to live. Ontario's unemployment rate is the lowest of the ten provinces. Workers also get paid more. In terms of access, its medical system is the most highly rated in Canada. Furthermore, a higher percentage of people in Ontario have university degrees, and, when one considers housing, the best housing is available in Ontario. However, Ontarians pay a price for these advantages. The divorce rate in Ontario is high. Housing is expensive, even though more families in Ontario own their own home. Those individuals seeking a less stressful lifestyle might opt for Prince Edward Island.

Improving Coherence through Parallel Structure:
Sample Paragraph Discussion

Improving coherence through parallel structure requires first that the writer consider the ideas in the paragraph carefully. Sentences should not be made parallel at random: parallel structure coheres by establishing for the reader the relationship between sentences, so, obviously, sentences that do not have some form of parallel relationship should not be made parallel.

If we consider the sample paragraph, we can see that the writer is clearly listing reasons for encouraging community newspapers. There seem to be three reasons listed: that newspaper coverage will be better, that profit will increase, and that community spirit will be created. The paragraph could be improved just by creating parallel sentences that state these reasons. Here is a possible partial revision:

> There are several excellent reasons for encouraging community newspapers. *First, reporting improves.* Newspapers that focus on the interests of a small group of people can cover many issues well. *Second, profit increases.* As Hendricks claims, people are more likely to subscribe to a newspaper that has articles on people they know (342). It also is not very profitable for a small town business to advertise in a large-circulation newspaper when its advertisements are aimed only at the local market. *Finally, community spirit is created.* Interest groups can be formed and issues raised through the newspaper itself.

The first two reasons are expressed through identical grammatical structures: transition modifying sentence, noun, verb in present tense. The last reason also follows this order approximately: transition modifying sentence, (adjective), noun, verb (in present progressive tense). Note that we have had to pull sentences apart to get the reasons. The first two reasons are not stated explicitly in the original paragraph, but are implied. The last reason is stated explicitly, but we had to break the final sentence in two to create the parallel structure we wanted.

Further work can still be done on this paragraph. We can also see that support for the claim accompanies each reason listed. When there is more than one supporting statement (as in the two sentences about profit), it would be helpful to express the pair in parallel structure as well. With some thought, we were able to make the following additional revision:

> There are several excellent reasons for encouraging community newspapers. First, reporting improves. Newspapers that focus on the interests of a small group of people can cover many issues well. Second, profit increases. *People are more likely to subscribe to a newspaper that has articles on people they know (Hendricks 342); businesses are more likely to purchase advertising when they know they are reaching their market.* Finally, community spirit is created. Interest groups can be formed and issues raised through the newspaper itself.

The two supporting claims now have openings that parallel each other: *people are more likely to* and *businesses are more likely to.* Note that we have changed the sentence so that reference to Hendricks is included only in the parenthetical documentation; this is a tricky revision that might not have occurred to you. We also had to shift the focus of Sentence Five away from what a large-circulation newspaper could not offer businesses toward what a community newspaper could. As you can see, creating parallel structures is an imaginative process.

Read through the two exercises and determine how each paragraph might benefit from having certain ideas expressed in parallel structure. Revise accordingly.

TRANSITIONS

While introductory and topic sentences direct the reader to an understanding of the main thought in a paragraph, transitional words and phrases lead the reader through the ideas, indicate shifts, maintain movement, and create what is often referred to as "flow." As the topic is developed, the supplementary information forms a relation with the primary information. The relation may be supportive, contrary, temporal, causal, or sequential. In each relation, a conjunctive word or phrase can signal the shift in thought: the transition. Conjunctives act like transformers; they act on a thought to alter it in some way. In a paragraph, or between paragraphs, the information relayed to the reader in one sentence is stored, and the transition allows the reader to add to and alter the stored material.

Imagine that a paragraph is a kind of tour—a tour of a developed thought. The writer is the tour guide, and transitions move the reader from one exhibit, or idea, to another, gracefully and easily. Transitions can transport the reader through time, space, or logic. Logically, the reader is taken through the expansion of an idea; through similarities or differences; or through causes and effects. Transitions point out concessions or reassure the reader that he or she is on the right track, and they can signal that the tour is coming to an end, that a concluding or summary sentence is to follow. When a paragraph is unified and coherent, the reader may even feel like giving the writer a well-earned tip— not loose change but a substantial mark.

¶ ¶ ¶ Movement through space is indicated (in the manner of the skillfully guided tour) by phrases like *on the top, on the bottom, to the right, to the left, to the east, to the west, within,* and *outside.*

Movement through time is indicated by words and phrases like *yesterday, today, tomorrow, a thousand years ago, in the last century, now, during, later,* and *before.*

Transitions that enlarge are expressed by words and phrases like *moreover, again, in addition, furthermore,* and *besides.*

Transitions that indicate order or rank are *first, second, third, most, least, best,* and *worst.*

Transitions that express similarities are *thus,* (which means *in like manner*), *likewise, similarly,* and *in the same way.*

Transitions that point out differences, contrasts, and conflicts are expressed in words and phrases like *nevertheless, however, on the other hand, on the contrary, in contrast, yet, but, otherwise,* and *alternatively.*

Transitions that lead the reader from cause to effect are *consequently, because, hence, since, so, as a result,* and *therefore.* (*Therefore* means *for this reason* or *as a result of.* Note the different meanings of *thus* and *therefore.*)

Transitions that concede and reaffirm are *certainly, naturally, to be sure, of course, indeed, even though, although,* and *admittedly.*

Transitions that signal a conclusion or summary are *in conclusion, finally, as a result, in sum, in short,* and *hence.*

Analyze the paragraphs that you write. Do you tend to compose your thoughts by stating a series of facts or ideas? You might argue that your paragraphs are coherent because all the facts and ideas each paragraph contains relate to one main thought. Look at your paragraphs again, this time more critically. Would readers lose their way through the series of ideas? Would they know the direction you have taken, or would they feel a little like a tourist without a guide in the National Art Gallery? Such a tourist has an abundance of information and much to look at but has no sense of direction or of how all the exhibits add up in either space or time. Whenever it seems appropriate and necessary, practise adding accurate, clear transitions that show the direction of your thought and link your ideas. A paragraph without transitions implies that the reader should know the connections that the writer has not made explicit. Sometimes, no transitions are necessary because the writer has used other coherence devices like repetition and parallel structure. Often, however, transitions are needed. The reader cannot see connections; he or she can only guess, and chances are the reader will take a wrong turn, make a wrong connection, or lose the way entirely.

Exercise Four: Transitions

The following sentences are the result of some brainstorming on the subject of detergent. They could make up the sentences of a paragraph, but because they are only a list of ideas, their context and relation to each other is unclear. Transitional words, phrases, and sentences must be added, so readers can follow the logical sequencing of the ideas.

Create a paragraph that includes the ideas expressed in the list. Begin by identifying a main idea, and, with the use of appropriate transitions, guide your reader through the ideas of a unified, coherent paragraph. Do not hesitate to add sentences of detail and support as well. Link each supporting idea to the main idea.

1) Detergent is an important cleansing agent.
2) It comes in many forms.
3) Detergents are a cause of water pollution.
4) Many detergents contain phosphates.
5) Many detergents also contain perfume.
6) Some consumers prefer non-scented detergent.

EFFECTIVE ORGANIZATION

Think for a moment about how you might arrange a set of books, all on the same general topic, on a shelf. There are many possibilities: you might arrange the books by colour, by size from biggest to smallest, by title or author in alphabetical order, by subject from general to specific, by subject from specific to general. The list is almost infinite.

Likewise, there are many ways to organize the ideas of a paragraph. You can probably guess some of the more common ones: organizing chronologically, organizing from specific to general or from general to specific. Descriptive paragraphs are often organized spatially: the writer describing a mountain might begin with its peak and work toward its base. When you write, you will rarely ask yourself whether a paragraph should be in spatial or chronological order: these forms usually evolve as you draft the paragraph. Indeed, in long paragraphs, you may arrange ideas in more than one order, perhaps having an overall spatial order with a particular set of details within the paragraph arranged from general to specific. As long as the reader can perceive how sentences relate to one another, can see <u>some</u> method of organization that can be described, any method of organization will be acceptable. Think about the following paragraph, for example:

> The biologist whose husband I am sometimes says to me: "All right, so where do we go when Montana's been ruined? Alaska? Norway? Where?" This is a dark joke between us. She grew up in Montana, loves the place the way some women might love an incorrigibly self-destructive man, with pain and fear and pity, and she has no desire to go anywhere else. I grew up in Ohio, discovered home in Montana only fifteen years ago, and I feel the same. But still we play at the dark joke. "Not Norway," I say, "and you know why." We're each half Norwegian and we've actually eaten lutefisk. "How about Antarctica," I say. "Antarctica should be O.K. for a while yet."[12]

This paragraph opens with a series of questions and closes with an answer to them. There are other questions and answers within the paragraph, as well. We are told that the biologist grew up in Montana, which leads us to ask the question: where did the narrator grow up? In Ohio. Why not go to Norway? Because they are both half Norwegian and, having eaten the exotic lutefisk, want to avoid eating it as a steady diet. (Note as well the cognitive link created with the repetition of *this is a dark joke* and *we play at the dark joke*.) As readers, we predict, when we see questions, that answers will follow, so this well-organized paragraph meets our expectations.

---

[12] David Quammen, "Strawberries Under Ice," *The Best American Essays 1989*, ed. Geoffrey Wolff (New York: Ticknor & Fields, 1989) 224.

Some handbooks will direct you to choose methods of organization for each paragraph. We have not found this advice particularly useful because organization need not always be predetermined; topic controls organization. Problems will arise, however, if a paragraph departs from an organizational pattern that the writer sets up and therefore the reader expects. Think about the books on the shelf again. Let's say you choose to arrange them by colour: red, blue, orange, and black. Someone looking at the bookshelf can see easily the organizational method by which the books are arranged. A mysterious visitor comes and places three purple books on the shelf: one between two red books, one between two orange books, and one at the end of the shelf, rather than placing all the purple books together. Now, although the books are still arranged primarily by colour, the purple books make that organization much more difficult to see.

So it is with paragraphs. If a paragraph starts with a sentence about 1914 and moves forward to 1918, but contains one unrelated sentence in the middle about 1962, it is disorganized. If a paragraph describing the plant life of a pond begins with plant life on the surface and proceeds to plant life on the bottom of the pond, but has one sentence in the middle about plant life on the shore, it is disorganized. In both cases, the paragraphs initiate a method of organization that the reader will expect to be followed throughout, and each paragraph will need to be revised to conform to the organizational pattern that the reader expects.

Another organizational problem that a writer might encounter is choosing an inappropriate method of organization. Arranging books by colour is not useful if the person using the books wants to know if a book by a particular author is on the shelf. The person would have to search the whole shelf for the book. Likewise, a writer discussing the images in a sonnet would not necessarily want to work through the poem line by line. A better order might be to focus on the image when it appears, rather than using an organizational pattern that would force the writer to discuss irrelevant lines.

¶   ¶   ¶

Improving Organization

Sample Paragraph:

1. Women's fashions changed greatly during the period between 1900 and 1920. **2.** Dresses during the early part of this era were soft and full. **3.** Designers chose fabrics like tulle, organdy, and velvet; sleeves were puffed, and skirts were made using generous amounts of material. **4.** These styles of dresses reappeared in the 1960s. **5.** When the war began, fashion trends shifted. **6.** Garb became more practical, less feminine, with sleeves going back to an average size and skirts narrowing. **7.** The extreme of this development came after the war, in the Flapper era. **8.** The Gibson-girl look epitomized fashion for the early part of the century, and the Flapper image represented fashion in the 1920s.

Exercise One:

A detailed description of this potential landfill site will help to establish important features. First, the soil type throughout the location is appropriate for a landfill site. A small creek runs alongside the northwest corner of the property. The property slopes gently downward from southeast to northwest, and there is a school in the southwest corner. A subdivision is being built on the other side of the creek.

Exercise Two:

Life on the prairies demanded that the farmer have a certain resilience or toughness in order to survive. There were constant uncertainties about the outcome of natural events: the unpredictability of the weather, the yield of the crops, the price of grain. Then there were the trials created by human folly: isolation, poor medical care, crops lost to storms and fire. In spite of all the farmer's efforts, success was constantly dependent on the will of the wind.

Improving Organization: Sample Paragraph Discussion

You probably had little difficulty recognizing the organizational problems in this paragraph. Sentences One and Two work together to suggest to the reader that the paragraph has a chronological order, that it will be discussing fashion trends between 1900 and 1920, and, because Sentence Two mentions *the early part of this era*, we expect the paragraph to discuss trends as they happened in time.

For the most part, the paragraph does do this. Sentence Two discusses dresses in the early part of the era, and Sentence Three provides specific details about the dresses mentioned in Sentence Two. Sentence Five mentions the changes that occurred during the First World War (1914-18), and Sentence Six gives concrete examples of the kinds of changes that were made. Sentence Seven moves the reader into the 1920s.

Sentence Four, however, with its reference to the 1960s, violates the reader's expectations because the chronology is broken. Sentence Eight, too, because it focuses in part on the early part of the era, seems out of place.

One strategy for dealing with Sentence Four might be to place it in an explanatory footnote. Explanatory footnotes are great places to put sentences containing important information that doesn't fit in the paragraph. The two clauses of Sentence Eight could be separated and relocated to the appropriate chronological spots in the paragraph.

Here is the revised paragraph:

> Women's fashions changed greatly during the period between 1900 and 1920. Dresses during the early part of this era were soft and full. Designers chose fabrics like tulle, organdy, and velvet; sleeves were puffed, and skirts were made using generous amounts of material.* The Gibson girl epitomized this fashion era. When the war began, fashion trends shifted. Garb became more practical, less feminine, with sleeves going back to an average size and skirts narrowing. The extreme of this development came after the war, in the Flapper era. Indeed, the Flapper girl represented fashion in the 1920s.

> * It is interesting to note that this style of dress reappeared in the 1960s, another decade of affluence.

Examine the two exercise paragraphs. Determine what organizational order would be appropriate for each paragraph and revise any sentences that seem to violate this order, either by eliminating them or moving them. Add words, phrases, and sentences that help to establish the organizational pattern if necessary.

MAKING CHOICES ABOUT PURPOSE: PARAGRAPH DEVELOPMENT

As our thoughts are shaped and organized in language, we find we have to be twin visionaries, one writer-self looking inward to discover what we want to say, the other writer-self looking outward to communicate with a reader. Purpose in writing acknowledges both the writer looking inward and the imaginary reader looking over our shoulder; it develops thought in the context of self, subject, and audience.

Rendering thought into written language is a process that occurs simultaneously on two levels. On one level **we compose meaning** to reveal not only what we want to say but also to find the best way of saying it. On another level **we construct structure** so the reader can recognize and decipher our meaning.

Constructing Paragraph Structure

The simple sentence has a subject and a verb, but is there a simple paragraph? We can parse a sentence, but can we "parse" a paragraph? The answer is yes to both of these questions. If we study paragraphs closely, we find that, as in sentences, the structure of a paragraph indicates movement: there is the equivalent of the move from subject to verb in a sentence. The main thought is undergoing change, becoming more focused, refined, and developed. If we were to analyze many paragraphs, we would find also that there is what could be called a simple paragraph, comprised of a topic and its supporting details, that is, of a main thought developed with reasons and explanations.

There is a structural model of sorts that can be followed for simple paragraphs, and it is helpful to keep this model in mind when we revise our paragraphs for development and completeness. The model is derived, just as all grammatical conventions are derived, from rhetorical tradition and usage. A simple paragraph, following this model, would focus on a single point or topic, develop that point with examples and illustrations, take the point to a different level of generality, and finally, in a sentence or two, summarize the point and conclude.

From our study of paragraphs, we know that the model is infinitely flexible and is adaptable to limitless forms of thought patterns, from the most simple to the most complex. Within this flexibility, certain functional types of sentences can be identified. Not all paragraphs contain all types, and some paragraphs contain several sentences of one type. Nevertheless, the structural model is a useful standard against which to measure our problem paragraphs when we revise.

Here is a list of the types of sentences to be found in a paragraph:

Lead Sentences

— point or direct the reader to the topic sentence
— may ask a question
— indicate the shift in focus to the thought expressed in the paragraph
— may provide a transition from the point made in the preceding paragraph

Topic Sentences

— may be explicitly stated or implied
— contain the main idea of the paragraph
— define the limits of the paragraph — the borders

Restricting Sentences

— refine the topic
— take the topic to another level of generality
— make the topic more specific
— make the direction taken more clear
— are marked by openings such as *in other words, specifically*
— focus the controlling idea of the paragraph

Supporting Sentences

— supply all the needed information to develop the topic fully
— may begin with a phrase such as *for example*
— may follow a wide variety of methods of development

Concluding Sentences

— bring the topic to a point of closure
— confirm the limits of the paragraph
— may provide a transition to the paragraphs that follow
— may be shared by two paragraphs
— may be the last sentence of one paragraph or the first sentence of the
  following paragraph

This arrangement of sentences, from lead sentence to concluding sentence, is the sequence most frequently followed in paragraph construction. Whether to include each type, and how many of each type to include, varies with purpose and style. The writer begins with a general proposition and proceeds to a particular aspect of the general proposition. Most frequently the writer is either giving reasons or explaining. In the well-developed paragraph, the movement of thought and the connections between ideas are clearly indicated in the relationship of the general statement to the specific statements.

DEVELOPMENT OF IDEAS

The relationship between ideas may be described as coordinate or subordinate. To make choices about how to develop the ideas in a paragraph, the writer simply asks the following questions:

What is the most important idea in this paragraph?
Is the most important idea indicated in my arrangement?
Are the supporting ideas indicated by their relation to the main idea?

In a **coordinate relationship**, two or more ideas are presented. The paragraph contains one topic with several considerations of equal importance.

In a **subordinate relationship**, the subordinate ideas are expressed in a series of statements, each of which is of lesser importance than the main proposition.

To be able to discern and make clear the relations between the main proposition and the subordinate ideas, ask the following questions:

Why am I emphasizing this point and not this other point?
How can I show these different degrees of importance?

To be able to discern and make clear the general and specific levels of propositions, ask these questions:

Is there a broad general statement of the topic?
Have I refined the general statement with specific statements, and have I focused the topic?

If, when you are revising your paragraphs, you feel that it would help immensely if you had an opportunity to explain your writing to your reader, look carefully at the structure. Developed paragraphs are self-explanatory. More than likely your uncertainty about your writing stems from poorly developed paragraphs. One or more of the sentence types may be missing. Ideas may not be properly introduced or related. Perhaps all the ideas are at the general, abstract level, or, conversely, maybe all the statements are at the specific, concrete level. At such times of uncertainty, think of the sentence types that shape the well-developed paragraph. Add, delete, rearrange, until the text of your paragraphs needs no explanation and no apology.

Exercise Five: Detecting Development and Purpose

The following sentences make up a paragraph. Find the main point of the paragraph and its supporting ideas. Rearrange the sentences into a well-developed paragraph. Identify the role each sentence plays in the paragraph (lead sentence, topic sentence, restricting sentence, supporting sentence, concluding sentence).

1) In two particular novels, George Eliot's The Mill on the Floss and Charles Dickens's Our Mutual Friend, principal characters represent typical gender roles.

2) In <u>Mill on the Floss</u>, Tom leaves home, is educated, and takes on the world, while Maggie stays by the hearth and acts with her heart.

3) In the literature of the nineteenth century, gender roles are very distinctly represented in brother-sister relationships.

4) Likewise, in <u>Our Mutual Friend</u>, it is Charley who leaves "the old life" (Dickens 117), and it is Lizzie who plays the nurturing role and occupies herself with household duties.

5) The brother represents the struggling party, the one who uses his head not his heart, while the sister represents the submissive party, the one who retreats rather than rebels.

6) In both novels, the female sibling works to preserve the loving relationship despite excessive hardship and conflict, while the male sibling works to preserve the family honour and is the one who heartlessly, almost selfishly, ends the loving relationship.

COMMON CAUSES OF UNDERDEVELOPMENT

Learning Prompt

Study the list of four instances when underdevelopment might occur. From the list, create a personal checklist to follow when you revise your own writing.

The main paragraphs of an essay must be developed enough to give the reader needed information. Support for the topic of a paragraph will be in the form of examples, illustrations, details, and statistics. Whether development of the topic is sufficient for the writer's purpose and the reader's full understanding is never completely certain. However, if the writer is thinking critically while revising and is attuned to the needs of the reader, instances of underdevelopment of meaning can be avoided. Here are some of those instances:

1) The writer may be unaware of any omissions, or is aware but assumes the information to be self-evident. In other words, the writer has never approached the written passage as a new reader would.

2) The writer may be uncertain of the way points relate to other points and will fail to make connections and transitions. In some cases, the paragraphs may be little more than annotated lists. To complete the thoughts expressed in a paragraph, additional sentences and transitions are needed.

3) The writer may not have made a decision about the main topic of the paragraph. Unless the topic is stated or sufficiently emphasized, the writer will lose the reader; the reader will be unable to sense the direction the writer has chosen or if, indeed, the writer has chosen.

4) The writer has not asked probing questions about the thoughts presented, and therefore the embedded questions go unanswered. On the other hand, the writer may have raised questions, but, as in the first instance, failed to answer them.

Revising Underdeveloped Paragraphs

Sample Paragraph:

1. Beads played an important role in both the Iroquois and the Algonquian cultures. **2.** Originally, beads were made from quills, shells, or animal bone. **3.** The colouring of the beadwork had great symbolic significance.

4. Embroidery was done with glass beads during the eighteenth century, replacing bone, quills, and small shell disks. **5.** The natives acquired commercial glass beads by trading with Europeans, and although the materials used changed, the ancient quill patterns were still used.

Exercise One:

The Canadian West offers several types of summer employment, and each has advantages and disadvantages. Many nature-loving students choose to plant trees for a few months. Others work in restaurants in Banff or make beds in its expensive hotels. In Vancouver, there are the employment possibilities that all large cities offer: students can work in summer theatres or on construction sites, at service industry jobs or at factory work. If a student is strong and hard-working, he or she should be able to stay employed.

Exercise Two:

To provide the necessities of life, the majority of women in Nicaragua of lower- and middle-class origin must work outside the home in addition to being responsible for the family's well-being and for the carrying out of all domestic labour.

Many rural women must endure the proverbial "double day." Not only must a woman work in the fields with her husband—clearing land, planting, or harvesting—but in conjunction with these chores, she is responsible for cooking the family dinner, caring for the children, and doing the domestic chores such as laundry, shopping, and household maintenance.

Some women continue, after all these tasks are completed, to do crafts and handiwork which may be sold in the markets to provide the additional income needed for survival.

Revising Underdeveloped Paragraphs: Sample Paragraph Discussion

The paragraphs contain several ideas but the ideas are slightly out of order and undeveloped. Here is a list of the ideas as they appear in the original paragraph:

1) Beads played an important role in Iroquois and Algonquian cultures.
2) Originally, beads were made from quills, shells, or animal bone.
3) The colouring of the beadwork had great symbolic significance.
4) Embroidery was done with glass beads during the eighteenth century, replacing bone, quills, and small shell disks.
5) The natives acquired commercial glass beads by trading with Europeans.
6) Although the materials changed, the ancient quill patterns were still used.

Note that all of the sentences say something about beads and beadwork. Sentences One and Three focus the topic of the role beads played, and Sentences Two, Four, Five, and Six focus the topic of the materials used for beads. Could these two topics make two new paragraphs, or could they make up one coherent paragraph? Note that chronological development takes place. Perhaps that development could help us to compose two paragraphs.

Sentence One tells the reader that *Beads played an important role in both the Iroquois and the Algonquian cultures.* The reader needs to know why; therefore, the sentence that follows should supply this information. It is found in Sentence Three: *The colouring of the beadwork had great symbolic significance.* This piece of information could be followed by examples that would substantiate or qualify the topic sentence. The sentence might begin, *For example. . . .* Or the paragraph could develop further the ways that beads played an important role; that is, beads might have also been a form of currency, or the beadwork patterns might have designated tribe. The writer's research would help to supply this additional information. After developing the paragraph, the writer might want to write a concluding sentence. Following these considerations, the first paragraph might look like this:

> Beads played an important role in both the Iroquois and the Algonquian cultures. The colouring of the beadwork had great symbolic significance. For example, [examples here of the significance of bead colours]. Beads, therefore, were not only decorative and attractive; their colours had deep religious and spiritual meaning.

One sentence, *Originally, beads were made from quills, shells, or animal bone,* is not linked to the topic of the first paragraph. We can experiment with making it the lead sentence of the second paragraph, a paragraph that might develop the topic of how beads and beadwork changed over time. Here is a possible revision of the second paragraph:

> Originally, beads were made from quills, shells, or animal bone. Later, during the eighteenth century, these beads were replaced with the commercial glass beads acquired by trade with the Europeans. Although the materials used in beadwork embroidery changed with the introduction of glass beads, the ancient quill patterns were still used.

The writer should anticipate the questions left unanswered: Did the native cultures permit embroidery that combined shells, quills, and the newer commercial glass beads? Did the advent of glass beads have an impact on the symbolic significance of beadwork? These questions may not have to be answered in this essay, but the writer should be aware that the information given has these (and, no doubt, other) questions embedded in it.

Now, attempt to organize the sentences and develop the thoughts expressed in the exercise paragraphs.

Composing Patterns of Meaning

Familiarity with the grammatical development of paragraphs, with paragraph construction, gives you a strategy with which to revise your writing. But we know that grammar does not exist for its own sake. Knowing the grammar of a paragraph does not mean that we know all we need to know about paragraphing any more than knowing the structure of a house means that we know all we need to know about building a home. A grammar of paragraphs gives us insight into the conventions that describe paragraphing, but does not tell us how to think our way through the paragraph. Let us look more closely at the meaning-making thought process that shapes this grammar. We will be looking at the creative process of composing, at how ideas are developed to reflect meaning.

PATTERNS OF DEVELOPMENT

¶ ¶ ¶

Writers compose paragraphs to fulfil many different purposes: to introduce a topic; to describe a person, place, or event; to narrate the episodes of a story; to define a term; to make a comparison; to evaluate options; to explain a process; or to draw conclusions.

At some point in the composing process, the writer must think about how best to express his or her thoughts. Just as there are sentence patterns, there are paragraph patterns — long-standing functional approaches to creating and communicating meaning. These patterns are so commonplace that we use them unconsciously every day in speech, yet when we write, we must practise using them consciously to be most effective. Telling a bedtime story, arguing the merits of waste reduction, describing a trip to a heritage park, explaining how to install floor tile: all require that the speaker choose at least one pattern of thought development. Essentially, the speaker is creating order out of many chaotic details and, in the process, is gaining control over thought.

All writers experience periods of chaotic confusion as thoughts, ideas, and details converge. At times like these, it is wise to consciously summon forth the strategies we employ to do a simple thinking task like explaining where we left our car in the parking lot. Here are some of the main patterns of thought used in any thinking task.

Description

What does it look like? Tell what it looks like, using simple description, or using figures of speech such as analogy, metaphor, or simile. For example:

> I cannot find my car. It is a 1982 grey Chrysler Cordoba, a two-door coupe with grey cloth interior. The roof is covered with black vinyl, the tires have white rims, and the wheels have wire-rimmed hub caps. My friend tells me that it resembles a proper Victorian lady wearing black silk blouse, grey bustled skirt, and black patent slippers.

Description often includes other methods of development such as definition, analysis, and synthesis.

Definition: What is it? Tell all the features that define it, indicating the boundaries or limits of the definition: what it is, what it is not, what is included, and what is excluded.

Analysis: Is the topic made up of sections or parts? Can you examine each of the separate parts, describe them, and show how they add up to the whole?

Synthesis: How does the whole compare with other known facts and how do these connections change things? This thinking task requires describing and explaining, putting ideas together, transforming them, and discovering new insights. The original ideas undergo change, and, by making choices and connections, they become something new.

Narration

What happened? Tell what happened progressively or chronologically. This thinking task might involve showing how something evolved or developed; it might outline a process. How did it come about? In other words, it might require that you look at causes and effects. What caused it? What led up to the occurrence, incident, or event? Tell about the effects, the results, the aftermath, and show the relation between the cause and the effects. This thinking task may involve description, narration, and definition.

> I cannot find my car. I entered this huge parking lot by the North Gate off Dundas Street, and I remember being struck immediately with the difficulty of trying to find a vacant space in a lot that seemed filled with endless rows of cars. I finally found an empty spot between a red Honda Civic and a blue Ford Tempo. Before getting out of the car, I looked up, and I saw the supermarket entrance in the distance. The spot where I parked might have been about five rows from the entrance. If I had not been in such a hurry, I think I would have taken more notice of the exact location. I know that I remembered to turn the lights off and lock the doors.

Classification

Can the parts or the whole be grouped into categories? Can you note common characteristics or features? This thinking task requires that the writer see the topic from various points of view. Once the topic is grouped into categories, can you compare and contrast the categories? Can you point out the similarities and differences? The writer tells, shows, makes connections, and indicates how the parts relate to each other and to the whole. Classification requires knowing the features and characteristics of the things under discussion.

> The grey two-door 1982 Chrysler Cordoba has features that distinguish it from other cars. It's a big North American car with a large wheel base: it easily fills a single parking space. The red Honda Civic, on the other hand, is a peppy little two-door hatchback sports car, hot-off-the-lot, and the beat-up dark blue Ford Tempo is a four-door sedan. The Honda occupies only half the parking space of the Cordoba, and the Tempo about two-thirds.

Writing Prompt

Asking questions takes the writer-thinker deeply and fully into the topic. How do you know what questions to ask? You do this by varying your point of view.

1) Write a list of questions about the practice of using chemical sprays to control weeds. Begin with the question: Why do we use chemical sprays to control weeds? Make a long list. Twenty-five questions should be about right.
2) Write several paragraphs defending the practice. Probe the questions. Think about the need to spray grain crops, market gardens, private lawns, and roadsides. Make claims for the values of spraying and back them up with evidence. Include qualifications (instances when spraying might be harmful), but override the qualifications with your defence.
3) Next, take the opposing view. Write several more paragraphs, this time making the qualifications mentioned in your first series of paragraphs your main argument. Argue persuasively for the banning of chemical sprays. The main arguments of your first series of paragraphs will become the qualifications mentioned in the second set of paragraphs.

1) **In a paragraph or two, describe your favourite place to go for a walk. Your audience is a friend, and you want this friend to accompany you on your walk.**

2) **In a paragraph or two, narrate the events of the past week to your friend as you go on this imaginary walk.**

3) **In a paragraph or two, classify all the ways walking will benefit one's health.**

4) **In a paragraph or two, evaluate the importance of regular exercise.**

Evaluation

How does the topic measure up against a standard? Evaluation is the most complex thinking task because it involves knowing, telling, showing, inferring, reasoning, and drawing conclusions. You may explain an ideal situation or solution and show how the existing conditions compare with the ideal. What happened? Why did it happen? What does this mean? Why is it important? What are the results? Where do we go from here?

One would expect that progress in technology would make life easier. However, losing one's car in a parking lot is just one example of the failure of progress to meet our expectations. Heavily reliant on the car as a means of transport to and from the supermarket for the weekly supply of groceries, we are confounded by the way shopping mall planners have sought to establish order out of chaos. Population density and the norm of the two-car family have ruled out random parking by the roadside. The other extreme, the one we find ourselves in, is the one where parking is a multi-million dollar industry entailing paving, curbs, ramps, lighting, signals, signage, alarms, computerized coin machines, the friendly attendant in the kiosk, and finally, the sign that exhorts you to have a nice day and to be sure to return next week so you can repeat the shopping ritual again. Yes, a driver needs to know the rules of the road, but technology has also made it necessary for her to have the skills of a cartographer to locate her car in the parking lot.

Paragraphs are developed using one or several of these thinking patterns. The writer either consciously decides or subconsciously forms the pattern of development that is most effective. He or she makes a choice based on which pattern suits best the purpose dictated by subject and audience. Usually there is no single right pattern, but there is nearly always one that is clearly effective.

Critical Thinking

There is a progression in patterns of thought, from showing, telling, pointing out differences and similarities, to evaluating. Once we have identified a subject, we look at it more closely. We become more critical, asking questions and making comparisons. We begin to assert our point of view and to see our point of view in relation to other points of view. Associations are made, and we compare what we are learning with things already known. Gradually, the thought patterns become more and more complex, and thus more interesting. The thoughts that make up our paragraphs become more creative, more accurate, and more developed.

The life and work of a scholar brings individuals into contact with vast amounts of knowledge. As we study, we are able to see things in abstract and in concrete terms. Our skills in analysis increase as we are able to break a topic into parts so that we can examine them in isolation from the whole, and, as we bring the parts together again, new connections are made, new ideas revealed. The greater the depth of knowledge and the wider and more diversified the learning experience, the greater the possibility for new insights.

New discoveries transform "showing and telling" into complex patterns of thought and meaning. This does not imply that all thinking tasks must be taken to the level of evaluation to be "good." Since the topic and the writer's purpose shape the thinking process, frequently the most complex thoughts can be expressed in simple, direct language. Description of the topic suffices. However, in order to achieve <u>accurate</u> description and <u>accurate</u>, simple, direct language, we need to have probed deeply into a subject. The paintings of Picasso illustrate this point well: they help us to see that abstraction is the result of precise selectivity and clarity of vision. Simple and direct can be complex. For the student writer who works at adopting more complex patterns of thought and more critical approaches to meaning, the rewards are great. As one would expect, the writer becomes more confident as he or she gains experience in developing ways to express complex ideas and make meaning clear.

Writing Prompt

1) Think of a recent learning experience. If you can think of several, list them and select one to write about. Create several paragraphs about this learning experience using different patterns of development singly or in combination.

2) Study the paragraphs you have written and try to identify the essential points you have made. Write one more paragraph that expresses the essence of your first set of paragraphs. Aim at precision in diction and meaning; be clear, correct, and creative.

¶ ¶ ¶

Chapter Three discusses the use of punctuation in creating variety and emphasis. In that chapter, we focused on the art of punctuation, showing you how to work with or even violate punctuation conventions to create a particular meaning or effect. In your own prose, you will use punctuation for variety and emphasis occasionally.

For the most part, however, you will want to create a clear style in your academic prose, a way of writing that does not draw attention to itself. That style, in terms of punctuation, is marked by the attempt to follow conventions consistently, inserting commas and dashes and semicolons where the reader expects them and leaving them out of places where they call attention to themselves. The focus of this chapter, therefore, is on the conventions: letting you know where punctuation marks belong. You will find that once you have learned the conventions (and there aren't very many), it will be much easier to make decisions not only about where particular punctuation marks should be placed but also about when conventions can be violated.

Commas

Commas are perhaps the most complex of all punctuation marks, primarily because they are used in a number of different ways for a number of different purposes. For this reason, we often make errors when using commas, applying the wrong principle at the wrong time. For example, many of us have been taught to put commas "where we pause" in reading a sentence, which is true frequently enough to be slightly useful but not frequently enough to keep us from making errors. People often pause when speaking, but comma conventions cover only a narrow range of these pauses.

To learn how to use commas, it is probably most helpful to think of commas as punctuation marks used either to separate items (words, phrases, clauses) within a sentence or to set off items (words, phrases, clauses) from the rest of a sentence. Under these two categories, there are still variations, but once you understand that commas are used to set off and separate, it becomes much easier to see where commas belong in a sentence and where they do not.

COMMAS THAT SEPARATE

Commas separate various things: items in a series, independent clauses, co-ordinate adjectives. For each of these separations, there are certain conventions to be followed.

Commas Separating Items in a Series

Put more simply, we are talking about lists (of three or more items). The following examples show where commas are placed in a list.

Learning Prompt

To test your innate punctuation sense, try the following exercise. Tape a five-minute political speech from television or radio. Then transcribe it, placing commas, periods, semicolons, colons, quotation marks, and dashes where you think they belong. What do you discover? Review your transcript again when you have finished this chapter. Where is your sense of punctuation accurate? Where does your innate sense vary from what conventions dictate?

Between words:

Rowboats, canoes, kayaks, and other motorless watercraft are welcome.

Three canoeing books are the ones by Mason, Morse, and Hodgins and Hobbs.

Between phrases:

White-water canoeing in Northern Ontario, taking a sailing course at RCYC, and swimming in the Muskokas: so the summer passes for the youth of the Canadian elite.

Graffiti was everywhere: on the walls, on the ceilings, on the desks, and in the halls.

Between clauses:

What I feel can have little impact, what I say can make a difference, but what I write can change the world.

The new prime minister faces three challenges: the split between Quebec and English Canada must be healed, the inflation rate must be reduced, and the tax burden must be shifted to the wealthy.

Three mistakes are made frequently when separating items in lists. First of all, note that we have placed a comma in all three sentences after the next-to-last item in the list (and before the conjunction in the list, for example, before *and* or *but*). Often, writers omit this last comma, and that can be a mistake. In some sentences, the comma isn't crucial to meaning, but see how important it becomes in the sentence about canoeing books: without the commas dividing the authors listed, the reader would not be sure that the third book was co-written by Hodgins and Hobbs. You can always be certain that your meaning will be more clear if you follow the convention of placing the comma after the next-to-last item in the list.

Secondly, writers often mistakenly place a comma between **two** items.

Incorrect: Strawberries, and cherries are necessary ingredients in summer wine.

Incorrect: There are strawberries in the basket, and cherries in the orchard.

A list is defined as three or more items, so no commas are necessary when only two items are listed.

Corrected: Strawberries and cherries are necessary ingredients in summer wine.

Corrected: There are strawberries in the basket and cherries in the orchard.

Finally, writers sometimes incorrectly place a comma before the list begins, interrupting the natural flow of the sentence.

Incorrect: The utensils we will need are, a paring knife, a large bowl, and a wooden spoon.

Remember, the commas separate only the items in the list; they do not separate the list from the rest of the sentence.

Corrected: The utensils we will need are a paring knife, a large bowl, and a wooden spoon.

Commas Separating Independent Clauses

You may remember from Chapter One that compound sentences consist of two or more independent clauses (clauses that could be sentences on their own). These clauses are often joined by a coordinating conjunction (*and, or, nor, so, but, for, yet*). The convention for this type of compound sentence is to place a comma before the coordinating conjunction:

Canadians could choose to support the CBC, or they could ask that it be abolished.

Deregulation of airlines has created safety problems in the United States, so other countries are considering it cautiously.

Crown corporations are often criticized by the general public, and this negative response contributes to a poor image.

If the two clauses are really short—say, less than five words each—you can probably omit the commas:

The CBC is informative but it's expensive.

Executives fly frequently so they demand convenience.

Bakers sell bread and grocers sell produce.

The mistake usually made by people who have trouble with commas is to put the comma after the conjunction:

Incorrect: We love Peter Gzowski but, we abhor Cross-Country Checkup.

Corrected: We love Peter Gzowski, but we abhor Cross-Country Checkup.

Incorrect: Dead air was common in early radio and, listeners expected it.

Corrected: Dead air was common in early radio, and listeners expected it.

Commas Separating Coordinate Adjectives

Coordinate adjectives are equal adjectives: each describes the same noun independent of the other. You can move them around, let them trade places, and the sentence will still make sense. Here's what we mean:

Alice Munro has a *gracious, gentle* style.
She uses *precise, penetrating* adjectives.
Her characters are *curious, intelligent* people.

These sentences could also be expressed in the following way without any change in meaning:

Alice Munro has a *gentle, gracious* style.
She uses *penetrating, precise* adjectives.
Her characters are *intelligent, curious* people.

Since each pair of sentences has the same meaning despite the adjectives being rearranged, the adjectives are considered coordinate, and commas are used to separate the two adjectives. However, not all adjectives are coordinate:

Trudy is a *typical young* woman.
She rents a *large bachelor* apartment.
It is furnished with *many potted* plants.

Shifting the adjectives in this case does not produce the same meaning:

Trudy is a *young typical* woman.
She rents a *bachelor large* apartment.
It is furnished with *potted many* plants.

In these sentences, the adjectives cannot be moved without loss of meaning. The adjectives, therefore, are not coordinate, so no commas are required.

Many coordinate adjective decisions are judgment calls. Since our language is evolving toward less punctuation, leave the comma out if you are doubtful about whether it is necessary.

Writing Prompt

Think about your favourite article of clothing or possession. Make up sentences about that possession that illustrate the comma conventions for separating items.

Using Commas to Separate

Sample Paragraph:

1. This pervasive, continuous-growth mentality in food production ultimately cannot succeed on our, finite earth. **2.** Our current system of agricultural subsidy is only prolonging the inevitable, imminent need to change our attitude about agriculture. **3.** The subsidies supplied to farmers by the government in order that the farmer can produce cheap, raw materials are enormous, and the effects of this system of agriculture on the environment (depletion of aquifers, erosion of soil, pollution of water, and food, and depletion of large amounts of non-renewable resources) are undeniably detrimental. **4.** Canada must begin to look for an alternative, agricultural system.

Exercise One:

The aboriginal language also reflects an elaborate, fundamental and complex kinship system. This system expresses not only numerous, kinship terms but a complex system of language sharing across the country. It was created in part as a result of laws requiring interclan, and interlanguage marriage. Languages of the Australian aboriginals also reflect a number of other characteristics: their unique understanding of land ownership and economics, and their values and beliefs as established by their laws. They are a people who see things in a very different way from us, and who have subsequently developed appropriate words to express this view.

Exercise Two:

Caribou have adapted to many limiting factors determined by the geography and biology of their range, and the seasonal variability of weather affecting the health of the herd. The distance between the calving grounds and the winter range, the energy exerted in migration and in the search for food if the snow is deep in late spring, the extent of insect harassment, and of energy expended in seeking refuge from bugs, are among the many, unpredictable variables which can significantly influence the herd's ability to cope with various additional stresses.

Using Commas to Separate: Sample Paragraph Discussion

This sample paragraph models the work of someone who has gone "comma happy": there are many more commas in the paragraph than are needed. The trick in comma conventions is being able to distinguish where convention dictates a comma from where it does not. Begin your work, therefore, by testing the comma placement in the passage against your knowledge of conventions.

Commas Separating Items in a Series

Let's begin this paragraph by looking for lists. Remember that a list is defined as three or more items, whether those items are words, phrases, or clauses. Remember also that two items are not a list.

The only list, then, is in Sentence Three: *depletion of aquifers, erosion of soil, pollution of water, and food, and depletion of large amounts of non-renewable resources.* The commas should be placed between the items in the list, and, if you read carefully, you will see an unnecessary comma. *Pollution of water and food* is one item, not two, so there should be no comma after *water.* The revised list reads as follows:

> depletion of aquifers, erosion of soil, pollution of water and food, and depletion of large amounts of non-renewable resources.

Commas Separating Independent Clauses

Begin by looking for coordinating conjunctions (*and, or, nor, for, but, so, yet*). The passage contains only three *ands*, the last two of which are used in the list in Sentence Three as conjunctions joining words, not clauses. The first *and*, however (*and the effects of this system . . .*), does join two independent clauses: (1) *The subsidies supplied to farmers by the government in order that the farmers can produce cheap, raw materials are enormous,* and (2) *The effects of this system on the environment . . . are undeniably detrimental.* Since *and* joins the two clauses, there should be a comma before it.

Commas Separating Coordinate Adjectives

Adjectives modify nouns, so begin by looking for two words placed before a person, place, or thing. You then need to decide if the words are coordinate adjectives, using the litmus test described on the previous page. If they can be turned around, they are coordinate, and therefore require commas; if they can't, they aren't and don't.

In Sentence One, the first set of adjectives is *pervasive, continuous-growth*: together they modify *mentality.* Can they be turned around? *Continuous-growth pervasive mentality* makes no sense, so the comma in place is unnecessary. Next we have *our, finite earth.* Since *finite our earth* does not convey the same meaning, again the comma is unnecessary.

In Sentence Two, there is no comma between *our* and *current* in the phrase *our current system.* Since *current our system* makes no sense, no comma would be required, so the punctuation is correct as is. Sentence Two also contains the next adjective set, *inevitable, imminent need.* This time, the adjectives are reversible: we can say *imminent, inevitable need* and arrive at the same meaning. The comma between the two adjectives is, therefore, necessary.

How about *cheap, raw materials* in Sentence Three? *Cheap* in this case modifies the words *raw materials*: the farmers do not produce any other kind of cheap material. The adjectives are not coordinate, so no comma is necessary.

Finally, consider *alternative, agricultural system* in Sentence Four. An *agricultural alternative system* conveys a different meaning, suggesting the possibility of a system that is not agricultural, so again the comma must be eliminated.

Here is the revised paragraph:

> This pervasive continuous-growth mentality in food production ultimately cannot succeed on our finite earth. Our current system of agricultural subsidy is only prolonging the inevitable, imminent need to change our attitude about agriculture. The subsidies supplied to farmers by the government in order that the farmer can produce cheap raw materials are enormous, and the effects of this system of agriculture on the environment (depletion of aquifers, erosion of soil, pollution of water and food, and depletion of large amounts of non-renewable resources) are undeniably detrimental. Canada must begin to look for an alternative agricultural system.

The revised passage shows that only a few commas are dictated by convention. Now the paragraph reads smoothly, and the reader is not distracted by commas that slow comprehension.

Work through the two exercise paragraphs, examining each comma. If the comma is correctly placed, explain why. If the comma is incorrectly placed, explain which convention it violates. Also add any commas still needed, and explain the convention you are following.

COMMAS THAT SET OFF

To understand commas that set off, it is useful to think about what might be called the usual or natural order of a simple sentence (a sentence consisting of one independent clause). A simple sentence in usual order begins with a subject followed by a verb. An object or complement (and possibly an indirect object) may follow the verb:[1]

Recipes and advice in cookbooks   can reveal   a great deal of social history.
     subject   *verb*   *object*

When a simple sentence is in its natural order, nothing is set off, so commas that set off will be unnecessary and incorrect. For this reason, commas are almost never placed between subject and verb or between verb and object:

Incorrect: The simple staples and hot spices of traditional Cajun food, establish its connections to French and Caribbean cuisine.

Corrected: The simple staples and hot spices of traditional Cajun food establish its connections to French and Caribbean cuisine.

Incorrect: The combination of beans and rice in many Cajun dishes intrigues, the less adventurous.

Corrected: The combination of beans and rice in many Cajun dishes intrigues the less adventurous.

This convention is useful to remember if you are one of those people who place commas "where you pause." Often writers pause for thought between subject and verb or between verb and object, but a comma is used to indicate a pause in syntax, not in thought.

However, many sentences do have disruptions in this natural order. When order is disrupted, commas are used to help the reader recognize the disruption. Commas can set off elements that come before the subject, elements that interrupt the subject and the verb or the verb and object, or elements that are added to the end of the sentence.

Commas Setting Off Introductory Elements

It is often possible to "hear" the pause between an introductory element and the complete subject. Read the following examples aloud:

, , ,

However, cookbooks predating the 19th century are scarce. (single word preceding subject)

By the turn of the century, the more advanced cookbooks showed evidence of the interest in domestic science. (prepositional phrases preceding subject)

---

[1] For more information about the patterns of simple sentences, see Chapter One.

When an introductory element is very short (particularly when it is an adverb or short prepositional phrase), a comma placed after the element can slow the reader down unduly. Often, the writer may omit this comma to keep the pace of the reading brisk:

In 1929 the stock market crashed.

Usually funds are secure in banks.

Here, your judgment is required. If the particular passage already has several commas, you might omit a few in cases like the ones above. If your sentences are fairly long and contain few commas, you may wish to retain the commas after short introductory elements.

Because refrigerated freight cars made the transportation of fruits and vegetables possible, Canadian cuisine became more diverse. (subordinate clause preceding subject)

Do you hear the pauses? They are needed to make meaning in the sentences; without them, the last words in the introductory element would seem attached to the subject.

As these examples indicate, various sorts of introductory elements might precede a subject: single words, prepositional phrases, subordinate clauses, gerunds. Fortunately, it is not important to identify precisely what precedes the subject, only the point at which the introductory element ends and the complete subject begins. Usually, this is not difficult. When you use an introductory element, you are placing something before the subject. After the introductory element, therefore, you still have an independent clause, a complete sentence:

Cookbooks predating the 19th century are scarce.

The more advanced cookbooks showed evidence of the interest in domestic science.

Canadian cuisine became more diverse.

Look for introductory words, phrases, and clauses in your sentences. Place a comma before the beginning of the independent clause, and you will have applied this comma convention correctly.

Commas Setting Off Mid-Sentence Interrupters

Often a writer may wish to include information in a sentence that is extraneous to the primary meaning of the sentence (in that the sentence would still have the same basic meaning without the information). When this syntactical situation arises, commas are used to enclose the information.

The extra information might be a directive to the reader—a transitional word or expression—or a phrase or clause that acts as a conversational aside—an appositive or some other non-essential phrase or clause. For example, consider this sentence:

Figure skating, a sport usually dominated by females, was not always deemed an appropriate occupation for women.

If we omit the information enclosed in commas, the sentence still carries the same basic meaning:

Figure skating was not always deemed an appropriate occupation for women.

Because this extra information can be omitted without substantial loss of meaning, it is enclosed in commas.

A broad range of sentence elements can be set off by commas, as the following examples indicate:

The early Canadian attitude toward ice skating, nevertheless, upheld the traditional beliefs about women in this era. (single word set off)

Dr. Kellogg, a prominent figure in the controversy over women participating in sports, influenced many adolescents. (appositive set off)

These physicians, who were mainly men, were allowed to provide the definition of a healthy woman. (non-essential or non-restrictive clause set off)

The key element to note here is that, when an interruption occurs in the middle of a sentence, **two commas** are employed, one to signal the beginning of the interruption, the other to indicate its close. The most common mistake made in placing commas around mid-sentence interruptions is to omit the second comma:

Incorrect: The sport of cycling, albeit at a primitive stage was taken up by many women.

Corrected: The sport of cycling, albeit at a primitive stage, was taken up by many women.

Think of brackets or parentheses; you would never use an opening bracket without eventually using a closing one.

RESTRICTIVE AND NON-RESTRICTIVE MODIFIERS

As we have noted, interrupting elements that need commas are characterized by a certain dispensability. They add extra information in the sentence, but that information is not integral to the sentence. If they were eliminated, the sentence would not have as much meaning, but it would have the same essence.

Johnny Wayne, whom I liked immensely, died in 1990.

Johnny Wayne died in 1990.

We call these dispensable elements non-restrictive or non-essential modifiers. There are, however, strange animals called restrictive or essential modifiers that do help to define part of a sentence. When restrictive or essential elements are employed, commas are not used (a tricky distinction to make but an important one in terms of meaning). Consider this sentence:

Women who did choose to wear bloomers were accused of wanting to be like men.

The Essential *That*

Here is a useful tip when you are trying to decide if a clause is restrictive or non-restrictive, essential or non-essential to the sentence: a clause beginning with *that* is <u>always</u> restrictive because *that* is always used to introduce a restrictive or essential modifier. For this reason, it is unusual to have a comma before a clause beginning with *that*.

Restrictive or Essential Appositives

You should be aware that appositives, as well as phrases and clauses, can be restrictive. For example, think about this sentence:

The famous photographer Diane Arbus killed herself.

Here, *Diane Arbus* identifies the famous photographer. Without her name, the sentence would refer to some unnamed photographer and would not have the same meaning: hence, no commas. However, consider the following:

Sylvia Plath, the famous poet, also committed suicide.

This appositive is non-restrictive, not essential, because the phrase merely adds additional information; without it, we would still know that Sylvia Plath killed herself. Commas are therefore necessary.

Writing Prompt

Learning to distinguish between essential and non-essential modifiers is difficult. To obtain some practice, compose three sentences which contain a clause that could be either restrictive or non-restrictive. For each sentence, explain the difference in meaning obtained when the clause is enclosed in commas.

Here, you lose the essence of the sentence if you omit *who did choose to wear bloomers*.

Women were accused of wanting to be like men.

Not all women were accused of wanting to be like men, only the women wearing bloomers. (See how the clause <u>restricts</u> the number of women accused of wanting to be like men?) Because the clause *who did choose to wear bloomers* does restrict the subject *women*, commas are not permitted. With commas, the sentence would have a different meaning:

Women, who did choose to wear bloomers, were accused of wanting to be like men.

Here, the author would be saying that all women were accused of wanting to be like men, and that, incidentally, women chose to wear bloomers.

Using commas to distinguish between restrictive and non-restrictive modifiers makes sense if we think of commas in terms of indicating pauses in speech. When we add additional information, we often pause before or after the information to indicate that the information is an aside.

My sister, who likes bowling, is coming to Peterborough.

We don't pause in the same way when we are adding vital information that identifies the subject:

My sister from Toronto likes bowling; the sister who is from Ottawa plays golf.

The pairs of commas that are used to indicate mid-sentence interruptions, therefore, do help to indicate speech patterns, and they also contribute to meaning, allowing the reader (as opposed to the listener) to recognize that the information enclosed in the commas is a non-essential addition to the sentence.

Commas Setting Off Concluding Elements

The same rules apply to concluding elements as govern mid-sentence interrupters. If the concluding element is non-essential, a comma at the close of the independent clause is necessary. If the concluding element is essential, no comma is required.

Correct: Fancy skating eventually emerged as an appropriate sport for women, allowing them to maintain a feminine image.

In this sentence, although the participial phrase *allowing them to maintain a feminine image* describes what the emergence of fancy skating as a prominent sport did, it does not restrict meaning. In the following sentence, however, meaning is restricted by the subordinate clause:

Correct: Fancy skating eventually emerged as an appropriate sport for women because it allowed them to maintain a feminine image.

In this sentence, the writer is saying that fancy skating became an appropriate sport for women only because of a certain condition; otherwise, it might have remained a sport for men. The meaning of the first clause is thus restricted by the second clause. To determine if a subordinate clause is restrictive, try reading the independent clause alone. If all essential meaning is conveyed in the independent clause, the subordinate clause is not restrictive, and a comma is required.

Also, when trying to set off concluding elements, be careful not to set off modifiers that are clearly a part of the independent clause, modifying the verb or the object, rather than the whole sentence. Consider the following:

Incorrect: This feminine image was dominant, in Canada, in the late nineteenth century.

Corrected: This feminine image was dominant in Canada in the late nineteenth century.

Two prepositional phrases (*in Canada* and *in the late nineteenth century*) end this sentence. However, both phrases are attached to the word *dominant*. Dominant when? In the nineteenth century. Dominant where? In Canada. Here, then, there is no need for a comma because the phrases are not modifying the sentence in its entirety. Indeed, the two phrases actually <u>restrict</u> what *dominant* means. Conversely, in the following example, the conjunctive adverb modifies the whole sentence, so a comma is required:

Correct: This feminine image was dominant in Canada, nevertheless.

However

Punctuating around *however* is complicated. Usually, *however* is a non-restrictive modifier interrupting a sentence.

I like cabbage rolls. However, I hate perogies. (introductory)

Enchiladas, however, are delicious. (mid-sentence)

Quiche Lorraine is my favourite, however. (concluding)

At other times, *however* is simply an adverb meaning *regardless of how* and needs no comma.

However expensive they are, sun-dried tomatoes are worth every penny.

Finally, *however* sometimes appears between two clauses joined by a semicolon, acting as an introductory element for the second clause. In this case, *however* is preceded by a semicolon that indicates the end of the first clause and is followed by a comma that indicates the beginning of a second complete subject.

Gourmet pizza is a gastronomical delicacy; however, a strong argument can be made in favour of pepperoni and double cheese.

Remember when you use *however* in this way that *however* is not a conjunction like *but* or *and*: it cannot join two independent clauses. The semicolon performs this function and is essential to grammatical correctness in this construction.

Using Commas to Set Off

Sample Paragraph:

1. Although still unable to make any headway in the establishment of aboriginal rights to unceded title, the Lubicon continued to endure court battles and government negotiations. **2.** In 1984 with growing international concern over the plight of the Lubicon people of Canada David Crombie was appointed as Minister to the Department of Indian and Northern Affairs. **3.** Crombie in turn appointed The Honourable Davie Fulton as Special Lubicon Negotiator to compile a report outlining areas of conflict, positions taken by each party, and suggestions for the resolution of differences. **4.** Fulton studied the situation for a year and came up with a discussion paper confirming that oil and gas development in the area had disastrous consequences for the people of Lubicon Lake. **5.** Fulton's report also supported many of the band's grievances, discussing them eloquently.

Exercise One:

The dilemma brought into focus by the conflicting values of development versus conservation and preservation raises serious questions. Not only must we ask what our society is doing to reduce our dependency on non-renewable energy sources; more significantly, we wonder what the point is of Environmental Impact Assessments when they are repeatedly overridden by political and economic "imperatives." While pressures for resource development in the North escalate annually, our valuation of wilderness ecosystems and their biological components seems to remain somewhat fixed. Conservation interests as a result appear to have become devalued against the inflation of economic necessities. In order to protect significant unique biological environments effectively it is necessary that we continually assess, as legitimate values, wilderness interests, and act to increase the effectiveness of our voice in a political/economic environment.

Exercise Two:

Although native women in the Canadian fur trade, during the eighteenth century were sometimes exploited and dominated by European traders, there are many reasons to suggest that the tremendous involvement of these women in the trade benefited North Americans, for both social and economic reasons. Despite the fact that some women were victimized, marriage between the native women and the traders was common across the country, allowing peaceful bonds to develop between these different societies. As well, during the fur traders' journeys, women assisted by supplying knowledge of the land and useful methods of trade. Some women even participated in the fur trade directly. Another area where women continued to be important, was in providing essential domestic skills that helped the fur traders and their families, to have a more enjoyable life. Finally, native women were often visible at trading posts, occupying numerous economic positions which were required for the successful system of trade.

Using Commas to Set Off: Sample Paragraph Discussion

You can conduct a search for interrupting phrases in an orderly fashion by focusing on the "natural order" of the independent clause. As we have noted, the natural order follows a subject-verb-object pattern. To check for correct placement of commas that interrupt, you must begin by looking for this pattern (and the variations on it) in the passage being examined.

Commas Setting Off Introductory Elements

The sample paragraph is typical of academic prose in that not all the sentences it contains begin with the subject of the independent clause. The last three sentences do: in Sentence Three, *Crombie* is appointing; in Sentence Four, *Fulton* is studying; and in Sentence Five, *Fulton's report* is supporting.

However, Sentences One and Two have introductory elements. Remember, the comma needs to come immediately before the commencement of the complete subject. In Sentence One, the complete subject is *the Lubicon*; they are continuing to endure. The comma placed after *title* is therefore correct: the introductory element is *Although still unable to make any headway in the establishment of aboriginal rights to unceded title.*

In Sentence Two, *David Crombie* is the complete subject; he is appointed. A comma should follow *Canada*, since the introductory element is *In 1984 with growing international concern over the plight of the Lubicon people of Canada.*

Commas Setting Off Mid-Sentence Interruptions

Astute comma users will detect a problem with Sentence Two: shouldn't there be a comma after *1984?* In fact, there should. Sentence Two could read: *In 1984, David Crombie was appointed as Minister to the Department of Indian and Northern Affairs.* This fact establishes that the phrase *with growing international concern over the plight of the Lubicon people of Canada* is a mid-sentence interrupter, an unusual one placed between an introductory element and a complete subject. The phrase, therefore, needs commas around it.

Sentence Three also contains a mid-sentence interrupter. Here, the interruption comes between subject and verb: Crombie *in turn* appointed. Commas are needed around *in turn*.

Commas Setting Off Concluding Elements

In Sentence Four, *confirming that oil and gas development in the area had disastrous consequences for the people of Lubicon Lake* looks like it might be a concluding element. However, it is only the *discussion paper*, not the entire sentence, that does the *confirming*, so the clause modifies only part of the sentence and does not need a comma.

Only Sentence Five in the sample passage has a concluding element that is non-restrictive. *Discussing them eloquently*, a participial phrase modifying the sentence, needs a comma preceding it because it adds non-restrictive or non-essential information.

The revised paragraph reads more clearly:

Although still unable to make any headway in the establishment of aboriginal rights to unceded title, the Lubicon continued to endure court battles and government negotiations. In 1984, with growing international concern over the plight of the Lubicon people of Canada, David Crombie was appointed as Minister to the Department of Indian and Northern Affairs. Crombie, in turn, appointed The Honourable Davie Fulton as Special Lubicon Negotiator to compile a report outlining areas of conflict, positions taken by each party, and suggestions for the resolution of differences. Fulton studied the situation for a year and came up with a discussion paper confirming that oil and gas development in the area had disastrous consequences for the people of Lubicon Lake. Fulton's report also supported many of the band's grievances, discussing them eloquently.

Work through the two exercise paragraphs. When you feel a comma is correctly placed, give an explanation for its correctness. When you feel a comma is not necessary, explain why not. When you feel a comma needs to be added, defend your addition.

Notes

My writing strengths:

Things I need to remember:

Things I need to check:

General Use of Commas

Exercise One:

Beginning in 1942 attempts were made by a federal government employee Malcolm McCrimmon, to decrease the number of registered Indians in Northern Alberta for the purpose of "tightening the budget" and by so doing he effectively limited potential future demands of these Indians. These measures removed ninety band members from the Lubicon membership list. After a court hearing in 1943 and a formal judicial inquiry in 1944 both of which discounted McCrimmon's actions, McCrimmon himself was left to act on these rulings at his own discretion. The result was that only eighteen Lubicon and relatively few Northern Alberta Indians were reinstated.

Exercise Two:

The Lubicon settlement at Little Buffalo is located, 240 miles north of Edmonton, and although this land is south of the 60th parallel, the development pressures and development impacts upon it are very similar to those felt in the North. The people are quite isolated, resources are extracted for external markets with no local input, resource extraction is based on non-renewable resources, and the social, land claim settlement may be delayed for an unreasonably long time partially because of the extensive bureaucracy inherent in tri-party negotiations, that have existed since the transfer of crown lands from the federal to the provincial government in 1930.

Exercise Three:

Feelings of vulnerability and dependency in the developed countries are being realized, as the genetic resources of the world dwindle. Ironically, developed countries are beginning to show an interest and appreciation in traditional farming techniques because, they nurture genetic diversity while allowing for a continual evolution of that genetic diversity. The problem of genetic erosion is being magnified by the movement from these traditional ecosystems to the adoption of modern cropping techniques and commercial agricultural practices including most importantly the use of hybrid seeds.

Commas for Clarity

What you have learned about commas thus far are the conventions, all of which are based on one important principle: the comma is used, in general, to avoid confusion. Commas separate or set off elements of sentences from each other so that the reader cannot inadvertently connect two groups of words that were not intended to be connected. Commas make meaning for the reader precisely because they indicate which words are to be grouped together.

Once you understand this principle, you can use the comma effectively, not only where the conventions dictate but in another way: where your own prose demands a comma for clarity. A comma may be entirely necessary in an unconventional location because two items need to be separated so the reader, who might have a tendency to link the two items, does not do so:

> Correct: Some doctors expected patients to be uninformed, and treated them
> as ignorant.

Were this comma not in place, the reader might link *uninformed and treated*: *Doctors expected patients to be uninformed and treated*. Obviously, this is not the meaning the writer intended.

Misusing Commas: Comma Splices

Although commas can be used both to separate and to set off items, there is one grammatical function they cannot be used for: joining sentences. A very common comma error is to place a comma between two complete sentences (the comma splice):

> Incorrect: Johnson also describes the main diseases which are affecting society today, here he explains how diseases have moved away from infectious diseases to chronic and degenerative diseases.

Commas cannot be used to join independent clauses. Only colons, semicolons, conjunctions, and the three end punctuation marks can perform that task. To correct the error, you can substitute an appropriate punctuation mark for the comma or combine the two sentences to make one (either by adding a conjunction or by reworking the sentence):

> Corrected: Johnson also describes the main diseases which are affecting society today. Here he explains how diseases have moved away from infectious diseases to chronic and degenerative diseases.

> Corrected: Johnson also describes the main diseases which are affecting society today by explaining how diseases have moved away from infectious diseases to chronic and degenerative diseases.

For more information about comma splices, see Chapter Two.

On the adjacent page are three more comma exercises, ones encompassing the entire range of comma possibilities. Use your good judgment to decide which commas are correctly placed, which are incorrectly placed, and what additional commas are needed.

Learning Prompt

Now that you are familiar with the conventions governing comma use, review one of your old essays. When do you use commas correctly? What comma errors do you make?

Semicolons, Colons, and Dashes

Most students don't use these marks incorrectly because they don't use them at all. Commas and periods, the meat and potatoes of punctuation, are hard to do without, but other punctuation marks are often viewed as more foreign, more exotic, by many writers, and we seem frightened by them, lest they add a bit too much spice to our prose.

But ordering squid or sushi at a restaurant can suggest sophistication, and so can using semicolons and colons. These devices permit you to express slightly more subtle relationships between ideas, and they appeal to your reader because they add variety to your prose. They have an additional advantage: the conventions governing their use are relatively straightforward. If you can learn when the use of semicolons, colons, and dashes is deemed appropriate and can avoid using them otherwise, you will have substantially increased the flexibility with which you can express relations between ideas.

SEMICOLONS

Conventionally, semicolons can be used for only two purposes: to join independent clauses and to separate items in a series when the items are already punctuated by commas or are particularly long.

Semicolons to Join Independent Clauses

Semicolons are best thought of as similar to periods and conjunctions. Like them, semicolons have the ability to join independent clauses, clauses which could stand on their own as sentences. The writer need only determine when a semicolon is a more appropriate choice than a period or a conjunction for joining the two clauses to use the semicolon with skill.

The standard textbook distinction in this case, that a semicolon is used when the two clauses are very closely related in meaning, is insufficient. How closely related is very closely related? Try to think of it in this way. If you place a period between two sentences, you are saying to the reader, "These ideas are completely separate. I choose to put one sentence immediately after the other, so they do have some connection, but there is a distinct gap between them."

We went to New York. We visited Cleveland.

Conjunctions can connect two independent clauses, but using a conjunction eliminates the pause between the two ideas. The two ideas are made into one, in fact, using the conjunction to show how they connect:

New York is cosmopolitan, but Cleveland is industrial.

A semicolon allows the reader to do more work. The nature of the connection is not made evident by the semicolon, but there is a connection implied:

New York swings; Cleveland rocks.

Here, the connection is a comparison. The writer is letting the reader know subtly the difference between the two cities. Note the use of parallel structure, another common feature of sentences joined by semicolons. Parallelism helps to make the close connection between the two sentences more explicit.

Semicolons are frequently used incorrectly to join an independent clause and a subordinate clause:

Incorrect: New York swings; whereas Cleveland rocks.[2]

Corrected: New York swings whereas Cleveland rocks.

The subordinating conjunction already does the work of joining the two ideas, and, in terms of meaning, makes a clear connection between the two sentences. A semicolon, therefore, is superfluous. (Even a comma would be unnecessary here since a subordinating conjunction is used.)

Semicolons to Separate Items in a Series

This use of the semicolon deals with a particular semantic problem, a lack of clarity caused either by comma confusion or lengthy items. Consider the following sentence:

Poor: Tourists avoid New York for several reasons: many people, who are probably accurate in their view, consider it unclean, parts of the city, including a large section of the subway system, are unsafe, and accommodation, at a reasonably comfortable hotel at least, is very expensive.

All the commas here are necessary, but they confuse the reader, making it difficult to separate the items being listed from the interrupting elements. In an instance such as this, the semicolon is used to separate the items:

Better: Tourists avoid New York for several reasons: many people, who are probably accurate in their view, consider it unclean; parts of the city, including a large section of the subway system, are unsafe; and accommodation, at a reasonably comfortable hotel at least, is very expensive.

In this revision, the items of the series immediately become more apparent to the reader. The same would hold true even if no commas were necessary in the list; semicolons hold items apart more clearly than do commas.

COLONS

Colons, like semicolons, have a limited number of uses. In all circumstances, however, they direct the reader's attention to what follows, providing an impetus that compels the reader forward. What can follow a colon is fairly wide-ranging: an individual item or series of items, examples illustrating or explaining the idea contained in the clause preceding the colon, and even complete independent

---

[2] For further comments on the use of the semicolon in this instance, see the section on violating punctuation conventions in Chapter Three.

clauses. Frequently, the material after the colon is an appositive, restating or clarifying the material preceding the colon and therefore giving it greater emphasis. (For this reason, a good litmus test for proper use of the colon is to substitute *namely* for the colon; if the sentence retains the same meaning, the use of a colon is appropriate.) However, because a colon is interpreted by the reader as directing attention forward, the writer can also use it simply as a means of providing emphasis.

Proper form must be followed when a colon is used, and there are places where a colon is considered grammatically inappropriate. The colon indicates a definitive pause. In grammatical terms, this means that usually there is an independent clause (a complete sentence) before the colon, and that what follows the colon does not flow syntactically with what preceded it.[3]

Colons to Introduce Items

This use of the colon is probably the most common in academic writing:

> The emergence of the paperback brought several changes to the publishing industry: sales increased, mass marketing became more important, and royalty regulations had to be altered.

A common mistake is to use a colon to introduce lists when there is no complete stop, no gap in syntax:

> Incorrect: The paperback can be: carried easily, printed cheaply, and thrown away.

> Corrected: The paperback can be carried easily, printed cheaply, and thrown away.

Since *The paperback can be* is not an independent clause, no complete stop is needed, so no colon is permitted. You can see also that the sentence would flow syntactically without the colon, again indicating that the colon is not allowed.

Another common mistake is to use a semicolon instead of a colon to introduce a list:

> Incorrect: Hardbacks have three advantages; durability, attractiveness, and value.

> Corrected: Hardbacks have three advantages: durability, attractiveness, and value.

---

[3] A colon does not need to be preceded by an independent clause if it introduces material set off from the main text, such as a block quotation.

Colons are allowed to introduce such lists, but semicolons are not, because semicolons must separate independent clauses. As you can see, *durability, attractiveness, and value* do not form an independent clause.

Colons to Introduce Examples and Explanations of Ideas

The principle at work here is much the same as the one for introducing items in a series. Again, there must be an independent clause (a complete sentence) before the colon. What follows the colon is an example or an explanation very closely related to the sentence preceding the colon:

> Hardbacks are now very expensive: the average price of a hardback novel is $24.95.

You can see that substituting *namely* for the colon here would work, so we know the punctuation choice is appropriate. It is also possible to recognize that a semicolon might be inappropriate. We are not inviting readers to make a connection, to balance one clause against the other, because the relation between the two ideas is clear: one clarifies the other. The colon thus prepares the reader to know that a clarification will follow.

You should also note, as is evident in the example above, that an independent clause can follow a colon and that no capital letter is required when the material following the colon is an independent clause. However, the explanation or example does not have to be an independent clause:

> Eventually, only one thing occupied my every thought: eating.

> What we wanted was what every child wanted: to play all day, every day.

In both these instances, the clarification is not an independent clause.

As a final note, you should not overuse the colon. Too many colons can be like a bus that stops at every railroad track. The reader becomes irritated at this interruption in rhythm if it occurs too often.

THE DASH

To a certain extent, dashes play the same role both as commas that set off and as parentheses: they set off asides or added information. The three are not interchangeable, however; each mark has its own connotative meaning. Sheridan Baker says that "the dash says aloud what the parenthesis whispers," and calls the dash "a conversational colon."[4] The dash is at once both casual and emphatic: it draws attention to what it encloses forcefully, but casually. Because the dash creates a stream-of-consciousness effect, at times it seems almost too impromptu for a formal essay, especially since the formal essay, of course, is the result of careful thinking, not casual conjecture. Dashes are

---

[4] Sheridan Baker, *The Practical Stylist,* 2nd Can. ed. (New York: Harper & Row, 1986) 230.

also said to be the most emphatic of those punctuation marks indicating interruptions, so, like exclamation marks, they need to be used sparingly. However, you will find that there are occasions when only a dash can achieve the effect you want. What follows is a list of those possible occasions.

Dashes to Indicate a Sudden Shift in Direction

Sometimes, you may have a phrase which contradicts or negates what has gone before, and a dash is a useful way of drawing the reader's attention to the contradiction:

Teachers can win over their students with tactics of affection — or of terror.

Dashes to Emphasize a Phrase

Occasionally, you will have a particularly clever turn of phrase, sometimes even in a thesis statement, upon which you want the reader to focus. Since the dash is interpreted as emphasizing what it encloses, it can bring that phrase to the fore:

There is a certain type of teaching that can bring out the best in a student — the boot camp method of instruction.

Dashes to Introduce a List

Dashes, like colons, may be used to introduce lists. As you might guess, the dash is less formal, so the choice between the dash and the colon will depend on the effect desired:

That professor lectures students on a variety of matters — their stupidity, their indolence, their general sloth.

Dashes to Incorporate End Punctuation

Occasionally, you may want to ask a question or make an exclamation in the middle of a sentence. Dashes permit you to accomplish this engineering feat of punctuation:

Students dread these lectures — who would not? — but they attend every week.

Parentheses can also be used to incorporate end punctuation, but they will de-emphasize the material they enclose.

Writing Prompt

Write a letter to a friend. In the letter, model correct use of the colon, the semicolon, and the dash. Try to use each of these punctuation marks at least twice in the letter. Once you have finished, photocopy the letter. Mail the original to your friend, but keep the photocopy for your own reference.

Common Dash Errors

The first common mistake made with dashes is to use them too often. Used sparingly, dashes are effective and pleasurable to encounter. If used too often, the reader will sense a sloppy writer, someone "dashing off" an essay, rather than contemplating it seriously.

The other common mistakes all involve technicalities. When dashes interrupt in mid-sentence, you need an opening dash and a closing dash:

Incorrect: Kind teachers—and they are common, can build our self-esteem.

In this sentence, the comma after *common* should be replaced with a dash.

Corrected: Kind teachers—and they are common—can build our self-esteem.

Any sentence in which dashes are placed should be complete without the material indicated by the dash(es). Consider the following example:

Incorrect: Fierce teachers—and they are rare—and have a different effect.

It doesn't work, does it? *Fierce teachers and have a different effect* isn't a sentence, so we need to revise:

Corrected: Fierce teachers—and they are rare—have a different effect.

Using Semicolons, Colons, and Dashes

Sample Paragraph:

1. Through such issues, doctors became increasingly aware that women could do physical damage to their bodies during sporting events. **2.** A prominent figure in this area was; Dr. T.S. Clousten. **3.** Dr. Clousten could be termed an early "sports physician": he claimed that if a woman participated in physical exercise and overexerted herself, she would suffer tremendously through: stunted growth, headaches, hysteria, and even insanity. **4.** Nonetheless, Clousten also felt that women needed to be directed toward physical exercise—exercise that would harden their muscles, add fat to their bodies, and soften their skin; such as outdoor play and moderate but vigorous gymnastics. **5.** However, he strongly emphasized that such activities needed to be regulated by a practising physician, as women—still viewed as hopeless and naive idiots—had the tendency to carry their exercises too far and cause damage to themselves.

Exercise One:

Other factors caused parents to put their children in orphanages: rampant disease, a high mortality rate, and year-round poverty. Childhood disease, in particular, was a problem. Statistics in 1867 show that: two out of every five children died within a year of birth. Infant illness was caused primarily by intestinal diseases, largely because babies were not breastfed; rather, they were given unpasteurized or diluted milk. Older children were often victims of smallpox, a fatal disease in this era. When children became ill, parents could not cope—they had no resources to deal with the illness, and so they gave their children to hospitals, hoping they would receive adequate care there.

Exercise Two:

It is also apparent that hierarchies among students are based on dominant middle-class values. Frideres offers an explanation for this in his study of native education in Canada: he recognizes the fact that schools emphasize the need to teach students the ways in which they can gain power and success. Teachers and faculty take on the function of; instilling business creeds and competitive qualities in their students. Schools—thought to be liberators— become the places in which students are taught to behave in such a way that they will obtain the ability to integrate themselves into the dominant middle- class value system (Frideres, 1987:284). It thus becomes vital that students accept and adapt to this system; otherwise, they will find classroom time boring and of little use (Frideres, 1987:284).

Using Semicolons, Colons, and Dashes: Sample Paragraph Discussion

In this exercise, we want to determine if the punctuation being used is correct. We will work through the sample passage, checking the placement of each semicolon, colon, and dash against the conventions we have learned.

Semicolons

The first semicolon occurs in Sentence Two. Always begin by checking to see if there are independent clauses on either side of the semicolon; if not, the placement is incorrect. Here we can see easily that *Dr. T.S. Clousten* is not an independent clause, nor is *A prominent figure in this area was*. What can we use instead? In fact, the sentence requires no internal punctuation at all, because it follows the simple order of subject to verb to complement.

The next semicolon occurs in Sentence Four. Here again, the words following the semicolon do not form an independent clause: *such as outdoor play and moderate but vigorous gymnastics* could not be a sentence on its own. In this instance, the punctuation needed is a closing dash, but we will discuss that in the section on dashes.

Colons

There are two colons in Sentence Three. The placement of the first is technically correct, since we do have an independent clause before the colon: *Dr. Clousten could be termed an early "sports physician."* Nonetheless, the colon is misused here. If we substituted "namely" for the first colon, the sentence would not have the same meaning: *Dr. Clousten could be termed an early "sports physician." Namely, he claimed that if a woman participated in physical exercise . . . she would suffer tremendously. . . .* The second clause does not restate or emphasize or clarify the first. Even a semicolon would be suspect here, because although we do have two independent clauses, the content of each is not so closely related that the reader needs to hold the two together. Probably it would be best to join the two sentences with the conjunction *and*.

The second colon in this sentence is also inappropriate. Here, the colon is breaking the natural flow of the sentence, coming between the preposition *through* and the objects of the preposition, *stunted growth, headaches, hysteria, and even insanity*. No punctuation at all is needed here, even though there is a list.

Dashes

When considering the placement of dashes, remember that, if a dash comes in the middle of a sentence, two dashes are needed, one to open and one to close the material. In Sentence Four, therefore, another dash is needed. What is intended to be enclosed in the dash is appropriate; *exercise that would harden their muscles, add fat to their bodies, and soften their skin* could be information that the author wishes to emphasize. However, a dash immediately after *skin* should close the material, rather than the semicolon which is there currently.

The pair of dashes in Sentence Five models the correct use of the dash. Here, two dashes are placed around the material that interrupts so that the contrasting comment is framed nicely.

The revised paragraph looks like this:

Through such issues, doctors became increasingly aware that women could do physical damage to their bodies during sporting events. A prominent figure in this area was Dr. T.S. Clousten. Dr. Clousten could be termed an early "sports physician," and he claimed that if a woman participated in physical exercise and overexerted herself, she would suffer tremendously through stunted growth, headaches, hysteria, and even insanity. Nonetheless, Clousten also felt that women needed to be directed toward physical exercise—exercise that would harden their muscles, add fat to their bodies, and soften their skin—such as outdoor play and moderate but vigorous gymnastics. However, he strongly emphasized that such activities needed to be regulated by a practising physician, as women—still viewed as hopeless and naive idiots—had the tendency to carry their exercises too far and cause damage to themselves.

Consider the use of semicolons, colons, and dashes in the two exercise paragraphs. Which punctuation marks are used correctly? Which are used incorrectly? Are any additional ones needed or permitted? Defend your answers.

Other Punctuation

There are other punctuation marks, of course, besides the comma, colon, semicolon, and dash. Some of these marks, like parentheses, are used so infrequently that they cause few problems. Others, like end punctuation, are used so often that most native speakers know the conventions governing their use. The following two sections on parentheses and end punctuation should answer any questions you might have about unusual usage circumstances.

THE PARENTHESIS

The parenthesis, like the dash, indicates an interruption or shift in thought, but rather than drawing attention to the interrupter as dashes do, the parenthesis downplays it, saying to the reader that the enclosed material is not that important:

( ) ( ) ( )

> He complained (as we all do) of underfunding.

The writer, by using parenthesis, is signalling to the reader that *as we all do* is an aside, not intended to be of the same import as the rest of the sentence.

The parenthesis, by definition, causes some readers concern. If a comment is not important, these readers ask, why write it? There are sound responses to this query: the parenthesis can lighten tone, present queries and exclamations, add information that some but not all readers might be looking for. However, when you use the parenthesis, keep the questioning reader in mind. Do you need the parenthetical comment? Is the comment parenthetical?

You may also run into a few punctuation problems when using other punctuation with the parenthesis. The only punctuation marks that should be permitted inside a parenthesis are those needed to punctuate the parenthetical material:

> The smile on LeeAnne's lips (a smug, conceited grin) stalled me for a moment.

> I longed to kiss those lips (who would not?) but felt she might betray me.

> Suddenly, we were interrupted (my opportunity was lost) by a knock at the door.

The second and third examples model a tricky punctuation nicety. When the parenthetical material inside a sentence is an independent clause requiring an exclamation or question mark, the end punctuation is included. When the material is an independent clause requiring a period, the period is not included. Note in all cases that capital letters are not required.

Sometimes, parenthetical material is not contained within a sentence but is a sentence on its own. In this instance, capitals and end punctuation are required:

> It was John. (He was a man whom I had always feared.)

> He shook my hand, and his cool skin repelled me. (Why?)

Writing Prompt

Write your own soap opera scene, creating sentences that model correct use of parentheses. Keep in mind that the material contained in the parenthesis should be an aside, not more important than the other parts of the sentence.

It is also important to remember that other punctuation marks may be needed in addition to the parenthesis: a parenthesis does not replace commas or periods. If a sentence would require a comma or a period without the parenthetical material, the comma or period is still required with that material.

> While he spoke to LeeAnne (his phoney British accent well modulated), I played with the crystal decanter.

> Nonetheless, I listened closely to their conversation (straining to hear romantic undertones).

Note that the comma or period is always placed <u>after</u> the closing parenthesis, never before.

END PUNCTUATION

End punctuation is necessary in a way that no other punctuation is; the breaking of thoughts into sentences gives an essential order and meaning to prose. Even Gertrude Stein is forced to admit, "Inevitably no matter how completely I had to have writing go on, physically one had to again and again stop sometime and if one had to again and again stop some time then periods had to exist."[5] Fortunately, because end punctuation is so essential to meaning, few writers have problems with it. We instinctively recognize that the close of a sentence is indicated by one of three punctuation marks: the period, the question mark, or the exclamation mark. Most of the time, we have very little difficulty deciding which of the three is the most appropriate. Periods close declarative statements and mild commands; question marks end questions; and exclamation marks end exclamations. However, there are a few fine points that may cause you to hesitate occasionally. The following section directs your attention to these instances.

Reported Questions

Reported questions are not actually questions at all but rather declarative statements reporting questions. A scientific think tank might ask, "Is objectivity possible?" A reported question would read:

> Some scientists ask whether objectivity is possible.

A Pollution Probe press release might pose the question, "Is the development of nuclear energy necessary?" A writer reporting the question could write:

> Pollution Probe researchers wonder if the development of nuclear energy is necessary.

---

[5] Gertrude Stein, "Poetry and Grammar," *Gertrude Stein: Writings and Lectures 1911-1945*, ed. Patricia Meyerowitz (London: Peter Owen, 1967) 128.

As these examples establish, reported questions are closed with periods. It is incorrect to end such questions with question marks. Either the question mark should be changed to a period or the indirect question should be made direct.

Incorrect: This paper will focus on the question of what has NATO accomplished?

Corrected: This paper will focus on the question of what NATO has accomplished.

Corrected: This paper will focus on the following question: what has NATO accomplished?

Note in the second corrected version that the first independent clause— *This paper will focus on the following question*—is a statement and the second— *what has NATO accomplished?*—is a question. In sentences where there is more than one independent clause, the final independent clause determines closing punctuation.

Courtesy Questions

Business writing (memos and letters) often contains courtesy questions, polite questions that are usually intended to be interpreted by the reader as polite commands:

Correct: Would you please forward this material to the Dean.

Correct: Could you provide a written response by the first of December.

Courtesy questions are usually closed with a period, perhaps to indicate that the writer does not intend the reader to give a response, but rather to comply with the request.

Double End Punctuation

Using two end punctuation marks to close a sentence is considered incorrect. When a sentence ends with an abbreviation, therefore, the second period should be deleted.

Incorrect: Elly went to Edmonton to begin her M.A..

Corrected: Elly went to Edmonton to begin her M.A.

Writing Prompt

Write three declarative sentences ending with an abbreviation, three indirect questions, three direct questions, and three courtesy questions so that you can practise end punctuation.

THE APOSTROPHE

The apostrophe serves several functions in the English language. It can indicate contraction, plurality, or possession. Most writers find using an apostrophe for the first two functions relatively easy, but many have difficulty with the possessive construction. For this reason, our section on apostrophes will deal only briefly with contraction and plurality and will focus on the possessive form.

Apostrophes to Indicate Contraction

An apostrophe can be used to indicate that a letter has been omitted: *I'm* for *I am, don't* for *do not, it's* for *it is*. Most writers have no problem indicating contractions successfully; the one important rule to remember is that the apostrophe must be placed where the letter has been omitted:

Incorrect: It is Jane whos' leaving.

Corrected: It is Jane who's leaving.

Apostrophes to Indicate Plurality

There is only one circumstance when the apostrophe, combined with an *s*, can be used to indicate a plural form: when it is used to form the plural of letters, figures, or words used as words:

Correct: Tony got three C's and two B's.

Correct: Elizabeth scored three 87's.

Correct: The paragraph contained too many or's.

Some writers also use the apostrophe to indicate a plural date: the 1970's, the 1800's. However, usage is evolving toward simply an addition of *s* in this instance: 1970s, 1800s. You will notice that this textbook uses the latter form.

Apostrophes to Indicate Possession

Many writers occasionally omit apostrophes needed to indicate possession, so that what should read *women's issue* is transcribed as *womens issue*, or so that *family's priorities* is wrongly recorded as *families priorities*.

Writers make these errors partially because they write what they hear, and what they hear is the sound of *s,* not the apostrophe. However, apostrophes are also omitted because writers have difficulty recognizing possessives: they confuse the *s* that is a plural or an *s* verb ending with the *s* used to indicate possession.

DEFINING THE POSSESSIVE

A possessive is one form of a noun, in the same way that a plural is one form of a noun. In the possessive form, an apostrophe or an apostrophe and an *s* is added to a noun to indicate possession (just as we add an *s* to a noun to indicate a plural). Furthermore, when a possessive form is created, the noun will function as an adjective: it will modify another noun.

But what is possession? The lay definition might be something belonging to someone, and it works well enough when the construction deals with individual people owning material objects:

Toby's BMW
Suzie's Honda
Alison's bicycle

However, often possession applies to much more abstract forms of belonging:

the candidate's bias
Canada's foreign policy
my parents' relationship

These forms are difficult to recognize if you are thinking only in terms of ownership. You might find defining the possessive easier if you remember that the other method of indicating possession is to use the preposition *of*: the bias of the candidate, the bicycle of Alison, the relationship of my parents. The dictionary defines *of* in this usage as meaning possessing, belonging to, or pertaining to, and the possessive form of the noun can have any of these meanings.

One word of caution: many readers believe that inanimate nouns (things having no life of their own – paper, books, desks) cannot take a possessive form. These readers claim that the *of* construction is the only acceptable indication of possession in this case: the cover of the book, the colour of the paper, the drawer of the desk. Although the language is evolving toward accepting a possessive form of inanimate nouns, you might wish to avoid creating this construction.

You may have guessed that if nouns can have a possessive form, pronouns can as well. In fact, there are two possessive forms for pronouns: pronominal adjectives (my, your, his, her, its, their) and possessive pronouns (mine, yours, his, hers, its, theirs). Note that these forms do not require apostrophes.

IDENTIFYING THE POSSESSIVE

Now that you know what a possessive is, the matter of identifying possessives becomes relatively simple. A possessive is always a noun and its last letter is always *s*. Furthermore, it always modifies another noun. If you have trouble identifying possessives, you might begin by underlining all nouns ending in *s* in your work.

Once you have sorted out the nouns ending in *s,* you need to decide which are possessives. (Some will be plurals—cats, dogs; others will be nouns that normally end in *s* —Chris, grass.) A couple of litmus tests will be useful here to determine the real possessives.

First, since one means of indicating possession is to use a prepositional phrase beginning with *of,* you can determine a possessive by checking to see if it can be expressed in this form.

Correct: *Colville's* paintings are usually done in muted colours.

This use of the possessive is correct because the sentence can be rephrased using the preposition *of* and still retain the same meaning:

The paintings of *Colville* are usually done in muted colours.

If the possessive is incorrect, this rephrasing will not be possible, as in the following example:

Incorrect: Magic *realists'* play an important role in Canadian art.

When this sentence is rephrased, the result is nonsense:

The play of magic *realists* an important role in Canadian art.

In this sentence, *realists* is just a plural form and thus doesn't need an apostrophe.

Corrected: Magic realists play an important role in Canadian art.

Here, then, is a useful litmus test for possessives. If you are in doubt about whether a word ending in *s* is actually a possessive, try expressing it in a phrase beginning with *of.* If the sentence makes sense that way, you need an apostrophe.

Remember also that the possessive form of a noun usually occupies the position of an adjective in a sentence: it occurs in the list of modifiers before a noun:

Monroe's desperate suicide
Garbo's plea for privacy
Garland's addiction

A final litmus test is to substitute a pronominal adjective (my, your, his, her, its, their) for the word you are wondering about. Since pronominal adjectives indicate possession too, if one makes sense as a substitute, the word being replaced is probably a possessive:

Correct: *Robinson's* views challenge even the more radical positions.
His views challenge even the more radical positions.

In the preceding example, the pronominal adjective *his* fits beautifully. In the example that follows, however, substituting the pronominal adjective *its* reveals an incorrect possessive:

Incorrect: His *view's* challenge even the more radical positions.
His *its* challenge even the more radical positions.

The second sentence is nonsensical because *views* is a plural noun in the sentence, not a possessive. No apostrophe is needed.

CORRECT POSSESSIVE FORM

Now that you can recognize your possessives, you need to know the proper placement of the apostrophe. Only two options are available to the writer: an apostrophe can be added, or an apostrophe plus an *s* can be added.

If the original noun does not end in *s*, an apostrophe plus an *s* is added:

Toby's BMW
family's beliefs
the candidate's bias

If the noun does end in *s*, an apostrophe plus an *s* is added when the noun is singular:

Chris's Accord
Yeats's poem

However, only an apostrophe is added when the noun is plural:

bosses' employees
candidates' bias
families' beliefs

The one exception to this rule occurs when a polysyllabic singular word ends in *s*; then, the writer may choose to add only an apostrophe to avoid confusion about pronunciation:

Archimedes' principle
Diogenes' sun

To decide which option is correct, you must determine the original noun form by changing the possessive construction to an *of* phrase. Let's work with this example:

He looked deeply into the *girls eyes*.

If you change the expression of the possessive into an *of* phrase, here is the result:

He looked deeply into the *eyes* of the *girl*.

Girl does not end in *s*, so the apostrophe is formed by adding an apostrophe plus an *s*:

He looked deeply into the *girl's eyes*.

Using the same construction in another context gets a different result:

All the *girls eyes* were infected.
All the *eyes* of the *girls* were infected.

In this case, the original noun is *girls*, not *girl*, so the correct possessive form dictates adding only an apostrophe:

All the *girls' eyes* were infected.

One more example is useful at this point. Consider this sentence:

Jess's eyes were full of tears.

Here the correct possessive form was modelled. We could write:

The *eyes* of *Jess* were full of tears.

This construction establishes that the noun already ends in *s* but is singular, so adding an apostrophe and an *s* is correct.

ITS

Everyone involved in producing this text agreed that the use of *its* demanded a separate section. By far the most common apostrophe error (and the one that irritates instructors most easily) is placing an apostrophe in the pronominal adjective *its*:

Incorrect: The dog wagged it's tail.

Corrected: The dog wagged its tail.

It's always means *it is*; the word can never be used to indicate possession. Likewise, *her's, their's,* and *your's* are also always incorrect.

Notes

My writing strengths:

Things I need to remember:

Things I need to check:

Using Apostrophes Correctly

Sample Paragraph:

1. One final set of **reviews**, those of Marian **Engels** infamous <u>Bear</u>, are worth discussing here. **2.** French, of <u>The Globe and Mail</u>, considers the work the epitome of Canadian cultural **distinctiveness**: "At **its** most elemental level, the bear represents the primitive society of Canada" (Rev. of <u>Bear</u> 38). **3. Humans** relationship to the **wilderness** is recognized as Canadian by every critic from Northrop Frye to Margaret Atwood, but such an assessment seems not to have penetrated foreign **reviewers consciousness. 4.** Possibly foreign **reviewers** do not see <u>Bear</u> as representing **Canadas** cultural **distinctiveness** because, as Frye argues, the Western world is becoming Canadianized: that man is out of synch with nature is no longer recognized only by **Canadians** but also by the rest of Western civilization.

Exercise One:

The second study was based on the fathers family of origin. Most theories concerning personality consider the family of origin to be critical to the formation of life-long behaviour patterns. In the development of a role such as fathering, ones family of origin seems important as the setting for both the process of identification that is the core of the psychological theories and the model of parenting behaviour that is stressed in cognitive and learning theories (Levinger and Mole, 1979: 310). One specific question concerns the strength of the fathers childhood relationships to each of his parents. Men with custody were more likely to be middle- or last-born children and were significantly more likely to have both brothers and sisters rather than siblings of only one sex. Men with custody described a more intense relationship with their mothers and a more distant one with their fathers. The mothers of men with custody were more likely to be employed outside the home.

Exercise Two:

In modern art, since this revolution in colours importance, there have been uncountable new experiments with its power. Each member of the colourist freedom revolution should be recognized as playing a vital role in the renovation of Western arts decor. Colour is crucial psychologically as its a primary factor in ambience. Anyone who fails to appreciate its worth (such as those who tried to repress Kandinsky and Delaunay in their freeing of colour from form) needs further education.

Using Apostrophes Correctly: Sample Paragraph Discussion

In the passage opposite, all the nouns and pronouns which end with *s* have been highlighted. If the use of apostrophes is a severe problem in your writing, underlining all nouns and pronouns ending in *s* is a sound strategy for eliminating error. The technique forces you to consider each noun independently to determine whether it is in possessive form. We will work through the highlighted words, first eliminating nouns that normally end in *s*. Next, using the various litmus tests mentioned to determine which *s* words are possessives, we will eliminate the plurals and, finally, we will add apostrophes to the words remaining — those that are possessives.

Words That Normally End in *S*

Some nouns end with *s* simply because that is the way they are spelled. The *s* doesn't indicate plural or possessive; it just indicates the *s* sound. These nouns can be possessives, but only if they occupy the modifier position in a sentence. Otherwise, they do not indicate possession. The following nouns in the passage ordinarily end in *s*, but are not in a modifier position in the sentence.

distinctiveness: This word occupies the place of a noun in the sentence. It is not a possessive.

wilderness: This word occupies the place of a noun in the sentence. It is not a possessive.

consciousness: The word occupies the place of a noun in this sentence. It is not a possessive.

distinctiveness: Again, this word occupies the place of a noun in this sentence. It is not a possessive.

Plurals

Plurals require a little more thought because a plural can be a possessive when it holds an adjective, or modifying, position. However, if a plural occupies a noun position in a sentence, it will not be a possessive. The following words are plurals that do not occupy a modifier position in a sentence.

reviews: The word occupies a noun position in this sentence as the object of an *of* phrase. It therefore is not a possessive.

reviewers (in Sentence Four): This *reviewers* is identical in appearance to the *reviewers* which preceded it, but does not play the same role. Here it is in a noun position: we can't say *the do of the reviewers* or *foreign their do*. The *s* simply indicates a plural form, more than one reviewer, not possession.

Canadians: The word is not in a modifier position, and the *s* indicates the plural. It is not a possessive.

Possessives

What remains are the possessives. You now must decide where to place the apostrophe that indicates possession.

Engels: With a name, you must always determine first whether the name actually ends in *s*. The author's name is Marian Engel. When we look further, we see that *Engels* does occupy a modifier position; it is in front of the noun <u>Bear</u>. Two other litmus tests work as well: we can say *her infamous <u>Bear</u>* (although it sounds odd) and we can at least form the phrase *the infamous <u>Bear</u> of Marian Engel*. This one passes the tests, so we need an apostrophe. The next question is where it should go. In the *of* phrase, Engel does not end in *s*, so the correct response is to add *'s*: *Engel's infamous <u>Bear</u>.*

its: As you should know by now, an *its* that occupies the modifier position in a sentence is a pronominal adjective, a possessive that does not require an apostrophe. THE WORD IS CORRECT AS IS.

humans: *Humans* is a noun, and the word *humans* is in the modifier position, in front of the noun *relationship*. We can say *the relationship of humans* and we can say *their relationship*. We have a possessive form. Since *humans* ends in *s* in the *of* construction, we add an apostrophe: *humans' relationship*.

reviewers (in Sentence Three): *Reviewers* is a noun, and *reviewers* is in the modifier position, describing *consciousness*. We can say *the consciousness of the foreign reviewers* and we can say *their consciousness*. Another possessive established. Since *reviewers* ends in *s* in the *of* construction, we add an apostrophe: *reviewers' consciousness*.

Canadas: *Canada* is a noun; *Canadas* is in a position to modify *distinctiveness,* and we can say *the cultural distinctiveness of Canada* or *its cultural distinctiveness*. We need an apostrophe, and since Canada does not end in *s* in the *of* construction, we write *Canada's cultural distinctiveness*.

The corrected paragraph would look like this:

One final set of reviews, those of Marian Engel's infamous <u>Bear</u>, are worth discussing here. French, of <u>The Globe and Mail</u>, considers the work the epitome of Canadian cultural distinctiveness: "At its most elemental level, the bear represents the primitive society of Canada" (Rev. of <u>Bear</u> 38). Humans' relationship to the wilderness is recognized as Canadian by every critic from Northrop Frye to Margaret Atwood, but such an assessment seems not to have penetrated foreign reviewers' consciousness. Possibly foreign reviewers do not see <u>Bear</u> as representing Canada's cultural distinctiveness because, as Frye argues, the Western world is becoming Canadianized: that man is out of synch with nature is no longer recognized only by Canadians, but also by the rest of Western civilization.

Work through the two exercise paragraphs, underlining every noun and pronoun ending in *s*. Indicate possessives correctly where necessary.

Punctuating Quotations

Many students who can follow standard punctuation conventions with ease falter when they must incorporate quotations into their prose. Here, a series of punctuation conventions apply that, while following the principles of general punctuation use, also have little quirks of their own. These quirks, however, can be reduced to a list of approximately a dozen conventions that are easy to memorize and use.

INCORPORATING QUOTATIONS

“   ”

Before beginning to discuss the punctuation of quotations, we think it is important to say a few words about incorporating them into one's own prose. Many writers err by plunking quotations down in their text without bothering to introduce them or explain their significance. One way or another, you should always make clear to the reader the connection between your prose and the quotations in it. What you want to avoid is prose such as this discussion of a Virginia Woolf novel:

Poor: The lighthouse is the central symbol of the novel. “It satisfied him” (231). It is significant that To the Lighthouse closes with a journey to it.

The reader is left helpless with this quotation: no signals are given about its context either before or after the quotation, so there is no way of understanding the connection it has to the writer's argument.

In the following quotations, however, the reader can see much more easily the relevance or context of the passage being quoted:

Better: The lighthouse, the central symbol of the novel, is particularly important to James. Woolf writes that “[i]t satisfied him” (231), and the journey to the lighthouse at the end of the novel reveals a great deal about his relationship with his father.

Better: “It satisfied him,” Woolf writes, reflecting on James's feelings about the lighthouse (231). The symbol helps the reader to interpret the role of James in the novel.

As the third example shows, it is not always necessary to explain a quotation before quoting. The reader will stay attentive until the end of a sentence or even the end of a paragraph to determine meaning. Sometimes, a quotation will need very little introduction because what precedes it will make clear the significance of the quotation. Nonetheless, when you review your prose, make sure that no quotations are left entirely stranded or unexplained. Otherwise, the reader may not know how to interpret them.

Secondly, when incorporating quotations, especially when reporting quotations indirectly, make certain that they align in terms of syntax and tense with your own prose. Use square brackets (see the section on square brackets) if necessary to alter the quotation so that it matches your own prose.

Incorrect: Woolf's fiction has been described as "weave stream-of-consciousness style with unusual imagery" (28).[6]

Corrected: Woolf's fiction has been described as "weav[ing] stream-of-consciousness style with unusual imagery" (28).

Incorrect: Edgerton believes that "The Waves (1931), the best-realized of her novels" (71).

Corrected: Edgerton believes that "The Waves (1931) [is] the best-realized of her novels" (71).

The reader should be able to read the quotations you use without sensing any disruptions at all: the prose should flow smoothly from your own work through the quotation and back to your own work.

Once you are sure your quotations are well incorporated, you are ready to check punctuation. A good place to begin is by noting that there are two types of quotations: **short** ones (no more than four typed lines of prose or three lines of poetry) and **long** ones (more than four typed lines of prose or four lines of poetry). Each type has its own series of conventions.

PUNCTUATING SHORT QUOTATIONS

A short quotation is signalled to the reader by the use of double quotation marks:

In To the Lighthouse, Lily thinks of "a large kitchen table" (27) when she contemplates Mr. Ramsay's work.

As Turner notes, "Lily is a visual thinker" (18).

Opening Punctuation

There are three common means of introducing a short quotation: with no punctuation, with a comma, or with a colon. The choice you make depends on the way in which the quotation is incorporated into your prose.

---

[6] All quotations from secondary sources in this section of the text are fabricated. Primary quotations are accurate. When quoting, we have opted to use a parenthetical method of documentation because it is the preferred method in most disciplines. If you are using an endnoting/footnoting method, remember that all superscript numbers are placed after final punctuation.

NO PUNCTUATION

In many cases, the quotation will be reported as if it were a part of your prose. It will fit neatly into your sentence as part of a clause or phrase; only the quotation marks will establish for your reader that you are quoting, not paraphrasing:

Minta is described as one of "those golden-reddish girls" (ll4).

Serpa argues that "Minta is a minor character" (34).

In the first example, the quotation is part of a prepositional phrase and consequently any punctuation mark would be unacceptable. In the second example, the quotation is part of a subordinate clause and again no punctuation is needed or permitted.

COMMAS TO INTRODUCE

In other situations, you may introduce a quotation as if you were recording a conversation. This style of incorporation is often signalled by the use of a verb of speaking (for example, says, notes, asks, replies) and requires a comma:

Eliot said, "I like Woolf's style" (32).

According to Johnson, "Woolf's style is unrivalled" (97).

COLONS TO INTRODUCE

Colons can also be used to introduce short quotations. As in any other instance, the colon draws attention to what comes after it: in this case, the quotation. When you want the reader to notice your quotation, to consider it carefully, use a colon.

When Woolf describes the dinner, she writes: "Now all the candles were lit, and the faces on both sides of the table were brought nearer by the candlelight" (112).

Here, the reader is given more of a pause to reflect on the quotation than a comma would make possible. As you can see, choosing between a comma and a colon is largely a stylistic choice.

Colons are also used when an independent clause (a complete sentence) precedes the quotation:

Here is what Woolf wrote: "Some change at once went through them all" (112).

In this instance, a comma would be incorrect since a comma cannot join two independent clauses. (See the section on comma splices in Chapter Two.) A semicolon would be inappropriate since your intent is not to have the reader balance the two statements. You want the reader to focus on the quotation, so a colon, which directs attention forward, works well.

Quotation Marks to Indicate Irony

Occasionally, double quotation marks are used around a phrase to establish that the author is using the term ironically, as in the following sentence:

These "lifestyle accessories" are the ultimate form of consumer indulgence.

Here, the author indicates that he or she is not the creator of this distasteful phrase by enclosing it in quotation marks. Provided you are being ironic, this use of quotation marks is acceptable. Do not, however, use quotation marks freely to indicate emphasis or slang. Rely on forceful words to give evidence; avoid using slang unless you are using it ironically.

INTRODUCTORY CAPITALIZATION

When you quote, the passage quoted must be reproduced exactly down to the last detail. Accordingly, a word should be capitalized only if it was capitalized in the original, and original capitals should not be made lower case. If you need to create a capital, use square brackets (see page 248) to indicate that you have changed the text.

Closing Punctuation

Almost any type of punctuation can close a quotation, depending on circumstance.

If the quotation itself ends in a question or exclamation, you should preserve the end punctuation:

"How did one judge people, think of them?" Lily asks (29).

Lily asks, "How did one judge people, think of them?" (29).

Note in the second example that a period is required to close the sentence completely after the parenthetical citation. End punctuation is always placed after the closing parenthesis of a parenthetical citation. The period would not be required in the second example were there no parenthetical citation, nor would it be necessary if a footnote had been used.

If your sentence is coming to a close after the quotation, you will need a period or some other full stop to close the quotation (whether or not the actual quotation has an end punctuation mark):

Woolf writes, "The wonder is that I've any clothes on my back" (334).

How can we interpret Woolf's reference to "perpetual waste and repair" (336)?

Note that when the writer's prose demands a question mark, the question mark is placed outside the quotation marks, not within, as it is when the quoted material contains a question mark.

If your sentence does not come to a close after the quotation, you should use whatever punctuation is required by your own prose. Remember that, in most cases, commas and periods go inside closing quotation marks; semicolons and colons go outside:

"How childlike, how absurd she was," Lily observes (116).

Lily observes, "How childlike, how absurd she was"; nonetheless, she still admires Mrs. Ramsay (116).

Punctuation within Short Quotations

A quotation should preserve the text of the original, even to the details of punctuation. Even when there is an error in the text, it should not be corrected but rather followed by *(sic)* to indicate that the error was not made by the writer, but rather was present in the original text.

However, there are occasions when altering the text is necessary. Single quotation marks, ellipsis dots, and square brackets are used to make these alterations clear to the reader.

SINGLE QUOTATION MARKS ' '

Occasionally, the original material being quoted may contain double quotation marks already:

Original:
  Woolf has been called "a bluestocking."

When such material is quoted in a short quotation, the original double quotation marks are changed to single quotation marks:

Quotation:
  Ryerson notes, "Woolf has been called 'a bluestocking'" (120).

Note the closing punctuation. The single quotation is closed first, then the double quotation.

ELLIPSIS DOTS . . .

Ellipsis dots are used to indicate omitted text. When the omission is within one sentence, three well-spaced ellipsis dots are appropriate:

Original:
  To the Lighthouse was published in 1927 and is an important work of the modern period.

Quotation:
  Ecclestone notes, "To the Lighthouse . . . is an important work of the modern period" (514).

When the omission is at the end of a quoted sentence or extends over more than one sentence, use a period and three ellipsis dots:

Original:
  Woolf has written several other novels, including Mrs Dalloway and The Waves. In addition, she is well known for her account of women's writing experience, A Room of One's Own.

Quotation:

 DeVries writes, "Woolf has written several other novels, including <u>Mrs Dalloway</u>. . . . In addition, she is well known for her account of women's writing experience, <u>A Room of One's Own</u>" (22).

SQUARE BRACKETS [ ]

Square brackets indicate information that has been added by the writer to the quotation, information not in the original text. Usually, the information is added to make some sort of clarification, either adding a detail to or commenting on an error in the original. Square brackets may also be used, as we have shown above, to alter the text so that tense and syntax in the quotation align with the writer's prose. Finally, they may be used sparingly to replace a portion of the original text when it is necessary to paraphrase either for the sake of brevity or clarification.

Original:

 Leslie Stephen had a significant impact on Virginia Woolf.

Quotation:

 According to Padolsky, "Leslie Stephen [Virginia Woolf's father] had a significant impact on Virginia Woolf" (78).

Original:

 Woolf's private life has intrigued many scholars and researchers both in England and the United States. As a consequence, several good biographies have been written.

Quotation:

 Harding notes, "Woolf's private life has intrigued many scholars and researchers. . . . [and] several good biographies have been written" (22).

THE SLASH /

When more than one line of poetry is quoted in a short quotation, a slash must be used to indicate line ends:

 Yeats writes of Maud Gonne, "Why should I blame her that she filled my days / With misery" ("No Second Troy" 1-2).

PUNCTUATING LONG OR BLOCK QUOTATIONS

Long or block quotations are not indicated by quotation marks; rather, they are set off from the text of an essay: a double-space is inserted (a triple-space if you intend to double-space the quotation itself), a new line is begun, and the left margin is indented. The quotation may be single-spaced or double-spaced.[7] When the quotation is ended, another double-space is inserted, and the reader returns to the prose of the text.

Example:
John Stuart Mill makes the following remark about Byron in his Autobiography:

> As might be expected, I got no good from this reading [of Byron], but the reverse. The poet's state of mind was too like my own. His was the lament of a man who had worn out all pleasures, and who seemed to think that life, to all who possess the good things of it, must necessarily be the vapid, uninteresting thing which I found it. (J.S. Mill, Autobiography 103)

If the quotation is of poetry, line ends must be preserved:

Example:
These lines from "To a Sky-Lark" establish Shelley's recognition of the tension between joy and sorrow:

> We look before and after,
>   And pine for what is not —
> Our sincerest laughter
>   With some pain is fraught —
> Our sweetest songs are those that tell of saddest thought.   (86-90)

Note that, as much as possible, the writer should try to preserve the way the poem is arranged on the page. Here, various indentations have been retained.

Opening Punctuation

Usually, as in the examples above, a long quotation is introduced by a colon. The use of this punctuation mark makes sense, since most of the time the reader must come to a fairly definitive pause before starting to read the quotation, and often an independent clause precedes a block quotation.

---

[7] In this book, all examples of long quotations are single-spaced. Check the relevant style guide for the preferred spacing in your discipline.

However, there are occasions when no punctuation is needed before a long quotation. Again, if the quotation seems to become part of your prose, any punctuation is inappropriate:

Example:
Shelley writes that

> The pale purple even
>   Melts around thy flight,
> Like a star of Heaven
>   In the broad day-light   (16-19)

A colon would be incorrect here, since it would interrupt the regular order of the sentence. The words of the verse have been incorporated into the writer's prose, so there is no need for punctuation.

Other punctuation marks — the comma, for example — can also be used to introduce a block quotation, depending on what is being said or quoted. Sometimes a comma or a dash is either more effective or necessary to meaning. However, if you use punctuation other than a colon to introduce a block quotation, be sure to have a reason for doing so. Remember as well that a semicolon will almost never introduce a quotation, since semicolons invite the reader to balance two clauses against each other, and the focus in a sentence containing a quotation is inevitably on the quotation, not on the signal words.

Closing Punctuation

The long quotation should be closed with whatever punctuation ends the material being quoted (even if that is no punctuation at all). Parenthetical references are not enclosed by punctuation as they are in short quotations. Instead, after the quotation is ended, the writer skips two spaces and begins the reference. No punctuation is placed after the reference. See the examples above for demonstrations of this form.

Punctuation within Long Quotations

As with short quotations, for the most part, the original text should be preserved in the block quotation. The regulations governing the use of square brackets and ellipsis dots are just about identical. The only difference is that ellipsis dots may be used slightly differently with verse:

Example:
Shelley writes:

> We look before and after,
>   And pine for what is not —
> . . . .
> Our sweetest songs are those that tell of saddest thought.   (86-90)

In verse, a row of ellipsis dots is used to indicate missing line(s) of poetry.

Slashes, of course, are not used at all in long quotations since line ends are replicated exactly.

As we have noted, double quotation marks are not used to set off block quotations. For this reason, when block quotations contain quotation marks, they are retained as double quotation marks, not altered to single quotation marks as they are in short quotations.

Punctuating Short Quotations

Sample Paragraph:

1. The myth of biculturalism, therefore, did not survive the sixties. **2.** Many explanations have been offered for its demise. **3.** Sandra Gwyn argues that Diefenbaker's attempts to: "replace discrimination with unhyphenated Canadianism" touched off a series of protests that eventually led to the formation of a multicultural policy ("Multiculturalism: A Threat and a Promise" 15). **4.** There have been other views, too. **5.** "When Trudeau became Prime Minister and adopted Marshall McLuhan as one of his advisors, Canada reverted to tribalism" (Northrop Frye, "Culture as Interpenetration" 16). **6.** It seems likely that the new interest in ethnicity and regional diversity was as much a product of a global village vision as of domestic cultural policy. **7.** Whatever its origin, the outcome was this: on October 8, 1971, Prime Minister Trudeau, "rose in the House of Commons to tell Canadians they were now a multicultural nation". (Gwyn, "Multiculturalism: A Threat and a Promise" 17) **8.** By the early seventies, then, ethnicity and regionalism were key factors in the constitution of Canadian culture.

Exercise One:

To ensure that the reader recognizes these two opposing worlds, Marvell uses further contrasts in the second stanza to distinguish between the busy world and the calm world. Again, the choice of words serves Marvell's purpose successfully. Here, the "busy companies of men" (12) are contrasted to the "delicious solitude" within the natural world. The key words "delicious" and "busy" definitely suggest that the natural world would be superior to the social world, "all but rude" (15). Even the soft flowing rhythm of the poem suggests a world of relaxation and peace. Marvell, then, not only introduces two worlds, but also gives the reader a clear impression of the one he favours: the world of nature.

Exercise Two:

MacLennan's Two Solitudes is the most celebrated fictional representation of Canadian culture during this era. As William Arthur Deacon, literary editor of The Globe and Mail, rhapsodises, "In Two Solitudes MacLennan is a Canadian . . . Ideas and feelings are expressed that would occur to nobody except a Canadian." (Rev. of Two Solitudes 18) The novel is primarily a discussion of Anglo-French relations in Canada, so evidently Deacon believes this theme embodies the essence of Canadian life. J. Donald Adams, the New York Times reviewer and also a Canadian, is in accord; he claims that the reader, "puts it [the book] down with a better knowledge of Canada's central difficulty as a nation. (Rev. of Two Solitudes 2)" Similarly, the anonymous reviewer in the Times Literary Supplement praises MacLennan for offering to the world "a careful and scrupulously fair picture of the conflict which arises" from Canada's bicultural situation, and readily interprets the union of Paul Tallard and Heather Methuen at the close of the novel as symbolizing, "the mutual understanding which is needed between the two races" (317).

Punctuating Short Quotations: Sample Paragraph Discussion

This sample passage contains three short quotations. Let's work through the passage by considering how each quotation is introduced, whether any internal punctuation is needed, and whether the closing punctuation is appropriate.

Introducing the Quotation

All three of the quotations in this passage are introduced incorrectly. In Sentence Three, the writer uses signal words correctly, since we know both who made the remark and who the remark was made about. However, the use of a colon to introduce the quotation disrupts the sentence, actually splitting the infinitive *to replace*. No punctuation is needed to introduce this quotation.

Sentence Five obviously needs signal words. Here, the reader has no idea who is responsible for this quotation or how the quotation is to be interpreted, other than that it expresses a different view from the previous quotation. Using the information in the parenthetical citation and adding a little background, you might write: *Northrop Frye, attributing the shift to the Liberals, notes, "When Trudeau. . . ."*

The quotation in Sentence Seven is introduced adequately in terms of signal words, for we know that the quotation is connected to Trudeau (although we do not know who made this particular remark). However, the comma used to introduce the quotation separates a subject from its verb, interrupting the flow of the sentence. Again, no punctuation is needed to introduce the quotation.

Internal Punctuation

None of the quotations in this paragraph requires internal punctuation. For practice in checking internal punctuation, try Exercise Two.

Closing the Quotation

The first quotation, in Sentence Three, is closed appropriately. No punctuation is needed because the end of the quotation fits into the prose of the essay.

The second quotation is also punctuated properly in terms of closure; the period is placed after the parenthetical citation. However, the final quotation in Sentence Seven is not punctuated properly. Here, the period needs to be placed after the parenthetical citation.

The revised paragraph is much cleaner:

> The myth of biculturalism, therefore, did not survive the sixties. Many explanations have been offered for its demise. Sandra Gwyn argues that Diefenbaker's attempts to "replace discrimination with unhyphenated Canadianism" touched off a series of protests that eventually led to the formation of a multicultural policy ("Multiculturalism: A Threat and a Promise" 15). There have been other views, too. Northrop Frye, attributing the shift to the Liberals, notes, "When Trudeau became Prime Minister and adopted Marshall McLuhan as one of his advisors, Canada reverted to tribalism" ("Culture as Interpenetration" 16). It seems likely that the new interest in ethnicity and regional diversity was as much a product of a global village vision as of domestic cultural policy. Whatever its origin, the outcome was this: on October 8, 1971, Prime Minister Trudeau "rose in the House of Commons to tell Canadians they were now a multicultural nation" (Gwyn, "Multiculturalism: A Threat and a Promise" 17). By the early seventies, then, ethnicity and regionalism were key factors in the constitution of Canadian culture.

Rewrite the two exercise paragraphs, correcting incorrect punctuation where appropriate.

Punctuating Long Quotations

Sample Paragraph:

1. To sum up, the protagonists of both <u>A Jest of God</u> and <u>The Fire-Dwellers</u> struggle with mother-daughter relationships, but only Rachel resolves her situation. **2.** Rachel comes to self-realization by understanding her relationship with her mother

> It isn't up to me. It never was. I can take care, but only some.
>
> I'm not responsible for keeping her alive (<u>Jest of God</u> 195).

3. Rachel does not reconcile with her mother, but in this passage she comes to understand the degree to which she is responsible for her, and thus sets herself free from some obligations. **4.** In <u>The Fire-Dwellers</u>, Stacey also reconciles with her daughter, Katie, but the revised relationship is still restricting. **5.** Consider this passage:

> Katie, I'm sorry. I guess I didn't hear. I only heard what was pertinent to you
>
> or what I imagined to be pertinent to you. (<u>Fire-Dwellers</u> 270)

6. Stacey's reconciliation still involves trying to be a good mother, so she is still attempting to conform to traditional expectations of a mother-daughter relationship.

Exercise One:

At the beginning of <u>Northanger Abbey</u>, Catherine is clearly shown to be in a state of naiveté. She is presented as everything but moronic

> "She never could learn or understand anything before she was taught; and
> sometimes not even then, for she was often inattentive, and occasionally stupid.
> Her mother was three months in teaching her only to repeat the "Beggar's
> Petition" . . . not that Catherine was always stupid—by no means." (38)

Catherine should not be condemned for her ignorance, however. As Austen tells the reader: "her mind was about as ignorant and uninformed as the female mind at seventeen usually is (41)".

Exercise Two:

The poem "Trees at the Arctic Circle" reflects Purdy's view of Canada. At first, Purdy is scornful of the eighteen-inch trees. He thinks of them as "coward trees" (<u>North of Summer</u> 29) in comparison to Douglas firs and feels contempt for them. However, at the close of the poem, Purdy recognizes that the trees are not cowardly. Rather:

> They have about three months
> to ensure that the species does not die
> and that's how they spend their time
>
> . . .
>
> just digging in here and now.
>
> (<u>North of Summer</u> 29)

The parallels between the trees in the poem and the Canadian-American situation are obvious.

Punctuating Long Quotations: Sample Paragraph Discussion

This sample passage contains two long or block quotations. Let's consider how effectively the quotations are punctuated by looking at opening, internal, and closing punctuation.

Opening Punctuation

Both quotations have a sufficient number of signal words to introduce the quotation. In the first, we recognize that the quotation reflects Rachel's thought about her mother. In the second, Sentence Four lets the reader know that the quotation should establish some proof that the new relationship Stacey has developed is restricting, and Sentence Five directs us toward the passage where evidence for the claim is found.

The first quotation, however, is punctuated poorly. The introductory words and the quotation cannot flow together (the introductory words form an independent clause), so the reader needs a punctuation mark that indicates a stop: a colon is required. The colon introducing the second quotation works quite well.

You will also notice that the spacing around the block quotations is incorrect. A single-spaced block quotation should be set off from the text by a double-space, both at the beginning and at the end of the quotation.

Internal Punctuation

No internal punctuation is necessary in these quotations. To test your knowledge of internal punctuation of block quotations, try Exercises One and Two.

Closing Punctuation

In the first quotation, the punctuation is inappropriate. The parenthetical reference (*Jest of God* 195) should be placed outside the period, not inside. The second quotation illustrates proper form for closing punctuation.

The corrected paragraph looks like this:

> To sum up, the protagonists of both A Jest of God and The Fire-Dwellers struggle with mother-daughter relationships, but only Rachel resolves her situation. Rachel comes to self-realization by understanding her relationship with her mother:
>
> > It isn't up to me. It never was. I can take care, but only some.
> > I'm not responsible for keeping her alive. (Jest of God 195)
>
> Rachel does not reconcile with her mother, but in this passage she comes to understand the degree to which she is responsible for her, and thus sets herself free from some obligations. In The Fire-Dwellers, Stacey also reconciles with her daughter, Katie, but the revised relationship is still restricting. Consider this passage:
>
> > Katie, I'm sorry. I guess I didn't hear. I only heard what was pertinent to you or what I imagined to be pertinent to you. (Fire-Dwellers 270)
>
> Stacey's reconciliation still involves trying to be a good mother, so she is still attempting to conform to traditional expectations of a mother-daughter relationship.

Revise the two exercise paragraphs, correcting the punctuation of the quotations where necessary.

Writers love words. They love the sound of words like concatenation, funicular, golden, and shining. They love the look of words, the graphic symmetry of words like murmur, pip, thrush, and wallow. They love to play with words, to stretch and shrink a word's meaning in the pursuit of humour or poetry or truth. But most of all, writers love to choose words, to browse through their memories in search of that perfect word—the word whose meaning exactly matches thought, whose choice will seem appropriate and natural to readers, and whose effect is evocative and artistic. These, then, are the three considerations of word choice, of diction: accuracy, propriety, and efficacy.

Choosing Accurate Words

With more than a half million English words to choose from, it is likely that every writer will make an inaccurate word choice at some time. In fact, it is a great tribute to the flexibility of the English language that writing is not consistently misunderstood. In general, writers select wrong words in three different circumstances. They may confuse words that sound the same but are different in meaning (homonyms like *flare* and *flair*), and ones that sound similar but are dissimilar in meaning (near homonyms like *applicable* and *explicable*). They may interchange words that are nearly synonymous: *accuracy* and *truth*. And they may confuse words that are technically synonymous but that suggest or imply different things: *rot* and *decompose*. This section will deal with each of these tendencies in turn, with confusing homonyms and near homonyms, with mixing words whose denotations are nearly synonymous, and with using words having inaccurate implications, in other words, inaccurate connotations.

HOMONYMS AND NEAR HOMONYMS

One group of words causes more markers to scribble "wrong word" in the margins of students' essays than any other: homonyms. Homonyms are words that sound the same but have different meanings, and spellings. When proofreading, check to see that you haven't, in a fit of absent-mindedness, confused homonymous words. Following is a list of the most frequently misused homonyms and near homonyms. (Near homonyms are words with different meanings and only slightly different sounds, like *than* and *then*.) The proper usage of these and other homonyms or near homonyms is untangled in the glossary.

Homonyms and Near Homonyms	Remembering the Difference (Mnemonic Tricks)
Accept is a verb meaning to acquire. *Except* is a verb meaning to exclude.	Remember that *except* can *exclude* or *x* out something.
Affect is usually a verb meaning to influence. *Effect* is usually a noun meaning result, but may be a verb meaning to cause.	Remember that *affect*, which starts with *a* usually denotes an *action*.
Its is the possessive form of it. *It's* is the contraction of it is.	Remember to read *it is* when you see *it's*.

Principal usually means chief and is used either as an adjective or, in the case of a school principal, as a noun. As a noun, it can also mean an amount of money on which interest is earned or paid.
Principle is a noun meaning a basic truth or belief.

Remember that the *chief* is your *pal*.

Than is used when making a comparison.
Then is an adverb meaning at that time, next, or in addition.

Remember that *then* can tell us *when*.

Their is the possessive form of they.
There is used either as an adverb meaning in or at that place or in an expletive phrase such as "There is a cat."
They're is the contraction of they are.

Remember that *there* contains *here* and refers to a place, and that *they're* reads *they are*.

To is a preposition meaning the opposite of from, or it is part of an infinitive (e.g., to go, to finish).
Too is an adverb meaning in addition, excessively, or extremely.
Two is an adjective or noun meaning the number 2.

Remember that there are always *two twins*, both words containing a *w*. Also, remember that *too,* meaning in addition or excessively, has an additional or excessive *o.*

Your is the possessive form of you.
You're is the contraction of you are.

Remember to read *you are* for *you're*.

Weather is used to refer to the climate.
Whether is used to introduce an alternative.

Remember that *whether* implies a choice and sports an *h* after the first *w* like *which,* another word useful in describing a choice. Also, *weather* contains the letters *eat* which appear in the word *heat*, another word relating to the climate.

Whose is the possessive form of who or which.
Who's is the contraction of who is or who has.

Remember to read *who is* or *who has* for *who's*.

It is impossible to list all the homonyms or near homonyms that bewilder word searchers. Each writer should make a personal list of words that have caused confusion in the past and develop strategies for remembering how these words are different. Even after a writer has done this, the quest for accuracy is not complete.

DENOTATION

Words that have similar sounds but dissimilar meanings are not the only perils awaiting those in pursuit of exact diction. Words completely unalike in sound but alike in meaning are also hazardous. The danger in selecting from a group of such words lies in the various and divergent shades of meaning each is capable of expressing, in the fact that, while listed as synonyms in a dictionary or thesaurus, these words are seldom completely synonymous. To avoid misusing nearly synonymous words, examine dictionary entries carefully to determine all the possible denotations a word can have.

The denotation of a word is its precise definition, the particular person, object, concept, sensation, feeling, act, or condition a word names. Dictionaries catalogue the denotations of words. Each dictionary entry usually lists multiple definitions of a word, as well as numerous contexts in which it is possible to use this word to denote or indicate a certain meaning. That an English word can denote many things at once allows for the creation of powerful poetry and prose. Since it embraces multifarious meanings, one single word carefully chosen can charm and convince many different readers. As Joseph Conrad wrote, "He who wants to persuade should put his trust not in the right argument, but in the right word. . . ."[1] Although a word can indicate a variety of meanings to a variety of people, it cannot mean all things to all people; freedom does not equal licence. Writers must accept the responsibility of deciding how much a word can denote before it means so much that it means nothing. Shakespeare, a master of word play, warns that those who "dally nicely with words may quickly make them wanton."[2] It is important, then, to recognize in which circumstances one word may be substituted for another having a synonymous or nearly synonymous denotation. *Awe* and *fear* are described as synonyms in a thesaurus because both denote an overwhelming and distressing emotion. However, a careful writer wouldn't substitute one word for the other in all situations.

Let's examine another word and its possible alternates more carefully. *Dry* can mean indifferent, cold, or unemotional when used in some contexts: *Canadians, being reserved, are often thought excessively dry by their more exuberant American neighbours. Dry* can also mean not sweet: *Chablis is a dry white Burgundy which sells well in Europe because Europeans like dry wine.* In the first circumstance, *cold* or *unemotional* could be used in place of *dry: Canadians, being reserved, are often thought excessively cold or unemotional by their more exuberant American neighbours.* Confusion would result, however, if a writer used *unemotional* or *cold* as synonymous with *dry* when referring to wine: *Chablis is an unemotional white Burgundy which sells well in Europe because Europeans like cold wine.*

---

[1] Joseph Conrad, "A Familiar Preface," *A Personal Record: Some Reminiscences* (London: Dent, 1912) xi.

[2] William Shakespeare, *Twelfth Night* 3.1.16-18.

Although a writer would not normally mistake the contexts in which *dry* is synonymous with *cold*, many inaccurate word choices do occur when words that are synonymous only in particular circumstances are used interchangeably in others. Academic writers must be especially vigilant about making such mistakes because one word may denote one thing to the general reading public and quite another to a professor. While *insurrection, rebellion,* and *revolution* are often used interchangeably by the press to mean acts of resistance against constituted authority, these words have different denotations and using them as synonyms in a politics essay would let loose a flood of red pencil marks. To confuse things even further, one word may denote different things to professors in different fields of study. For example, the simple word *cell* might mean a device for producing electrolysis to a physical chemist, a structural unit of plant and animal life to a biologist, or a small group acting within a larger organization to a political historian.

While the glossary lists words in the general vocabulary which writers frequently misuse, it cannot begin to cover the discipline-specific denotations of a word like *realism, irony, alienation,* or *peripheral.* When writing for a particular discipline, therefore, consult dictionaries and encyclopedias written to explain the terminology of that discipline. Also, when searching your brain or any dictionary or thesaurus for synonyms, pay close attention to the range of denotations each word has and to the contexts in which a particular denotation will be understood.

Writing Prompt

Write a sentence in which the paired words could be interchanged without significantly altering the sentence's meaning and another in which they could not. Use a dictionary.

stoical/stolid	peculiar/unique
obdurate/hardened	remark/notice
peruse/survey	destitute/poor
suspicion/suggestion	faithful/staunch
groundless/false	ponder/wonder

✔   ✔   ✔

Revising Considering Homonyms and Denotations

Sample Paragraph:

1. While the hypothesis that ecological diversity parallels ecological stability has been generally excepted for sometime, mathematical models supportive of this theory first gained fame in the 1950s. **2.** During that decade, McCarther introduced a mathematical model that defined community stability in terms of quantifiable trophic diversity. **3.** His study was the beginning of many attempts to apply mathematical models to communities in order to find empirical evidence for the stability-diversity hypothesis. **4.** Many of these mathematical models were fixated on proving or refuting two suppositions specially: one, that agro-ecosystems are less stable than natural ecosystems because man-made monoculture is more vulnerable to diseases and to pestilence, being less divers; and two, that tropical ecosystems are more stable than temperate ecosystems.

Exercise One:

There have been both biological and cultural differences among men and women since the growth of *homo sapiens*. Cultural differences are easy to document and readily apprehended after an examination of the cannons of Western civilization. In Western literature and philosophy, women have been accorded unequal status. According to the Christian principals enunciated in the Bible, a man was the first human created, and a woman was constituted from this man's rib. In other words, men are preponderant to women. Because men have been considered superior to women for so long, it is strenuous to pinpoint the exact biological dissensions between the sexes. Take the concept of strength, for example. While it is possible to investigate weather it is men or women who are generally more capable of lifting heavy weights, this definition of strength favours the biological capabilities of men. Women would receive a higher ranking in tests of strength predicated on the base of endurance rather than on the ability to lift. Put simply, a woman's capabilities are not measured in equilibrium to a man's because of traditional beliefs about woman's inferiority.

Exercise Two:

In "The Garden," Marvell attempts to show the precedence of the natural over the civil. To demonstrate this elevation of the life of nature, Marvell uses description and images to contrast two peculiar societies. He exploits appropriate words to differentiate between the busy, hustling world of society and the solitary, tranquil world of the garden. Even more creatively, Marvell changes mythology in order to associate solitude more closely with the natural state of man. No Eve is present in Marvell's Eden. The poem follows a cyclical image, one that can be contrasted with the cycle of nature's seasons. At the end of this cycle, the reader is returned to the conflicting images that began the poem, to the conflict between the busy world and the tranquil world. However, Marvell does not try to effect the reader's choice regarding which world is more desirable by being dogmatic and proscriptive. Rather the decision to except his elevation of one world over the other is left to each individual reader.

Revising Considering Homonyms and Denotations: Sample Paragraph Discussion

The sample paragraph typifies the writing of students who have trouble choosing words accurately; it shows a writer using complicated, discipline-specific terminology correctly while misusing simple common words.

A good way to begin revising this paragraph (or any other) for accurate word choice is to read it aloud, making sure to pronounce all words precisely. One way to encourage an exact reading is to read sentence by sentence from the end to the beginning of the paragraph. Doing this helps us to read what is written by making it difficult to gauge the context in which each sentence appears, thus preventing us from substituting the words the writer meant to write for the words he or she actually wrote. Reading a piece of writing aloud from the finish to the start is particularly useful for catching errors made through the confusion of homonyms and near homonyms.

Homonyms and Near Homonyms

Let us begin, then, with the last sentence of the paragraph so that we may catch errors more easily. When Sentence Four is read aloud, two words seem inaccurate: *specially* and *divers*.

Specially is pronounced spesh′əl ē and makes us think of the adjective *special*, which means *distinctive*. Change the word *specially* to *distinctively*. Does this substitution work? Do you think that the writer wanted to say that the mathematical models tried to prove or refute two suppositions in a distinctive way? Probably not, given the list that follows the colon. In this case, a more accurate word would be *especially* (pronounced e spesh′əl, ē), meaning *particularly*. Because the phrase *suppositions especially* sounds a little like a tongue twister, it would be even better to substitute *in particular* rather than *especially* for the word *specially*.

The word *divers* (pronounced dī′vərz) is usually used to mean *several*. In this case, the writer probably meant to use the word *diverse* (pronounced də vʉrs′), which means *different*. Here is a partial revision of Sentence Four:

> Many of these mathematical models were fixated on proving or refuting two suppositions in particular: one, that agro-ecosystems are less stable than natural ecosystems because man-made monoculture is more vulnerable to diseases and to pestilence, being less diverse; and two, that tropical ecosystems are more stable than temperate ecosystems.

When we read Sentence Three and Sentence Two aloud, neither appears to contain any wrong words. Two words catch our attention in Sentence One, however: *excepted* and *sometime*.

Excepted is pronounced *ek sept′ed* and means *excluded*. This isn't the meaning required. The writer should have written the word *accepted*, which is pronounced *ak sept′ed* and which means *agreed to*.

The imprecision of the second word (*sometime*) is more difficult to hear; the reader would have to make a distinction between the pronunciation of the word *sometime* and the words *some time*. *Sometime* means *once* and the words *some time* mean *an indeterminate amount of time*. Of course, the writer of this sentence means *for an indeterminate amount of time*, not *for once*. Here is a partial revision of Sentence One:

> While the hypothesis that ecological diversity parallels ecological stability has been generally accepted for some time, mathematical models supportive of this theory first gained fame in the 1950s.

There are still inaccurate words in the sample paragraph. We have not searched for and revised words that, in certain contexts, have synonymous denotations but that should not have been considered synonymous in the context of this paragraph.

Denotation

Denotation can only be recognized in context, so this time we will work through the sentences of the paragraph in chronological order. The first word of Sentence One poses a problem: do the words *while* and *although* have the same denotation? In some circumstances, these words are synonymous and can be used interchangeably: *while* (meaning *at the same time as*) could be used instead of *although* (meaning *for all that*) in the following sentence, for example. *Although (While) I admired her eloquence, I disliked her verbosity.* In Sentence One, however, the more accurate word is *although* because one cannot substitute the phrase *at the same time as* for the word *while*.

There is another word choice problem in Sentence One: the word *fame* is used to describe what mathematical models achieved in the 1950s. *Fame* means *the state of being widely noticed and recognized,* in other words, *the state of being renowned.* Do you think these mathematical models became renowned? Another word denoting the *state of being noticed and recognized* is *recognition.* This word is more accurate. Here is one possible revision of Sentence One:

> Although the hypothesis that ecological diversity parallels ecological stability has been generally accepted for some time, mathematical models supportive of this theory first gained recognition in the 1950s.

The other instance in which two words with similar denotations are confused is in Sentence Four. Although the word *fixated* can mean *concentrated,* it usually denotes *being obsessively concentrated.* The mathematical models in question probably did not have an obsessive preoccupation with the proof or refutation of two suppositions. They probably <u>concentrated on</u> proving or refuting these suppositions. Better still, they probably <u>were created to prove or refute</u> these suppositions. Here is Sentence Four revised:

> Many of these mathematical models were created to prove or refute two suppositions in particular: one, that agro-ecosystems are less stable than natural ecosystems because man-made monoculture is more vulnerable to diseases and to pestilence, being less diverse; and two, that tropical ecosystems are more stable than temperate ecosystems.

Here is one revision of the whole paragraph:

> Although the hypothesis that ecological diversity parallels ecological stability has been generally accepted for some time, mathematical models supportive of this theory first gained recognition in the 1950s. During that decade, McCarther introduced a mathematical model that defined community stability in terms of quantifiable trophic diversity. His study was the beginning of many attempts to apply mathematical models to communities in order to find empirical evidence for the stability-diversity hypothesis. Many of these mathematical models were created to prove or refute two suppositions in particular: one, that agro-ecosystems are less stable than natural ecosystems because man-made monoculture is more vulnerable to diseases and to pestilence, being less diverse; and two, that tropical ecosystems are more stable than temperate ecosystems.

Work through the two exercise paragraphs considering all words carefully. Look first for homonym or near homonym errors and revise these accordingly. Then think about word choice in terms of denotation. Use a dictionary to ensure that all words chosen are accurate. Where it is necessary, revise to improve denotation.

CONNOTATION

Just as a word denotes more than its constituent letters, it expresses more than its numerous denotations. Words not only have denotations or definitions, but also connotations or associations. When I write the word *home*, it calls forth a myriad of mental images. One reader might associate *home* with *hearth* and imagine a cosy fire casting honeyed light into the corners of a room at dusk. Another might recall waking up to the smells and sounds of an early morning breakfast. The point is that words, like smells, sounds, and sights, have the power to summon ideas and emotions not directly expressed by them. And a writer can use the correct word as a sorcerer uses an incantation, to conjure up the shadow world of suggestion.

An awareness of the connotative ability of words is essential to accurate word choice. Writers who choose words that imply as well as declare more readily convince. In the following passage, Farley Mowat, arguing that the North is not a lifeless land, uses words that denote and connote procreation, plenty, and permanence.

> Birds *breed* almost *everywhere*. Mammals of *many* species, ranging from *squat, rotund* lemmings to *massive* muskox *occupy* the *lands*. The *seas* are *home* to whales, seals, *obese* walrus and *sinuous* white bears. The *seas* are also *rich* in fishes as are the *numberless* inland lakes. For those with eyes to see, the North is *vitally* and *vividly alive*. *Long, long ago,* men of other races out of another *time* recognized this truth and learned to call the northern regions "*home*."[3]

While this passage explicitly expresses the idea that the North is teeming with life, it also implies, through the selection of modifiers with connotative power, that this life is stable and enduring. The words *squat, rotund, massive, obese,* and *sinuous* suggest that those who have occupied these *lands* since a *time long, long ago* will not be easily removed from their *home*.

There is another reason why writers should pay attention to a word's connotations. Choosing a word whose connotations oppose the writer's purpose undermines meaning. For example, selecting the word *home* when you want to describe a cold, unfriendly habitat would elicit the wrong responses in a reader. In this instance, the connotative ability of the word *home* works against your meaning by suggesting a warm, friendly dwelling place.

---

[3] Farley Mowat, *Canada North* (Toronto: McClelland and Stewart, 1967) 27.

Learning Prompt

Rank the words in the following groups as having positive, negative, or neutral connotations. Be prepared to explain and defend your rankings to others. Next, compare your findings with those of others. Are there similarities that point to commonly held ideas about the connotations of these words? In collaboration with others, rank the words a second time. Then, compare the group's ranking with any information concerning the connotations of these words that you can find in dictionaries. If you are working alone, compare your subjective ranking of these words with a dictionary's description of their denotation and connotation.

1) guilt/blame/culpability/fault/ onus/responsibility
2) crazed/demented/lunatic/un- balanced/unsound/deranged/ disturbed
3) categorize/sort/classify/group/ pigeon-hole/label/discriminate
4) pile/heap/mass/stack/mound/ hoard/collection/accumulation/ aggregation/jumble/load
5) harmless/innocuous/innocent/ nontoxic/inoffensive/innoxious /safe
6) revive/renew/resuscitate/ revivify/resurrect/rekindle/ reactivate
7) surrogate/substitute/alternate/ backup/replacement/stand-in
8) inconclusive/open/uncertain/ undecided/indecisive/unsettled
9) conflicting/disconsonant/ discordant/incongruent/dis- sonant/incompatible/incon- sonant
10) absent-minded/bemused/pre- occupied/inconscient/heedless/ abstracted/inattentive
11) pure/unadulterated/unmiti- gated/utter/absolute/sheer/ perfect/plain
12) definite/circumscribed/ determinate/limited/precise/ narrow/restricted/fixed

Think about the words *understanding, agreement, bargain, deal,* and *pact.* All five words have similar denotations; all can mean an arrangement that is accepted by all parties. Yet all have different connotations. *Understanding* makes me think of familiarity and tolerance. I imagine all parties to an arrangement knowing and accepting one another's concerns. For me, this word has positive connotations. *Agreement* makes me think of agreeable things, of an arrangement that is to the liking of all. It also has a positive connotation. *Bargain,* on the other hand, is associated with the concept of haggling and of cheapness. The word may be said to have a positive connotation when it is used in the context of getting a bargain. In the context of striking a bargain, however, the word's connotation is less positive since it suggests the give and take of a fist fight rather than the agreement and harmony of a consensus. *Deal* sounds even less agreeable than *bargain.* People who wheel and deal meet in back rooms to concoct underhanded arrangements with the purpose of delivering raw deals to those not privy to these discussions. And what about *pact*? While *pact* once had a neutral connotation, it now evokes images of soul-selling, of making an agreement with the devil. For me, *pact* has a very negative connotation.

If I had to rank each of these words according to whether its connotation was positive or negative, I would order them, from most positive to most negative, as follows: understanding, agreement, bargain, deal, pact. Your arrangement might differ. However, there would probably be some similarities. Because of these similarities, because some of the connotations of some words are widely accepted, writers can mistakenly use a word whose connotation undermines its denotation. They can err by using the word *agreement* when they mean to describe a behind-the-stairs *deal.* Watch for words having connotations that undercut meaning. Don't use *model* to mean *a bad example* or *quell* to mean *crush.*

Slanted Language

Before leaving our discussion of connotation, we must deal with one other misuse of the connotative power of words: writing slanted, exaggerated prose. While academic writers may legitimately use words whose connotations add texture, weight, and depth to their arguments, they must try to avoid a dependence upon implication and suggestion, upon the ability of certain words to call forth certain responses. Choosing a word whose connotations are too strong or too immoderate to communicate effectively produces prose that is unconvincing because it is manipulative rather than expressive.

Avoiding slanted language is difficult because there is a fine line between exaggeration and emphasis. What seems overdrawn to one person appears compellingly delineated to another. As Goebbels recognized, the big lie is often mistaken for eloquent truth.

One way of recognizing slanted diction is that it suggests more than it explains. Look for sentences and words that play on the emotions. Ask yourself if there is enough proof or logical argument in a passage to justify the sorts of words used. Since we usually write slanted prose when excited to anger or to joy, look for writers whose outrage or enthusiasm seems disproportionate to their exposition, for those who find everything deplorable and those who are perpetual enthusiasts. Both err in the same way; they do not choose words that allow for understanding. By choosing loaded words, they arrest analysis.

Notes

My writing strengths:

Things I need to remember:

Things I need to check:

Revising Disproportionate and Slanted Language

Sample Paragraph:

1. Technically, the poem is a masterpiece: the most original, economical, labour of love created in the century. **2.** Just as children's hearts revel uncomprehendingly in the sing-song of nursery rhymes, so too is the reader swept away by Hopkins's love affair with words. **3.** From the initial reading, the reader is dancing to the sound, gracefully waltzing to the melodious, harmonious music woven with such consummate artistry. **4.** Hearts soar, glide, and dive with the falcon's flight. **5.** From beginning to end, Hopkins serves up a feast of wondrous words calling forth the sound of flight. **6.** However, it is in his exceptionally original, peerless use of rhythm that Hopkins masterfully weaves his illusion. **7.** Like the titled subject of the work, the poem offers a constantly changing pattern of flight.

Exercise One:

In the period beginning with the leaked documents outlining Carter's coal conversion plans and continuing into the environmental dark ages of the opportunistic Reagan Administration, two things became abundantly clear: the astonishing level of American ignorance regarding acid rain and the complete indifference accorded to this grave issue by the reactionary, money-mad ultra-conservatives of the Reagan Administration. Of the four-fifths of Canadians who know about acid rain, ninety per cent feel the problem is serious; on the other hand, a staggering eighty per cent of Americans are completely oblivious even to the simple fact that their country produces acid rain. It has been noted that Americans, once believers, are completely unreasonable. They hold on to the most ludicrous fabrications with the tenacity of a fractious Peter Pan, refusing to grow up. One shared fairy-tale worthy of a Disney movie is that the United States leads the way with the toughest environmental legislation in the world. All who have tried to remove the rose-coloured glasses which miraculously blind American citizens to smog and acid rain, Canadians included, have been viciously slandered by being labelled anti-American communists or outright liars.

Exercise Two:

What Mary Wollstonecraft demonstrates ably and eloquently in Vindication of the Rights of Women is that men, being lazy louts unwilling to work at anything unless pestered or coerced, become married to slavish women who endure their husbands' idleness without a murmur of complaint. Men call this bondage love and the vassals they attach to themselves virtuous wives. While virtue in a wife may mean passivity and powerlessness, it does not mean indolence. These frail faultless wives are forced to work hard at pleasing and serving their lordly, domineering husbands. To conclude, Wollstonecraft amply proves that a man does not marry a woman because of what she is, but because of what she will let him get away with.

Revising Disproportionate and Slanted Language: Sample Paragraph Discussion

When trying to eliminate slanted language, put aside your knowledge of the topic under discussion; what matters is not whether you know the writer to be correct or incorrect, but whether he or she has used loaded language. It follows that, although you might agree with the writer of the sample paragraph, although you might think Gerard Manley Hopkins's poem "Windhover" a technical masterpiece, you can only judge and revise the paragraph on the basis of what has been written.

What has been written in the sample paragraph? Other than a glowing recommendation of Hopkins, not much. The enthusiastic praise of Hopkins masks not only a lack of proof for the series of statements made but also a lack of analysis of the poem in question. In fact, the reader is never told which of Hopkins's poems is worthy of such praise. In order to recognize when slanted language has been used, let's strip the paragraph down to its bones. Let's try to determine the main point of each sentence.

The main point of Sentence One is that the poem is a technical masterpiece. Most of the information imparted after the semicolon is secondary to the purpose of the paragraph; the writer doesn't continue by comparing Hopkins's poem with those of other nineteenth-century poets or by discussing the poem's economy or creation. The originality of Hopkins's use of rhythm is mentioned again, but the writer doesn't tell why this use of rhythm should be considered original. One possible revision follows:

> Technically, the poem is a masterpiece.

The main point of Sentence Two is difficult to see. The writer links Hopkins's love affair with words to children's appreciation of nursery rhymes, which is characterized as uncomprehending. The sentence seems to say that Hopkins is more concerned with the sound and rhythm of words than with their sense. Here is a revision:

> The sound and rhythm of Hopkins's words appeal to the senses the way the sing-song words of nursery rhymes appeal to children who have no idea of their meanings.

There doesn't seem to be any point to the next sentence except perhaps that the poem's effect can be likened to that of music. Likewise, the only point of worth in both Sentence Four and Sentence Five is that the poem's words emulate the sound of a falcon's flight. We will just note these two points briefly in our revision:

> This poem's effect is similar to that of music. Its words sound like a falcon's flight.

Once the verbiage of the next two sentences has been eliminated, we can see that they concern Hopkins's original rhythms, which emulate the changing pattern of flight:

> Hopkins's original rhythms emulate the changing pattern of flight.

Now let's see what is left:

> Technically, the poem is a masterpiece. The sound and rhythm of Hopkins's words appeal to the senses the way the sing-song words of nursery rhymes appeal to children who have no idea of their meanings. The poem's effect is similar to that of music. Its words sound like a falcon's flight. Hopkins's original rhythms emulate the changing pattern of flight.

Of course, the revised paragraph is not better. However, having created it, we can now see how little the original paragraph actually meant. We can also make some guesses as to how the meaning of the original might be expanded. How was the poem original? How was it economical? The writer might have meant that the poem's rhythms were original and that its words, being onomatopoeic, were economical. We can only guess as to how the poem's rhythms were original. Did the writer mean to discuss "sprung rhythm" or what Hopkins called "counterpoint"? Perhaps onomatopoeic words were not the only reason this writer considered the poem economical. Maybe the writer wanted to examine Hopkins's concept of "passionate condensation."

The examination of the effects of the poem might also have been expanded. What connections can be made between the way the poem affects readers, the way nursery rhymes affect children, and the way music affects listeners?

Two other ideas should be connected, the ideas expressed in Sentences Four and Five of the revised paragraph: *Both the sound of Hopkins's words and the original rhythm Hopkins uses emulate the sound and changing pattern of a falcon's flight.* In other words, is the poem's design uniquely suited to its theme, achieving the stylistic quality Hopkins called "inscape"?

You may respond to the preceding questions by thinking that you cannot answer them. Of course, without some knowledge of Hopkins, of the poem, or of the mind of the writer of the sample paragraph, no accurate revision is possible. In your own writing, however, you will be able to pose similar questions and improve your writing by adding concrete details and explanations.

For now, let's just tidy up our first revision attempt:

> Technically, the poem is a masterpiece. The sound and rhythm of Hopkins's words appeal to the senses the way the sing-song words of nursery rhymes appeal to children who have no idea of their meanings. In this regard, the poem's appeal is similar to that of music. Hopkins uses words and original rhythms that emulate the sound and changing pattern of a falcon's flight.

Strip away the excessively condemnatory language of the two exercise paragraphs. What information remains? What argument? Revise these paragraphs so that the language of each is appropriately objective for an academic audience. Remember, you do not need to eliminate all words that have negative or positive connotations. Your revised paragraph should still be lively, but it should be fair.

GENERAL AND SPECIFIC/ABSTRACT AND CONCRETE WORDS

Just as words can be arranged along a spectrum of connotation, ranging from very positive to extremely negative, they also can vary in terms of abstraction and concreteness and of generality and specificity. Let's consider the generality/specificity spectrum first. Think of the word *spectrum* itself. As a series of colours, the word *spectrum* is more general than the word *colour*. However, *colour* is still quite a general word; we can all, for example, think of specific colours that would offer a more detailed description of a sunset than the word *colourful*. *Red* might suffice, but perhaps *crimson*, an even more specific shade of red, would be more precise.

The abstract/concrete spectrum works much the same way. Abstract words name concepts, thoughts that are in some way separate from concrete, visible reality. Concrete words, on the other hand, frequently denote solid, perceptible objects. For example, if I wrote to tell you that I had just bought a Harley-Davidson, you would be able to picture it, and if you came to visit, you could ride it. Like the word *motorcycle*, the proper noun *Harley-Davidson* symbolizes an actual object. If, however, I wrote to say that I had purchased a new form of transportation, no concrete thing would be brought to your mind, and *transportation* is a lot harder to ride than a *motorcycle*. The noun *motorcycle* is concrete while the noun *transportation* is abstract.

As you might have guessed, the two spectrums often overlap. *Motorcycle* is also more specific than *transportation*. However, you will have noticed that there are degrees of specificity among concrete words, that while a *Harley-Davidson* is no more concrete than a *motorcycle*, it is more specific.

Obviously, accuracy means more than correctness; it means precision. While it might be correct to say that a particular sunset displayed the colours of the spectrum, or was colourful, or red, or crimson, accuracy demands choosing the word most suited to the circumstances, be that word general or specific. Academic prose needs a mixture of specific and general and concrete and abstract words. A writer who expresses only abstract generalities is open to accusations of vagueness while one who writes using only specific, concrete words risks not being able to communicate any thought or argument, not being able to describe or consider the forest because of being too concerned with portraying the trees.

Certain academic writing tasks seem to call forth prose that is either overly general or overly specific. Many philosophy students, for example, have complained that a philosophy essay demands the use of abstract, general words. Although there is truth in this, it is also true that philosophers use concrete analogies, allegorical stories, and parables to convey their messages. And if philosophy students think about the philosophical texts they have read, they will probably realize that, most often, they have come to an understanding of a complex, abstract idea through a concrete exemplification of this idea rather than through its direct expression. Look at the mixture of concrete and abstract and specific and general words in the following passage, taken from David Hume's An Inquiry Concerning Human Understanding.

Learning Prompt

Using each of the eight words in the first list as starting points, provide eight series of associated words moving from the specific or concrete to the general or abstract. Reverse the process for the words in the second list; move from the general or abstract to the specific or concrete.

1) **Lake Ontario**
   maple tree
   Atwood and Laurence
   cocker spaniel
   a slice of cake
   the Free Trade Agreement
   aspirin
   to launch

2) **religion**
   to move
   an environmental issue
   to say
   art
   education
   to act
   normal

I shall venture to affirm, as a general proposition which admits of no exception, that the knowledge of this relation [between cause and effect] is not, in any instance, attained by reasonings *a priori,* but arises entirely from experience, when we find that any particular objects are constantly conjoined with each other. Let an object be presented to a man of ever so strong natural reason and abilities—if that object be entirely new to him, he will not be able, by the most accurate examination of its sensible qualities, to discover any of its causes or effects. Adam, though his rational faculties be supposed, at the very first, entirely perfect, could not have inferred from the fluidity and transparency of water that it would suffocate him, or from the light and warmth of fire that it would consume him.[4]

In this passage, Hume commences with very general, abstract language in the first sentence—*knowledge of this relation, arises entirely from experience*—when he is introducing his topic. However, as he explains this idea, his terms become more specific. A man is introduced, and the abstract concept of cause and effect is elaborated in the concrete and specific example of the dangers of water and fire.

While philosophy students claim that they need to write in generalities, science students say that they need to abjure all generalizations. Unfortunately, as any philosopher will tell you, this is impossible. All thought and language is abstraction, generalization. Relative to the philosophy paper, however, the science paper should probably contain more concrete, specific words. Yet a compilation of statistics, details, "facts" is not an essay, or even a report. Some summary, inference, or hypothesis, some generalization, must be included. The science writer who produced the following passage knew this.

Our difficulties in understanding or effectuating communication with other animals may arise from our reluctance to grasp unfamiliar ways of dealing with the world. For example, dolphins and whales, who sense their surroundings with a quite elaborate sonar echo location technique, also communicate with each other by a rich and elaborate set of clicks, whose interpretation has so far eluded human attempts to understand it. One very clever recent suggestion, which is now being investigated, is that dolphin/dolphin communication involves a re-creation of the sonar reflection characteristics of the objects being described. In this view a dolphin does not "say" a single word for shark, but rather transmits a set of clicks corresponding to the audio reflection spectrum it would obtain on irradiating a shark with sound waves in the dolphin's sonar mode. The basic form of dolphin/dolphin communication in this view would be a sort of aural onomatopoeia, a drawing of audio frequency pictures—in this case, caricatures of a shark.[5]

---

[4] David Hume, *An Inquiry Concerning Human Understanding* (New York: Bobbs-Merrill, 1955) 42.

[5] Carl Sagan, *The Dragons of Eden: Speculations on the Evolution of Human Intelligence* (New York: Ballantine, 1977) 113-114n.

Although the content is quite different, Sagan's paragraph follows much the same pattern as did the passage from Hume. The opening sentence uses general words (*communication, animals, reluctance, unfamiliar ways*). As Sagan develops his idea, his language becomes much more concrete (*sonar echo, dolphins, elaborate set of clicks*). Sagan closes, however, by moving toward slightly more general language, thereby helping the reader to pull the concrete, specific information together to form a general point.

Revising Considering General and Specific/Abstract and Concrete Words

Sample Paragraph:

1. Most nations are currently composed of different people. **2.** Canadians are particularly proud of their state's diversity. **3.** The Canadian nation encompasses individuals with divergent ethnic and cultural backgrounds. **4.** Because our governments have given official sanction to the policy of multiculturalism, our citizens are encouraged to preserve their heritage. **5.** In 1986, Toronto was home to 1,372,185 people whose mother tongue was English, 10,395 whose mother tongue was French, and 216,640 who were originally speakers of a language other than English or French. **6.** Statistics from the same year show that 15.7 per cent of Canada's people were foreign born.

Exercise One:

Some native women would trap rabbits and martens seasonally in order to trade them for beads and lace. Most, however, would prepare pemmican and collect berries and wild rice for white fur traders who, in return, would give them copper pots and kettles. Heating stones to add to bark cooking pots rapidly became unnecessary. Native women also prepared pelts. Mending the tents and clothes of fur traders was another of their tasks. They also provided moccasins and snowshoes for the men of the Hudson's Bay Company and the Northwest Company.

Exercise Two:

Pollution is one of the larger global problems and affects many aspects of our lives. The dictionary might define pollution as the state of being impure or unclean, or the process of reaching that state. However, in environmental terms, pollution is the term for a man-made phenomenon which is harmful to the environment. Pollution results from numerous things, many of which can be regulated or modified so that we can still enjoy the benefits of industrial society without suffering its consequences. We can and should control pollution by eliminating or at least severely reducing use.

Revising Considering General and Specific/Abstract and Concrete Words: Sample Paragraph Discussion

The writer of the sample paragraph has used a strange combination of general and specific and of abstract and concrete words. Over all, the first four sentences seem too general to introduce the last two adequately. Let's look at these sentences one by one.

Sentence One seems to be too vague to mean much of anything. Which nations are composed of different people? How are the individuals who compose a nation different? Are not all nations made up of individuals? Is not each individual different in some way from another? Since the focus of the paragraph seems to be the Canadian nation, which is composed of individuals from different ethnic and cultural backgrounds, Sentence One could be revised like this:

> Canada, like most nations, is composed of individuals from different ethnic and cultural backgrounds.

Sentence Two tells us that Canadians are proud of Canada's diversity. Which specific diversity makes Canadians proud? Regional diversity? Economic diversity? Presumably the writer means that Canadians are proud of the ethnic and cultural diversity of Canada's people. This raises another question: are all Canadians proud in this way? Probably not, considering recent battles over language rights. Here is a revision of Sentence Two:

> Many Canadians are proud of this ethnic and cultural diversity.

After the revision of Sentence One, Sentence Three is redundant. We can eliminate it.

Sentence Four does not adequately specify which governments have sanctioned the policy of multiculturalism. Does the writer mean that the federal government and all the provincial governments encourage this policy? From the statistics that follow in Sentences Five and Six, it would appear that the writer is focusing on the Ontario government and the federal government. This might have been what was meant:

> Because both the federal government and the Ontario government have given official sanction to the policy of multiculturalism, a large number of Canadian citizens have been encouraged to preserve their heritage.

Now there is a jump. What abstract ideas are suggested by the statistics given in Sentences Five and Six? Sentence Five implies that Toronto has a multilingual heritage, but doesn't say anything about the preservation of this heritage. Sentence Six tells us that a large percentage of Canadian citizens are immigrants. Perhaps this is the missing link. Maybe the writer wanted to say that many languages and cultures are represented in Canada because so many Canadians are immigrants.

Here is one, possibly far from perfect, revision of the whole paragraph:

> Canada, like most nations, is composed of individuals from different ethnic and cultural backgrounds. Many Canadians are proud of this ethnic and cultural diversity. Because both the federal government and the Ontario government have given official sanction to the policy of multiculturalism, a large number of Canadian citizens have been encouraged to preserve their heritage. There are many different languages and cultures to preserve. Toronto, for example, has a multilingual heritage. In 1986, Toronto was home to 1,372,185 people whose mother tongue was English, 10,395 whose mother tongue was French, and 216,640 who were originally speakers of a language other than English or French. Toronto's multilingual heritage is not surprising considering that statistics from the same year show that 15.7 per cent of Canada's people were foreign born.

Most writers would still be dissatisfied with this paragraph because, while the first three sentences discuss the abstract concept of multiculturalism, the sentences that follow make concrete statements, not about the abstraction multiculturalism, but about multilingualism. As a result, the paragraph seems to break down in the middle. Often, revising for more precise wording will point out faulty connections in your work which you will need to revise.

Work through Exercise One, which suffers from a lack of general, abstract diction, and Exercise Two, which suffers from a lack of specific, concrete diction. Notice that, in these paragraphs at least, revising for accurate diction necessitates re-thinking. Overly general or overly specific word choice, then, often indicates more than a stylistic problem. Feel free, as you revise, to add details and alter the paragraph to make it mean what you imagine the writer wanted it to mean.

Choosing Appropriate Words

As we have seen, accurate word choice is informed by the writer's purpose, that is, by the conceptual and emotional meanings a writer wants to convey. When choosing words for their appropriateness, a writer's focus shifts away from self and toward audience. The question becomes what sort of communication the reader will find acceptable rather than what the writer wants to communicate. In this light, choosing appropriate words can be seen as fine-tuning; the writer is already sending an accurate message, having selected meaningful words, but now is trying to eliminate static. To put this another way, the choice confronting a writer concerned with appropriateness is often between two words or phrases meaning essentially the same thing. Whether I choose to write *kind of a drag* or *fairly boring* does not affect my meaning so much as my tone. But as anyone who has trained dogs (or children) can tell you, tone is at least as important as sense.

Because appropriate diction is a concept defined by audience rather than by individual writer, it is difficult to explain. While glaring errors in suitability are as apparent as a man dressed in a bikini at the opera, it is as hard to describe what sort of prose fits each particular academic writing task as it is to clarify exactly what is meant by *dress casually*. To diplomats, casual dress might mean that neither black-ties nor evening gowns are required while among my friends, it means—*wear shoes*.

This being said, we must try to analyze the sort of diction generally accepted at Canadian high schools and universities. From the preceding analogies, it is obvious that one of the important determinants of acceptability involves level of formality. How dressed-up, how formal or informal should academic prose be? Other related questions must be answered as well. For example, what objectivity or subjectivity, what polite indirectness or direct impoliteness, what exclusiveness or inclusiveness is expected by our academic audience?

LEVEL OF FORMALITY

As stated, it is easier to identify inappropriately informal or formal diction than to define an appropriate level of formality. For this reason, we will first concentrate on prose that is either under-dressed or over-dressed in the hopes that a useful dress code will emerge.

We all use informal words to speak to one another. Most people, when confronted with an impertinent sales clerk, for example, would not say, "You are ostensibly one of the most officious individuals I have ever encountered." However, they might say, "You seem to be one of the biggest jerks I've ever met." Of course, transferring such informal language to academic prose is unfitting. You might want to tell your professor that a certain politician seems to be the biggest jerk alive, but a more formal, and a more analytical, description is necessary in an essay.

In an academic context, two categories of expression indicate inappropriately informal diction: slang and colloquialisms.

Obviously, slang says a great deal about culture. Write slang that corresponds to the following words. Can certain themes or images be discerned? Look for words having to do with food, drink, or dirt, for example. Do particular sounds seem to be associated with specific attributes? Can you categorize the slang you have written as that of a particular group or time? If so, what does this suggest about these groups and their histories?

lover	music
stupid	car
walk	idiot
inebriated	good
talk	bad
child	fashionable
parent	police officer
criminal	modern

Informal Words

SLANG

Slang is not only one of the most informal levels of language but also one of the most creative, colourful, and personal. When an individual or a group feels the need to express an idea in a novel, vivid way, slang is often the result.

Many words that began as slang gradually became accepted into standard English. The word *mob,* for example, was a slang term of the eighteenth century coined from the Latin phrase *mobile vulgus,* which means the movable or inconstant common people. *Mob* is now a part of our standard vocabulary. Other words born as slang hover for centuries in the purgatory between acceptable and overly informal prose. For example, the word *nerve,* meaning courage, was once slang but is now considered either acceptable or colloquial, depending upon who is doing the considering. Contrarily, some slang words stick around as slang for years. Take the British word *blighty. Old Blighty* has meant England since it was first used by the British in India who couldn't pronounce the Hindu word for home, *bilayati.* During World War I, the meaning of *blighty* grew; it also came to mean a wound or furlough that allowed a soldier to escape the trenches and return to England. As slang goes, however, the word *blighty* is ancient. Most slang has about the same life span as a May fly, a fact which causes people trying to use current slang words no end of embarrassment. Imagine a poor high school student using the word *neat* to mean great or wonderful. She would probably be considered a *dizzbrain dweeb,* a *nitwitted nerd,* or a *zapped zod,* whichever derogatory slang expression was current at the precise second of her gross error in judgment. Slang, then, should be avoided not only because it is too informal but also because it is frequently out of date the minute it is written down and defined.

Slang can also create confusion; a slang word may be imprecise or inaccurate as well as old-fashioned and under-dressed. Much slang develops as an almost private language used between members of an exclusive group. Hockey enthusiasts, reporters, criminals, soldiers, and adolescents all have their own slang, which they use as a litmus test to recognize one of their own and as a way of communicating with group members without fear of being understood by outsiders. Slang, then, often develops as an attempt to hide meaning from certain people, parents, for example. Because of its function as a mask for meaning, slang should be avoided by writers striving for clarity. Also, since different groups may use the same slang word to mean different things, choosing a slang word can be inaccurate as well as unclear.

Think of the word *hacker.* To most, this word describes an individual who does something without talent or skill. To a computer whiz, however, a *hacker* is a David-like hero who tries to gain unauthorized access to a Goliath-like computer system. What about the word *grounder*? A baseball player thinks of a ball that rolls or bounces along the ground when hearing this word while a hobo dreams of a half-smoked cigarette lying on the street. The word *punk* also means different things to different groups of people. To cops, a *punk* means a petty criminal; to circus people, a *punk* is a child; and to writers for Rolling Stone, a *punk* is someone who performs or listens to punk rock.

To conclude, even though slang is often vivid and expressive (I can't think of a word that sounds more like a dull, foolish, out-of-step teenager than *dweeb*), it should be avoided in academic writing.

COLLOQUIALISMS

While not as informal as slang, colloquial language is characteristic of familiar conversation rather than of formal speech or writing. Widely accepted short forms (*prof, rev, mom, phone, photo*) are considered colloquial and unacceptable in academic prose. Contractions (*can't, don't, didn't, haven't, it's, they're, who's, wasn't, you're*) are equally unsuitable. Luckily, most students composing on word-processors can catch contractions with a computer program that checks spelling. Other words and phrases (*awful, funny, out loud, relate to*) either are colloquialisms or can be used in a colloquial way.

There is a reason to avoid colloquial language beyond considerations of appropriateness. Consider the word *awful.* Informally, this word can mean *very bad, very ugly,* or *extremely.* In formal usage, it means *inspiring fear or awe.* Because, outside of spoken English, it is hard to distinguish between this word's possible meanings, using *awful* in an informal way might confuse your reader. The same point holds true for *funny.* A reader might well ask, "What do you mean, funny? Funny-peculiar or funny-ha-ha?"

Following is a list of informal or colloquial expressions that should be avoided in academic prose. This list is not comprehensive; see the glossary for a more complete listing and for more information about the words and phrases listed.

Informal or Colloquial	Acceptable Alternative
a lot	many, much, numerous, abundant
all right	satisfactorily, well
around	about, approximately
awful	bad, sick, very ugly, extremely
blame on	blame
bust	burst
can't, don't, haven't, etc.	cannot, do not, have not
each and every	each, every
expect (I expect you want a job)	suppose, suspect, imagine
figure	believe, think
fix	repair, mend, predicament
funnily enough	oddly
funny	odd, strange, unusual
get a handle on	understand, decipher
lifestyle	life, style of living
nowhere near	not at all, not anywhere close to
off (I got the book off her)	from
off of	off
okay	satisfactory, correct
on account of	because of
out loud	aloud
over with	over, finished, done
phone	telephone
photo	photograph
reckon	believe, think, calculate
relate to	like, have an affinity with
right away, right now	immediately

shape (He's in bad shape)	condition
show up	come, appear, arrive, prove to be better than
size up	judge, examine, estimate the value of
someplace, everyplace, anyplace	somewhere, everywhere, anywhere
sort of a, kind of a	sort of, kind of
TV	television

Formal Words

Although the words chosen for essays should be more formal than those used in formal, polite conversations, they should be less formal than those found in some speeches. Funerals, wars, natural disasters, and other solemn occasions require exceptionally formal diction. Words are chosen for their sound and sense, for their cadence and core; the speaker's purpose is to assuage grief or inspire conviction by choosing timeless words and weaving them into a totemic pattern that parallels ritual and ceremony. Here is an example.

> For heroes have the whole earth for their tomb; and in lands far from their own, where the column with its epitaph declares it, there is enshrined in every breast a record unwritten with no tablet to preserve it, except that of the heart. These take as your model, and judging happiness to be the fruit of freedom and freedom of valour, never decline the dangers of war. For it is not the miserable that would most justly be unsparing of their lives; these have nothing to hope for: it is rather they to whom continued life may bring reverses as yet unknown, and to whom a fall, if it came, would be most tremendous in its consequences. And surely, to a man of spirit, the degradation of cowardice must be immeasurably more grievous than the unfelt death which strikes him in the midst of his strength and patriotism![6]

Obviously, such words and such a style should be reserved for ceremonial occasions or to emphasize the extraordinarily significant points of an essay. If you continually affect this tone, you will wear your readers out rather than impress them. You will resemble an operatic soprano constantly belting out high C's or a baseball pitcher throwing nothing but fastballs. Initially, people may be amazed that you can sustain this level of intensity, but they will certainly become bored or familiar with it; they will tune out your piercing arias or they will learn to hit you out of the park.

Besides lacking variety, diction that is overly formal for its purpose is irritating. It sounds pompous and ponderous. Its reader feels that its writer is either being condescending or crafty, is either laying down the law from atop a mountain of disdain (rather than bringing it down to the people) or dressing up simplistic notions (rather than expressing simple truths). So avoid using inflated, exaggerated diction. Simple, small words are often as expressive as

---

[6] The funeral oration of Pericles as reported by Thucydides in *The Peloponnesian War,* trans. Crawley (New York: Random House, 1951) 107-108.

elaborate big ones. *Relation* means *interrelationship*. *Rank* says as much as *prioritize*. There is no need to call a *reward* an *emolument*. As the Shaker song says, "'Tis the gift to be simple." Of course, this doesn't mean that your prose must be Quakerish, only that it should be functional, that is, truly meaningful and evocative. As George Orwell says, "If you simplify your English, . . . when you make a stupid remark, its stupidity will be obvious, even to yourself."[7]

Unfortunately, making foolish statements is just what many students fear; believing themselves to be more than capable of writing nonsensical prose, they shun simplicity. The secret is to think again, to revise silly thoughts before your reader has the chance to recognize them, not to try to hide a paucity of logic behind an abundance of ostentation. A great irony is apparent here: an insecure student, one who fears being thought simple-minded, is most susceptible to over-writing. This student's readers, after struggling through piles of words to discover a meaning the size and significance of a pea, think the student egotistical and pompous, as well as foolish. So take courage and write using plain English. After all, it is better to be honest.

The Middle Level of Diction

We have learned that an essay should not read like a friendly conversation nor like the Sermon on the Mount. What should it read like? Like an essay. Being a serious, analytical work, an essay should be written for an intelligent, critical reader. The words used in an essay should be precise, intelligible to most educated people, and evocative. Essayists should observe the golden mean by striving for a level of diction midway between high formality and commonplace casualness. Remember that you are not writing for yourself or for your best friend. Neither are you writing for an omnipotent, omniscient being. You are writing for a professor, for a well-educated intellectual who may or may not know as much about your chosen topic as you do. Consider the following passage to see how one student maintains the proper level of formality, the middle level of diction.

Both war and revolution *require* the use of *political force*: the first is a *demonstration* of an authority's *acknowledged prerogative* to *use* force, and the second is a *violent challenge* to that authority's *legitimacy*. War and revolution are *related* in another way as well; when a *government* is *defeated* in a war, its political legitimacy, its acknowledged *right* to the *exclusive* use of force, is *weakened*, allowing *revolutionary groups* challenging that legitimacy either to *grow* in *strength* or to *succeed*.

What words are used? Can you think of more formal and less formal equivalents for each of the words in italics?

Before we leave level of formality behind, the question of whether it is appropriate to use pronouns like *I, you, we,* and *us* in academic prose must be considered. Different academic writing tasks allow for more or less familiarity

---
[7] George Orwell, "Politics and the English Language," *The Penguin Essays of George Orwell* (Harmondsworth, Middlesex: Penguin, 1984) 365.

between writer and reader. If, for example, you are asked to write an autobiographical piece that relates your experiences to the themes of the course, a friendly, personal tone would be suitable, and it would be difficult to avoid the pronoun *I*. In general, however, using *I* in an essay is redundant because all of the opinions, analyses, and descriptions not attributed to others are yours. You sometimes need *I* to distinguish your ideas from those of others whom you have quoted or paraphrased. Also, you occasionally need an *I think* or an *I believe* for emphasis.

Regarding the use of *you, we,* and *us,* more definite conventions exist. Using these pronouns is almost always presumptuous. *I,* the writer, presume to tell *you,* the reader, what to do, think, or feel. When *I* use *we* and *us, I* not only presume to know your reactions and direct your actions, but also to eliminate all distinctions between *us,* to make *you* a part of *we* and to tell *us* what *we* are. Notice that we, the writers of this book, use all these familiar pronouns. This text is not an essay but a handbook, and its writers hope to bridge the gulf between teacher and learner by building familiarity. We want our tone to say, "*We* are all in this together, *you* and *I,* working to improve *our* writing."

Notes

My writing strengths:

Things I need to remember:

Things I need to check:

Revising to Achieve the Middle Level of Diction

Sample Paragraph:

1. Pre-impressionist artistic representations were predicated upon professedly homogeneous but de facto heterogeneously constituted apprehensions of the macrocosmos, a macrocosmos composed of transcendental and substantial constituents alike. **2.** Impressionism, antithetically, was emulous of actualizing a homogeneity that was wholly and purely ocular. **3.** Pre-impressionist art, the art of synthesis, was diametrically antipodal to impressionistic artistic renderings, which exteriorized the art of analysis. **4.** The dissemblance between pre-impressionist art and impressionism is concretized in the dissimilar brush-work of a Leonardo and a Manet.

Exercise One:

Gradgrind can't relate to people well because he's been taught to put on a poker face. We see this face when his daughter comes out with the fact that Bounderby has popped the question. Their whole chat is unemotional; Gradgrind has his "unbending, utilitarian, matter-of-fact face" on, and she seems kind of flat as well (135). The whole scene of the room that they get together in also feels dead. We hear the ticking of "a deadly statistical clock . . . which measured every second with a beat like a rap upon a coffin-lid" (132).

Exercise Two:

Joseph Conrad was excruciatingly cognizant of the circumscriptions of auditory and written symbols of communication. Despite the subtle, rationalistic craftsmanship evinced in his multifarious novels and stories, and the potency and aesthetic excellence of many of the prose passages they harbour, units of symbolic expression failed the author. They oft disintegrated under the burdensome weightiness of his conceptions. "I can't find the words to match my thought," Conrad lamented while conversing with an acquaintance on a meander through the dimly illuminated streets of Ajaccio, Corsica.[1] Conrad should have sought solace in his own counsel, bestowed upon Hugh Clifford, that there are circumstances in which "no word is adequate."[2]

Revising to Achieve the Middle Level of Diction

The sample paragraph is too formal and contains too many unnecessarily big words. It is, in fact, an example of what some style manuals call "purple prose." Its words seem meant to impress readers rather than to communicate with them. We will work through the passage sentence by sentence trying to lower the level of formality and increase comprehensibility. As we work, we must continually ask, "Does the choice of a more formal word help the writer to obtain a more precise meaning?" If the answer is affirmative, of course the word may remain. Some very formal and large words will be appropriate because they are precise. Only the overly formal vocabulary that does not contribute to meaning needs to be eliminated.

In Sentence One, the phrase *pre-impressionist artistic representations* is probably a fancy way of saying *pre-impressionist art*. The words *based on* can be substituted for the words *predicated upon*, *supposedly* can replace *professedly*, and *actually* can replace *de facto*. Next, we come to the phrase *heterogeneously constituted*. What's wrong with *heterogeneous*? It parallels *homogeneous*. Now, what could *apprehensions of the macrocosmos* mean? Maybe the writer meant *views of the world*, but to be safe, let's substitute the phrase *visions of the universe*. After all, *macrocosm* means *the great world* or *the universe*. Should the phrase *composed of transcendental and substantial constituents alike* be revised? Probably the words *transcendental* (meaning *beyond the natural*) and *substantial* (meaning *having substance*) are accurate and appropriate, but there is no need to say that the universe is composed of constituents. Here is the first sentence revised:

> Pre-impressionist art was based on supposedly homogeneous but actually heterogeneous visions of the universe, a universe composed of both the transcendental and the substantial.

In Sentence Two, the phrase *on the other hand* can replace the word *antithetically*. But how to revise the rest of the sentence? Perhaps *was emulous of actualizing a homogeneity* means *tried to achieve a homogeneity*. Could *that was wholly and purely ocular* be replaced by *that was solely visual*? We just have to make an informed guess:

> Impressionism, on the other hand, tried to achieve a homogeneity that was solely visual.

The phrases that need translating in Sentence Three are *diametrically antipodal* and *impressionistic artistic renderings*. The first might mean *the opposite of* and the second *impressionistic art*. If the parallel structure of the sentence is improved, some of the inflated diction will be eliminated: *which exteriorized the art of analysis* becomes *the art of analysis*. Here is one revision of Sentence Three:

> Pre-impressionist art, the art of synthesis, was the opposite of impressionistic art, the art of analysis.

Now for the last sentence. *Dissemblance* means *difference*, and *is concretized,* in this instance, means *can be seen*. The phrase *of a Leonardo and a Manet* should also be revised because it gives the impression that there were many Leonardos and Manets to choose from:

> The difference between pre-impressionist art and impressionism can be seen in the dissimilar brush-work of Leonardo da Vinci and Edouard Manet.

Here is one revision of the sample paragraph. Is it easier to understand? How does it compare with the revision you made in your head during your first reading of this paragraph?

Pre-impressionist art was based on supposedly homogeneous but actually heterogeneous visions of the universe, a universe composed of both the transcendental and the substantial. Impressionism, on the other hand, tried to achieve a homogeneity that was solely visual. Pre-impressionist art, the art of synthesis, was the opposite of impressionistic art, the art of analysis. The difference between pre-impressionist art and impressionism can be seen in the dissimilar brush-work of Leonardo da Vinci and Edouard Manet.

Revise Exercise One by raising and Exercise Two by lowering the level of formality. Notice how the quoted passages in both exercise paragraphs stick out. When standard English seems unusual in this way, the writer has probably used an inappropriate level of formality.

JARGON

Both informal and overly formal words are inappropriate in essays because, by using them, writers demonstrate that they have an inaccurate picture of their readers. Using informal language treats the reader like a pal; using overly formal language treats the reader like an all-knowing, all-powerful being, like a mind-reader. The writer who uses jargon also makes inaccurate assumptions about the reader. Frequently, the use of jargon shows a writer assuming, incorrectly, that the reader has either a knowledge or an acceptance of the terminology used in a discipline outside the reader's domain.

What is jargon? Originally, the word *jargon* travelled to England from France, where it meant "the chattering of birds." This fact is significant because, while we can't understand the language of birds, birds seem to have no trouble communicating with one another. Jargon, then, although it has come to denote an unattractive, specialized language that is hard to understand, may be completely straightforward to those within a certain group, to birds talking bird-talk, for example. Look at the following passage.

> To prepare camera-ready art, drop in halftones using rubylith overlays rather than pasting in PMT halftones. Cutlines should be set at 7 points with an x-height of at least 4 points, and they should be no longer than 13 picas in a suitable serif face.

While the general reader would probably find these instructions impossible to follow, they would make perfect sense to a graphic designer or printer. Of course, using words like *rubylith, cutlines,* and *x-height* without explanation in an essay on the history of poster art in North America would be risky. Although the professor reading the essay might be expert in the language of art history or art criticism, she or he is probably not knowledgable about the language used by people working in a printshop.

Whether words are considered jargon, then, is determined by your audience's knowledge. One person's jargon is another person's discourse. And each discipline will have its own discourse, its own words and ways of using them. The most effective writers, however, don't rely too heavily upon a common discipline-specific vocabulary. When they use a technical term, they tend to surround it with words the non-expert can understand; they use the term in a context that makes its meaning plain. The following passage, taken from a computer manual, exemplifies this strategy.

> Your computer equipment, called *hardware,* probably includes a keyboard, display, printer, and one or more disk drives. The purposes of the first three are straightforward: You type instructions at the keyboard, and the system responds by displaying or printing messages and results.
>
> The purpose of a disk drive isn't quite so obvious, but it quickly becomes apparent as you use the system. A disk drive records and plays back information, much as a tape deck records and plays back music. The computer's information is recorded in files on disks; you'll find that disk files are as central to your computer work as paper files are to more traditional office work.[8]

Now we know the meaning of *hardware, display, disk drive,* and *disk file,* without having suffered through a series of boring definitions.

---

[8] Van Wolverton, *Running MS-DOS,* 3rd ed. (Washington: Microsoft, 1988) 4.

Revising Jargon

Sample Paragraph:

1. Herbert Pocket is not a memorable character, yet he functions as a foil for the protagonist, and he advances the bildungsroman by playing a strong role in Pip's developmental sequence. **2.** One reason for Herbert's seeming insignificance is that he is ahistorical. **3.** The reader knows almost nothing about his past except that he was an unsuccessful candidate for a position with Miss Havisham. **4.** In addition to his lack of history, in a sense, Herbert lacks bonding. **5.** The reader knows who Herbert's parents and siblings are and how Herbert is related to Miss Havisham, but not how he conducts interpersonal interactions within his nuclear family. **6.** Herbert is always alienated from his family; the only reference to his visiting them is that he often goes to Hammersmith with Pip.

Exercise One:

The utilization of negative and positive feedback correlates with creativity. Nonsupportive feedback impacts negatively while favourable feedback impacts positively. Parents, therefore, should utilize encouraging output in interactions with their children. This output, which children receive as input, is causative of a chain reaction; it is itself stimulative of creativity, and it sustains an environment in which children's receivers will be attuned to further stimuli, which will, in turn, stimulate creativity. By neglecting to provide an atmosphere in which a child can find a niche, parents sending only negative signals neutralize creativity.

Exercise Two:

During the recent prioritization and rationalization of our Health and Safety Code, three recommendations were made. First, the ergonomic difficulties consequent on long periods of concentrated work with VDT's should be ameliorated by the provision of break periods of no less than fifteen minutes after every two hours of VDT work. Second, atmospheric examinations should be conducted where aerobiosis is necessary, especially in climatically sensitive areas such as sealed, climate-controlled, or air-conditioned offices. Third, the accessing of antitoxic medicaments by laboratory staff handling toxicogenic ophidians should be easily facilitated.

Revising Jargon: Sample Paragraph Discussion

The sample paragraph was written for an English literature course, so all terminology specific to this discipline should not be considered jargon. This condition exempts both *protagonist* and *bildungsroman*.

Some jargon, borrowed from psychology, mars Sentence One, however. There is no reason to use the term *developmental sequence*; *development* will do.

> Herbert Pocket is not a memorable character, yet he functions as a foil for the protagonist, and he advances the bildungsroman by playing a strong role in Pip's development.

In Sentence Two, *ahistorical* might be considered too jargon-like, since it has a very specific meaning in the discipline of history. To be safe, substitute *without a history*. This description seems more accurate as well as more appropriate.

> One reason for Herbert's seeming insignificance is that he is without a history.

Sentence Three seems jargon-free, but in Sentence Four, the word *bonding* grates. The writer probably meant to say that Herbert is without strong connections to others and used a psychological term instead of plain English. Here is a revision:

> In addition to his lack of history, in a sense, Herbert lacks strong connections to others.

Psychological terms are also evident in Sentence Five. In fact, the phrase *conducts interpersonal interactions within his nuclear family* contains sociological as well as psychological terms. The use of this terminology in an English literature essay is inappropriate. The phrase can easily be replaced with *acts within his immediate family*.

> The reader knows who Herbert's parents and siblings are and how Herbert is related to Miss Havisham, but not how he acts within his immediate family.

The use of sociological terminology in Sentence Six confuses the writer's meaning; to a sociologist, *alienated* means to feel estranged or withdrawn from, but the writer seems to mean something different. Perhaps she means that Herbert is always seen apart from his family.

> Herbert is always seen apart from his family; the only reference to his visiting them is that he often goes to Hammersmith with Pip.

With these minor revisions accomplished, we have a more appropriate paragraph, one that uses plain English and the terminology specific to English literature. Here is a revision of the complete paragraph:

> Herbert Pocket is not a memorable character, yet he functions as a foil for the protagonist, and he advances the bildungsroman by playing a strong role in Pip's development. One reason for Herbert's seeming insignificance is that he is without a history. The reader knows almost nothing about his past except that he was an unsuccessful candidate for a position with Miss Havisham. In addition to his lack of history, in a sense, Herbert lacks strong connections to others. The reader knows who Herbert's parents and siblings are and how Herbert is related to Miss Havisham, but not how he acts within his immediate family. Herbert is always seen apart from his family; the only reference to his visiting them is that he often goes to Hammersmith with Pip.

Work through the two exercise paragraphs, eliminating unnecessary jargon. You will discover that you need to identify the discipline for which the passage has been written before you can determine which words are jargon and which words are appropriate terminology.

DIRECT AND INDIRECT LANGUAGE

Most of the time, when we address people, we try to meet their gaze directly. Indeed, "looking someone straight in the eye" is considered an indication of honesty. Likewise, in language, it is usually more appropriate to use direct and active language, to avoid euphemistic diction, weak verbs, and passive sentences, especially in cases where the prose is made more honest by the omission of these constructions. As in other considerations of appropriate diction, however, a correct appraisal of the reader is necessary to determine how direct or indirect your language should be.

Euphemisms

Euphemisms are everywhere: wherever people *perspire* rather than *sweat*, wherever they *rinse their mouths* to prevent *morning-breath* rather than *gargle* to mask *bad breath*, wherever *false teeth* are *dentures*, *dyed* hair is *highlighted*, and *constipation* is *irregularity*. At their least offensive, euphemisms are polite or agreeable words which substitute for impolite or disagreeable ones.

Perhaps because sweat and sex and other natural bodily functions or activities remind us that we too are animals, for all our powers of rationalization, many euphemisms developed to express indirectly these necessary animalistic actions or behaviours. *Copulation*, from the Latin word meaning *a binding together*, once meant *a joining together or coupling*. Now it means *sexual union* or *sexual intercourse*, primarily. *To defecate* once meant *to purify or refine by the clearing of dregs*. Now we would rarely refer to defecating the wine because *to defecate* means *to void excrement from the bowels through the anus*. So even the words we now consider direct often originated as euphemisms, and, according to a process which Hugh Rawson defines as Gresham's Law, the "bad" or euphemistic meanings of these words drove out their "good" or direct meanings.[9]

Euphemisms, however, are not all "bad." They have a place. To avoid using euphemisms when talking to someone who has experienced pain or grief would be not only impolite but insensitive. Flip through a newspaper to the *death announcements*, often called *obituaries*, and you will see what I mean. In this section of the paper, people don't die from *cancer* or *heart disease* but *after a lengthy illness* or *suddenly*. After death, they are placed in a *casket* not a *coffin* and *interred* in a *cemetery* rather than *buried* in a *graveyard*. Certain events are too painful to name in a direct and clear way. We often need to shield our emotions and thoughts by using indirect, euphemistic language when discussing death.

We also use a sort of euphemism to avoid unfair judgments, to show that, while individuals are different from one another and have unequal abilities, they are equally human and valuable. In this context, the phrase *persons with special needs* is a euphemism for *disabled people* which is a euphemism for *the handicapped* which, if one goes back in time far enough, is a euphemism for *the halt and the lame* of the Bible. Each euphemism is more inclusive, less pejorative, and more sensitive to people as people. Similarly, we try to coin euphemisms

---

[9] Hugh Rawson, "Euphemisms," *About Language: A Reader for Writers*, ed. William Roberts and Gregoire Turgeon, 2nd ed. (Boston: Houghton-Mifflin, 1989) 247.

which categorize societies, cultures, and nations without judging one to be better than another. Look at the history of terms used in comparative economics: *backward nations, underdeveloped nations, developing nations, emergent nations*. Obviously, euphemisms have a place in academic prose, even though, from certain perspectives, a person who has a special need might be more accurately described as deaf, even though the economy of an emergent nation, being based on barter, might still seem primitive or backward to the average Canadian.

In the preceding cases, euphemisms may help the reader to think more deeply and positively about a person or a group of people. But some euphemisms are dangerous, especially when they have exactly the opposite effect. Because the words we use influence our thoughts as much as our thoughts influence the words we use, euphemisms can reflect and encourage a way of thinking and writing that is not only vague, but also dishonest. In Nineteen Eighty-Four, Orwell calls this way of thinking Doublethink and this way of communicating Newspeak. Newspeak, he writes, is intended "to diminish the range of thought,"[10] and Doublethink is a mental process which allows one to "be conscious of complete truthfulness while telling carefully constructed lies."[11] This sort of language and thought communicates and causes ethical bankruptcy. It is Watergate language, as John W. Dean III makes clear:

> If Bob Haldeman or John Ehrlichman or even Richard Nixon had said to me, "John, I want you to do a little crime for me. I want you to obstruct justice," I would have told him he was crazy and disappeared from sight. No one thought about the Watergate coverup in those terms — at first, anyway. Rather it was "containing" Watergate or keeping the defendants "on the reservation" or coming up with the right public relations "scenario" and the like.[12]

Newspeak was also the language of the Holocaust.

> Jews were not executed, let alone killed or murdered; they were only "resettled", "evacuated", "removed", "deported" or at worst given "special treatment". "Special treatment" was, however, too outspoken for the sensitive Himmler; when Korherr, the chief statistician of the SS submitted to him an interim report about the progress of the "final solution" — yet another of these euphemisms — Himmler ordered him not to use this term any more but simply to refer to the "transport of Jews".[13]

We would all like to think ourselves immune to the use of these euphemisms which make murder sound attractive, as if someone is doing us a particular favour by gassing us. However, as Dean attests, we are influenced by the expressions of others who may not call a crime a crime, and we deceive

---

[10] George Orwell, *Nineteen Eighty-Four* (New York: New American Library, 1961) 247.

[11] Orwell, *Nineteen Eighty-Four* 32.

[12] John W. Dean III, "Haldeman Is No More Innocent Than I Am," *New York Times* 6 April 1975: D25.

[13] Walter Laqueur, *The Terrible Secret* (Harmondsworth, Middlesex: Penguin, 1982) 17-18.

ourselves when we try to make the realities of life and death more bearable (or appealing) by using indirect words as symbols. Self-deception and the unrecognized deceits of others make Doublethink and Newspeak common. Again, look in any newspaper. Phrases and words like *pregnancy termination* (abortion), *revenue enhancement* (taxes), *genuine naugahyde* (real fake leather), *protective custody* (imprisonment), and *pacification* (war) abound. We live in a world of *custodial engineers* (janitors) and *cost effective promotional offerings* (little plastic toys given away with each burger purchase). It is hard not to think and write using these lying euphemisms when they surround us, forming the vocabulary through which we make sense of the world.

Weak Verbs

Weak verbs, or more precisely verbs like *to be* and *to have* used weakly, communicate indirectly, vaguely, and tentatively. They cause actions to go unnoticed or to seem beyond control by allowing them to become things in their own right, by encouraging the transformation of verbs into nouns. *Jane runs quickly* becomes *Jane is a quick runner* or *Jane has the skills of a quick runner*.

Of course, *to have* is a strong verb when expressive of ownership: *I have you now*. And *to be,* when used to show equality or identity, is very powerful: *War is hell*. But *to have* and *to be* frequently stand in for verbs of action. If you can replace a verb of *having* or *being* with a verb of action, do it.

Poor: Shakespeare's Hamlet is a close following of the conventions of a revenge play.
Better: Shakespeare's Hamlet closely follows the conventions of a revenge play.

Poor: Also, by questioning the attendant, Socrates is helping him realize how little he is actually remembering; thus, the attendant is realizing that he is not finished searching for and learning of that which his soul knows but has forgotten in the process of being reborn.
Better: Also, by questioning the attendant, Socrates helps him realize how little he actually remembers; thus, the attendant realizes he must search for and learn of that which his soul knows but has forgotten in the process of being reborn.

Because using weak verbs causes wordiness, there is more information on replacing these verbs in the next chapter entitled "How Many Words Are Enough?"

The Passive Voice

While we say that verbs have either active or passive voices, the best way of determining which voice a verb is speaking in is to see whether the subject of that verb is acting or being acted upon. An acting subject indicates an active voice, and a subject that is acted upon indicates a passive voice. Here are some examples of active and passive constructions of the same idea.

Active: Rules and models destroy genius and art.
Passive: Genius and art are destroyed by rules and models.

Active: Little Jack Horner sat in a corner.
Passive: A corner was sat in by Little Jack Horner.

As you can see, in these two instances, the passive construction makes meaning unnecessarily indirect.

Although there are occasions when the passive construction is appropriate, the usual counsel is to prefer the active to the passive voice. There are good reasons to heed this advice. First, the active voice forces a writer to name names, to assign responsibility or blame. The passive voice, on the other hand, allows the actor in a sentence to remain invisible, to escape responsibility.

An error was made.
Bombs were dropped.
People were killed.

These passive sentences don't tell us who made the mistake, dropped the bombs, killed the people. Active sentences would. Second, even if the actor is present in a passive sentence, he, she, or it seems not particularly responsible for the action because distanced from it, divorced from it by being positioned after its expression, after the verb.

An error was made by two Canadian pilots.
Bombs were dropped on Kashgar by them.
People were killed by these bombs.

Notice how changing these passive sentences into active sentences enhances not only their directness but also their brevity. Passive constructions, as well as being indirect, are also wordy.

Two Canadian pilots made an error.
They dropped bombs on Kashgar.
These bombs killed people.

The active voice allows us to ditch words like *was, were,* and *by.*[14]

However, there are reasons for choosing the passive voice. Use the passive voice when the actor is unknown or irrelevant.

---

[14] For more information on eliminating wordiness caused by the use of the passive voice see pages 333-334 in the chapter "How Many Words are Enough?"

It may be that in a time of widening uncertainty and chronic stress the historian's voice is the most needed, the more so as others seem inadequate, often absurd.[15]

Although this sentence doesn't tell us who needs the historian's voice, we assume that all people, humanity at large, have this need. Because we are able to make this assumption, the passive voice is useful here; it allows Tuchman to concentrate on her topic, the historian's voice, without allowing the expression of who needs this voice to distract her or her readers.

Use the passive to avoid shifting your focus or subject when describing someone or something both acting and being acted upon.

I am enjoying the publicity attendant on this disaster, particularly the idea which I have put abroad that if it had not been for a chance decision to go to Aldershot for the night I should have been killed. I should probably only have been cut about or bruised.[16]

Ritchie keeps our attention on himself as subject by using the active voice to explain what he is feeling and doing (enjoyment and starting rumours) and the passive voice to describe what things might have happened to him (death or injury).

Use the passive also to stress that your subject is more acted upon than acting, when your subject is a victim. Here is Ritchie again.

The attacks on London have only been going on for ten days. So far people are steady; there has been no panic. But they are depressed.[17]

While the thought that Londoners are steady is expressed using the active voice, their lack of panic and depression is expressed in passive constructions. Also, the attacks on London are treated like acts of God; they are not being made by anyone, but have simply been going on. Look at what happens if the active voice is used.

German bombers have attacked London for only ten days. So far people are steady; they are not panicking. But the bombing has depressed them.

The focus has shifted subtly; now these sentences seem as concerned with bombing and with German bombers as with London and Londoners.

In academic prose, occasions will often arise when you wish to stress that someone or something is being acted upon. For example, in sociology, individuals are often seen as being controlled by society; sociologists frequently reject the notion that the individual may act entirely of his or her own accord.

[15] Barbara Tuchman, "The Historian's Opportunity," *Practising History: Selected Essays* (New York: Ballantine, 1982) 50.

[16] Charles Ritchie, *The Siren Years: A Canadian Diplomat Abroad, 1937-1945* (Toronto: Macmillan, 1974) 77.

[17] Ritchie 66.

There will also be times when the actor is irrelevant, when the action itself needs to be the focus of a sentence. Look at the following sentence written using the passive voice.

Automobiles, symbols of power and sexual prowess, are often stolen because of feelings of powerlessness and sexual insecurity.

This sentence focuses on the act of stealing cars rather than on the thieves. It seems to let the thieves off the hook. However, a sociology student might write this sentence precisely because he believed that the individual thieves were not responsible for their actions, that the stealing took place because of societal expectations, that, indeed, the thieves should be let off the hook. The student might also write this sentence because he determined that the causes of the action were more important than naming the actor. Here is a more direct expression of a similar thought.

Frequently, teenage boys who feel powerless and sexually insecure in a society that values male power and sexual aggression steal automobiles because cars are symbols of power and sexual prowess.

The subject of this sentence is teenage boys who feel a certain way in a particular society. When the construction is active, the reader knows that teenage boys are stealing and may focus on this fact rather than on the reasons cars are stolen. Because the first, passive sentence emphasizes why cars are stolen by not mentioning who does the stealing, it may be more appropriate to the writer's purpose, even though it is less precise than the second, active sentence.

In the context, then, of seeing people or objects as agents that are acted upon, the passive may be acceptable. It may also be acceptable to use the passive voice when you want to concentrate on an action or on the causes of an action. However, do not get carried away with passivity, as the writer of the following sentence did.

Automobiles, symbols of power and sexual prowess, are often stolen because of feelings of powerlessness and sexual insecurity felt by teenage boys who exist in a society that values male power and sexual aggression.

While a case could be made for the first passive sentence, there is no excuse for this one. The writer has named the boys, albeit indirectly, and thus has negated any useful effect the passive construction might have had.

Finally, use the passive when grammar forces you to put the actor at the end of a clause so you can gracefully attach long modifiers or qualifiers.

> Reaching the village of Kotali with the cargo of laughing children, Mr. Chaudhuri still pedalling some distance behind, Miss Crane was met by the chaukidar and the headman and several men and women who had been on the point of setting out to bring the children back from school.[18]

Here, the two initial phrases are linked to the sentence's subject (Miss Crane), which, for clarity, must be positioned where it is. This placement forces the use of the passive voice. Otherwise, the sentence's complete subject would be the *chaukidar and the headman and several men and women who had been on the point of setting out to bring the children back from school.*

In most other circumstances, use the active voice. It is more concise, direct, and vivid than the passive voice. It also helps you to avoid ambiguity or dishonesty by forcing you to know and state who is doing what to whom.

---

[18] Paul Scott, *The Jewel in the Crown* (London: Granada, 1973) 59.

Notes

My writing strengths:

Things I need to remember:

Things I need to check:

Revising for Appropriately Direct or Indirect Prose

Sample Paragraph:

1. In 1986, there was the explosion of the space shuttle "Challenger." **2.** After this occurrence, questions were asked. **3.** What was this anomaly a function of? **4.** Why did it happen in the first place? **5.** By looking at the performance of NASA's administration using four perspectives, it is possible to see that this circumstance was assisted by NASA's management style or, more accurately, by the fact that many management styles were extant. **6.** The four perspectives to be utilized will be the political perspective, the organizational perspective, the human resource perspective, and the symbolic perspective. **7.** This is because NASA is a political entity, an organization, an employer, and an American symbol of progress.

Exercise One:

NASA was started by the American government with the goal of creating a symbol of technological excellence. It was hoped by the government that soon NASA would "be in a position second to none" (303). Awareness of this goal was known by NASA's administrators, but, to them, the most important goal was the development of technology to its full potential; to be first was not as important as to progress. This goal was somewhat open-ended. Therefore, many intermittent goals were set in order to maintain direction within the organization. Apollo was the first goal of NASA. The focus given by Apollo was pleasing to NASA, and the goal itself was pleasing to the government. The way the goals had been adapted was satisfying to both parties.

Exercise Two:

NASA was not managed very effectively. There were few single, clear goals. Past experience was relied upon when structuring this organization and deciding upon its goals; however, this experience was not very relevant to the circumstances of the eighties. The organization's human resource perspective was off-base for the type of work that was required. There were problems being created by human error, and an attempt to solve them should have been made before non-performance resulted in a dangerous situation. In the future, an evaluation of goals and organizational structures should be undertaken in order to align them with present management concepts. This restructuring will permit a more effective response to problems as they arise.

Revising for Appropriately Direct or Indirect Prose:
Sample Paragraph Discussion

Presumably, the writer of the sample paragraph (and of the two exercise paragraphs) wants to determine the causes of the explosion of the space shuttle "Challenger." To do this, she must show that certain people acted in certain ways causing certain results. The indirect language of the three paragraphs masks not only the seriousness of the accident but also its causes.

According to the previous discussion, there are three main characteristics of indirect language: euphemisms, weak verbs, and the passive voice. We will revise the sample paragraph considering each of these in turn.

Euphemisms

Throughout the paragraph, the writer tries to avoid calling the explosion of the space shuttle an explosion. In Sentence Two, she calls it an *occurrence*; in Sentence Three, it is an *anomaly*; and in Sentence Five, it is a *circumstance*. To eliminate these euphemisms, let's ask ourselves a few questions. First, what occurred? An *explosion*. Second, what does the writer mean by an *anomaly*? Well, in the context of this paragraph, perhaps she means an *accident*. Third, what *circumstance* is she talking about? Probably the *explosion* or the *accident* again. Here are the three sentences partially revised.

After this explosion, questions were asked.

What was this accident a function of?

By looking at the performance of NASA's administration using four perspectives, it is possible to see that this accident was assisted by NASA's management style or, more accurately, by the fact that many management styles were extant.

The partial revision of Sentence Five allows us to see one other euphemism. Was an accident really *assisted* by NASA's management style? *Assisted* is a less direct word for *caused*. Here is Sentence Five again:

By looking at the performance of NASA's administration using four perspectives, it is possible to see that this accident was caused by NASA's management style or, more accurately, by the fact that many management styles were extant.

Weak Verbs

Weak verbs are a major problem in this paragraph. Look at how many times the verb *to be* is used weakly. It is the verb in all but one clause. The use of this verb deadens the first sentence. Look at how much more effective the active verb *to explode* makes the sentence:

In 1986, the space shuttle "Challenger" exploded.

Another weak use of the verb *to be* occurs in Sentence Three. If something is a function of something, it is caused by that second thing. Maybe the writer was trying to avoid the verb *to cause* again. Here is a second revision of Sentence Three:

What caused this accident?

In Sentence Five, the verb *to be* is again used unnecessarily. There is no reason to write that *many management styles were extant. Many management styles existed* is sufficient. Here is a third revision of Sentence Five.

> By looking at the performance of NASA's administration using four perspectives, it is possible to see that this accident was caused by NASA's management style or, more accurately, by the fact that many management styles existed.

In Sentence Six, the phrase *to be utilized will be* is definitely weak. If the sentence is rewritten so that it can use the more active verb *to use,* it becomes not only direct but also clear:

> Four perspectives will be used: the political perspective, the organizational perspective, the human resource perspective, and the symbolic perspective.

Passive Voice

The first passive sentence is Sentence Two. Here, the passive voice allows the person or people asking the questions to remain unnamed. Because it is possible that the writer wants to focus the reader's attention on the fact that questions were asked rather than on the people doing the asking, this passive construction might be considered acceptable. Let's leave this passive sentence because the most likely revision (*The explosion raised questions*) is worse: Explosions raise a lot of dust, but can they raise questions?

There is also a passive construction in Sentence Five. Instead of NASA's management style causing the accident, the accident is caused by NASA's management style. Now the writer could make a case for this passive structure as well; after all, it allows her to tag on the long qualifier *by the fact that many management styles existed.* The whole sentence could be rewritten using the active voice, however.

> By looking at the performance of NASA's administration using four perspectives, it is possible to see that NASA's management style or, more accurately, the fact that many management styles existed at NASA, caused this accident.

It is probably best to rewrite Sentence Five in this way for two reasons. First, unless the student is writing for NASA, it is probably best to use the active voice so that she firmly establishes NASA's guilt. Secondly, Sentence Six is also passive, and should most likely remain passive. In this sentence, the writer used a passive construction to avoid writing *I will use four perspectives.* Because using the first person is often considered too informal for academic prose and because there is no reason for the writer to call attention to herself or to her opinions here, her use of the passive voice is justifiable.

Here is one revision of the whole paragraph:

> In 1986, the space shuttle "Challenger" exploded. After this explosion, many questions were asked. What caused this accident? Why did it happen in the first place? By looking at the performance of NASA's administration using four perspectives, it is possible to see that NASA's management style or, more accurately, the fact that many management styles existed at NASA, caused this accident. Four perspectives will be used: the political perspective, the organizational perspective, the human resource perspective, and the symbolic perspective. This is because NASA is a political entity, an organization, an employer, and an American symbol of progress.

To revise Exercise One and Exercise Two, identify euphemisms, weak verbs, and passive constructions, and then revise those that are inappropriate.

Choosing Words for Special Effects

While prose that is precise and kind to its readers is effective prose, sometimes writers want to create special effects by choosing words that are particularly evocative and memorable. Since sound and sight have a great deal to do with memory, writers tend to choose words and phrases that are attractive to the ear and suggestive to the eye when they want to make the reader notice and remember some idea. The techniques of constructing memorable prose through the selection of appealing, expressive words have acquired labels over the years. We will concern ourselves with five of these labelled strategies, which can be grouped into two categories: choosing words for their sound and choosing words that are figurative, that communicate through the figures or sights they make readers see.

THE SOUND OF WORDS

As children, we all played with the sounds of speech. We babbled *ba ba da da ma ma ma*, creating our first rhyme. When we learned that meaningful words also rhymed, we spent hours singing simple songs like *bail male pail sail dale whale*. Later, as sophisticated word players, we probably joked with the sounds words make: *Ned Ned bo bed, banana fana foe fed, fee fie mo med, Ned*. Of course, as adults we learned to control our youthful exuberance. We probably also learned that writing an essay is not fun and that choosing words for essays is work, not play.

Many stylists agree. Poetry, not prose, Sir Herbert Read orders, is the place for word play. "The art of prose is not creative, but constructive, or logical," he states.[19] Prose shouldn't be playful and poetic but practical and prosaic. While the words chosen to communicate an idea to an academic audience must not be so fanciful or florid that they lack clarity, there is no reason to abandon fun. Playful creativity and the ability to relax and enjoy words are as essential to a writer's education as to a child's language acquisition.

Alliteration

One tip from poets is to emphasize the similarities or differences between two concepts by expressing them in words beginning with the same letter or sound. Think of the pairs of words which are now clichés because they once attracted our attention by pleasing our ear: murder and mayhem, death and destruction, good as gold, clear as crystal, blushing bride, ardent admirer. While these combinations are now hackneyed, the technique that oversaw their creation can still be used to create special effects. This particular technique is called alliteration and is defined as the repetition in successive words of the same sound or letter. Most grammar books advocate using alliteration sparingly in descriptive writing and not at all in expository writing. However, many respected prose writers, even those who write expository prose, do emphasize key points by selecting alliterative words. The author of the following passage does.

---

[19] quoted in F.L. Lucas, *Style* (London: Cassell, 1955) 191.

In attending so *tenaciously to the tight-fisted*, unyielding, and proud *Scottish spirit*, Laurence tapped a major nerve in the Canadian sensibility. The Stone Angel is unabashedly middle-class, *Scottish*, and *small-town* in its emphases. As such, it captures something *essential* about the *energy, enterprise*, mood and pattern of the settlement and development that have characterized not only the growth of Manitoba but of Canada as a whole.[20]

Of course, a little alliteration goes a long way; the boundary between effective and excessive alliteration is difficult to see and easy to cross. Look at the following monstrous deformation of the first sentence of the preceding passage.

> Tending tenaciously to the tight-fisted, stiff, and superior Scottish spirit, Laurence struck a significant source of Canadian sensibility.

Here alliteration distracts us from meaning, and the meaning of the original sentence is altered. Alliteration, like the brush strokes of a painting, is not an end in itself but a means to a meaning. You would never write phrases such as *the fecund, febrile females of factitious fiction* in an essay (or anywhere else for that matter). However, alliteration should not be completely avoided. Even F.L. Lucas, who wrote that obscurity in prose "comes not so much from incompetence as from ambition — the ambition to be admired for depth of sense, or *pomp of sound* or wealth of ornament," does not eschew alliteration.[21]

> In short, it is usually the pretentious and the egotistic who are obscure, especially in prose; those who write with wider sympathy, to serve some purpose beyond themselves, must usually be *muddy-minded* creatures if they cannot, or will not, be clear.[22]

Some types of non-fiction can make more frequent use of alliterative words than others. Autobiographical writings, personal narratives, learning logs, and other subjective pieces that are required of university students enrolled in certain courses can be more poetic than the typical academic essay. Following is Dylan Thomas's description of an August holiday spent by the sea, taken from one of his autobiographical sketches.

> Lolling or larriking that unsoiled boiling beauty of a common day, great gods with their braces over their vests sang, spat pips, puffed smoke at wasps, gulped and ogled, forgot the rent, embraced, posed for the dicky bird, were coarse, had rainbow-coloured arm-pits, winked, belched, blamed the radishes, looked at Ilfracombe, played hymns on paper and

Learning Prompt

Examine the works of your favourite poet, novelist, and writer of non-fiction for alliteration. Make judgments about when and how the alliterative words you find add to or detract from meaning.

Writing Prompt

Describe a scene from your childhood, your current surroundings, or your favourite view. Try to use alliteration to good effect.

[20] Michael Peterman, "'All That Happens, One Must Try to Understand': The Kindredness of Tillie Olsen's 'Tell Me a Riddle' and Margaret Laurence's *The Stone Angel*," *Margaret Laurence: An Appreciation*, ed. Christl Verduyn (Peterborough: The Journal of Canadian Studies and Broadview Press, 1988) 78.
[21] Lucas 76.
[22] Lucas 77.

comb, peeled bananas, scratched, found seaweed in their panamas, blew up paper-bags and banged them, wished for nothing. But over all the beautiful beach I remember most the children playing, boys and girls tumbling, moving jewels, who might never be happy again.[23]

Notice the alliteration: boiling beauty, great gods, beautiful beach. What I like especially is the way in which alliterative words are separated with commas: sang, spat pips, puffed smoke at wasps; belched, blamed the radishes. Now this is prose as poetry or poetry as prose, a difficult and not always appropriate thing for a student writing an essay to create. However, student writers should know that if they can manage to express logic with clarity and with a playfulness that pleases the ear, their communications will be well received.

Onomatopoeia

Another strategy for achieving pleasing sounds in prose, which is also functional, is onomatopoeia. Onomatopoeic words sound like what they mean. Dylan Thomas's passage exemplifies onomatopoeia as well as alliteration. Lolling, larriking, boiling, spat, puffed, gulped, belched, and most of the other verbs or verbals it contains sound like the actions they symbolize. A writer doesn't have to go to such extremes with onomatopoeia; a writer of academic prose rarely should, in fact. However, choosing a strong, expressive verb whose meaning and sound conjoin is a way of avoiding wordiness. For example, writing that the character Stanley *bellowed* in a certain scene in Streetcar Named Desire would be more concise than writing *Stanley spoke in a loud and deep voice*. Because *bellows* sounds like what it is (a deep, angry sound), we don't need further adjectives to describe Stanley's manner of speaking. Look at the following sentence.

Gangs of Hitler Youth rushed through Berlin's streets, shattered shop windows, and burst into Jewish businesses.

The verbs *rushed, shattered*, and *burst* are onomatopoeic; they do a lot of work in this sentence. Imagine the sentence without these verbs.

Gangs of Hitler Youth walked hurriedly or ran through Berlin's streets, fragmented shop windows causing the sound of breaking glass, and entered Jewish businesses suddenly, noisily, and violently.

Wordy and tuneless.

Learning Prompt

Circle every onomatopoeic word you find in the sports section of a newspaper. Are these words useful and effective? Have they become clichés? Do you think the writers of these articles used onomatopoeia consciously?

Writing Prompt

Imagine that you are witnessing a current or historical event. You may decide to witness anything from a recent trial or disaster to an event that was news many years ago (e.g., the Battle of Queenston Heights, Riel's hanging, the Winnipeg General Strike, the October Crisis of 1970). Describe the event using onomatopoeia.

---

[23] Dylan Thomas, "Holiday Memory," *Quite Early One Morning* (London: Dent, 1954) 34-35.

FIGURATIVE LANGUAGE

While alliteration and onomatopoeia appeal to the ear, figurative language appeals to the eye. It creates pictures in the mind that enable readers to see abstract ideas made concrete. But do analogies, similes, and metaphors have a place in academic prose? Yes. Even Metternich, a very practical man, recognized that figurative language promotes brevity and clarity of expression. He writes, "In politics calm clarity is the only true eloquence; but, to be sure, this clarity can at times be best gained by an image."[24] Look at the images created by Margaret Atwood in her discussion of writing.

> Readers and critics both are still addicted to the concept of self-expression, the writer as a kind of spider, spinning out his entire work from within.[25]

This sentence, by comparing readers and critics to addicts, the writer to a spider, and writing to spinning a web, shows us that writing is not solely self-expression.

In fact, comparisons are the essence of figurative language. The most useful figures—analogies, similes, and metaphors—compare one thing to another.

Analogies

Analogies are obvious, explicit comparisons; they compare the similarities of two fairly dissimilar things to promote understanding of both. The following analogy compares the evolution of language to biological evolution.

> The evolution of language can be compared to the biological evolution of species, depending on how far you are willing to stretch analogies. The first and deepest question is open and unanswerable in both cases: how did life start up at its very beginning? What was the very first human speech like? . . . The fossils of human language are much more recent, of course, and can only be scrutinized by the indirect methods of comparative philology, but they are certainly there.[26]

Similes

A simile is an explicit comparison as well. When we write that something is *like* or *similar* to something else, we create a simile.

> Ants are so much like human beings as to be an embarrassment. They farm fungi, raise aphids as livestock, launch armies into war, use chemical sprays to alarm and confuse enemies, capture slaves.[27]

Notice that the words *like* and *as* often signal similes.

---

[24] quoted in Lucas 205.

[25] Margaret Atwood, "An End to Audience?" *Second Words: Selected Critical Prose* (Toronto: Anansi Press, 1982) 342.

[26] Lewis Thomas, "Leech Leech, Et Cetera," *A Long Line of Cells: Collected Essays* (New York: Viking Penguin, 1990) 225-226.

[27] Lewis Thomas, "On Societies as Organisms," *A Long Line* 10.

Metaphors

Metaphors, being implicit rather than explicit comparisons, leave out *like* and *as*. Something is said to be something else rather than to be like something else. The Atwood passage already quoted uses a metaphor, as does the following selection about writing.

> When you compose, you are the shepherd and the sheep dog and it's up to you to decide whether you want the sheep in fold, flank, or field and to know how to get them there.[28]

Misusing Figurative Language

Anything that can be used can be misused, and figurative language is no exception. Generally, writers misuse figurative language in four ways: the figures they use are inappropriate, strained, inconsistent, or clichés.

INAPPROPRIATE FIGURATIVE EXPRESSIONS

An inappropriate figurative expression is one that doesn't suit the writer's purpose. It is inept. It just doesn't fit. When a metaphor, simile, or analogy calls attention to itself rather than to the writer's intended meaning, suspect inappropriate figurative language. Following, two examples of inappropriate figurative language are explained and revised.

> Inappropriate: The term *Industrial Revolution* is an unhappily chosen *epitaph* for a singularly productive era.

In this sentence, the term *Industrial Revolution* is likened to an inscription on a tomb. The writer probably wanted to say that the word *revolution* was too destructive to describe the creative era in which modern industrialism was born. The metaphor used does not work, however. Because *epitaph* brings the image of a tombstone to mind, it suggests that the Industrial Revolution somehow died. Although a revolution can be violently destructive, it is anything but dead.

> Revised: The term *Industrial Revolution* is unhappily chosen, for it suggests that a singularly productive era was violently destructive.

Here is another inappropriate figurative expression to consider.

> Inappropriate: The political engine moves slowly, like a locomotive without fuel.

Writing Prompt

Write a paragraph using figurative language to describe writing. If you want, start your paragraph with the sentence "Writing is _____."

---

[28] Ann Berthoff with James Stephens, *Forming/Thinking/Writing: The Composing Imagination*, 2nd ed. (Portsmouth, N.H.: Boynton/Cook, 1988) 49.

Of course a locomotive without fuel wouldn't move at all. This simile is not only inappropriate, it is stale. In this case, elimination of the simile would probably be the best revision strategy. However, here is a more appropriate, if no less hackneyed, simile:

> Revised: The political engine moves slowly, like a locomotive running short of fuel.

Writing Prompt

Revise the metaphor of writing that you created in response to the previous writing prompt so it contains examples of inappropriate, strained, and inconsistent figurative language. Be sure to include some mixed metaphors. If you did not write in response to the previous writing prompt, write a paragraph about one of the following subjects (or about a subject of your choice) that misuses figurative language in the ways examined to this point.

writing	economic recessions
reading	vacations
listening	illness
speaking	tourists
professors	death
students	work
universities	photography

STRAINED FIGURATIVE LANGUAGE

A writer often strains a figurative expression when he or she becomes fond of it and extends it beyond the point where it is useful. Again, when a metaphor, simile, or analogy takes over a writer's prose, when figurative language causes the reader to lose sight of the writer's purpose, it is probably strained. Figurative language should be a means to an end, not an end in itself. Here is an example of an overextended, strained metaphor.

> Charles Dickens is a master chef, who can throw together a sumptuous feast from left-over ingredients. In Oliver Twist he sifts through the forgotten of London, mixes choice characters together, and cooks up a hearty meal. The book's short chapters dish the plot out in tasty mouthfuls, allowing readers to savour Dickens's blend of the spicy and the bland, the sweet and the sour, the fat and the lean. In all, Dickens creates a remarkable concoction, which resembles the cornucopia of London. This varied diet is washed down by the healthy dram of romanticism Dickens provides.

This writer should have taken the advice Sir Arthur Quiller-Couch gave to his students: "*Murder your darlings.*"[29]

INCONSISTENT FIGURATIVE LANGUAGE

Inconsistent figurative language leaves the reader with a confused rather than a clear picture by bringing together images that pull against one another. For example, if someone describes a speech as *a beacon orchestrating the thoughts of the oppressed,* the reader envisions both a lighthouse and a composer; the writer has created a confused picture in the reader's mind.

The most common sort of inconsistent figurative expression is the incongruently mixed metaphor. Most writers happen into this stylistic fault when they use tired or dead metaphors, in other words, metaphors that, because they have been so frequently overused, are not thought of as metaphors. Here is an example:

> Mixed Metaphor: Clyde Wells bit off more than he could chew when he nipped Meech Lake in the bud.

The writer obviously did not visualize Clyde Wells biting or pruning anything. For him, both phrases had lost their metaphoric force.

---

[29] Sir Arthur Quiller-Couch, *On the Art of Writing Well* (New York: Putnam, 1943) 281.

OVERUSED FIGURATIVE EXPRESSIONS (Clichés)

Now we must examine the most common misuse of figurative language: the use of overused figurative expressions. Most of the clichés that clutter our language are tired or dead figurative expressions. Think of the clichés used to describe people. We have *as busy as a bee, as clear as mud, as cool as a cucumber, as gentle as a lamb, as good as gold, as sharp as a tack, as smart as a whip, as strong as an ox,* and *as weak as a kitten.* I'm sure you could add to this list. All of these clichés were once effective figurative expressions. Now, they are *as dead as a doornail,* whatever that means. Sometimes an overused figurative expression becomes so meaningless that a writer jumbles its sense. A minute ago, I almost wrote *as dead as a dormouse,* for example. Maybe I was thinking of *as poor as a church mouse.*

Whether writers twist clichés is not important, however. The point is that this sort of figurative language is not effective and should not be used. To improve style, follow the first of George Orwell's rules for writers: "Never use a metaphor, simile or other figure of speech which you are used to seeing in print" (or hearing in speech, I might add).[30]

The following clichés appear frequently in academic prose and should be avoided.

beat a hasty retreat	the moment of truth
the bottom line	nipped in the bud
bring to a head	on the right track
by leaps and bounds	par for the course
by no manner of means	perfectly clear
call a spade a spade	ripe old age
corridors of power	rears its ugly head
crystal-clear	rude awakening
from dawn till dusk	see the light
doomed to failure	strike while the iron is hot
fly off the handle	time immemorial
hit the nail on the head	toe the line
in one ear and out the other	to the bitter end
in the nick of time	vicious circle

Writing Prompt

Select a paragraph from one of your old essays. Rewrite it misusing figurative language in any way you can.

Learning Prompt

After examining the adjacent list, select from it those clichés you most commonly use. Add any other clichés you recall using. Then, consult a dictionary, like the Oxford English Dictionary or a dictionary of common phrases, to determine the origins of these clichés.

---

[30] Orwell, "Politics" 365.

Revising Misused Figurative Language

Sample Paragraph:

1. As soon as feminists seem to get their act together, the issue of pornography rears its ugly head throwing them into disarray. **2.** Should pornography be censored? **3.** Should some forms of pornography be censored, and what is pornography anyway? **4.** Liberal and socialist feminists tend to disagree on the answers to these and other questions concerning pornography. **5.** While many liberal feminists agree wholeheartedly with socialist feminists about the definition of pornography, they generally disagree as to how or whether pornography should be controlled. **6.** The concept of freedom of speech is so deeply entrenched in the minds of liberal feminists that censorship is usually regarded as evil incarnate. **7.** Some socialist feminists believe that pornography, because it portrays women's bodies as exploitable commodities, plants the seeds of violence in men which blossom into the bitter fruit of sexual abuse.

Exercise One:

Twelfth Night is a play divided into many compartments, but the bottom line is that it has a plot and a subplot. The main characters, those tangled up in the web of the plot, usually speak using mannered and decorative words. Shakespeare puts the words of poetry into their mouths. Contrarily, the characters of the subplot express themselves using prose. The rough conversations of Maria, Sir Toby, and Sir Andrew, which are chock-full of quick retorts, are par for the course. Just as these conversations, carried out in irreverent prose, highlight the solemn romanticism of the poetic speeches, so the subplot throws the main plot into the limelight. As Charles Prouty writes, "In direct contrast with the whimsical attitudes of the high comedy, we have the schemes and plots of the lower comedy . . ." (307). Shakespeare contrasts the plot with the subplot to the benefit of each.

Exercise Two:

Change in Arembepe, Brazil arrived like a speeding locomotive. In less than twenty years, the small village was transformed. In 1973, there was a good road into Arembepe, an obvious indication that progress had not passed by the fishing community. Refrigeration also reached Arembepe in that year. Thereafter, fishermen could peddle their wares in Salvador as well as in the village, a far cry from the days when they had to sell their fish right out of their boats. Because of such modern conveniences, fishermen were able to fish from dusk till dawn for several days at a time. In the long run, this ability destroyed community spirit. In the olden days, the whole town would turn out to give the returning fishermen a warm welcome after their day at sea. After the introduction of refrigeration, no one noticed the fishermen's return from the sea because boats came in at all times of the day and night.

Revising Misused Figurative Language:
Sample Paragraph Discussion

Most of the figurative expressions in the sample paragraph are clichés. Sentence One contains three: *get their act together, rears its ugly head,* and *throwing them into disarray.* To revise, simply substitute plain English for these figures of speech:

> As soon as feminists seem to reach a consensus about the goals of the feminist movement, the issue of pornography creates dissension.

The next figurative expression, occurring in Sentence Five, is also a cliché. Why must all agreements be described as *wholehearted*? This figure of speech is so common that it will probably be acceptable to the reader. However, the sentence can be revised in this way:

> While many liberal feminists agree completely with socialist feminists about the definition of pornography, they generally disagree as to how or whether pornography should be controlled.

Sentence Six contains two clichés: *deeply entrenched* and *evil incarnate.* The first is passable, but do any feminists really *regard censorship* as *evil incarnate*? The following revision avoids both overused metaphors.

> Liberal feminists believe so strongly in the concept of freedom of speech that they usually regard censorship as an evil.

The last metaphor, the one in Sentence Seven, is the most problematic. It is inappropriate, inconsistent, and hackneyed. Should we think of *sexual abuse* as a *fruit*? Can a *blossom* become a *fruit*? Hasn't the metaphor that likens planting seeds to something's origin been overused? Here is a revision.

> Some socialist feminists believe that pornography, because it portrays women's bodies as exploitable commodities, induces men to sexually abuse women.

Here is one revision of the whole paragraph:

> As soon as feminists seem to reach a consensus about the goals of the feminist movement, the issue of pornography creates dissension. Should pornography be censored? Should some forms of pornography be censored, and what is pornography anyway? Liberal and socialist feminists tend to disagree on the answers to these and other questions concerning pornography. While many liberal feminists agree completely with socialist feminists about the definition of pornography, they generally disagree as to how or whether pornography should be controlled. Liberal feminists believe so strongly in the concept of freedom of speech that they usually regard censorship as an evil. Some socialist feminists believe that pornography, because it portrays women's bodies as exploitable commodities, induces men to sexually abuse women.

Revise Exercise One and Exercise Two by eliminating or improving the figurative expressions used in each.

Learning Prompt

Become familiar with patterns of wordiness by devising wordy equivalents for the following common expressions. Use as many words as you can without altering meaning.

1) **A stitch in time saves nine.**
2) **Waste not, want not.**
3) **Look before you leap.**
4) **Haste makes waste.**
5) **You can't judge a book by its cover.**

Wordiness irritates. It irritates the listener, who begins to suspect trickery and betrayal behind embellished turns of phrase. It irritates the reader who, having laboured through a turgid passage, discovers the point made trivial. It irritates the instructor, who responds by slashing words, phrases, sometimes even whole sentences and paragraphs, leaving the few grains of meaning bleakly exposed. There is nothing technically wrong with wordiness, but it wastes time and space and causes confusion. Furthermore, the ultimate goal of writing is to express meaning with clarity, and any form of wordiness works counter to that goal since extra or redundant words almost inevitably obscure meaning.

Wordiness can be defined as the habit of expressing an idea with more words than necessary. "Close the door" is not wordy; "It would be preferable if the door could be placed in a closed position" is. The second sentence not only uses more words, but also confuses meaning by phrasing the command in terms that obscure rather than clarify. No one would say or write such a preposterous statement, you argue? Perhaps not. Certainly, however, students and professional writers everywhere often use more words than they need, and often with as negative an outcome.

Reasons for this are easy to infer. In the first place, models of wordiness flourish in our language: statesmen, politicians, lawyers, and civil servants actively and adeptly employ empty phrases to obscure, disguise, or exaggerate meaning. Even though the writing of these professionals may defy comprehension, it is imitated, primarily because it sounds impressively intellectual. We tend to admire the verbal dexterity of someone who claims, "It is financial deprivation that I lament" and not the forthrightness of the individual who bluntly says, "I'm broke."

What impresses in a court room or on a convention floor, however, can fail dramatically in an academic setting. Academic writers must <u>deliver</u> intellectual goods: weighty meaning must underlie weighty sentences. Writers must therefore guard against imitating the prose of civil servants and politicians; caution must be exercised even when following academic models. The elaborate turns of phrase and intricately worded sentences found in the work of good professional writers are often necessary because the ideas being considered are complex. However, if the concepts under discussion are straightforward (as they often are both in undergraduate and professional writing), an elaborate style is no longer justified: the writer captures style without substance.

Not all wordiness problems, however, result from imitating the wrong model. Some wordiness occurs simply because the writer is unsure of meaning. Writers use drafting as a means of making meaning clear to themselves, so most drafts are full of repetitions. As we rewrite, we come closer to understanding, and it may take three or four drafts before we can clearly communicate an idea without being redundant. Experienced composers learn to delete these repetitions as they revise, but novice writers may not even recognize them.

In this chapter, you will read about several strategies for eliminating wordiness from your prose. Remember, as you read, that eliminating wordiness is a revision step. It is unwise to try to trim excess prose as you draft. Thinking about redundancies when you are trying to find expression for your thought will only slow you down. Once you have a draft on paper, then begin pruning.

Forms of Wordiness

Revising for wordiness demands that you acquire two skills. First, you must learn to recognize standard patterns of wordiness and revise them as a matter of course. Secondly, you must learn to recognize your own meaning so that you may delete redundancies, phrases and sentences and passages which needlessly repeat that meaning. The first five sections of this chapter are intended to help you recognize standard patterns of wordiness; the last section focuses on eliminating redundant content. As you read through this chapter, you will discover that eliminating any form of wordiness demands above all that you think about the words you use, examining each sentence carefully for obvious (and often not-so-obvious) instances of repetition and redundancy.

NON-CONTRIBUTING WORDS

Often when students write essays or reports, they are very aware of the number of words required and are fearful that they may not be able to write that much. Putting aside the point that this anxiety is misplaced, since the real challenge of writing is to tighten prose, we can still acknowledge that one common, if faulty, response to this worry is simply to add as many words to each sentence as possible – not words that develop the idea in the sentence or that add details, but words that just occupy space. These we call non-contributing words.

Eliminating these non-contributing words requires the writer to pay careful attention to the meaning of individual words and phrases. Sometimes words don't contribute because two words are supplying the same information in a sentence:

Poor: *Also,* Monet was concerned with the use of colour *as well.*

Better: Monet was concerned with the use of colour *as well.*

In other instances, an elaborate phrase may need to be replaced by a shorter expression:

Poor: Earl is absent *due to the fact that* he is ill.[1]

Better: Earl is absent *because* he is ill.

To eliminate non-contributing words, look at each sentence carefully. Are there words which repeat meaning? Are there phrases or expressions which could be replaced by single words? Watch in particular for tautologies, double modifiers, redundant intensifiers, overused modifiers, and formulaic phrases.

---

[1] See the glossary for a further explanation of the grammatical problems that can be caused by the expression *due to the fact that.*

Tautologies

In grammar, tautology is defined as the unnecessary repetition of the same idea in different words. Many grammarians expand this definition to cover virtually any redundancy, but a tautology is a specific sort of repetition. In a tautological expression, one word or group of words usually contains the essence of the meaning expressed by the second word or group of words. Think about the words *yellow in colour*. Because the word *yellow* is a colour, the *colour* meaning is already contained in the word *yellow*. The reader knows, then, that *yellow* means *yellow in colour*.

You can probably see from this example that a tautology is not always a straightforward repetition. Because tautologies are not straightforward repetitions, they demand that you think carefully about the essence of the words you are using. You must be able to recognize the deep meanings of words, the structures they imply.

The following list highlights some common tautologies to guard against:

actual fact	each separate word
other alternatives	refer back
several different ways	centres around
repeat again	final outcome
consensus of opinion	narrow in width
past history	mix together
blue in colour	continue on
small in size	necessary requirement
at this point in time	widow woman
her own autobiography	more preferable
but nevertheless	general consensus
new innovation	each and every one
because of these reasons	both together, both . . . alike
advance planning	opposed against

Think about each of these expressions. Why is each a tautology? What meaning is being repeated? The inventive word spinner can create an infinite number of tautologies, so it is important not only that you learn to recognize the common tautologies listed here but also that you come to an understanding of how a tautology is created. You will then be able to analyze your own work for any tautologies which might appear there and decide whether they must be eliminated. (Keep in mind that occasionally you may want to preserve a tautology either because it adds emphasis or because the context demands it. Not all tautologies must be eliminated, only those that serve no purpose.)

Double Modifiers

Another type of redundancy can occur when the writer, striving to make a sentence more substantial, adds an adjective or an adverb that is synonymous with one already written:

Poor: The speech she gave was *vague* and *unexplicit*.

Poor: Furthermore, she spoke *rapidly* and *quickly*.

In each case, the author is using two modifiers that have almost the same meaning. One modifier, usually the least precise, should be eliminated:

Better: The speech was unexplicit.

Better: Furthermore, she spoke rapidly.

If you tend to be wordy, you will need to examine all double modifiers carefully. Of course, most will be completely acceptable because the two modifiers will have different meanings:

Correct: The speech she gave was *vague* and *boring*.

Correct: Furthermore, she spoke *rapidly* and *monotonously*.

If necessary, use a dictionary to determine whether you are adding information by adding a modifier.

Redundant Intensifiers

Intensifiers are words (usually adverbs) which add emphasis to an expression. For example, in the sentence "I am *very* upset," *very* is an intensifier ensuring that the reader knows the speaker is more than mildly upset. Intensifiers have an important function in prose, but they can be used incorrectly, especially by people who tend to be overly emphatic. The dialogue of the young women billed by the media as "Valley Girls" a few years ago exemplifies the use of redundant intensifiers: "Her Vuarnets are, like, you know, *really genuine*." In this example, the intensifier *really* is used incorrectly to modify *genuine*, a word that cannot be intensified. The intensifier has no meaning: something is either genuine or it is not. The following example presents the same problem:

"Voice of Fire" is a *very unique* work of art.

Again, something is either unique or it is not, since unique means the only one of a kind; the word *very* in this instance cannot intensify meaning.

Other words that rarely benefit from intensifiers are:

crucial	universal	necessary
essential	perfect	empty
full	straight	wrong
round	square	complete
correct	real	genuine

Overused Intensifiers and Modifiers

Furthermore, some intensifiers and modifiers are used so frequently in everyday language that they have lost their power to add emphasis:

Paul McCartney is *absolutely* fantastic.

If the writer had penned, "Paul McCartney is fantastic," the reader probably would take exactly the same meaning from the sentence.

Other overused modifiers include:

really	actually	simply
quite	incredibly	pretty
rather	sort of	somewhat
awfully	very	
absolutely	basically	

Formulaic Phrases

Because so much prose in popular media is wordy, when we write, the phrases that occur to us immediately are often the least concise. *Due to the fact that* flows from the pen even though *because* would carry the same meaning. Indeed, to our distorted senses, the longer phrase sounds more professional, primarily because we hear many professionals use it. However, in an academic essay, these formulaic phrases are considered trite and unoriginal. In particular, avoid the following patterns.

1) Do not use an elaborate phrase when a subordinating conjunction is adequate.

Poor: *At the same time that* students rebelled in Paris, Prague Spring occurred in Czechoslovakia.

Better: *While* students rebelled in Paris, Prague Spring occurred in Czechoslovakia.

Here are some commonly used phrases listed with a subordinating conjunction that could replace them.

due to the fact that	because
except for the fact that	except
because of the fact that	because
being as/being as how	since
seeing that/seeing as how	since
in the case that	if
despite the fact that	although
in the way that	since/because
for the simple reason that	because

2) Avoid using a verb with an adverb or preposition, or using a series of verbs, when one, more accurate, verb will suffice. When we are speaking casually, we often use these wordy verbal expressions, partially to avoid sounding overly formal but also because the simple words occur to us more readily. In academic prose, the more formal, less wordy choice is usually preferable.

Poor: Stella *brought up* an interesting point.

Better: Stella *raised/introduced* an interesting point.

Again, here are some common wordy phrases listed with a less wordy verb substitute. (The substitute is only a suggestion and may not always be appropriate.) Remember again that sometimes the wordy expression will convey your precise meaning; do not eliminate it if this is the case.

point out	illustrate
put down	criticize
going on	continuing
get across	establish, show
caught up	involved
look at	consider
set up	create, form
turns out	happens
found out	discovered
have got to	must
had ought to	should
took place	occurred
came in	was
put forth	presented

Writing Prompt

Pretend for a few minutes that you are a candidate running in a provincial election. You must speak for five minutes on low-income housing, even though you know little about the issue and your party's record in this area is abysmal. Using redundant intensifiers, tautologies, and formulaic phrases, write a five-minute speech which says nothing.

Eliminating Non-Contributing Words

Sample Paragraph:

1. In the case of <u>Peace Shall Destroy Many</u>, Wiebe makes two elements of the Canadian West absolutely real. **2.** First of all, by setting his novel in a Mennonite community, he has pointed out that the West is actually not a culturally pure homogeneity. **3.** It is, in true fact, a combination of many different and diverse cultures, all of whom share with the Mennonites the confusion and difficulties of adjusting to each other. **4.** In addition, Wiebe furthermore puts across an extremely genuine picture of racial prejudice, and of the hard difficulties involved in coming to terms with it.

Exercise One:

Through the years, the labour force in which men and women participate has been researched, and researchers have accepted false stereotypes. There is much controversy over whether or not women have progressed. One misleading belief is that women have in fact advanced their position in the workforce (especially in comparison to men). This in actual truth is not a correct statement. Women have suffered tremendously and find themselves in degrading, deskilling, and alienating jobs. This essay attempts to demonstrate the negative and unfair aspects of women's work. It goes on further to support the fact that there is little hope for women's escape from the double ghetto.

Exercise Two:

Other developments have also been negative factors in women's work. For example, the expansion of hospitals opened the doors for numerous nurturing jobs which were quickly filled by women. However, it was soon to be found out that this type of work was exhausting, frustrating, and, of course, alienating. As Shapiro points out, nurses have fairly low status in the hospital hierarchy. He also goes on to say that nurses are allowed to make very few decisions and must follow orders by the physicians. Doctors further alienate nurses by seeing them as dull and dumb; many don't even recall the nurses' first names. In the end, women in the field of hospital nursing hold jobs which require demanding shift work but provide very little opportunity for advancement.

Eliminating Non-Contributing Words: Sample Paragraph Discussion

The sample paragraph is typical of the prose written by students who want to get 2500 words on paper.

Tautologies

Let's begin revising the paragraph on Rudy Wiebe's work by finding the tautologies it contains. There are several:

1) *First of all.* By definition, the word *first* means to precede everything else. The *of all* can be eliminated.

2) *Pure homogeneity. Homogeneous*, meaning *of one kind*, does the work of *pure*. We can eliminate *homogeneous* and revise the expression to read *actually not culturally pure*.

3) *True fact.* Facts that are not true are fiction, so we can eliminate *true*.

4) *Different and diverse cultures. Diverse* implies *different*. We can eliminate *different*.

5) *Confusion and difficulties.* The revision here is a judgment call. *Confusion* is a difficulty, so it might be possible to eliminate it. However, if the writer wanted to stress *confusion* as a particular *difficulty*, both nouns should stay.

6) *In addition, Wiebe furthermore.* Here we have two transitions indicating addition in one sentence. We can eliminate either *in addition* or *furthermore*.

7) *Hard difficulties. Difficulties* are *hard*, so the *hard* can be eliminated.

Here is what the paragraph looks like now:

> In the case of <u>Peace Shall Destroy Many</u>, Wiebe makes two elements of the Canadian West absolutely real. First, by setting his novel in a Mennonite community, he has pointed out that the West is actually not culturally pure. It is, in fact, a combination of many diverse cultures, all of whom share with the Mennonites the difficulties of adjusting to each other. In addition, Wiebe puts across an extremely genuine picture of racial prejudice, and of the difficulties involved in coming to terms with it.

Redundant Intensifiers and Overused Modifiers

Look through the passage for instances of words that rarely benefit from intensifiers and for overused modifiers. (See the lists on page 312.) You should be able to spot three instances of this form of wordiness. We can eliminate the unnecessary modifier or intensifier.

1) *Absolutely real* to *real*

2) *West is actually not* to *West is not*

3) *Extremely genuine* to *genuine*

Formulaic Phrases

Finally, let's delete all formulaic phrases. In Sentence One, it is not necessary (or graceful) to write *In the case of.* This phrase could be shortened to *In*. In Sentence Two, a verb like *established* seems a good substitute for *pointed out*, since Wiebe is not literally pointing at anything. In Sentence Four, we find another wordy phrase, *puts across. Presents* would be a more accurate choice. Finally, the expression *coming to terms* is also a little wordy and imprecise. *Coping* could carry the meaning intended.

These additional revisions create a clear, concise paragraph:

In Peace Shall Destroy Many, Wiebe makes two elements of the Canadian West real. First, by setting his novel in a Mennonite community, he has established that the West is not culturally pure. It is, in fact, a combination of many diverse cultures, all of whom share with the Mennonites the difficulties of adjusting to each other. In addition, Wiebe presents a genuine picture of racial prejudice and of the difficulties involved in coping with it.

You may see other possible revisions to make this paragraph even more precise. Our revisions have focused on non-contributing words, but you will learn shortly that many other constructions also contribute to wordiness.

Examine the sentences of the two exercise paragraphs carefully. What tautologies, double modifiers, redundant intensifiers, overused modifiers, and formulaic expressions can you find? Revise the paragraphs, eliminating non-contributing words where possible.

WHICH AND THAT AFFLICTION: OVERUSE OF SUBORDINATE CLAUSES BEGINNING WITH RELATIVE PRONOUNS

These subordinate clauses, also known as adjective clauses because they modify nouns and pronouns, can usually be easily identified in a sentence since they begin with relative pronouns (*which, who, whom, whose, that*). These clauses cannot be eliminated entirely, nor should they be. However, an excessive number of *which, who,* and *that* clauses slows the reader's progress through a passage and consequently impedes comprehension. When a passage contains too many subordinate clauses beginning with relative pronouns, therefore, some should be eliminated to make meaning more accessible.

In your editing, you should consider consciously the adjective clauses used and decide whether they must remain as is or be eliminated. Usually these clauses can be revised in one of five ways:

1) The clause may be replaced by an adjective.

Environmental disasters, *which threaten our very existence*, are occurring with more frequency in Canada.
Life-threatening environmental disasters are occurring with more frequency in Canada.

The cumulative effects of the disasters *that continue to happen* are unknown.
The cumulative effects of these *recurring* disasters are unknown.

2) The relative pronoun and the verb that follows it may be omitted, creating an appositive.

David Suzuki, *who is an expert on the environment*, believes the disasters will ultimately lead to the destruction of the planet.
David Suzuki, *an expert on the environment*, believes the disasters will ultimately lead to the destruction of the planet.

The Green Party, *which is a relatively new political creation*, agrees.
The Green Party, *a relatively new political creation*, agrees.

3) The relative pronoun and the verb which follows it may be replaced by a participle.

Environmental activists *who focus on fostering awareness of environmental issues* may need to change tactics.
Environmental activists *focusing on fostering awareness of environmental issues* may need to change tactics.

Big businesses *that have no environmental policy* will need to develop one.
Big businesses *having no environmental policy* will need to develop one.

4) The clause may be replaced by a possessive.[2]

The concerns *which are of interest to the public* are not being addressed.
The *public's* concerns are not being addressed.

The opinions *that Suzuki expresses* are shared by others.
Suzuki's opinions are shared by others.

5) The clause can be eliminated altogether to create one main clause.

He is a man *who values education*.
He *values education*.

When eliminating subordinate clauses beginning with relative pronouns, you should be sure not to get overzealous. Relative pronouns are often needed to make meaning clear. If deleting such a clause seems to make meaning hazy, re-insert it.

---

[2] Be careful here. Avoid using an apostrophe to make an inanimate noun possessive. See the section on apostrophes in Chapter Five for more information.

Notes

My writing strengths:

Things I need to remember:

Things I need to check:

Eliminating Subordinate Clauses Beginning with Relative Pronouns

Sample Paragraph:
1. Moving on to a later work, **which was written by McNaught**, called <u>The Winnipeg General Strike: 1919</u>, one sees the emergence of the first major text in a new generation of material. **2.** McNaught's book, **which was co-written with Bercuson**, is really one of two primary sources written in preparation for Bercuson's later work, **which is called <u>Confrontation at Winnipeg</u>.** **3.** This work, **which looks at a new wealth of primary material on the topic that was unavailable to Logan and Masters (which included government papers and documents about the strike)**, downplays the political dimensions of the strike, **which are looked at by Masters and Logan**, and emphasizes the significance of the structural issues of the labour organization, further legitimizing the strike. **4.** In doing this, McNaught does a good job of breaking down the elements of the strike, looking at the machine shops, railways, and private pressures of the strike, and contrasting them with traditional craft conservatism, industrial radicalism, and the "exotic" O.B.U. radicalism.

Exercise One:

To make it appear as if only the French made grave mistakes during this time would be wrong, for Moltke made just as many serious errors; however, they did not appear to be mistakes when all went well. The mistake that was to cost the Germans the most was not having the First Army take the channel ports during the French retreat when they were left undefended. The price would be heavy and they would fail during "the race to the sea." The other grave mistake which was made by Moltke was to send seven regular divisions to mask Antwerp, instead of using Landwehr as Schlieffen had proposed. Thus he reduced his offensive strength for little gain. However, the move that proved to be the most useless was that of taking two corps from the right wing and transporting them to meet an emergency in the East which was over by the time they had arrived: Moltke had once again reduced his fighting strength for no gain.

Exercise Two:

These women who arrived on the prairies found a situation which did not come close to meeting their expectations. Expectations which had been cultivated by fertile imaginations, supported by advertising images, and embellished by their dreams and desires had grown to utopian proportions. The response of these women, who had little sense of control over their situation and little or no money, was that of resignation. Essentially, they felt that they had no choice but to stay and do what was necessary for survival.

Eliminating Subordinate Clauses Beginning with Relative Pronouns: Sample Paragraph Discussion

If you read through the sample paragraph, you will immediately see the dangers of overusing subordinate clauses beginning with relative pronouns. The excessive number of *which* clauses focuses the reader on extraneous information and detracts from the main point, the contribution that McNaught's book makes. Let's work through the passage, sentence by sentence, eliminating and revising as we go.

Sentence One

This sentence contains one adjective clause, *which was written by McNaught*. The *which was written* can easily be eliminated, since the reader will assume that *by McNaught* means written by McNaught.

> Moving on to a later work by McNaught called <u>The Winnipeg General Strike</u>: 1919, one sees the emergence of the first major text in a new generation of material.

Sentence Two

Here we have two adjective clauses, *which was co-written with Bercuson* and *which is called Confrontation at Winnipeg*. In both cases, the *which was/which is* can simply be eliminated to create an appositive, and in the second instance, *called* can be deleted as well.

Note that this sentence also contains a meaningless intensifier, the word *really*. We'll eliminate this word too.

> McNaught's book, co-written with Bercuson, is one of two primary sources written in preparation for Bercuson's later work, <u>Confrontation at Winnipeg</u>.

Sentence Three

There are four adjective clauses in this sentence, three beginning with *which* and one beginning with *that*: *which looks at a new wealth of primary material on the topic*; *that was unavailable to Logan and Masters*; *which included government papers and documents about the strike*; *which are looked at by Masters and Logan*.

The first adjective clause probably needs to remain, since none of the possible revisions creates the same meaning. The clause contains too much information to be reduced to an adjective; *looking* in this instance does not carry the same meaning as *which looks at*, and the verb cannot be eliminated since it adds meaning. However, you will remember that *looks at* is a formulaic expression; it can be replaced with *examine*.

The second adjective clause, *that was unavailable*, can survive without *that was*.

In the third, *which included* can be shortened to the participle *including*. Finally, *which are looked at* can be replaced by the participle *considered*, eliminating both the adjective clause and a formulaic expression.

> This work, which examines a new wealth of primary material on the topic unavailable to Logan and Masters (including government papers and documents about the strike), downplays the political dimensions of the strike considered by Masters and Logan, and emphasizes the significance of the structural issues of the labour organization, further legitimizing the strike.

This sentence is free of adjective clauses, but *looking at* might again be replaced, this time by *mentioning*.

In doing this, McNaught does a good job of breaking down the elements of the strike, mentioning the machine shops, railways, and private pressures of the strike, and contrasting them with traditional craft conservatism, industrial radicalism, and the "exotic" O.B.U. radicalism.

What remains is clearer and easier to read:

Moving on to a later work by McNaught called The Winnipeg General Strike: 1919, one sees the emergence of the first major text in a new generation of material. McNaught's book, co-written with Bercuson, is one of two primary sources written in preparation for Bercuson's later work, Confrontation at Winnipeg. This work, which examines a new wealth of primary material on the topic unavailable to Logan and Masters (including government papers and documents about the strike), downplays the political dimensions of the strike considered by Masters and Logan, and emphasizes the significance of the structural issues of the labour organization, further legitimizing the strike. In doing this, McNaught does a good job of breaking down the elements of the strike, mentioning the machine shops, railways, and private pressures of the strike, and contrasting them with traditional craft conservatism, industrial radicalism, and the "exotic" O.B.U. radicalism.

You may see other ways of revising this paragraph, particularly if you consider combining sentences. As long as you have faithfully preserved meaning, other revisions are acceptable.

Read through the two exercise paragraphs, underlining the clauses beginning with relative pronouns in each. Which clauses could be revised? Rewrite each paragraph, eliminating these clauses where possible and appropriate.

OVERUSE OF PREPOSITIONAL PHRASES

Most academic prose is full of prepositional phrases: prepositions help us to make connections, and academic writing is primarily concerned with making connections.[3] However, academic prose marked by long strings of prepositional phrases is difficult to read: all the little prepositions (to, in, on, at . . .) and the articles which usually follow them (a, an, the) help to create distance between important words, and this distance prevents the reader from seeing those important connections quickly. Furthermore, prepositional phrases add more nouns to a sentence, and nouns tend to weigh ideas down, rather than move them forward.

There are several means of connecting ideas without using prepositional phrases. What follows are some suggestions for revising sentences to eliminate prepositional phrases. Again, we must stress that not all prepositional phrases are wordy and that many will be necessary to your meaning. Do not eliminate prepositional phrases unless the revision expresses your intent more concisely without loss of meaning.

1) Substitute an appropriate adjective.

The novelist *from Japan* read at Harbourfront.
The *Japanese* novelist read at Harbourfront.

Elgin draws our attention to an item *of interest*.
Elgin draws our attention to an *interesting* item.

Bats are creatures *of the night*.
Bats are *nocturnal* creatures.

2) Substitute an appropriate adverb.

She plans to return to Tokyo *in the near future*.
She plans to return to Tokyo *soon*.

He notes that meals were served *in an informal manner*.
He notes that meals were served *informally*.

Bats fly *at great speeds*.
Bats fly *quickly*.

3) Substitute an appropriate verbal.

In light of these facts, the historian must conclude that the War Measures Act was unnecessarily invoked.
Considering these facts, the historian must conclude that the War Measures Act was unnecessarily invoked.

---

[3] For further information about prepositional phrases, see the section on "Modifying Phrases" in Chapter One.

Nutritionists were consulted *in connection with vitamins*.
Nutritionists were consulted *concerning vitamins*.

Some people love to watch *the flight of bats*.
Some people love to watch *bats fly*.

4) Substitute an appropriate possessive.

The priorities of Donald Trump are sadly misplaced.
Donald Trump's priorities are sadly misplaced.

The meals *of the president* were carefully prepared.
The president's meals were carefully prepared.

The *behaviour of bats* inspires fear.
Bats' behaviour inspires fear.

Exercise some caution when replacing a prepositional phrase with a possessive. Not all readers accept inanimate possessors, so if the object of your preposition is an inanimate object, you may want to retain the phrase. See Chapter Five for more information on possessives.

Writers should also be aware that many formulaic expressions are prepositional phrases. Substitute a shorter version when possible. Watch in particular for the use of compound prepositions (two prepositions together). As the list below shows, often an appropriate single-word substitute can be found.

in order to	to
by means of	by
in all likelihood	probably
in connection with	with, about
in relation to	with, about
so as to	to
inside of	inside
off of	off
in between	between
above and beyond	beyond
on the basis of	from
as a result of	because
in the case of	in this case
in so far as	while, although
in terms of	about, in

Finally, watch for pronouns that may also be used as adjectives, usually eliminating the need for the preposition *of*. These are usually words of measurement.

all of my life   all my life
several of the items   several items
many of the problems   many problems
some of the pie   some pie

Remember, however, to revise for meaning. *Some of the pie* does not always mean *some pie,* because the prepositional phrase can imply reference to a specific pie.

Eliminating Prepositional Phrases

Sample Paragraph:

1. In retrospect, we can see that the prohibition movement was supposed to solve the problems **of** society. **2.** Many temperance people felt, **before** the introduction **of** prohibition legislation, that alcohol was the cause **of** the ills **of** society. **3.** Others felt that the introduction **of** prohibition could solve many **of** the problems **of** the urban society. **4.** Some **of** the elite **of** the temperance movement felt that prohibition would help to assimilate a growing non-British population, and still others believed that prohibition would help **with** all **of** these things. **5.** However, many became aware **at** a later time that abstinence alone would not solve all **of** the problems **of** society, and a select few came to realize that the elimination **of** poverty and **of** social inequities would solve more **of** the problems **of** Canada.

Exercise One:

Realist directors, according to Giannetti, employ the camera so as to perpetuate the illusion that there is no camera. Angles, lighting, and editing are all put into execution so as to keep cinematic intrusion at a minimum. Realist directors, for example, usually prefer to do most of their shooting at eye-level, five to six feet above the ground. The viewer therefore sees incidents as she would were she a participant in the action, and is therefore less conscious of the aesthetic distance between herself and the film. Medium to long shots are favoured by Realist directors for the same reason; because these shots provide details of background, they preserve what Giannetti terms "spatial integrity." Again, the viewer, because she can understand the physical context of the scene, does not feel distanced from it.

Exercise Two:

By the end of the 1960s, there had been a radical alteration in opinion as to the provision of contraceptive services as part of domestic health programs. The initiative for change, however, did not come from state-sponsoring of domestic programs; rather, it was a result of the changed attitude in the United States toward sponsoring birth control programs in other countries. Leading Americans felt that the United States had a responsibility to keep other nations from suffering from starvation and poverty. The United States, then, saw its duty to promote policies of international family planning, and what was applied to the international sphere ultimately became important within the country as well.

Eliminating Prepositional Phrases: Sample Paragraph Discussion

Begin eliminating wordy prepositional phrases by identifying them. All prepositions in the sample paragraph are highlighted. The sample shows some common wordiness patterns in the use of prepositional phrases: few possessives, overuse of *of,* two prepositional phrases in a row. Many of the twenty-odd prepositional phrases in the passage can be eliminated through simple revision.

Replacing Prepositional Phrases with Adjectives and Adverbs

In Sentence One, *In retrospect* is not only a prepositional phrase but is also a formulaic expression that could be replaced by an adverb. However, possible substitutes (retrospectively) would sound awkward, so the phrase should remain. *Of society,* on the other hand, can easily be revised by substituting an adjective: *societal problems*.

The second double prepositional phrase in Sentence Two, *of the ills of society,* can be revised in part by using an adjective. *Ills of society* can be transformed to *societal ills*. Then, if one changes the verb *was* to the more active verb *caused*, the sentence can read . . . *alcohol caused societal ills.* (See the section on "Passive Construction" for further explanation of this revision.)

In the third sentence, *many of the problems of the urban society* can be revised in two steps. First, the second phrase can be eliminated by using an adjective: *many of urban societal problems*. Secondly, since *many* can be an adjective as well as a pronoun, the preposition can be deleted: *many urban societal problems*.

In Sentence Four, *Some of the elite of the temperance movement* can be shortened somewhat by using *temperance movement* as a compound adjective: *Some of the temperance-movement elite.* Make this type of revision with caution, however. Turning nouns into adjectives in this manner can add to the heaviness of a passage.

The remaining prepositional phrase is difficult to eliminate since *some of* carries meaning: it shows that the item being measured (the elite) can be counted (as opposed to *some sugar*). We will leave it as is.

Finally, in Sentence Five, *At a later time* can be replaced by the adverb *later. All of the problems of society* can be revised to *all societal problems. All,* like *many,* can be either a pronoun or an adjective in this case.

Replacing Prepositional Phrases with Verbals

The first double prepositional phrase of the second sentence, *before the introduction of prohibition legislation,* can be revised to one prepositional phrase using a verb: *before prohibition legislation was introduced.* Since the preposition *before* adds meaning to the sentence, that phrase need not be eliminated. Also, in this sentence we have already replaced *was the cause of* with the verb *caused*.

In Sentence Five, the compound prepositional phrases *the elimination of poverty and of social inequities* can be revised by changing *elimination* to the verbal *eliminating*: *eliminating poverty and social inequities*.

Replacing Prepositional Phrases with Possessives

In Sentence Three, *introduction of prohibition* might be revised by using a possessive: *prohibition's introduction.* However, many readers would consider *prohibition* an inanimate object, so the cautious writer would leave this phrase as is.

In Sentence Five, *of the problems of Canada* can be revised to *of Canada's problems*.

Eliminating Unnecessary Prepositions

We have already eliminated unnecessary prepositions in two instances: in Sentence Three, we have changed *many of the problems* to *many problems,* and in Sentence Five, we have changed *all of the problems* to *all the problems.*

In Sentence Four, *help with all of these things* employs words so vague that it contributes almost no meaning. The *of* can simply be eliminated: *help with all these things.* However, what remains is still unsatisfactory. Try revising *things* by replacing it with the noun it represents, and a slightly more meaningful phrase emerges: *help with all these difficulties.*

Now let's look at the revised paragraph:

> In retrospect, we can see that the prohibition movement was supposed to solve societal problems. Many temperance people felt, before prohibition legislation was introduced, that alcohol caused societal ills. Others felt that the introduction of prohibition could solve many urban societal problems. Some of the temperance-movement elite felt that prohibition would help to assimilate a growing non-British population, and still others believed that prohibition would help with all these difficulties. However, many became aware later that abstinence alone would not solve all societal problems, and a select few came to realize that eliminating poverty and social inequities would solve more of Canada's problems.

You will probably notice, as you review the revised paragraph, that it still doesn't read very gracefully. The phrase *societal problems* has been used repeatedly, and the repetition makes the passage read awkwardly. The recurrence of the phrase signals an underlying problem: the paragraph contains too many general points and very few specific details. The writer should revise again to include more concrete explanations and facts. Often wordiness can disguise other writing problems. Be sure in your own writing to look for other problems after wordy expressions have been eliminated.

Read through the two exercise paragraphs, underlining the prepositional phrases in each. Rewrite the paragraphs, making appropriate substitutions for the prepositional phrases to avoid wordiness.

DEADENING THE VERB

In Chapter Six, you were made aware of the advantages of active verbs. They keep sentences alive, making the ideas move forward and helping the reader to progress through a passage. In wordy prose, verbs are often replaced by nouns or adjectives: the net effect is that the sentence slows down, and occasionally the reader is stopped completely, prevented from forging ahead by a mass of words which seem to go nowhere.

Most commonly, verbs are turned into nouns or adjectives. To avoid dead prose, revive the verb.

1) Turn nouns into verbs.

The Finance Minister gave *a summary of* the budget.
The Finance Minister *summarized* the budget.

A member of the opposition *made a short speech* outlining her objections.
A member of the opposition *spoke briefly* outlining her objections.

A backbencher *took a nap* while the debate raged.
A backbencher *napped* while the debate raged.

Note in these three examples that nouns cannot simply be exchanged for verbs. When a noun is used instead of a verb, often a whole group of words – articles, prepositions, non-active verbs – become necessary to make meaning clear. Turning nouns into verbs, therefore, often eliminates not one but several words.

2) Turn modifiers into verbs.

He *thought deliberately* and *carefully* about the matter.
He *pondered* the matter.

The bill *progressed slowly* through the Legislature.
The bill *inched* through the Legislature.

Activists *lined up around* the building.
Activists *circled* the building.

Again, using modifiers instead of lively verbs often adds several unnecessary words. In the first example, you can see clearly that two adverbs and a non-active verb are eliminated when an active verb is substituted. A little careful thought (or thesaurus-skimming) to obtain an appropriate verb can often eliminate extra words. (For more information about revising modifiers, see "General and Specific/Abstract and Concrete Words" in Chapter Six.)

Turning Modifiers and Nouns into Verbs

Sample Paragraph:

1. It **is also apparent** that such hierarchies at Lakeshore High **operate within a framework of** dominant middle-class values. **2.** Frideres's study of native education in Canada recognizes that schools **put emphasis on** the need **for instruction of** students in ways in which they can gain power and success. **3.** Teachers and faculty **take on the function of instilling** business creeds and competitive qualities into their students. **4.** Schools become the places in which students are taught how to behave in order **to obtain the ability to integrate themselves** into the dominant middle-class value system (Frideres, 1987:24). **5.** It thus becomes vital that students **have acceptance of and adaptation to** this system; otherwise, they **will find classroom time boring** (Frideres, 1987:284).

Exercise One:

Not only was the physician the determining factor in terms of whether the private-duty nurse could obtain employment; he also had control over her work. Again, this control was not physical. Because the private-duty nurse did not work with the doctor on a day-to-day basis, she did not provide him with service as the hospital nurse did. However, if the actions of a private-duty nurse displeased the physician, he could terminate her position immediately. In addition to losing that particular job, the nurse might discover that the physician never called on her again. Far worse, the physician might take the initiative to place her on a blacklist within the community.

Exercise Two:

The Applebaum-Hébert Report (1982), like the Massey Commission, serves as an accurate reflection of the prevalent attitudes toward Canadian culture during the period of 1974-83. The Report often puts emphasis on Canada's multicultural aspects; indeed, the chapter on international cultural relations makes the recommendation that "Canadian artists and performers representing the cultural traditions of Canada's Native peoples and ethnic communities" should be given priority to be the recipients of federal support for artistic projects (Applebaum-Hébert Report 322). Ethnicity is granted recognition in the report; likewise, regional culture gains status. In the 1950s, the differences among the regions were granted only grudging acknowledgement. Regionalism has always existed in Canada, but only since the 1960s have its cultural influences been given encouragement. Regionalism, along with ethnicity, is now understood as an aspect of Canadian cultural distinctiveness.

Turning Modifiers and Nouns into Verbs: Sample Paragraph Discussion

Highlighted in the sample passage are several phrases that can be replaced by active verbs. Revising these phrases often requires some thought since the sentence may need to be restructured.

Replacing Nouns with Verbs

Let's look first at the phrases in which nouns can be changed into verbs.

1) *Operate within a framework of.* Here, the noun *framework* can be expressed as a verb, eliminating the need for *operated*: *hierarchies at Lakeshore High are framed by dominant middle-class values.*

2) *Put emphasis on.* Again in this instance, we have a verb and a noun when an action verb would be preferable: *schools emphasize the need.*

3) *For instruction of.* Replace with the infinitive: *to instruct.*

4) *Take on the function of instilling. Instill* would be an excellent alternative here.

5) *To obtain the ability to integrate themselves.* By replacing the noun *ability* with the verb *enable*, we can eliminate *obtain*: *to enable them to integrate.*

6) *Have acceptance of and adaptation to.* Change *acceptance* and *adaptation* to verbs: *accept and adapt to.*

Replacing Modifiers with Verbs

The phrases remaining require that we turn modifiers into verbs, eliminating the weak verb in the process.

1) *It is also apparent.* Using the verb *appears* allows more action in the sentence: *it also appears.*

2) *Will find classroom time boring. Find* is not a very descriptive verb and thus requires a modifier. If we focus on the modifier *boring*, and determine what verb could replace it, we can eliminate wordiness. *Classroom time will bore them,* for example, is one, more active, alternative.

The revised paragraph reads much more energetically:

It also appears that such hierarchies at Lakeshore High are framed by dominant middle-class values. Frideres's study of native education in Canada recognizes that schools emphasize the need to instruct students in ways in which they can gain power and success. Teachers and faculty instill business creeds and competitive qualities into their students. Schools become the places in which students are taught how to behave in order to enable them to integrate into the dominant middle-class value system (Frideres, 1987:24). It thus becomes vital that students accept and adapt to this system; otherwise, classroom time will bore them (Frideres, 1987:284).

The two exercise paragraphs also contain many dead sentences in which nouns and modifiers replace verbs. Breathe some life into these passages by substituting active verbs where appropriate.

OVERUSE OF THE VERB *TO BE*

To be or not to be — that is the question. In the context of wordiness, it is usually preferable to take arms against a sea of troubles and eliminate at least a few instances of this unexciting verb from your prose. *To be* is a useful verb, one of the most frequently used verbs in the English language. It appears often as an auxiliary verb (*is* helping), as a linking verb (he *is* tall), and as a substantive verb, meaning to exist (the book *is* on the table). No writer can avoid using the verb *to be,* and no writer needs to. However, there are certain *to be* constructions which, when abused, contribute to wordiness.

Expletives

Expletives are words or phrases that carry no meaning but are needed to make a sentence grammatically complete. *There is* and *it is* are common expletive phrases.

> *There is* nothing left.
> *It is* difficult to sail.

Expletives are not faulty in themselves, but they are easy to construct, and lazy writers may become overly dependent on them. When they occur in excess, they should be eliminated.

> Nothing is left.
> To sail is difficult.

Particularly wordy are the expletive constructions that necessitate the use of a relative pronoun:

> *It is* attitude *that* is important.
> Attitude *is* important.

> *There are* several issues *which* must be considered.
> Several issues *must* be considered.

In these sentences, deleting the expletive makes no difference at all to meaning or sentence completion. Note that eliminating the expletive permits the elimination of a relative pronoun as well.

Overuse of Auxiliary Verbs

The most common wordiness tendency in this case is using the progressive tense which contains a *to be* auxiliary (*was cooking, is cooking*) when the past or present tense (*cooked, cooks*) would be equally or more appropriate. Writers also may overuse the perfect tense which contains the *to have* auxiliary (*has cooked, has been cooking*). Both perfect and progressive tenses indicate an action that continues for a period of time, while the present and past tenses indicate an action that happens at a particular time. When the past or present will convey your meaning, use one of them.

> The king *was reigning* for twenty-five years.
> The king *had reigned* for twenty-five years.
> The king *reigned* for twenty-five years.

In this example, the past tense is more appropriate than the progressive or the perfect since the prepositional phrase *for twenty-five years* makes clear that the king's reign continued over a period of time.

> She *is living* at 24 Sussex Drive.
> She *has been living* at 24 Sussex Drive.
> She *lives* at 24 Sussex Drive.

In this case, the verb *lives* implies an ongoing process, so use of the progressive or perfect tense seems redundant.

Any attempt to change tenses requires that you think carefully about meaning, since shifting tense inevitably alters the sense of the sentence. Do not change tenses without contemplating your intention. If you tend to be wordy, you probably use perfect and progressive tenses when the simple past or present would better meet your purpose. However, never change tense if changing the tense means losing meaning in the process.

Passive Construction

Passive construction is thoroughly explained in Chapter Six, but since it also often contributes to wordiness, we are including a brief note about it here as well. When expressing an action, a writer can choose between an active voice, which emphasizes the actor, or a passive voice, which emphasizes the person or thing being acted upon:

> Active: Marcelle *spoke* to Gerard.
> Passive: Gerard *was spoken to* by Marcelle.

> Active: An ambitious colleague *victimized* Gavreau.
> Passive: Gavreau *was victimized* by an ambitious colleague.

Writing Prompt

Try to obtain some committee minutes (from your student council or Senate). Usually they will be written in passive voice. Rewrite them in active voice. How do meaning and emphasis change?

Pretend you are a sportscaster describing a home run or a goal being scored in hockey. Write an account of the incident first in active voice, then entirely in passive. Exchange both versions with a learning partner. Ask your partner to comment on the change of tone between the two passages.

We often use the passive when we want to avoid writing *I* or *we*. (These problems must be addressed/We must address these problems.) The writer can use *we* or *I* occasionally, but some passives may be necessary to avoid too many first-person pronouns.

In the first example, in the active sentence, Marcelle gets the reader's attention; in the second, passive sentence, Gerard is the focus. Note that the passive voice is formed by using the verb *to be* and a past participle, and that it adds extra words (often prepositions) to the sentence.

The passive voice is appropriate when you want to emphasize the person or thing being acted upon: it is often the preferred construction in scientific experiments and committee minutes for that reason. In the second example, the writer probably does want to focus on Gavreau, not the ambitious colleague, so the passive is an appropriate choice. However, the active is more direct, more exciting, and less wordy. Try to eliminate the passive unless you have a sound reason for using it.

Using *To Be* Instead of an Active Verb

This revision may not always help you eliminate words, but it will make your prose more active. When you are writing, examine the instances of *is* and *are* in your prose. Could another verb convey more meaning?

This matter *is important to* us.
This matter *concerns* us.

Grammar *is* important.
Grammar *remains* important.
Grammar *seems* important.
Grammar *stays* important.
Grammar *appears* important.

You will recognize immediately that the meaning of the sentence changes when *is* is replaced, but as long as the meaning changes to something that more accurately reflects your intent, the substitution is appropriate.

For more information about active verbs, see Chapter Six.

Notes

My writing strengths:

Things I need to remember:

Things I need to check:

Eliminating *To Be* Constructions

Sample Paragraph:

1. Although numbers are more easily attacked than people, it is not solely the number of people which is the problem, but rather the impact of each individual on the ecological system. **2.** A destructive impact on the global environment is created by the strain that each individual puts on his or her personal environment. **3.** It is at this point that it is important to recognize that the environment is not strained by the people in poor, underdeveloped countries, but by the people in industrialized nations where resources are overused. **4.** It is on this issue that Ehrlich notes, "Resource consumption in rich nations threatens earth's capacity to sustain us all" (1988:943).

Exercise One:

Ehrlich does not address the fact that, while population control might be a necessary evil in developing countries, the growth rate in industrialized countries is at or near the zero level. In most industrialized countries, if it were not for immigration, there would be no increase in population. It is not the number of people in industrialized countries that is the problem; rather, it is how and what they consume that results in environmental decline. Rather than having one birth control policy for all countries, what is needed are birth control policies in developing and underdeveloped countries and consumption policies in developed countries.

Exercise Two:

One of Ehrlich's suggestions is to withhold aid from poor nations who are still in the position of being able to rehabilitate themselves in their own cultural way. It is when underdeveloped countries are helped by industrialized countries that the former become dependent, and their own traditional ways of securing resources are abandoned. Once industrialized countries have solved or are well on their way to solving their problems, they are then in the position to advise other more slowly moving countries.

Eliminating *To Be* Constructions: Sample Paragraph Discussion

If you glance through the sample paragraph, you will spot immediately the tell-tale signs of passive and expletive constructions: many instances of *is,* and *which* and *that,* the pronouns that often accompany passive construction, dot the passage. You probably also recognize a few other wordiness problems in the sample, including an overabundance of prepositional phrases and several nouns replacing verbs. Although we will focus on revising *to be* constructions, we will not neglect eliminating these additional wordy structures.

Sentence One

Numbers are more easily attacked is a passive construction; the active revision would read *We can more easily attack numbers.* However, the intent here is probably not to draw attention to the reader or writer (to *we*); *numbers being attacked* is the focus of the sentence. Since we want to draw attention to the object, the passive construction should remain.

It is not solely the number of people which is the problem. In this case, the *it is* construction does add words without adding much meaning to the sentence. We can revise by eliminating the *it is* and the *which*:

... the number of people is not solely the problem, but rather the impact of each individual on the ecological system.

Sentence Two

This sentence could be changed to the active voice: *The strain that each individual puts on his or her personal environment creates a destructive impact on the global environment.* (However, a writer who wished to emphasize the environment might retain the passive so that the reader focused on the environment, not on individuals.) Further wordiness might be eliminated by changing the noun *strain* into a participle and by finding a verb form to replace *creates a destructive impact*:

Each individual straining his or her personal environment helps to destroy the global environment.

Sentence Three

The sentence begins with two expletives, *It is at this point that,* and *it is important to recognize that.* Both can be eliminated. In the first instance, *at this point* can stand alone or, better still, be deleted altogether since it adds no meaning. In the second case, a subject (*we,* or *one,* or *the reader*) can be used to make an alternate construction: *we must recognize that.* Your choice of subject will be dictated by the formality of the essay. Here, the author is making a personal appeal, so *we* is appropriate. In other cases, you might want to use the more formal *one.*

The adjective clause (beginning with *that*) in this sentence is constructed passively, and can be made active by making *people* the subject of the clause: *We must recognize that people in poor, underdeveloped countries do not strain the environment.* As a final note, the wordy auxiliary construction *where resources are overused* could be revised to *but people in industrialized nations who overuse resources do.* Here, however, we need to add the verb *do* to the end of the sentence to retain the parallel structure found in the original.

We must recognize that people in poor, underdeveloped countries do not strain the environment, but people in industrialized nations who overuse resources do.

Sentence Four

The expletive *it is* can be deleted. Once the expletive is eliminated, it is possible to replace the wordy phrase *on this issue* with the more concise *as*:

> As Ehrlich notes, "Resource consumption in rich nations threatens earth's capacity to sustain us all" (1988:943).

The revised paragraph reads as follows:

> Although numbers are more easily attacked than people, the number of people is not solely the problem, but rather the impact of each individual on the ecological system. Each individual straining his or her personal environment helps to destroy the global environment. We must recognize that people in poor, underdeveloped countries do not strain the environment, but people in industrialized nations who overuse resources do. As Ehrlich notes, "Resource consumption in rich nations threatens earth's capacity to sustain us all" (1988:943).

When you read this paragraph, you probably recognize that there are still redundancies here at the level of meaning. Sentences One and Two, for example, might be combined because the ideas they contain overlap. After you read the next section, you might want to return to this paragraph and revise it for redundancy in content.

Work your way through the two exercise paragraphs. Begin by underlining all *to be* constructions. Decide which serve a useful function in the passage and which can be replaced. Revise each passage to eliminate wordiness.

REDUNDANCY IN CONTENT

This chapter has discussed word choices and syntactical patterns which lead to wordiness: these types of redundancies are easy to recognize and eliminate. However, wordiness often results from simple repetition of ideas and points. As Chapter Four has already established, selective repetition can help keep a paragraph on track. Needless repetition, however, merely bores and confuses the reader. Unfortunately, this variation of wordiness is easy to produce, since we all are repetitious as we find our way through a first draft. It is also more difficult to eliminate, for it requires careful thought about the content of the paper and the points being made.

Chapter Four has already acquainted you with some strategies for recognizing meaning within paragraphs. When you are revising for redundancy in content, these strategies come into play again. Begin by inspecting all your paragraphs carefully, searching for the controlling idea of each. Study how each sentence within the paragraph relates to that idea. Then, look for redundancy. Often, at least one clause doesn't add much meaning to a paragraph. Revise by deletion.

Deletion eliminates redundancy quickly, but often you may need to rework a paragraph completely to make meaning precise. Sometimes a single idea is presented over the course of three or four sentences, little pieces of meaning scattered throughout an entire passage. In this case, begin by considering what elements in each sentence need to be preserved. Then, ignoring the original completely, work to fashion a sentence or series of sentences which contain the key point but do not restate it or inflate it.

Eliminating redundancy in content helps to highlight flaws in unity, so once you have cut redundancies, you may need one more revision, this time adding words that create meaning. The procedure takes some skill, but through deletion and revision, much extraneous text can be eliminated.

A final word of caution: do not cut transitional words, pronouns, or repeated ideas that show progression or that achieve cohesion. Redundancy is not as serious a writing flaw as incoherence or lack of cohesion.

Learning Prompt

Redundancy in content occurs most frequently when you are not sure of the direction of your thought. Examine several of your essays, considering several paragraphs in each. Find the controlling idea of each paragraph. Do any of the passages contain redundant content? Revise the wordiest of the paragraphs to eliminate redundancy.

Eliminating Redundancies in Content

Sample Paragraph:

Anne of Green Gables appears to be a careful imitation of other popular orphan novels of the time in that it shares many elements in common with other orphan novels. In particular, the work bears some resemblance to Rebecca of Sunnybrook Farm, although it is not identical in nature. The title of the latter work is now a catch phrase for excessive and sickening goodness; the same image is not evoked by Montgomery's novel. Montgomery makes use of the conventions of the orphan story, but she is not consistently faithful to its standards. She departs from the sugar-coated conventionality of the genre in order to explore, humorously but seriously, the darker implications of an outsider entering an established community and of an exceptionally creative child coming to terms with that community's conventions.

Exercise One:

The second way that population can be controlled is through a system of financial rewards and penalties. It would be a method of giving to people who controlled population and penalizing those who did not. This is the opposite to the system that we have now, which rewards on the basis of having children both through baby bonuses and tax deductions for children. Taxation of specific items which are necessities for small children, such as diapers and baby bottles, would be another possible form of penalty. The last form is one of education, specifically sex education in schools, which would emphasize to children the importance of the lowering of the birth rate and how this lowering can be accomplished. It is external pressures such as these which would have a negative effect on the size of the population in a way which for the most part would be positive.

Exercise Two:

Implicit in all that Bruce writes about the Maritimes is a statement about community — about the Maritime community. There cannot be an overestimation of the Maritime community's power. A simple examination of the topography shows why. The Maritimers of the Channel Shore live in isolated communities, separated from other villages by bays, coves, and religious prejudice. As a result of their isolation from others, it is the community which acts as a judge of all actions, and determines guilt or innocence.

Eliminating Redundancies in Content: Sample Paragraph Discussion

When revising for redundancy, it is not possible to revise sentence by sentence, because often sentences need to be combined. There is a two-step revision process involved in eliminating redundancy of content. First, the writer must determine the controlling idea of the paragraph and then must eliminate redundant information.

Finding the Controlling Idea

Fortunately, the controlling idea is fairly evident in this passage: Anne of Green Gables follows some conventions of the orphan story genre, but also departs from that genre.

Redundant Information

Sentences One, Two, and Three all focus on the first part of the controlling idea, that Anne of Green Gables follows some of the conventions of the orphan story genre. If you consider the first three sentences carefully, you will see that the writer tends to articulate an idea in the abstract first (the novel imitates other novels) and then follows it with the same idea stated more concretely (it shares elements with them). This creates some redundancy because the concrete ideas contain the abstract idea, and for such a clear, simple point, the reader does not need the abstraction. Consider this revision of the first three sentences:

> Anne of Green Gables appears to imitate other popular orphan novels of its time. In particular, the work bears some resemblance to Rebecca of Sunnybrook Farm, although the title of the latter work is now a catch phrase for excessive and sickening goodness, and the same image is not evoked by Montgomery's novel.

Here, we have eliminated the clause describing Anne of Green Gables as *sharing some elements,* because that is evident in the word *imitate.* We have also eliminated the subordinate clause *although it is not identical in nature* because, once again, the clause following establishes that the two works are not identical.

Sentences Four and Five develop the second part of the controlling idea, that the novel departs from orphan story conventions. Once again, we see redundancy in content, particularly in the clause *but she is not consistently faithful to its standards.* Sentence Five makes this point adequately, so the entire clause can be omitted.

> Montgomery makes use of the conventions of the orphan story, but she departs from the sugar-coated conventionality of the genre in order to explore, humorously but seriously, the darker implications of an outsider entering an established community and of an exceptionally creative child coming to terms with that community's conventions.

Here is the revised paragraph:

> Anne of Green Gables appears to imitate other popular orphan novels of its time. In particular, the work bears some resemblance to Rebecca of Sunnybrook Farm, although the title of the latter work is now a catch phrase for excessive and sickening goodness, and the same image is not evoked by Montgomery's novel. Montgomery makes use of the conventions of the orphan story, but she departs from the sugar-coated conventionality of the genre in order to explore, humorously but seriously, the darker implications of an outsider entering an established community and of an exceptionally creative child coming to terms with that community's conventions.

The small changes make the passage tighter, but the meaning is still retained.

Study the two exercise paragraphs. What is the controlling idea of each? Rewrite each paragraph, making the controlling idea, and the points that support and develop that idea, clear. Eliminate any redundancies in content.

Now that you are familiar with standard patterns of wordiness, take the time to examine one of your old essays. Do you see any wordy expressions? What patterns of wordiness do you frequently use? Take two of your most wordy paragraphs and edit them to eliminate wordiness.

CONCLUDING NOTE

You have revised your rough draft, ruthlessly deleting all forms of wordiness. Now, after revision, you are left with a scant thousand words—and the assignment requires at least fifteen hundred. What can be done?

Rather than reinserting all the wordy expressions you just eliminated, think about developing your ideas more fully. Can you add more examples? Expand on the implications of a point? Explain a concept more fully? Show connections more clearly? Qualify assertions? Too short essays usually suffer from lack of development: expand your ideas, not the words used to express those ideas.

Be careful, too, as you revise for wordiness, to avoid being overzealous. Prose that is entirely stripped of unnecessary words begins to sound like a telegram. Retain rhythm and meaning: eliminate redundancies only, not words and phrases that add grace or emphasis or information.

a/an

In choosing to use either **a** or **an** before a word, the sound of that word is more important than its spelling. The **a** is used before all consonantal sounds, and **an** is used before all vowel sounds (*a poem* but *an ode; a university* but *an undergraduate; a eulogy* but *an epitaph; a U.E.L.* but *an M.P.P.; a SALT treaty* but *an S.S. victory*). Words beginning with a silent unaspirated *h* are preceded by **an** (*an honour, an hour*). Because the pronunciation of words beginning with *h* varies, some Canadians, especially those whose speech patterns are close to those of the British, use **an** before words like *history* and *hotel*. However, it is more usual for Canadians to sound the *h* in such words, so *a history* is more common than *an history*. **An** is still used frequently before an aspirated but unaccented syllable starting with *h* (*an historian, an habitual drunk*).

a lot

There is no such word as *alot*. If you want to write that someone has **a lot** of gall, you have to use two words. Even then, it is often more graceful to use words like *many, numerous, abundant, plentiful,* or *copious* instead of **a lot**.

Poor: **A lot** of times he took **a lot** of notes at lectures and shared them with **a lot** of people.
Better: **Many** times he took **copious** notes at lectures and shared them with **numerous** people.

able; able to

While the phrase **able to** has made its way into our vocabularies, **able** is the correct form for referring to people or things that possess ability, as in the following palindrome about Napoleon: *Able was I ere I saw Elba.* The phrase **able to** is wordy and can usually be replaced by the word *can* or *could*.

Poor: She was **able to** play tennis.
Better: She **could** play tennis. She **can** play tennis.

above; below

Using the terms **above** and **below** in such statements as *the above* quotation or *the map appearing* **below** should be avoided. After all, in your final draft, the map may not appear on the same page as your sentence of direction, let alone below it. The word *preceding* or *foregoing* may be substituted for the word **above**, and the word *following* can stand in for the word **below**. Note that overuse of the term **above** or **below** in a first draft may signify poor organization; there may be too much distance between related points if you frequently have to direct your audience to past or upcoming discussions.

accept/except

Accept is a verb meaning *to agree to* or *to receive*. **Except** can be a verb meaning *to exclude* or *to leave out*. It can also be a preposition meaning *leaving out* or *other than*. *Accept the* **acceptable;** *except the* **unacceptable except** *for the unavoidable.*

access

This word is a noun and usually means *the freedom or ability to approach, to enter, to communicate with, or to use: The Prime Minister had ready* **access** *to the latest intelligence reports.* In computer-related texts, **access** is also used as a verb meaning *to get at: He* **accessed** *the computer's memory banks.* Avoid using **access** as a verb in any context other than this one; there are other perfectly serviceable verbs to use instead, and they frequently are more expressive and direct.

Poor: The researcher **accessed** the appropriate information.
Better: The researcher **found** the appropriate information.

according to

This phrase is often misused to refer to general concepts or fields of study (**according to** *geography, science, research, time*) or to particular written works (**according to** *Hamlet, this article, reports*). While it is acceptable to write **according to** *the Bible,* **according to** should refer to a person or a group of people whenever the authors of texts or originators of ideas are known.

Poor: **According to** history, the ideas of the Enlightenment were epitomized in the Declaration of the Rights of Man.
Better: **According to** historian Georges Lefebvre, the ideas of the Enlightenment were epitomized in the Declaration of the Rights of Man.
Poor: **According to** the novel A Bird in the House, Vanessa's maturation resulted from her discovery that things are seldom what they seem.
Better: The novel A Bird in the House **demonstrates** how Vanessa matures through discovering that things are seldom what they seem.

accurate

See **true/valid/accurate**.

achievement

This noun should not be used as a direct object after verbs like *to make, to do,* or *to accomplish*. When **achievement** is used erroneously as a direct object, the sentence containing it can usually be corrected by replacing **achievement** used as a noun with the verb *to achieve*.

Poor: Capitalism has **accomplished** many **achievements** and left many **achievements** unaccomplished.
Better: Capitalism has **achieved** many things and left many things **unachieved**.

adapt/adopt; adaptation/adoption

Adapt and **adopt** are often confused. **To adapt** is a verb meaning *to make fit or suitable* or *to adjust*. This verb implies a modification according to circumstances. **To adopt** is also a verb, meaning *to take or receive as one's own* or *to accept. Canada World Youth participants usually* **adapt** *well to their new environment,* **adopting** *the customs and mannerisms of their new community.*

Remember as well that the noun derived from **adapt** is **adaptation**, and the noun derived from **adopt** is **adoption**. The two are not interchangeable.

Incorrect: The **adoption** to the Arctic climate was slow for the teachers from Southern Ontario.
Corrected: The **adaptation** to the Arctic climate was slow for the teachers from Southern Ontario.

adjectives and adverbs

Adjectives modify nouns; adverbs modify verbs, adjectives, and other adverbs. In North American colloquial speech, however, adjectives are often used to modify other adjectives and verbs, particularly in some formulaic expressions like *real slow* and *real loud*. While this may sound Texan and friendly, the construction is completely unacceptable in academic prose. Use adverbs instead.

Incorrect: John Wayne moves **real slow**.
Corrected: John Wayne moves **really slowly**.

Incorrect: The announcer spoke **loud** and **quick**.
Corrected: The announcer spoke **loudly** and **quickly**.

Another common adjective/adverb error arises in the use of linking verbs. When a linking verb is used, the complement after it modifies the subject (a noun or pronoun), not the verb: *Carmen is extravagant*. In this sentence, *extravagant* describes Carmen, not *is*. Since only adjectives can modify nouns, the complement, *extravagant*, must be an adjective, not an adverb.

To determine if a verb is acting as a linking verb, ask yourself whether the word or word group following the verb relates to the subject or to the verb. If your answer is the subject, you have a linking verb, and you should use an adjective. If your answer is the verb, the verb is active and requires an adverb: *Carmen is extravagant, so she buys goods extravagantly.*

Verbs like *feels* or *smells*, which can be linking verbs or non-linking verbs depending on context, cause most adjective/adverb problems.

Correct: Doctors report that patients suffering from this nasal problem often **smell badly**; these patients have problems identifying sour odours.

Correct: Compost heaps rarely **smell bad**.

Incorrect: One might associate pulp and paper mills with air pollution since they **smell badly**.

Corrected: One might associate pulp and paper mills with air pollution since they **smell bad**.

adverse/averse

Adverse means *opposing, contrary*, or *unfavourable*. Think of the noun **adversary**. **Averse** means *disinclined, unwilling*, or *having a strong feeling of repugnance or distaste*. Think of the noun **aversion**. *I am averse to long cycling trips, especially in adverse weather conditions*.

advice/advise

Advice is a noun meaning *guidance*, and **advise** is a verb meaning *to give guidance, to counsel, to recommend*, or *to notify*. The two words cannot be used interchangeably.

Incorrect: Few Canadians under thirty seek personal **advise** from a minister or priest.

Corrected: Few Canadians under thirty seek personal **advice** from a minister or priest.

affect/effect

These two words are often confused, particularly in their most common usage. Although **affect** can be used in other senses (for example, psychologists use **affect** as a noun meaning *emotion* or *feeling*), the word is usually a verb meaning *to influence*: *Alistair Horne's experiences during World War II affected his perception of the First World War*. **Effect** is most commonly used as a noun meaning *result* or *consequence*: *The effect of these experiences is most visible in his book The Price of Glory: Verdun, 1916*. However, **effect** can also be used as a verb meaning *to cause, to bring about, to accomplish*, or *to perform*: *A good manager will effect necessary changes without adversely affecting employee morale*. Avoid using the noun **effect** when your meaning requires the verb **affect**, and vice versa.

Incorrect: The recital **effected** me deeply.

Corrected: The recital **affected** me deeply.

Incorrect: The decision to strike had serious **affects**.

Corrected: The decision to strike had serious **effects**.

afflict

See **inflict/afflict**.

afraid of/frightened by

Use **at** or **by** after **frightened** and **of** after **afraid**. *One of Freud's patients was afraid of horses; he was frightened by the possibility that they would bite him.*

afterward/afterwards

See **toward/towards**.

agree on/agree to/agree with

Try to use the correct preposition with **agree**. People **agree on** the details of something or **on** a particular course of action after consulting one another. They **agree to** a proposal or a request for action. Often, this proposal or request has been framed by individuals outside of the group doing the agreeing. People **agree with** other people or another person on an opinion or on an interpretation of reality. Also, we sometimes say that the weather, the food, or another circumstance **agrees with** us. *While some truckers agree with government officials concerning the importance of drug testing, few will agree to support testing of all truckers, especially since unions have not agreed on their official reaction to a drug-testing policy.*

all of

Of can be eliminated after the adjective **all** when it adds no meaning.

Poor: **All of** the machinists are on strike.

Better: **All** machinists are on strike.

However, when the reference is to a single whole, the **of** will be necessary: *All of me, why not take all of me?*

all right/alright

Never use **alright**; most readers consider it an incorrect spelling of **all right**. **All right** can be used to give assent or to mean *correct, safe, unharmed*, or *without fail*. However, avoid using **all right** to mean *satisfactorily* or *well* in academic writing.

Poor: While approximately sixty per cent of Switzerland's people speak German, a large number of these German speakers also speak French and Italian **all right**.

Better: While approximately sixty per cent of Switzerland's people speak German, a large number of these German speakers also speak French and Italian **well**.

all together/altogether

These terms are not interchangeable. **All together** should be used to refer to things or people grouped together in one place: *The necessary information was all together in a file in the Director's Office*. **Altogether** usually means *wholly* or *entirely*: *Never put off till tomorrow what you can avoid altogether*. However, it can also mean *in all*: *Altogether, eighteen Prime Ministers have served Canada between 1867 and 1987*.

allow

See **make/allow/make possible**.

allude/refer/elude

When you **allude** to something, you call attention to it indirectly. When you **refer** to something, you call attention to it directly. To distinguish between **allude** and **refer**, remember that an allusion is an indirect reference: *The speaker referred frequently to Milton's propensity to allude to the Bible.*

Do not confuse **elude** with **allude**. When you **elude** something, you avoid it or escape from it by using your cunning or quickness.

allusion/delusion/illusion
See **illusion/allusion/delusion**.

along the line; along this line
Both **along the line** and **along this line** are usually used as filler and can easily be replaced by a more precise word or phrase.

Poor: Somewhere **along the line**, Jennifer lost interest in film.
Better: **At some point**, Jennifer lost interest in film.

Poor: Please compose your essay **along these lines**.
Better: Please compose your essay **in this way**.

aloud/out loud
Both expressions mean *audibly*, but **aloud**, being shorter and less colloquial, is preferable.

already/all ready
The adverb **already** means *previously, by now*, or *earlier*. The phrase **all ready** is used as an adjectival modifier meaning *completely prepared*. *They were **all ready** for battle, but the armistice had **already** been signed.*

alternate/alternative
The verb **alternate** means *to change back and forth* or *to occur by turns*, and the adjective **alternate** means *succeeding each other by turns* or *referring to every other item in a series*. **Alternative** implies *the idea of making a choice*.
*A manic depressive **alternates** between delirium and depression.*
*The hidden message is discernible only by reading **alternate** lines of the poem.*
*To live is great, considering the **alternative**.*
*An **alternative** interpretation of Balzac's The Girl with the Golden Eyes is possible.*
Because **alternate** can also be used as a noun meaning *a substitute*, it is sometimes used incorrectly as an adjective when **alternative** would be correct.

Incorrect: An **alternate** solution would be to penalize the offenders.
Corrected: An **alternative** solution would be to penalize the offenders.

alternately/alternatively
Alternately and **alternatively** are also frequently confused. Again, remember that **alternately** implies *by turns* and **alternatively** implies *choosing*. *The water ran **alternately** hot and cold, so we could risk being scalded in the shower or, **alternatively**, we could remain dirty.*

altogether/all together
See **all together/altogether**.

among/between
Many texts counsel writers to use **among** when discussing relationships involving three or more people or things and to use **between** when discussing relationships involving two people or two things. This advice is sometimes useful. *The Supreme Court judges discussed the case **among** themselves and decided **between** the defendant and the plaintiff.* However, when an individual or an object is involved in a relationship characterized by obligations or associations with each of the other two, three, or more individuals or objects, **between** is preferred. *Negotiated trade agreements **between** Canada, America, and Mexico could create an American trading zone.*

amount/number
Amount is used when the thing or concept being described is considered as a total or mass, when it is uncountable. **Number** is used with countable things or persons. *A small **number** of environmentalists did a large **amount** of political lobbying.*

and/as well
See **as well/and**.

anti-/ante-
The prefix **anti-** means *against* or *opposite of* while the prefix **ante-** means *before*. ***Anti**-slavery agitators were not well received in the **ante**bellum South of the 1840s.*

anticipate/expect
Anticipate and **expect** are often used interchangeably. However, **anticipate** implies that an event or circumstance is not only being foreseen but also being met. *A perfect friend, he **anticipated** all her needs and desires; she came to **expect** this sensitivity of him.*

anybody/any body; anyone/any one
Both **anybody** and **anyone** mean *any person at all* or *any person not specified*. They are both singular. **Any one** refers to *a specific person, thing, or group* and **any body** to *a specific body*. *The mercury level of **any body** of water should be tested before **anybody** consumes its fish. **Anyone** who has studied film knows the names Charlie Chaplin, Buster Keaton, and Harold Lloyd; **any one** of these comedians has influenced the comedic film genre.*

anxious/eager
Anxious means *worried* or *uneasy*. **Eager** means *keen* or *enthusiastic*. Avoid using **anxious** when the connotation should be positive, and **eager** when the connotation should be negative.

Poor: The newly elected M.P.P. was **anxious** to please her constituents.
Better: The newly elected M.P.P. was **eager** to please her constituents.

appraise/apprise
Appraise is a verb meaning *to estimate the value or nature of something*. The verb **apprise** means *to inform* or *to advise*. It is often followed by *of*. *The manager was **apprised** of her department's financial problems, and hired an accountant to **appraise** the department's efficiency.*

apt/liable/likely
Apt and **likely** have similar meanings. **Apt**, however, is best used to indicate *a tendency or the state of being fit to do something* while **likely** is best used to indicate *a probability*. *Being absent-minded, the professor was **apt** to forget which of her classes she was addressing. She is **likely** to deliver a lecture on Plato's Republic to today's class.* In a legal context, **liable** means *legally responsible*. Generally, however, **liable** is used to mean *exposed to risk* or *in danger of*. When distinguishing between **liable** and **apt**, remember that **liable** always implies a negative outcome: it would be appropriate to write *Nick is **liable** to become a criminal* but inappropriate to write *Nick is **liable** to get the job he has always wanted*.

are/our
See **our/are**.

as, as if, as though/like
See **like/as, as if, as though**.

as far as...is concerned

Avoid confusing this expression with *as for*. *As for* does not require a verb to complete it, but **as far as...is concerned** needs the **is concerned** to be complete.

Incorrect: **As far as vegetarians**, subsidization of the beef industry should be halted.

Corrected: **As far as vegetarians are concerned**, subsidization of the beef industry should be halted.

The expression **as far as...is concerned** can also often be wordy. When possible, try to replace it with a more concise expression.

as well/and

Although these expressions both imply *addition*, they are not interchangeable grammatically. Do not use **as well** as a conjunction between two clauses; if you do, you will create a comma splice.

Incorrect: Thatcherism has left its stamp on the British, **as well** it has affected Western politics in general.

Corrected: Thatcherism has left its stamp on the British, **and** it has affected Western politics in general.

assure/ensure/insure

Assure means *to promise* or *to give an assurance*. Both **ensure** and **insure** can be used to mean *to guarantee* or *to make certain*. However, the use of **insure** is often limited to discussions of financial or legal guarantees while **ensure** is used in broader contexts. *The union leader **assured** his constituency that the company would **ensure** that the workers were **insured**.*

averse

See **adverse/averse**.

awhile/a while

The adverb **awhile** modifies a verb and means *for a while*. It is therefore incorrect to write *for **awhile***. In any prepositional phrase, the correct form is **a while**: *for a while*, *in a while*, *after a while*. *Hitler abided by the terms of the Russo-German non-aggression pact **awhile**, since safeguarding his eastern frontier was worth his **while**. After a **while**, however, he changed his strategy.*

backward/backwards

See **toward/towards**.

bad/badly

See **adjectives and adverbs**.

barely

See **can't hardly; can't scarcely**.

be/become

The verb **to be** indicates *existence*; the verb **to become** indicates *the process of coming to be, of changing*.

Incorrect: After the end of the Mau Mau uprising, it took Kenya four years **to be** independent.

Corrected: After the end of the Mau Mau uprising, it took Kenya four years **to become** independent.

because, for/since

See **since/for, because**.

because of

See **due to, owing to/because of**.

because/reason is because

Sometimes, **because** is incorrectly used to mean *that*. The result is a **reason is because** sentence, a construction that is both redundant and grammatically incorrect.

Incorrect: The **reason** for the Conservatives' introduction of Bill C-54 **was because** a Gallup poll indicated that Canadians wanted strict anti-pornography legislation.

Corrected: The **reason** for the Conservatives' introduction of Bill C-54 **was that** a Gallup poll indicated that Canadians wanted strict anti-pornography legislation.

Better Still: The Conservatives introduced Bill C-54 **because** a Gallup poll indicated that Canadians wanted strict anti-pornography legislation.

become

See **be/become**.

belabour/labour

People often **labour** a point: they overdo their explanation or proof of it. It is difficult to **belabour** a point, to beat it soundly.

below; above

See **above; below**.

beside/besides

Currently, a distinction is made between **beside** and **besides**. **Beside** is always used as a preposition meaning *next to* or *out of contact with*. As a preposition, **besides** is used to mean *in addition to* or *other than*. In informal writing, **besides** can also be an adverb meaning *moreover, also*, and *as well*. *Putting a tire dump **beside** a populated area is dangerous. **Besides** a risk of chemicals leaching into the area's water supply, there is the danger of fire. **Besides**, living next to an unsightly pile of tires is unpleasant. For most people, these drawbacks are **beside** the point. They worry more about the consequent decrease in the property value of their homes.*

better/best

See **worse/worst**.

between/among

See **among/between**.

between...and.../between...to...

When using the preposition **between**, the two items should be joined with **and**, not **to**.

Incorrect: **Between** 1960 **to** 1965, universities expanded.

Corrected: **Between** 1960 **and** 1965, universities expanded.

Another possible revision would be to change the preposition **between** to *from*, thereby retaining the *to*.

Corrected: **From** 1960 **to** 1965, universities expanded.

bring/take

In speech, **bring** and **take** are often used interchangeably, but they have different connotations. **Bring** implies *movement toward a place, to come here with*; usually, the place is one associated with the speaker. **Take** implies *to go away from a place, to go there with*; usually the place is not associated with the speaker. *The Prime Minister **brings** his aides home for a party, but he **takes** them to Europe for summit meetings.*

Poor: Joe Clark tries to **bring** his luggage to foreign countries but often fails.

Better: Joe Clark tries to **take** his luggage to foreign countries but often fails.

can/may

Can means *to be able to* or *to be capable of.* **May** means *to be permitted to* or *to be allowed to.* In other words, **can** indicates ability or capacity and **may** indicates permission (although in speech the two are often used interchangeably). **May** can also be used to indicate possibility. *Although American icebreakers can negotiate Arctic waters, Canada has stated that the United States may not use this route. Further negotiations may be necessary to resolve this issue satisfactorily.*

cannot help but

This phrase is not considered standard by many readers. To avoid problems, substitute a gerund (a verb form ending in *-ing*) for **but** and the verb that usually follows it.

Poor: The historian **cannot help but be** astonished at this odd interpretation of General Lee's motives.
Better: The historian **cannot help being** astonished at this odd interpretation of General Lee's motives.

can't/cannot/can not

While we have used contractions such as **can't** in this book in an attempt to make the text seem less formal, contractions should generally be avoided in academic writing because they are considered too colloquial. **Cannot** is usually preferable to **can not**; use **can not** only when you want to be emphatic.

can't hardly; can't scarcely

Words like **hardly**, **barely**, and **scarcely** can cause problems if they are linked with a negative. They are themselves negatives, so linking them with a negative creates a faulty double negative. Use **can hardly** and **can scarcely**.

Incorrect: Many low-income families **can't hardly** pay rent.
Corrected: Many low-income families **can hardly** pay rent.

capital/capitol

We can write about a **capital** letter, the **capital** of a country, the **capital** collected by **capitalists**, and the **capital** or top part of a building's column. We can also discuss **capital** punishment with a **capital** fellow who is the **capital** proponent of prison reform. However, the U.S. Congress holds its sessions in the **Capitol**, and any other edifice housing a legislature might be called a **capitol**. To summarize, use **capitol** when naming these buildings, and **capital** in all other circumstances.

Incorrect: The **capitol** of Canada is Ottawa.
Corrected: The **capital** of Canada is Ottawa.

careless/uncaring

Careless can be defined as the opposite of careful. **Uncaring** can be defined as the opposite of caring. *A careless man might misplace his bus fare; an uncaring woman would not help him find it.*

censor/censure

Censor and **censure** are often used and confused. **Censor** can be a noun meaning *an official who examines books, films, and other materials for the purpose of suppressing parts deemed objectionable* or a verb meaning *to examine and suppress or delete, to expurgate.* As a verb, **censure** means *to find fault with, to criticize in a harsh manner, to reprimand.* The noun **censure** means *blame* or *disapproval.* *Feminists have trouble deciding whether pornography should be censored. Most support freedom of expression but also censure those who depict violence against women and children.*

centre on/centre around, centre about

Centre around and **centre about** are redundant because to **centre** already means *to collect around a central point* or *to focus on a central point.* To **centre** is not synonymous with *to gather.* Therefore, it is logical and economical to write **centre on** rather than **centre around** or **centre about**.

Poor: The debate **centred around** supplying birth control to teenagers.
Better: The debate **centred on** supplying birth control to teenagers.

character

The word **character** is often used needlessly. Try to avoid expressions such as *of a _____* **character** or *the _____* **character of the _____** when they are not essential to your meaning.

Poor: According to George Carlin, football is a game **of a barbaric and ruthless character**.
Better: According to George Carlin, football is **a barbaric, ruthless game**.

cite/sight/site

Cite is a verb meaning *to refer to, quote, or bring forward as an example, proof, or precedent.* **Site** is most frequently a noun meaning *the location of an actual or planned structure,* but it can be a verb meaning *to situate or place in position.* To **sight** means *to see* or *to spot.* *Once Fraser had skimmed the horizon and sighted the rowers moving toward the site of the new building, he returned to the work at hand: citing sources for his essay.*

compare/contrast

To **compare** is *to examine in order to perceive similarities,* although in the course of perceiving similarities, one might perceive some differences. A **comparison** is the act of comparing. To **contrast** is *to examine only differences.* A **contrast** is a striking difference.

complement/compliment

Complement implies *completion.* As a verb, it means *to bring to complete perfection,* and as a noun, it means *the quantity or number required to make a thing complete.* **Compliment** implies *flattery* or *praise.* As a noun, it means *an expression of praise, respect, admiration, or best wishes,* and as a verb, it means *to make such an expression.* *Lewis complimented the host on providing the perfect complement to the evening meal: chocolate mousse.*

compose/comprise/include

Compose means *to form by putting together, to constitute or form the substance of something by composing.* **Comprise** means *to contain* or *to include.* The difference between these two words is one of perspective; a whole is **composed** of its parts, and these parts **comprise** it. Also, **compose** implies the act of putting the whole together. *A Bloody Mary is composed of vodka and tomato juice; vodka and clamato juice comprise a Bloody Caesar.* When only some parts of the whole are being examined, use **include** rather than **comprise**: *The ingredients for a Marguerita include tequila and salt.*

conscience/conscious/conscientious

Because these words sound alike, they are frequently confused. The noun **conscience** means *a personal guide or inner voice which helps determine right from wrong*. **Conscientious** is the adjectival form of **conscience** meaning *governed by conscience*. The adjective **conscious** means *aware* or *capable of perceiving, apprehending, or noting*. *Criminals are often* **conscious** *of laws, but their* **conscience** *does not seem to help them act* **conscientiously**.

consequently

See **subsequently/consequently**.

contact

This verb means *to make a connection*. It is too frequently used when other verbs (*to telephone, to write, to consult, to speak to, to meet with*) would be more exact.

Poor: Please **contact me in person** regarding your proposal to reduce our company's overhead costs.

Better: Please **meet with me** regarding your proposal to reduce our company's overhead costs.

continual/continuous

Continual implies *a steady and sometimes infinite reoccurrence*, while **continuous** suggests *an uninterrupted duration, a continuity*. *The professor delivering a* **continuous** *monologue remained undisturbed by the* **continual** *opening and closing of the door*. Avoid using the terms in reverse.

Poor: The meeting was **continuously** interrupted by phone calls.

Better: The meeting was **continually** interrupted by phone calls.

contrast/compare

See **compare/contrast**.

could of

See **of/have**.

council/counsel

The noun **council** means *an assembly which discusses, decides, and advises*: *The Canada* **Council** *makes many decisions about arts funding in Canada*. As a verb, **counsel** means *to advise*, and as a noun, it means *advice given* or *an adviser (lawyer, consultant)*. The terms cannot be used interchangeably.

Incorrect: The planning **counsel** plays a key role in municipal affairs.

Corrected: The planning **council** plays a key role in municipal affairs.

credible/creditable/credulous

If something is **credible**, it is *believable*. If something is **creditable**, it *deserves commercial credit* or *is good enough to bring praise or esteem*. A **credulous** individual is *too ready to believe*: he or she is gullible. *Though the witness gave a* **creditable** *performance, her story was incredible. The* **credulous** *jury, however, thought her fiction* **credible**.
Writers occasionally confuse **credulous** with **credible**.

Incorrect: The stories in the National Enquirer hardly seem **credulous** to most critical readers.

Corrected: The stories in the National Enquirer hardly seem **credible** to most critical readers.

criteria/criterion

Criteria is plural; **criterion** is singular.

Incorrect: The committee used the following **criterion** for judging the applications: applicability to target groups, contribution to community, and cost.

Corrected: The committee used the following **criteria** for judging the applications: applicability to target groups, contribution to community, and cost.

critique

While gradually gaining in acceptance, the practice of using **critique** as a verb is still regarded as non-standard. In the strictest sense, **critique** is a noun meaning *a critical estimation or discussion*. When you require a verb, use *evaluate* instead.

Poor: The guest lecturer **critiqued** current trends in sociological theory.

Better: The guest lecturer **evaluated** current trends in sociological theory.

data/datum

Data is the plural of **datum**, a word rarely seen these days. Although **data** is often treated as a singular noun in informal speech and writing, it should be treated as a plural in academic prose.

Incorrect: The statistical **data** on bankruptcy **has** shocking implications for small business.

Corrected: The statistical **data** on bankruptcy **have** shocking implications for small business.

decimate

Strict usage calls for the use of **decimate** only when a tenth of a whole is destroyed or deducted. Do not use **decimate**, therefore, when you mean *annihilate*. For example, it is often said that the North American native population was **decimated** after European contact, but such a statement does not accurately convey the severity of the impact of disease.

decrease

See **increase; decrease**.

deduction

See **induction/deduction; induce/deduce**.

delusion

See **illusion/allusion/delusion**.

dependent/dependant

Dependent is an adjective which means *contingent, subordinate*, or *relying on another person or thing for support*. **Dependant** is a noun meaning *one who is dependent*, especially *one who relies on another for financial support*. *For income tax purposes, most children under eighteen are classified as* **dependants**, **dependent** *on their parents or guardians for financial support*.

dialogue

Dialogue is a noun meaning *an exchange of ideas and opinions, a conversation between two or more people*, or *a communication between two or more computers or between a computer and a person*. Although the verb **dialogue** has existed since 1597, its current popularity is considered a result of the increasing encroachment of computer terminology upon English diction. Avoid using **dialogue** as a verb in academic writing.

Poor: The American president **dialogued** for several hours with United Nations representatives.

Better: The American president **talked** for several hours with United Nations representatives.

differ from/differ with

Differ from means *to be unlike* while **differ with** means *to disagree with*. *The debaters **differed with** one another to provide a lively discussion, although they didn't **differ from** one another substantially in economic and social background.*

different than/different from

While **different than** is becoming acceptable, **different from** is still preferred in academic writing.

Poor: Marx's perception of the effects of the industrial revolution is **different than** Weber's.

Better: Marx's perception of the effects of the industrial revolution is **different from** Weber's.

However, when a clause follows the expression of difference, **different than** is acceptable, particularly if using **different from** would encourage wordiness.

Poor: Fredericton had a **different** atmosphere **from what** the travel agent had expected.

Better: Fredericton had a **different** atmosphere **than** the travel agent had expected.

discreet/discrete

Both are adjectives. **Discreet** means *having or showing discretion*. A **discreet** individual is tactful, unpretentious, modest, and sensible enough to remain silent and unnoticed when necessary. **Discrete** means *having a separate or discrete entity, one that is distinct or unconnected*. *Discreet Lester saw his lovers as **discrete** entities and met each one separately.*

disinterested/uninterested

A **disinterested** person is *impartial, unbiased, objective*; an **uninterested** person is *not interested* or *indifferent*. *The Human Rights Committee requires **disinterested**, but not **uninterested**, members.*

Incorrect: His bored facial expression suggested that Chris was completely **disinterested** in the subject.

Corrected: His bored facial expression suggested that Chris was completely **uninterested** in the subject.

disorient/disorientate

See **orient/orientate**.

distinct/distinctive

Distinct implies *discreteness* or *separateness* while **distinctive** implies *stylishness* or *worthiness*. *Quebec is and wants to be perceived as a **distinct** society, recognizably different from the rest of Canada. The women of Montreal dress comfortably yet with a **distinctive** flair seldom seen in Toronto.*

do

This verb is frequently used as a substitute for a more precise verb, and the result is awkward and unclear: *I will **do** my essay tomorrow; the private investigator will **do** his presentation next; the subjects should have **done** their sleeping before the experiment began.* Revise and tighten by using a more accurate verb: *I will **write** my essay tomorrow; the private investigator will **present** next; the subjects should have **slept** before the experiment began.*

due to, owing to/because of

Due to and **owing to** are used to mean *traceable to, resulting from*, or *the result of*; they always introduce an adjectival phrase, never an adverbial phrase. **Because of** is used to mean *as a result of*. Many careful editors object to the use of **due to** or **owing to** for **because of**. A good rule of thumb is to use **due to** and **owing to** only after a form of the verb *to be* and never at the beginning of a sentence. *Excessive tooth decay is often **due to** bulimia and is caused by contact with gastric juices during self-induced vomiting. **Because of** this contact, tooth enamel is eroded.*

Incorrect: **Owing to** his lack of entrepreneurial experience, the Soviet businessman had difficulty entering the European market.

Corrected: **Because of** his lack of entrepreneurial experience, the Soviet businessman had difficulty entering the European market.

due to the fact that; owing to the fact that

See **owing to the fact that; due to the fact that**.

each other/one another

Strict grammarians use **each other** when referring to two people or things and **one another** when referring to more than two people or things. *The husband and wife loved **each other**, but their three children hated **one another**.*

eager/anxious

See **anxious/eager**.

easy/easily

See **adjectives and adverbs**.

ecology/ecosystem

Ecology is *the branch of science which studies inter-relationships in the biological world*. An **ecosystem** is *a set of inter-related biological elements*. Be careful not to use **ecology** when you mean **ecosystem**.

Incorrect: The marshland **ecology** is worth studying.

Corrected: The marshland **ecosystem** is worth studying.

effect/affect

See **affect/effect**.

e.g./i.e.

See **i.e./e.g.**

either; neither

Either means *one of two*, and **neither** means *not one of two*. Therefore, it is usually considered an error to make either **either** or **neither** refer to more than two things, people, or actions.

Incorrect: She has studied piano, violin, and voice, but is expert at **neither**.

Corrected: She has studied piano, violin, and voice, but is expert at **none**.

either...or; neither...nor

Either goes with **or**, and **neither** with **nor**. When these correlative conjunctions are used, it is considered proper form to make the portion of the sentence coming after the **or** or **nor** parallel to that which is after the **either** or **neither**.

Poor: Canada's North is viewed as either **a wasteland** or **it is treated like a storehouse**.

Better: Canada's North is viewed as either **a wasteland** or **a storehouse**.

elicit/illicit

See **illicit/elicit**.

elude

See **allude/refer/elude**.

emigrate/immigrate

To **emigrate** is *to leave one's country for another.* To **immigrate** is *to enter a new country to live.* Consequently, one **emigrates** <u>from</u> somewhere, and one **immigrates** <u>to</u> somewhere. *Many Chinese wish to **emigrate** from Hong Kong before 1997; some have already **immigrated** to Canada.*

eminent/imminent/immanent

An **eminent** person is *distinguished* or *outstanding* in some way. An **imminent** thing is *ready to take place.* **Immanent** means *inherent* and is used primarily by philosophers and theologians to refer to the idea that God or a spirit pervades the world. *That God is **immanent** in all things was argued by an **eminent** pantheist whose death was **imminent**.*

endless/innumerable

See **innumerable/endless**.

enervate/invigorate

To **enervate** means *to sap the vitality* or *to reduce the strength of someone or something.* To **invigorate** means almost the opposite, *to animate.* Because writers associate **enervate** with *energy*, the term is often used incorrectly.

Incorrect: After a long day of study, the student needed an **enervating** walk in the fresh air.

Corrected: After a long day of study, the student needed an **invigorating** walk in the fresh air.

ensure

See **assure/ensure/insure**.

envelop/envelope

The verb **envelop** means *to cover* or *to surround.* **Envelope** is a noun meaning *something to mail a letter in. The scented **envelope** appeared to **envelop** a love letter.*

especially/specially

These two words are so close in meaning that many dictionaries regard them as synonyms. Some, however, think that **especially** indicates *preeminence* and means *particularly* while **specially** stresses *having a unique character* and means *for a special or certain reason. I **especially** value the cradle which my husband made **specially** for our first child.*

etc.

In the interests of clarity, this abbreviation of the Latin phrase *et cetera*, which literally means *and other things*, should be avoided unless it appears at the end of a list that demonstrates a logical progression (*2, 4, 6, etc.*). In other circumstances, finish your list by naming its other members. Notice that when the abbreviation is used, a comma precedes it. Remember also that *and* **etc.** is redundant since *et cetera* already means *and other things*. Finally, keep in mind that **etc.** should not be used at the end of lists introduced by phrases like *for example* or *such as* because these introductions already imply that there are other items in the list.

every one/everyone; every body/everybody; every day/everyday

Everybody and **everyone** are indefinite pronouns meaning *every individual. **Everyone** knows fairy tales in which **everybody** lives happily ever after.* Note that some readers would consider **everybody** too informal for academic prose.

The phrase **every body** has an adjective (**every**) modifying a noun (**body**) while the phrase **every one** has an adjective (**every**) modifying a pronoun (**one**). Both of these combinations refer to each of the things or people mentioned following them: *every body of literature, every one of the books.*

Everyday is an adjective meaning *daily* or *ordinary.* The phrase **every day** has an adjective (**every**) modifying a noun (**day**) and means *each day. Television advertisements tell us every day to buy **everyday** wear.*

evoke/invoke

To **evoke** is *to call forth, to bring to mind,* or *to recreate imaginatively.* To **invoke** means *to petition for help, to appeal to an authority,* or *to put into practice. The scent of pine cones **evoked** the summers spent at camp where we **invoked** the powers of heaven to keep the weeks sunny and the tents dry.*

example/instance

Example refers to *a typical person or thing that is representative of a group or type.* **Instance** applies to *a single person or thing offered to illustrate a concept.* Although *for instance* and *for example* are considered interchangeable, **example** and **instance** often are not.

Poor: One **instance** of a bird is the red-headed woodpecker.

Better: One **example** of a bird is the red-headed woodpecker.

except

See **accept/except**.

expect

Expect means *to look forward to as certain or probable.* In academic writing, therefore, do not use **expect** to mean *suppose, think, presume,* or *imagine.*

Poor: I **expect** Bergson is correct in his analysis of determinism.

Better: I **believe** Bergson is correct in his analysis of determinism.

expect/anticipate

See **anticipate/expect**.

explicit/implicit

These two adjectives are antonyms. **Explicit** means *fully expressed* or *explicated* and **implicit** means *capable of being understood though unexpressed* or *implied. While the **explicit** sex of pornographic films offends some people, most are more disturbed by the **implicit** messages such films communicate.*

extant/extent/extend

The adjective **extant** means *currently existing*: *Heather Cooper is one of the most famous Canadian graphic designers **extant**.* **Extent** is a noun meaning *scope* or *range*: *The **extent** of Cooper's fame is limited, however.* The verb **extend** means *to spread, stretch, advance,* or *prolong*: *The journal* <u>Communication Arts</u> *has helped to **extend** the influence of commercial artists like Cooper.*

the fact is

See **the truth is; the fact is**.

factor

Expository writers tend to overuse this word meaning *an element that contributes or promotes, an ingredient*. Very often, **factor** is unnecessary and should be eliminated.

Poor: A contributing **factor** in the popularity of soccer is the World Cup.

Better: The World Cup contributes to the popularity of soccer.

farther/further

Further and **farther** are both comparatives of the word *far*. In formal writing, **farther** is used to refer to distance and **further** to quantity, time, or degree. Further, **further** can be used as a conjunctive adverb meaning *besides*, or as a verb meaning *to advance*. *The farther Napoleon's army marched, the more important it became to receive further supplies so further victories could be secured and Napoleon's reputation as a victor could be furthered.*

Incorrect: The map is not drawn to scale, and, in fact, Edmonton and Calgary are much **further** apart than the map would suggest.

Corrected: The map is not drawn to scale, and, in fact, Edmonton and Calgary are much **farther** apart than the map would suggest.

fatal/fateful

Fatal means *deadly* while **fateful** means *momentous*. These two adjectives are often confused. *The Brahmin was not concerned when on a fateful day he was diagnosed as having a fatal disease.*

feature

Like *factor*, this word often creates wordiness rather than meaning. See if your sentence can do without it.

Poor: A **feature** of Heart of Darkness which must be discussed is Marlow's role as narrator.

Better: Marlow's role as the narrator of Heart of Darkness must be discussed.

feel

Feel is frequently used in informal speech and writing to mean *think* or *believe*. In the interests of precision, it is best to limit the use of **feel** to the description of emotional or physical reaction.

Poor: I **feel** that Schlesinger's biography of John Kennedy has been a best-seller.

Better: I **think** that Schlesinger's biography of John Kennedy has been a best-seller.

few/a few

Sometimes **few** implies fewer than **a few**. Consider these sentences. *Where his political ambition was involved, Nixon had few scruples. Where his political ambition was involved, Nixon had a few scruples.* The former sentence suggests that Nixon had next to no scruples, the latter that Nixon had enough scruples to be counted.

few/a little; fewer/less

Few and **fewer** are used with countable nouns while **a little** and **less** are used with uncountable (mass) nouns. *Few cats will refuse a little milk, although less milk and more water would mean fewer trips to the veterinary.*

Frequently, **less** is used incorrectly with countable nouns.

Incorrect: **Less** people are attending community college.

Corrected: **Fewer** people are attending community college.

figuratively

See **literally/virtually/figuratively**.

figure

Using **figure** to mean *calculate*, *think*, or *believe* is considered a colloquialism. Avoid it.

Poor: Copernicus **figured** that the earth rotated daily on its axis.

Better: Copernicus **thought** [or **estimated**] that the earth rotated daily on its axis.

finalize

This relatively new verb is often deemed unnecessary by strict grammarians. Since there are other words to use in its place (*complete, conclude, finish, approve*), it is probably best to avoid it.

first/firstly; second/secondly

As well as being an adjective, **first** is an adverb in its own right, so there is no need to add the *-ly*. It is proper and economical to write **first, second, third,** etc., but **first, secondly, thirdly, etc.** is also acceptable. **Firstly**, however, is considered pedantic. Use **first** in all cases.

fix/repair

Using **fix** to mean *repair, organize*, or *prepare* is too informal for academic prose. Stick to the long-established meaning of **fix**: *to make stable* or *to give permanence to*. *The Canadian government tried to repair the economic damage done by the 1990 constitutional crisis by fixing interest rates well above those in the United States to attract foreign investment.*

flaunt/flout

These verbs have different meanings. **Flaunt** means *to show off* and **flout** means *to treat contemptuously* or *to disregard*. *Lord Byron flaunted his individuality by flouting the conventions of English society.*

Incorrect: A common strategy among activists is to **flaunt** authority by breaking laws.

Corrected: A common strategy among activists is to **flout** authority by breaking laws.

following

See **above; below**.

for/since/because

See **since/for, because**.

foreseeable future

If the **future** were **foreseeable**, everyone from weather forecasters to astrologers would be out of a job. Just write *the future* or *the near future* and forget **foreseeable**.

foreword/forward

A **foreword** is *a prefatory comment*, like the **foreword** of a book. This word is always a noun. **Forward**, however, can be an adjective (meaning *in advance, brash, precocious*, or *radical*), an adverb (meaning *toward what is in advance*), or a verb (meaning *to advance* or *send onward*). *"Forward to the future," commanded the forward young author who wrote the book's foreword to advocate that the city move forward.*

former/latter

When two things are listed, **former** refers to the *first* and **latter** to the *second*. This is easy to remember by associating **former** with *first* and **latter** with *last*. If more than two items comprise your list, however, use neither **former** nor **latter**. Sometimes *first, second, third,* and *last* will do as substitutes. Whenever you use referents like this, or like **former** and **latter**, make sure that no confusion regarding what is being referred to exists.

forward/forwards

See **toward/towards**.

frightened by/afraid of
See **afraid of/frightened by**.

from/off
See **off/from**.

further/farther
See **farther/further**.

genuine/real
See **real/genuine**.

good/well
Good is always an adjective; **well** can be used as an adjective or an adverb. Errors arise when **good** is used as an adverb.

Incorrect: Joan Armatrading sang **good** at the concert.
Corrected: Joan Armatrading sang **well** at the concert.

Be careful not to over-correct here. When **good** completes a sentence with a linking verb, it functions as an adjective and is perfectly acceptable: *I feel good; that news is good; souvlaki tastes good*.

gotten/got
Gotten and **got** are both past participles of *get*, and either is acceptable. However, **gotten** is usually considered the more archaic of the two.

See also **have got to; have got to get**.

had ought to; hadn't ought to
Ought in the past tense is the same as in the present. **Had ought** should be corrected to **ought**, and **hadn't ought** to ought not.

Incorrect: The government **had ought** to have regulated investments in savings and loans companies.
Corrected: The government **ought** to have regulated investments in savings and loans companies.

Incorrect: The skyscraper **had not ought** to have been built on Yonge Street.
Corrected: The skyscraper **ought not** to have been built on Yonge Street.

Ought is always used with an infinitive, so problems also arise when the verb **ought** is used in conjunction with other auxiliary verbs. Remember to tack **to** onto **ought**: *I ought to and will visit my friend*. Another easy solution is to substitute the word *should*: *I should and will visit my friend*.

half a/a half/a half a
Avoid writing **a half a**. Write **a half** or **half a**: not *a half a loaf*, but *a half loaf* or *half a loaf*.

hanged/hung
The past tense of the verb *to hang* is **hung**: *Tom Dooly hung down his head*. The past form **hanged** refers to execution by hanging: *He was hanged from the old oak tree*. Do not use **hanged** when you mean **hung**.

Incorrect: Lester **hanged** his coat by the door.
Corrected: Lester **hung** his coat by the door.

hardly
See **can't hardly; can't scarcely**.

have got to; have got to get
These expressions are colloquial and should be avoided in formal writing because the **got** or **got to get** is redundant, since **have**, like **got**, can mean *to be obliged to* or *to possess*. Depending on context, you may either delete the **got** or substitute *must, should*, or *ought to* for the entire phrase.

Poor: Researchers **have got to** invent a better disposable diaper.
Better: Researchers **have to** invent a better disposable diaper.

Poor: Terry **has got to get** admitted to medical school.
Better: Terry **must** be admitted to medical school.

See also **gotten/got**.

herself; himself; myself
These reflexive pronouns are customarily used in sentences following a particular pattern: *Alex hurt himself; I told myself to stop; Erica made herself eat*. These words should not be used as subjects of sentences or objects of prepositions.

Incorrect: Alex and **myself** ate at Charlotte Anne's.
Corrected: Alex and **I** ate at Charlotte Anne's.

Incorrect: The governor-general asked the premier to attend a meeting with the prime minister and **himself**.
Corrected: The governor-general asked the premier to attend a meeting with the prime minister and **him**.

Incorrect: The matter pertains only to my lawyer and **myself**.
Corrected: The matter pertains only to my lawyer and **me**.

historic/historical
There is a clear distinction between these two words. **Historic** refers to *something of timely or great significance*: *This is an historic moment*. **Historical** means *concerned with or a part of history*: *They have recovered all the lost historical documents*. Avoid confusing the two.

Poor: The file on Louis Riel contains useful **historic** material.
Better: The file on Louis Riel contains useful **historical** material.

hopefully; thankfully
Hopefully means *full of hope*, and it should not be used to mean *it is hoped* or *I hope*. **Hopefully** should be used only to modify a verb: *The fans looked hopefully at the clock*. The word cannot be used to modify an entire clause. In such cases, use *I hope* or *it is hoped* instead.

Incorrect: **Hopefully**, this experiment will support the theory that sleep disruption interferes with dream patterns.
Corrected: **It is hoped** that this experiment will support the theory that sleep disruption interferes with dream patterns.

Note that another adverb that creates a similar problem is **thankfully**; it also cannot modify an entire clause.

Incorrect: **Thankfully**, the experiment was a success.
Corrected: We are **thankful** that the experiment was a success.

however

Because **however** has two distinct meanings that require different punctuation, it causes many problems. **However** is most commonly used as a conjunctive adverb meaning *nevertheless*: *I would like to attend; however, I cannot. I am, however, free next Thursday.* Note that when **however** is used as a conjunctive adverb, it requires punctuation marks enclosing it. **However** can also be used as an ordinary adverb indicating degree. In this use, it means *no matter how, no matter how much, in some degree,* or *in some way*: *However difficult it may be for them to travel, they will make the trip.* When **however** functions as an ordinary adverb, no punctuation is needed. Confusion results when the punctuation around **however** is incorrect.

Incorrect: **However** the course presents an interesting addition to the study of anthropology.

Corrected: **However**, the course presents an interesting addition to the study of anthropology.

human/humane

Human means *of, or belonging to the human race.* **Humane** means *possessing kind, highly civilized characteristics.* Do not use **human** when you mean **humane**.

Poor: Maslow's theory concerning a hierarchy of needs is more **human** than Taylor's principles of scientific management.

Better: Maslow's theory concerning a hierarchy of needs is more **humane** than Taylor's principles of scientific management.

I; you; we

See **you; I; we**.

i.e./e.g.

The abbreviation **e.g.** stands for the Latin phrase *exempli gratia*, which means *for example.* The Latin phrase *id est* is abbreviated to **i.e.**, and means *that is.* Don't confuse the two.

Incorrect: Some animals are more susceptible to fatal illnesses when confined in zoos, **i.e.**, whales, pandas, and dolphins.

Corrected: Some animals are more susceptible to fatal illnesses when confined in zoos, **e.g.**, whales, pandas, and dolphins.

Punctuate these abbreviations carefully (following the models above) and use them cautiously. Many readers would prefer that you avoid them altogether by introducing your examples and qualifications formally with the words *for example* and *that is.*

illicit/elicit

Elicit is a verb meaning *to bring out.* Someone might **elicit** a response, a truth, or anything latent. **Illicit** is an adjective meaning *not permitted* or *unlawful. The **illicit** gambling house was doomed to **elicit** a strong reaction.*

illusion/allusion/delusion

These terms are frequently confused. An **allusion** is an indirect reference or mention: *Biblical **allusions** pepper the works of English literature.* The words **delusion** and **illusion** are sometimes interchangeable; however, there is a subtle distinction between their meanings. **Delusion** can mean *a false belief that has been accepted.* **Illusion**, on the other hand, can mean *a false impression or idea that has not been completely or permanently accepted. While summer days give us the **illusion** of permanence, we must not suffer under the **delusion** that we are immortal.*

immanent/imminent/eminent

See **eminent/imminent/immanent**.

immigrate/emigrate

See **emigrate/immigrate**.

impact

As a noun, **impact** means *the striking of one object against another: The **impact** of the ball against the window shattered the glass.* Problems arise when **impact** is used as a verb. While **impact** can be used as a verb meaning *to pack firmly* (*The painter will **impact** the caulking around the window*), **impact** is often used as a verb when the meaning is clearly that of the noun form. This latter use of **impact** as a verb has become commonplace; nevertheless, it is best to avoid this usage in academic writing.

Poor: The high cost of living **impacted** on their savings.

Better: The high cost of living made **an impact** on their savings.

Better Still: The high cost of living **decreased** their savings.

implicit/explicit

See **explicit/implicit**.

imply/infer

To **imply** is *to suggest*; to **infer** is *to draw conclusions.* One **implies** when one hints at something not clearly evident: *She **implied** that the exam would be difficult when she urged everyone to study.* One **infers** when one is able to draw conclusions from evidence presented: *I **inferred** that this year's exam would be difficult when I saw a copy of the one the students wrote last year.* A standard rule of thumb is that the transmitter of an idea **implies** and the recipient of an idea **infers**.

importantly

This adverb is often tucked into prose without an explanation of how or why a thing, person, or concept is important. The reader is left begging for more information.

Poor: **Importantly**, the figures show that the depletion of the caribou herd was not abrupt, but spread over a period of years.

Better: It is **important** that the figures show that the depletion of the caribou herd was not abrupt, but spread over a period of years, because an abrupt depletion would indicate the presence of disease.

in/into

In indicates *position in time or space: He enrolled **in** several courses to complete his degree.* **Into** implies *movement from out to in, from outside to inside: He moved all his possessions **into** the dormitory.* Avoid using **in** when you mean **into**.

Poor: He walked **in** the room and removed his coat.

Better: He walked **into** the room and removed his coat.

incidents/incidence

These homonyms can be confused. **Incidents** are *events or occurrences: **Incidents** that happen in our youth leave lasting impressions.* **Incidence** usually means *the degree or rate of occurrence: The **incidence** of a complete solar eclipse is very low.*

Incorrect: The **incidents** of AIDS is still on the rise.

Corrected: The **incidence** of AIDS is still on the rise.

include

See **compose/comprise/include**.

increase; decrease

Only numbers or nouns which refer to quantities can **increase** or **decrease**. You can **increase** the number of sweaters you own, but you cannot **increase** sweaters. You can **decrease** the number of errors on a test, but you cannot **decrease** errors.

individual/person

The word **individual** is used properly when the intent is to consider a human being who stands out in contrast to his or her group or society: *Many Canadians had concerns about the development of natural resources in the North, but few* **individuals** *reflected on the matter as carefully as Thomas Berger did.* **Person** should be used instead of **individual** when no contrast is involved.

Poor: Picasso's biographers have portrayed him as a self-absorbed **individual**.

Better: Picasso's biographers have portrayed him as a self-absorbed **person**.

induction/deduction; induce/deduce

These are two common methods of reasoning. **Induction** is *reasoning from facts or premises to a general principle or conclusion.* Many pieces of information add up to something: *After observing the migratory patterns of hundreds of Canadian geese, we* **induced** *that these birds fly north in the spring and south in the fall.* **Deduction** is *reasoning from a general principle to a specific case or fact: Since all bears hibernate in winter, we* **deduced** *that we would not encounter any in the park in January.*

infer/imply

See **imply/infer**.

inflict/afflict

These two verbs have the same Latin root, *fligere*, which means *to strike*, but they have slightly different idiomatic usages. **Inflict** means *to burden or bear down on someone or something* and is used with the preposition *upon* or *on*: *We tried not to* **inflict** *our unhappiness on the rest of the group.* **Afflict** means *to bring pain to someone or something* and is used with the preposition *with*: *During the camping trip, we were* **afflicted** *with insect bites.* Note that **inflict** often implies an action caused by the subject, while **afflict** usually implies an action received by the subject.

Incorrect: Many children are **inflicted** with AIDS.

Corrected: Many children are **afflicted** with AIDS.

information

Just remember that you give, not tell, **information**. **Information** is something given by telling. The telling is implied.

Poor: She **told** me the **information**.

Better: She **gave** me the **information**.

innumerable/endless

Do not confuse **endless** with **innumerable**. **Endless** means *infinite*, or *without end*. **Innumerable** means *too many to be numbered*. These words can be, and often are, used interchangeably. Knowing their distinct meanings allows you to choose the most accurate word.

Poor: Procuring a student loan involves **endless** steps.

Better: Procuring a student loan involves **innumerable** steps.

inside of/the inside of, inside

Inside can function as a noun: *He is going to paint* **the inside of** *the box.* It can also be a preposition: *He is going to paint* **inside** *the box.* Sometimes, writers combine the two phrases awkwardly and the result is the imprecise **inside of**, which confuses the reader and creates a wordy double preposition. Always revise **inside of** to express your meaning precisely.

Poor: He is going to paint **inside of** the box.

Better: He is going to paint **the inside of** the box.

Better: He is going to paint **inside** the box.

instinctive/instinctual

Both words are adjectives, but they are used in slightly different ways. **Instinctive** means *of or having a natural or inborn tendency* and is synonymous with *involuntary*. **Instinctual** means *to possess or display instincts. The trainer reacted* **instinctively** *when the tiger displayed* **instinctual** *aggressive behaviour.*

insure

See **assure/ensure/insure**.

interested/interesting/interestingly

Interested is an adjective meaning *having an interest, concern, or bias*: *He was an* **interested** *bystander.* **Interesting** is also an adjective, meaning *exciting interest or curiosity*: *He was an* **interested** *bystander of the* **interesting** *events.* **Interestingly** is the adverbial form of **interesting**. *He was an* **interested** *bystander of* **interesting** *events, and the plot of his story unfolded* **interestingly**.

invigorate/enervate

See **enervate/invigorate**.

invoke/evoke

See **evoke/invoke**.

irregardless

Irregardless has made its way into the dictionary, but its usage is not standard form. Avoid using it in all written work. **Regardless** is sufficient.

Incorrect: **Irregardless** of the outcome, Andrea will attempt to write the exam.

Corrected: **Regardless** of the outcome, Andrea will attempt to write the exam.

is when; is where

These constructions sometimes slip into speech when something is being defined or described. To eliminate them, try to reconstruct your sentence so that it has only one clause, not two.

Poor: Fraud **is where** people carry out deceptive, illegal activities.

Better: Fraud **is** a deceptive, illegal activity.

it is I/it is me

It is I is correct, not **it is me**. *Is* is a linking verb, so what follows it will be in subject form (**I**), not in object form (**me**). To avoid sounding overly stiff and formal, try *This is Alfred* (or whatever your name is) instead.

its/it's

Its is the possessive form of **it**, in just the same way that *his* is the possessive form of *he*: *The species has been identified, but* **its** *characteristics have never been recorded.* **It's** can only be one thing: a contraction of **it is** or **it has**: *It's a lovely day*; *It's been sunny all day.* If you want to check your prose for the correct usage of **its**, substitute **it is** for every occurrence of **it's**. If a nonsensical construction is created, you will know that the possessive is what you want. *The species had been identified, but* **it is** (!) *characteristics have never been recorded.*

judicial/judicious

Although both words are adjectives, **judicial** is usually used only in reference to the legal system; **judicious** means *having shown sound or fair judgment. The Canadian* **judicial** *system has made many* **judicious** *decisions.*

kind of

Kind of, meaning *rather* or *somewhat*, is considered slang: *rather* or *somewhat* is preferable.

Poor: Patricia Hearst was **kind of** influenced by terrorists.
Better: Patricia Hearst was **somewhat** influenced by terrorists.

labour/belabour

See **belabour/labour**.

laid/lain

See **lay/lie/laid/lain**.

last/latest

Both words are superlative forms of the word *late* (*late, later, latest*; *late, later, last*), and both mean *coming after all others*, but they have different connotations. **Latest** implies *most recent* or *most current*; **last** implies *final* or *conclusive, at the end*. *The* **latest** *broadcast reported that the Canadian soccer team placed* **last**.

later/latter

Weak spellers frequently confuse these words. **Latter** means *the last item mentioned of two items*: *The issues of economic independence and natural resource exploitation both must be considered, but this paper will focus on the* **latter**. **Later** means *subsequently* or *after some time*: *Economic independence will be considered* **later** *in the paper, after the more pressing issues have been addressed*.

latter/former

See **former/latter**.

lay/lie/laid/lain

To lay is *to place*: *I* **lay** *the clothes down, I* **laid** *the clothes down, I* **have laid** *the clothes down*. **To lie** is *to recline*: *I* **lie** *down, I* **lay** *down, I* **have lain** *down*. **To lay** always takes a direct object; **to lie** never does. Confusion arises when tenses are changed: note that the present tense of **to lay** is also the past tense of **to lie**. Be careful, therefore, to determine which verb you are using.

Incorrect: It would be best to **lie** the fabric near the counter.
Corrected: It would be best to **lay** the fabric near the counter.

Incorrect: She **laid** down half an hour ago.
Corrected: She **lay** down half an hour ago.

Incorrect: I have **lain** the clothes on your bed.
Corrected: I have **laid** the clothes on your bed.

lead/led

Lead pronounced with a long *e* (as in *beet*) is the present tense of the verb *to lead*: *The Liberals* **lead** *in popularity today*. **Lead** pronounced with a short *e* (as in *bed*) is a heavy metal: **lead** *pencils*, **lead** *weights*. **Led** is the past tense of the verb *to lead*: *The Conservatives* **led** *in popularity last month*. A common mistake is using **lead** as the past tense of *to lead*.

Incorrect: The orienteer **lead** us to the cave entrance before beginning to speak.
Corrected: The orienteer **led** us to the cave entrance before beginning to speak.

lend/loan

See **loan/lend**.

less/fewer

See **few/a little; fewer/less**.

liable

See **apt/liable/likely**.

liaise

Liaise is a verb created from the noun *liaison*, but it is not recognized as standard in most dictionaries. Academic readers consider it bureaucratic jargon. Replace it with a less offensive verb, or use the noun *liaison*.

Poor: Doctors wish **to liaise** with chiropractors.
Better: Doctors wish **to consult** with chiropractors.
Better: Doctors wish **to form a liaison** with chiropractors.

lighted/lit

Both these verbs can be used to form the past tense or past participle of the verb *to light*: *The lab technician* **lit** *[***lighted***] the fire*. However, **lighted** is more commonly used when the past participle is being used as a modifier: *The* **lighted** *match initiated a chain reaction*.

like/as, as if, as though

Avoid using **like** as a conjunction to join two clauses. **Like** is a preposition and is therefore considered incapable of joining clauses. Either **as**, **as if**, or **as though** is an appropriate substitute.

Correct: She is **like** a spoiled princess.

Incorrect: She acted **like** she didn't know me.
Corrected: She acted **as if** she didn't know me.

Incorrect: She acted **like** my teenage sister would.
Corrected: She acted **as** my teenage sister would.

like what

In this expression, **like** is usually being used incorrectly as a conjunction to join two clauses. Revise by changing the clause so that a prepositional phrase beginning with **like** can be used or by preserving the clause and replacing **like** with *as*.

Incorrect: To complete the equation, use a formula **like what** the textbook uses.
Corrected: To complete the equation, use a formula **like** the one in the textbook.

Incorrect: Canadians long to be powerful, **like what** Americans are.
Corrected: Canadians long to be powerful, **as** Americans are.

likely/liable/apt

See **apt/liable/likely**.

line

Using **line** to mean *field* or *area* or *department* is considered inappropriate in academic prose.

Poor: Bob White's **line** of work is union activism.
Better: Bob White is a union activist.

literally/virtually/figuratively

Literally means *exactly to the letter*; **virtually** means *practically, almost to the letter*. **Figuratively** stands in opposition, meaning *metaphorically, but not in actual fact*. Writers often use all three interchangeably and thus sometimes confound their meaning.

Incorrect: Rena, the beauty queen, was **literally** a goddess.
Corrected: Rena, the beauty queen, was **virtually** a goddess.

Incorrect: The concert hall **literally** exploded when Wynton Marsalis began to play.
Corrected: The concert hall **figuratively** exploded when Wynton Marsalis began to play.

a little/few

See **few/a little; fewer/less**.

loan/lend

Although many people use both these words as verbs, purists define **loan** as a noun. When in doubt, use **lend** if a verb is required.

Poor: Canadians will **loan** money to Germany.
Better: Canadians will **lend** money to Germany.

loath/loathe

Loath is an adjective meaning *reluctant*; **loathe** is a verb meaning *to despise or hate*. *Although many professionals loathe living in large urban centres, they are loath to give up the creative opportunities available in Toronto or Montreal.*

loose/lose

These words are frequently misspelled. **Loose** means *not tight*; **lose** means *to misplace*. Remember that **loose** has a double *o* by remembering that it rhymes with *moose, goose,* and *noose,* all of which also have two *o's*. **Lose**, on the other hand, has lost an *o*.

loud/loudly

See **adjectives and adverbs**.

mad

Use **mad** to mean *insane*; avoid using it to mean *angry*. When you change **mad** to *angry*, change the preposition too; you can not be *angry at* someone, only *angry with* someone.

Poor: Many American authors are **mad at** Tom Wolfe for criticizing their work.
Better: Many American authors are **angry with** Tom Wolfe for criticizing their work.

make/allow/make possible

All three verbs can mean *to cause a result*, but their connotations are different. **Make** used in this context implies force; **allow** and **make possible** suggest permitting something that someone already wants to do. Guard against using **make** when your meaning does not connote force.

Poor: Lowering tuition will **make** lower income students attend university.
Better: Lowering tuition will **allow** lower income students to attend university.

mandate

Mandate is almost always a noun, meaning *an authoritative requirement*. However, it can be a verb meaning *to assign a territory or region to a nation under a mandate*. Restrict your use of **mandate** as a verb to discussions of territorial responsibility.

Poor: The federal government **mandated** the provincial government to be responsible for education.
Better: The federal government gave the provincial government the **mandate** for education.

may/can

See **can/may**.

material/materialistic

Both **material** and **materialistic** can be used as adjectives denoting *interest in physical, rather than in spiritual or intellectual, matters*. However, the two have different connotations. **Material** is used to describe objects or items associated with physical needs or pleasures: *The couple had achieved a significant degree of material success.* **Materialistic** is closely associated with *materialism*, a philosophical doctrine that places the highest value on physical well-being and material possessions. **Materialistic**, therefore, should usually be used in association with people or cultures who might follow such a doctrine, either consciously or unconsciously: *Their materialistic values were evident in the number of appliances and gadgets in their home.* **Materialistic** is not usually used to describe objects.

Poor: The home computer is another **materialistic** object that many middle-class people purchase but few actually need.
Better: The home computer is another **material** object that many middle-class people purchase but few actually need.

maybe/may be

The single word **maybe** is an adverb meaning *perhaps*. As two words, **may be** forms the verb, or part of the verb, of a sentence.

Correct: **Maybe** Elvis is alive.
Correct: Elvis **may be** alive.

Incorrect: Elvis **maybe** living in Arkansas.
Corrected: Elvis **may be** living in Arkansas.
Corrected: **Maybe** Elvis is living in Arkansas.

me

As children, we are corrected so often by our parents for saying *Ralph and me are going to play* (*Ralph and I*) that we begin to believe that all compound uses of **me** are incorrect. It is true that **me** is incorrect as the subject of a sentence. However, **me** is correct as the object of any sentence or preposition.

Correct: Come to the store with Ralph and **me**.
Correct: Help Edie and **me** clean up this mess.

Incorrect: Ralph and **me** are going to the store.
Corrected: Ralph and **I** are going to the store.

meaningful

As an adjective, this term is useful, but can often be used imprecisely. **Meaningful** means *to be full of significance or import*. In instances in which the reader needs to know what type of significance or import something has, it is preferable to use a more concrete word or phrase.

Poor: The results of the trial experiment were **meaningful**.
Better: The results of the trial experiment were **statistically significant**.

meantime/meanwhile

Meantime is a noun; **meanwhile** is an adverb. **Meantime** therefore must usually be used in phrases such as *in the meantime*; **meanwhile** can be used alone.

Incorrect: **Meantime**, the Senate was stalling.
Corrected: **Meanwhile**, the Senate was stalling.
Corrected: **In the meantime**, the Senate was stalling.

medium/media/mediums

Medium is the singular form, **media** the plural, of the noun meaning *an agency through which things are communicated or transferred*. Make sure that the verb of your sentence agrees with the form you are using, and be sure to use the form appropriate to your intent.

Incorrect: The American **media is** biased against activists.
Corrected: The American **media are** biased against activists.

Incorrect: The **media** of radio is not as popular as that of television.
Corrected: The **medium** of radio is not as popular as that of television.

Mediums is the correct plural form for individuals who commune with the spiritual world.

meet up with

This is an awkward, wordy phrase that can usually be replaced by some form of the verb *to meet*.

Poor: When union **meets up with** management, conflict ensues.
Better: When union **meets with** management, conflict ensues.

minimal/minimum

Minimal is an adjective; **minimum** is conventionally a noun. The careful writer should avoid using **minimum** for **minimal**.

Poor: The provincial government spent the **minimum** amount of funds possible on preventative health care.
Better: The provincial government spent the **minimal** amount of funds possible on preventative health care.

momentarily

Avoid using **momentarily** to mean *in a moment*. **Momentarily** means *for a moment*: *The speaker seemed momentarily at a loss for words*.

Incorrect: It was expected that the ambassador would arrive **momentarily**.
Corrected: It was expected that the ambassador would arrive **in a moment**.

moral/morale

Moral is an adjective or noun concerned with *judgments about right and wrong*; **morale** is a noun concerned with *state of mind, confidence, hope. The troops have low **morale** because their actions have not been in accordance with their **morals***.

Incorrect: The **morale** of "The Paper-Bag Princess" is that girls should be independent.
Corrected: The **moral** of "The Paper-Bag Princess" is that girls should be independent.

more; most

More means *greater in amount, degree, or number*; **most** means *greatest in amount, degree, or number*. **More** is a comparative, and **most** is a superlative. Avoid using **more** with another comparative or **most** with another superlative.

Incorrect: Regina was her **most happiest** when alone.
Corrected: Regina was her **happiest** when alone.

Incorrect: In this case, Napoleon was **more smarter** than his opponents.
Corrected: In this case, Napoleon was **smarter** than his opponents.

motive/motif

Although these two words look alike, they do not have similar meanings. A **motive** is *a reason for action*; a **motif** is *a recurring subject or theme, a pattern. The quilter had a strong **motive** for using the leaf **motif***.

myself

See **herself; himself; myself**.

the nature of

Be judicious in your use of expressions beginning with **the nature of**. They may be wordy.

Poor: **The nature of** Freire's work is to teach about education.
Better: Freire's work is to teach about education.

need/want

Be judicious in your use of the word **need**. **Need** implies *necessity*, something that one cannot survive without, so if you use **need** when you mean **want**, you are in danger of exaggeration. *The lobby group **wants** the support of the entire Cabinet, but **needs** the support of only three cabinet ministers to halt the legislation*.

neither

See **either; neither** or **either…or; neither…nor**.

nice

Once upon a time, **nice** meant only *suitable* or *exact*. Now, everyone is **nice**, from the mass murderer down the street (he seemed like such a **nice** boy) to the woman someone considers too young to date (she's a **nice** kid). The term is used too vaguely and too often. Try for something more precise, like *pleasant*, or *disarming*, or *sincere*, or *agreeable*, or *honest*.

none…is

Although **none** can take either a singular or a plural verb depending on context, in instances in which **none** means *not one*, it should take a singular verb.

Incorrect: **None** of the celebrities mentioned in the article **are** sincerely interested in the cause discussed.
Corrected: **None** of the celebrities mentioned in the article **is** sincerely interested in the cause discussed.

nor

See **either…or; neither…nor**.

not…no; not…nothing; not…nobody; not…nowhere

The lyrics of many popular songs aside (*I **ain't** got **no** money*; *We **don't** need **no** education/We **don't** need **no** thought control*; *Baby, you **ain't** seen **nothing** yet*), it is not currently considered correct to use two negatives in one statement. We call this structure a double negative, and, as in mathematics, double negatives make positives (*I have money*; *We need education/We need thought control*; *Baby, you've seen it all*). Use *any* instead of **no**, *anything* instead of **nothing**, *anybody* instead of **nobody**, *anywhere* instead of **nowhere** in cases where one negative is already in place.

Incorrect: We **don't** need **no** thought control.
Corrected: We **don't** need **any** thought control.

number

See **amount/number**.

obsolete/obsolescent

An **obsolete** item is completely outdated and not in use, but an **obsolescent** item is in the process of becoming obsolete, though not quite there yet. *Eight-track tapes are **obsolete**; records are **obsolescent***.

of

Try not to overuse **of**. Often, in conversation, people will unnecessarily use **of** to follow another preposition, but this **of** is considered redundant in academic prose.

Poor: Passengers were directed to get **off of** the train while the police checked for bombs.

Better: Passengers were directed to get **off** the train while the police checked for bombs.

Poor: The bomb was eventually discovered **inside of** a suitcase.

Better: The bomb was eventually discovered **inside** a suitcase.

of/have

Avoid using **of** when your meaning requires the auxiliary or helper verb **have**. In speech, **have** sounds like **of** when we say *would've, should've, could've,* but what we are saying are the contractions of *would have, should have,* and *could have.* Never write *could of, should of, would of.*

Incorrect: Benjamin Franklin **could of** chosen not to go to France.

Corrected: Benjamin Franklin **could have** chosen not to go to France.

of which/whose

Normally we think of **who** and its derivatives as referring only to people. However, since **which** has no possessive form, we are permitted to borrow the possessive form of *who,* **whose,** to avoid wordy and awkward phrasing.

Poor: The book, **the back of which** was missing, was returned.

Better: The book **whose back** was missing was returned.

off/from

Off as a preposition means *no longer on.* Therefore, one can get a cup **off** a shelf because the cup can be *on* a shelf. However, people do not usually have items *on* them, so one cannot get items **off** people as one would get items **off** a shelf. Use **from** instead.

Incorrect: Restaurants usually buy produce **off** wholesale suppliers.

Corrected: Restaurants usually buy produce **from** wholesale suppliers.

off of

See **of** or **off/from**.

on

The preposition **on** implies a physical location: *London is situated on the Thames.* Avoid using **on** when you mean *about* or *concerning.*

Poor: Givner's book is **on** Katherine Anne Porter.

Better: Givner's book is **about** Katherine Anne Porter.

on account of

This is a wordy expression that can often be replaced with *because.*

Poor: I am writing **on account of** my interest in recycling.

Better: I am writing **because of** my interest in recycling.

Especially avoid using **on account of** in a sentence which already contains the word *cause.* The expression will be redundant since you will have two words or phrases meaning *cause* in it.

Poor: The **cause** for my writing is **on account of** my interest in cars.

Better: My interest in cars **causes** me to write.

one another/each other

See **each other/one another**.

one of the...if not the

This type of construction can often lead to faulty parallelism. Consider this sentence: *One of the first, if not the first, explorers was Leif the Lucky.* In this sentence, the word *explorers* does not agree grammatically with both phrases. It is possible to say *One of the first explorers was Leif the Lucky,* but it is not possible to say *The first explorers was Leif the Lucky.* Avoid this incongruity through rephrasing: *One of the first, if not the first, of the explorers was Leif the Lucky.*

opposed against/opposed to

Since **opposed** contains the idea of **against**, **opposed against** is a redundancy. Use **opposed to** instead.

Poor: Britain has occasionally been **opposed against** economic sanctions.

Better: Britain has occasionally been **opposed to** economic sanctions.

oral/verbal

Oral means *spoken* ; **verbal** means *connected with words.* A person who cannot speak might have excellent **verbal** skills, even though she might be unable to communicate **orally**. Although idiomatic expressions, such as *a verbal agreement,* contradict this definition, in strict usage, the distinction between the two terms should be preserved.

Incorrect: The urban planner spoke effectively in her **verbal** presentation.

Corrected: The urban planner spoke effectively in her **oral** presentation.

orient/orientate

-Ate may be added to nouns to form verbs (*invalid, invalidate* ; *orchestra, orchestrate*) or to nouns to form adjectives (*passion, passionate* ; *foliage, foliate*). However, writers make their prose sound verbose when unnecessary syllables are added, when **orient** becomes **orientate**, **disorient** becomes **disorientate**, and so on. All these words are words, but in academic writing, it is preferable to avoid the more convoluted form.

Poor: This map will help visitors to **orientate** themselves.

Better: This map will help visitors to **orient** themselves.

-oriented; -related

Avoid attaching these hyphenated suffixes to the end of words, since the result sounds awkward and convoluted.

Poor: Stephanie is a very **goal-oriented** worker.

Better: Stephanie is very concerned with working toward goals.

ought

See **had ought to; hadn't ought to**.

our/are

A common spelling mistake involves interchanging these two words. **Our** is a pronoun and occupies an adjectival position in a sentence (before a noun): *our house, our dog, our car.* **Are** is a form of the verb *to be,* and therefore will often follow a noun or pronoun: *they are going* ; *rattlesnakes are deadly.*

out loud

See **aloud/out loud**.

owing to, due to

See **due to, owing to/because of**.

owing to the fact that; due to the fact that

Both *owing to* and *due to* are acceptable adjectival expressions; **owing to the fact that** and **due to the fact that** are overly wordy.

Poor: The steady decline in the birth rate is often **due to the fact that** birth control devices are readily available.

Better: The steady decline in the birth rate is often **due to** the ready availability of birth control devices.

partially/partly

Partly has only one meaning: *not complete or total*. **Partially** can mean *not complete or total*, but it can also mean *showing favour* or *with bias*. For this reason, **partly** is preferable to **partially** in cases where meaning might be made ambiguous by the use of the latter word.

Poor: The decision to build the shopping mall was made **partially** by the developers.

Better: The decision to build the shopping mall was made **partly** by the developers.

passed/past

These homonyms are frequently confused. **Passed** is the past tense or past participle of the verb *to pass*: *I passed the Fiat*; *I passed the exam*. **Past** can be a noun or a preposition, an adjective or an adverb: *She spent the past few days of her life running past the golf course*. Since *past* is never a verb, make sure you always use **passed** in a verbal construction, and **past** everywhere else.

people/persons

These terms are synonymous; **persons** are **people**. **People**, however, usually connotes a large group seen as a collective whereas **persons** connotes a small group composed of individuals. *The people at the concert could barely hear the persons on the stage.*

per cent/percent; percentage

Both spellings, **per cent** and **percent**, are acceptable; however, **percentage**, a singular noun, must be spelled as one word.

person/individual

See **individual/person**.

personal/personnel

Personal means *connected to a particular person*; **personnel** is *the staff of an office or business*. *My personal secretary has worked for our Personnel Department.*

personalize

Personalize, unlike *priorize* or *prioritize*, does have an acceptable use as a verb; it means *to mark with one's initials*, as in *personalized stationery*. However, using **personalize** to mean *marked by one's personality* is considered jargon.

Poor: The Delarouxs **personalize** their bathrooms with designer hand soaps.

Better: The Delarouxs **decorate** their bathrooms with designer hand soaps.

personally

Personally is a useful adverb when your meaning demands that you separate the experience of one individual from that of a group or society as a whole: *My sister, a broadcaster, has been personally affected by cutbacks at the CBC*. However, avoid using **personally** as an absolute or intensifier. It is usually redundant.

Poor: **Personally**, I have little interest in jazz.

Better: I have little interest in jazz.

phase

Because **phase** comes from the Greek word for *appear*, in strict usage, it should refer only to changes that can be seen: *phases of the moon, phases of a construction project*. It should not be used to denote sections or parts of a whole.

Poor: In this **phase** of the text, Mailloux outlines his central argument.

Better: In this **section** of the text, Mailloux outlines his central argument.

phenomena/phenomenon

Phenomena is the plural; **phenomenon** is the singular. *A comet is an interesting phenomenon, but meteorites are interesting phenomena*. When using these terms, make sure that you use the accurate term, and that the verb of the sentence agrees with the subject.

Incorrect: The flying-saucer **phenomena is** not new.

Corrected: The flying-saucer **phenomenon is** not new.

plenty

Plenty is a noun meaning *an abundant supply*. Do not use it as a substitute for *very* or *extremely*.

Poor: Sylvester was **plenty tired** after chasing his tail all day.

Better: Sylvester was **very tired** after chasing his tail all day.

plus

Avoid using **plus** as a substitute for *and* or *in addition* in instances in which sums are not involved. **Plus** denotes numerical addition and should not be used figuratively.

Poor: Yeats was a mystic **plus** a poet.

Better: Yeats was a mystic **and** a poet.

population/populace/populous

The **population** of a locale is the number of residents in it. The **populace** of a locale, however, usually refers to the commoners of the locale and sometimes has a negative connotation implying mob. **Populous** is an adjective, meaning well-populated. *Ontario is a populous province, its population exceeding nine million. The populace of Toronto, however, dictates its will to the rest of the province.*

posses/possess

Posses is the plural form of the noun meaning *a band of men gathered to assist a sheriff*, a term that rarely appears in academic prose. **Possess** means *to own* or *to hold*. Individuals who depend on spell-checkers to proofread for errors need to remember that the spell-checker will recognize **posses** as a word.

practical/practicable

Something that is **practicable** is something that can be put into practice: *Ending drug wars by executing all dealers is not practicable: there are too many dealers*. However, **practical**, meaning *sensible*, could be substituted here: *Ending drug wars by executing all dealers is also not practical: it would cost too much*. Whereas **practicable** refers to the possibility of practising something or to the state of being able to put something into practice, **practical** implies that something is useful or sensible. Note also that only **practical** can apply to people.

practise/practice

These homonyms are often confused. In standard Canadian English, **practice** is a noun and **practise** is a verb. *At piano practice, Jake practised his scales.*

precede/proceed

Precede means *to go before*; **proceed** means *to commence, to begin*. *In a typical Christian wedding ceremony, a young woman, called a maid-of-honour, **precedes** the bride down the aisle before the religious ceremony can **proceed**.*

precedence/precedent

Both these words are derived from Latin terms meaning *to go before*, but they have different purposes. **Precedence** refers to who or what goes first: *In People magazine, movie stars take **precedence** over novelists.* **Precedent** has a legal connotation: **precedents** are set, meaning that a case or incident which has gone before will determine how a current case is viewed. Avoid confusing the two.

Incorrect: Most medical scientists believe that cancer research should take **precedent** over reproductive technology studies.
Corrected: Most medical scientists believe that cancer research should take **precedence** over reproductive technology studies.

preclude

Preclude means *to make something impossible because of another act already done*. Remember that people, therefore, cannot be **precluded**.

Incorrect: Folger's focus **precludes him** from investigating other possibilities in the novel.
Corrected: Folger's focus **precludes** his investigating other possibilities in the novel.

predominate/predominant

Predominate is a verb; **predominant** is an adjective. Both mean *to be superior in power*. *The **predominant** animals **predominate** in the desert.*

prescribe/proscribe

Prescribe means *to give directions in one way or another*. **Proscribe** means *to condemn* or *to outlaw*. *Although the headmistress had **prescribed** appropriate behaviour for the young women, many persisted in indulging in the **proscribed** activity of smoking cigarettes.*

presently

Presently means *in a short time* or *soon*. It is sometimes used to mean *currently* or *at this time*, but this usage can be considered an error. *Currently* is probably a better choice if you mean *at this time*.

Incorrect: **Presently**, Edgar is enrolled at Western.
Corrected: **Currently**, Edgar is enrolled at Western.

presumably/supposedly

See **supposedly/presumably**.

presumptuous/presumptive

Presumptuous means *arrogant* or *bold, presuming too much*; **presumptive**, usually a legal term, means *based on inference*. *It is **presumptuous** of the Secretary of State to make a decision about women's centres based only on the **presumptive** evidence that these centres are no longer needed.*

principal/principle

These two homonyms are often confused. **Principal** as a noun means *the head of a school*; as an adjective, it means *primary or chief*. **Principle** means *a general truth or law*. *The **principal** of Laurentian High was a **principal** influence on my life, primarily because of his **principles** regarding education.*

Incorrect: The **principle** reason for obeying traffic rules is safety.
Corrected: The **principal** reason for obeying traffic rules is safety.

priorize; prioritize

Both these words represent attempts to make a verb from the noun *priority*. Neither is acceptable in academic prose.

Poor: The newly elected government must **prioritize** its concerns.
Better: The newly elected government must **set priorities**.

prophecy/prophesy

Prophecy is the noun; **prophesy** is the verb. *The Sphinx **prophesied** a dreadful **prophecy**.*

proposition/proposal

Both words mean *plan*, but **proposition** has a negative connotation suggesting shadiness that **proposal** does not. *Shysters have **propositions** to make (or they **proposition** people); arbitrators and judges have **proposals**.* An exception to this is the use of the term **proposition** in logic and math: here it is a neutral term meaning *statement* or *operation*.

proved/proven

Both **proved** and **proven** can be used as past participles, although **proven** is considered the more standard form: *Alice has **proven** [**proved**] her worth.*

purposely/purposefully

Purposely means *intentionally* or *not accidentally*; **purposefully** means *to be infused with purpose, to be very deliberate*. The distinction is subtle, but **purposefully** is definitely the stronger and less common of the two words. *Chris worked **purposefully** to find a home that had not been **purposely** stripped of character.*

quality

Lately, **quality** is being used as an adjective: *Fathers want to spend more **quality** time with their children.* Like any current catch phrase, this expression sounds awkward in academic prose, so you should avoid it by substituting a more precise term.

Poor: Industries need to discover a **quality** solution to waste management.
Better: Industries need to discover a **viable** solution to waste management.

quick/quickly

See **adjectives and adverbs**.

quite

Quite, as an adverb, means *to the fullest* or *to a considerable extent*; it cannot be used as a synonym for *rather* or *somewhat*.

Poor: The two computer programs are **quite** similar, sharing one feature.
Better: The two computer programs are **somewhat** similar, sharing one feature.

quote/quotation

Quote is a verb: *Didion **quoted** Yeats.* **Quotation** is a noun: *The **quotation** was from "The Second Coming."* A common error involves using **quote** as a noun.

Incorrect: The following **quote** illustrates Bookchin's concern.
Corrected: The following **quotation** illustrates Bookchin's concern.

raise/rise

The verb **raise** is transitive: it requires an object. The verb **rise** does not. A common mistake is to use **raise** instead of **rise** in a sentence where there is no object.

Incorrect: The audience will **raise** from their seats to give a standing ovation.

Corrected: The audience will **rise** from their seats to give a standing ovation.

rational/rationale

Rational is an adjective meaning *reasonable*; **rationale** is a noun meaning *the logical basis of an idea or action*. *Placing her child for adoption was a **rational** choice based on the **rationale** that she could not raise the child on her own.*

ravish/ravage

Although both words come from the same root, do not use **ravish** unless you are talking about rape or rapture. If you are simply referring to destruction, use **ravage**.

Incorrect: The soldiers **ravished** the city, destroying all statues.

Corrected: The soldiers **ravaged** the city, destroying all statues.

real/genuine

Some writers use **real** incorrectly to mean **genuine**. **Genuine** means *authentic*: something **genuine** is not fake. **Real** means *existing*. A counterfeit bill, therefore, is always **real**, but it is not **genuine**.

real/really

See **adjectives and adverbs**.

reason is because

See **because/reason is because**.

reason why

This expression contains a redundancy since both **reason** and **why** indicate a cause and effect relationship. Usually the **why** can simply be omitted.

Poor: That's the **reason why** she quit school.
Better: That's the **reason** she quit school.

refer

See **allude/refer/elude**.

regarding

Regarding in some instances can be ambiguous, as it often is not clear whether the writer means *looking at* or *about*: *I am writing **regarding** the flowers* (writing while looking at the flowers? or writing about the flowers?). **Regarding** is also considered a little business-like for academic prose; it can usually be replaced with *about* or *concerning*: *I am writing **concerning** the flowers*.

Poor: He has misconceptions **regarding** the environment.
Better: He has misconceptions **about** the environment.

regardless/irregardless

See **irregardless**.

regretful/regrettable

Usually, a person is **regretful** (sorry about something) and an event is **regrettable** (we wish it hadn't happened). *The students were not **regretful** about their party, but they found the fire alarm incident **regrettable**.*

Incorrect: The accidental death of the diver was **regretful**.
Corrected: The accidental death of the diver was **regrettable**.

relate to

In speech, people often use expressions like *I can **relate to** the music of Bruce Cockburn*, meaning that they have an affinity for the subject under discussion. This expression is considered too informal in academic writing. Try *I **like** the music of Bruce Cockburn* or *I **have an affinity for** the music of Bruce Cockburn* instead.

-related

See **-oriented; -related**.

relation/relationship

Technically, **relationship** is necessary only when family connections are being discussed; otherwise, **relation** is simpler. However, most people use **relationship** to describe connections between people: *John and Mary have a good working **relationship***. Try to avoid using **relationship** when discussing objects.

Poor: The **relationship** between Wordsworth's "Intimations of Immortality" and Coleridge's "Dejection: An Ode" is immediately evident.

Better: The **relation** between Wordsworth's "Intimations of Immortality" and Coleridge's "Dejection: An Ode" is immediately evident.

relative/relevant

Because, in some usages, these words have similar meanings, they are often confused. **Relative** means *related to* or *regarded in relation to*; **relevant** means *pertinent to*. *The **relative** warmth of the house was **relevant** only to those who were cold*.

Incorrect: The information about Mayan ceremonies was **relative** to the topic of New World customs.

Corrected: The information about Mayan ceremonies was **relevant** to the topic of New World customs.

repair/fix

See **fix/repair**.

respectfully/respectively

Respectfully means *with respect*: *Alice spoke **respectfully** to her grandparents*. **Respectively** means *in the order given*: *Alice spoke to her grandmother and grandfather **respectively*** (grandmother first, grandfather second).

say/state

See **state/say**.

scarcely

See **can't hardly; can't scarcely**.

second/secondly

See **first/firstly; second/secondly**.

seeing that; seeing as how

These two awkward and wordy expressions can usually be replaced with *because, if,* or *since*.

Poor: **Seeing as how** the meeting is scheduled for Friday, perhaps the agenda should be set now.

Better: **Since** the meeting is scheduled for Friday, perhaps the agenda should be set now.

sensory/sensuous/sensual

The term **sensual** applies primarily to physical appetites — eating, drinking, sex — and tends to have a carnal connotation. **Sensuous** more broadly pertains to the senses; **sensuous** is the appropriate term to use when discussing poetry or art. **Sensory** also means *pertaining to sensation*, but only in terms of physiology or biology. *After months of **sensory** deprivation, I craved the **sensual** pleasures of food and drink and the **sensuous** pleasures of art and music.*

shall/will

Shall traditionally has been considered the appropriate indicator of the simple future in the first person: *Tonight I shall go to sleep.* **Will** has customarily indicated willingness or resolve in the first person: *I will go whether you want me to or not.* For second and third person, the reverse is true: *He will go to sleep; he shall go whether you want him to or not.* Such usage is still appropriate, but rare: most Canadian speakers now use **will** in all cases to indicate the simple future and **shall** either for formal circumstances requiring politeness (*We shall expect you for dinner at one*) or to indicate emphasis (*We shall overcome*). In academic prose, writers should follow the traditional conventions to be correct.

should have/supposed to

See **supposed to/should have**.

should of

See **of/have**.

sic

Sic is a phrase borrowed from the Latin meaning *thus* or *so*. It is used in academic work to indicate that an error or oddity in a quoted passage was in the original and is knowingly quoted verbatim: *Stevens writes, "We has (sic) no money."*

sight

See **cite/sight/site**.

simple/simplistic

Simple means *straightforward, not complex.* **Simplistic** has a negative connotation, implying *overly simple: Millhouse's argument was **simplistic** in that it overlooked several fundamental principles.*

since/for, because

As a subordinating conjunction, **since** can refer to time or to cause: *Since the invention of the automobile, oil and gas have become important natural resources; Since little thought was given to the pollution caused by the automobile, a substantial amount of environmental damage was sustained before car manufacturers modified design.* In a sentence where the meaning of **since** might be ambivalent, where **since** could refer either to time or to cause, use **because** or **for** to achieve greater precision.

Poor: **Since** the trees were cut in the area, tourism has declined.
Better: **Because** the trees were cut in the area, tourism has declined.

site

See **cite/sight/site**.

slow/slowly

See **adjectives and adverbs**.

so

When **so** is used to indicate degree or extent, it needs to be accompanied by *that*. Do not use **so** interchangeably with the intensifier *very*.

Incorrect: The Haida culture is **so** rich.
Corrected: The Haida culture is **very** rich.
Corrected: The Haida culture is **so** rich **that** art critics are often amazed by the complexity and sophistication of its art.

some one/someone

Some one and **someone** are not interchangeable. **Someone** should be used only if *somebody* can be substituted for it. Consider this sentence: *I would like **some one** person to be honest with me.* Obviously, saying *I would like **somebody** person to be honest* makes no sense, so the two-word version of **some one** should be used. On the other hand, if the sentence read *I would like **someone** to be honest with me, somebody* could be substituted readily, therefore the one-word **someone** would be appropriate.

some time/sometime/sometimes

Sometimes means *occasionally*, **sometime** means *at some indefinite point in the future*, and **some time** means *a quantity of time: **Sometimes**, I **sometime** think I would like to take **some time** from work to visit my uncle.*

somehow/somewhat

Don't confuse **somehow** with **somewhat**. **Somehow** means *in some way*; **somewhat** means *in some degree. I must **somehow** accept his **somewhat** unusual habits.*

sort of/sort of a

It is considered correct to use **sort of** when you are naming a specific species or type. However, avoid using the expression **sort of a**. The indefinite article confuses the reader, since it lessens the emphasis on *species* or *type*.

Poor: What **sort of an** artist is Emily Carr?
Better: What **sort of** artist is Emily Carr?

Also, avoid using **sort of** in sentences where you mean *rather* or *somewhat* and are not trying to name a specific type.

Poor: The Mexicans seem **sort of** ambivalent about expanding tourism.
Better: The Mexicans seem **somewhat** ambivalent about expanding tourism.

specially/especially

See **especially/specially**.

state/say

Since **state** is a stronger verb than **say**, use it primarily when you want to give emphasis.

Poor: He **stated**, "Let's drive to Toronto."
Better: He **said**, "Let's drive to Toronto."

Poor: He **said**, "I categorically forbid shorts to be worn in school."
Better: He **stated**, "I categorically forbid shorts to be worn in school."

stimulant/stimulus

Both these words mean *something that quickens action.* **Stimulant**, however, is usually used to describe something that quickens a physiological process: *Alcohol is a **stimulant**.* **Stimulus** can refer to anything that excites the mind or the spirit: *My interest in quilting served as a **stimulus** to buy a new sewing machine.*

subsequently/consequently

Subsequently and **consequently** are easily confused because both usually suggest the passage of time. The meaning of **subsequently**, however, is confined to time; **consequently** also indicates cause and effect. Avoid using **subsequently** when you want to show a causal relationship.

Incorrect: The temperature dropped below freezing; **subsequently**, the water froze.
Corrected: The temperature dropped below freezing; **consequently**, the water froze.

substitute for/substitute with/substitute by

One *replaces* one item **with** another, but one **substitutes** one item **for** another. The preposition **for**, therefore, is used with **substitute**. Do not use **with** or **by**, as you would with *replace*.

Poor: Trudeau **substituted** youth **with** charm.
Better: Trudeau **substituted** charm **for** youth.
Better: Trudeau **replaced** youth **with** charm.

suppose to/supposed to

Some people misspell **supposed to** by dropping the final *d* on **supposed**. The mistake is not surprising since the *d* cannot be heard in speech; nonetheless, it belongs there. *I was supposed to attend Queen's, but chose Trent instead.*

supposed to/should have

Supposed to and **should have** are often used interchangeably, most times with success. But be careful. **Supposed to** means *to be expected to, or required to* ; **should have** means *being under obligation*. **Supposed to**, therefore, should not be used to discuss an action that is not expected or required.

Poor: The prank was silly, but the girls were not **supposed to** be expelled.
Better: The prank was silly, but the girls **should** not **have** been expelled.

supposedly/presumably

When someone says *He is supposedly an expert*, that person is implying that perhaps the man in question is not an expert, since **supposedly** means *imagined to be*. When someone says *He is presumably an expert*, the sentence carries a much more positive meaning, since **presumably** means *reasonably expected*, rather than just *imagined to be*. *Elvis is supposedly still alive, but presumably is buried at Graceland.*

sure/surely

See **adjectives and adverbs**.

sure and/sure to

See **try and/try to**.

suspicious

The sentence *Renata was a very suspicious person* can have two meanings: either that Renata is **suspicious** of other people or that other people are **suspicious** of Renata. If the meaning is clear from context, you need not worry about the distinction. However, where meaning might be unclear, it is preferable to use **suspicious** to mean *distrustful of other people*. If you mean that the person's behaviour is questionable, make that meaning clear: *I am suspicious of Renata; Renata's actions are suspect.*

tack/tact

These two words are commonly confused by people using the expression *taking a different tack*. Although *taking a different tact* has a weird sort of logic (trying to be tactful, or diplomatic, in a different way), *taking a different tack* is the correct expression because the phrase comes from sailing, where **tack** means *a ship's course, especially a course run crosswind.*

take/bring

See **bring/take**.

than/then

These two words are not interchangeable. **Than** indicates a comparison: *The Diviners is a more ambitious novel than A Jest of God*. **Then** is associated with time: *Because Florida is warm in winter, my parents will return there then*. Proofread by substituting *when* for **then** to frame a question: *My parents will return when? Then*. If the substitution doesn't work, **than** is probably correct.

thankfully

See **hopefully; thankfully**.

that/this

See **this/that**.

that/which/who

Determining which of these relative pronouns is appropriate in a particular circumstance is not easy, especially because there are two separate matters to consider. First, the writer must decide whether the pronoun is being used to attach information to an animate or inanimate antecedent. **That** can be used with either an animate or inanimate object: *The man that sits in this chair is important* ; *The car that I prefer has standard steering*. **Which** is used exclusively with inanimate objects: *The necklace, which hung around her neck, was gold.* **Who** is used exclusively with animate objects: *Fred, who is my favourite uncle, has a large dairy farm*. A common error here would be to use **which** when referring to a person or to use **who** when referring to an inanimate object.

Incorrect: The Japanese ambassador, **which** was from Tokyo, spoke eloquently.
Corrected: The Japanese ambassador, **who** was from Tokyo, spoke eloquently.
Incorrect: The red Honda, **who** is sitting in the garage, has no brakes.
Corrected: The red Honda, **which** is sitting in the garage, has no brakes.

Once you have decided whether you are using the pronoun in connection with an animate or inanimate object, you need to think about another matter: whether the relative pronoun is being used to open a clause that contains essential information. In strict usage, **that** is used only to open restrictive clauses (clauses containing information essential to the meaning of the sentence): *The photograph that I will use is not developed yet.* **Which** and **who** are also sometimes used to open restrictive clauses, but they are most often used to open non-restrictive clauses (clauses that add information that is not essential to the meaning of the sentence): *The photograph, which I will use, is not developed yet.* Note how the meaning shifts in the sentence about the photograph when **which** replaces **that**. Note also the commas surrounding the **which** clause. When a clause is non-restrictive, it is enclosed in commas; when it is restrictive, no commas are used.

A common error made in this second choice is to use **that**, which indicates a restrictive clause, in conjunction with commas, which indicate a non-restrictive clause. The combination, because it sends contradictory signals, makes it difficult for the reader to determine meaning.

Incorrect: The vacuum cleaner, **that** is used in Act V, needs repair.
Corrected: The vacuum cleaner **that** is used in Act V needs repair.
Corrected: The vacuum cleaner, **which** is used in Act V, needs repair.

For more information on punctuating restrictive and non-restrictive clauses, see the chapter on punctuation.

then/than

See **than/then**.

there/their/they're; there's/theirs

Errors frequently result when these homonyms are used, so writers must learn to distinguish among them. **There** has several uses in a sentence. Most commonly it is used as an adverb indicating place: *The submarine is going there.* However, it is also often used as an expletive: *There are several items to consider.* **Their** is a possessive form of the pronoun *they*: *The women retrieved their possessions.* **They're** is a contraction standing for *they are* or *they were*. Try to associate **there** with *here* and *where*, which also end in *ere*, and **their** with *her, his,* and *its* (all of which do not use an apostrophe). Always read *they are* for **they're**. **There's** is also a contraction, standing for *there is*: *There's a hummingbird!* **Theirs** is another possessive form of the pronoun *they*: *The birdcage was theirs.*

To proofread for correctness, you can try the following substitutions.

Here or *where* for **there**:

There is a nice boy. *Here* is a nice boy.
I am sitting over *where*? I am sitting over **there**.

His, her, hers, or *its* for **their** or **theirs**:

It is **their** car. It is *her* car.
The child is **theirs**. The child is *his*.

If the substitution doesn't work, you are probably using the wrong word.

therefore/thus

See **thus/therefore**.

they

Remember that **they** is a pronoun and therefore by definition must stand in place of a group of people. That group of people should be clearly defined, although in conversation, we often use **they** vaguely: *They say it is going to rain.* (Who are **they**? Weather forecasters? People on the street?) In academic prose, avoid using **they** as a noun implying *society* or *the powers that be.*

Poor: **They** claim that a political crisis is unavoidable.
Better: **Foreign correspondents** claim that a political crisis is unavoidable.

this/that

Use **this** when referring to an item, concept, or person that is nearby in time, space, or thought. Use **that** when referring to an item, concept, or person at a distance in time, space, or thought. *This concept, which we discussed today, I understand, but that formula we learned last week seems unclear to me.*

thus/therefore

Thus means *in this manner*; **therefore** means *for this reason.* Although often both words may work in a particular passage, they are not always interchangeable.

Incorrect: Newcastle had no hotels; **thus** we continued our journey.
Corrected: Newcastle had no hotels; **therefore** we continued our journey.

thusly

Adding an *-ly* ending is a means of turning an adjective into an adverb: *slow/slowly, thorough/thoroughly.* **Thus** is already an adverb; adding *-ly* is the equivalent of writing *slowlyly* or *thoroughlyly.* Use **thus** instead.

tiring/tiresome

Lifting heavy objects is **tiring**; whiny three-year-olds are **tiresome**. Many activities are both **tiring** and **tiresome** — both exhausting and irritating.

to/two/too

Two is a number: *I have invited two people for brunch.* **Too** is an adverb, meaning either *in addition* (*Susan will probably come too*) or *in excess* (*She spends too much time with me*). Using **too** correctly is easier if you remember that it has an additional or an excessive *o* to match its meaning. **To** is usually a preposition (*She comes to my house at all hours*) or part of an infinitive (*She wants to drink coffee or gin*).

to/toward

To and **toward** are not interchangeable terms. **Toward** suggests moving in the direction of, but **to** hints at the possibility of arrival. In the sentence *We drove toward Toronto*, the reader knows that the car is somewhere outside of Toronto, and that Toronto is not necessarily the driver's destination. In the sentence *We drove to Toronto*, the reader knows that the car is within city limits.

toward/towards

Toward and **towards** are both acceptable. The former is the American spelling, the latter, British. Whatever spelling you choose, be consistent: always retain or drop the *s*. Be consistent as well in your spelling of **afterward/afterwards**, **backward/backwards**, and **forward/forwards**.

tortuous/torturous

Tortuous means *twisted*, either figuratively or literally. **Torturous** is an adjective meaning *to cause severe pain.* *European roads are often **tortuous** because they move with the contours of the land. As a result, they are **torturous** driving for the faint-hearted.*

transpire

The dictionary definition of **transpire** is *to give off waste products, to exhale,* or *to become known by degrees*: *As events **transpired**, the need for military action became evident.* However, **transpire** is often used informally as a synonym for *occurred*: *What **transpired** at the meeting?* In academic prose, this usage is considered inappropriate.

Poor: The witness described in great detail what had **transpired**.
Better: The witness described in great detail what had **occurred**.

true/valid/accurate

A **valid** statement (or argument, or point) is one that is believable or based on convincing evidence. A **true** statement is one that is faithful to reality, and that reality may be determined by the speaker. An **accurate** statement, however, is faithful to objective facts. *While it may be **true** that New Kids on the Block are like the Monkees, it is not **accurate** to say that they have no musical knowledge, so I do not find your argument that the group is fraudulent to be **valid**.*

true facts

What would a false fact be? A fact is a fact, and **true** adds no meaning here. The same holds true for *certifiable* and *accurate* in the expressions *certifiable **facts*** and *accurate **facts***.

the truth is; the fact is

These expressions are wordy expletives and usually unnecessary. We use them when speaking to give emphasis, but in academic prose they will sound slangy and redundant.

Poor: The **truth is** that the word professional has lost meaning.
Better: The word professional has lost meaning.

try and/try to

Avoid using **try and** as a substitute for **try to**. When you substitute **try and**, you create a compound verb that usually does not relay your intended meaning. *The NDP will **try and** enact socialist policies* means that the NDP will try socialist policies, and that they will enact socialist policies. *The NDP will **try to** enact socialist policies* means that they will make an attempt to enact socialist policies, and does not suggest that they will be successful in enacting them.

Incorrect: The government will **try and** reduce the deficit.
Corrected: The government will **try to** reduce the deficit.

two

See **to/two/too**.

type/type of

In written work, avoid using **type** immediately before a noun. Use **type of** instead.

Poor: An old-fashioned **type** rocker sat on the back porch.
Better: An old-fashioned **type of** rocker sat on the back porch.
Better Still: An old-fashioned rocker sat on the back porch.

-type

Avoid creating adjectives by ending words with **-type**.

Poor: She has an **electronic-type** sewing machine.
Better: She has an electronic sewing machine.

As the preceding example suggests, using **-type** not only creates jargon, but is often unnecessary.

uncaring

See **careless/uncaring**.

unexceptional/unexceptionable

Unexceptional means *ordinary*; **unexceptionable** describes *a person or object to whom none can take exception, something very nearly perfect. His **unexceptional** middle-class childhood was found **unexceptionable** by his new in-laws.*

uninterested/disinterested

See **disinterested/uninterested**.

upward/upwards

Upward and **upwards** are interchangeable only when used in the expression *upwards of/upward of*. Otherwise, use **upward**.

usage/use

Usually **usage** refers to custom: *"You all" is standard **usage** in the South*. Do not try to use **usage** interchangeably with **use**.

Incorrect: The **usage** of advertising in political campaigns is excessive.
Corrected: The **use** of advertising in political campaigns is excessive.

use/utilize, utilization

All sorts of possibilities for wordiness are provided by these words. **Utilize** and **utilization** should be used with caution. Since both mean *to make use of*, often the simpler term, **use**, in either a noun or verb form, can be substituted.

Poor: I will **utilize** Rousseau's ideas in my paper.
Better: I will **use** Rousseau's ideas in my paper.

Poor: The **utilization** of chemical fertilizers is prohibited.
Better: The **use** of chemical fertilizers is prohibited.

use to/used to

Occasionally writers will misspell **used to** by dropping the final *d* on **used**. Since the *d* cannot be heard, the error is understandable, but nonetheless incorrect.

Incorrect: Canada **use to** have nine provinces.
Corrected: Canada **used to** have nine provinces.

valid/true/accurate

See **true/valid/accurate**.

varied/various

Varied connotes *one whole consisting of different parts*; **various** connotes *several different wholes. My **varied** background has permitted me to meet **various** types of people.*

verbal/oral

See **oral/verbal**.

via

In strict usage, **via** is a preposition meaning *by way of* or *by a route passing through*: *I travelled to Vancouver **via** the Crowsnest Pass*. It does not mean *by means of* and in academic prose should not be used to refer to the means of travel.

Poor: Himmler received his orders **via** Hitler.
Better: Himmler received his orders **from** Hitler.

virtually/figuratively/literally

See **literally/virtually/figuratively**.

wait for/wait on

Waitresses **wait on** customers in that they serve them. Mothers **wait for** their children to finish basketball practice in that they sit patiently in a car watching the clock. The two expressions cannot be used interchangeably.

Incorrect: Canada **waited on** a reaction from the United States before lifting sanctions.
Corrected: Canada **waited for** a reaction from the United States before lifting sanctions.

want/need

See **need/want**.

was/were

Although many forms of the subjunctive are no longer in use, one that still remains is the convention of changing **was** to **were** to indicate subjunctive mood. The OED defines subjunctive as a verb form used to denote an action or a state as conceived (and not as a fact), and [expressing] a wish, command, exhortation, or a contingent, hypothetical or prospective event. Put more simply, the subjunctive is used to express a possibility or supposition, not to state an actual fact. In academic prose, this form appears most often in conditional sentences containing *if* (*If he were alive today, he would condemn this policy*) and in sentences expressing a desire (*I wish he were alive*). Do not use the indicative form of the verb *to be* when the subjunctive is necessary.

Incorrect: If one household **was** to change all its lightbulbs to low-wattage bulbs, a good deal of energy would be saved.

Corrected: If one household **were** to change all its lightbulbs to low-wattage bulbs, a good deal of energy would be saved.

way/ways

When discussing distance, always use **way**.

Poor: We still have a long **ways** to go.

Better: We still have a long **way** to go.

we

See **you; I; we**.

well/good

See **good/well**.

were/where

A common spelling mistake involves confusing these two words. **Where** is always connected to location or direction: *Where are the grapes? They are where the salad is.* **Were** is a form of the verb *to be*: *They were planning to attend the party but were delayed.*

whether/whether or not

Often **whether or not** is a wordy way of saying **whether**. In these instances, the less wordy form is preferable.

Poor: **Whether or not** the witness lied has not yet been determined.

Better: **Whether** the witness lied has not yet been determined.

However, there are occasions when you will want to use **whether or not** to emphasize the notion of giving equal attention to possibilities: *We will go whether or not it rains.* In this case, the *or not* cannot be omitted without losing the intended meaning of the sentence.

which/that/who

See **that/which/who**.

which means that

This is an awkward and wordy construction that can usually be replaced by *so, therefore,* or *thus*.

Incorrect: Montgomery died in 1941, **which means that** she did not live to see the war end.

Corrected: Montgomery died in 1941, **so** she did not live to see the war end.

while

While, used as a conjunction, can mean *during the time that* or *whereas* or *although*. Strict grammarians would prefer that **while** be used only in the first sense, but **while** can be used to mean *although* provided no ambiguity is created. Ambiguity will arise if the content of the sentence is such that **while** could mean either *during the time that* or *although*. If the reader might not be able to determine that *although* is the meaning you intend for **while**, use *although* instead of **while**.

Poor: **While** Sinclair Ross worked as a bank teller, he also wrote short stories and novels.

Better: **Although** Sinclair Ross worked as a bank teller, he also wrote short stories and novels.

who/which/that

See **that/which/who**.

who/whom

Writers often make mistakes in using **who** or **whom**. **Whom** seems more formal, so writers use it when formal prose is demanded rather than when grammatical convention requires it. Both **who** and **whom** have specific grammatical functions: **who** is used in a subject position or as a predicate pronoun; **whom** is used in an object position. You will use **who** and **whom** correctly if you think of them this way: *who/he, whom/him*: **Who** *is going? He is going.* **Whom** *are you cheering for? Are you cheering for him?*

Incorrect: The mayor, **who** constituents elected last term, will not run again.

Corrected: The mayor, **whom** constituents elected last term, will not run again. (Constituents elected him.)

Incorrect: **Whom** is the governor?

Corrected: **Who** is the governor? (He is the governor.)

whose/of which

See **of which/whose**.

whose/who's

These two words are frequently confused. **Who's** is a contraction for *who is*: **Who's** *going to graduate school?* **Whose** is the possessive form of *who*: **Whose** *socks are these?*

will/shall

See **shall/will**.

-wise

Avoid this hyphenated suffix in academic writing. It sounds immature or bureaucratic.

Poor: **Cost-wise**, I came out ahead.

Better: **In terms of cost**, I came out ahead.

Better Still: I did well financially.

worse/worst

Good, better, best; bad, worse, worst: think of these parallel sets of words and you can check your usage. *Stephen is a bad boy; his brother Michael is worse, but Patrick is the worst Wilson brother.* The common error is to use the comparative form, **worse**, when the superlative, **worst**, is required.

Incorrect: Patrick is the **worse** boy I have ever met.

Corrected: Patrick is the **worst** boy I have ever met.

Careful writers should also note that **worst** and **best** should not be used when only two items are being compared.

Incorrect: This banana is the **worst** of the two.

Corrected: This banana is the **worse** of the two.

These conventions also apply to other comparatives and superlatives such as *more/most* and *better/best*.

would of

See **of/have**.

you; I; we

Students often wonder when it is appropriate to use **you**, **I**, and **we** in academic prose. **You** is almost always too informal for an essay, since one is expected to respect the reader and maintain a certain distance. Sentences like *You can easily see why Hamlet is indecisive* should therefore be avoided.

The use of **I** is a little more difficult. All the opinions stated in your essay are yours, all the structures are your creations, so saying *I will first discuss* or *I believe that* is redundant. However, using **I** for emphasis, to stress your viewpoint, is perfectly acceptable in most disciplines.

The acceptability of **we** usually depends on context. When **we** is used, it implies a shared opinion: *We know that grass is green*. When you have no doubt that your opinion will be shared (after all, grass is green), you may use **we**. However, do not use **we** when there is some doubt as to whether the reader will agree with your statement.

Poor: **We** know that Milton made a greater contribution to literature than did Shakespeare.

Better: Milton made a greater contribution to literature than did Shakespeare.

For most of the exercises in <u>Clear, Correct, Creative</u>, there is no one correct answer. Passages can be revised several ways. For each exercise, we present one possible revision and an explanation of the choices made in that revision. Do not assume your revision is incorrect if it is not exactly like the one provided.

Chapter One: Composing Sentences

EXERCISE ONE: NONSENSE SENTENCES

What follows are a few examples of sentences created from the nonsense sentences in the exercise. You might like to compare your sentences to see if they match the typical pattern we describe.

1)

A brepling vlatage stuzlled quirmorly to haddle a floupen, zledful whurt.
A caring child struggled determinedly to rescue a sodden, beautiful kitten.
A strapping quarterback reached quickly to grab a floating, speeding ball.
A strong mule struggled agonizingly to pull a heavy, colourful cart.
A trembling youth struggled bravely to land a strong, beautiful fish.
A frightening dog barked loudly to scare a rotten, wilful sheep.
A braying donkey tried repeatedly to summon a drunken, neglectful farmer.
Typical Pattern:
Article / Adjective / Noun as Subject / Verb / Adverb / Infinitive / Article / Adjective / Adjective / Noun.

2)

Glump the meklest pizt.
Grab the biggest pie.
Make the best pizza.
Eat the biggest fish.
Grab the mustard pickle.
Jump the biggest fence.
Kiss the nicest girl.
Typical Pattern:
Verb / Article / Adjective / Noun.

3)

Did the woozes flek the chumped boph greeperly?
Did the dogs eat the chopped beef eagerly?
Did the painters sand the chipped wall properly?
Did the Jays win the big game easily?
Did the children eat the roasted pig eagerly?
Did the wives fluff the flattened pillows joyfully?
Did the walkers reach the covered bridge quickly?
Typical Pattern:
Auxiliary Verb / Article / Noun as Subject / Verb / Article / Adjective / Noun / Adverb.

4)

Ip's glipperful!
He's wonderful!
George is wonderful!
She's wonderful!
Music is beautiful!
It's wonderful!
That's sensational!
Typical Pattern:
Pronoun as Subject and Verb Contraction / Adjective.
OR
Noun as Subject / Verb / Adjective.

5)

To bech is to trackle Jenny's fleab.
To belch is to tickle Jenny's fancy.
To laugh is to deny Jenny's problem.
To eat is to offend Jenny's sensibility.
To be frustrated is to tackle Jenny's car.
To bend is to survive Jenny's temper.
To etch is to enter Jenny's world.
Typical Pattern:
Infinitive as Subject / Verb / Infinitive / Possessive Pronoun / Noun.

6)

Crafing crums crouster crets.
Drinking drives mother crazy.
Leaving crumbs creates dirt.
Eating hamburgers causes boils.
Crying makes mother fret.
Choking causes sister pain.
Quaffing wine creates drunks.
Typical Pattern:
Noun (Gerund) as Subject / Verb / Noun / Noun.
OR
Noun (Gerund) as Subject / Noun / Verb / Noun.

EXERCISE TWO: SENTENCE PATTERNS

1) There are only verbs in the predicates of these sentences. The pattern could be diagrammed like this:

SUBJECT + VERB.

2) The verbs are *suffered, reconsidered, influenced,* and *encouraged.* The phrases *an acute mental crisis, his philosophy, this new philosophy,* and *Mill's interest in humanity* all name something that answers the question *what.*

> What did John Stuart Mill suffer? *an acute mental crisis*
> What did he reconsider? *his philosophy*
> What did the poetry of Wordsworth influence? *this new philosophy*
> What did it encourage? *Mill's interest in humanity*

The pattern could be diagrammed like this:

SUBJECT + VERB MADE MORE MEANINGFUL BY AN ANSWER TO THE QUESTION WHAT + ANSWER TO THE QUESTION WHAT.

3) The verbs are *gave, promised, promised,* and *sold.* These verbs are also made more meaningful by an answer to the question *what.*

> What did Chinese labourers give? *bonds*
> What did these companies promise? *passage to North America*
> What did they promise? *cheap labour*
> What did they sell? *a virtually enslaved labour force*

Notice that the answers to these questions come at the end of the predicates and that other words intervene between the verbs and these answers. These intervening words answer the question *to whom.*

> To whom did Chinese labourers give bonds? to *Chinese companies*
> To whom did these companies make promises? to *indentured workers*
> To whom did they promise cheap labour? to *North American businesses*
> To whom did they sell a virtually enslaved labour force? to *railway contractors*

The pattern could be diagrammed like this:

SUBJECT + VERB MADE MORE MEANINGFUL BY AN ANSWER TO THE QUESTION WHAT + ANSWER TO THE QUESTION TO WHOM + ANSWER TO THE QUESTION WHAT.

4) The verbs are *considered, made, labelled,* and *thought.* Again, an answer to the question *what* makes the predicate mean more. But look what happens when we attempt answers.

> What did Freud consider? *every dream*
> What did dreams make? *dangerous impulses and experiences*
> What did Freud label? *this job*
> What did he think about? *this dream work*

The answers don't seem very complete. We need to pose the question *what* one more time.

What did he consider every dream? *a piece of hard work*
What did dreams make dangerous impulses and experiences? *harmless*
What did Freud label this job? *dream work*
What did he think this dream work? *essential*

The pattern might be diagrammed like this:

SUBJECT + VERB MADE MORE MEANINGFUL BY AN ANSWER TO THE QUESTION WHAT + ANSWER TO THE QUESTION WHAT MADE MORE MEANINGFUL BY AN ANSWER TO THE QUESTION WHAT + ANSWER TO THE QUESTION WHAT.

5) The verbs are *is, is, includes,* and *are.* Notice that three of the verbs are variations of the verb *to be.* The words following all four verbs answer the question *what.*

What is the company's solar heating system? *automatic*
What is it? *efficient*
What does it include? *several components*
What are these components? *piping, a storage tank, a water pump, a heat exchanger, and a solar collector*

At first, these sentences seem to follow a pattern similar to that of the sentences in group two: both patterns have verbs followed by answers to the question *what.* However, there are subtle differences between the two patterns. These differences are clear when we examine the nature and requirements of the verbs in each pattern. For example, it is the nature of most of the verbs in pattern five to allow us to answer the question *what* by renaming the subject.

What is the company's solar heating system? *the company's solar heating system*

In pattern two, however, the verb does not allow for this sort of substitution.

What did John Stuart Mill suffer? It was not John Stuart Mill.

Also, the verbs in pattern five seem to <u>require</u> answers to the question *what.* The following combinations of subject and verb appear incomplete.

The company's solar heating system is.
It is.
The system includes.
These components are.

The pattern of the sentences in group five might be diagrammed like this:

SUBJECT + VERB REQUIRING AN ANSWER TO THE QUESTION WHAT + NOUN OR ADJECTIVE ANSWERING THIS QUESTION THAT COULD BE REPLACED BY THE SUBJECT.

REVISING EXCESSIVE AND ILLOGICAL COORDINATION

Exercise One:

Courtesy was a necessary attribute in King Arthur's court. King Arthur had developed the Knights of the Round Table knowing that the people of his kingdom were important assets. All knights were to be courteous because these knights were to protect the people, and in no way were they to make the people uncomfortable. Obviously, since the only reason the knights existed was to protect and keep the people of the kingdom secure, they had to be courteous. Courtesy worked both ways: the knights were expected to be courteous to the people, and the people were expected to be courteous to the knights in return. We especially see this courtesy in the relationship between Sir Gawain and the people; the people respected Sir Gawain and Sir Gawain was very considerate and caring of the people.

You may have found this paragraph difficult to revise. When a writer uses excessive or illogical co-ordination, the reader has to determine what the actual relationships between sentences are. The first sentence of the original paragraph links two ideas that are not coordinate: the first clause operates on a more general level than the second. In our revision, we have separated the original first sentence into two sentences. The second sentence of the original seems to show illogical coordination; our revision uses the subordinating conjunction *because* instead of *so,* and moves *All knights were to be courteous* to the beginning of the sentence to improve coherence. (Note that, when ideas are connected using only coordination, it is easy for a writer to accidentally place ideas in the wrong order.)

In our revision of the third original sentence, we change the *so* to *since* to show connections more clearly. Shortening *and thus the kingdom would be strong* to *keeping the kingdom strong* improves coherence and emphasis.

The last sentence of the original paragraph is revised by replacing *for* and the comma preceding it with a semicolon. Although doing this does not reduce the number of coordinate independent clauses, it does help to separate the general idea (in front of the semicolon in the revision) from the more specific one.

You may have revised quite differently, especially if your interpretation of the passage was different from ours.

Exercise Two:

The cost of preventative medicine is low because there is no need for technological research. Many of its methods, having been in practice since the beginning of civilization, have already had many years of testing and have proven to be effective. Consequently, there is no money needed for testing procedures. Also, because these methods do not rely on the technology and equip-ment usually found in a hospital located in an urban centre, they are more accessible to a greater portion of the public. Preventative medicine can easily become a part of everyone's life, for it is so accessible and costs little. If this were to happen, less money would have to be put into curative medicine because fewer people would get sick.

The original paragraph is difficult to revise because we can only guess its author's intentions. Is the first sentence an example of illogical coordination? Should the author have used *because* instead of *and*? We guessed yes. We also thought that the last sentence incorrectly preferred coordination to subordination, and we revised accordingly. As for other changes, one of the coordinate clauses in the first half of the very long second sentence was eliminated by using a participial phrase beginning with *having.* Also, this long sentence was divided into two sentences, which were related logically by the adverb *consequently.* In the next sentence, *and thus* was eliminated, the first clause was made subordinate to the second, and, for coherence, *also* was added. It might be useful to note that double conjunctions, like *and thus, and so,* or *and therefore,* often signal illogical or excessive coordination.

REVISING EXCESSIVE, ILLOGICAL, AND UPSIDE-DOWN SUBORDINATION

Exercise One:

More common than Dutch barns in Ontario are the Pennsylvania German barns. These barns can be distinguished from Dutch barns by their size, their cantilevered forebay, and their hillside setting. The German barn is very large. It is typically sixty feet wide by one hundred feet long, more than double the size of the voluminous Dutch barn. Although both barns have a lengthy gable roof, the German barn's roof is sometimes distinguished by the asymmetry of its two slopes. Viewed from the outside, the German barn stands much taller at its eaves than does the Dutch. Its most characteristic feature, however, is its cantilevered forebay. This forebay overhangs the upper mow, protecting the windows and walls of the lower storey and making the German barn an improvement upon the Bavarian prototype in which the upper storey was cantilevered a mere foot or so. Because the practice of building barns into the sides of hills originated in the hilly country of Upper Bavaria, the Southern Black Forest, and Switzerland, it was followed in the building of Pennsylvania German barns.

The main problem with the original paragraph is excessive subordination. Notice how excessive subordination makes it difficult for the reader to determine what the paragraph is about. Which differences between the two types of barn does the writer want to emphasize? The reader can't distinguish between essential and tangential information because ideas are strung together with relative pronouns. In fact, the three main differences appear in a relative clause in the original paragraph: *which are characterized by their size, their cantilevered forebay, and their typical hillside setting.* The revision attempts to emphasize main points by expressing them in shorter independent clauses. The last sentence of the original paragraph is an example of illogical subordination; Pennsylvania German barns were built into the sides of hills because (not *even though*) this practice originated in the old country.

Exercise Two:

The reason some issues divide Canadians and become the subjects of political debates while other issues do not is simple: the group with economic or political power furthering concerns that are not too delicate for politicians, who will not deal with sensitive problems, will make its concerns the subjects of debate. If an issue is supported by a group that does not have any power, or if supporting an issue is considered political suicide, the chances of that issue becoming the subject of debate are almost non-existent. In conclusion, whether an issue is considered political or not depends on how volatile it is and on how much money is behind it. An issue that is too emotionally charged or that does not have any money pushing it has little chance of becoming political, and an issue that is both volatile and unbacked by capital is not even an issue in the political sense of the word.

This revision is very similar to the original paragraph; only two sentences have been changed. Of course, you may have rewritten this paragraph differently. But you probably changed the first and the last sentence, regardless of what other revisions you made. In the first sentence of the original paragraph, relative clauses again get in the way of clear expression. This revision eliminates one of these relative clauses (*which is either economic or political*) by using modifiers (*the group with economic or political power*), and another (*that wants to further concerns*) by using a participial phrase (*furthering concerns*). These changes emphasize that a group must have power and the right sort of concerns to make its concerns political issues. The revision also changes the *although* of the last sentence to an *and*. Coordination is more logical than subordination in this instance because the two ideas expressed on either side of the comma are of equal importance.

EXERCISE THREE: COMBINING SENTENCES

Of course, there are as many ways to combine the sentences in these two writing samples as there are writers and editors. In the following revision of the first writing sample, the strategy of turning some sentences into modifying words and phrases is used more frequently than either the strategy of coordination or of subordination. In the revision of writing sample number two, all three strategies are used.

1)   Acid rain, or unnaturally acidic precipitation, falls to earth downwind from industrial sources of sulphur dioxide and nitric oxides. Composed of approximately two parts sulphuric acid to one part nitric acid, it is formed when SO_2 and NO_x are dispersed into an atmosphere containing water vapour and dust. Heavy metals and other inorganic pollutants are transported along with acid rain, compounding the ecological damage it does.

Canadian sources of the primary pollutant, SO_2, differ from American sources in their geographic concentration and in the absolute quantity of their emissions. In Canada, large non-ferrous metal-smelting industries emit the bulk of SO_2. In America, the sources of SO_2 are more widely dispersed and represent smaller, less easily regulated private-sector industries. In 1980, in the area east of Flin Flon, Canada's contribution to the acid rain problem was over four and a half million metric tons of SO_2. Canadian acid rain, coming from a metallurgic source, has a higher concentration of heavy metals than American acid rain. American SO_2 emissions, originating primarily from coal-fired electric generating stations, are about five times the Canadian total, adding up to roughly 26 million metric tons.

2)   The expansion of hospitals created numerous nurturing jobs which were quickly filled by women. In fact, the nursing profession became dominated by women. However, it was soon found that this type of work was exhausting, frustrating, and, of course, alienating. As Shapiro points out, because nurses have a fairly low status in the hospital hierarchy, they are allowed very limited decision-making powers and must follow orders given by physicians.

The expansion of the government created clerical jobs, which also pulled women into the labour force. These occupations offered women low wages and required low skill levels, limited responsibility, and few hours of work. Women entered and were trapped in these degrading jobs, which were further degraded by the development of highly specialized machines.

Another factor drawing women into the job market was that the number of teaching jobs available expanded to meet the demand created by the baby boom of 1946-1964. The majority of these new teaching positions were soon filled by women. In general, women did well in this profession. As Armstrong points out, they held most of the full-time jobs, men being hired on a part-time basis. Women today still occupy elementary and secondary school teaching jobs, although a low percentage of females teach in higher education facilities.

Chapter Two: Common Sentence Problems

REVISING SENTENCE FRAGMENTS

Exercise One:

In looking at the actions taken by Germany in 1914, one must examine the German Army in the age of Moltke. By doing this, one will come to an understanding of why Germany acted the way she did and of what the military believed was possible in the Great War. In looking at the German Army in the age of Moltke, one must first look at Clausewitz, because Moltke claimed to be his student. Then the theories of Moltke have to be examined, and finally the theories of Schlieffen and the plan that bears his name.

The original paragraph has four fragments. All were probably created because the writer was worried that his sentences were getting too long. All but one begin with coordinating conjunctions. Of course, it is possible to begin a sentence with a coordinating conjunction. However, the two word groups beginning with *and* are definitely fragments; the first *and* is followed by a dependent clause, and the second *and* introduces two nouns and their modifiers. These fragments have been connected to the appropriate sentences in the revised paragraph.

The word group beginning with *for* should also be considered a fragment. In it, the *for* acts almost like the subordinating conjunction *because*; therefore, the clause it introduces seems logically incomplete when it is grammatically separated from the first sentence of the paragraph. To shorten the sentences of the original paragraph, *for* has been eliminated. It is unnecessary because the prepositional phrase *by doing this* already establishes a conceptual (if not a grammatical) connection to the thought that one must examine the German Army in the age of Moltke.

The other fragment in the original paragraph is a dependent clause fragment beginning with the relative pronoun *whom*. The revised paragraph eliminates the awkwardness of this dependent clause. Another minor addition has been made to enhance the symmetry of the revised paragraph: an *of* has been added before *what the military believed . . .* to make it parallel *of why Germany acted the way she did. . . .*

Exercise Two:

John Maynard Keynes, in a book entitled <u>The General Theory of Employment, Interest and Money</u>, provided a solution to high unemployment. The government could mechanize the business cycle by means of monetary and fiscal policy. When times were bad, it could increase public spending and decrease taxes; when times were good, it could decrease public spending and increase taxes to acquire a surplus to compensate the economy in the future. When the system reached full employment, it would be able to regulate itself. In Keynes's theory, social programs provide the immediate stimulus to the economy because they provide a way of transferring purchasing power to those willing to spend.

The original paragraph has four fragments. The first, beginning with *in effect,* has neither a subject nor a verb relating to that subject. It consists of two prepositional phrases (starting with *in* and *by*) and one dependent clause (starting with the subordinating conjunction *when*). The second fragment follows the same pattern except it starts with the coordinating conjunction *and.* The third fragment is an infinitive phrase fragment; it contains two verbals (*to acquire* and *to compensate*) but no verb. These three fragments, coming one right after the other, were no doubt created because the writer thought her sentences were getting too long. The revision eliminates the first two fragments by giving them subjects (the pronoun *it* in both cases) and verbs. Notice that the dependent clauses beginning with *when* have been moved in front of the independent clauses and that the two sentences created from the two fragments have been made coordinate. This reordering allows the third fragment to be easily joined to the end of the sentence.

The fourth fragment in the original paragraph is a dependent clause fragment beginning with the subordinating conjunction *because.* The revision simply joins this dependent clause to the independent clause that precedes it.

REVISING COMMA SPLICES AND FUSED SENTENCES

Exercise One:

The courts' predilection to grant divorced mothers custody of children stems from a variety of factors. In most cases, the mother has already been the primary child-rearer. This circumstance usually means that the mother has better child-care skills and that her dependence on the children is greater, regardless of the father's emotional attachment to his children. It has also established patterns within the family that would require a major adjustment for all family members if they were to change. Men are more likely to be employed full time, to be making a larger income, to have higher status jobs, and to be in career progression. Thus, following the divorce it is usually easier for the father to continue his occupation than for a non-working mother to leave the home and start a new career. In addition, the social pressures on mothers to take custody are overwhelming.

There are four comma splices in the original paragraph. The first three were probably a result of this writer's attempt to place all the reasons divorced mothers are usually granted custody of children in one sentence. The revision separates these reasons into three sentences. Notice that the first of these separated sentences begins with a transitional phrase (*in most cases*) and that the next two begin with pronouns (*this* and *it*). Perhaps the writer also had difficulty recognizing that transitional phrases and pronouns are capable of beginning complete sentences. The next comma splice seems to verify this thought; the transitional phrase *in addition* is used as if it had the conjunctive power of an *and*. Again, this comma splice is revised by separating the two spliced sentences. Another minor point: in the revision, we have added *circumstance* after the demonstrative pronoun *this* in our third sentence to avoid ambiguity.

Exercise Two:

Because there are vast differences among all the major regions of Canada, these regions are brought into conflict. Some reasons for conflict are as simple as the terms under which provinces entered Confederation. Such was the case with the Western provinces. When they entered Confederation, the federal government kept control over natural resources. In the Maritime provinces, the story is different. They joined Confederation in order to boost the sagging industrial sector, but this did not happen.

The original paragraph contains four comma splices and one fused sentence. The first comma splice occurred because the writer misused the conjunctive adverb *therefore*. The revision preserves the logic of the original; *therefore* has been omitted, and the first of the spliced sentences has been turned into a dependent clause. The next splicing comma appears before the pronoun *such,* which is the subject of the second spliced sentence. In the revision, these sentences are separate. Although *such* is an unusual pronoun, it is probable that this writer does not easily recognize any pronoun as a subject; the next two splicing commas occur before pronoun subjects (*they* and *this*). Separation is used to correct the first, and coordination to correct the second.

The fused sentence begins with *when*. The writer may have thought that the adverb clause *when they entered Confederation* could provide a bridge between independent clauses. Although it is possible to join this adverb clause to either of the independent clauses surrounding it, it is not possible for it to be joined to both at the same time: *Such was the case with the Western provinces when they entered Confederation* is correct, and *When they entered Confederation, the federal government kept control over natural resources* is correct, but the writer can't have it both ways.

You will note that we have added two commas, one after the prepositional phrase *when they entered Confederation* and one after the prepositional phrase *in the Maritime provinces*. Once the faulty commas are eliminated from a passage, a writer can see more clearly where there might be a need for properly placed commas.

REVISING FOR SUBJECT-VERB AGREEMENT

Exercise One:

It has been suggested that the disparity between costs and benefits underlies the difficulty in arriving at a comprehensive agreement. Two camps, each composed of memberships that cut across party, national, and even ideological lines, have been unable to reconcile their different perspectives. Both seek to avoid the costs; neither quantifies the benefits. One of the sides seems to enjoy a burgeoning mass support while the other fights a holding action of counter-information and relies on the prevalence of conservative economic attitudes during periods of economic downturn.

There are five instances of subjects not agreeing with verbs in the original paragraph. The subjects and verbs that do not agree are *disparity* and *underlie*, *that* and *cuts*, *neither* and *quantify*, *one* and *seem*, and *other* and *rely*. Most of these errors occur because words intervene between subject and verb. For example, the plural verb *underlie* is far away from its singular subject *disparity*. Two errors may have been caused because the writer was not sure of the number of the pronoun subject. The relative pronoun *that* takes on the number of its antecedent. In this case, the antecedent (*memberships*) is plural, so the verb (*cuts*) is incorrect. The pronoun *neither* is singular. (We can remember this if we read *neither one nor the other* whenever we see *neither*.) The verb *quantify*, being plural, is therefore incorrect. The revisions change the number of the verbs to match the number of their subjects.

Exercise Two:

Uncertainty regarding the costs of abatement is dwarfed by the great controversy over quantifying the environmental costs of inaction. In many ways, the problem of proving dose-response relationships is analogous to the difficulties encountered in proving cigarettes cause cancer. In the same way that the tobacco industry challenged medical evidence, many industrial polluters hope to defeat the issue by funding "research" that fails to make the obvious conclusions. Equally dishonest are the rearguard actions fought by such groups as the Coalition for Energy-Environment Balance. This group runs full page ads in major American daily newspapers calling into question Canadian motives for opposition to coal-fired plant emissions. In providing a position paper on the Clean Air Act, the National Environmental Development Association, whose members include the Allied Chemical Corporation, Standard Oil, General Electric, and General Motors, makes the case for more research.

The original paragraph has six subject-verb agreement errors. The first two incorrectly pair singular subjects with plural verbs: (*uncertainty* and *are*; *problem* and *are*). These mistakes probably occurred because the writer lost sight of the subject. The third error may have happened either because the writer did not know that a relative pronoun takes the number of its antecedent, or because he didn't realize that *research* is singular. A similar misunderstanding may have occasioned the fifth error; here a collective noun denoting a single unit (*group*) is treated as if it were plural. The subject and verb are inverted in this instance, making the mistake even more difficult to catch. The fourth error probably occurred because the subject (*actions*) comes after the verb (*is* in the original). We have revised so that the verb (*are*) aligns with the subject. You may not have seen the sixth error at all. More than likely, it was made because a list of the members of *the National Environmental Development Association* obscures the fact that this single association is the subject of the sentence; the verb (*make*) is incorrect, being plural.

REVISING FOR PRONOUN-ANTECEDENT AGREEMENT

Exercise One:

Every woman of this period became alienated from physical exercise because society and the medical profession took it upon themselves to tell her what she could and could not participate in. Medical experts directed females toward a safe recovery from the menstrual cycle. They believed that because women experienced menstruation, a time of physical renewal was absolutely necessary. For this, outdoor exercise was of utmost importance. Consequently, doctors advised women in both Canada and the United States to partake of fresh air and moderate physical activity to allow for a healthy alleviation of the emotional and physical stress brought on by menstruation. Improving women's emotional well-being became as important as developing their physical strength in doctors' decisions regarding exercise. Physicians believed light exercise was an absolute necessity in order to develop a healthy character and a strong mind, attributes that would make a woman into a "fit mother." This attitude pushed women into believing that their only purpose in life was to bear children. As a result of this belief, a woman's exercise was curtailed, and social and medical attitudes toward a woman's biological and psychological make-up made overexertion or competitive sports impossible since they might damage her capacity to fulfil her primary role.

Because the author alternates between discussing *women* (plural) and *a woman* (singular), there are many pronoun-antecedent agreement errors in the original paragraph. The revision uses the plural unless the singular is more emphatic (as in the first sentence) or more logical (as in the sentences concerned with what makes *a fit mother* and what constitutes a woman's *primary role*). Of course, many different revisions are possible, so let's just identify what must be changed.

There are seven errors in the original paragraph, three in the first sentence alone. *Itself* should be *themselves* because the antecedent is a compound (*society and the medical profession*). Of course, *every woman* is singular; the phrase could be replaced with *every single woman*. Therefore, *them* and *they* should be *her* and *she*. In the second sentence, the pronoun (*her*) does not agree with the antecedent (*females*). In the revision, the pronoun is deleted; it is unnecessary. The next error also involves a compound antecedent; *fresh air and moderate physical activity* should be represented by a plural pronoun instead of by *it*. Again we have revised to eliminate the pronoun altogether. Error six occurs in the second to last sentence; the antecedent *women* should not be referred to using *her*, a singular pronoun. You may not have caught the last error, which occurs in the last sentence. Here an alternative antecedent is mistaken for a compound antecedent. *Competitive sports or overexertion* should take a singular pronoun in the original sentence because the pronoun is closer to the singular noun *overexertion*. The revision switches the order of the nouns in the alternative antecedent and preserves the plural pronoun.

Exercise Two:

During the 13th century, the jury had two functions: it presented the accused to the bench, and it tried him on his conviction. Each jury was formed of twelve men of stature from the community it served. These men took an oath before becoming jury members, and they were kept honest by being subjected to fines and imprisonment for concealment of pleas. The trial was simple; the jury members informed themselves. No evidence was presented and no witness was called, because the jury's job was to discover the facts of each case without either. Jury members judged the accused based on his character and his reputation within the community. By considering the offense committed and by witnessing the prisoner's confrontation with the bench, they determined the verdict. If anything was unclear, they asked questions. One can only marvel that despite the paucity of protection afforded the accused, neither the prisoner nor the judge usually challenged the jury's verdict; each considered most judgments fair. We can surmise that this arose more from the fact that the jury held the majority of power within the system than from its effective dispensation of justice.

Most of the pronoun-antecedent agreement problems in the original paragraph result from a sliding understanding of the number of the collective noun *jury*. The revision considers *jury* to be singular when it means a single, legal entity, in other words, when the jury functions as a single unit. However, the word is treated as a plural when it means the members of the jury. Because it is always possible to question the number of this noun, revisions of this paragraph may vary greatly. This revision changes ten pronouns.

The first three pronouns referring to the jury (*they* in all cases) are changed to *it*. The next change was made because it seemed to us that *jury members* informing *themselves* was more logical than *the jury* informing *itself*. Next, *it* is replaced by *either* because *it* does not adequately refer to the antecedent *no evidence . . . and no witness*. The following *it, its,* and *it* are also changed to emphasize that jury members are doing the considering, witnessing, and questioning as individuals, not as a single unit. In the second-to-last sentence, *they* is changed to *each* in order to refer more appropriately to the alternative noun antecedent *neither the prisoner nor the judge*. Again, because we feel that the jury is considered as a unit in the last sentence, *their* has been replaced by *its*.

REVISING FAULTY AND FALSE PARALLELISM

Exercise One:

The late nineteenth century brought many changes to Alberta. The coming of the North-West Mounted Police did not end the misfortunes of the Indians and Métis. Their strength and spirit had been taken away by the white man's ways. In 1876 and 1877, the Indians signed away their heritage of parklands, plains, and freedom. In exchange, they were given small amounts of treaty money, forced onto reserves, and compelled to farm instead of hunt. With the bison gone and the Indians on reserves, Alberta was ready for settlement. At first, growth was slow; a few settlers ranched in the south and others lived around Fort Edmonton, Fort Saskatchewan, Fort Calgary, and Fort Macleod. According to the Dominion census of 1881, there were only 18,072 whites and Métis living in what would soon be Alberta. Nonetheless, surveyors and scientists were reporting on routes for roads and railways, investigating the fertility of the soil, and prospecting for coal, oil, gas, and minerals. During this time, thousands of square miles of prairie were divided into neat square parcels of 160 acres, free to any male over eighteen or to any widow who was head of a family (Hardy, 1967, 310-12).

The original passage suffers primarily from faulty parallelism. The first two sentences read gracefully, but the syntax of the third sentence is difficult to follow. We have revised *the way they had spirit* to parallel *their strength*.

You may argue that *parklands, plains, and freedom* in the fourth sentence is a clear example of false parallelism: *freedom* does not equal *parkland* or *plains.* Because we liked the dramatic effect, we retained the sentence.

The fifth sentence, beginning with *in exchange*, contains a list of items that must all start with a past participle (*given, forced, compelled*) to be parallel. In the sixth sentence, we have revised *now that the Indians were on reserves*, a subordinate clause, to *the Indians on reserve.* This revision permits *the Indians on reserve* to be the object of the preposition *with*, as *the bison gone* is. Verbs are changed to tighten parallelism in the next sentence (*tried ranching* to *ranched*). In the sentence beginning with *nonetheless*, we have made sure that all items in the list begin with a present participle (*reporting, investigating, prospecting*). In the final sentence, we have repeated the words *for any* to tighten parallelism.

Exercise Two:

The possibilities of the Western genre become most apparent when films within the genre are compared. <u>My Darling Clementine</u> (1947), <u>The Man Who Shot Liberty Valance</u> (1962), and <u>The Left-Handed Gun</u> (1959) are essentially the same film in terms of plot. In each, a stranger enters a town, decides to act in accordance with his own moral code, effects some change, and then leaves the town. Nonetheless, the films are not indistinguishable. If the earliest of the three, <u>My Darling Clementine</u>, is taken as the prototype by which the other two can be considered, it soon becomes apparent that John Ford's <u>Liberty Valance</u> is a self-conscious commentary on the nature of the Western hero, while Arthur Penn's <u>The Left-Handed Gun</u> is a sharp criticism of the manner in which society understands that hero. <u>Liberty Valance</u> rises above its restricted structure to comment on the form itself; <u>Left-Handed Gun</u> reaches underneath this limited structure to examine its darker origins. The artistry in these two films, then, is created by each director's exploration of the possibilities within the genre, not simply by each director's variation of a standard theme.

Small errors in parallelism make the original passage read awkwardly. A minimal amount of revising produces a more graceful passage. For example, eliminating *the work* from the second sentence makes the list of films parallel. The third sentence, however, requires more extensive revision. We have revised the list of the stranger's actions so that each item describes an action by beginning with a verb in the present tense (*enters town, decides to act, effects some change, leaves the town*).

The next sentence compares <u>Liberty Valance</u> and <u>The Left-Handed Gun</u>. To make the comparison more effective, we have made the two clauses parallel (one film *is a self-conscious criticism of . . .*; the other *is a sharp criticism of . . .*). The clauses of the next sentence, which also compares the two films, have likewise been made parallel. In the final sentence, *not simply are variations on a standard theme demonstrated* has been revised to begin with the preposition *by* to parallel the other prepositional phrase in the sentence.

REVISING MISPLACED AND DANGLING MODIFIERS

Exercise One:

Consequently, it would seem that because Fulton had not maintained an impartial position, it was decided that he was no longer needed by the federal government, and, subsequently, Crombie was also shuffled out of Indian and Northern Affairs to another ministry. Roger Tasse, appointed as the new Federal Negotiator soon after Fulton's departure, decisively limited the possibility of fruitful discussion by refusing ever to work from the discussion paper compiled by Fulton or to involve him as a mediator. Once again, no headway was made in negotiations until a couple of years had passed.

Although short, the original paragraph contains one dangling and five misplaced or awkwardly placed modifiers. The participial phrase *having not maintained an impartial position* dangles because it cannot attach itself to the pronoun *it*. The revision turns this phrase into a subordinate clause. It also adds punctuation and changes the position of the modifier *no longer* in order to avoid a reading that links this modifier with *subsequently*. We don't want the reader to think that Fulton was needed *no longer and subsequently*. Besides these changes, *also* was moved closer to *shuffled out*, which it modifies. Two modifiers were moved in the second sentence: *decisively* was placed in front of *limited*, and *ever* in front of *to*, to revise the split infinitive *to ever work*. The last misplaced modifier is the prepositional phrase *for a couple of years*. The writer wants to say that no headway was made for a couple of years, but, as the original sentence stands, *for a couple of years* seems to attach itself to *negotiations*. Because it is difficult to move this modifier (an introductory element occupies the place it might be moved to) we have left it at the end of the sentence, but changed its initial preposition to *until*, a word that doesn't attach itself as easily to *negotiations*.

Exercise Two:

There are several reasons that the character of Herbert is not memorable. First, we are introduced to Herbert in an incident comprising only one and a half pages. Encountering a "milk toast" young man referred to as the "pale young gentleman" (70), readers consider the first meeting memorable only because of the occurrence of a fight, which is unprovoked and unimpassioned. In fact, an exchange of pleasantries, showing Herbert's distinct lack of passion, follows the fight. Second, Herbert is equally unimpassioned and unmemorable in his love relationships. Clara seems only moderately enamoured of Herbert, although the two are supposed to marry eventually.

The original paragraph has one dangling modifier and five misplaced or awkwardly placed modifiers. The correct placement of *only* seems particularly hard for this writer; she misplaces this adverb three times. In the revised paragraph, *only* has been moved closer to the following three sentence elements: *one and a half pages, because of the occurrence of a fight,* and *moderately enamoured of Herbert.* The prepositional phrase *in fact* is also misplaced in the original paragraph. A lack of punctuation makes this modifier squint; it could modify *pleasantries* or *showing Herbert's distinct lack of passion.* The revision moves *in fact* to the beginning of the sentence, making it modify the whole sentence. An awkward split infinitive (*to eventually marry*) is also revised. The dangling modifier, a participial phrase beginning with *encountering*, occurs in the third sentence of the original paragraph. In the revision, the clause following the participial phrase is in the active voice; therefore, the phrase has the noun *readers* to modify.

REVISING AWKWARD SENTENCES

Exercise One:

From this it is clearly seen that, in the future, the number of elderly people within the province will increase. At the same time, the number of younger people will rapidly decrease. This is because couples, if they choose to have children, believe that the ideal family contains one or two children, or three at the most. In 1901, seniors made up 5.5 per cent of the total population in Ontario, and, as the baby boom hit the nation, Ontario's senior population increased to 8.7 per cent. During the 1970s, the number of people of the younger generation decreased because of two simple facts: parents were reducing the size of their families and the baby boom generation was getting older. It seems evident, then, that the average age of people in Ontario will increase in the next twenty years.

Much of the awkwardness of this paragraph results from non-alignment of meaning. The student is working with numbers and percentages, and often (in Sentences One, Two, Five, and Six), she makes people and places increase or decrease, rather than correctly making amounts or percentages increase or decrease. Also, the student's use of figurative language (*the future holds, couples view*) often does not align in a meaningful way with what follows. Our revisions eliminate the figurative turns of phrase and substitute more concrete words. Occasionally, as in the fourth sentence, the student omits necessary information (the word *senior* must be repeated so the reader knows that the senior population increased, not Ontario's population). As our discussion of this passage indicates, when you are using statistics in prose, you should strive for precision of expression.

Exercise Two:

It is still important to consider how education was viewed in the pre-industrial period. All education was conducted within the walls of a child's home. In fact, many parents believed that the things a child needed to learn were sewing, farming, and other such skills. However, with the emergence of industrialization, Canadians became more aware of the importance of education in this technological era. The attitudes of parents who did not have their children enrolled in schools changed, and they began to feel that it was very important for a child to grow and develop through formal education. Another factor contributing to the expansion of schools was the growing concern about street urchins. In the 1840s and 1850s, social leaders feared social disorder because so many young adolescents were idle.

The first sentence of the original passage is an awkward match of statement and question; we have restructured it as a statement. In two sentences (the second and the sixth), the paragraph suffers from the form of awkwardness in which the complement in a linking verb sentence does not align with the subject of that sentence. The writer does not mean that education was within the walls of the home; she means that education was conducted within those walls. Neither does she mean that street urchins promoted schools. You may not agree with our revision of the fourth sentence. It is difficult to determine from the original what the writer meant by *empowered*; in our revision, we guessed that it meant that Canadians became more aware of the importance of education.

Sentence Five is also a difficult revision. Read aloud, it sounds awkward; because the sentence begins with *for parents who did not have their children enrolled in schools,* we expect a clause like *times were changing,* not a clause that repeats a reference to the parents (*their attitudes changed*). We have revised the sentence so that there is no need for this repetition. Sentence Five also contains another awkward non-alignment of meaning. Does the writer mean literally that parents wanted their children to grow and develop *inside* a classroom? Surely they expected them to grow outside the classroom too. By changing the prepositional phrase from *inside a classroom* to *through formal education,* we have eliminated the awkwardness.

Chapter Three: Creating Interesting Prose: Variety, Clarity, Emphasis

EXERCISE ONE: DISCOVERING SENTENCE VARIETY

Here are some stylistic elements you might have noticed about each author's prose.

Annie Dillard uses many commas, interrupting her main thought to add ideas and information. Her sentences are constructed simply — many begin with *I* — but are fairly long, and she uses short, familiar words. The overall effect is that of a casual conversation.

E.M. Forster is much more formal. His sentence structure is more complex; the sentences don't usually begin with *I* or even with the subject. He asks questions. Most of his sentences are very long, but two are dramatically short.

Joan Didion's prose seems conversational, too, but it is much more dramatic than that of Dillard. Part of the drama seems to be created through parallel structure. Didion's passage is also much more varied in terms of punctuation: she uses italics, dashes, and colons.

Bronowski seems to us the most poetic of the five writers. His sentences add details by using *and* or *or*: he doesn't use interrupters as Dillard does. The effect is a soft accumulation of details.

Atwood's prose reads like a comic routine. She uses parallel structure and repetition as Didion does, but creates a more lively tone with short, almost choppy, sentences.

VARYING SENTENCE LENGTH

Exercise One:

The railway lines had enlisted men to kill the buffalos, and these men spared few herds. In fact, often they killed needlessly. It is true that buffalo were killed for their meat and for their fur, which was used to make practical and fashionable robes, and that supplying people with robes contributed greatly to the extinction of the buffalo. However, not all buffalo hunters were interested in economic gain. Some killed for the mere joy of watching the beasts fall.

The original paragraph has too many short sentences, creating a choppy effect. Since the vocabulary of the passage is simple and the ideas it contains are relatively straightforward, the writer can easily afford longer sentences. Our revision combines the first two short sentences and places the main focus of the paragraph — the needless killing of buffalo — in a short, emphatic sentence. We also combine the next four sentences because they make one point — that, although there were economic reasons for killing buffalo, these were not the only reasons for buffalo extinction.

The important idea that some buffalo hunters killed for recreation is lost in the original paragraph because it is contained in an unemphatic sentence that seems like an afterthought. In our revision, the added transitional sentence helps to highlight the idea, now contained in a short emphatic sentence that closes the paragraph.

Exercise Two:

Meanwhile, in January 1980, a move by Jimmy Carter caused some concern. Carter announced his support for the EPA plan to force a ten-billion-dollar conversion from oil to coal-fired electric generation. The lack of provisions for pollution abatement equipment attached to these mandatory conversions aroused suspicions in Canada. The Carter Administration seemed to be promoting relaxed air quality standards while appearing to move toward an international agreement. Despite immediate concern over this apparent contradiction, there was little doubt that if Reagan were elected a much more pronounced retreat would be in the offing. As one American environment official, reacting to the strong lobbying of coal producers and utilities, said, "It's a good time to circle the wagons and protect what environmental legislation we have." This choice of a homespun metaphor would be one that the next holder of the Oval Office could understand if not appreciate. It clearly reflects the fact that the environmentalists were shifting to the defensive.

The sentences in the original passage are quite long, and the difficult vocabulary adds to the density of the passage. Within the body of the paragraph, we have broken the second sentence in two and tightened the wording of the third. However, our focus has been on shortening sentences at the beginning and end of the paragraph. Short sentences at the beginning ease the reader into the paragraph. You will notice that we have omitted some information altogether, including the prepositional phrase *in the United States.* In the context of this paragraph, this information seemed obvious and unnecessary.

The final sentence contains the point that the paragraph has been building toward: that the stance of environmentalists is changing. In the original, the point gets lost because of the lengthy subordinate clause, *that the next holder of the Oval Office could understand if not appreciate,* intervening between the subject and the verb of the independent clause. The revision separates the two clauses, allowing the more important point to be emphasized.

VARYING SENTENCE FUNCTION

Exercise One:

By reflecting on the various comments made by these authors, it is possible to infer the following two points. First, society has viewed learning-disabled individuals as undesirable deviants from the norm. Secondly, the lack of a positive self-image and self-esteem is a major problem for these individuals. These observations led to the formation of this study, which will consider this question: how is the behaviour of learning-disabled students modified by their perception of how society views them?

The original paragraph concludes with a statement; our revision changes that statement to a question. The revision allows us to bring the central concern into focus for the reader—using a question emphasizes the problem being addressed. Remember, if you use this rhetorical strategy, the reader will expect an answer to the question posed. Don't forget to answer the question.

Exercise Two:

Hamlet does undoubtedly delay. Whether he delays consciously or not, one cannot ascertain. There is significant evidence that Hamlet has other matters to think over as well. J. Dover Wilson, for example, has convincingly shown that the perplexing question of the ghost's true nature was a real enough concern. Elizabethans themselves were in disagreement about this issue: were apparitions really ghosts or merely devils trying to confuse the living? In this light, Hamlet's recourse to the play as a means of getting at the truth seems not as ridiculous as Dr. A.C. Bradley would have us believe. Consider Bradley's assertion: "It is an unconscious fiction, an excuse for his delay—and for its continuance" (104). Although there is some truth in Bradley's comment, it would seem unwise to dismiss Hamlet's plan as purely "fiction."

Although the passage reads well (note its excellent variation of sentence length), varying grammatical function can add even more life to the paragraph. We have added a question and a command. The question brings the issue debated by Elizabethans into focus; the command helps to direct the reader's attention to the quotation from Bradley.

VARYING GRAMMATICAL STRUCTURE

Exercise One:

The whole work environment at university was very impersonal. Human relations were not considered important, as the student identification system showed. All correspondence was conducted by means of the student identification number, and the number was the only personal identification required on assignments and exams. Clearly, students were numbers, not names. Prisoners are likewise identified by a number. Guards do not generally know every prisoner by name but rather identify them by the numbers stitched on their uniforms.

The original paragraph consists of nine simple sentences. Although meaning is clear, emphasis is difficult to determine. The paragraph also seems choppy because the simple sentences are short. In our revision, we have retained three simple sentences: the first sentence, which introduces the main idea explored in the first part of the paragraph; the sentence introducing the subject of prisoners, the comparison; and the emphatic *students were numbers, not names* (made more emphatic by the transition *clearly*). These short sentences allow the reader to focus on the key concepts in the paragraph, while supporting details are now contained in longer compound and complex sentences.

Exercise Two:

The book reviews of the era, both native and foreign, reflect these assumptions about national culture. Most reviewers of this era supposed Canada to have its own culture; that the New York Times employed Stuart Keates, a Canadian and the editor of the Victoria Times, to write most of its Canadian literature reviews, supports this statement. The assumption that only a Canadian could fully comprehend the subtleties of Canadian literature is implicit in this action. Evidently, because the Americans saw Canadian culture as an unknown entity, they considered native journalists too ignorant to provide knowledgeable reviews. The action of the New York Times not only indicates a willingness to admit ignorance of Canadian culture, but also suggests Canada to be different in some vital way from the United States. The nation should have its own culture; it should have a national literature.

The original passage consists mainly of compound sentences joined by semicolons. (The writer evidently liked this punctuation mark!) Creating a few complex sentences improves clarity since subordinate conjunctions more clearly show the relationships between ideas than do semicolons. For example, the reader now will understand better that Americans considered native journalists too ignorant to review Canadian literature because they viewed Canadian culture as an unknown entity. Note that the last sentence retains its semicolon. We liked the way the closing sentence pulls the two strands of the paragraph together. However, we did revise the clauses into a tighter parallel structure to make the connection between a national culture and a national literature more obvious.

VARYING RHETORICAL ARRANGEMENT

Exercise One:

At one time, the bricklayer/stonemason and carpenter/joiner represented the apogee of artisanal autonomy. The long craft traditions of these two trades meant that both carpenters and bricklayers, without perceiving their actions as class-oriented or radical in any way, were able to react to threats of craft degradation. During the 1880s, the carpenters first encountered threats to their craft autonomy; two decades later, the bricklayers began their relatively slow decline. Determined in part by the persistence of producer-conscious unionism, this gradual yet differential rate of degradation also seems to have been dictated by the building aristocracy's craft-conscious reaction to technological change. Alone, these peculiar strains of "consciousness" might not have been enough to stay the building trades from resorting to confrontational class-conscious action; however, the town's leading promoters had adopted an industrial strategy that successfully stabilized the normal boom-and-bust building cycles. The context within which these aristocrats of the building trades operated determined the range of possible responses to changes in the industry.

The original paragraph does exhibit some variety: sentences vary in length and in grammatical type. However, the passage does not have much variety in terms of sentence openings or interrupters. The structure of the sentences in the passage does not allow for many mid-sentence interrupters, but we were able to vary the opening of four sentences in this revision, changes that make the paragraph less forbidding. For example, *once* in the first sentence becomes *At one time,* creating an opening that eases the reader into the paragraph. Note also that the tightening of parallel structure in the third sentence improves the grace and coherence of the paragraph. In our revision, the reader can see much more easily both the subjects (carpenters and bricklayers) and the point being made (both trades went into decline, but at different times).

Exercise Two:

The majority of Canadians against conscription were from Quebec, but other people, such as farmers and municipal officers, also opposed it. Farmers could not afford to have their sons, who were an economic asset, do the actual fighting: crops could not be grown if the sons were sent to war. Municipal officers felt that conscription was interfering with their economies and their regular duties.

There are a few interrupters in the original paragraph, but no variety in opening, no parallel structure, no variation of sentence type. In the revision, some sentences have been combined so that information is given in interrupting clauses and phrases rather than in individual sentences. These clauses and phrases (*such as farmers and municipal officers, who were an economic asset*) create emphatic interrupters, adding to variety. Note the partial parallel structure in our revised second sentence created through the repetition of the words *could not.* The desperate situation of the farmers is now stated more forcefully.

VARYING PUNCTUATION: WORKING WITHIN CONVENTIONS

Exercise One:

My Darling Clementine is not a simple film, but its presentation of the typical aspects of the Western plot is precise and vivid. Wyatt Earp is the usual Western hero: he simultaneously upholds violence and law by becoming marshal in order to avenge the murder of his younger brother. Earp takes the law into his own hands – both figuratively and literally – and shoots the Clanton brothers, who are the archetypal Western bad guys. The Clanton family obviously represents the savagery of the West which must be quelled and conquered; its members are unkempt, illiterate barbarians. The Earp family, conversely, is good; the brothers are clean (in fact, Wyatt is quite preoccupied with baths and shaving), neat, and, above all, fair. When the shoot-out at the O.K. Corral is over, and the dust settles on dead Clanton bodies, no viewer would dispute that justice has been served.

The original paragraph creates a voice through parallel structure and good use of interrupters, but the prose still seems a little dead. The addition of parenthesis and dashes livens the passage somewhat. In this revision, note that the added semicolons aid in reinforcing parallel structure in the sentences on the Clanton and Earp families. You will also see that the clause about Wyatt's cleanliness has been put in parenthesis and moved closer to *clean,* the word it elaborates. This revision adds clarity as well as variety.

Exercise Two:

Joseph Conrad's Victory is a novel about belief – belief, trust, faith, confidence, and fidelity – all those qualities that give life meaning and purpose when the necessary knowledge, evidence, and hard facts do not exist. It is a novel about those things upon which belief is founded: a word, an instinct, a smile, a code, a tradition, a religion, a voice. It is also a novel about those things that destroy belief: a word, many words, gossip, doubt, suspicion, fear, apathy, and cynicism. Finally, it is a novel about the absence of belief, about a man (to paraphrase Professor Frye) who attempts to live directly, nakedly in nature without illusions, myths, religions, or beliefs; it is about a "disarmed man." Wandering Heyst substitutes detachment for piety; the island Heyst substitutes need for love; and, in both cases, he endures by stoically, fastidiously, refusing to surrender to belief.

The original paragraph uses parallel structure to very good advantage to create interest. However, alternative punctuation is badly needed in this passage since it contains so many lists: commas used to set off in the first three sentences seem confusing when so many commas are being used to separate. Dashes, semicolons, and colons are used to good effect in the revision, both to give the passage a reflective tone and to augment parallel structure. Placing *to paraphrase Professor Frye* in parenthesis also helps to create that reflective tone.

MAKING CHOICES ABOUT VIOLATION OF PUNCTUATION CONVENTIONS

Exercise One:

Gigantism was close to the Russian heart — and who represented the Russian heart and soul better than that Georgian, Joseph Stalin? Whether it was a hydro-electric dam, the numbers in its standing army, the ego of its leader, or merely the plans on paper, the Stalinist regime admired size in a way that would have done America proud; like Texans, only bigger! The rich ores and hydro potential of the Ural-Kuznet area, lacking only good coking coal, were developed in plans of gigantic scale. Workers went hungry, disastrous accidents occurred, but the work went on.

The original paragraph contains several punctuation violations, some that work well and others that do not. The dash in the opening sentence of the original is used appropriately to set off an interrupting question. In this revision, a comma has been inserted after *paper* in the second sentence; without it, the reader would have difficulty separating subject from introductory element. The revision has also retained the semicolon in this sentence, even though it is technically incorrect. The violation sets off the writer's humorous aside nicely. Note that this is one of the rare occasions when an exclamation mark seems appropriate in academic prose.

Exercise Two:

It seems inappropriate to attribute human susceptibilities to Stalin, but both the Soviet planners and their leader were unexceptional in one respect: they, like everyone else (Canadians often exhibit this quality), could not leave a resource untapped — it seemed to burn a hole in the national pocket. The reason "because it is there" seems enough for most progressive-minded materialist developers; and, if anything, the five-year planners were developers. Economic planners in their establishment of a centralized, hierarchical bureaucracy were forced to look beyond economics. Military and especially ideological imagery became a powerful inducement for the exploitation of immense resources of hydroelectricity, oil, copper, gold, lead, nickel, zinc, platinum, and coal.

Two punctuation violations in the original paragraph are unacceptable. The interrupter *like everyone else* needs commas around it so that *like* is not read as a verb. The dash in the last sentence is inappropriate, because the information added is more integral to the meaning of the text than a dash would suggest. However, other violations, such as the omission of commas around the interrupter *and especially ideological,* are acceptable because they do not confuse the reader, and they improve the movement through the passage. Some readers might find the semicolon before the independent clause *and, if anything, the five-year planners were developers* unconventional, but it does give the second independent clause more emphasis than a comma would.

Chapter Four: Paragraphing

REVISING IRRELEVANCIES AND DIGRESSIONS

Exercise One:

Native people have lived in Canada for thousands of years, and they know how to survive in the Canadian environment. When Europeans set out to discover the New World in the early sixteenth century, they landed in Canada and found the native people already there. In order to survive, the Europeans had to depend on the natives to show them how to live off the land, to kill animals, and to fish for food.

The original paragraph seems to have two topics: general information about native people and the ability of native people to survive in the Canadian environment. To revise, one must first decide which topic is the focus of the paragraph. We selected the natives' ability to survive as the focus. (If you selected general information about native people, your revision will differ substantially.) When the natives' ability to survive is the focus, the third sentence of the original paragraph becomes irrelevant: the structure of native political organizations has no connection to the topic. The first sentence of the original seems like a stray point too; we added the clause about survival in the Canadian environment to demonstrate the focus of the paragraph.

Exercise Two:

When the Europeans decided to remain in the New World, they formed their own government, which would take an active role in assimilating natives through education. Likewise, soon more missionaries joined the Europeans already there and without hesitation set up residential schools for native boys and girls. Sharing an attitude of racial and cultural superiority, both the government and the missionaries decided they were going to assimilate the Indians, through education, to European government, religion, and culture. They went about this by forcing Indian families to give up their children, telling them that truant children would be put in jail. Native parents wanted their children to have an education but were not aware of the complications involved.

The original paragraph is particularly difficult to comprehend because the first sentence (which the reader would expect to introduce the topic) does not seem clearly connected to the rest of the paragraph. We decided that the topic of the paragraph was the manner in which the European government and the missionaries tried to assimilate Indians through education. This decision necessitated a complete reworking of the first sentence. We had to eliminate the clause *which included an Indian agent who organized the fur trade* because it was now a digression. We also added the clause *which would take an active role in assimilating natives through education.* The addition helps to connect the revised sentence to the rest of the paragraph. Adding *likewise* as a transition further strengthens the connection. Note that we have also added *through education* to the third sentence. Again, the addition connects the sentence more clearly to the topic.

EXERCISE ONE: CREATING PARAGRAPH BREAKS

Here is one way the paragraph might be revised. This example is by no means the only revision possible:

1. The entrance of Lady Macbeth in Scene 5 comes as a strong dramatic contrast to all the preceding scenes. **2.** Until this scene, we have had only the vaguest mention of her, and her appearance is all the more forceful because of this. **3.** Alone on the stage, she has a chance to state her frankest and most hidden thoughts, uncomplicated by the social compromises of dialogue. **4.** In this appearance, Shakespeare reveals not only her intentions, but also the flaw in them.

5. She begins to speak by reading Macbeth's letter aloud. **6.** In the letter's opening line, Shakespeare subtly reveals the crucial flaw in the couple's plans: "They met in the day of success . . ." (Macbeth 1.5.1). **7.** There is no mention here of Banquo, and it is his presence at the meeting with the witches that so undermines the couple's success. **8.** The audience is made more aware that Lady Macbeth does not realize Banquo's full involvement in Macbeth's plans.

9. Finishing the letter, Lady Macbeth then begins a forceful soliloquy in which she discusses her husband's character, inadvertently revealing through this discussion her perception of her own role. **10.** Apparent here is her repressed disgust and automatic assumption of superiority over him. **11.** In this passage, she categorically outlines his flaws and his obvious inadequacy to fulfil their shared ambitions. **12.** In doing so, she is unconsciously convincing herself that only she is capable of perpetrating the murder of Duncan. **13.** In her mind a vision is already forming of herself as controller of their joint destiny. **14.** The clarity of her vision and the completeness of her commitment to this destiny have strong dramatic impact, for she is not once besieged by the moral doubts which have left Macbeth completely indecisive. **15.** Plainly she sees action rather than passivity as the only means to the throne, and it is this preference which determines the role she will play in the struggle.

16. Shakespeare reveals this passionate intent in a brilliantly subtle stroke. **17.** When the messenger interrupts her reverie with the words "The King comes here tonight" (Macbeth 1.5.29), he is referring to Duncan. **18.** For Lady Macbeth, who already is unconsciously associating Macbeth with the throne, it is as though someone read her innermost thoughts. **19.** Her amazed reaction, "Thou art mad to say it!" is hastily covered up with the weak rejoinder, "Is not the master with him?" (Macbeth 1.5.30-31), for she quickly realizes whom the messenger really means. **20.** This nervous misjudgment plainly reveals the depth of her guilty thoughts and the earnestness of her intent.

The student who wrote this passage obviously enjoyed digging into Shakespeare's tragic drama. Interest and excitement of discovery made the writer forget about the poor reader. Notice that the original paragraph makes you, the reader, struggle to find the main topic. Rather than sharing the writer's enjoyment, you may well ask, "Why is the writer telling me all this?" This is exactly the kind of ruthless inquiry the writer should expect of the reader. The reader will always want to have at least a sense of where the writer is going and why.

In our revision, we have tried to create that sense of direction in two ways. First, we have made paragraph breaks according to shifts in chronology. The first paragraph serves as a general introduction to the subsequent paragraphs on the scene. The second paragraph focuses on the first section of the scene, the reading aloud of Macbeth's letter. The third paragraph discusses the soliloquy itself, and the final paragraph discusses the interruption of the soliloquy by the messenger.

These breaks make sense only because, in each of these paragraphs, the writer is advancing a different point. In the first paragraph, the topic is the introduction of the focus of the rest of the passage. In our revision, we have stated this focus explicitly, that *in this appearance, Shakespeare reveals not only her intentions, but also the flaw in them.* The second paragraph establishes that *Shakespeare subtly reveals the crucial flaw in the couple's plans*; the remainder of the paragraph develops this idea.

Both the third and the fourth paragraph focus on the revelation of Lady Macbeth's vision of her destiny. You might have chosen to keep these paragraphs together for that reason. We decided to split the two, having the first focus on this revelation through the soliloquy and the second through the interruption of the messenger. Our choice makes sense because of our emphasis on chronology; however, if you weren't concerned about chronology, you might have created two different paragraphs, the first one encompassing Sentences Nine to Thirteen and focusing on Lady Macbeth's response to her husband's inadequacies, the second encompassing Sentences Fourteen to Twenty and focusing on Lady Macbeth's passionate intent.

In our revision, all four paragraphs are now fairly short. An astute writer would now proceed to develop the paragraphs more fully by incorporating more details and evidence to support points.

EXERCISE TWO: REPETITION AND SUBSTITUTION

The comparatively sudden appearance at the turn of the seventeenth century of the novel as we know it was a manifestation of a marked **change** in the direction of men's interests. Comparable and related **changes**, sometimes resulting in new forms in art and literature, had of course occurred in the arts before. Until about the fifteenth century, for instance, there was no such thing as portrait **painting** as we know it. It began as representations of the **Virgin** or the Holy Family. Then, as the Renaissance advanced, the **painter's** attitude to his subject **changed**; he went on **painting Virgins**, but more and more his model is obviously a flesh-and-blood and not-at-all-**virginal** peasant girl or great lady. After a space of years the pretext disappeared entirely: to **paint** a woman it was no longer necessary for the **painter** to pretend that he was **painting** the **image of the Mother of God.**[7]

There are many instances of repetition and substitution in this paragraph; we have focused on three key ones. Because the opening sentence of the paragraph is about novels, while the remainder of the paragraph focuses primarily on painting, the repetition of various forms of the word *change* helps to connect the first sentence to the remainder of the passage. The writer's use of *paint, painter,* and *painting* also helps keep the paragraph coherent, as do the continual references to *virgins*. Note the elegant substitution of *the image of the Mother of God* for *Virgin* in the final sentence.

There are several pronouns in the paragraph, including two instances of *we*. You will have noted that there is no antecedent for either *we*; the author does not tell us whom exactly *we* is. Does this make you feel included in the paragraph or excluded from it? Your answer will depend on whether or not you agree that the author speaks for you. The other pronouns in the paragraph, *he, his,* and *it,* substitute nicely for *the painter* and *painting*.

REVISING PRONOUN REFERENCE

Exercise One:

Vienna, during Franz Schubert's short life, experienced major political, economic, and social upheavals. The Holy Roman Empire, which was ruled from **this city** for at least one thousand years, effectively came to an end in 1806, when Emperor Franz II relinquished his title to Napoleon. Vienna's aristocracy had lost much money and status since the abolition of serfdom and the institution of new land taxes in the 1780s. Consequently, **aristocratic Viennese** were no longer in a position to patronize musicians as extensively as in the past. As a result, the middle class emerged as a new factor in the music industry of Vienna. **Middle-class patrons** desired

---

[7] Walter Allen, *The English Novel: A Short Critical History* (Harmondsworth, Middlesex: Penguin, 1954) 21.

published music that could be performed by small groups of amateur musicians. This **demand** increased the number of publishing houses and made composing certain types of music a viable occupation. Beethoven, who settled **in Vienna** in 1792, lived through **these political, economic, and social changes**. So did Haydn. **Both** were older men, however, with defined personalities and musical styles. Unlike **these two men**, Schubert was born into **the unsettled and dynamic Vienna of 1797**, and his personality and musical talent were defined by **this period of transition**. Musical historians argue that his music can only be correctly understood and interpreted when placed in this historical context: he lived and matured in Vienna between 1797 and 1828, when **the conditions governing the composition and production of music** were in a state of flux.

We have highlighted the changes made to the paragraph. Because this paragraph is quite lengthy, pronoun references become more tangled toward the close of the passage as the writer tries to unite ideas. At the opening, the reader may have little difficulty discerning that the *it* in the second sentence refers to Vienna (you may not even have changed this pronoun). However, what the *this* refers to in the last sentence is quite unclear. We had to re-read the paragraph before we could substitute *the conditions governing the composition and production of music*. The revision of this passage establishes clearly that writers must use *this* carefully; it is easy to write *this* and avoid thinking about what the *this* actually refers to.

Exercise Two:

Alcohol profoundly alters the structure and functioning of the central nervous system. It interferes with the supply of oxygen to the brain, sometimes causing blackout or temporary amnesia. It destroys brain cells, causing the deterioration and atrophy of the brain. It is possible that this **damage to the brain caused by alcohol's destruction of brain cells** can be reversed, but research is insufficient to prove **this hypothesis**. Also, **alcohol** alters the brain's production of RNA, an important genetic "messenger." Finally, **alcohol** causes vitamin B deficiencies, **a nutritional problem** that can result in a neurological disorder called Wernicke-Korsakoff's syndrome. **This syndrome**, whose symptoms include amnesia, loss of short-term memory, disorientation, hallucinations, double vision, and loss of muscle control, may also be a result of the direct action of alcohol on the brain. **The serious damage alcohol can do to the central nervous system** should make one think very carefully about even moderate alcohol consumption.

The author of this paragraph probably wanted to avoid repeating *alcohol*, possibly having been told by someone never to use the same word twice in a paragraph. (Any time you are worried about repetition, remember that "Home, Sweet Home" sounds much better than "Home, Sweet House.") Using *it* instead of *alcohol* is fine in the second and third sentences, where parallel structure helps the reader see clearly to what the *it* is referring. However, by the fifth and sixth sentence, the reader needs the noun *alcohol* for clarity. Note our extensive revisions to several of the sentences. We often had to combine two sentences to improve pronoun reference. Be prepared in your own revisions to make substantial changes occasionally; sometimes, just substituting the word the pronoun refers to will not improve clarity.

EXERCISE THREE: RECOGNIZING PARALLEL STRUCTURE

Personal alienation is compounded by the inability of the characters portrayed in the stories to communicate their feelings. (1) **They construct** mental walls which confine and distort their sense of reality. (1) **They struggle** like some forgotten race (2) **for perpetuation** and (2) **for freedom** to reveal the truth that lies just beneath the surface of their prosaic lives. The brief exposure of the characters (3) **in single episodes**, (3) **in mere fragments** of commonplace "adventures," intensifies the portrayal of isolated, unhappy souls. (1) **They do not grow or change**. The reader leaves many of them as they are found: (4) **Wing Biddlebaum will continue** to walk his veranda, (4) **Enoch Williams will remain** alone with the phantom people of his dreams, (4) **the Reverend Curtis Hartman will continue** to preach. (5) **Only George Willard**, as the one who sees and listens, is present in every episode; (5) **only he** passes the milestones of growth from adolescence to young adulthood. The presence of George unites the separate lives. (6) **He is the natural confidant** of all the lonely people of the town; (6) **he is "the young thing"** referred to in "The Book of the Grotesque" (Anderson 24). (6) **He is the singular manifestation** of (7) **renewal**, (7) **rebirth**, and (7) **hope**; even so, Elmer Cowley feels that George Willard "(8) **belonged to the town**, (8) **typified the town**, (8) **represented** in his person **the spirit of the town**."

We have highlighted the examples of parallel structure in this passage, numbering them so that you can see how they align. Once parallelism is highlighted in this way, you can see easily how it works to create coherence. The first sentence, which is the first claim of the paragraph, stands alone. Once the writer begins to develop the paragraph, she uses parallel structure to keep the evidence for a single claim united. The sentences beginning with *they* (parallelism #1), all develop the first claim. When the writer moves to a new claim, that *the reader leaves many of them as they are found*, we see a new set of parallel structures (parallelism #4) to develop that claim. Likewise, parallelism #6 develops the final claim of the paragraph. Within each of these subpoints, supporting details in sentences are held together through parallel structure as well.

IMPROVING COHERENCE THROUGH PARALLEL STRUCTURE

Exercise One:

The adolescent female wants both security and freedom, and therefore demands made by her are often contradictory. One week, she might request a personal set of keys for the family car, but the next, she might want one of her parents to arrange an oil change for that same car. Similarly, one night, she might insist that she be allowed to stay out until two a.m. But the next night, she might become angry because her parents didn't wait up for her. These fluctuations in mood are to be expected. Parents will often find them irritating, but must learn to endure them.

The writer of the original paragraph often misses the opportunity to emphasize contrasts through parallelism. There are several places in the paragraph where the writer could use parallelism to create links between sentences. Because the points being made are general and hypothetical, we can create parallelism by making changes like substituting *the next [week]* for *later* and adding *one night* to the opening of the third sentence. Likewise, we can rewrite the third sentence of the original so that it has a different emphasis in our revision, stressing the demand placed on the parents. These changes do not alter meaning but do improve coherence. (In some prose, changes similar to the ones we have made might alter meaning and would be unacceptable.)

Exercise Two:

When all indicators are taken into consideration, Ontario emerges as the best province in which to live. Of all the ten provinces, Ontario's unemployment rate is the lowest, its wages are the highest, and its medical system is the most accessible. Furthermore, Ontario offers the best housing and the best-educated neighbours—a higher percentage of people in Ontario have university degrees. However, Ontarians pay a price for these advantages. The divorce rate is high, and, even though more families own their own home, housing is expensive. Those individuals seeking a less stressful lifestyle might opt for Prince Edward Island.

In the first exercise paragraph, we tended to preserve sentences and make them parallel. In this revision, we combine sentences to create parallelism. This paragraph establishes clearly the advantages of using parallel structure when listing items. The benefits of living in Ontario sound rather lame in the original; when listed in parallel form, they seem more emphatic. You will note, however, that to achieve parallel structure, we had to revise extensively, changing *workers also get paid more* to *its wages are the highest,* for example. When you are trying to achieve coherence through parallel structure, you may have to revise in a similar manner. Be sure that you do not lose meaning when you create parallelism.

EXERCISE FOUR: TRANSITIONS

Here are two examples of paragraphs composed from the list of six sentences about detergent.

Detergent is an important cleansing agent. **Nonetheless**, it is also a cause of water pollution. Because it comes in many forms, it can contain many kinds of pollutants. **For example**, many detergents contain harmful phosphates. Others may **also** contain perfume, another pollutant. **For this reason**, ecologically-minded consumers usually prefer non-scented detergent.

Detergent is an important part of one of the everyday rituals of our lives. In the form of granules, a liquid, or a bar, it is used for numerous purposes and seems an innocuous necessity, like water which is an indispensable adjunct to detergent's use. "Cleanliness is next to godliness" our grandmothers told us, and we carried this adage into adult life like a talisman—scrubbing and cleaning our way to respectability. **However**, detergent, misused and overused, pollutes the environment and is not the harmless washday helper it has been made out to be. Many detergents contain phosphates and perfumes which contaminate water. **Even though** scented detergent has been widely accepted as a necessary part of maintaining personal hygiene, as grey, foul-smelling effluent in lakes, streams, and even drinking water, it endangers our health and threatens the purity of one of our most important natural resources. **Indeed**, it is this image that has made many consumers switch to non-scented detergent, sacrificing that fresh laundry smell that our grandmothers taught us to love.

The two paragraphs are very different: one is short and to the point; the other is quite interesting and elaborate. However, each relies on transitions to signal direction of thought to the reader. For example, both paragraphs use a transition that signals a conflicting direction (*nonetheless, however*) when they move from discussing detergent as a cleanser to detergent as a pollutant. Both paragraphs also use a transition when they begin to discuss consumer purchase of non-scented detergent. In the first paragraph *for this reason* conveys cause and effect; in the second, *indeed* emphasizes and affirms the effect.

IMPROVING ORGANIZATION

Exercise One:

A detailed description of this potential landfill site will help to establish its important features. Beginning at the northwest corner of the site and moving clockwise, we spot several items worthy of consideration. First, a small creek runs alongside the northwest corner of the property. A subdivision is being built on the other side of this creek. From the northwest, the property slopes gently upward to the southeast. There are no remarkable features along the east side of the site at all, but there is a school in the southwest corner. Finally, if we consider the location as a whole, we can note that the soil type throughout is appropriate for a landfill site.

The writer of this passage had a difficult task; she needed to describe the site in a way that would permit the reader to picture it clearly. In our revision, we decided that an appropriate method of organization would be to move clockwise around the site because that was one way that a viewer might inspect the area. Note that we informed the reader of our organizational strategy in the second sentence. We also added a sentence about the east side. Even though there is nothing of importance there, the reader needs to know this "negative" piece of information to follow the paragraph. We placed the sentence about soil type at the end of the paragraph because the information it contains doesn't align well with our chosen method of organization. Note that we alerted the reader that we had finished our clockwise tour and were now considering the site as a whole.

Exercise Two:

Life on the prairies demanded that the farmer have a certain resilience or toughness in order to survive. There were the trials created by human folly: isolation, poor medical care, the price of grain. Then there were constant uncertainties about the outcome of natural events: the unpredictability of the weather, the yield of the crops, crops lost to storms and fire. In spite of all the farmer's efforts, success was constantly dependent on the will of the wind.

The original paragraph is interesting because, although it doesn't have a method of organization that can be easily named, there is a logical way that the sentences must be organized. *The will of the wind* refers to natural events, so we rearranged the paragraph to place the other sentence about natural events near it. There is also a logical inconsistency in the original within each of the two lists. *The price of grain* is a human folly; *crops lost to storms and fire* is an outcome of a natural event. We reorganized to correct this problem.

EXERCISE FIVE: DETECTING DEVELOPMENT AND PURPOSE

Lead Sentence: In the literature of the nineteenth century, gender roles are very distinctly represented in brother-sister relationships. **Topic Sentence:** In two particular novels, George Eliot's The Mill on the Floss and Charles Dickens's Our Mutual Friend, principal characters represent typical gender roles. **Restricting Sentence:** The brother represents the struggling party, the one who uses his head not his heart, while the sister represents the submissive party, the one who retreats rather than rebels. **Supporting Sentence:** In Mill on the Floss, Tom leaves home, is educated, and takes on the world, while Maggie stays by the hearth and acts with her heart. **Supporting Sentence:** Likewise, in Our Mutual Friend, it is Charley who leaves "the old life" (Dickens 117), and it is Lizzie who plays the nurturing role and occupies herself with household duties. **Concluding Sentence:** In both novels, the female sibling works to preserve the loving relationship despite excessive hardship and conflict, while the male sibling works to preserve the family honour and is the one who heartlessly, almost selfishly, ends the loving relationship.

This paragraph, once arranged properly, reads as a graceful mini-essay. Not all the paragraphs you write will follow this order. Some may have no lead sentence, others no concluding sentence. Some may have five supporting sentences, but no restricting sentences. Many may have only an implied topic sentence, not one that you can clearly label. But that sense of movement between abstract claim and concrete detail is what defines a paragraph.

REVISING UNDERDEVELOPED PARAGRAPHS

Exercise One:

The Canadian West offers several types of summer employment, and each has advantages and disadvantages. Many nature-loving students choose to plant trees for a few months. This work pays very well, usually over ten dollars an hour, but it is backbreaking; the weak and the wimpy should avoid it. Other students work in restaurants in Banff or make beds in its expensive hotels. The social person will like this work; there are plenty of opportunities to meet people and enjoy nightlife. There is one drawback, however: accommodation for hotel and restaurant workers is cramped and limited. People who need privacy will be unhappy working at the summer resorts. In Vancouver, there are the employment possibilities that all large cities offer: students can work in summer theatres or on construction sites, at service industry jobs or at factory work. Vancouver is a great summer city with wonderful beaches and lots of things to do, but housing is quite expensive. Students who need to save money would be better to look for work outside the city. In short, there is work to be found, but deciding what work to look for and where to live depends on the individual's priorities.

The original paragraph would not be underdeveloped if the introductory sentence simply stated that the Canadian West offered several types of summer employment to students. However, the opening sentence makes an additional promise, to discuss advantages and disadvantages, and that aspect of the paragraph is undeveloped. We have added sentences about advantages and disadvantages after each of the supporting sentences. Note that we replaced the last sentence with another, more appropriate, concluding sentence. Once the paragraph had been fully developed, the original closing sentence no longer made sense.

Exercise Two:

To provide the necessities of life, the majority of women in Nicaragua of lower- and middle-class origin must work outside the home in addition to being responsible for the family's well-being and for the carrying out of all domestic labour. The cost of living in Nicaragua is such that a family of three or four simply cannot survive on one income; the average cost of housing and food exceeds the average wage. As in most societies, however, the necessity of both parents working for wages has not changed the traditional assumption that women complete all domestic work, and most men perform less than ten per cent of all household tasks.

Many rural women in particular must endure the proverbial "double day." Not only must a woman work in the fields with her husband—clearing land, planting, or harvesting—but in conjunction with these chores, she is responsible for cooking the family dinner, caring for the children, and doing the domestic chores such as laundry, shopping, and household maintenance. Some women continue, after all these tasks are completed, to do crafts and handiwork which may be sold in the markets to provide the additional income needed for survival.

In the original, the first paragraph is nothing more than an assertion, a claim. It contains no evidence at all to persuade the reader that women in Nicaragua must work both in the paid labour force and inside the home. We have added two sentences in our revision that explain and defend the claim. The other two paragraphs we simply combined. Both paragraphs help to develop the assertion that opens the second paragraph, that rural women must endure a double day.

Chapter Five: The Conventions of Punctuation

USING COMMAS TO SEPARATE

Exercise One:

The aboriginal language also reflects an elaborate, fundamental, and complex kinship system. This system expresses not only numerous kinship terms but a complex system of language sharing across the country. It was created in part as a result of laws requiring interclan and interlanguage marriage. Languages of the Australian aboriginals also reflect a number of other characteristics: their unique understanding of land ownership and economics and their values and beliefs as established by their laws. They are a people who see things in a very different way from us and who have subsequently developed appropriate words to express this view.

The original paragraph needs one comma added and four commas deleted. In the first sentence, a comma should be placed after *fundamental* because it is in a list of coordinate adjectives. In the second sentence, because *numerous* and *kinship* are not coordinate adjectives, the comma between them should be deleted. The comma after *interclan* in the third sentence should also be deleted, because the two items *interclan and interlanguage* do not constitute a list. Likewise, *their unique understanding of land ownership and economics and their values and beliefs as established by their laws* is only two items, so no comma. Finally, the comma before the *and* in the last sentence might have been placed there because the writer thought it was separating two coordinate clauses. The *and* separates two items, so no comma.

Exercise Two:

Caribou have adapted to many limiting factors determined by the geography and biology of their range and the seasonal variability of weather affecting the health of the herd. The distance between the calving grounds and the winter range, the energy exerted in migration and in the search for food if the snow is deep in late spring, and the extent of insect harassment and of energy expended in seeking refuge from bugs are among the many unpredictable variables which can significantly influence the herd's ability to cope with various additional stresses.

This paragraph amply illustrates the challenge of punctuation: the reader must examine sentences carefully to determine sentence construction before revising. Careful scrutiny reveals that the original paragraph contains four extra commas. No comma is needed after *range* in the first sentence since only two items are listed. No comma is needed after *harassment* in the second sentence since the final *and* joins only two items (prepositional phrases modifying *extent*), not the entire series of items. Note that we added another *and* after *spring* to improve clarity. Furthermore, no comma is permitted after *bugs* since such a comma would separate the subject of the clause from the verb. Many writers would be tempted to put one there since the list of items in the subject is very lengthy. A better solution might be to revise the sentence by shortening the list. Finally, *many* and *unpredictable* are not coordinate adjectives, so no comma is needed there.

USING COMMAS TO SET OFF

Exercise One:

The dilemma brought into focus by the conflicting values of development versus conservation and preservation raises serious questions. Not only must we ask what our society is doing to reduce our dependency on non-renewable energy sources; more significantly, we wonder what the point is of Environmental Impact Assessments when they are repeatedly overridden by political and economic "imperatives." While pressures for resource development in the North escalate annually, our valuation of wilderness ecosystems and their biological components seems to remain somewhat fixed. Conservation interests, as a result, appear to have become devalued against the inflation of economic necessities. In order to protect significant unique biological environments effectively, it is necessary that we continually assess, as legitimate values, wilderness interests and act to increase the effectiveness of our voice in a political/economic environment.

If you like using commas, you probably found this paragraph difficult to revise. Although the sentences in it are long and complex, very few phrases or words need to be set off. The first three sentences, for example, are fine as is. Commas should be placed around *as a result* in the fourth sentence to set off the interjection, and in the fifth sentence, a comma is needed before *it* to set off the introductory element. No comma is needed after *wilderness interests* since the words following are an essential component of the predicate, not a non-essential or non-restrictive piece of information.

Exercise Two:

Although native women in the Canadian fur trade during the eighteenth century were sometimes exploited and dominated by European traders, there are many reasons to suggest that the tremendous involvement of these women in the trade benefited North Americans for both social and economic reasons. Despite the fact that some women were victimized, marriage between the native women and the traders was common across the country, allowing peaceful bonds to develop between these different societies. As well, during the fur traders' journeys, women assisted by supplying knowledge of the land and useful methods of trade. Some women even participated in the fur trade directly. Another area where women continued to be important was in providing essential domestic skills that helped the fur traders and their families to have a more enjoyable life. Finally, native women were often visible at trading posts, occupying numerous economic positions which were required for the successful system of trade.

In the first sentence, the initial comma after *trade* is incorrect, as is the final comma after *Americans,* both for the same reason. Each comma precedes a prepositional phrase that is directly connected to what precedes it. Since *during the eighteenth century* and *for both social and economic reasons* are essential modifiers, they should not be set off by a comma. In Sentence Five, the comma following *important* should also be deleted since it separates the subject from the verb. Likewise, the comma after *families* in the same sentence separates an infinitive phrase beginning with *to have* from the verb it modifies, *helped.* All other commas in the passage are placed correctly.

GENERAL USE OF COMMAS

Exercise One:

Beginning in 1942, attempts were made by a federal government employee, Malcolm McCrimmon, to decrease the number of registered Indians in Northern Alberta for the purpose of "tightening the budget," and, by so doing, he effectively limited potential future demands of these Indians. These measures removed ninety band members from the Lubicon membership list. After a court hearing in 1943 and a formal judicial inquiry in 1944, both of which discounted McCrimmon's actions, McCrimmon himself was left to act on these rulings at his own discretion. The result was that only eighteen Lubicon and relatively few Northern Alberta Indians were reinstated.

In this paragraph, extra commas are needed in several spots to set off interrupting elements. In the opening sentence, the introductory element *beginning in 1942* and the interrupters *Malcolm McCrimmon* and *by so doing* all need commas to set them off. Because *beginning in 1942* starts the sentence, it requires only one comma, but the other phrases need to be enclosed by a pair of commas. You will notice that we have also placed a comma before *and* in the first sentence to separate two independent clauses. The second sentence is fine as is, but the third requires some thought (and some commas). Both an introductory element and a mid-sentence interrupter precede the subject, *McCrimmon.* The final sentence does not require commas.

Exercise Two:

The Lubicon settlement at Little Buffalo is located 240 miles north of Edmonton, and, although this land is south of the 60th parallel, the development pressures and development impacts upon it are very similar to those felt in the North. The people are quite isolated, resources are extracted for external markets with no local input, resource extraction is based on non-renewable resources, and the social land claim settlement may be delayed for an unreasonably long time partially because of the extensive bureaucracy inherent in tri-party negotiations that have existed since the transfer of crown lands from the federal to the provincial government in 1930.

The first sentence of the original contains two comma errors. Since *240 miles north of Edmonton* is an essential modifier of *is located,* no comma should be placed between the two. We have also added a comma after *and,* a revision that is technically correct because *although this land is south of the 60th parallel* is a mid-sentence interrupter and should be enclosed in commas. Probably you found the last sentence in this passage difficult to read because of its length; however, to be correct, it needs two fewer commas. (The comma after *social* and the one after *negotiations* should be deleted because *social* and *land claim* are not coordinate adjectives and because the information following *negotiations* is restrictive, as the *that* indicates.) The author probably included these incorrect commas in an attempt to give the reader a break. However, because the sentence is a list of independent clauses, the only commas required are those between the items in the list. Nonetheless, because the items are so lengthy, the reader finds it difficult to retain the information in the sentence. A better revision might have been to break the sentence into two or three complete sentences.

Exercise Three:

Feelings of vulnerability and dependency in the developed countries are being realized as the genetic resources of the world dwindle. Ironically, developed countries are beginning to show an interest and appreciation in traditional farming techniques because they nurture genetic diversity while allowing for a continual evolution of that genetic diversity. The problem of genetic erosion is being magnified by the movement from these traditional ecosystems to the adoption of modern cropping techniques and commercial agricultural practices including, most importantly, the use of hybrid seeds.

This paragraph requires few commas even though its sentences are long and complex. The comma before *as* in the first sentence is inappropriate since the clause is restrictive. The writer may have included the comma for clarity; another possible revision that would avoid any possible confusion would be to change the *as* to *while*, still deleting the comma. In Sentence Two, the comma after *because* is completely incorrect, first because commas precede conjunctions rather than follow them. Secondly, the *because* clause is restrictive, so no comma is necessary. The commas we have placed around the phrase *most importantly* in the final sentence set off the interrupter and help to break a long sentence.

USING SEMICOLONS, COLONS, AND DASHES

Exercise One:

Other factors caused parents to put their children in orphanages: rampant disease, a high mortality rate, and year-round poverty. Childhood disease, in particular, was a problem. Statistics in 1867 show that two out of every five children died within a year of birth. Infant illness was caused primarily by intestinal diseases, largely because babies were not breastfed; rather, they were given unpasteurized or diluted milk. Older children were often victims of smallpox, a fatal disease in this era. When children became ill, parents could not cope — they had no resources to deal with the illness — and so they gave their children to hospitals, hoping they would receive adequate care there.

Sentence One models a proper use of the colon. The colon is preceded by an independent clause and followed by a list that does not flow syntactically from the first clause. In the third sentence, there is no need for a colon to introduce the list since the sentence flows grammatically and since the information preceding the colon does not form an independent clause. The semicolon in the fourth sentence is used correctly: it joins two independent clauses that are closely related. A final dash is needed in the last sentence after *illness* to close the aside properly.

Exercise Two:

It is also apparent that hierarchies among students are based on dominant middle-class values. Frideres offers an explanation for this in his study of native education in Canada: he recognizes the fact that schools emphasize the need to teach students the ways in which they can gain power and success. Teachers and faculty take on the function of instilling business creeds and competitive qualities in their students. Schools — thought to be liberators — become the places in which students are taught to behave in such a way that they will obtain the ability to integrate themselves into the dominant middle-class value system (Frideres, 1987:284). It thus becomes vital that students accept and adapt to this system; otherwise, they will find classroom time boring and of little use (Frideres, 1987:284).

The colon in the second sentence can remain, since what follows it is an example of what the main clause introduces. The semicolon after *of,* however, is incorrect since the semicolon does not join independent clauses. No punctuation is needed in this sentence at all. The dashes around *thought to be liberators* are correctly placed, but they could be replaced by commas with little ill effect. In the final sentence, the semicolon is correctly placed. What precedes it and what follows it are independent clauses that are closely related.

USING APOSTROPHES CORRECTLY

Exercise One:

The second study was based on the father's family of origin. Most theories concerning personality consider the family of origin to be critical to the formation of life-long behaviour patterns. In the development of a role such as fathering, one's family of origin seems important as the setting for both the process of identification that is the core of the psychological theories and the model of parenting behaviour that is stressed in cognitive and learning theories (Levinger and Mole, 1979: 310). One specific question concerns the strength of the father's childhood relationships to each of his parents. Men with custody were more likely to be middle- or last-born children and were significantly more likely to have both brothers and sisters rather than siblings of only one sex. Men with custody described a more intense relationship with their mothers and a more distant one with their fathers. The mothers of men with custody were more likely to be employed outside the home.

The difficulty in this passage lies in separating the plurals (brothers, sisters, parents, fathers) from the possessives. In all, there are three possessives. The first sentence contains one. Since *the fathers family of origin* can be read as *the family of origin of the father,* we need an apostrophe and an *s.* In the third sentence, we have added an apostrophe to *ones.* We can say *his family of origin* easily, so *ones* clearly should be a possessive. In the fourth sentence, *fathers* should be a possessive because we can say *the childhood relationships of the father.* All the other words ending in *s* are plurals, verbs, or words that always end in *s.* You might have had difficulty with *parents* at the end of Sentence Four. If you read the sentence carefully, however, you will see that *parents* is a noun, an object of the *of* phrase; it does not modify another word.

Exercise Two:

In modern art, since this revolution in colour's importance, there have been uncountable new experiments with its power. Each member of the colourist freedom revolution should be recognized as playing a vital role in the renovation of Western art's decor. Colour is crucial psychologically as it's a primary factor in ambience. Anyone who fails to appreciate its worth (such as those who tried to repress Kandinsky and Delaunay in their freeing of colour from form) needs further education.

Sentence One of the original contains two words we must consider, *colours* and *its.* Since we can say *the importance of colour,* we know that we need to write *colour's.* The several *its* in this passage are a little difficult, but if you remember that *it's* always means *it is,* correction is easy. The one in the first sentence and the one in the fourth are possessives; only the *its* in Sentence Three needs an apostrophe. *Art's* in Sentence Two is a judgment call. It is definitely a possessive, but it is difficult to determine where the apostrophe should be placed. Did the writer mean *the decor of Western art* or *the decor of Western arts*? We guessed the former.

PUNCTUATING SHORT QUOTATIONS

Exercise One:

To ensure that the reader recognizes these two opposing worlds, Marvell uses further contrasts in the second stanza to distinguish between the busy world and the calm world. Again, the choice of words serves Marvell's purpose successfully. Here, the "busy companies of men" (12) are contrasted to the "delicious solitude" (16) within the natural world. The key words "delicious" and "busy" definitely suggest that the natural world would be superior to the social world which is "all but rude" (15). Even the soft flowing rhythm of the poem suggests a world of relaxation and peace. Marvell, then, not only introduces two worlds, but also gives the reader a clear impression of the one he favours: the world of nature.

There are no glaring technical errors in this passage, but the quotation *all but rude* is poorly signalled. The added *which is* improves the flow of the sentence. Also, the quotation *delicious solitude* requires a parenthetical citation. Note that when these words are re-quoted in the next sentence, they do not need to be documented again.

Exercise Two:

MacLennan's Two Solitudes is the most celebrated fictional representation of Canadian culture during this era. As William Arthur Deacon, literary editor of The Globe and Mail, rhapsodizes, "In Two Solitudes MacLennan is a Canadian. . . . Ideas and feelings are expressed that would occur to nobody except a Canadian" (Rev. of Two Solitudes 18). The novel is primarily a discussion of Anglo-French relations in Canada, so evidently Deacon believes this theme embodies the essence of Canadian life. J. Donald Adams, the New York Times reviewer and also a Canadian, is in accord; he claims that the reader "puts it [the book] down with a better knowledge of Canada's central difficulty as a nation" (Rev. of Two Solitudes 2). Similarly, the anonymous reviewer in the Times Literary Supplement praises MacLennan for offering to the world "a careful and scrupulously fair picture of the conflict which arises" from Canada's bicultural situation, and readily interprets the union of Paul Tallard and Heather Methuen at the close of the novel as symbolizing "the mutual understanding which is needed between the two races" (317).

All quotations are well signalled in the original, but the punctuation is poor. The first problem in this passage is that the writer tends to use a comma to introduce all quotations whether there is a break in the syntax or not. These extra commas (the one after *reader* in the fourth sentence and the one after *symbolizing* in the final sentence) have been omitted. Also, in the second sentence, it seems likely that, since *Ideas* begins with a capital, a sentence has been omitted in the first quotation. Four ellipsis dots are therefore necessary. Finally, the writer needs to enclose some of the parenthetical citations within sentences. The correct form for this enclosure is modelled by the last citation in the original: *races" (317)*. Note also the correct use of square brackets to insert information that clarifies in the second quotation.

PUNCTUATING LONG QUOTATIONS

Exercise One:

At the beginning of <u>Northanger Abbey</u>, Catherine is clearly shown to be in a state of naiveté. She is presented as everything but moronic:

> She never could learn or understand anything before she was taught; and sometimes not even then, for she was often inattentive, and occasionally stupid. Her mother was three months in teaching her only to repeat the "Beggar's Petition" . . . not that Catherine was always stupid — by no means. (38)

Catherine should not be condemned for her ignorance, however. As Austen tells the reader, "her mind was about as ignorant and uninformed as the female mind at seventeen usually is" (41).

The revisions to be made here are primarily technical. The block quotation is well introduced but is punctuated poorly. Since the introduction to the block quotation is an independent clause, a colon is required to indicate the break in syntax. The quotation marks around the block quotation are unnecessary and incorrect, and the ellipsis dots should be better spaced. Finally, the block quotation needs to be set off by a double space from the text of the paper. You can also see that we have revised the punctuation of the short quotation. The comma is a more appropriate, less forceful introduction to the quotation. The parenthetical citation is now correctly placed outside the closing quotation mark.

Exercise Two:

The poem "Trees at the Arctic Circle" reflects Purdy's view of Canada. At first, Purdy is scornful of the eighteen-inch trees. He thinks of them as "coward trees" (<u>North of Summer</u> 29) in comparison to Douglas firs and feels contempt for them. However, at the close of the poem, Purdy recognizes that the trees are not cowardly. Rather,

> They have about three months
> to ensure that the species does not die
> and that's how they spend their time
>
> . . . .
> just digging in here and now. (<u>North of Summer</u> 29)

The parallels between the trees in the poem and the Canadian-American situation are obvious.

Only a few technical problems here. The missing line(s) should be indicated by a row of well-spaced ellipsis dots, and the parenthetical citation for the block quotation should appear on the last quoted line. The colon following *Rather* has been replaced by a comma because the text of the essayist here is grammatically aligned with the text of the poet. You may believe that *rather* is a weak signal for the introduction of a quotation. The word could be replaced with a slightly more detailed introduction to the quotation.

Chapter Six: Choosing Words

REVISING CONSIDERING HOMONYMS AND DENOTATIONS

Exercise One:

There have been both biological and cultural differences **between** men and women since the **evolution** of homo sapiens. Cultural differences are easy to document and readily **comprehended** after an examination of the **canons** of Western civilization. In Western literature and philosophy, women have been **afforded** unequal status. According to the Christian **principles of** the Bible, a man was the first human created, and a woman was **fashioned** from this man's rib. In other words, men are **predominant** to women. Because men have been considered superior to women for so long, it is **difficult** to pinpoint the exact biological **differences** between the sexes. Take the concept of strength, for example. While it is possible to investigate **whether** it is men or women who are generally more capable of lifting heavy weights, this definition of strength favours the biological capabilities of men. Women would receive a higher ranking in tests of strength **based** on endurance rather than on lifting ability. Put simply, a woman's capabilities are not considered **equal** to a man's because of traditional beliefs about woman's inferiority.

The homonym errors in this passage—*cannon* for *canon*, *principals* for *principles*, *weather* for *whether*—are easier to spot than the denotation problems. Some denotation mistakes—*strenuous* for *difficult*, for example—are obvious because the reader realizes immediately that *strenuous* denotes physical difficulty and the writer is discussing mental difficulty. However, most readers will not immediately recognize all the denotation problems. For example, you may not have known that *among* generally denotes more than two parties, while *between* is used when discussing only two parties (men and women in this case). Look up the words you missed (and their replacements) in a dictionary. The dictionary definitions should help you to see why the revision was necessary.

Finally, note that in the second last sentence, we changed the wordy *predicated on the base of* to the more accurate and concise *based*. This prompted another change, *the ability to lift* to *lifting ability*, a revision that seems unconnected to homonym or denotation errors. Remember, when you change one part of a sentence, you must often change another to keep elements balanced.

Exercise Two:

In "The Garden," Marvell attempts to show the **superiority** of the natural over the civil. To demonstrate the **pre-eminence** of the life of nature, Marvell uses description and images to contrast two **distinct** societies. He **uses** appropriate words to differentiate between the busy, hustling world of society and the solitary, tranquil world of the garden. Even more creatively, Marvell changes mythology in order to associate solitude more closely with the natural state of man. No Eve is present in Marvell's Eden. The poem follows a cyclical **pattern**, one that can be **compared** to the cycle of nature's seasons. At the end of this cycle, the reader is returned to the conflicting images that began the poem, to the conflict between the busy world and the tranquil world. However, Marvell does not try to **affect** the reader's choice regarding which world is more desirable by being dogmatic and **prescriptive**. Rather the decision to **accept** his elevation of one world over the other is left to each individual reader.

The unusual use of *peculiar* in this passage is probably the result of over-reliance on a thesaurus. *Peculiar* and *distinct* are occasionally synonymous, but not in this passage. If you write English literature essays, you probably were interested in the change of the word *image* to *pattern*. Be careful when you are using literary terms to use them precisely. Cyclical images cannot exist because an image is a picture fixed in time.

Did you spot the *effect/affect* error? This homonym confusion is perhaps the most common of all homonym problems in academic prose, probably because academic essays often require the writer to consider effects. If you have problems with this error, you might use the word-search function of a computer to locate all instances of *effect* and *affect* in your prose so that you can correct your usage.

REVISING DISPROPORTIONATE AND SLANTED LANGUAGE

Exercise One:

In the period beginning with the leaked documents outlining Carter's coal conversion plans and continuing into the era of the Reagan Administration, two things became clear: the level of American ignorance regarding acid rain and the indifference accorded to this issue by the Reagan Administration. Of the four-fifths of Canadians who know about acid rain, ninety per cent feel the problem is serious; on the other hand, eighty per cent of Americans are unaware of the fact that their country produces acid rain. It has been noted that Americans, once believers, are difficult to dissuade. One shared belief is that the United States leads the way with the toughest environmental legislation in the world. Many who have tried to challenge this belief by pointing out the amount of smog and acid rain that originates in the United States, Canadians included, have been accused of anti-Americanism or misrepresentation.

It is when a writer feels particularly strongly about an issue that he or she is most likely to use slanted language. In the unrevised passage, the writer's disgust at the American response to acid rain is evident. However, the language would fail to persuade the sceptical reader because it seems motivated by emotion rather than reason. The revised passage, which eliminates such loaded expressions as *complete indifference, completely unreasonable,* and *reactionary money-mad ultraconservatives,* and which deletes the fairy-tale analogy entirely, will more easily convince the objective reader because the slanted language has been toned down.

Exercise Two:

What Mary Wollstonecraft demonstrates in <u>Vindication of the Rights of Women</u> is that men, being unwilling to work unless forced, become married to women who accept their idleness without complaint. Men call this arrangement love and the women they attach to themselves virtuous wives. While virtue in a wife may mean passivity and powerlessness, it does not mean indolence. These virtuous wives are supposed to work hard at pleasing and serving their husbands. To conclude, Wollstonecraft argues that a man does not marry a woman because of what she is, but because of what she will let him be.

Mary Wollstonecraft herself is no slouch when it comes to using slanted language, so it is perhaps not surprising that a student writing about Wollstonecraft's ideas might also indulge in this practice. In the revised passage, we have tried to eliminate the excessively negative language used to characterize men (*lazy louts,* for example) and the overdramatization of women's condition (*without a murmur of complaint*). Even when this language is deleted, the contradictory and powerless position of the virtuous woman is still clearly outlined.

REVISING CONSIDERING GENERAL AND SPECIFIC/ABSTRACT AND CONCRETE WORDS

Exercise One:

Some native women participated directly in the fur trade, trapping rabbits and martens seasonally in order to trade them for beads, lace, and other luxury items produced in Europe. Most, however, were only indirectly involved in the fur trade. They would provide white fur traders with food and other necessities in order to obtain useful European goods. For example, native women provided moccasins and snowshoes for the men of the Hudson's Bay Company and the Northwest Company, and they mended the tents and clothes of fur traders. They also frequently traded pemmican, berries, and wild rice for copper pots and kettles. Having European goods affected the lives and the work of native women. Copper pots and kettles, for instance, made heating stones to add to bark cooking pots unnecessary. Native women also prepared pelts for their men to trade, thus participating in the fur trade in a somewhat invisible (and often unrewarded) way.

In the original paragraph, one can see clearly the problem of writing that relies too heavily on concrete and specific language. The reader has difficulty determining the point of the passage; the sentences seem unconnected. When the abstract ideas are added (women participating directly, indirectly, and invisibly in the fur trade), the paragraph becomes more ordered and coherent. Adding the abstract ideas, however, reveals that some of the concrete details are digressions. The unity of the revised paragraph could be improved by moving the sentences about European goods affecting the lives and work of native women to another paragraph.

Exercise Two:

Although the dictionary defines pollution as the state of being impure or unclean, or the process of reaching that state, in environmental terms, pollution, a significant global problem, is defined as a man-made phenomenon which is harmful to the environment. Many human activities create pollution: overpackaging of consumer goods, excessive dependency on automobiles, industrial dumping of chemicals. Many of these activities can be regulated or modified so that we can still enjoy the benefits of industrial society without suffering its consequences. Big Macs need not disappear—only the cartons that hold them. Cars do not have to be eliminated, but public transit should be improved. We can and should control pollution by eliminating or at least severely reducing our use of natural resources and our creation of "unnatural" wastes.

The original paragraph suffers from too many general and abstract words and phrases. Some of the abstract phrases in the passage are simply redundant: for example, if pollution is a global problem, obviously it affects our lives. You might also think that the general definition of pollution is pointless if the paragraph focuses only on the more concrete environmental definition. It would be possible to eliminate the general definition altogether. Note that the concrete examples of pollution help to make the abstract definition more vivid. Furthermore, specific suggestions on regulation help to make the writer's argument more convincing.

REVISING TO ACHIEVE THE MIDDLE LEVEL OF DICTION

Exercise One:

Gradgrind cannot establish and maintain relationships easily because he has been taught to hide his emotions behind a mask of indifference. We see this mask when his daughter tells him that Bounderby has proposed marriage to her. Their whole conversation is unemotional; Gradgrind wears his "unbending, utilitarian, matter-of-fact face" (135), and she seems depressed and unenthusiastic. The room in which they meet also feels dead. We hear the ticking of "a deadly statistical clock . . . which measured every second with a beat like a rap upon a coffin-lid" (132).

The very casual diction in this passage is a disservice both to Dickens and to the writer's good ideas. The tone needs to be elevated somewhat. The first step taken in this revision is to eliminate all contractions (*can't, he's*). Grating slang such as *popped the question* and *can't relate to people* has also been eliminated. The resultant tone is more appropriate for an academic essay, especially because the writer now seems to be considering the novel much more seriously.

Exercise Two:

Joseph Conrad was painfully aware of the limitations of words. Despite the subtle, reasoned craftsmanship of his many novels and stories, and the power and artistry of many of the prose passages they contain, words failed the author. They often disintegrated under the burden of his thoughts. "I can't find the words to match my thought," Conrad complained while talking with an acquaintance on a stroll through the dimly lit streets of Ajaccio, Corsica.[21] Conrad should have taken his own advice, which he gave to Hugh Clifford, that there are circumstances in which "no word is adequate."[22]

The writer of the original passage seems to have tried to use the most elaborate nouns, adjectives, and adverbs possible. In many cases, the more complex word adds little to meaning, and in some instances it confounds meaning entirely. Few readers, even academic ones, would easily recognize *rationalistic* as meaning *reasoned*. A reader might also be confused by the use of *units of symbolic expression* for *words*. "If the writer meant *words*," we might ask, "why didn't she just say so?" Note, however, that a few formal words, such as *disintegrated* and *acquaintance* remain in our revision. These words contribute to the precision of the passage and therefore are essential to meaning.

REVISING JARGON

Exercise One:

Negative and positive responses correlate with creativity. There is a negative correlation to non-supportive responses and a positive correlation to supportive responses. Parents, therefore, should give supportive responses to their children. Such responses produce chain reactions; they stimulate creativity, and they sustain an environment in which a child will be ready for further stimuli, which will, in turn, stimulate creativity. By neglecting to provide an atmosphere in which a child can feel comfortable, non-supportive parents limit creativity.

In the original passage, computer terminology (or perhaps the terminology of radio—*receivers, feed-back, signals*) is combined with the discourse of psychology. The result is a paragraph in which a simple point, that parents should be supportive, is needlessly obscured. In our revision, we preserve the language of psychology, retaining such terms as *correlate, response,* and *stimuli,* but omit the terminology related to computer use.

Note in particular our omission of the term *utilize,* a word that is nearly always considered jargon. We have substituted *give,* but often *utilize* can be replaced by *use.*

Exercise Two:

During the recent review of our Health and Safety Code, three recommendations were made. First, to avoid the health problems that arise when computers are used, a break of no less than fifteen minutes should be allowed after every two hours of work with a Video Display Terminal (VDT). Second, the air should be tested where people work, especially in areas such as sealed, climate-controlled, or air-conditioned offices. Third, the laboratory staff who handle the snakes should have easy access to antitoxins.

In our revision of this passage, we decided that the readers of the passage were workers, people who could be unfamiliar both with the bureaucratic language of middle management and with the scientific terminology used in the original. For this reason, we tried to rewrite all sentences using lay terminology. For example, we changed *ophidians* to *snakes* and *atmospheric examinations* to *testing air.* We also changed the long phrase *where aerobiosis is necessary* to make the meaning depend less on the reader having knowledge of word *aerobiosis: aerobiosis* means breathing and obviously people breathe where they work. Note that we have given the complete term *Video Display Terminal* and then followed it with the acronym *VDT.* You should never use an acronym without indicating what it stands for; an overuse of acronyms is jargon at its worst.

REVISING FOR APPROPRIATELY DIRECT OR INDIRECT PROSE

Exercise One:

The American government started NASA with the goal of creating a symbol of technological excellence. The government hoped that soon NASA would "be in a position second to none" (303). NASA's administrators, although aware of this goal, nonetheless believed that NASA should place greatest emphasis on developing technology to its full potential; making progress took precedence over being first. Since this goal lacked definitive parameters, NASA administrators set many intermittent goals in order to maintain direction within the organization. Apollo was the first goal. The focus Apollo gave pleased NASA, and the goal itself pleased the government. NASA's adaptation satisfied both parties.

The original paragraph contains no euphemistic language but is riddled with needless passive constructions and many weak verbs. Most of these passive constructions are signalled by *to be* verbs and the preposition *by* and can be easily eliminated. For example, in the first and last sentences, we have shifted to the active voice by making the subjects of the original sentences objects. However, as you can see from the extensive revision, eliminating *to be* constructions often requires rewriting. In the third sentence, for example, eliminating *was the development* and *was not as important* required introducing the active verbs *place* and *took.* When these verbs are introduced, many other elements of the sentence need to be shifted as well.

Exercise Two:

NASA's managers were ineffective. They had few single, clear goals. Also, although they relied upon past experience when structuring the organization and deciding upon its goals, this experience lacked relevance in the eighties. This type of work required a different approach to managing staff. The mistakes made by workers were causing problems, and NASA's administration should have tried to solve these problems before human error resulted in danger. In the future, NASA's administration should evaluate the organization's goals and structures and align them with present management concepts. This restructuring will permit a more effective response to problems as they arise.

The indirect language used in the original passage seems bureaucratic and evasive. Of course, there are circumstances when such indirect prose might be appropriate — if the writer wanted to avoid placing blame on the NASA managers, for example. In our revision, we have opted for a more critical view and accordingly have placed more focus on NASA's managers by making many passive constructions active. We also use words and phrases that are less euphemistic, that more clearly denounce these managers. For example, rather than softening the description of the managers' ineffectiveness by using the passive voice and many modifiers (*NASA was not managed very effectively*), we choose to use the active voice and one telling adjective (*NASA's managers were ineffective*). Likewise, we substitute *human error* for *non-performance* and *danger* for *a dangerous situation*, thus stating the problems more directly.

REVISING MISUSED FIGURATIVE LANGUAGE

Exercise One:

Twelfth Night is a play of great diversity, but two of its main features are its plot and its subplot. The main characters, those of the plot, usually speak using mannered and decorative words. Shakespeare writes their speeches in verse. Contrarily, the characters of the subplot express themselves using prose. The rough conversations of Maria, Sir Toby, and Sir Andrew, which are full of quick retorts, exemplify this prose. Just as these irreverent conversations highlight the solemn romanticism of the poetic speeches, so the subplot illuminates the main plot. As Charles Prouty writes, "In direct contrast with the whimsical attitudes of the high comedy, we have the schemes and plots of the lower comedy . . ." (307). Shakespeare contrasts the plot with the subplot to the benefit of each.

If you have an ear for language, you probably cringed reading the original version of this passage since it contains several figurative expressions quite inappropriate to a discussion of Shakespeare. The clichés *chock-full* and *par for the course,* for example, bring to mind bottles and golf, certainly items that have little connection to Twelfth Night. Other misused figures are less obvious. For instance, we have changed *puts the words of poetry into their mouths* to *Shakespeare writes their speeches in verse.* The original gives the reader the impression that Shakespeare is acting upon living people, not characters he invented. Finally, the idea of a subplot *throwing* a main plot into *the limelight* just does not work; we can imagine throwing, and we can imagine illuminating, but the two together conjure up an image that one might see only in animated cartoons.

Exercise Two:

Change in Arembepe, Brazil arrived quickly. In less than twenty years, the small village was transformed. In 1973, there was a good road into Arembepe, an obvious indicator of progress. Refrigeration reached this fishing community in the same year. Thereafter, fishermen could market their fish in Salvador as well as in the village instead of having to sell their fish right out of their boats. Because of such modern conveniences, fishermen were able to fish all day for several days at a time. Eventually, this ability destroyed community spirit. In the past, the whole town would come down to the harbour to greet fishermen returning from their day at sea. After the introduction of refrigeration, no one noticed the fishermen's return because boats came in at all times.

The writer here is dealing with a serious — indeed, almost tragic — subject, the disintegration of community spirit in a fishing village. The use of clichés makes the passage seem imprecise and glib, thereby lessening its impact on the reader. In our revision, we eliminated such trite phrases as *like a speeding locomotive* and *peddle their wares* in order to grant the subject the kind of attention it deserves.

Chapter Seven: How Many Words are Enough?

ELIMINATING NON-CONTRIBUTING WORDS

Exercise One:

Through the years, the labour force in which men and women participate has been researched, and researchers have accepted false stereotypes. There is much controversy over whether women have progressed. One misleading belief is that women have advanced their position in the workforce (especially in comparison with men). This is not a correct statement. Women have suffered tremendously and find themselves in degrading, deskilling, and alienating jobs. This essay attempts to demonstrate the negative aspects of women's work. It proceeds to argue that there is little hope for women's escape from the double ghetto.

The original paragraph contains a tautology, a double modifier, and several formulaic phrases. The phrase *whether or not,* as used in the second sentence, is a tautology: *whether* contains the meaning of *or not.* We have eliminated *unfair* from the penultimate sentence since an *unfair aspect* is a *negative aspect.* (In your own writing, you may be unwilling to delete in cases like this one because you may have a special reason for including the extra adjective.) The formulaic phrases *in fact* and *in actual truth* have simply been deleted. *Goes on further to support the fact that* requires a little more work. We have replaced it with *proceeds to argue that,* a revision that omits four needless words.

Exercise Two:

Other developments have also been negative factors in women's work. For example, the expansion of hospitals opened the doors for numerous nurturing jobs which were quickly filled by women. However, it was soon discovered that this work was exhausting, frustrating, and alienating. As Shapiro establishes, nurses have fairly low status in the hospital hierarchy. He also says that nurses are allowed to make few decisions and must follow orders by the physicians. Doctors further alienate nurses by seeing them as dull and dumb; many don't even recall the nurses' first names. To conclude, women nursing in hospitals hold jobs which require demanding shift work but provide little opportunity for advancement.

In this paragraph, revision has focused on replacing formulaic phrases with more concise substitutes. In the third sentence, *to be found out* has been replaced by *discovered* and *type of* has been eliminated entirely. *Points out,* in the fourth sentence, has been replaced by *establishes*; *goes on to* has simply been deleted in the fifth. In the final sentence, *to conclude* is a more precise substitute for the formulaic *in the end,* and *nursing in hospitals* is more concise than *in the field of hospital nursing.*

ELIMINATING SUBORDINATE CLAUSES BEGINNING WITH RELATIVE PRONOUNS

Exercise One:

To make it appear as if only the French made grave mistakes during this time would be wrong, for Moltke made just as many serious errors; however, they did not appear to be mistakes when all went well. The most costly mistake for the Germans was not having the First Army take the channel ports during the French retreat when they were left undefended. The price would be heavy and they would fail during "the race to the sea." Moltke's other grave mistake was to send seven regular divisions to mask Antwerp, instead of using Landwehr as Schlieffen had proposed. Thus he reduced his offensive strength for little gain. The most useless move, however, was taking two corps from the right wing and transporting them to meet an emergency in the East, already over by the time they had arrived: Moltke had once again reduced his fighting strength for no gain.

Because the sentences in this passage are fairly long and describe complex details, there is a need to eliminate extraneous words. Several of the adjective clauses in this passage have therefore been changed to other forms of adjectival modifiers (*mistake that was to cost the Germans the most* = *most costly mistake; the move that was to prove the most useless* = *the most useless move*) or possessives (*the other grave mistake which was made by Moltke* = *Moltke's other grave mistake*). The *that of* and the *which was* of the final sentence have simply been deleted.

Exercise Two:

These women arriving on the prairies found a situation which did not come close to meeting their expectations. Expectations cultivated by fertile imaginations, supported by advertising images, and embellished by their dreams and desires had grown to utopian proportions. The response of these women, who had little sense of control over their situation and little or no money, was resignation. Essentially, they felt they had no choice but to stay and do what was necessary for survival.

In the revised passage, a few adjective clauses remain. These clauses, because they contain fairly subtle ideas, are not easily replaced by a few words. For example, consider *who had little sense of control over their situation and little or no money.* Far too much qualified information is contained here for the passage to be replaced, and the clause cannot be made into an appositive, so it must remain. The same is true of *which did not come close to meeting their expectations.* We have, however, eliminated *who arrived on the prairies* by substituting a verbal, and we have dropped the *which had been* in the second sentence altogether. We also dropped *that of* in the third sentence and *that* in the fourth because meaning is still clear without the relative pronoun.

ELIMINATING PREPOSITIONAL PHRASES

Exercise One:

Realist directors, according to Giannetti, employ the camera to perpetuate the illusion that there is no camera. Angles, lighting, and editing are all executed to keep cinematic intrusion minimal. Realist directors, for example, usually prefer to shoot at eye-level. The viewer therefore sees incidents as she would were she an active participant, and is therefore less conscious of the aesthetic distance between herself and the film. Realist directors likewise favour medium to long shots; because these shots provide background details, they preserve what Giannetti terms "spatial integrity." Again, the viewer, because she can understand the physical context of the scene, does not feel distanced.

The original paragraph illustrates several standard patterns of prepositional-phrase overuse. We have eliminated two prepositional phrases by substituting verbals: *put into execution* becomes *are executed*; *to do most of their shooting* becomes *to shoot*. Several prepositional phrases have been replaced by adjectives: *at a minimum* becomes *minimal*; *a participant in the action* becomes *active participant*; *for the same reason* becomes *likewise*; and *details of background* becomes *background details*. Finally, a few prepositional phrases are simply dropped because they are redundant. For example, *five to six feet above the ground* has been omitted entirely; *at eye-level* means *five to six feet above the ground* for most adults, so the information is unnecessary. Likewise, the closing *from it* is unnecessary. We also shortened the formulaic *so as to* to *to* twice. Note also that we did not revise *physical context of the scene* to *the scene's physical context*. Since *scene* is inanimate, some readers might consider the possessive an error in this case.

Exercise Two:

By the late 1960s, opinion about providing contraceptive services through domestic health programs had radically altered. The initiative for change, however, did not come from state-sponsored domestic programs; rather, Americans changed their attitude toward sponsoring foreign birth control programs. Leading Americans felt that the United States had a responsibility to prevent starvation and poverty internationally. The United States, then, saw its duty to promote international family-planning policies, and what was applied internationally ultimately became important nationally as well.

Some of the changes we have made to the original passage are relatively straightforward. Many prepositional phrases have been replaced by adjectives and adverbs: *by the end of the 1960s* has been changed to *by the late 1960s*; *state-sponsoring of domestic programs* has been altered to *state-sponsored domestic programs*; *in other countries* has been replaced by *foreign*; *to the international sphere* has been changed to *internationally*, and *within the country* has been changed to *nationally*. Other revisions, however, have involved much more extensive changes, and you may not agree with some of ours. For example, *a changed attitude in the United States* might not have the same meaning as *Americans changed their attitude*. In your own revisions, be wary of these substitutions. Make sure you are not losing your meaning in the attempt to eliminate words.

TURNING MODIFIERS AND NOUNS INTO VERBS

Exercise One:

Not only did the physician determine whether the private-duty nurse could obtain employment; he also controlled her work. Again, this control was not physical. Because the private-duty nurse did not work with the doctor on a day-to-day basis, she did not serve him as the hospital nurse did. However, if the actions of a private-duty nurse displeased the physician, he could dismiss her immediately. In addition to losing that particular job, the nurse might discover that the physician never called on her again. Far worse, the physician might blacklist her within the community.

The process of revising this paragraph probably made you realize that the wordiness of the original was created by inactive verbs. Look at what happens when we revise. In the first sentence when we use the active verb *determine,* we eliminate not only *factor,* but *in terms of.* Likewise, when we replace *had control over* with the verb *control, had* and *over* disappear as well. Watch in your own revisions for instances paralleling *take the initiative to place her on a blacklist.* The revision here makes clear that the extra verbs and noun are unnecessary to convey meaning.

Exercise Two:

The Applebaum-Hébert Report (1982), like the Massey Commission, accurately reflects the prevalent attitudes toward Canadian culture during the period of 1974-83. The Report often emphasizes Canada's multicultural aspects; indeed, the chapter on international cultural relations recommends that "Canadian artists and performers representing the cultural traditions of Canada's Native peoples and ethnic communities" should be given priority to receive federal support for artistic projects (Applebaum-Hébert 322). Ethnicity is recognized in the report; likewise, regional culture gains status. In the 1950s, the differences among the regions were acknowledged only grudgingly. Regionalism has always existed in Canada, but only since the 1960s have its cultural influences been encouraged. Regionalism, along with ethnicity, is now understood as an aspect of Canadian cultural distinctiveness.

This paragraph shows how easy it is to deaden verbs by using nouns as substitutes for them. In our revision, for example, *reflects* replaces *serves as an accurate reflection of; emphasizes* replaces *puts emphasis on*; *recognizes* replaces *granted recognition*; and *been encouraged* replaces *been given encouragement.* Note in this passage that *given priority* was not replaced with *prioritized.* This verb, although less wordy, is considered bureaucratic jargon by many writers, so we avoid it.

ELIMINATING *TO BE* CONSTRUCTIONS

Exercise One:

Ehrlich does not address the fact that, while population control might be a necessary evil in developing countries, the growth rate in industrialized countries remains at or near the zero level. Without immigration, the population of most industrialized countries would not increase. Environmental decline results not from the number of people in industrialized countries, but from how and what they consume. Rather than having one birth control policy for all countries, we need birth control policies in developing and underdeveloped countries and consumption policies in developed countries.

The author of the original paragraph is far too fond of the expletive constructions *it is, it were,* and *there would.* We have eliminated all these constructions, thereby making substantial changes in Sentences Two and Three. We have also replaced some *to be* verbs with more active verbs: *is = remains.* Note that the revision contains the pronoun *we* in the final sentence. The change gives more passion to the sentence but is not a strategy that can be used throughout the entire paragraph since it would make the argument too personal.

Exercise Two:

Ehrlich suggests withholding aid from poor nations who can still rehabilitate themselves in their own cultural way. When industrialized countries help underdeveloped countries, the former become dependent and abandon their traditional ways of securing resources. Once industrialized countries have solved or almost solved their problems, they can advise other more slowly moving countries.

In the first sentence, we have replaced *one of Ehrlich's suggestions* with *Ehrlich suggests,* a revision that allows us to eliminate *is.* Many other extraneous words have been deleted from the first sentence simply by replacing the lengthy *to be* phrase *are still in the position of being able to* with a verb (*can*). The second sentence is made less wordy by eliminating the expletive *it is* and by making the second clause active instead of passive. *Almost solved* may be an inappropriate substitute for *well on their way to solving*: one would have to know context to be sure the revision is appropriate.

ELIMINATING REDUNDANCIES IN CONTENT

Exercise One:

A second method of controlling population would be a system of financial penalties for people who had children. Currently, our system rewards couples who do have children through baby bonuses and tax deductions. Instead, we could tax items such as diapers and baby bottles, thereby penalizing parents. We could also control population by educating children both about sex and about the importance of lowering the birth rate. These external pressures would decrease population in a primarily positive way.

The controlling idea of this paragraph is that population can be controlled through a system of rewards and penalties and through education. The idea of rewards and penalties is spread through the first two sentences of the original. We have tightened the redundant content in these sentences by making the revised paragraph refer only to penalties (rewards are implied). The writer also takes too much space writing in general terms about concepts that are easily understood through examples. For instance, the reader knows that baby bottles and diapers are necessities for small children, so the clause *which are necessities for small children* can be eliminated. When these explanations are eliminated, meaning becomes much more clear. Note that *we* has been used in the revision to improve coherence and eliminate wordiness. Again, the use of *we* is acceptable in these circumstances because the paragraph is a personal appeal, but it would not always be appropriate.

You will notice that we have also revised this paragraph for ordinary wordiness. In particular, we have revised the last sentence to eliminate the expletive and unnecessary prepositional phrases.

Exercise Two:

Implicit in all that Bruce writes is a statement about the absolute power of the Maritime community. A simple examination of the topography shows why. The Maritimers of the Channel Shore live in isolated communities, separated from other villages by bays, coves, and religious prejudice. As a result of its isolation from others, the community acts as a judge of all actions.

The controlling idea here is that the Maritime community, because it is so isolated, has absolute power. In the first two sentences of the original paragraph, the writer uses a good many words to express a simple concept, that Bruce is writing about the Maritime community's power. In our revision, the first two sentences have been compressed into one. You might not have made this revision if you believed that the repetition was effective. The final clause of the last sentence has also been deleted since it adds no new meaning; obviously a judge would determine guilt or innocence.

EXERCISES

REVISION WORKSHEETS

The page reference listed directs the reader to the passage in the text that covers most thoroughly the item in question. Readers desiring further information should consult the index.

COMMON SENTENCE-LEVEL COMMENTS

Symbol	Meaning	Pages
√sent	effective sentence	
awk	awkward sentence	109-116
coord	illogical or excessive coordination	25-28
√coord	good coordination	22-24
cs	comma splice	51-62
sf	sentence fragment	40-50
fs	fused sentence	51-62
mix	mixed construction	109-112
run-on	run-on sentence	51-62
shft	inappropriate sentence shift	109-112
sub	illogical or excessive subordination	33-38
√sub	good subordination	29-33
sv agr	incorrect subject-verb agreement	63-72

COMMON PARAGRAPH-LEVEL COMMENTS

Symbol	Meaning	Pages
√	good point; well expressed	
?	unclear	
¶	paragraph needed here	168-169
no ¶	no new paragraph needed here	168-169
¶ coh	problem with paragraph coherence	170-193
¶ dev	paragraph poorly developed	194-202
√ dev	good development	
¶ org	paragraph poorly organized	190-193
¶ un	paragraph not unified	160-167
√ un	good unity	
dig	digression	164-167
e.g.	example needed	194-199
emph	good use of emphasis	
log	faulty logic	
purp	purpose unclear	194-202

Symbol	Meaning	Pages
red	redundant information	339-341
rep	monotonous repetition	339-341
trans	ineffective or missing transition	188-189
√trans	good transition	
vag	vague expression of ideas	194-199
var	passage needs variety	117-156

PUNCTUATION AND MECHANICS COMMENTS

Symbol	Meaning	Pages
√punc	effective use of punctuation	
∧	comma needed	204-221
no ∧	no comma needed	204-221
⊙	period needed	
∨	apostrophe needed	234-242
no ∨	no apostrophe needed	234-242
∧	colon needed	223-225
no ∧	no colon needed	223-225
∧	semicolon needed	222-223
no ∧	no semicolon needed	222-223
abbr	abbreviation incorrect	
cap	capital letter needed	
hyph	hyphen needed	
lc	lower case letter needed	
poss	incorrect form of possessive	234-242
sp	spelling error	

OPERATIONAL COMMENTS

Symbol	Meaning
⌣	close up space
⊓⊔	reverse order of two elements
∧	something has been omitted
ℓ	delete
#	space needed

DICTION AND STYLE COMMENTS

abst	expression too abstract	269-274
choppy	sentences too choppy	120-124
cl	cliché	305
coll	expression too colloquial	277-278
con	word has inappropriate connotation	263-268
√conc	concisely worded; no wordiness	
d	poor diction; poor word choice	256-307
√d	good word choice	
emph	weak or inappropriate emphasis	117-118
euph	euphemism	288-290
exact	more exact or precise word needed	269-274
fig	inappropriate figure of speech	303-307
fl	language too flowery	278-284
inf	expression too informal	275-284
jarg	jargon	285-287
√ lev	good level of diction	279-284
mix met	mixed metaphor	304
nsw	no such word	
pass	inappropriate use of passive voice	291-298
pret	pretentious word	278-279
sent l	sentence length ineffective	120-124
sl	inappropriate use of slang	276
sl lang	language too slanted	264
sxl	sexist language	77-78
t	tone inappropriate	275-284
us	usage questioned — check glossary	343-367
wc	ineffective word choice	256-307
wdy	wordiness problem	308-342
wv	weak verb	290
ww	wrong word	256-274

PARALLEL STRUCTURE COMMENTS

false ||	false parallelism	85
faulty ||	faulty parallelism	83-95
√ ||	effective use of parallel structure	138-142; 181-187

MODIFIER ERRORS

dm	dangling modifier	102-106
mm	misplaced modifier	96-101
spl in	split infinitive	100
sq m	squinting modifier	98-99

QUOTATION ERRORS

mq	misfitted quotation	243-244
q punc	quotation incorrectly punctuated	243-255
quot	faulty quotation form	243-255
" "	add quotation marks	243-255
no " "	no quotation marks needed	243-255

PRONOUN ERRORS

pr agr/g	pronoun-antecedent agreement — gender	73
pr agr/n	pronoun-antecedent agreement — number	74-78
pr agr/p	pronoun-antecedent agreement — person	73-74
pr ca	pronoun case error	366
pr ref/amb	ambiguous pronoun reference	176
pr ref/ant	no antecedent for pronoun	175
pr ref/rem	remote pronoun reference	175
pr ref/vag	vague pronoun reference	176-177